THE CONSERVATIVE FRONTIER

THE CONSERVATIVE FRONTIER

TEXAS AND THE ORIGINS OF THE NEW RIGHT

JEFF ROCHE

University of Texas Press   *Austin*

Copyright © 2025 by the University of Texas Press
All rights reserved
Printed in the United States of America
First edition, 2025

Requests for permission to reproduce material from this work should be sent to permissions@utpress.utexas.edu.

♾ The paper used in this book meets the minimum requirements of ANSI/NISO Z39.48-1992 (R1997) (Permanence of Paper).

Cataloging-in-Publication Data is available from the Library of Congress.
 ISBN 978-1-4773-3264-1 (cloth)
 ISBN 978-1-4773-3265-8 (PDF)
 ISBN 978-1-4773-3266-5 (ePub)

doi:10.7560/332641

THE UNIVERSITY OF TEXAS PRESS GRATEFULLY ACKNOWLEDGES THE CLIFTON AND SHIRLEY CALDWELL TEXAS HERITAGE ENDOWMENT FOR ITS SUPPORT OF THIS PUBLICATION.

CONTENTS

BOOK THREE. COWBOY CONSERVATISM

INTRODUCTION

Imagine yourself as a small hopeful immigrant family, alone on the Staked Plains, with the Comanche and the Kiowa still on the loose. The power of such experience will not sift out of the descendants of that venturer in one generation and produce Middletown. Elements of that primal venturing will surely inform several generations.

LARRY MCMURTRY

In 2015, Hereford, a small feedlot-stockyard town in West Texas, was named the number one most conservative place in America by Crowdpac, a startup data analysis and fundraising organization. Also making its Top Ten list were West Texas towns Monahans, Dalhart, and Childress. Crowdpac's second tier included the Panhandle towns of Canyon and Plainview and West Texas's biggest cities: Amarillo, Lubbock, Midland, and Odessa. Around that same time, a couple of political scientists crunched their numbers and calculated that Amarillo was the nation's most conservative big city. And Smart Asset, a data-mining company in the financial advising/real estate/relocation world, sliced its research a little thinner and named Midland as the best *overall* city for conservatives, but suggested Amarillo as the best place for the purely ideologically motivated. Lubbock also made everyone's short list.[1] For over twenty years, Cook's Partisan Voting Index, a go-to tool for political operatives, has ranked the Texas 13th Congressional District (the Panhandle) as the most reliably Republican district in the nation. Joining it in the Top Five were the Texas 19th (southern plains) and the Texas 11th (Permian Basin). The three men who served those districts for most of those years, Mac Thornberry, Randy Neugebauer, and Mike Conaway, all earned a lifetime conservative rating from the Conservative Political Action Committee (CPAC) of over 90 percent.[2] If these three contiguous districts were their own state, it would be the reddest in the country. And it wouldn't be close.

It was the sheer starkness of this political geography that drew me in. Look at any county-level map of West Texas votes after any election of the last generation and see for yourself: your screen glowing deep-crimson pixels. Over an area the size of Wyoming, you will not find a single blue county. It's so red that the pinkish counties stand out. What was it about this place, this huge place, that could produce such a uniformity in political thought and behavior? How does a place produce politics and politicians so far to the edges of the national median? I am a historian, so I looked to the past for answers. I went back to the beginning, back to the days when West Texans developed their own society, their own politics, their own culture. And here's the story.

The Conservative Frontier follows two interwoven narrative strands, the double helix of the region's DNA, consisting of politics rather than polymers. The first is a history of West Texas. The second is a history of its politics. Let me say from the onset: a comprehensive history of West Texas is beyond the scope of this book. Because I sought to explore and explain how and why this place produced such a unique political culture, the book illuminates distinct moments and movements and characters. It is a chronicle told through vignettes and episodes that reveal a larger history of the region. Even so, the narrative that emerges from those accounts, which covers roughly a century, tells a story much different than those told in most of the scholarly and popular histories and studies of West Texas.

As a political history, well, it's a bit different there as well. While most sections of the book are anchored by some form of electoral contest or another, for the most part, *The Conservative Frontier* concentrates on the conditions (especially the social and cultural conditions) in which certain political events took place rather than on narrowly focused analyses of voting data or campaigns. This book also features a different cast of characters than one might expect in a political history; alongside such recognizable national figures as George H. W. Bush and Barry Goldwater we have beauty queen political operatives, historian/polemicists, lumber barons, rebellious football coaches, small-town newspaper editors, politically minded brine brokers, activist grammarians, and the breakfast cereal tycoon who founded America's only capitalist utopia.[3] The Republican Party is important and the site of much of the action of this book, but so are church congregations and sororities and sewing and book groups and historical organizations and chambers of commerce, especially chambers of commerce. Well-known national right-wing organizations and activists like the John Birch Society and Dan Smoot are here, but so are the Texans for America and J. Evetts Haley.

One of the other attractions of West Texas, besides its obvious outlier status, is its short political history. The National League is older. So is the telephone. The whole place was controlled by the Comanche Nation until the mid-1870s. When the first white settler set up a ranch in Palo Duro Canyon in 1876, during that summer of the nation's Centennial Exposition, there wasn't a road, a settlement, or a fort for over a hundred miles in any direction. For someone interested in how conservatism developed over the twentieth century, West Texas was like a cleanroom, an engineered isolated space where airborne political and historical particles had been filtered out. Unlike other large ultraconservative western spaces like eastern Wyoming or the western half of Oklahoma, the federal government had played little role in the economic, cultural, or political development of West Texas. There were no long-standing military installations, no federally subsidized railroads or federally granted homesteads, no federal land or Native American reservations, or experience with territorial government. Unlike other southern places (including the eastern half of Texas), there was no legacy of slavery or the Civil War. The region wasn't settled by Anglo-Americans until long after Reconstruction in Texas had ended. The agrarian uprisings that roiled Texas, the South, and the prairie and mountain states of the American West, had little impact in the western half of the state. It was still too sparsely settled and still too focused on cattle for Populist arguments over free silver and programs for stabilizing cotton prices to make much of an impact.[4]

As an agricultural frontier, West Texas developed with extraordinary quickness. Led almost exclusively by real estate developers selling off the massive holdings of large ranches and railroads, the first quarter of the twentieth century witnessed the region moving from a raw cattle frontier to the most productive agricultural section in the nation. A new land and a new people developed a new politics. Grounded in the reality of settlement and a local political economy organized around the expansion of small-scale commercial agriculture, a lot of the political action took place within local civic and business organizations. It was a politics of growth, of modernity. And it was a politics wrapped in a new national narrative that positioned small-town businessmen and commercial farmers as the heroes of the story of Modern America.

I also need to acknowledge the possibility that West Texas might be so different from the rest of the country that its political advance is an outlier. Historically and right up until the present, the region has had one of the most monochromatic and uniform populations in the country: overwhelmingly white, native-born, Christian (primarily fundamentalist and evangelical Christian), middle-class, and educated. Since the 1930s, most West Texans have been born and raised in West Texas. Its cities and towns are ruled by a class of small-scale capitalists who have never faced any real threat to their cultural or economic hegemony. With no industrial development to speak of, there's never been a labor movement. West Texas has, until very recently, never had large-scale foreign immigration. The region mostly missed out on any drastic Sunbelt growth.[5] There are no huge cities. Its largest metropolitan area, Lubbock, is only the tenth-largest city in Texas. (Nationally, its population falls between Toledo, Ohio, and Hialeah, Florida.) Like the other cities of the region—Amarillo, Abilene, Midland, and Odessa—Lubbock grew over the twentieth century, but mostly at the expense of nearby small towns and villages. With little in-migration, West Texas cities exhibit a provincial nature one might expect from a smaller town. And they function the way they always have, serving as hubs of the regional economy, run by and for the business class. Outside the cities, West Texas is among the most rural places in the United States; most of its hundred-odd counties have populations that average fewer than two people per square mile, literally the old official American definition of "unsettled." It is, to put it simply, a population prone to conformity.

While there's no universally accepted demarcation of the borders of "West Texas," for this account, I rely on the boundaries of the 11th, 13th, and 19th Texas congressional districts as drawn in 2015.[6] While some geographers split West Texas into three sections, the Panhandle, the southern plains, and the Permian Basin, I've folded all three into the larger region and included counties of the western Cross Timbers. This West Texas contains a little over one hundred counties, four metropolitan areas, and a lot of small towns. Its economy is largely extractive—wheat, cotton, cattle, oil, and gas. The history and demography are consistent across the region and distinct from the rest of the state. Overlay any number of maps of the natural world—ecology, soils, native plants, average annual rainfall, average wind speed, average monthly temperatures—and the region's geographic distinctiveness shows through clearly. Broadly speaking, this West Texas is the southernmost section of the American Great Plains and has much in common with the rest of the prairie states and provinces of North America.

Particularly, and interestingly, it is closer to the political culture of the rest of the Great Plains as well.[7] Widening our view of the Cook's Partisan Index rankings of the mid-2010s, we see another regional political geography, this one linking the western half of the Lone Star State with the western halves of Oklahoma, Kansas, and Nebraska. The western congressional districts of those states rank just below West Texas in their partisan rankings.[8] Looking over county voting data from the single-district plains states of Montana, Wyoming, and the Dakotas, the same pattern appears: the prairie counties of each are among the most reliably Republican places in the country. After the 2016 presidential election, I could have driven my pickup from Guthrie, Texas, to Portal, North Dakota, and not passed through a single zip code where Donald Trump won by fewer than 63 points.

These are places dominated by a belief system that I call *cowboy conservatism*. An ideology born on the old cattle frontier and that spread across the North American prairies with the cattle business, cowboy conservatism was a powerful formative influence on the development of the politics of these places. Founded in the entrepreneurial and protolibertarian culture of nineteenth-century Texas ranchers and boosted by the cult of the cowboy that dominated American popular media in the first half of the twentieth, cowboy conservatism draws on the mythology, iconography, and language of the Texas-western frontier to express a long and complicated set of ideas, including white supremacy; hyperpatriotic nationalism, often expressed through a unilateralist view of foreign policy and intense militarism; religious fundamentalism; an antistatism that regularly veers into a paranoid fear of government power; an unreconstructed devotion to the free market; a set of ideas about gender forged during battles over prohibition and woman suffrage; and a fierce devotion to both individualism *and* small-town ideas about responsibility to community. At its foundation is a commitment to values long associated with the American frontier myth: individualism, self-reliance, equality (for white men), honesty, thrift, a strong moral code, hard work, modesty, and faith in God. Cowboy conservatives also regularly wrap their philosophy in frontier mythology, language, and iconography. It's often easy to focus on the costumes (the boots and buckles and Levis and Stetsons) or the props (ranches and pickups and rifles), but cowboy conservatism is more than image or rhetoric; it is the articulation of a political philosophy born in a place and reflects the history and reality of West Texas and large swaths of the rest of the American West.[9]

That a place as big as West Texas should continue to be dominated by the cultural values of a ranching frontier that was settled over a hundred years ago should not surprise us. Sharp-eyed observers of America's cultural development have long recognized that people of a particular place tend to "take their colouring" from "the peculiar manners of the first settlers." This process was just "natural," Jedidiah Morse suggested in 1789.[10] In West Texas, though, ranchers and their culture have dominated West Texas to a degree far beyond their economic power, which is itself significant. The most successful of the pioneer ranching class went into real estate, town building, oil and gas, media, railroads, and banking, literally dictating regional development and recruiting settler/investors who shared their entrepreneurial vision. Their daughters and sons and granddaughters and grandsons built multi-hyphenate empires. As important, ranchers and cowboys and the entire cattle frontier enjoyed a dominance in popular imagination and cultural media across most of the twentieth century. Texas and its cattle frontier were the subjects of an unknowable number of movies, plays, musicals, films, novels, short stories, comic books, television shows, poetry, and popular music. At one point in the 1950s, eight of the Top Ten–rated shows on television were Westerns. Louis L'Amour, who set many of his most popular novels on the Texas frontier, sold 200 million books.

The argument of this book is simple. When it comes to political behavior, place matters and the past matters and people matter. Most voters don't create their political identity or make their electoral choices in a vacuum. And in West Texas, an overwhelming majority of the electorate has made right-wing conservatism an essential part of their identity, political and otherwise. Why? As this book shows, West Texas, particularly in the wheat and cotton counties, was (and is) one of the last places in the nation where the agricultural fundamentalism that all but defined the nineteenth century still serves as an organizational principle for society. It's an ethos founded on the principle that a nation's economic and moral health depends on protecting and promoting the values of its rural and small-town farming and ranching communities. While much of the rest of the nation urbanized, industrialized, and experienced mass immigration over the twentieth century, West Texas remained largely native-born, white, rural, and small town. With great advances in technology and improvements in farming practices, along with federal programs and subsidies, many of the risks borne by earlier generations of farmers were removed (with the obvious exception of extreme weather events), leaving behind a politics that has trended toward cultural issues and the protection of long-standing ideas about morality and the proper functioning of society and democracy. One result is a political culture preternaturally attuned to abstract and often distant threats: the dangers of organized labor, mass immigration, federal power, internal subversion, communism, and those who would challenge traditional ideas about gender and sexuality, racial hierarchies, or local customs or social codes. Another result is that despite an overall outmigration from the region—particularly in the less populated counties—commercial family farms have remained the foundation of local economies simply because fewer people have been needed to bring wheat or cotton or cattle to market. Which left an aging and homogenous population prone to conformity and with an even greater sense of responsibility to protect the status quo.

West Texans' right-wing ideology didn't materialize all at once, of course, but rather emerged over the twentieth century in stages that roughly correspond to the three main sections of *The Conservative Frontier*. The first was the creation of a separate regional identity. From the beginning, West Texans saw themselves as a people apart, the fulfillment of the nation's destiny, the final stage of a two-century process of pioneering that had honed the "American" into the perfect democratic creature. They had tamed the wildest frontier on the continent and transformed a desolate wilderness into something close to a utopia—the Agricultural Wonderland. They had built a different economy, a different society, and a different culture out on the Texas prairies—an entire nation, really, of white, Christian, commercial family farmers and the small-town professionals and entrepreneurs who tended to their financial, technological, consumer, educational, spiritual, and other needs. In the early years of the century, it was the whitest, most middle-class, most gender-balanced agricultural frontier in the nation. It was also the fastest growing. Recognizing their unique economy and society, West Texans built out their own regional institutions and organizations. The West Texas Chamber of Commerce became one of the most powerful lobbying groups in Texas. Its distinct politics was founded on the typical booster ideals of growth—improved transportation systems, pro-business local governments, better and more state services, greater representation in Austin. But they were also noticeably progressive, seeing prohibition and women's suffrage as logical next steps in a frontier narrative founded on literal progress. By the 1920s, West Texas voters had begun to pull away from the Democratic Party and the rest of Texas to embrace the small-town and Middle West Republicanism of Herbert Hoover.

The dust, drought, depression, and desperation of the 1930s broke the dream. The Agricultural Wonderland became the Dust Bowl, a national problem to be solved. Their own federal government blamed West Texans for their plight and threatened to take control of local farms and ranches. The national press treated them as objects of scorn. Or worse, pity, and portrayed their home as a desolate hellscape. The dizzying array of projects initiated by the New Deal left many confused and many others angry and frightened about what effect a powerful new federal government might mean for local systems of power. Scattered widely across Texas, like-minded reactionaries against the New Deal found one another and formed the first right-wing organizations in the state. Those early efforts were led by a collection of paranoiacs; antigovernment, anti-Catholic, and antilabor zealots; rabid segregationists; and early-adopting anticommunists brought together by an intense distrust and even hatred of Franklin Roosevelt and the New Deal. By the 1950s, a growing number of ultraconservatives had coalesced under the standard of Americanism and had begun to view any unwelcome change in society as evidence of a possible communist plot to overthrow America from within. Anticommunism began to animate the booster classes and dominate the editorial focus of almost every single news outlet in the region. By 1960, West Texas was already recognized as a right-wing stronghold.

Starting in the early 1960s, right-wing activists moved into the largely empty shell of the state's Republican Party, seeing it as a logical vehicle for the promotion of their political worldview. Since the beginning, then, the modern GOP in Texas has been dominated by those on the far right. In other states—California, for example—the ultraconservatives who began to flood the Republican Party in the 1960s had to challenge an existing leadership and were forced to coexist (and convert) long-standing Republicans. In Texas, right-wing activists created their local GOP from scratch and in their image. And they built it with great speed and unbridled enthusiasm. Within a decade of the first important Republican effort of the postwar years, the senatorial campaigns of conservative John Tower in 1960 and 1961, the West Texas GOP would come to dominate much of the region. Its embrace of the cultural politics of the late sixties and early seventies—coming out against student activism and other challenges to unquestioning patriotism, rejecting any new constructions of gender or sexuality, questioning the directions and motives of a new generation of civil rights activists, and ferociously defending the local cultural, economic, and social status quo—helped determine its success.

A word about the title. From the beginning, the U.S. federal government has conducted a census every ten years. As it quantified the spatial distribution of its population, the census took care to identify those places where there were fewer than two people per square mile. This distinction helped to visualize the difference and distance between the "settled" and the "unsettled" sections of the country. The line between these spaces was known as the frontier. Over time, the movement of this frontier line showed a clear chronicle of settlement, a literal mapping of American movement. Those on the unsettled side were far (often very far) from the comforts and conveniences of civilization: organization and infrastructure, dependable communication, consumables, and capital. Frontier folk were literally way out there. As I considered the emergence and spread of a form of right-wing politics that was, for most of the twentieth century, way out there and focused my attention on a place where frontier mythology stands for local history, the metaphor was obvious and delightfully apt. It was easy to imagine the activists and officeholders and the intellectuals and ideologues as some sort of pioneers who had staked their futures far from political settlement. They certainly saw themselves that way; their primary spokesman, an activist-intellectual named J. Evetts Haley, blended his entire political message and persona around the fact that he was a well-respected historian of the frontier.

To continue the metaphor, if one were to map out American political thought from any time in the 1930s to the 1980s, conservative West Texas voters would occupy spaces far distant from the more settled sections of American ideology. Isolated from the comforts of political civilization, our metaphorical pioneers did what actual pioneers did. They built out their own systems and organizations and media. Much of the work of developing and promoting their brand of politics took place within the mundane all-but-invisible world of the small-town or small-city civic elite and wannabe civic elite. Much also happened in national organizations with cultural and social power in West Texas: groups like the American Legion, the Daughters of the American Revolution, and the Farm Bureau—all of which would come to occupy far-right positions. It happened in the media, with right-wing ideologues occupying central positions in the regional programming of television and radio and dominating the Opinion pages of almost every single newspaper. Once a form of right-wing political thought emerged in the 1950s, under the guise of "Americanism" and under the banner of fighting the Cold War, the conformist nature of the region's homogenous population took over.[11]

Not surprisingly, then, *The Conservative Frontier* borrows its basic narrative structure from this omnipresent story of settlement. It ends the way all frontier stories end. Where once there were few, there are now many. Where once was nothing, now there is everything. The story begins in 1876 when the first white settler moved into the Panhandle and ends at the 1976 Republican National Convention in Kansas City, when cowboy conservatives failed in their attempt to name Ronald Reagan their party's candidate for president. They would not lose a fight of this importance for the next four decades.

EXPOSITION
THE DESPOBLADO

Its sublimity arises from its unbounded extent, its barren monotony and desolation, its still, unmoved, calm, stern, almost self-confident grandeur, its strange power of deception, its want of echo, and in fine, its power of throwing a man back upon himself and giving him a feeling of lone helplessness, strangely mingled at the same time with a feeling of liberty and freedom from restraint.

ALBERT PIKE, 1831

He was just another young New Englander out for adventure when Albert Pike found himself stranded on the Texas High Plains in the fall of 1831. It had been a miserable year so far. Hired a few months earlier as part of a security detail for a trade caravan on the Santa Fe Trail, Pike's party endured disaster after disaster: they ran out of food and water; so many of its oxen died, the caravan was tailed across several states by packs of wolves feasting on the carcasses; horses ran away, including Pike's, forcing him to walk the last several hundred miles; then, almost within sight of Santa Fe, the party got caught in a horrific blizzard where it was so cold that horses froze to death. Once in Santa Fe, all Pike could find for work was a part-time retail gig. So, after just a few weeks in Nuevo México, he signed on to a beaver-trapping expedition on the Canadian River, deep in Comanche territory. This was an equally miserable experience: game and water were scarce, hunger and thirst common, beaver nonexistent. Those six fruitless and miserable weeks on the strange landscape of the Llano Estacado made a lasting impression on the twenty-one-year-old Pike, though. For him, raised in a wooded and wet northeast corner of Massachusetts, it was an almost indescribable land. "Broad, level, gray and barren, the immense desert which extends thence westwardly almost to the shadow of the mountains is too grand and too sublime to be imaged. . . . The eye," he wrote, once he was safely tucked away at Fort Smith in the weeks after his adventures, "can see no bounds. Not a tree, nor a bush, not a shrub, not a tall weed lifts its head above the barren grandeur of the desert; not a stone is to be seen on its hard beaten surface; no undulation, no abruptness, no break to relieve the monotony; nothing save here and there a deep narrow track worn into the hard plain by the constant hoof of the buffalo."[1] No landscape he could possibly imagine could have made so "vivid" an impression on an American.

Pike, who would go on to become one of the nineteenth century's best nature writers, regularly used the word "sublime" as he described the prairies of West Texas. At the height of the Romantic Era, Pike's use of the word takes on a special meaning. "Sublime" was a way to convey the feelings conjured when confronted with a landscape that overwhelms the senses, a place where beauty and dread are interwoven into a confusing and terrifying tapestry. As Edmund Burke (coincidentally also the intellectual founder of modern conservative thought) put it in his landmark work of art criticism, the sublime landscape invokes such feelings of astonishment that reason becomes impossible and all the motion of the soul is "suspended, with some degree of horror." For Pike, the terror and beauty of the plains lay in their ability to stir both feelings of supreme independence and naked vulnerability. He wouldn't be the last to feel that way.[2]

It starts with the land. Some 75 million years ago, at the birth of the Rocky Mountains, now long-lost rivers and streams flowing between the gaps of adolescent peaks drew away the flotsam and jetsam of mountain making eastward, creating a nation-sized swamp across the middle third of North America. Over millennia, the gradient flattened, the mud thickened, and the swamp became the plains—at over a million square miles, one of Earth's most magnificent prairies. At the southern end of those plains, calcium-rich springs built a towering mesa. Made from millions of wafer-thin layers of erosion-resistant rock and topped by rich grasses feeding from even richer soil, the tabletop now stretches over hundreds of square miles and looms hundreds of feet above the surrounding plains. The Spanish would call it the Llano Estacado, the

"Staked Plains." Albert Pike called it sublime. South and east of the Llano, an even older tale, a region of rolling plains and rich grasslands, sitting atop the worn-down limestone remnants of the ancient edges of an Appalachian range that began to collapse along with Pangea.

The western half of Texas has no forests or navigable rivers and is all but defined by its lack of topographic or environmental variation. The few European and American explorers, soldiers, and traders who encountered it between 1541 and 1875 mostly hated and feared the place. For generations of people emotionally and economically wedded to wooded, well-watered, and hilly spaces, West Texas was a worthless and terrifying hellscape, a land without visual respite from a stupefying horizontal monotony. Until the twentieth century, a layer of prairie grasses two feet high and crowned with airy seedheads covered almost everything. There were three colors: the pale blue crown of an ever-present sky, the grayish greens of the grasses, and the chalky reddish browns of the dirt. The Llano was bigger than Pennsylvania and as flat as a dining room table. To imagine the disorienting feeling of those Europeans who first encountered the space, it would be helpful to visualize a man on horseback with his stirrups brushing the tops of caterpillar seeds of the two-feet-tall grasses. To get a sense of scale, picture our mounted traveler as only two inches tall from hoof to hat. Holding this image of a teeny explorer in your head, think of an empty 1970s living room replete with pale avocado shag carpet and your tiny figure in the middle of that room. At scale, the living room would be twice the size of Houston. It was more than a little discomforting.

On average, the region enjoys a pleasant climate. January temperatures range from the thirties to the fifties, though the wind usually makes it feel colder. Summer temperatures average seventy to eighty degrees, and near-constant breezes and a lack of humidity make it comfortable. The sun shines almost every day. The one or two yearly snowfalls rarely add up to more than three or four inches and melt away in a matter of days. Overcast days are few and far between and happen mostly in May. It rains typically in mid- to late spring and early fall and averages between fifteen and twenty inches a year, but commonly enough far more or far less. It isn't the averages that define West Texas weather, but the extremes. Summer days can clock in over a hundred degrees for a week or more at a time. In the winter, wind-chill temperatures can force schools to close. Long periods of well-above-average rain are accompanied by intense droughts, some lasting years. Violent and terrifying thunderstorms, too often accompanied by deadly tornadoes, rip through the region with little warning, destroying communities in their wake. Blue northers, enormous and fast-moving cold fronts accompanied by driving snow and heavy winds, can cause temperatures to plummet forty or fifty degrees in less than an hour.[3]

The harshness of the weather, the sheer distance between sources of water and wood, and the lack of easily recognized natural resources (apart from bison) limited human habitation across the southern plains for most of its prehistory. Over the centuries, various nomadic bands built small societies that trailed buffalo herds, which numbered in the millions, and used the animal for protein, shelter, tools, and trade goods, but few lasted more than three or four generations.[4] When the Spanish finally reached the Texas plains in the mid-sixteenth century, the region was all but free of human habitation.

We can trace the first European feelings about this part of Texas back to history's most famous accountant. The short version goes like this: Assigned to keep the books for an expedition that put the ill in ill-fated, Álvar Núñez Cabeza de Vaca was shipwrecked on the Texas Coast in 1528 and, mostly by convincing the indigenous peoples that he met that he was a deity or least a mystic, he steadily worked his way down the Texas coast toward Mexico. After eight years and a ridiculously long detour to the eastern shore of the Gulf of California, he managed to make his way back to Mexico City. Along the way, he even, miraculously, met back up with the other three survivors of his original six hundred-man expedition. The men were easily the biggest celebrities in the New World, dining out on the stories of their astounding adventures for months. As their star began to dim, however, the stories grew more fantastic, finally reaching the realm of golden cities, Amazon women, and fantastical creatures and landscapes. The place, they said, was called "Cíbola." The tales drew the attention of Viceroy Antonio de Mendoza, then locked in a power struggle with Hernán Cortés for control of New Spain. Mendoza believed that the discovery of a new source of wealth for the kingdom might help him cement his hold on power. After a hasty thousand-mile reconnoitering mission to the north seemed to confirm the stories, the viceroy mounted the largest expedition in the short history of the New World.

In April 1540, led by Francisco Coronado, three hundred novice conquistadors hungry for adventure and even hungrier for gold, dozens of priests eager to spread the word, a thousand Native slaves, and enough livestock to feed them all trekked north from Culiacán toward glory. Of course, when Coronado arrived at the place that the prior year's scouting had identified as Cíbola, he found only the mud structures of a people scratching out an existence on a hardscrabble high-desert plateau. Desperate, angry, but still hopeful, the expedition marched east from pueblo to pueblo, inquiring about cities of gold. Quickly catching on, Pueblo people learned to play along and pointed Coronado farther down the road.

The Spanish wintered near present-day Albuquerque. Their arrogance and violence toward the locals led Pueblo leaders to launch a scheme to get rid of Coronado's party for good. They planted a jailhouse snitch who strategically (and seemingly unwillingly) parsed out information about a place he knew called Quivira, also a kingdom of gold, but many, many leagues to the east. The Spanish pressed their informant, whom they called "The Turk," into service, ordering him to lead them to Quivira in early spring 1541, before the Rio Grande had even thawed. The Pueblo's plan was simple. The Turk would lead the expedition deep into the flatlands of the present-day Texas Panhandle, slip away, and the Spanish, with no geologic features to guide them, would get desperately lost and wander the trackless prairies until they all died. They would not have been the first. The place was so disorienting that even the Pueblo avoided it.

The plan failed. The Spanish did get hopelessly lost but figured out how to blaze trails with cairns of buffalo chips and use bugles as sonic markers. They soon recognized that the Turk was leading them in circles and confronted him before he had a chance to flee. They forced a confession and then killed him. Coronado, hopeful to the end, finally discovered "Quivira," a small settlement of straw-thatched huts along the Arkansas River in present-day southwestern Kansas. He returned to Mexico City in disgrace. He was broke and had suffered brain damage from a horse accident. Mendoza stripped him of his titles and put him on trial. He died in shame in 1554.

The reports from the Coronado expedition described the Llano as a nightmarish cacotopia where a human felt adrift and meaningless, where loneliness pressed down like a weight. Coronado compared it to being "swallowed up by the sea."[5] Pedro Castañeda, the expedition's able chronicler, recalled a constant dizziness and disorientation in which he and the others felt physically ill and in almost constant terror. He labeled the whole region a *despoblado*, a word with no direct contemporary English translation but that roughly means a place where human habitation is impossible—a name on a map both descriptive and prescriptive.[6] The Spanish took the name to heart and avoided the Despoblado for almost three centuries. The empire built no roads, founded no missions, and established no presidios.

American explorers would come to agree with Castañeda. Zebulon Pike, reporting on a calamitous 1806 expedition to the headwaters of the Arkansas, described the entire region south of the river as the "Great Sandy Desert." The maps produced after the Stephen H. Long expedition in 1819–1820 stamped "Great American Desert" across most of the Great Plains. That term would be reprinted on maps and in textbooks for decades. In 1854, the U.S. Boundary Commission described the Texas prairies as a "sterile, barren plain without water or Timber producing a few stunted shrubs which are insufficient to sustain animal life."[7] Sidestepping ongoing debates about the accuracy of these claims or the motivations behind perpetuating the idea that the plains were an honest-to-goodness desert, or the degree to which contemporary Americans bought into that idea, instead it's probably more useful to simply recognize that men like Pike and Long and agencies like the Boundary Commission represented a nation of farmers and measured landscapes by their agricultural potential. Desert or no, Long was unequivocal on this account: the plains were "unfit for cultivation" and "uninhabitable by a people depending upon agriculture for their subsistence." It was a place best served "as a barrier to prevent too great an extension of our population westward, and secure us against the machination or incursions of an enemy."[8] An American despoblado.

Ultimately, until 1875 at least, it didn't really matter whether or not Americans believed that the Texas prairies were an uninhabitable and unfarmable desert, because settlement was out of the question. That entire part of the world was the heart of the most violent, most powerful, and least understood empire in North America, the Comanche, who had controlled the region since the mid-eighteenth century.[9] When the Spanish abandoned their New Mexico settlements after the Pueblo Revolt in 1680, the horses they left behind spread and multiplied across the entire Arkansas Valley. This massive horse herd formed the basis of an entirely new sort of Native society—mounted nomadic groups capable of thriving on the American prairies. And no group prospered like the Comanche, whose economic and military empire dominated the Southwest from San Antonio to Santa Fe. The Comanche controlled the key markets: horses, slaves, and buffalo hides. Their military prowess was unmatched and their key alliances, particularly among Northern Plains tribes, gave them tactical advantages that neither the Spanish nor the Americans could match. They were the greatest cavalry the world has perhaps ever seen: ruthless, efficient, and creatively violent in combat. It was the Comanche that frustrated the expansion of the restless Republic of Texas, and the decades-long war between the two helped define both civilizations. During and immediately after the Civil War, the Comanche Empire expanded its territorial influence across Texas and posed a legitimate threat to American expansion. An 1868 treaty, meant to bring the Comanche into Indian Territory, was largely a failure, a consequence of U.S. treaty negotiators' complete misunderstanding of the Comanche's decentralized political structure. Some bands settled in Oklahoma, but most remained on the Texas and New Mexico prairies and even opened lucrative new markets in stolen Texas cattle.

In 1871, the United States launched an insurgency military campaign to take the Comanche down. Its multipronged guerilla strategy was necessary because the Comanche were too powerful, too entrenched in their strange homeland, too connected, and too wealthy for the U.S. Army to attack head on. A relentless harassment campaign against the Comancheros, who traded horses and hides with the Comanche in eastern New Mexico, was the first step, and by 1873, the western markets of Comanchería lay in shambles. The next year, the U.S. Army, led by Nelson Miles, launched a perpetual badgering campaign against the Comanche up on the High Plains. Operating out of a series of forts that bordered the edges of Comanchería in Texas, soldiers attacked camps and caravans not to claim territory but to disrupt routines and destroy seasonal camps. The idea was to keep the Comanche on the move and make the Fort Sill Reservation the only respite. More and more bands, weary and hungry, trickled into Indian Territory.

In 1874, a large Comanche offensive ended in disaster. A 700-strong party of Comanche and Kiowa led by young war chief Quanah Parker and a spiritual leader named Esatai took off from the reservation in June, determined to reclaim the Llano. Their first target was Adobe Walls, an abandoned trading post on Bent Creek in present-day Hutchinson County, where a group of buffalo hunters were holed up. Attacking a group of professional marksmen bunkered down in an adobe structure with three-feet-thick walls of dried Texas clay and laid in with ungodly amounts of ammo and guns powerful enough to take down a 1,500-pound buffalo proved to be, not surprisingly, a mistake. The yellow paint that the young men had smeared all over their bodies to make them bulletproof didn't work. Fifteen lay dead and several more, including Quanah, were wounded after the first assault on the compound. After a couple of days of siege and a few more reckless charges on the buildings, the group scattered. Quanah and about 400 followers took off for the south. In September, the Fourth U.S. Cavalry, led by a brilliant and perpetually angry colonel named Ranald Mackenzie, launched a daring and dangerous predawn raid on several bands that had set up winter camp at the bottom of Palo Duro Canyon. The men charged into the campgrounds, and rather than follow the Comanche and Kiowa who fled deeper into the canyon, Mackenzie simply ordered the destruction of the camp's winter supplies (food, blankets, and teepees) along with all but 300 of its 1,400-pony remuda. Over the next few weeks, those who had hoped to winter in the canyon had no choice but to make their way to Fort Sill. Quanah Parker and his warriors spent a few dispirited months wandering the old trails into Mexico and showed up in Indian Territory in May.

If this is a book about twentieth-century conservative politics, which it assuredly is, a reader might be wondering why it begins with stories of cartography, conquistadors, and Comanchería. There are two reasons: space and time. This large area, controlled by the Comanche, dismissed by American explorers, and rejected by the Spanish, is unique in that for most of its history it has been defined by its geology and geography far more than its politics or economics or populations. Its internal environmental logic demands imagination, technology, and ambition to make it work for humans. The Comanche, thanks to the technology of the horse, which collapsed space and time, were the first to successfully harness the energy of the Llano's flora and fauna and create a new kind of economy and empire. As they exited its stage, suddenly one of the last great "blank spaces" on the American map was now open for settlement, another chance for another people to bring creative energy and tech together and reimagine the Despoblado.[10]

Which brings us to time. While the rest of the nation had grown up around it, negative perceptions of this part of the world and the reality of Comanche control had kept Europeans and Americans out of this 100,000-square-mile section of North America. Almost 350 years after Coronado, a century after the establishment of the United States, 40 years after Texas independence, here was a place the size of Alabama and North Carolina combined without a road, a store, a house. It was a place, in the white American mind at least, without a history. A place whose story had not even begun.

So our story of how West Texas became the most conservative place in America starts with a blank page.

BOOK ONE

WONDERLAND

The Utopia of a modern dreamer must needs differ in one fundamental aspect from the Nowheres and Utopias men planned before Darwin quickened the thought of the world. . . . The Modern Utopia must be not static but kinetic, must shape not as a permanent state but as a hopeful stage, leading to a long ascent of stages. Nowadays we do not resist and overcome the great stream of things, but rather float upon it. We build now not citadels, but ships of state.

H. G. WELLS, 1905

I

THE RISE AND FALL OF THE CATTLE KINGDOM

We were solitary adventurers in a great land as fresh and new as a spring morning, and we were free and full of the zest of darers.

When the ranch is in peace, no other life is as perfect.

CHARLES GOODNIGHT

Once established on the Fort Sill Reservation, Quanah Parker proved a smart and savvy politician. Within just three years he was recognized as the head of the Comanche and was able to negotiate permission to lead a small band of hunters out onto the Panhandle Plains for a buffalo hunt. Setting out in a bitterly cold March in 1878, the party crossed two hundred miles of barren plains before finally arriving at Palo Duro Canyon's eastern rim. They saw no buffalo along the way. Strange. Peering into the canyon, the party was stunned. Where buffalo should have been were only hundreds of rangy lowing longhorns. Surprise turned to anger. The warriors charged to the bottom of the canyon and began slaughtering cattle.

Watching the carnage from the canyon's opposite rim was a small group of terrified cowboys. They didn't hang around long before hightailing it back to ranch headquarters. "Indians are coming," they breathlessly warned the boss, "in considerable numbers." The man who ran the ranch, legendary cattleman Charles Goodnight, mounted his fastest horse and flew down the canyon to stop Quanah and his band. He arrived at a bloodbath; forty beeves lay butchered on the canyon floor, its brown dust soaked in red. The Comanche were, as Goodnight remembered, "in an ugly mood." The rancher calmly approached the party and offered parley at his home at dawn.[1] A few hours later, Goodnight found himself sitting in a giant circle surrounded by angry and well-armed warriors. He did his best to explain that he didn't know where the buffalo had all gone, as he had driven them from the canyon two years earlier.[2] He left out the part about how buffalo hunters had practically wiped the beasts off the face of the earth. Parley was reached. The Comanche were free to hunt for buffalo on Goodnight's range, and in exchange they would not kill Goodnight or his men or any more cattle than they needed to eat. The Comanche lingered in the Panhandle for a few dispiriting days before limping back to Fort Sill. They never saw a buffalo.[3]

The Goodnight-Quanah meeting is one of the great legends of the American West; at the bottom of the achingly beautiful Palo Duro Canyon, the great Comanche leader passes control of West Texas to the great American rancher. Literally and figuratively, the past of the Indian and buffalo peacefully gives way to the future of ranchers and cattle. A perfect Turnerian segue captured in a single identifiable moment.[4] The summit also fits a modern historical narrative: as the final act in those stories of the industrial annihilation of the bison, the state-sponsored destruction of Plains Indians, and the opening scene in the tale of how the western plains were transformed into one of the world's most profitable, productive, and ruthlessly exploitive sites of corporate agriculture. I would suggest yet another way to understand the importance of the moment—as a transition from one culture that had figured out how to exploit the limited resources of the Despoblado to another. From an environmental and economic standpoint, this transition perhaps suggests more continuity than drastic change, a middle chapter in the larger story about the constant reimagining of landscape, energy, space, technology, commerce, and culture in West Texas. Goodnight, and the ranchers who followed him to the Panhandle, wanted what the Comanche had built: an economic empire built from a land no one else wanted.

I

In 1876, when Charles Goodnight, the Panhandle's first white settler, drove a small herd of 1,600 cattle into Palo Duro Canyon, he was alone, smack-dab in the middle of the last great blank space in America. The nearest military fort was ten days away. The nearest supply depot three weeks. The Despoblado was even emptier than it had been when Coronado crossed it three centuries earlier. Goodnight was hoping (even banking) on it staying that way. The odds were with him: since the days of Coronado, white observers spoke in near unanimity about that part of the world—"civilized" people just couldn't live here. Americans were a forest and river and farming people. They were never going to settle a vast grassland with no trees, no rivers, and no rain. Goodnight saw what they couldn't; rather than a terrifying empty prairie, he gazed on an ocean of grass, the biggest pasture in the country, maybe the world, big enough and rich enough to support enough cattle to feed that world. But first, he would have to reinvent one of humankind's oldest industries.

For centuries and everywhere, stock raising had always been local: herders operated on society's geographic fringes where they could count on cheap and abundant land and still walk their product to local markets.[5] Goodnight, however, was a disrupter. He and the other ranchers who would soon follow him into these newly opened prairies saw the chance to scale up this ancient industry, to imagine a new business model. Together they would raise hundreds of thousands of cattle on millions of acres thousands of miles from markets. They would take advantage of an expanding railroad system, a newly industrialized form of meat packing, and an exploding and concentrated set of consumers to transform beef production. Costs were so low, and prices so high, that Goodnight could calculate something close to a 100 percent profit every season.

Rather than seeing Goodnight and the other pioneer ranchers through a gauzy lens of fawning nostalgia, I would suggest we think about that first ranching class in West Texas in more contemporary terms—they were entrepreneurs. They revolutionized an industry and created an entire culture to service it. They took over most of western Texas and most of the prairie lands of the rest of North America. In less than a generation, they transformed the middle third of the continent into a Cattle Kingdom. They were bold and reckless, and their adventures would, as we shall see, end in heartbreak and economic and environmental collapse. The tenets that guided ranchers in those years were those found in all entrepreneurial cultures: an internal suspicion of outsiders and a built-in antistatism; a competitive and self-reliant ethos buffered by a clear-eyed recognition of the value of industrial cooperation; a rough commitment to equality of opportunity; and an enthusiasm for experimentation and risk taking coupled with a stoic acceptance of luck, good and bad. They were, in their own minds and as described by most of the chroniclers since, highly individualistic. For most of them, stock raising was just one path to wealth, and they tended to dabble in all kinds of ventures: real estate, media, banking, transportation, law, mining, pretty much anything but farming or heavy industry. They were dealmakers who saw their industry as *the* foundation of regional wealth. And they built West Texas in their image.

Goodnight, arguably the best rancher in American history, was the best of them, standing comfortably among the pantheon of western legends. In Texas, he ranks with the gods, the "Father of the Panhandle."[6] His life story really was the stuff of legend. It started when he was just ten years old and rode a horse bareback from Illinois to Texas in 1845. When he was a boy, local Caddo Indians taught him how to hunt, trap, and track. He started his first ranch when he was still a teenager. He perfected the chuck wagon, blazed cattle trails, and was among the first Texans to raise cattle in the Cross Timbers. He served in the Frontier Regiment during the Civil War and supplied the military with beef. No one built a better fence. No one knew cattle or the country as well. He founded schools, towns, colleges, and banks. He experimented with breeding, crops, and irrigation. He was married to his childhood sweetheart for fifty-six years. Goodnight's private herd was used to reintroduce bison to Yellowstone National Park.[7] He was an inaugural member of the Cowboy Hall of Fame.[8]

With his thick, shaggy hair, pointed beard, and barrel chest, Goodnight looked like a human buffalo. His black-eyed stare could make Phil Ivey blink. He was a quiet man by nature, and his primary form of verbal communication was mumbling streams of vulgarities around a cigar jammed in the corner of his mouth. As a boss he was a demanding perfectionist who would tolerate neither laziness nor insubordination. But he never asked his employees to do any job that he would not do himself (usually better). And hidden by the short-tempered and frightening exterior was as savvy and scientific a businessman as any in the American West.[9]

He had been pushing innovation on the industry since the 1850s. Along with ranching icons C. C. Slaughter and Oliver Loving, he developed the range system that allowed cattlemen to operate on the very edges of the world. Recognizing new and critical markets emerging in the mining towns and military forts in New Mexico and Colorado, he blazed vital trails to reach them. After the Civil War left the Texas cattle business in shambles, with 4 million head scattered, corrals and fences destroyed, and ranch houses burned, he not only rebuilt his stake but reestablished the industry, one new market and one brutal drive at a time. In 1869, he left Texas for Colorado to establish a ranching operation in the rich Arkansas River valley. He put everything he had learned about ranching into his Rock Canyon Ranch, a model operation with upgraded herds, stone corrals, a stone barn (which still stands), irrigated hay fields, and an orchard. Clearing almost $10,000 a year (the equivalent of $250,000 in 2024), he poured his profits back into the ranch and used the rest to build up Pueblo, the nearest town. He started a demonstration farm, founded the local bank, opened a flour mill, established a meat-packing business, and sold commercial real estate. He even helped finance Pueblo's new opera house. He was the very model of a successful and diversified western rancher and investor.

But even the greatest cowman of his day was not immune to the Panic of 1873, the worst economic depression of the century. "It wiped me off the face of the earth," he once said.[10] Goodnight went broke and was forced to sell off or sign off his assets for pennies on the dollar, leaving him with nothing but a small herd of 1,600 cattle. At thirty-eight, America's best rancher had to start over, again. He gambled on the Panhandle, literally staking his life on his belief that the Comanche were on the reservation for good. Right after the spring thaw in 1876, he pushed his herd straight into the Comanche's traditional winter campgrounds in Palo Duro Canyon, just miles from the site of Mackenzie's raid eighteen months earlier. He wanted the canyon for the same reason that the Comanche had: it was the best-watered and best-sheltered location for three hundred miles in any direction—in the middle of the best grasslands anywhere. What Goodnight was proposing, namely, building an industry in a new location with no established transportation, financial, or political infrastructure, was going to require a great deal of creativity. And money.

John Adair was probably the most hated man in Ireland. Although educated to become a diplomat, he was ill-suited to a life governed by polite words and gentle compromise. Landlordism was more his style. He built a massive fortune in real estate by buying up landed estates during the potato famine on the cheap and wrenching every shilling out of the

Charles Goodnight as a young man.

peasants on his land. When they couldn't keep up with his outrageous rent increases, he had them thrown in the street by actual goon squads. In Derryveagh on St. Patrick's Day in 1861, his "crowbar brigade" launched a three-day eviction campaign that left 244 people homeless; 159 were children. And that was just to make room for his private hunting preserve.[11] Once the estates were producing again, "Black Jack," as the locals called him, sold them off for large profits. Looking to get into finance, he came to the States in 1866 and set up a shop selling commercial paper at 10 percent. It was backed by his own millions and a generous line of credit from London banks at 4 percent. America's latest venture capitalist found Gilded Age America a welcoming place. Adair dined in the finest establishments and stayed in elite hotels. He met his wife at a Republican Party fundraiser, and the U.S. Army gave him a personal escort on a western hunting trip. In 1875, lured by the incredible stories of instant wealth and the silver rush in Colorado, Adair opened a bank in Denver. And met Goodnight.

Goodnight had come to Denver looking to borrow around $30,000 and was willing to pay 18 percent interest. He made his pitch to Adair for the Palo Duro ranch: sheltered, watered, easy to defend, and the best grass in the country. Adair, familiar with Goodnight's reputation for making money, had been looking to add cattle to his portfolio. After a tour of the Palo Duro site, Adair proposed that the men become partners. Much has been made of the ruthlessness of the deal, and understandably so: In exchange for Adair's financial backing, Goodnight would put up his herd, secure the site, hire and manage the staff, fight off "hostile Indians" and criminals, protect his cattle and range from competitors, expand the herd, figure out a way to get it to market, and basically run a business three weeks from anywhere. The ranch name would bear Adair's initials and Goodnight had to submit regular detailed reports. For his part, Adair put up the necessary capital for Goodnight to start and run the "JA Ranch." He also agreed to pay Goodnight an annual salary that instantly made the rancher a wealthy man. It was a five-year deal. After Adair had recouped his entire investment plus 10 percent, the two men would split the remaining profits, with Goodnight getting a third. If the operation went bust, Goodnight would be left with nothing—even his starter herd would go to Adair. But, for the cost of 1,600 cattle and his expertise, he would have the opportunity to build a ranch the way he thought it should be built.

This was a typical sort of arrangement in an entrepreneurial culture. Especially for a startup. Goodnight, leveraging his reputation and experience, pitched a new enterprise to an investor, and Adair constructed an agreement that would limit his risk and maximize his return. If it worked the way Goodnight suggested that it would, they would make a ton of money. And they did.

By the mid-1870s, one fundamental feature of the new model for the cattle business had already emerged—the range system, a creatively practical approach for stock raising on the distant peripheries of Texas. Emerging first in the Cross Timbers of central North Texas in the 1850s, where Goodnight and others had first set up shop, the range model was a twist on the Spanish mega-ranch as it was practiced across the Southwest. In this model, cattle are free to wander across huge swaths of territory, lightly tended by a small and mobile workforce. Spanish ranches were part of massive land grants bestowed on individuals by the crown, but in Texas, ranching was conducted on the millions of acres of unclaimed public lands. Twice a year, cattle were gathered to brand newborn calves and castrate young bulls. After the fall roundup, a selection of stock would be taken to market.[12] Cattle, normally docile and lazy creatures with huge dietary needs, could be expected to stay within a particular range. With good grass and a reliable water source, they don't wander far, rarely more than eight miles, which was how ranchers measured a claim—eight miles in every direction from a good spring or reliable creek. Ranchers filed their claim with an announcement in a newspaper. Not surprisingly, inventory loss was acute: bad weather, theft, wolves, cows wandering off. It was thus a business that needed to accommodate a scale that could withstand such losses, and it did. Ranchers claimed humungous ranges, tens or hundreds of thousands of acres. And they ran thousands and thousands of head of cattle.[13] They hired mostly restless young men as seasonal labor to keep track of their herds.

Designed to operate on distant frontiers, on land years from the surveyor's glass and unfit for the plow, the range system was based solely on the geographic realities of the cattle business. It worked like this: Upon arriving in a new country, often recently vacated by Plains tribes, a rancher scouted the land, looking for a specific physical "range" where his cattle would graze. He would also be on the lookout for a good place for a ranch headquarters. The system centered on access to reliable water. Once the rancher found his ranch, cattle would be moved onto the range and legal notice would be placed in surrounding newspapers. The whole enterprise held together through an explicit, if legally dubious, agreement between ranchers to respect the boundaries of each range. Violations could and did end in violence. It absolutely depended on the integrity and cooperation of every rancher and cowboy to make it work. And it did. Well enough for Goodnight to stake his new ranch and the future of the cattle business on the model.

But Adair had been clear: the ranch must own at least several thousand acres outright. A landlord at heart, he was understandably leery about the long-term viability of a property with no title, so Goodnight had to find out who owned the land he wanted, not as easy as it might sound. The legal status of a particular parcel of Panhandle land in 1876 was an abstract notion at best. For decades, perpetually broke Texas had used its western lands as a kind of bond, rewarding unspecified and unsurveyed land certificates to encourage railroad building or other large-scale infrastructure projects and in lieu of pensions to veterans.[14]

Land scrip for territory controlled by the Comanche, and by all accounts uninhabitable, created, not surprisingly, a high-risk futures market for aggressive investors. Texas land scrip traded for less than ten cents an acre at a time when Kansas farmland sold for over a hundred times that amount. Among the biggest players in the market was the lawyer/surveyor team of Jot Gunter and William Munson, which had recently started working Panhandle claims. They met with Goodnight and spirited negotiations began. The brokers had the scrip and the surveying equipment, and Goodnight "wanted that canyon!" The two sides settled on a deal wherein Goodnight agreed to purchase 12,000 acres at 75 cents an acre. But, once the terms were struck, Goodnight unveiled his "crazy quilt" strategy. At no time had the rancher agreed to purchase 12,000 contiguous acres, as Gunter and Munson had assumed. Instead, Goodnight selected a bunch of isolated but choice parcels where he could establish various ranges. "Every good ranch in the country, every place a man was liable to come, I took."[15] Goodnight ran Gunter and Munson ragged pointing out his parcels. A few hundred shaded and watered acres here, a few hundred there, and a nice big spread between the forks of the Prairie Dog River as it snaked into Palo Duro Canyon. Goodnight did not bother with any of the thousands of acres between his new holdings, because he knew that under the range system, they were his anyway. His 12,000-acre quilt netted a ranch ten times that size. Over the next few years after his range was established, Goodnight snapped up the acres in between his holdings for pennies. By the early 1880s, the JA owned a third of a million acres outright and had a range almost twice that big. How the wily cowpuncher put it over on the city slicker lawyers became essential to the Goodnight legend, but it's also a good example of the kind of dealmaking common in entrepreneurial cultures. Even at 75 cents an acre, Goodnight was paying way above any demonstrated market value, guaranteeing Gunter and Munson a spectacular windfall. He got what he wanted, and they got what they wanted. The three businessmen would collaborate on real estate and cattle deals for years afterward. Munson even became Goodnight's closest neighbor when he bought the T Anchor Ranch (only forty miles away).[16]

Within five years of the founding of the JA, there were twenty-four other huge ranches and half a million cattle in the Panhandle. Ranges spread across every valley of the Canadian, Pease, Red, and Brazos rivers. Smaller outfits worked pocket-sized ranges in the creeks and breaks and draws. Railroad cattle towns moved closer every year and the demand for beef rose. Texas, looking to cash in on this surge of interest in its western lands, offered them up at 50 cents an acre in what was known as the Fifty Cent Act. Ranches, led by the largest operations, bought up millions, but the range system remained intact. Cows outnumbered people 200 to 1.

II

With no real government to speak of, the political economy of cattle country worked under an extralegal system called the cow custom or the code of the West, of which the range and land policies were just a part.[17] Often misinterpreted, misapplied, or wrapped up in misty-eyed nostalgia and manufactured myth, the code was a set of unwritten rules and expectations that governed personal behavior, defined and defended physical space and property, and regulated business transactions—a set of industry standards wrapped up in a package of societal norms.[18] It also reflected American Victorian beliefs, especially concerning issues of race, gender, and class. The code/custom also, as in many new business climates, was vaguely utopian, especially among those who viewed cattle country as an antidote and alternative to the industrial and urban East or a way to preserve the ideals of the independent and egalitarian society of previous frontiers.[19]

The code reflected its entrepreneurial origins with its openness to innovation, acceptance of failure, and focus on personal responsibility. Its intense individualism was slightly balanced by a recognition of collective goals. In the decades before any actual state power operated in the region, the code served as its legal and political system, enforced and interpreted through local stock associations. Without almost universal acceptance of their authority, the cattle business simply could not have operated. And it's not as if the philosophy that undergirded the cow code was some alien construct. The opposite was true: it was based on widely accepted notions about the purposes and organization of the political economy.[20]

When it came to personal behavior, everyone was expected to be honest, self-reliant, tough, and hardworking and to assume everyone they met shared those qualities. Polite hospitality in such a sparsely populated country was essential, and travelers could expect a welcome, a meal, and a place to bed down at any ranch or cowboy camp. On the job, men were expected to maintain self-control in word, deed, and habit, and women were to be good-natured, tough, and motherly. The code also promoted a coarse brand of social equality (for white men); status was earned by skill on the job and modesty. No loudmouths or show-offs or hotheads would ever be promoted to Top Hand, no matter their skill. Regardless of wealth, respect for a rancher still depended on their understanding of the business, including knowing how to cowboy. The regulations surrounding interpersonal behavior were meant to reduce the propensity for deadly violence among a population of young, armed, single men. Custom demanded that men exhibit an outward calm and cheerful demeanor, especially when dealing with strangers. They were also expected to pull their share and be brave and true to their word, thus eliminating many of the catalysts that could lead to violence.[21] Most ranches, including Goodnight's, had regulations against alcohol, gambling, and fighting, further reducing potential sources of contention. That said, an extralegal form of dueling allowed men with unreconcilable differences to fight to the death, with little fear of criminal charges. Even if brought to court, the code dictated that juries and judges acquit men acting in self-defense or fighting on equal ground. It was, as cowboy chronicler Eugene Manlove Rhodes described it, a "queer, lop-sided, topsy-turvy, jumbled and senseless code—but a code for all that."[22]

Protecting access to opportunity (again, for white males exclusively) was also built into the ranching system, both in spirit and policy. Ranchers lent their cooperation and support to their ambitious and hardworking employees who sought to work their way into the property-owning class. In those early years, the cattle business worked as a variation on the republican vision of a free society where men had the opportunity to accumulate property and practice equality. It was an attempt, as folklorist Mody Boatright, who grew up on a West Texas ranch, put it, "to organize a society in which human needs would be superior to special privilege."[23]

In an almost exclusively male environment in cattle country's first two decades, traditional notions of masculinity were baked into every aspect of the culture. A property owner with land and cattle was a catt*leman*; his employees were cow*boys*. The former was expected to invest in the industry and take responsibility for the land and its environs. The

*Molly Goodnight as a
young woman.*

latter were supposed to value the freedom that came with seasonal work.
Growing into manhood meant sacrificing freedom and making a stake
in the country. Women were stuck in a stunted Victorian stage of femi-
ninity and pedestals, but with one important addition—the ranch wife.
In cattle country, women had few opportunities to take part in the Cult
of True Womanhood; practicing purity, piety, and submissiveness and
maintaining a proper domestic home were simply unobtainable goals
in a dugout or ranch cabin tucked away in a draw twenty miles from
the nearest dwelling. Instead, a ranch wife was to be tough, tender, and
friendly, a surrogate mother and actual nurse to cowboys, a lover of
nature, and a hard-headed businesswoman.[24] Molly Goodnight was the
model. For years, from her home at JA headquarters she took care of
hundreds of cowboys, sewing their clothes and stitching their wounds,
reading them stories, and feeding them meals, nursing them back to
health from broken limbs and snakebites. Taking care of their money

and letters from home. She also had a business to run. With Charlie away for weeks at a time, it was Molly who tended to the everyday operation of the JA, making sure fences were mended and calves tended. She kept the books and ran several of her own businesses on the side. The famous Goodnight buffalo herd that would reinstate bison into Yellowstone was born from her careful raising of orphaned buffalo calves.[25]

While racial diversity tended to be the norm on most ranching frontiers with Latino, Native, and African American cowboys making up a large percentage of those punching cows, in the Panhandle most cowboys were white, and southern.[26] The handful of Latino families that had settled the region and were raising sheep near Tascosa were run off once ranching gained a foothold. On the few ranches that hired Black cowboys, only those truly exceptional at their job could win multiyear contracts and would never be considered for a Top Hand position.[27] As one longtime Black cowboy said later: "If it weren't for my damned old black face, I'd have been boss of one of these [XIT] divisions long ago."[28]

For white men, an equality of opportunity was built into the system; thanks to certain provisions in the code, a man could rise or fall based on his skill, willingness to work hard, intelligence, and luck. Low-cost legal methods to enter the ranching class were available to just about anyone. A remnant of pre–Civil War "cow catching" days of the business, Texas law stated that any calf not following a branded mother or any adult animal without a brand was considered unclaimed property, literally a "maverick." The animals were free to the first person lucky enough to find it, catch it, and brand it. Plenty of motivated cowboys spent their down time scouring the draws and breaks for stock that had managed to escape the branding iron, which they could use to either build a herd or sell off for a few fun nights in town. Cowboys could also ask for part of their wages in cattle, and some accommodating ranchers even gave them a wholesale rate. Most of the big ranchers allowed cowboys or even neighbors to run a few cattle on their range, what was called a shirttail herd. With a sharp stick and soft ground, a young man could calculate how a single bull and half a dozen cows could be a herd of fifty or sixty in just a few years. Some shrewd trading, a nice range, a couple of profitable drives—the chance to become a legitimate rancher was within reach. (And we should not be surprised when some men lived under a cloud of suspicion when their herds grew at a rate that defied basic arithmetic.)[29] For ranchers, these kinds of incentives helped them keep a

The Amarillo Daily News *captioned this photo "The Most Notable Group of Pioneers ever Assembled" when it was taken in 1925. Charles Goodnight is seated in the middle. T. D. Hobart is standing third from the left.*

workforce of responsible and hardworking cowboys, providing stability and leadership and, in time, building the industry and territory with such men.

For years, the Panhandle Stock Association (PSA) of Texas, formed in 1880, was the only political structure in that part of the world. It was one of the first cattlemen's groups anywhere. And it was open to every rancher, "whether he had one cow, ten cows, or many cattle." Goodnight, its founder and first president, insisted on it.[30] Its only real purpose was to tend to the collective needs of ranchers. It hired stock detectives to cut down on cattle theft (including the group that tracked down Billy the Kid), maintained a brand book, and published a range description guide. It organized Donley County so that ranchers could have a court to try cattle rustlers. It kept famed frontier lawyer Temple Houston on retainer. It organized roundups and drives and worked out trails and health standards. It pushed innovation like breeding programs, fencing, underground water exploration and exploitation, and experimentation with forage crops. It built the Panhandle's first school and hundreds of miles of drift fences to protect its winter grasses from cattle wandering down from the north. It kept its southern borders safe from potential diseased cattle through its "Winchester Quarantine." It lobbied in Austin on behalf of Panhandle ranchers and pushed its main message that the region was suitable *only* for cattle raising.

In addition to control of the levers of political and economic power, ranchers, as the founders of this new society, also enjoyed an almost unprecedented cultural power. What cultural geographer Wilbur Zelinsky identified as the Doctrine of First Effective Settlement meant that the first group of people who create a "viable and self-perpetuating society" would have an outsized impact on the society and culture of that place for generations.[31] But West Texas ranchers did more than just create a society; they controlled it for decades. These "colonizers" guided and controlled immigration into the region well into the 1920s: land sales, town sites, railroad routes, and road building. They controlled the real estate companies, the banks, and the media. As founders and patrons of the settler and historical societies, they controlled the official mechanisms for constructing historical memory, literally writing the history of West Texas with themselves as the heroes of the greatest frontier story ever told. Their entrepreneurial values and their primitive moral code would serve as a foundation of the political ideology of all of West Texas: entrepreneurial, individualistic, hypercapitalist, antistatist, and lodged in Victorian Era ideas about race and gender. They had effectively built, as historian Walter Prescott Webb, who grew up in West Texas, described, "a world within itself, with a culture all its own . . . complete and self-satisfying."[32]

III

The first challenge to the world the pioneer ranchers built was a sudden and enormous invasion of investment capital. In the early 1880s, it looked to the world as if Texas ranchers were printing their own money. The by now 700,000-acre JA Ranch was worth half a million dollars. Typical annual profits for well-run outfits hovered at close to 100 percent. The industry had spread from Texas to Alberta, 400,000 square miles of ranch country with solid transportation routes and hungry markets. In good years, it was as can't-miss a business as one was likely to find. A breathless financial media reported the industry. Even staid and responsible British outlets like the *Times*, the *Economist*, and the *Fortnightly Review* described western cattle as a necessary part of any shrewd gentleman's portfolio. Early versions of the sort of investment strategy guides that now crowd airport bookstores abounded. Especially popular was James S. Brisbin's *The Beef Bonanza; or, How to Get Rich on the Plains* from 1881. It promised a 10 percent annual return and doubling of investment every five years. Another popular guide, *Cattle Raising on the Plains* (1885), declared: "No business in the world has brighter prospects, both as to safety in investment and in the amount of profit it will secure."[33] Prominent investors abounded: Prime Minister Lord Rosebery (Archibald Primrose) and Charles Francklyn (who also founded Con-Ed and was the son-in-law of the founder-owner of the Cunard Steamship Line) were big in the Texas cattle business. The investments of the Earl of Aberdeen and the Lord of Tweedmouth were reported to have been made on behalf of Queen Victoria herself. The "mania for American ranching" was the biggest financial story of the time.[34] Cattle companies, led by some of the wealthiest and best-connected investors in London, Edinburgh, and New York, were all the rage. They called it the Beef Bonanza.

But Texas ranches weren't like other investments: there was no stock or shares to purchase; there were only dozens and dozens of independent outfits of all shapes and sizes operating a hundred miles from anywhere. Seeking to get in at scale, investors had two main options, both expensive. The first was to send a representative to Texas who would, relying on the testimony of experts in range grasses, locate an appropriate site, hire a capable and competent manager, buy a herd, purchase (or lease) the land under question (or buy the range rights), stock the ranch with the necessary equipment and supplies, and hire a labor force. This took time. The second method was faster but even more costly: a company representative would head to Texas and start buying up existing ranches lock, stock, and barrel until they ran out of money. Between 1881 and 1885, nine investment syndicates spent $8 million setting up Texas land and cattle companies (about $15 billion in 2024).[35] One by one they snapped up the pioneer ranches. The LIT, the LE, the LX, the Turkey Track, the Quarter Circle T, the Matador, the Rocking Chair. The Bonanza led to an immediate spike in both land and cattle prices. During one buying spree, the Prairie Land and Cattle Company was paying close to retail for its cattle, almost $30 a head. By 1885, the West Texas cattle business had all the looks of an investment bubble.

For the entrepreneur ranchers who had just settled the region, the Bonanza meant a huge windfall. The Ikard and Harrold brothers cashed in for $1.5 million. William Lee sold his half of the LE Ranch for almost $200,000. The always savvy George W. Littlefield held out long enough to scoop up $250,000 for a few thousand head and his range rights. Offered $175,000 for his Quarter Circle T Ranch in 1881, Thomas Bugbee sold the next year for twice that amount. Hank Campbell, who had built up the Matador Ranch to some 40,000 head of cattle and 100,000 acres (and whose range was a million acres), sold out for a cool $1.25 million. These men took the cash and invested in railroads, real estate, banks, and towns. Some started new ranches in calmer markets.[36]

Doomed from the start, the new syndicate ranches suffered from a fundamental misunderstanding of how and why the range model worked. Low costs in production and maintenance along with a lack of government oversight were big draws for investors, but the major attraction to them was the chance to correct what they saw as managerial inefficiencies in labor, inventory, and land use. Run properly, companies like the Prairie Land and Cattle Company believed, Texas ranches could produce even greater profits. What the syndicates failed to recognize was the symbiotic interconnectedness of the entire system. Changing any variable in the calculus of the business could destroy it. Take inventory management, for example. For the independent rancher, the actual number of animals (or their market value) on his range was an abstract figure at best. Only when the cattle reached market could a concrete number or value be determined. Any premarket value of a herd was no more than a guess; there was just too much unpredictability in a business in which the inventory wandered the Texas prairies. But the investment-driven syndicates demanded actual numbers when they bought ranches. When faced with questions about herd size, ranchers estimated using what they called book count, a back-of-the-envelope accounting system that calculated original herd size, multiplied by projected reproduction rate, minus estimated losses. It wasn't much of a bookkeeping system, but it gave ranchers a rough sense of the financial health of their operation as they planned each season. British buyers (answering to stockholders obsessed with herd size) took the book count as an absolute.[37] And in every auditor's worst nightmare, the ranch managers sent from

England or Scotland to oversee the syndicate's Texas holdings adopted book count into their own bookkeeping, listing guesses as assets in their financial statements. Needless to say, the books were a mess when as much as 80 percent of a syndicate's inventory might exist only in the columns of company ledgers.

Or consider the syndicates and labor. The Cattle Kingdom was one of the most egalitarian cultures (again, for white men) in the Western world. The typical English investor (imagine the Dashwoods from *Sense and Sensibility*) had a difficult time relating to this aspect of the business. Visiting the ranch, their haughty digressions from the code were hilarious and potentially dangerous: calling cowboys "cow servants," inspecting the range from the back of a shaded carriage, putting their boots outside the door at night expecting them to be polished by morning. Worse were the policy changes. Treating the ranch as a private estate, syndicate ranchers assumed sovereignty over everything: the grass, the water, and every animal on it, branded or not. Forbidding hunting by cowboys, they even claimed the wildlife. The syndicates prohibited mavericking and shirttail herds. Out to control a growing industry, they had no interest in encouraging entry into the ranching class or creating potential competitors. Cowboys weren't future neighbors or colleagues but a disposable and transient workforce. The syndicates froze wages and let most of their cowboys go after the fall roundups and drives. The workers would have to reapply for their jobs every spring. Chuck and bunkhouse privileges for those passing through were eliminated.[38]

The only cowboy strike in the history of Texas was a direct response to syndicate policies. In 1883, cowboys from the LE, LS, LIT, T Anchor, and LX ranches went on strike just before the spring roundup. It didn't get very far; management never seriously considered strikers' demands, and the cowboys burned through their meager strike fund on liquor and prostitutes in only a couple of weeks.[39] But sides were drawn. Goodnight quit the Panhandle Stock Association over the actions of the syndicates. Smaller ranchers and cowboys fought back by launching a cattle-rustling offensive against syndicate ranches. "It wasn't considered any crime to brand a syndicate calf," as cowboy legend Bones Hooks later explained. Even Billy the Kid got involved. Operating out of Tascosa, he set up an elaborate cattle theft operation where he and his gang stole syndicate cattle and drove them to a chop shop just over the New Mexico line. By the time a posse got there, Billy was gone, the cattle butchered, the hides buried, and sides of beef were on wagons on the way to a mining camp or army fort. The *Tascosa Pioneer*, the self-appointed voice of agrarian settlement, lambasted the syndicates in every editorial. The Texas legislature began debating laws making land ownership by foreign corporations illegal. The federal government began investigations into the syndicate ranches' use of public and reservation lands.

Maybe worse, the world's financial press began to question the stability and viability of an industry dependent on land that companies didn't own and inventory that they couldn't control. Investment slowed. Cattle prices flatlined. Having grown dependent on rising prices and the expansion of the bubble to pay their dividends, syndicates like the Prairie were forced instead to use money from new investment rounds, turning land and cattle companies into Ponzi schemes.

IV

A second threat to the hegemony of the ranching class was a growing clamor in Texas for the state to more closely regulate its public lands. By the mid-1880s, thanks to gifts to railroads, land brokers like Gunter and Munson, and legislation like the Fifty Cent Act, 30 million acres of West Texas land had fallen into private hands. All the state had left of its once nation-sized public land holdings were the "school lands," as they were called. In yet another quirk of Texas land law, in its 1876 constitution, the state had divided its western lands into two categories: those for sale or settlement (which included the railroad and veteran lands) and an equal number of acres set aside as a future source of revenue for Texas public schools. The reserved "school lands" and the land for sale were arranged in a checkerboard pattern, in which every square measured a square mile. The idea was to thwart the accumulation of huge contiguous estates and encourage equity. Remember, however, that when these land laws were written, West Texas was nothing more than an "imagined space"; for all the control the state had over its western acres, they might as well have been on Mars.[40] And the school lands model had been determined long before the establishment of large-scale ranching had demonstrated a profitable and practical use for what most saw as worthless scrub. Ranchers paid zero attention to the checkerboard; the range model insisted on control of contiguous parcels of land defined only by access to water sources. Politically, the matter of the school lands was tied up in an enduring fantasy, held by many in the state legislature and by influential media figures, that West Texas would eventually fill up with productive small-scale freehold farmers, working 80- or 160-acre operations. No lack of demand for these sorts of farms or recognition of the reality of just how ill-suited West Texas was to this sort of agriculture could shake loose the fantasy of family farms stretching across the width and breadth of Texas. Soon came the demands that ranchers stop using the "children's grass."

In 1883, a group of legislators in Austin, known as the Granger Bloc, who represented the interests of small farmers mostly in the eastern part of the state, wrote up a new set of land laws that, accompanied by a mind-blowing new piece of technology, set off the first major political struggle in West Texas.[41] Meant to replace the giveaways of the Fifty Cent Act and curb the ambitions of the "bullionaires," along with perhaps encouraging settlement in the Panhandle and plains, the 1883 Land Laws opened millions of acres of the previously unobtainable school lands for sale.[42] The price was set at between $2 and $3 an acre with good terms and capped at a maximum of 4,480 acres.[43] Sales went nowhere; no one was interested in paying six times the previous price. And the only ones who might, the syndicates and giant independents, weren't interested in seven measly sections. Smaller operators weren't going to pay for something they were using for free, and cotton farmers weren't ready to move to the Great American Desert, no matter how cheap the land.[44] More interesting was the lease option. The 1883 Land Laws also offered long-term leases on the school lands for 4 cents an acre. To run the program, Texas created a new bureaucracy, the Texas Land Board (TLB), and named its ambitious and aggressive attorney general, John D. Templeton, as its head.

Ranchers like Goodnight saw the new lease option as a win-win-win. With ranchers gaining legal and long-term control over crucial pastureland, the law offered stability to the industry, would keep reckless and desperate farmers from going broke trying to turn the semiarid grasslands into cotton farms, and would pump millions of dollars into the Permanent School Fund. Leases would also allow the bigger outfits to take greater advantage of the potential for range management offered by barbed wire.

Considering the astonishing technological innovations of the time—radio, telephone, electric lights, internal combustion engines—few think about barbed wire. But Joseph Glidden's invention allowed for cheap, strong, easy-to-build fencing in a part of the world with no timber and where property boundaries measured in miles. It was, as the pitch went, "lighter than air, cheaper than dirt, and stronger than whiskey." Glidden himself operated a massive barbed-wire demonstration ranch outside Amarillo that enclosed 60,000 acres within 120 miles of wire. It was a godsend for the large ranches that could afford it; fences offered the chance to control breeding, manage pastures, keep out diseased cattle, even cut down on theft. And the more you fenced, the cheaper it got.[45]

Templeton's Land Board greedily envisioned a windfall: British-backed syndicates locked in a bidding war for the school lands would drive lease prices up, fill School Fund coffers, raise property values on remaining state land, and soak the rich. He dispatched surveying teams to the Panhandle, where they couldn't help but notice that cattlemen everywhere were hard at work building fences around the school lands. On Bid Day, bids and parcel descriptions poured into the TLB offices. But each parcel received only a single bid, for the minimum of 4 cents an acre. Across the region, ranchers simply bid on school lands they were already using. Those committed to the range didn't bid at all, but rather depended on custom (and the real potential for violence) to protect their holdings.[46] Templeton raged and rejected all the bids. He announced a second round, arbitrarily doubled the minimum bid to 8 cents an acre, and, perhaps as a club to hold over the ranchers' heads, warned that some of the better-watered sections might not be available to anyone in any circumstances. Then he demanded that a grand jury convene to bring charges against the ranchers for illegally fencing the school lands.[47]

The press had a field day, accusing the bullionaires and European aristocrats of establishing a modern feudal system on the prairies. The *Marlin Ball* said that the big ranchers were intent on creating "principalities, pashalics and baronates." The *Dallas Herald* agreed: the syndicates were striding across Texas with "the sway of lords."[48] Goodnight lawyered up and launched a media blitz of his own, giving interviews to reporters from all over the state. He explained that the ranchers were not against settlement. In fact, he said long-term leases on the school lands would spur immigration to the region. Again and again, he hammered home the idea that "there's more money for the cattleman in a fair lease than in free grass." He made a very public display of paying for the land he had bid on (and had already fenced): Goodnight and William Munson (by then the owner of the T Anchor) took out a $100,000 loan from an Austin bank, loaded the cash in a wheelbarrow, hired a porter, drew their pistols, and accompanied the money across the street to the TLB offices. Along with their attorneys, they forced the agent to accept the cash as rent for the school lands and to provide a receipt for their tender offer. Then they wheeled the cash back to the bank, paid a day's interest on the money, and retired to the hotel bar.

In December 1885, Templeton (who was also Texas attorney general, remember) ordered W. H. Woodman, the newly named district attorney for far northwest Texas, to prosecute Goodnight, Munson, and the other big ranchers for preemptively and illegally fencing the school lands. Woodman was always good for a show. A grandstander by nature, he cut quite a figure; he dressed impeccably, maintained an equally immaculate head of long, black hair, and spoke every word as if he were a Shakespearean actor. He even had his own catchphrase: he was "an Englishman by birth, a Virginian by education, and a Texan by the Grace of God."[49] The trial was a circus; the defendants were actually members of the grand jury and, eager to clear their names and settle the leasing issue, returned seventy-six indictments against themselves. The prosecuting attorney, Woodman, was the general counsel for the Panhandle Stock Association. Templeton, at the time, was in the midst of an effort to replace the district judge, Frank Willis, with his own man, who happened to be the defendants' attorney. And the jury was made up of cowboys who worked for the defendants.[50] Once the ranchers established that they had fenced only the land that they had bid on before the TLB changed the rules, the outcome was never in doubt. Judge Willis let the jury foreman drone on for a few minutes with "not guilty" verdict after "not guilty" verdict before dismissing the remaining of the seventy-six charges and throwing in a few digs at Templeton, who was in the courtroom.[51] Historian J. Evetts Haley, who knew the cattlemen better than anyone, believed that the entire affair established among these "conservative cowmen" a distrust of government and perpetual fear of an "arbitrary usurpation of power and vacillating policy."[52]

V

The industry collapsed shortly thereafter. An extended drought over much of Texas that began in fall 1883 dragged on for two years. Already under duress from the expansion of herds, the land was showing signs of overgrazing by summer 1884. Fences went up around many of the better pastures, shrinking available acreage for those still working a range. In late summer 1885, President Grover Cleveland ordered Texas cattlemen to remove tens of thousands of cattle from Indian Territory. Most ended up in the dried-out Panhandle.[53] By November, grass was chewed to the roots and cattle starved. Snowstorms started in December, and a wave of blue northers culminated in one of the worst winter storms in American history.[54] A massive low-pressure system formed just north of Texas on the sixth of January, luring extremely cold temperatures and snow from Canada. As the system moved south, temperatures dropped from the forties to below zero in a matter of hours. Fifty-mile-an-hour winds drove heavy snow into banks eight feet deep. Locomotives froze to the tracks and chickens froze solid. Ice formed on the Gulf of Mexico. Keeping the storm at their backs and bunched together against the cold, hundreds of thousands of cattle walked south until blocked by a fence or a draw. Too close to one another to retreat and with no way forward, they froze to death, stuck together like a box of peas in the freezer.[55] Half a decade of disorderly accounting meant no accurate number of the dead was possible, but the best estimates are around 200,000 head. Spring's warm winds carried the stench of rotting corpses for miles and for weeks.[56] Cowboys joked that they could walk across Texas on the bloated, half-frozen bodies. Malnourished and exhausted cattle dropped dead into late summer. The calf crop was a fraction of normal, and with weakened mothers unable to produce milk, few of even these calves survived. Some companies estimated losses at 90 percent.[57] The next winter brought more storms. They called it the Great Die-Up.[58] A popular cowboy song captured the horror:

I may not see a hundred
Before I see the Styx,
But, coal or ember, I'll remember
Eighteen eighty-six.

The stiff heaps in the coulee,
The dead eyes in the camp,
And the wind about, blowing fortunes out
As a woman blows out a lamp.[59]

With dividends to pay and inventory wiped out, the syndicates dumped cattle onto the market at a suicidal pace. Prices went into free-fall, as the average per hundred weight dropped 400 percent.[60] Most of the big British outfits closed shop, taking tremendous losses. With cattle and land prices at rock bottom, quite a few of the old entrepreneurial pioneer ranchers got back in the game and reinvented the industry once again. A new stock-raising model emerged, which required much less land and was built around barbed wire, windmills, pasturing, and the expansion of the nation's railroads into West Texas. More exciting, however, were ranchers' plans to convert millions of acres of prairie into salable units suitable for farming. They were going to turn the Cattle Kingdom into the Agricultural Wonderland.[61]

2
AGRICULTURAL WONDERLAND

... I listen long
To his domestic hum, and think I hear
The sound of that advancing multitude
Which soon shall fill these deserts. From the ground
Comes up the laugh of children, the soft voice
Of maidens, and the sweet and solemn hymn
Of Sabbath worshippers. The low of herds
Blends with the rustling of the heavy grain
Over the dark brown furrows. All at once
A fresher winds sweeps by, and breaks my dream,
And I am in the wilderness alone.

WILLIAM CULLEN BRYANT, 1832

Timothy Dwight Hobart was a respectable and tidy man, an upstanding young citizen of an equally respectable and tidy New England village, Berlin, Vermont. Hobart men and women had been spreading across New England founding tidy towns, settling tidy farms, and founding respectable schools and churches since 1635. Almost all of them were farmers, preachers, or teachers, or some combination of the three. Timothy was born in 1855, the son of a farmer and a schoolteacher. He started his own farm in his teens. At twenty-nine he was running his farm, supervising Berlin's one-room school, and handling the village's finances. He was single and still lived with his parents.

One day in 1882, T. D.'s cousin, Ira Hobart Evans, a flamboyant wheeler-dealer from one village over, blew in from Texas, spinning thrilling tales of daring railroad and real estate deals. Timothy sat spellbound. Within weeks, Berlin's favorite son and most important bureaucrat ditched the do-gooder life and lit out for Texas. Unlike the thousands of other young men heading west those years, seeking adventure on the trails or in the mountains, Timothy wasn't going to be a cowboy or gold seeker; he was going to sell real estate in the nation's most speculative market and on its wildest frontier.[1]

A self-taught surveyor, Hobart spent his first four years in Texas living out of a tricked-out wagon, bringing tidiness and respectability to the lands of West Texas. With his tripod, transit, leveling rod, and compass Hobart imposed the geometry of real estate onto the intractable prairie. Day after day, and week after week, he neatly tallied up the holdings of the New York and Texas Land Company (NY&TLC) in leather-bound survey books.[2] He probably knew that part of West Texas better than anyone, even Goodnight. In 1886, Hobart earned a promotion to sales and took up an office in Mobeetie, still little more than a market for buffalo hunters. He shared the space with flamboyant frontier lawyer Temple Houston.[3] Hobart was entrusted with a portfolio of a million acres. Within a decade, he had them all surveyed, leased, or sold. At forty-one, he was a real estate legend. And he was just getting started.

I

When Hobart opened his Mobeetie shop, the local economy was in free fall. Tens of thousands of cattle corpses rotted on the prairies, victims of the previous winter's Die-Up. Syndicate ranches were falling apart; cattle and land prices were plummeting. There could not have been a worse market for real estate anywhere in the United States. But Hobart saw only opportunity. Like Goodnight, who had arrived in the Panhandle a decade earlier, Hobart thought differently about cattle and land. Whether it was the years viewing Texas through a surveyor's lens and arranging the countryside into logical and salable shapes, or some inborn Puritan compulsion to bring order from the wilderness, or just the necessity of finding a way to sell land no one seemed to want anymore, Hobart imagined ranching's next logical step and, once again, the physical and cultural landscape of the Texas prairies was rearranged.

First, he reordered the way ranchers understood land. Men like Goodnight saw the prairies as geography—water, shelter, weather, grass, trails, distance and direction and time. Hobart saw geometry—quadrilaterals,

Standing behind the tripod he used to bring order to the Texas prairies, T. D. Hobart poses with the staff of the White Deer Land Company.

angles, and lines—a landscape ready to be snapped into place by wire, roads, and rail. Where ranchers saw valleys and creeks, Hobart saw pastures and ponds. Where ranchers saw ranges, Hobart saw real estate. The beauty (and profit) of the range model had been a combination of its flexible sense of scale, its minimums of expense and maintenance, and its creative employment of the grass as the region's only recognizable natural resource. Too much of its functionality, however, depended on a uniform acceptance of the industry's code and an assumption that the range model could operate freely for the foreseeable future. But state action, fencing, syndicate behavior, and a growing interest in agricultural settlement posed threats to the system even before the Die-Up. Remaining, however, was still a common wisdom that the plains were best suited for raising cattle and an entrepreneurial willingness to try a different model. That's where Hobart came in. Utilizing three essential pieces of technology, Hobart helped reinvent ranching, spur greater settlement, and once again reconfigure West Texas. What he promised was a new type of ranching, a cattle version of the homestead farm, an even more egalitarian and democratic version of the industry than the range model.

The key to the new system, known as stock farming, was the pasture, a measurable unit of grassland with reliable water. And the key to the pasture was barbed wire. While varying in size and shape, pastures were fenced units of land meant to carry an environmentally appropriate number of animals. Limiting animal movement allowed better range management and cut down on theft. At first, Hobart created big, almost range-sized pastures mostly for lease. With the steady income provided by those leases, he upgraded the NY&TLC lands into excellent well-watered and fenced pastureland: if there were streams on a property, he dammed them for stock ponds; if there were none, he put in windmills and stock tanks. He fenced and watered to order. He was creative with financing. Before long, Hobart was converting even committed range ranchers to a more systematic approach to land and water. Ranchers could create different pastures for different needs: one for horses, one for weaning calves, one for finishing steers, one for winter forage. Greater control of movement allowed for upgraded breeds like Angus or Hereford that grew fatter faster and whose beef was gaining popularity among American diners. Behind a fence, it was also easier to keep cattle fed in the winter and improve the health and increase the size of the spring calf crop. While an average market-bound range steer required around 50 acres of land, Hobart's pasture-raised cattle needed only 10.

Although Hobart had plenty of customers who leased humungous pastures of more than 100 sections, he heavily marketed much smaller family-run ranchettes of 4 to 8 sections, the livestock version of a quarter-section freehold farm. It wasn't just Hobart; stock farming was becoming the hot thing in Texas agriculture.[4] A 2,500- to 5,000-acre property was the ideal size for a family to run an independent operation. Stock farmers could grow their own forage, put in orchards and vegetable gardens, keep chickens, and even raise a small cash crop like cotton or wheat. By 1895, stock farming was so popular in the Panhandle that its state representative, Amarillo's W. B. Plemons, pushed through a new land policy for the disposal of West Texas's remaining public lands. The Plemons Four-Section Act awarded 2,500-acre family homesteads on generous terms—$1.50 an acre and 3 percent interest on a forty-year note.[5] That single piece of legislation, one longtime resident mused, was largely responsible for the "settlement of West Texas."[6] Settlers gobbled up five million acres.

It was the windmills that made stock farming work. Sitting atop the 174,000-square-mile Ogallala Aquifer, an underground lake stretching from Texas to Nebraska, Panhandle ranchers had access to a steady water source that rarely lay more than a hundred feet below them. Drilling a well and installing a windmill were relatively cheap—a couple of hundred bucks, including the rig.[7] And despite cowboys' constant complaints about having to climb the forty or fifty feet to grease them, windmills were easy to maintain.[8] On the windy plains, windmills provided a reliable source of water not only for stock but also for irrigating gardens and orchards. Some were even set up for limited household use. Best of all, a windmill could bring water anywhere, even up on the great flatlands that had been too far from reliable surface water to profitably ranch.[9]

Railroads were the last piece of the stock farm puzzle. When they began crisscrossing western Texas at the turn of the century, smaller ranchers who lacked the resources to stage long drives had an easy way to get cattle to market. Within just a day or two, they could drive their herds to the local railroad depot and transport them by train to Kansas City or Chicago. By 1910, almost every county within two hundred miles had a railway line that connected it to Amarillo, which became the biggest cattle market in the country. A big-shot rancher like George Littlefield could even convince a railroad to put a depot on his property. Providing more than just ease of transportation, the railroads helped ranchers fetch higher prices. By eliminating the long drive, they could keep steers fat right up to the day of sale.

Hobart left his position at the NY&TLC in 1903 and took charge of selling off the White Deer Lands, three quarters of a million acres that stretched across Gray, Roberts, Carson, and Hutchinson counties, all that remained of the ill-fated Francklyn Land and Cattle Company. Hobart went all in on stock farms, actively seeking to build "a colony of contented and prosperous stock farmers."[10] There was plenty of interest from local cowboys seeking to settle down, farmers from the east looking for the next big thing, and others intrigued by possibilities in the Panhandle. The "hunger" for these kinds of arrangements among the "landless multitudes" seemed, to Texas land commissioner Richard Hall, boundless.[11]

Unlike the villains who populate the pages of pulp Westerns, most Panhandle ranchers viewed stock farms with the cold calculation of a banker. Holding millions of cheap acres that they had scooped up from the state or railroads, many were eager to get into real estate. Speaking to Texas cattlemen at their annual meeting in 1887, the head of the Continental Cattle Company, W. E. Hughes, who just happened to also be a banker, laid it out clearly. "Gentlemen, the ranchman of the plains is fast passing away," he told them. With rising land values, growing populations, and disappearing wild grasses, ranchers had to convert to stock farming or "cease to exist." The rancher had "redeemed the lands from savage occupancy," but it was now time for him to pass those lands "to his successor in the march of civilization."[12]

By the first decade of the twentieth century, stock farms were fast becoming the foundation of regional ranching. "Every man, as a rule, who settles this new region goes to work with an eye to the stock business," as one early railroad brochure explained without exaggeration.[13] The population exploded and, significantly, spread up from the shallow river valleys and crept onto the dry tablelands. By 1910, Castro County, only a few years removed from having been the loneliest outpost of the T Anchor Ranch, had 250 stock farms. Collingsworth County, home of the Rocking Chair (now in the hands of W. E. Hughes), had almost 500. Goodnight's Tule Ranch in Swisher County was now 400 stock farms.[14] The number of farms in Randall County quadrupled, and Wheeler County's population jumped by a factor of six. This growth was fueled primarily by young ranching families, giving the Panhandle the youngest and most gender-balanced population of any western frontier.

Hobart's next gambit was to carve up his properties into even smaller and more profitable chunks and attract actual farmers to the Texas prairies. It too was wildly successful. He and an entire generation of real estate developers would, over a quarter century, transform West Texas yet again. Within fifty years of the Battle of Adobe Walls, the region would be the fastest-growing, most productive agricultural area in the country. An entire Wonderland for farmers with hungry markets, reliable transportation, fertile soil, mostly terrific weather, modern and clean and moral towns. New schools and churches and neighbors, straight roads, and honest merchants. Hobart, it is important to note, wasn't marketing the White Deer Lands as homesteads, but rather as business opportunities. And the numbers spoke for themselves. In its first year, Hobart's Pampa demonstration farm produced twenty bushels of wheat an acre—on land that sold for a fraction of similar farmland in Iowa or Kansas. With no federal land in play and with millions upon millions of acres of railroad and ranch land in private hands, it was developers like Hobart who would create the foundation of the region's society, culture, and economy—one devoted to the needs of commercial family farming.

II

Timothy Dwight Hobart wasn't alone in imagining the Agricultural Wonderland. Joining him among the ranks of the major developers was the "Empire Builder" W. P. Soash of Waterloo, Iowa. Soash was a sixth-generation frontier child, a natural promoter, a salesman who could, as the idiom went, sell sawdust to a lumber mill. If Hobart's childhood was stern, Soash's was hard. Born on a just-scratched-into-existence Iowa homestead in 1877, his mother died when he was seven. His father, George Soash, was a railroad man, which meant that Bill bounced from Iowa relative to Iowa relative until he was old enough to join his father, on the Burlington and Missouri Railroad, living out of a suitcase and on the train. He slept in flophouses and wandered the notorious streets of its western terminals—Sheridan, Cheyenne, Deadwood—and reveled in the bright glories of Kansas City, St. Louis, and Chicago. Bill was fifteen when his dad died. After that, he grew up fast and he grew up tough, punching cattle and breaking horses, playing professional baseball and high-stakes poker. He was a decent carpenter, a great dancer, and a deputy U.S. marshal. He knew his way around a logging camp. He got married, had a daughter, opened a hardware store in Iowa, and then decided on real estate. It was 1900. He was twenty-three.[15]

He started as an agent, wrangling prospects and hustling contracts in the tough markets of the northern plains. But he was good at it. He kept his listings active and ran a respectable office. He knew his holdings and his customers. It didn't take the savvy Soash long to realize that the real money lay in colonizing and town building—carving up large units into individual farms and lots and creating entire communities from the dirt. He sent out a few feelers.

Any ranking of the largest and most outrageous Texas land deals is going to include the story of the XIT Ranch, the 3 million–acre property on the far western border of the Panhandle that Texas awarded to an investment syndicate in 1888 in exchange for the construction of its new state capitol building. The Capitol Lands—47,000 square miles, the size of two Delawares—had been set aside by the 1876 constitution for just that purpose, a built-in financial instrument to build a new capitol sometime in the future. When the existing capitol burned down in 1881, Texas began looking to swap those 3 million acres for a new building. A group of investors raised the cash and built the capitol, seeing the Capitol Lands as a solid investment in the rapidly growing Southwest.[16] While they waited for their windfall, the investment groups established a ranch on the property, the XIT. The largest cattle operation in the world, and among the best laid out and best organized, it ran 150,000 cattle on dozens of specialty pastures, watered by hundreds of windmills, and directly serviced by the railroads with depots at each division headquarters. It even had a sister operation in Montana. Even so, most years, the ranch only broke even. By 1900, impatient investors demanded that the syndicate begin to liquidate property, at a discount if necessary. It peddled some of its biggest pastures to neighboring ranchers, selling, for example, at cost, its entire Yellow House Division (312,175 acres) to George Littlefield in 1901. In 1905, the XIT opened a settlement office, headed by F. W. Wilsey, former head of land sales for the Northern Pacific Railroad, who was tasked with turning the ranch into farms.[17]

Passing off the Texas prairies as prime agricultural real estate was always going to be tough. Most Americans believed the Panhandle was dime-novel dangerous, full of bad men and bloodthirsty Indians. Farmers were, understandably, wary of the western prairies after a generation had trusted in God and busted in Kansas. And western land agents had a reputation somewhere between snake oil salesmen and card sharps. F. W. Wilsey, who knew the salesman from his Minnesota days, gave W. P. Soash first crack at colonizing the XIT, tasking him to develop a 30,000-acre tract in Dallam County. It was a good move; Soash had a vision. He knew that agricultural real estate had changed; the new buyer, with access to more acreage than ever before and almost all of it within a day of a railway depot, was savvy and discriminating. Today's customers were looking for more than just good soil and decent weather (which he promised) but also access to markets, thriving towns, and good roads. The modern farmer wasn't looking for just a homestead, but rather a new site for his business and a new home for his family. Soash would build out his new project to fulfill those needs and more—an entire community and infrastructure for modern family commercial farms.

Among Soash's many innovations in land development—in marketing, packaging, customer acquisition—nothing rivaled his promotion of the Agricultural Wonderland. Within just a few years, all the other great developers were offering versions of the same ideal. Whether in Canyon or Post City or Pampa, the biggest and best land companies were creating projections of their own ecospheres built around commercial family farming: railroads, modern towns, new crops, innovative technologies. They also promised a culture that attended directly to their prospects' social values: Christian, rural, capitalist, and white. In a nation undergoing a transformation into something close to unrecognizable to your average farmer or small-town professional, Soash and the others offered an alternative America: a new homeland, far from the crowded cities, the smells and the smokestacks, and the alien populations pouring into those cities. This was no backward-looking nostalgia trip, but quite the opposite. The Agricultural Wonderland was to be something new and modern, an entire agricultural community that represented the most up-to-date farming methods, transportation and distribution systems, and logically spaced population centers with all the requisite institutions to serve the population.

The W. P. Soash Company of Waterloo, Iowa, was easily among the most professional and well-run real estate businesses in America. Each of its main offices—scattered across ten states—was modeled to look like a bank with walnut desks and tables, high ceilings, lots of marble, and contemporary lighting. Employees wore polished shoes, fashionable neckwear, crisp suits, and fresh haircuts. They practiced "the Soash Way . . . the perfect blend of push, dash, tact, good judgement, and that go-to-it spirit, with honesty, sincerity, perseverance, and accomplishment."[18] In those years, most land companies used commissioned agents to track down prospects and get them to sign up for a tour of a land site. The company took over from there, taking care of the tours, sales, financing, and titles. It was a convenient arrangement, but one fraught with potential misunderstandings and poor messaging. Soash combined everything in one company. He hired his own agents and organized all the excursions to his sites. He not only saved money on commissions but also and more importantly delivered an integrated marketing and messaging campaign. By regularly inviting journalists from his primary markets on junkets, he enjoyed plenty of free publicity. Not that he

The offices of the W. P. Soash Land Company of Waterloo, Iowa.

needed it; the legendary Lord and Thomas Company out of Chicago handled his advertising. Soash himself—the Empire Builder—was central to the campaign. Customers were buying land from the landowner himself: "Trainloads going to the Texas South Plains! With Soash, the Man of the Hour!"[19] Knowing that Soash himself owned the land made the entire enterprise seem more trustworthy, everyone sharing an interest in further development. Soash made it perfectly clear that his lands were not just for farms but investment property. Soash even handled the financing. (He often bundled up the loans and sold them as mortgage-backed securities.)

The W. P. Soash Company targeted specific types of customers, mostly young farm families from agricultural areas in the Middle West, where land prices were skyrocketing.[20] He promised them a chance to get in early on the next great farm country, a chance to collapse generations of capital growth into a lifetime.[21] He had offices in Missouri, Kansas, Illinois, Iowa, Ohio, Wisconsin, and Indiana and spent between $2,000 and $4,000 a month advertising in local newspapers: "A tidal wave of eager homeseekers is sweeping down upon the rich, cheap lands of the South Plains of Texas," read one. "The exodus from the high-priced farming section of the Mississippi Valley to this new land of promise gains volume daily, hourly. The public has awaked to the startling fact that this is the LAST OF THE CHEAP LAND."[22] He was also always open to straight-up land swaps with customers from the more established farming communities.

In the past, frontier land agents built their pitch around the freedom of a family farm and the chance to develop new lands, create a garden from the wilderness. But Soash was selling a business opportunity, an investment. With the rapid growth of railroads and new tech emerging every year, agriculture was undergoing a tectonic shift, rapidly accelerating longtime trends toward the commercialization of the family farm. New farm buyers were factoring rising land values into their calculations. Soash understood this and always portrayed his lands as an "investment" in a place where an investor's "money will make large and quick profits." But he promised not just future gains but a place where the land was still cheap enough to pay for itself in just a couple of seasons.[23] Safer than the stock market, he said.

Controlling so much acreage allowed Soash to pitch his properties as more stable than a typical farming frontier. For three decades, the rise of commercial agriculture had been setting farmers in motion across the country, creating a cycle of boom and bust across the edges of agricultural settlement. In established communities, commercialization drove farm prices into the stratosphere. The better-capitalized operations and those with access to credit bought out their neighbors and scaled up their operations. Those who sold out headed west with a nice pile of start-up money; even a modest 160-acre Ohio homestead could fetch $20,000. New hot spots lured speculators, who then set off hundreds of localized bubbles. "These new investors made quick returns," one insightful farm economist explained, "for they sold out to those who followed, and the values in each case reached higher." In the more frenzied markets, parcels turned over every couple of years. One 240-acre farm sold seven times in eight years, the first time for $5,000 and the last for $30,000.[24] When the local bubbles burst, which they always did, the entire plains economy shuddered.[25]

West Texas land was not only cheaper but safer. Most developers were still in the early stages of land sales and were more focused on initial settlement than resales. The uniformity and volume of available land also kept prices down. The market was just too young for the kind of speculation running rampant in places like Kansas and too small to attract the real schemers. Even as land prices rose across the country, West Texas land remained a bargain well into the 1920s. In those years, proven cotton land in the area around Lubbock sold for a quarter less per acre than land in the eastern Cotton Belt. Panhandle wheat lands were much, much cheaper than similar lands of the Middle West.

Speaking to a new generation of professional farmers, Soash and the other promoters of the Agricultural Wonderland made sure to include plenty of hard data to support the by-then-standard marketing claims—perfect climate, mild winters, great soil—with statistics of production yields, rainfall, access to underground water sources, and commercial crop viability. While cattle, forage, winter wheat, and long-staple cotton would soon dominate the farm economy, developers promoted a variety of other possibilities: fruits and nuts, watermelons, corn, oats, alfalfa, rye, barley, potatoes, peanuts, and pigs. Marketing materials were stuffed with prices and production numbers, innumerable charts and graphs, and testimonials to the viability of one crop or another.[26] One promotional map divided Shackleford County's nine hundred square miles into various realms: "wheat land," "oats land," "rye land," "corn land," "cotton land," "potato land."[27]

Soash's marketing was particularly impressive. It started with his newspaper ads, spectacular full-page spreads that featured a giant Soash riding west wearing trains on his feet like roller skates. Resembling circus leaflets, they had plenty of short sections, cool images, and multiple fonts. The campaign was meant to generate excitement for the "Grand Excursions with the Empire Builder," when potential buyers would take a special and direct train from midwestern cities to Soash's properties in Texas. The idea of the excursion train was as old as the railroads and familiar to anyone who has sat through a time-share pitch: developers offer prospects a massively discounted trip to inspect far-off property where they find themselves at the mercy of their sales agent hosts. By the time Soash got into the game, the excursion train had developed a seedy reputation: crude boxcars full of men, free from the drudgery of the farm, sharing a flask, smoking cheap cigars, and playing cards. But the Soash Specials really were different: they were clean, cheap, direct, and private. The Empire Builder had special arrangements with the Rock Island Railroad and provided his own Pullman cars and comfortable

An advertisement that appeared in W. P. Soash's promotional magazine The Golden West, *probably in 1909.*

berths. The trains left Kansas City, Chicago, and Minneapolis on the first and third Tuesdays of the month. Soash agents would meet prospects in the lobbies of grand hotels and ferry them to the train station in shiny automobiles decked out in Soash banners. They pinned Soash Land Company buttons on everyone's chest and, with the help of a barbershop quartet, taught everyone the Soash Company jingle: "Oh Texas land, great Texas land / We look across the waving grain / and in our hearts we do proclaim / on a better land the sun never shown / We'll set our stakes and build our home."[28] Men were encouraged to bring their wives: "We want the ladies to realize the land we have for sale is located in God's country, where every influence for all that is good is as pronounced as at home."[29] A typical Iowa-based train would make a dozen or more stops for Soash buyers before leaving the state. In six years, Soash ran 87 trains with an average of 125 prospects per train. He claimed to have sold land to 20 percent of them.[30]

Running his own trains allowed Soash to control when his prospects arrived, which he always arranged for the middle of the night. This allowed their first waking impression to be West Texas at dawn, in most seasons the finest moment of the day: calm, cool, even dewy. After a quick breakfast and after the "camera fiends had been satisfied," land agents scooped up their prospects in yet more shiny new automobiles (also adorned with Soash banners) and did a quick lap around town, pointing out (often in the future tense) churches, parks, and commercial structures. They'd duck down a soon-to-be tree-lined residential street and roll past the modern bungalows under construction.[31] Then it was off to the demonstration farm, a promotional pamphlet brought to life. Parking under the canopy of shade trees that surrounded a lovely four-room farmhouse, agents encouraged prospects to wander. They fetched cool glasses of water drawn from the windmill pipe, pointed out the bright flowers in the window boxes, and led prospects down lined paths to large vegetable gardens and nearby ponds (stocked). All the water, a Soash agent would explain, was sourced from inexhaustible underground rivers just below their feet. A single fifty-dollar windmill provided water for the garden and household use, they'd say. Fences and walkways snapped the whole operation into rational grids: house, barn, chicken coop, pens, sheds, orchard, pasture, garden, and lush fields of cotton, wheat, or sorghum. (The logic of the operation was a far cry from the typical midwestern farm, whose ramshackle arrangements told stories of the spastic growth of the good years and the sad neglect of the bad years.) In the spotless barns sat fresh hay and a brand-new tractor. A wide, dry caliche road ran right in front of the estate. "Such a ride!" proclaimed one visitor. "Just imagine yourself in an auto going full speed over a splendid road, with no bridges, not a stone or a stump, absolutely rutless and straight course."[32]

Before the gleaming visage of the model operations could fade, prospects were back in the car touring available properties. Zipping down the arrow-straight roads at fifteen miles per hour, agents pointed out various lots and talked up the farms already up and running. Every single acre they saw was available on generous terms. The company could accommodate any size, any shape. Turnkey properties with a home, a barn, a windmill, and a stock tank sold for a premium, $20 or more per acre. The raw and remote land of the breaks sold for a quarter of that. Either was a steal—Iowa farmland was going for $255 an acre.[33] A typical payment scheme required a minimum of 10 percent down, 6 percent interest, and five to ten annual payments.

Once a prospect took notice of a parcel, agents gave them a shovel and left them alone. While company marketing materials certainly exaggerated rainfall and gilded descriptions of the weather, the soil spoke for itself: spectacularly rich, a nice and not too alkaline mix of clay and sandy loams. For millennia, megafauna had deposited fertilizer on these grasslands. "Take a spade and turn it anywhere," Soash urged. "Smell of it and you will find it reeks with vegetation. Feel of it and you will find that it has the 'good feeling' that one finds in handling the high priced earth of the older states."[34] Standing under the brilliant Texas sun, prospects looked over a flat and treeless plain and saw for themselves that the brochures hadn't embellished; the "virgin soil is ready for the plow, requires no clearing or draining, is easily cultivated and there is no waste land. . . . A plow can run for miles without obstruction and the productive sod crops require no cultivating, being free from weeds." No weeds, no bugs, no stumps, no rocks. Just rich farmland stretching to the horizon.[35] Soash had his original 30,000-acre portfolio sold off in a year. He continued to purchase land from the Capitol Syndicate and sold it off as fast as he could buy it.

Men like Soash weren't just selling rich farmland. They were selling a new world, a new white Christian homeland.[36] Texas land promoters, seeking to lure white southerners west after the Civil War, had been describing the state as a "Whiteman's Country" for decades. Texas was, as the *Austin Democratic Statesman* once defined it, "essentially a white man's country, won by the valor of white men, and ever to be ruled by white men."[37] West Texas developers like Soash not only echoed this language well into the twentieth century but also forbade African Americans and other people of color to purchase, lease, or rent any property or lot. From the beginning, most West Texas counties were exclusively and deliberately white.[38]

Ads from 1909 for Soash's Running Water Ranch properties made the point in twenty-point boldface, all-cap type: "A WHITE MAN'S TOWN. NO NEGROES CAN OWN OR OCCUPY LOTS." Every deed, he assured readers, contained a clause forbidding Black residents. As he explained: "We have a beautiful country and by preventing negroes from settling, we eliminate forever 'the race problem.'"[39] It wasn't just Soash; the Fort Worth and Denver Railway's newspaper ads assured prospective settlers that "Texas was a white man's country, and no effort was made to induce any negro immigration, as the Denver does not care about locating this class on its line."[40] A Hereford developer, F. W. Barber, wanted to hear from farmers who were looking for land in "white man's country where no negroes are found."[41] The North Texas Land Company stated simply, "Negroes and Mexicans are not allowed in the Panhandle and North Texas countries."[42] Short and Williams told prospects, "Our population is entirely white and we are glad that this is the case; for wherever we may be, if thousands of miles from home, we know of a certainty that our loved ones are safe and can rest with the calm assurance that our families have the protection of American men."[43] Town newspapers, usually an arm of the development company, pushed the same message. The *Hereford Brand*, one of the Panhandle's more booster-forward news outlets, promised that in addition to its cheap, fertile lands and magnificent weather, the Panhandle had "no Negroes, Mexicans, Chinamen or other undesirable foreigners."[44] In one piece that appeared all over Texas, the *Daily Panhandle* urged white Texans to "leave the mosquitoes, the chills, the buck ague, the alligators, the negroes and the yellow jaundice and head for the Panhandle, the rosy land of promises fulfilled."[45] Promoters in Lubbock County, who tended to focus sales campaigns on white southern cotton farmers, were among the most racist in their advertising. One Lubbock promoter described the town as a place "where there are no negroes and where you do not have to keep the door of your corn-crib and smokehouse locked, where you can leave your home and remain away for weeks at a time without fear of returning to find that a horrifying tragedy has befallen your loved ones in your absence."[46]

In wasn't just whiteness: developers also promised the Agricultural Wonderland was an upright, moral, and Protestant society. Testimonials about the variety and passion of the Christian denominations in their respective communities accompanied every form of real estate advertising, along with images of sparkling new churches. Developers themselves often footed the cost of construction of churches. Some even recruited specific religious communities. Advertising his Texas lands to the kaleidoscopic bevy of religious sects found in Iowa, Ohio, and Illinois, Soash reassured the midwesterners, "Churches of every denomination are to be found. The native Texans are very strong in their religious belief, and those from the North, East, and West who have settled there have contributed to the general promotion of the church. The religious and educational advantages are as prominent as can be found in any of the older settled countries of the North and East."[47] But every other land company and promoter promised the same thing. Spur Ranch developers avowed that "the people of the country are church-loving, law-abiding citizens and the incoming population will find every assistance from the resident population in the furtherance of church work."[48] The Lubbock Chamber of Commerce claimed "practically all the various churches are represented in the city. The nearest saloon is 95 miles away, and the people of the South Plains will measure to a higher standard intellectually and morally than many of the older settled communities."[49] None of the new developments allowed saloons or alcohol.[50]

In 1909, Soash went all in on 100,000 acres of former ranch land on the southern plains. He bought out his partners and cashed in his remaining holdings in Dalhart and Plainview. His called his new project the Big Springs Country and he "had big plans."[51] The new town of Soash would be at the center of it all. The nearest railroad was still twenty miles away, but Soash, confident it would arrive soon, advertised that his latest empire would be served by the "Gulf, Soash & Pacific Railway." He spent at least $10,000 in an attempt to get the Santa Fe Railroad to build through his properties. He launched a magazine, *The Golden West*, to market the Big Spring Country. While he waited for the railroad, he and his agents operated out of Big Spring, using a thirty-strong fleet of automobiles to ferry prospects out to farm lots. Soash town lots he sold as an investment, offering a pre-railroad special, each lot available for a dollar down and a dollar a month. He built the Lorna, one of the best hotels in West Texas, complete with electric lights and hot and cold running water. He laid out parks and church lots. He planted so many trees that the town had to hire a full-time crew just to keep them watered. He put in a telephone exchange, a post office, and an electric company. Road and construction crews were everywhere all at once. Soash started a cotton gin, a bank, a school, a canning factory for locally grown vegetables, and a cement plant.[52]

But then it stopped raining. The year 1909 was dry; so was 1910. And

1911. The drought kept the prospects away. The railroad never came. His buyers drifted away. Soash lost everything. Today, all that remains of the Empire Builder's dream town is a tumbled-down bank building long overtaken by a small copse of Soash's surviving trees.

III

As Soash learned the hard way, the Agricultural Wonderland was going to be built around the railroads.[53] With few landscape features to be negotiated and with the total cooperation of the land companies and ranches, railroads chose the shortest and straightest routes between major markets. Developers and railroads worked together to determine town sites, built around depots, and spaced the towns out so that local farmers would be less than a day's journey from a station. The spatial arrangement of any plains town tells the story. Take Littlefield, Texas, for example. Located up in Lamb County, the town would serve as the hub for a 300,000-acre land development project pursued by legendary cattleman and banker George W. Littlefield.[54] He had been running a successful cattle operation on the property since he'd bought it from the XIT back in 1901. When he found out in 1911 that the Santa Fe Railroad was looking for a cut-off to shave time on its Texas Gulf–to–Los Angeles route, Littlefield saw the chance to score a depot on his land and start selling off some of his acreage. He gave up a couple of hundred acres for the right-of-way and threw in $100,000 to make it happen. Then he formed the Littlefield Lands Company and put his nephew-in-law in charge.[55]

Littlefield is anchored by a magnificent prairie deco railroad depot that, at the Santa Fe's insistence, sits at the base of the town's main boulevard. Red brick and trimmed in white sandstone, the structure made a good impression on prospects. (Littlefield, like most, ran excursion trains.) Opposite the station was a lush and shaded green space that framed a prospect's view clear down Littlefield's primary commercial street. The ubiquity of this perpendicular relationship between a railroad line and the main street of any plains town cannot be stressed enough. It was *the* model for town building on the Great Plains, so dominant that city planners had to tweak Littlefield's geometry to make it work. Almost every town built on the plains in these years was "square to the world" with streets running north–south and avenues east–west. From above, they all look like graph paper. The railroad, which also ran as close to north–south and east–west as possible, formed one edge of the grid. The town's commercial district (usually three streets) ran at a 90-degree angle from the railroad, forming a T. But Littlefield was built along what they called the Texico cutoff, which ran at almost exactly a 45-degree angle from Earth's latitudes. No problem. The Littlefield design team still platted its three main thoroughfares at a 90-degree angle from the railroad; they just built the rest of the town around it. Most blocks and streets still run square to the world, but as the residential district meets the business district, there are, in addition to all the 90-degree angles and squares and rectangles, a few 45-degree and even 60-degree angles and some "blocks" that are triangles and polygons.[56]

Other than its odd spatial variance, Littlefield hewed to the model of a proper town in the Agricultural Wonderland. Its residential areas spread out from the central business district, and it had broad, tree-lined avenues and wide sidewalks. Perhaps more strictly controlled than other towns, there was a uniformity in housing style and lot size and arrangements. Forward-thinking planners established alleys and phone and power lines behind each lot. In the flood-prone playa on the west side of town, the company established Laguna Park as a cool and shady oasis. While decades have bleached out whatever originality and creativity most West Texas towns might have enjoyed in their early years, what remains is the spatial uniformity of a system built around the transportation, financial, professional, cultural, and social needs of a population of commercial family farmers.[57] Even the modern automobile- and truck-centered transportation structure runs, in most places, adjacent to the system established by the railroads. The basic layout of every town is the same.[58] Historian and geographer John Miller Morris calls this "the intersection of abstract place with corporate needs."[59]

Walking straight out of any railroad depot in West Texas meant heading straight down the main street, past the banks, law and land and newspaper offices, the nice hotel, the fancy barber, the biggest mercantile establishment, the finest dress shops and haberdashers. Streets were wide, and the buildings stone or brick. Large plate glass windows looked over the sidewalks. At the edge of the business district would be the red-brick and white-steepled churches and pride-of-the-town schools. Off to the right or left would be the residential neighborhoods spread out in quadrants of sixteen- or twenty-five-block squares. The houses sat off the street, small modern cottages with front porches and green lawns. Trees lined the sidewalks. Every town had at least one large city park. These were and are personal towns, walking and waving towns.[60]

They were designed by men like Littlefield and T. D. Hobart to be a new kind of town, more like a modern subdivision than the typical frontier community with its muddy streets, saloons, houses of ill repute, and ramshackle construction. These were towns designed for businessmen and families, ideal in their central vision. The speed and execution of town building, along with the centralization of capital and planning within a single development office, allowed these towns to look complete within just a couple of years from their founding. There were churches, schools, banks, retail shops, trees, sidewalks, and neighborhoods. Moreover, with the same aggressiveness with which they sold farmlands, land companies recruited professionals and business owners to their new communities by promising opportunity and growth—a good investment. Potential town growth itself became a commodity, a chance to leverage time and money and expertise and then, if the place took off, cash in.[61]

IV

This settlement-as-investment model was made possible by the reality that West Texas was the easiest agricultural frontier to settle in U.S. history. Twentieth-century pioneer farmers could literally load their entire household—family, furniture, clothing, farm equipment, even animals—onto boxcars and unload within only a few miles of their new frontier homestead. The "hardships of pioneering," as one Lubbock promoter put it, "have been rolled away on the chariot wheels of the modern railway train."[62] The towns grew quickly. In 1910, there was not a city in West Texas with a population over 10,000; twenty years later there were seven. Each anchored a strong local economy.[63] By 1930, Lubbock had a population of 20,000 and was the most important cotton center in Texas. Amarillo was the eleventh-largest city in the state with skyscrapers, suburbs, and 45,000 people. Distributed regularly along the railroads were county agricultural centers like Canyon, Floydada, Midland, Brownfield, Shamrock, Canadian, Tulia, Childress, Dalhart, Plainview, and Levelland. Each had grown from a real estate office to a real com-

A typical farm in the Agricultural Wonderland.

munity in just a few years. Periodic and localized droughts like those that had crushed the dreams of W. P. Soash were exceptions to a thirty-year rule of almost unchecked growth. By the 1920s, West Texas was, maybe except for Land Boom Florida, the fastest-growing place in the United States.

Commercial farming took off. The promises of Soash, Hobart, and the other developers were being fulfilled. Stock farms and cattle still dominated the economy of the Permian Basin (if not for long); cotton and cattle were the crops of the southern plains, and wheat and cattle in the Panhandle. Different versions of stock farming spread as families experimented with herd size and landholdings. With smaller, watered pastures and better breeds, it was possible for almost any well-run operation to make money no matter the size, from the two-section cow/calf outfit to the still-massive Matador Ranch. In Midland County, where stock farming flourished, three hundred families were running cattle operations worth a total of almost $1 million in value.

Ecologically appropriate production, new technologies, and machines fueled the growth on the southern plains and Panhandle.[64] In the former it was a new strain of cotton produced by the Texas Agricultural Experiment Substation at Lubbock. "Westex," a long-staple cotton like Pima, had a good yield, matured early, and was drought, wind, and weed resistant. Its short growing season meant it could be planted after the worst of the spring winds had subsided and harvested before fall's first frost.[65] More important, 98 percent of bolls could be reaped by a tractor pulling a stripper sled.[66] While the yield per plant was less than more common short-staple varieties, production costs were close to nothing. Just as Soash and the other promoters had promised, the cheap, flat land lent itself to larger spreads and mechanized farming. A family with regular access to a tractor could farm upward of 320 acres, eight times the size of a typical farm in the eastern part of the state. In the traditional Cotton Belt, production had always been limited by cotton's enormous labor demands. Spring days were slogs through the mud, wrestling an 80-pound plow and an 800-pound mule just to plant a crop. Summers were long hours under the brutal Texas sun, trying to beat back a relentless tide of weeds with nothing but a hoe, calloused hands, and a strong back. Harvests were eighteen-hour day after eighteen-hour day spent stooped, picking bolls with bleeding fingers and dragging a 50-pound bag through the dust. Even the largest family could only expect to farm twenty or maybe forty acres and scratch out only the slimmest of profits. But a southern plains tractor farmer could prep, plow, and seed a half section in a few weeks, all while seated atop a machine. There were no native weeds. At harvesttime, it was back on the tractor, pulling a sled down the rows, dumping it on the turn row, loading piles of cotton onto a wagon, and heading to the gin. By 1925, this mechanized, connected, tech-forward, specialized form of agriculture had transformed the southern plains into the cotton capital of the nation, dominated, just as planned, by owner-operated, large-scale commercial family farmers. Between 1920 and 1925, the number of farmers on the Littlefield Lands increased by a factor of five. Average farm size among its 632 separate operations was 246 acres. Average worth, $10,000. There were 30,000 acres planted in cotton (a number that would triple by 1930) worth $1.5 million. Ninety-five percent of farms were owner-operated, and most of those owners were either from Texas or elsewhere in the South. Every single county resident was white.[67]

The Panhandle was the wheat belt, and T. D. Hobart's Pampa was its buckle. Even as he developed the stock farm as a legitimate real estate product, Hobart had continued to search for a commercial crop that might spur even greater interest in the White Deer Lands, especially among the professional class of farmers in the Middle West. With his usual attention to detail, Hobart used his demonstration farms as exper-

The chaos of rapid growth: Childress, Texas, 1897.

imental stations and, as early as 1905, had started planting hard winter wheat, originally developed in the similar climates of eastern Europe. (Predictions of wheat's potential had been around a while. Legend had it that Goodnight himself had enjoyed such success with the crop that he plowed the whole thing under lest word get out and his ranch be overwhelmed by plowmen.) By 1912, Gray County farmers were shipping half a million bushels out of Pampa. By 1920, they had doubled it. Even more than cotton, high plains wheat farms were large-scale, capital-intensive, and tech-dependent. Rather than the traditional growing cycle of spring planting and fall harvest, winter wheat is planted in the fall, when it begins to germinate before the weather turns too cold. The plants lie dormant over the winter months and begin to shoot just as the Panhandle's predictable and mostly soft spring rains begin. The wheat finishes under the warm sun of early summer and is harvested before the Fourth of July. Even on the larger wheat farms, the work year was mostly two to three hard weeks in the fall and three or four more in early summer. Between planting and harvesting, there wasn't much to do. Wheat production costs were even cheaper than cotton, only 70 to 80 cents a bushel (in years when a bushel sold for over $2), and a Panhandle acre could produce forty or fifty bushels. Plenty of folks recognized a couple of hundred acres in wheat could produce a nice profit without much work, and lots of nonfarmers got into the business part-time. The lines between farmer and businessman, between town and country, blurred. During the First World War, wheat prices hit $3 a bushel. Hobart—or any other developer—couldn't sell land fast enough. By 1925, Gray County farms were some of the most valuable in Texas, averaging $20,768. There wasn't a single Black farmer in the county.

The Agricultural Wonderland fulfilled the rest of its promises. By 1925, there was an established state college in Canyon, a brand-new state agricultural university, and eleven denominational colleges. West Texas had its own Banker's Association, two Press Associations, and the most powerful regional Chamber of Commerce in the nation. It was the most gender-balanced spot in the West, right at 1:1. It was a young frontier with a majority population under thirty, most of them under fifteen. There was an almost equal balance of town and country folk. In Hale and Hall counties, for example, there was one town resident for every two in the countryside. (In older parts of the state the ratio was closer to 1:7.) In some counties, city residents outnumbered their country cousins.

It was the most homogenous population in Texas. Across the hundred counties and hundreds of square miles of West Texas, African Americans made up less than 1 percent of the population. Over a third of the counties had no Black residents at all. Sundown towns were the rule. In Wheeler County, sociologist Arthur Raper reported, Black passengers didn't even dare "stick their heads out of the train coaches."[68] West Texans weren't just white: even in the midst of one of the greatest immigration booms in history, they were 98 percent native-born white, almost to a person from either Texas, the South, or the Middle West.[69] They were almost exclusively fundamentalist, evangelical Protestants. And with only the exceptions of those who lived and worked in the fast-growing cities of Amarillo, Lubbock, or Abilene, they lived and worked on the region's commercial family farms or in the small towns that served them.

Summing up the world view of T. D. Hobart, his able biographer put it this way: "Any correct interpretation or evaluation, therefore, of the life and times of T. D. Hobart and his generation must be viewed from the standpoint of the capitalistic system."[70] Indeed.

3
CAPITALIST UTOPIA

They constantly try to escape
From the darkness outside and within
By dreaming of systems so perfect that no one will need
   to be good.
But the man that is will shadow
The man that pretends to be.

T. S. ELIOT

No person dreamt the infinite possibilities of the Agricultural Wonderland with the clarity of American businessman C. W. Post. Between 1906 and 1914, the cereal magnate poured millions into founding America's first and only capitalist utopia. By that point in his amazing career, Post was one of the wealthiest and most famous men in the world. Postum and Grape-Nuts were household staples. Advertisements for his products and his essays on political economy appeared in every newspaper in the United States. His Battle Creek, Michigan, factory, a prototype for the contemporary corporate campus, was so stunningly beautiful and well organized that he was forced to give tours of the property and publish a coffee-table book about it. Serious and sober people threw his name into conversations about potential presidential candidates. His opinions on currency, advertising, foreign trade, even yacht racing were widely sought. He was also the best-known antilabor zealot in the country.

His original plan was just to buy a West Texas ranch in the middle of nowhere where he could unwind and enjoy the "outdoor life."[1] Having mostly retired from the day-to-day running of his food company, Post dedicated himself to travel and public affairs. The ranch would be a place where he could escape. In 1906, he and a family friend, "Uncle" Tom Stevens, a savvy ranch broker from Fort Worth, went looking for land along the remote breaks of the Llano Estacado. After a few weeks considering properties, Post decided to buy the old Curry Comb Ranch, a pretty piece of well-watered property between Sweetwater and Lubbock. He snapped up a few adjoining parcels, bringing his total holdings to around 350 square miles spread across Lynn and Garza counties. He was now one of the largest landowners in Texas. If solitude was his wish, he couldn't have chosen better: across both counties (which he now owned most of) there were barely two hundred people. His new home was seventy miles from a railroad. Fort Worth, the nearest city, was 250 miles to the east.

Post celebrated the deal by throwing a huge party at his new ranch. Everybody within a two-day ride showed up. Beef, mutton, pies, cakes, breads, and pickled vegetables weighed down the tables Post had built for the occasion. Spirits flowed and the mood was cheerful. Post was riding high when the crowd asked him to give a short speech. Wearing black boots, black pants, maroon western shirt, and modestly clutching his white Stetson near his waist, the breakfast magnate faced the crowd as one of them.[2] Whether it was the anticipatory looks on the faces in front of him, or the morning's conversations, or just a burst of inspiration, we may never know, but as Post detailed his plans for the new property, he abandoned his ranch-as-refuge plan and instead vowed he would transform his new property into the greatest agricultural community in America. He would bring in a railroad and divide the dusty and underpopulated land into beautiful farms and ranchettes. As he got wound up, he grew more elaborate, promising a modern and stunning new town with a grand hotel, a waterworks, tree-lined streets, a telephone system, an electric company. The cowboys were skeptical.

They didn't know C. W. Post.

Within weeks, Post was promoting his project in the national media.[3] He formed a new company, the Double U (a play on his middle initial), to build the town, lay out the farms, and recruit buyers. He put his longtime right-hand man Wilbur Hawk in charge. There was, as we have seen, no shortage of hyperbolic visionaries working the West Texas real estate market in those years, but Post was playing at a higher level, something much more radical. He was going to build a literal capitalist utopia, a place where property ownership was required, labor unions prohibited, and every citizen owned a business. Post City, as he decided to call it, was going to be a model community demonstrating the value and logic of a new form of business conservatism, a community ideal predicated on an absolute devotion to what we now call a business-friendly environment: city government run by and for business owners, low taxes, no regulation, and absolutely no labor unions. It was to demonstrate the logic and equity of pure booster politics. And every business leader and political opportunist in West Texas would come to share his vision.

I

Post was born (1854) and raised in Springfield, Illinois, a city practically willed into existence by local businessmen and that had become the state's capital thanks to their ceaseless braying and politicking. His father was a serial entrepreneur who sold farm implements and dabbled in real estate.[4] The boosters of Springfield were a new breed of businessperson and a new type of frontier settler that had emerged in the mid-nineteenth century. These were townspeople, rather than agriculturalists, who settled into the new communities that served the agricultural frontiers of the Middle West and Upper South. While eager to sell their wares, practice their profession, preach, or publish, the collective goal was growth—to help foster the expansion of a village into a town and maybe even a city. With that growth would come personal and professional opportunities, business development, and wealth. Every venture saw itself as the next Cincinnati or Kansas City, an urban titan, holding an entire state's or region's worth of towns and villages, factories and farms within its gravitational pull. In the early years, these "go-getters," to borrow Daniel Boorstin's wonderfully apt phrase, hustled to lure some guarantor of permanence to their town: a railroad, a denominational college, a county seat. (The biggest prize was landing a state university or the state capital.)[5]

Post came of age during Springfield's greatest period of booster-driven growth. The city had been named the state capital just fifteen years earlier, and the surrounding area was booming, with new techniques, new lands, and new technologies transforming central Illinois into a major agricultural center. Corn, wheat, wool, and pork were the biggest commodities, and in Springfield's new mills and plants they were turned into valuable consumer goods. The thriving economy (and the business of state government) brought in a large professional class, plenty of merchants (Springfield had two dozen general stores), and the kinds of construction industries associated with rapid development.

At thirteen, a restless and ambitious Post left home to attend the new Industrial University in Urbana (now the University of Illinois). He hoped to become an engineer but lasted only two years. Back home, he helped his dad around the shop and joined up with the Springfield Zouaves, a ceremonial militia made up of teenagers who would get all kitted up in fancy uniforms and make appearances with the governor. He was gone again before he turned eighteen, lighting out for the Kansas prairies where he punched cattle and tried running a store. Two years later, he was back in Springfield, where he married Ella Merriweather, his childhood sweetheart. He took a job as a traveling salesman for a farm equipment company, covering the Iowa and Nebraska prairie frontiers. An itinerant tinkerer who had literally grown up in the ag machinery business, Post was soon designing custom rigs for his customers. At twenty-seven, with a couple of patents to his name, he founded the Illinois Agricultural Works to manufacture a new type of cultivator. It failed. Overwhelmed, Post went into a deep funk and the business collapsed. He lost everything, including the deed to his parents' homestead, when his business partners took over the company. Deciding a change was needed, the Posts set out for Fort Worth in early 1888.[6]

The whole Post clan—C. W., Ella, infant daughter Marjorie, C. W.'s parents, his brothers, aunts, and uncles—liquidated their Springfield holdings and relocated to Texas.[7] A booster's dream come to life, Fort Worth over the previous few years had grown from a prosperous town of 6,000 to an expanding city of over 20,000. Taking up offices at 610 Main Street, the Posts poured $100,000 into local real estate by July and had plans to invest at least that much more by year's end. Looking at Fort Worth in the late 1880s, Post saw Chicago just twenty years earlier, a flourishing city settled into the seam between a continent's worth of agricultural expansion to its west and a new and efficient transportation system and expanding markets to its east. Any man, he told a Fort Worth reporter, who could not see that the city offered the best chance to "turn an honest penny in city property" was simply "too short-sighted to be worthy of comment."[8]

The East Fort Worth Land Company was the Posts' biggest project.

The family bought four hundred undeveloped acres just across the Trinity River from downtown with plans to build a modern, upscale subdivision they called Sylvania, a planned community where every home would have electricity and running water.[9] Every street would have a sidewalk and be lit by electric streetlights. A streetcar, another Post Family project, would connect the neighborhood to downtown. C. W. attended to the smallest of details, right down to the types of electric bulbs used in each home. Concurrently, the hyperactive Post was also constructing an enormous woolen mill that he was importing brick-by-brick from Missouri and building a workingman's suburb on the southeast part of town.

The Posts were active boosters. They had been in Fort Worth about a year when the city put on its Spring Palace Exhibition, designed to show off the city's economic potential. C. W. donated land for the site and put together excursion trains to the Texas Panhandle (whose own boosters were all over the Spring Palace). Cousin Willis was the organization's event secretary. On another front, C. W. helped design and promote Fort Worth's Trinity Park project and was part of yet another venture, which hoped to channel the languid energy of the loping and sandy Trinity River into an electric power plant.[10]

When he wasn't boosting or selling real estate, Post was busy running a bunch of small companies he had created to hawk his various inventions: stationery made from cotton seed hulls, a "safety" bicycle wheel (the designs for which he would eventually just give to the Columbia Bicycle Company), a new form of sheet music for player pianos, and "scientific" suspenders that could be worn under a shirt. Keeping a coffee-fueled inhuman pace for thirty-seven months, he collapsed in a heap in January 1891. C. W. could barely walk or talk. Ella put her husband on a train to Battle Creek, Michigan—home of the finest health resort in the world.[11]

II

In those days, Battle Creek was the center of the health fad world, a Babylon of mesmerists, vegetarians, gymnasts, Christian Scientists, water therapists, and other half-serious charlatans promising miraculous cures for the ailments that plagued the Gilded Age's middle and upper classes. At the center of it all was the "San," run by Dr. John Harvey Kellogg, the nation's leading promoter of "biologic living" and one of its most respected medical men.[12] Patients at the San, which over the years included some of the wealthiest and most famous people in the Western world, were treated through a regimen of physical fitness, relaxation, a regular rotation of various therapies—hydrotherapy, phototherapy, electrotherapy—and with a particular attention to diet.[13] It was so well respected because the programming worked. Guests were forbidden meat, alcohol, and caffeine. A strict diet of grains, nuts, and fresh vegetables, often concocted into strange foodstuffs with even stranger names, was accompanied by an equally stern exercise routine. Days were to be spent in mostly quiet reflection with regular meditation worked in between various therapy sessions. Both breakfast and bedtime came early. Several times a week, guests gathered to hear Kellogg lecture on healthy living.[14] Not surprisingly, most of the San's stressed-out and out-of-shape guests felt much better after a few weeks of exercise, quiet, and a vegetarian, caffeine- and alcohol-free diet.

But not C. W. Post. The San almost killed him. In nine months, he lost ninety pounds, half his body weight. He had no energy or appetite. Most days he spent moping around in a wheelchair morbidly whining about his certain and impending death. He was in such pathetic shape that Dr. Kellogg consulted with Ella, urging her to get C. W.'s affairs in order, and quickly. He had maybe a week.[15] A desperate Ella turned to a local Christian Scientist, Elizabeth Gregory, and asked her to speak to C. W. about the miraculous power of positive thinking. The idea that people could recover their health through the power of their own mind was, after all, the kind of solution that a go-getter like her husband might respond to. Ella was right; C. W. took to Christian Science at once. After one session, he set himself up in Gregory's guest room, gobbling up her literature and everything in the icebox. Within weeks, he had regained much of his strength and vigor. And started his own health and wellness business.[16]

Post partnered with his old nurse from the San and bought a small farm on Battle Creek's outskirts and opened La Vita Inn, a knock-off of Kellogg's place.[17] It was cheaper, and guests were allowed to eat meat (Post loved a good steak). Post, of course, was no physician,[18] but that didn't stop him from imitating Kellogg's lectures at La Vita, with regular discourses on health, faith, and spirituality, most of it an incomprehensible mishmash of Christian Science, neurology, religion, and mesmerism drawn from a hodgepodge of sources. In 1894, he had choice selections collected in a book he self-published: *I Am Well! The Modern Practice of Natural Suggestion as Distinct from Hypnotic or Unnatural Influence.* Interspersed with stories about miraculous cures—a regular occurrence at La Vita, apparently—the book explained the Law of Harmony and described how to access the Universal Divine Mind. It read like this:

> It is only when the ignorance of intellect is displaced by the higher intelligence, the psychic sense, Soul, Life, or Divine Mind, whichever term seems best, that the being gains a knowledge of the plane of eternal principles and of man's connection with his cause. This knowledge unfolds the new man and brings with it, according to law, an endowment of the ponderous power of Life, dismissing the unreal breaking the mesmeric spell, and returning man to a natural, normal state, from the world of illusion to the world of eternal realities.[19]

For 150 pages.

La Vita never really caught on. Post stayed afloat largely because his "scientific suspenders" were selling well.[20] He began spending less time lecturing or attending to guests in favor of hours in La Vita's barn-turned–food lab, where he and his assistant tried to replicate various food and health products offered at the San. In 1895, he had his first great success, a coffee alternative made from grains and molasses that he called Postum. Like many Americans, Post tended to overindulge in coffee and had grown convinced that the drink lay at the root of his gastrointestinal problems. Gambling that he was not alone in his suffering, he set out to convince the nation that Postum was the solution to digestive discomfort.[21] Thanks largely to a well-conceived marketing campaign—including sampling stations (as at Costco), letting grocers sell on consignment, and the most aggressive and largest advertising campaign in American history—Postum took off. It was the very first health food, a grocery product that made blood red, nerves steady, and cured "coffee neuralgia" (a disease Post made up from whole cloth). Pouring his considerable profits right back into advertising, Post sought a universal demand for Postum. Thirty percent of his advertising budget—easily the largest in the nation—went for full-page ads in national magazines like *Collier's*, *McClure's*, and the *Saturday Evening Post.* The rest went to newspaper ads of every type and in every paper he and his marketing department could identify. These were critical years in the food industry, as the modern supermarket had begun to displace the shopkeeper as the primary place for selling foodstuffs. Post understood earlier than most that selling food directly off the shelves would depend on branding, packaging, and advertising. A food purveyor had to *create* demand for their particular product.[22] It worked. Post had created a new food category and enjoyed a huge financial windfall. By 1900, he was selling almost half a million dollars of Postum a year.

Then he reinvented breakfast with Grape-Nuts (1897) and Post Toasties (1906), two of the first ready-to-eat cereals. Post marketed Grape-Nuts like Postum, as a health food. Regular consumption of the cereal would make the blood stronger and the mind clearer; "pre-digested" sugars and "phosphate of potash" fed the nerve cells and could cure malaria or appendicitis. (The latter claim led to a nasty false-advertising fight with *Collier's* magazine, which Post lost).[23] He pitched his ads, which he wrote himself, to a growing middle-class segment of American consumer. Full-page magazine ads usually depicted some homey scene of everyday life, and the accompanying text spoke to the hopes, dreams, and fears of this huge and growing market. Post Toasties, for example, was mostly pitched to busy mothers as a healthy and nutritious morning meal option for children. Post's tagline "There's a Reason" appeared in every ad. Within a decade of going into business, Post ran one of the largest food companies in the world and had created two brand-new food categories that, thanks to his advertising, dominated the market. By 1903, his company was clearing over a million dollars a year in profit.[24]

By then, the Postum Food Company had long since eclipsed the San as the most important business in Battle Creek, and with dozens of imitators in operation at any one time, breakfast cereal had replaced the health business as the engine of the city's economy. C. W. Post was now the town's leading citizen. His manufacturing facility, built on the La Vita Inn property, was a marvel—America's first corporate campus: clean, modern, and technologically advanced. With its mani-cured grounds and every building painted the same shade of crisp linen white, locals called it the "White City." Covering several acres and with 2,500 employees, it was the largest food-processing center in the world. Dedicated buildings housed the dozens of massive and built-to-order ovens, grinders, kneaders, molders, slicers, carton makers, packer belts, rollers, evaporators, and roasters. Identically dressed employees, their uniform reflecting their specific position, tended to the machines. At the center of campus was a beautiful Elizabethan mansion that stood as the company headquarters (and the in-house advertising unit).[25] The company's delivery trucks were all new, sparkling, with clean lines and clear advertising. They were driven by scrubbed and fresh young men in sharp white uniforms. Post, who considered himself an enlightened and benevolent employer, paid higher-than-average wages, offered health insurance, and even established a bonus system. A firm believer in the value of homeownership for all, Post revived his Fort Worth plan for a working-class suburb and put in the Post Addition, a neighborhood of attractive custom homes available to his employees at close to cost. He even arranged the financing.[26]

Post became the city's biggest booster. He purchased Battle Creek's daily newspaper. He built the Post Tavern, the finest hotel between Detroit and Chicago, with private baths, electric lighting, in-room telephones, and a first-rate restaurant. He financed the construction of the two thousand–seat Post Theater. He donated land to factories that wanted to relocate to Battle Creek. The Marjorie Block, named for his daughter and built by Post, was the city's first high-rise business address. Most important, Post mapped out a plan that he believed would guarantee the continued growth of his adopted home—"The Battle Creek Way," a pledge among the city's business leaders to cooperate and keep labor unions out of their town and out of their industries. Boosterism became linked to opposing organized labor.

III

By 1902, a million boxes of cereal a day were shipping out of Battle Creek: Grape-Nuts of course, but also plenty of imitators: Golden Manna, Malta Vita, Nokra Oats, Mapl-Flakes, Grain-o, Grape Sugar Flakes, Ceroloa, and more. And the Kelloggs hadn't yet gotten into the game. The breakfast cereal industry employed over 70 percent of the city's workforce and Post was determined to keep organized labor out of every single company in town. The city already had a reputation as an antilabor stronghold; the Seventh Day Adventist Church, which called Battle

Creek home, actively discouraged its members from joining unions, and
the many farm implement manufacturers in the city were bitterly antilabor. But Post was particularly intolerant, viewing labor unions as a des-
ecration of the laws that governed the natural economy and the tenets
of the good society. It would be Post who would relentlessly work to
make opposition to organized labor the foundation of boosterism. What
would become known as "right to work" laws and "business-friendly"
climates, the hallmarks of business conservatism for most of the twentieth century, would become C. W. Post's lasting political legacy.

Even though he had been a businessman for two decades, Post
had never had a lot of employees until Postum took off. His views of
management and labor were still stuck in the booster ethic of mid-
nineteenth-century Springfield. In those years, before the widespread
emergence of industrial capitalism and wage labor, working for someone else was supposed to be a temporary condition. A young person
might apprentice for a few years as they learned a trade or work for
wages as they built a stake, but always toward a goal of independence.
Relationships between employer and employee were personal and often
meant working side by side, day after day. Even as industrial manufacturing came online, factories in places like Springfield or Battle Creek
maintained some semblance of that relationship. A factory owner was
on property, usually with an office just off the shop floor. Owners knew
their employees by name and had hired most of them personally. Men
like Post saw employment as a personal agreement between two independent individuals. At the dawn of the twentieth century, he still maintained faith that for most, wage labor was still just a temporary condition
and that these "working capitalists" would, after a time, gain the power
to control their own "matter and conditions."[27]

Labor unions fundamentally undermined Post's (and an entire
employer class's) understanding of labor markets. He saw workers the
same way that West Texas ranchers saw cowboys—as individual agents
who sold their labor for a certain price and for a predetermined period of
time. Employees were responsible for doing quality work. Owners were
responsible for paying good wages (Post paid better than most) and to
provide a safe, comfortable work environment. Further, an owner should
recognize talent and reward excellent performance, and a worker should
perform his or her tasks with efficiency and care. These two precepts,
Post believed, were the foundation of the laws that governed the natural

economy. Labor unions, by claiming the right to negotiate on behalf of a company's employees, effectively negated the rational operation of the labor market, disrupted the individualism on which it was based, and put in a dangerous barrier between workers and employers.

The only logical arrangement for Post was the open shop, an arrangement that precluded any employee from being forced to join a union in order to work in a particular factory or industry.[28] Post knew of course that a closed shop, where a labor union speaks for the entirety of a factory's (or industry's) workers, was the main source of power for organized labor, but for him it was not only a violent deviation from basic economics but also a threat to democracy. Like a lot of Americans, Post feared and loathed strikes and the bloody viciousness that they seemed to trigger. But as a producer of an easily replicated consumer good, his greatest concern was the threat of an organized boycott of his products. In 1902, when an obscure labor publication called for just such a boycott of Postum and Grape-Nuts, Post joined the National Association of Manufacturers (NAM), the "shock troop brigade" of the antilabor movement.[29]

Founded in 1895, the NAM had been mostly a sleepy organization of overstuffed small-city businessmen harrumphing about tariffs and trade agreements. But in 1902, when President Theodore Roosevelt refused to side with management during a massive coal strike and instead arbitrated an agreement that resulted in a partial victory for the United Mine Workers, the NAM's whole purpose changed. For decades, capital had come to see the federal government as a loyal and powerful ally in the fight against labor, but Roosevelt's position signaled a shift in the status quo. These were also years of aggressive expansion by the American Federation of Labor as it tried to organize craft unions among the thousands of independent factories in the small cities of the Middle West—including Battle Creek and Springfield. In 1903, NAM membership tripled, and new leadership emerged, mostly drawn from its violently antilabor faction. Post was the most prominent among them. His first speech before the group was titled "The Tyranny of the Trade Unions."[30]

He moved in as head of the Citizens' Industrial Association of America (CIAA), a NAM spin-off that organized local employers' associations. Starting at home, he founded the Battle Creek Citizens' Alliance (BCCA); every important employer in town joined. The group pledged to bar labor unions from their factories and shops. Post named the strategy the "Battle Creek Way" and explicitly linked the open shop to a booster philosophy of economic and demographic growth. Banning labor unions would "protect" the interests of the city and expand its economy by luring new industries to a place that guaranteed "immunity from labor troubles of every kind." BCCA members also promised to pay competitive wages and provide safe working environments. They still reserved the right to fire an employee for cause. Strikes and boycotts were strictly forbidden.[31]

As president of the CIAA, Post launched a national campaign. Working from a suite of offices in New York, he sent a small army of commissioned agents across the country to organize local affiliates. The coordinators, who gained a reputation for persuasiveness and aggression, helped make antipathy toward labor unions part of the booster creed. At their disposal was an astonishing volume of open-shop propaganda, much of it prepared by the CIAA's communication director, an up-and-coming Kansas City newspaperman named George Creel.[32] The centerpiece of CIAA marketing was the *Square Deal*, a monthly magazine. It was a slick, high-quality publication prepared by Post's marketing department back in Battle Creek. The magazine's philosophy was clear: organized labor was evil and the open shop was the only moral approach to the labor question. Each issue featured horror stories about labor violence and terrorism and a corresponding number of reasonable-sounding articles on the open shop, but the *Square Deal* also included news stories, general business advice, fun facts, jokes, cartoons, and the like. It was the sort of magazine that littered the reception areas of thousands of offices. Post wrote several essays a year, and the magazine also drew on a solid roster of other talent: business owners, economists, ministers, sociologists, politicians, political scientists, public figures, and public intellectuals. CIAA affiliates also received legal aid, management training, and access to the organization's network of strikebreakers and spies. By 1909, it represented more than four hundred local associations.[33]

Not content with preaching to the choir and organizing his fellow businessmen, in 1904 Post launched an all-out effort—at his own expense—to warn the American public of the dangers of organized labor and to articulate the logic of the open shop. For a decade, Post paid huge sums of money to regularly print his lengthy antilabor jeremiads in seemingly every newspaper in the country. His screeds, which ran to thousands and thousands of words, ran in major newspapers like the *New York Times* and the *Hartford Courant* but also tiny ones like the

Bronson (Kansas) Pilot and the Tuscumbia *North Alabamian*. He spent millions. While he made clear, in a *nota bene* that closed every ad, that he had purchased the space, it wasn't as if most newspapers could refuse to publish his broadsides. He made it clear to newspapers that refusing to publish his political statements meant losing the Postum account.[34] Even the shortest of his compositions took up a full quarter page. They were all pretty much alike, with lurid and gloomy tales of the damage labor unions had inflicted on the nation and vivid descriptions of public violence and devastation to innocent families. Unions, he would declare, were the real "trusts" and labor leaders were tyrants. "The great 90 percent of Americans do not take kindly to the acts of tyranny by those trust leaders openly demanding that all people bow down to the rules of the Labor Trust and we are treated to the humiliating spectacle of our Congress and even the Chief Executive entertaining these convicted law-breakers and listening with consideration to their insolent demands that the very laws be changed to allow them to safely carry on their plan of gaining control over the affairs of the people."[35] Using his considerable talents for advertising, Post pitched his message directly to the middle-class consumers who bought Grape-Nuts and Postum, a group scared of labor violence and confused by the strange new workings of the American economy.

IV

The most ambitious element in Post's antilabor boosterism was Post City, his capitalist utopia on the Texas plains. Here, he would "demonstrate that a city and a country made up of individual owners" could achieve "wealth, comfort [and] peace." Here, he would clearly and convincingly contrast "individualism" with "socialism." In Post City, residents would "stand on their own resources, to maintain their own homes, and to live their own lives as becomes independent American citizens."[36] Every member of the community would be a "a landed proprietor and a defender of peace and prosperity." He would create a place simply incapable of producing "socialists or anarchists."[37]

Post, who really did have remarkable vision, planned every detail: the architecture and amenities of individual homes, the number and types of businesses, the design and functions of the surrounding agricultural community, the layout and aesthetics of the city itself, the editorial stance of its newspaper, the structure of city government. He wrote the recipe for the beefsteaks served in his hotel and determined exactly where bowls of Grape-Nuts would be placed on its breakfast tables. He decided who could live in Post City, demanding references and interviews with potential residents. No renters or speculators were allowed. Newcomers were placed on a six-month probationary period. Farmers had to demonstrate previous success. He had veto power over the local government. Needless to say, labor unions were not permitted: "No man who comes into Post City will ever be tyrannized over by labor unions."[38]

Staking out the town started in late spring of 1906, less than half a year after his ranch-buying barbecue speech. Most of the major decisions and planning came out of Battle Creek, but Post chartered the Double U Company to run the day-to-day construction and operation. Post chose a site atop the caprock about forty miles southeast of Lubbock. A large tent city was in place before the year was out. Its white canvas structures could be seen for miles. He founded a quarry nearby to cut native stone and built a lumber mill on-site to cut material to order. A massive commissary served hundreds of workers. The nearest railroad was still seventy miles away in Big Spring, so Post had a road graded between his project and the depot and put together the largest supply train in Texas: twenty-four built-to-order Studebaker wagons and a seventy-two-mule team imported from Missouri. For four years, the team trudged back and forth over the four-day trek, hauling all he needed across the Texas prairie. Nothing was allowed to slow development; when a survey revealed that the town site wasn't close enough to the county's geographic center to be named the county seat, Post ordered a temporary halt in construction, hopped a train to Texas, and within a few days had picked out a new site, laid out its stakes, and resumed building. (Close City, Texas, named for Post's first son-in-law, sits on the old site.) He spent a fortune.[39]

By Christmas 1907, Post City was taking shape. A city-block building complex that would house, among other things, the largest general store in West Texas, was almost complete. Across the street, construction on the Algerita, which promised to be the finest hotel between Fort Worth and Denver, had begun. Scattered across various plats, there were fifty brand-new homes on site, almost all of them occupied. Double U construction crews were putting up a house every eleven days. Soon, they had it down to six. In 1908, the sewer and electric systems went in along with the telephone exchange. All the wire ran down the town's alleys. Main Street businesses were open and so were the school and a bank. The Double U built three churches. The Algerita Hotel opened and delivered as promised with well-appointed rooms, solid furnishings, and a good restaurant. By year's end there were nearly six hundred residents, a fire brigade, a men's baseball team, and a women's basketball team. The Masonic Lodge, a theater, a cotton gin and warehouse, a hospital, a grain elevator, and recreational lake came the next year. So did a golf course. Post himself designed the trophy for the club championship. Post spent several weeks a year on-site, and when away, he communicated regularly with his managers through the mail and by telegram and telephone. He insisted on regular and detailed reports from Wilbur Hawk and his team in Texas.

Post got creative promoting his town. There was the traditional pamphlet approach—like "Making Money in Texas," a short promotional brochure prepared by Wilbur Hawk and mailed out by the thousands. But more interesting were some of the other methods. Like the story about Coronado's silver that appeared in newspapers across the country in late 1907 and early 1908. The uncredited report told of how two and a half pounds of silver trimming (probably belonging to a member of the Coronado Expedition) had been found in a cave on Post's Texas property. Only the first two paragraphs (of thirteen) describe the unusual find; the rest of the article is an advertisement for Post City. Literally: its landscape ("a great smooth plain with rich grass-covered land"), its turnkey farms, its orchards, its government ("affairs are conducted in a thrifty, economic manner"), its retail establishments, its "beautiful stone court house," its water system, its climate ("air is dry, sweet and pure"), its potential for agricultural production (cattle, hogs, kaffir, alfalfa, cotton), its creed ("labor union tyranny is not permitted in Post City.")[40]

Not every flattering story about Post City originated in Battle Creek. His "model town" in Texas got plenty of good press. "Magical" was how a correspondent for the Maysville, Kentucky, *Public Ledger* described the town in 1908: "One is constantly rubbing his eyes and pinching himself to learn whether he is dreaming or not. Rows of beautiful dwellings, splendid reproductions of bungalows, Swiss cottages, half stone and half mansard effect, beautifully dressed stone cut into every imaginable effect, a panorama of fairy tale effects."[41] The *Abilene (Texas) Daily*

Reporter called Post City "without a doubt the most substantially built city west of Fort Worth."[42] A piece for *Hampton's Broadway Magazine* (picked up by the wire services) called it "a city free from the evils of speculation" and praised its intolerance for renters, land sharks, saloons, and "gambling dens," as well as its government, run by businessmen.[43] Perhaps the most fawning story was the one that appeared in the *Detroit Free Press* in April 1908. Written by journalist and poet Fannie Sprague Talbot who had joined C. W. and Marjorie for an extended visit to Post City a few months earlier, the article gushed: "The same brain that has evolved millions from the manufacture of foods has now undertaken the stupendous task of building an ideal city, a city that will be a credit to itself, to the state of its adoption and to the builder himself."[44]

Despite the rhetorical flights of fancy in these stories, the fact remained that Post City was, simply put, the prettiest town in West Texas. Post's attention and money compressed even the shortened developmental stages of planned communities like Littlefield or Pampa and established an aesthetic impossible without his obsessive attention to detail and demands for central planning. Every home was a version of a California cottage, the hottest architectural style going, and was wired and plumbed. The city's main street was divided by a handsome tree-filled median. At the town's main intersection stood the huge general store, the hotel, and the bank. Extending out five blocks from the central business district were residential neighborhoods laid out in two identical forty-block grids. He grew the 100,000 ash, poplar, catalpa, and locust trees planted along every street—including the roads in and out of town—in a nursery he built on-site. A modern waterworks brought water down from the caprock. He constructed his high school, courthouse, and hotel out of the lovely native sandstone from his quarry. Each was in the same classic prairie style. His liberal use of stone, which even made its way into home construction, gave Post City an immediate air of permanence.

At the center of Post's utopian vision was homeownership. He had always been interested in residential development (he viewed Postumville in Battle Creek as the centerpiece of his industrial benevolence), but Post City had even loftier goals, a way to conclusively demonstrate that a "prosperous community is best built by men who own their homes and their business buildings." Homeownership would be the key, he believed, to restoring peace and comfort to a nation disordered by the vagaries of industrial capitalism. The insatiable need for workers in the nation's new factories during the previous few decades had, Post believed, upended the trajectory of home- and landownership. The transitory millions who poured into the nation's cities, where they were forced to live in squalid tenements, had no commitment or attachment to their new communities. The cruel nature of this residential volatility was one of the reasons that so many were turning to labor unions and socialism. Consequently, employers had both a moral and an economic interest in improving the domestic stability of their employees. "A man without a home which he actually owns . . . feels that he is, in a way, only a transient, not really a part of the government, not one of the real solid oak timbers in the great structure, but that he is only one of the chips to be swept out when the owners wish." A homeowner, by contrast, "is a self-sustaining and self-respecting individual—to my mind the best type of citizen, the most reliable, and helps to form the most prosperous community."[45] Furthermore, he claimed, a workman, "who has been shown a way to pay for his home and practice thrift does not need poor laws, workhouses, old-age pensions, or charity of any kind."[46]

Post City bungalows sold for between $1,500 and $3,000. Buyers needed a healthy down payment and had four years to pay off the note. Homes were built to order and ranged in size from one-bedroom cottages to four-bedroom houses. Toilets, tubs, and sinks were installed even before the waterworks was up and running. They all had fireplaces and came painted and wallpapered. Many had basements, and some had summer kitchens and sleeping porches. There was plenty of curb appeal with charming front porches, dormers, custom-cut bargeboards, painted shutters, hedges, and plenty of windows. Every home sat on a nice-sized lot with both a front and a back yard. There was an annual contest for the prettiest yard and Post himself named the winner. Within four years, Post City had one thousand citizens.[47]

The farms proved a tougher sell. Post had, like everything else, particular ideas about agriculture. He had great faith in the commercial family farm where what he called "intensive farming" could be practiced on a suitable scale, where a "family can give farming ample attention."[48] He designed the farms of Post City to match that vision. But his way was expensive, several times the cost per acre elsewhere in the southern plains. And the land hadn't been broken. And it was still eighty miles from the railroad. And 1907 was a drought year.[49] Undeterred, Post took advantage of the slow pace of sales to conduct crop experiments on his farmlands. He subsidized renters who tried out different agricultural commodities: grains, vegetables, forage, cotton, sorghum, hogs. He also planted a massive town garden. He grew so deliberate in his study that he even took his farms off the market for a couple of years.

When the farms did go up for sale, they were spectacular. Each property was a turnkey operation, complete with a four-room house; a barn, stable, chicken house, and hog shed; a well, a three-acre orchard protected by hedgerows, and a windmill. The properties were already fenced. Like the houses, all the farm structures were built to spec by the Double U Company according to a standard set of plans. There was easy access to the latest agricultural technology (in their interviews, farmers had to demonstrate proficiency in the use of agricultural implements). Every farm was on a graded road with easy access to town. Ringing the half-section family farmlands were four-section ranchettes, all with windmills and water tanks.[50]

The *New York Tribune Farmer* raved: "I very much doubt whether the agricultural history of the United States records such a unique plan, so practical in its conception and so successfully carried out, of building up such a very large farm and highly intelligent community of farmers, and having every detail conducted according to the latest and most improved methods of farm life and practice." Post, the reporter continued, was helping Americans become "better citizens" and creating in West Texas "some of the best and most productive land in the country."[51]

Post even came to believe that he could transform the actual climate of his properties. Perhaps preternaturally drawn to pseudoscience, he became a convert to "pluviculture," the crackpot theory that one can make it rain on demand by blowing up dynamite in the atmosphere. For years the good folk of Post City endured their benefactor's "rain battle" experiments. When conditions were right—and his town managers were to keep him regularly updated on local weather conditions—Post would order up to three thousand pounds of dynamite to be launched into the skies from the caprock just west of town. Four in the morning, noon, supper time, midnight. Dogs howled, horses spooked, babies cried, windows rattled, and houses shook. Honestly believing that his experiments were yielding results, he spent $50,000 in dynamite over one summer. When Post died, there were still twenty-five tons of TNT stored in special caverns above the city. The good citizens of Post City, not surprisingly, had no interest in continuing the experiments. When the United States entered World War I, in a terrific display of paranoia and Yosemite Sam problem-solving, city leaders, terrified by what the potential German saboteurs in their midst might do with all that dynamite, attached a long fuse to the whole mess and blew it up.[52]

Post also took charge of finding buyers for the businesses of Post City. Like the farms, they were designed to be turnkey operations. Some, like the lumberyard and the stable, were up and running from the beginning. Others, like the barbershop and the tailor, he designed and advertised in trade magazines. When he failed to find one buyer for his gigantic general store, he split it into different businesses and sold them off to individual merchants: groceries, furniture, hardware, dry goods, confectionary, paint, shoes, drugs, stationery, and so forth. Each already had regular customers and inventory on the shelves. Depending on the size of the operation he demanded between $2,000 and $10,0000 as a down payment and offered reasonable terms and a "good opening to make money as the country grows."[53]

The town was effectively governed by the Double U, which took its direction from Post or Wilbur Hawk. Post planned eventually to implement a city commission–style system whereby the executive and legislative functions would be combined in a small, elected body of commissioners, each with a specific administrative role. Those commissioners would be drawn from the booster class. Often called the Galveston plan, it was already the most popular form of city government in West Texas. But, until the city population grew, Post ran the city according to a strict set of instructions he laid out in the city's "Dedication." There was an exacting code governing sanitation and property upkeep. No home or business was allowed to have alcohol on the premises. Prostitution and gambling were strictly banned. (Once, in his absence, overzealous town leaders prosecuted a pool hall owner for gambling because losers were expected to pay for the game. When he heard about this strict interpretation of his rule, Post paid the fine himself.) There was even a curfew. Land speculators were forbidden. No one was allowed to sublet their home or farm. Neither African Americans nor Mexican Americans were allowed to purchase land or lots.

Neither, obviously, were members of labor unions. Or socialists. The newspaper, naturally called the *Post City Post*, followed Post's views on "trade unionism, socialism, and anarchism." When its editor wrote—

at Post's urging—a full-throated condemnation of the pro-labor and socialist newspaper *Appeal to Reason*, Post paid to have it reprinted as an advertisement in the newspaper. For a full year, just in case his townspeople were unclear on the subject. And for good measure he also instructed the local post office to refuse to accept or deliver copies of the *Appeal to Reason*. Getting caught with a copy could get you kicked out of town.[54] When W. T. Estes, a socialist from Lubbock, took it upon himself to give away copies in Post City, Post, who happened to be in town, confronted the man and threatened him with jail or violence or both. The next time Estes showed his face, he was beaten up and chased out of town.[55]

In 1912, Post cranked up a new economic engine for his city. Up to that point, *he* had basically been the economy, spending upward of $36,000 a month and still micromanaging every detail of Post City. But that year he broke ground on the Postex Cotton Mills, a 136,000-square-foot facility, the first of its kind to spin local cotton into a product, in this case, bed linens. The mill produced two styles, luxury sheets (named Postex, no surprise there), among the finest linens available in the country, and the everyday brand (Garza), also popular. The mill employed 250 people and its power plant served the entire town. It would produce up to twenty thousand sheet sets a year until the 1940s.

By 1914, Post was ready to put his farmlands back on the market. Five hundred small truck farms were laid out on the very edges of the city, along with dozens of four-section stock farms just beyond. The biggest sales campaign in the city's history was set to start on April 1. For months, Post peppered Texas newspapers with stories and ads for the properties. Thirteen thousand copies of the Post-penned flyer "A Chance to Own a Fine Farm" were mailed out to prospects.[56] "Breaking Up a Great Ranch," another sales pitch,[57] started showing up in rural and agricultural newspapers across Texas and the Great Plains:

> I feel that we are offering such opportunities to deserving home seekers as assure the establishment and building up of a prosperous community. I am providing completed home farms for those who have a little money and are sufficiently enterprising to enter upon owning a home for themselves and their families. . . . There has been a substantial growth and development at Post during the few years of my ownership of property there, and I feel that the time has now come for me to share its future prosperity

with those who are in earnest about wanting to prosper. You will be greeted with hearty sincerity at Post and assisted in every reasonable way towards getting along. There is real happiness to be derived from fresh air and sunshine and growing crops and values, where the big part of the growth and increase comes to the man who is earning and getting it.[58]

Post wouldn't live to see the campaign's results. Laid low and holed up in a Santa Barbara mansion that he had recently built to spend his winters, Post had grown despondent and distressed by a crippling case of appendicitis. He grew convinced that the stomach troubles that had sent him to Battle Creek those many years ago had returned. Not even an emergency surgery at the Mayo Clinic relieved his fears. On May 9, he penned a short note to his daughter and wife (his second), put on one of his best suits, and took his own life with his prized Winchester .40-72 rifle. He was sixty years old. He was worth $50 million.[59]

Within hours of his death, the news reached Post City. The entire town turned out to mourn. A public meeting produced the proclamation that

we [who] have lost a friend and a benefactor, a man loved and respected by all, desire to show our appreciation of his many acts of kindness and generosity toward us and the community at large. Mr. Post, with unusual foresight and magnificent courage, planned and developed this city, providing employment to hundreds of people and arranging for their comfort and pleasure in many practical ways. . . . This city and surrounding county will feel his loss most keenly, as all felt his personality to be one of the great influences of good in the future development and prosperity of this section.[60]

On the day of his funeral in Battle Creek—attended by thousands—Post City held a simultaneous memorial service, and schools and businesses closed for the day.

Over two days in mid-September 1957, the city of Post celebrated its fiftieth anniversary.[61] Post's daughter, Marjorie, then the wealthiest woman in America, returned as the city's guest of honor. The celebration was about as West Texas an event as one might conjure: barbecue for four thousand (twenty beeves' worth of meat), a fiddle contest, a dominoes tournament, a beard contest, plaques for dignitaries, Boy Scouts doing "Indian dances," and a "cavalcade" of 350 people re-creating the history of Post.[62] Marjorie, who had fond memories of the town from her childhood, was a good sport. On the second day she even headed out in a dust storm to take her place in the parade.[63]

The keynote address for the dedication was given by former Texas Tech University president D. M. Wiggins, who laid out how Post's prairie utopia had perfectly captured the culture of the entire region. The town's founder was, as Wiggins illuminated, "a powerful exponent of the dignity of individualism and the concept of free enterprise."[64] Indeed, the twin ideals of free enterprise and individualism would animate the politics and culture of almost every town in West Texas for the rest of the century.

4
WEST TEXAS NATIONALISM

A place belongs forever to whoever claims it hardest, remembers it most obsessively, wrenches it from itself, shapes it, renders it, loves it so radically that he remakes it in his own image.

JOAN DIDION

West Texas was always supposed to be its own state. Maybe even two. That was its intent when Congress admitted Texas to the Union. With land claims that rivaled the area of the old Northwest Territory, no serious person in Washington could imagine a single state as large as Texas.[1] Which is why within the 1845 annexation resolution was a provision to allow Texas to split into five separate states—perhaps not coincidentally, the same number carved from the old Northwest Territory. The resolution left the task of division up to Texans, who never quite got around to it. Nowadays, the only folks who ponder the possibilities of this geopolitical meiosis are geography nerds or political junkies.[2] Occasionally, some striving Texas pol publicly muses about the power ten Texas senators might have on national policy, and the five-state factoid enjoys a quick run through the news cycle.[3] But in reality, in its entire 180-year history, there has only been one serious threat to split the state—that was when boosters of the Agricultural Wonderland threatened to secede from Texas.

By the mid-1910s, West Texas was a very different place from the rest of the state. It had a distinct history, its own unique economy, and a drastically dissimilar environment. Its population was almost all white, it was young, it was middle-class, had a significant nonsouthern population, and was growing at phenomenal speed. Though agricultural, it was a town-centered culture, dominated by a forward-looking, petite-bourgeois booster class primarily invested in the growth and expansion of the Agricultural Wonderland.

At the center of West Texas identity was its history. In the opening decades of the twentieth century, while white Texans in the eastern half of the state wallowed in the moonlight and magnolias of Lost Cause mythology, West Texans saw themselves as the last generation of pioneers who had conquered and settled the wildest of the western frontiers. These were the years when western expansion became the origin story of the nation and pioneering was seen as the basis of the American character and the source of American democracy. In real time, as West Texans brought their gardens from the desert, the frontier national narrative was gelling into common knowledge. Local lore was punctuated by tales of danger and excitement and the hardship of taming this new land, a place defined by strange weather and wild beasts and unimaginable distances.[4] The markers of their success—the opening of the first school and the coming of the railroad—were shared memories in every West Texas community. These were places that had come together quickly, within a generation, and regional identity was formed over a short and shared history. Comanche, cattle and cowboys, cotton or wheat, towns and tractors.[5] In most of the American West, with longer local histories and a larger federal presence, it often took two or even three generations to establish a regional identity. But, in West Texas, led by a pioneer generation eager to secure its cultural position in a society moving beyond a frontier stage of development, it happened much faster. Within twenty years of laying out towns like Post City and Pampa, West Texas already had its own regional chamber of commerce and a host of other regional business and professional organizations. There were two regional historical societies and a historical museum. West Texans had begun to set themselves against the rest of the state.[6]

I

In 1883, two Fort Worth bankers, looking to cash in on the cattle Bonanza, founded the Spur Ranch. They bought a quarter million acres from T. D. Hobart's New York and Texas Land Company in a four-county block on the southern plains. They sold out to a syndicate two years later and tripled their money. The new syndicate was called the Espuela Land and Cattle Company, though everybody still called it the Spur. It was a failure from the get-go. The company never recovered from the Die-Up. For twenty years it met disaster after disaster and it bled money.[7] Finally, in 1906, the company dumped the whole enterprise at $5 an acre to an investment group looking to get into agricultural real estate. The buyers, led by the Swenson ranch family, hired a professional manager, Charles A. Jones, away from the Armour Company in Kansas City to run the operation.[8] He was a good choice; within a couple of years, Jones scored an agricultural experiment station on the property, built several towns, founded a bank and a chamber of commerce, and lured a railroad. Recognizing his obvious talent, the company sent Jones to run its sulfur and mining interests on the gulf coast, where he would build the town of Freeport.[9] Taking over his duties on the Spur was Jones's twenty-four-year-old son, Clifford B. Jones.

Over the next sixty years, the younger Jones would become the most important booster in West Texas. He ranched, he banked, he developed real estate and founded towns. Mayor of Spur, founder and president of the West Texas Chamber of Commerce and the Spur Security Bank, vice-president of the Texas Highway Association, director of the Dallas Mercantile Bank, the Lubbock National Bank, and the Southwestern Public Service Company, and president and regent of Texas Tech University.[10] And in spring 1921, Clifford B. Jones found himself in Sweetwater, Texas, chairing a meeting where a fiery mob of hundreds of West Texas lawyers, newspaper editors, farmers, implement and insurance salesmen, auto dealers, movie house owners, and other businessmen were demanding that the region secede from the Lone Star State.

The idea of secession had been floating around for a few years. W. A. Johnson, a newspaper editor and Texas state senator originally from Memphis, had been stewing for half a decade over the fact that the state had not redistricted after the 1910 census. Furious over the fact that while the population of West Texas had doubled, the State of Texas had not increased the number of state representatives to the legislature, in 1915 Johnson introduced a bill that would split the state in two. The 106 westernmost counties would become the forty-ninth state, which he proposed would be called Jefferson. Mostly meaning it as a form of protest and a way to raise awareness of the inequity that failure to redistrict had created, Johnson had a little fun with the proposal.[11] He named himself one of Jefferson's U.S. senators as well as his choices for governor, lieutenant governor, ag commissioner, and other offices. Abilene, he said, should be the provisional state capital. He wrote a rough draft of a legal code and set dates for Jefferson's constitutional convention. The bill, which even made it out of committee, set off a flurry of other divisional proposals but ultimately went nowhere. Nevertheless, Johnson became the godfather of West Texas secessionists. Week after week, he used his editorial perch at the *Hall County Herald* to complain about the unfair nature of Texas's tax structure (West Texas farmers paid three dollars in taxes for every dollar they received in state services) and to criticize those land policies that had awarded millions of acres of West Texas to pay for institutions, railroads, and improvements in other parts of the state. Unstated in Johnson's criticisms, but a position widely held, was anger over West Texans being taxed to pay for the state's elaborate and expensive mechanisms of segregation, not an issue that applied in blindingly white West Texas.[12] Explicitly stated was that Texas would be better off with more representation from this modern, vibrant region, blessed with the nation's fastest-growing economy and population.[13]

More than anything, boosters like Johnson wanted a state agricultural college, an "A&M for the plains," like the one at College Station but for the "white boys" of West Texas.[14] Shortly after Johnson's original bill to divide the state was announced, Hugh Nugent Fitzgerald, the powerful publisher of the *Fort Worth Record*, began pushing for "West Texas A&M," borrowing many of Johnson's arguments. By the end of the year, the school was the talk of every local chamber of commerce and the subject of dozens of small-town newspaper editorials. A strong case emerged. Since it was West Texas land that had paid for so much of the state's educational institutions, the region had earned its own school. West Texas taxes were being used to pay for an agricultural college that was too far away for West Texas students to attend; most college-age West Texans lived closer to ag schools in Oklahoma, Kansas, and Colorado than they did to College Station. Also, the soils, climate, and crops of Brazos County were just too different. West Texas ag students needed a more environmentally appropriate place to learn modern farming and ranching techniques.[15] In April 1915, when Porter Whaley, Amarillo's head of development, called for a region-wide meeting to lobby for a West Texas A&M, 250 boosters from fifty different towns showed up.[16] They formed the West Texas A&M Association.

Within weeks, the Association had printed thousands of slick brochures peppered with photos, factoids, graphs, and a strong argument for a new agricultural college in the most productive farming region in Texas. Not surprisingly, the print campaign bore a striking resemblance to the real estate marketing materials put out by developers like W. P. Soash. The Association hired a full-time director and secretary and launched a statewide campaign, mailing sixty thousand promotional pieces to influencers and politicians. It took out regular ads and placed statements in newspapers across Texas. Every West Texas county had its own chapter of the West Texas A&M committee. Local editors went into overdrive hyping the college, and chambers of commerce pledged regular donations. An informal speaker's bureau gave talks to civic organizations and social groups, racking up endorsements. Insiders working the Democratic Party secured a plank for the school in the state's 1916 party platform. With "more of the wealth of West Texas than has ever before gathered," the Texas Democratic Party, meeting in Fort Worth and hosted by that city's Chamber of Commerce, made the creation of an A&M for West Texas a priority. As promised, a bill was introduced at the next session of the legislature, which passed easily. Governor James Ferguson signed the bill into law in February 1917. It had been less than eighteen months since Fitzgerald's editorial.[17] The West Texas A&M Association had one last meeting, where, at the encouragement of the Fort Worth Chamber of Commerce, it became the West Texas Chamber of Commerce, the voice of "West Texas patriotism."[18]

Then, the whole project collapsed.

"Farmer Jim" Ferguson was of a generation of "populist" governors who in various guises drew remarkable electoral strength by appealing directly to the dirt farmers of the American South, those unlucky multitudes left behind by the modern economy and still eking out a life on tiny plots at the creek branches and in the forest clearings. A lawyer/banker from Bell County and a political insider who had come up in the antiprohibitionist wing of the party, Ferguson was a fantastic stump speaker ("bad grammar, folksy stories, sarcasm, and slander in about equal proportions"[19]) and shrewd tactician. He had been elected governor in 1914 (his first run for office) by promising to cap farm rents and improve rural schools. He had a good first term and despite not-so-quiet rumors about unsavory dealings in the Governor's Mansion, he was reelected easily. He was *not* popular in West Texas, where there were few sharecroppers and where support for prohibition was close to universal.

Nevertheless, it was Ferguson who chaired the blue-ribbon committee charged with selecting the site of the new West Texas A&M.[20] The group also included Lieutenant Governor William Hobby, House Speaker Franklin Fuller, Agricultural Commissioner Fred Davis, and State School Superintendent Walter Doughty. The committee considered twenty-three different towns and cities, even visiting many of the potential sites. By June 1917, it had narrowed its choices to Amarillo, Snyder, Haskell, Abilene, and San Angelo. The men gathered in Austin to make their final selection. In the first round of voting, Abilene got two votes (Ferguson and Doughty), and Haskell, Snyder, and San Angelo received a vote apiece. After another round of discussion, a second vote was held; Abilene received three votes and Amarillo and Snyder each got one. With Abilene as the clear favorite, the five committee members agreed on one last vote to make the decision unanimous. That night, things got weird. Hobby and Davis told reporters that in the second vote they had chosen Amarillo and Snyder, respectively. As he read the evening papers, the fifth commission member, Franklin Fuller, was shocked; he had also voted for Snyder, which would have meant a tie between Abilene and Snyder. Fuller went public. The story blew up: either a committee member was lying, or someone had rigged the votes. Working in executive session, the committee had kept no written records. A janitor had conveniently cleaned the room after the men had left and had incinerated the paper ballots along with the trash.

Before anyone got to the bottom of the scandal, the A&M selection crisis got caught up in an entire tidal wave of accusations against Ferguson that swept over the state in the second half of June: mishandled appropriation bills, financial indiscretions, embezzlement, and misappropriation of funds. The embattled governor was also enmeshed in a vulgar fight with the University of Texas, where he was intimidating faculty and making accusations of graft. The Ferguson story dominated the state's politics and press. In July, a Travis County grand jury indicted the governor on nine counts. Then the Texas House of Representatives impeached him. On September 22, the Senate convicted Ferguson and threw him out of office.[21] In the wake of the irregularities surrounding Abilene's selection and the scandals that disrupted the creation of the new agricultural college, the committee withdrew its recommendation.

The West Texas Chamber of Commerce, whose own selection committee did *not* favor Abilene, tried in vain to get the new governor, William
Hobby—who had been on the committee—to call a do-over.[22]

For four years West Texas boosters tried to relaunch the process of
establishing an agricultural college. Finally, in early 1921, the legislature appropriated $50,000 to find a new site. That April, the West Texas
booster class gathered in different meetings called to coincide with the
Manufacturers' Merchants and Automobile Dealers' Exposition, a major
tractor and farm implement trade show, in Sweetwater. The new college
bill was all anyone could talk about. And everyone expected that the
governor, Pat Neff, who enjoyed huge support in West Texas, would be
signing it while they were at the convention. They waited anxiously.[23]

Then came the telegram—Neff had vetoed the bill. That's when the
convention took on a pitchfork-and-torch vibe. For two days, a decade's
worth of frustration poured out in speeches and condemnations. At
one point the lawyers, editors, and politicians ducked into a side room
and emerged with a set of demands: they wanted their agricultural college, immediate legislative reapportionment, compensation for land
giveaways, and tax reform. Without immediate redress, West Texans
would secede from the rest of the state: "We, the citizenship of West
Texas, stand united and cohesive in the determination to right these
wrongs."[24] Clifford B. Jones, the newly elected president of the West
Texas Chamber of Commerce (WTCC) and a practical man, released
his own statement. He ignored talk of secession but expressed shock
and dismay that Governor Neff would deny the education that the "the
youth of Texas" deserved by "every expectancy of heritage and justice."
The hot-headed president of the Young Businessmen's League, on the
other hand, announced a "Divide-the-State" conference for April 6.

Which is how Clifford B. Jones found himself at the head of a secession convention, just two months into his tenure as chamber president.
He had his hands full. Mitchell County delegates printed up badges
reading "Loraine, Mitchell County, State of West Texas."[25] There was
a lot of "Tea Party" talk. State representative R. M. Chitwood, who
had written the vetoed bill, declared that West Texans suffered under
a regime that "denies them the chance to realize their hopes and aspirations." For good measure, he added that they wanted a West Texas
A&M designed for "the training of the white boys of Texas . . . in the
white man's part of Texas."[26] Jones and other WTCC members worked

backdoor channels to keep a secession vote off the table as they negotiated with Neff to call a special session of the legislature to address
reapportionment and provide assurances that the West Texas A&M
proposal was not dead. Their semiofficial stance was that "it will take a
bigger man than Pat Neff to force us in a position where we will have to
divide Texas to get justice." The convention settled on the "West Texas
Declaration of Rights," in which the signatories reserved the right to
secede if those rights were denied. The document, a testament to West
Texas nationalism, demanded an immediate special session of the Texas
State Legislature to address redistricting and more equal representation,
a restructuring of taxes and state services to the region, and West Texas
A&M. "No free and vigorous people can be content to live under a
state government which denies them such rights and privileges." If their
demands were not met, the convention promised, "we will call for the
creation of a new state under which we may hope to have equal rights
and representation." There was not a single dissenting vote.[27]

As for Pat Neff, he never quite understood the hubbub. A staunch
conservative and prohibitionist, he was, until April anyway, incredibly
popular in West Texas. As he explained it, he vetoed the measure only
because he had promised in his campaign that as governor, he would
confine his work to fulfilling the state Democratic Party platform of
1920. Since that document did not include a plank for creating the new
college (despite an intense lobbying effort by the WTCC), he, a loyal
Democrat, was bound to the platform. (It should be noted that everyone
in the Texas house and senate was a Democrat and the bill had passed
easily.) Neff assured the WTCC that if the party had an A&M plank in
its next platform, he would gladly sign it. They did and he did in early
1922.[28] Eleven months to the day after Neff's original veto, seven thousand people showed up for a celebration in Sweetwater. The jubilation
was so intense, organizers finally abandoned the official program to let
the crowds mingle, yell, and backslap, all they apparently wanted to do.

Thirty-six towns and cities competed to be the home of what was
by then being called Texas Tech. They included San Angelo, Midland,
Amarillo, Sweetwater, Plainview, Snyder, and even Post, but it was
fast-growing Lubbock that won the prize.[29] The *Lubbock Avalanche* celebrated: "It is not alone the ambitious youth of West Texas who are to
be blessed. It is West Texas agriculture, West Texas manufacturers, West
Texas enterprise of every description. The technological college will

have as its business the training of minds for coping with the immediate problems of the territory it supplies, the installation of western ideals, the breeding of virile crops of typical western manhood."[30] The school's first Board of Regents was drawn from the region's booster class. Prominent among them was Clifford B. Jones, by then being hailed as "West Texas's Number One Citizen."

II

Hattie Mabel Anderson showed up in Canyon in fall 1920, the newest member of the West Texas State Normal College's department of history. A thirty-three-year-old, unmarried woman, Anderson was not a typical college professor. The daughter of Swedish immigrant farmers, the newly minted faculty member had grown up on the Missouri frontier near Sedalia, the one-time terminus of one of Texas's most important cattle trails. At sixteen, she had taken over the teaching duties at her local one-room school, a position she would hold even as she took degrees from Central Missouri State Teachers College and the University of Missouri. Curious, driven, and deeply intellectual, Anderson took the unusual step toward a PhD in history, starting her work at the University of Chicago and writing her dissertation at the University of Missouri. In those years, fewer than 15 percent of all doctorates were earned by women and in history, a discipline dominated by men, that number was even smaller.[31] Anderson was particularly interested in the emerging field of frontier history and was delighted to take a position in the Texas Panhandle, just then emerging from its "pioneer" stage of development. Established specifically to train the region's schoolteachers, West Texas State Normal (WT) also appealed to the schoolteacher in her. WT in those days was actually two schools: a two-year teaching college and a "demonstration school," essentially a high school academy for gifted local kids.[32] The two worked in tandem, the demonstration school offering a real-world training ground for future teachers, and the academy serving as a pipeline for students heading to college.[33] WT had hired Anderson to design and run the history department's teacher-training program. When one considers the fact that over her thirty-seven-year career at WT, Anderson was directly responsible for training thousands of schoolteachers, and further imagines how many hundreds of thousands of West Texas schoolchildren learned American history from those teachers, it's safe to say this former one-room school teacher had a greater impact on the way that West Texans understood their past than anyone. And Hattie M. Anderson, like everyone on the WT history faculty, had a particular way of understanding the American past.[34]

It was 1893 when Frederick Jackson Turner, a youngish history professor from Wisconsin, presented a paper at the youngish American Historical Association meeting at Chicago. He titled his essay "The Significance of the Frontier in American History," and his argument went like this: American exceptionalism (a given to a Progressive historian like Turner) was the evolutionary result of two centuries of Americans transforming rugged wilderness spaces into productive farming communities. The act of rebuilding society and reestablishing democracy on each successive frontier worked to hone a unique American character and develop America's high-functioning political economy. The money quote: "The existence of an area of free land, its continuous recession, and the advance of American settlement westward, explain American development."[35] Speaking in Chicago, a glowing, pulsating example of this type of frontier transformation—from muddy village to world city in less than a century—gave Turner's thesis obvious immediacy. Speaking to a generation that, like Turner, had in its lifetime borne witness to the transformation of the entire western two-thirds of the nation gave it intimate intellectual resonance. Presenting his testament to American exceptionalism in the midst of the World's Columbian Exposition, an outrageously over-the-top celebration of American greatness, gave it massive cultural power.[36]

Turner's Frontier Thesis, a story of process, and a progressive one at that, lent itself beautifully to narrative history. With a recognizable beginning, middle, and end, it brought American history right up to the moment of his essay. He laid out a generic set of historical stages easily applied across space and time: hunters, traders, stockmen, farmers, townsfolk, and city dwellers. Consequently, it could serve as national, regional, even local history. It was the history of every settlement, every community, every family. By the dawn of the new century, Turner's Thesis was not just *the* historical interpretation of national development but had also slipped the bonds of the academy to become America's origin story—its gamma ray accident, its radioactive spider bite. In academic circles, it served for a brief but crucial time as the Unified Theory of American Development, enjoying a status that bordered on the absolute, like Newton's laws of motion. The second-most influential American historian of the time, Charles Beard, famously believed that Turner's thesis enjoyed "a more profound influence on thought about American history than any other essay or volume ever written on the subject."[37]

That was certainly the case at West Texas State, where the history department organized around Turner's thesis. J. A. Hill, its first member and chair, said as much in the department's mission statement: "In the teaching of History events will be ignored except in so far as they throw light upon institutions and historical processes . . . the pupil will be led to appreciate the origin and growth of political, religious and social organizations as revealed in the unfolding of national life and the development of the human race as a whole."[38] Hill's first book, which he cowrote with WT president R. B. Cousins,[39] was a popular American history text that included this transcendent example of Turnerian influence:

> The careful student has already noticed the influence of the western frontier upon our national life. Not one great movement in the life of the American people has been unaffected by what the brave and strong pioneer has thought and felt and done. Indeed, the distinctive character of American civilization would have been lost long ago but for the free spirit and rugged strength of the Westerners; for into the West have always come the most freedom-loving members of a freedom-loving race; and the conditions of the frontier have not only tended to preserve liberty, but even to promote individual freedom. The Anglo-Saxon's instinct for a fuller life led him to brave the dangers of a savage land separated by three thousand miles of water from his mother country and plant himself permanently on the western shores of Atlantic; it carried him likewise through the narrow passes of the Alleghanies and established him in the rich valleys of the Ohio, the Tennessee, and the Cumberland it urged him to cross the great "father of waters" and take possession of the rolling prairies and fertile woodlands of the Louisiana Territory. To have stopped here would have been to reverse the order of nature.[40]

Hill was promoted to WT president in 1918 and hired Lester Fields Sheffy, a child of the Panhandle frontier, to fill his position. Sheffy, who had graduated from Clarendon College, was also a devoted Turner disciple. His best work, a biography of Timothy Dwight Hobart, placed his subject as the final chapter of a long frontier family history: "The work of pioneering on new frontiers, which the Hobarts had begun so auspiciously on the first American frontier in the seventeenth century, was now resumed in Texas on one of the last American frontiers."[41] Sheffy would go on to chair the WT history department for forty years. When he hired Anderson in 1920, she was still researching for her dissertation, a literal application of Turner's thesis: "A Study in Frontier Democracy: The Social and Economic Bases of the Rise of the Jackson Group in Missouri, 1815–1828." Also joining Anderson in those early years was the woefully underutilized Angie Debo, who would go on to an amazing career as a historian of Native America and who had trained under Edward Everett Dale, himself a student and acolyte of Turner.[42]

On the tenth anniversary of the founding of West Texas Normal, students, led by a group of history majors, put on a play: "Alma Mater the Immortal: An Allegorical Representation of the History and Growth of West Texas State Normal College." As insufferably precocious as its title might suggest, the play was written by one of the department's best and brightest, Mody C. Boatright, who would mature into one of the great folklorists and public intellectuals in Texas. The play was set at the last stage of the frontier process and opens with its protagonist "Quaesitor, the pioneer of the Plains," standing alone on a stage: "The savage and the beast before my might have fled, terrified to see their comrades slain before their eyes. I rejoice to beat them on the field of combat, for I am strong. I strike them down as loathful insects." But having defeated cruel nature and the "savages" who have roamed Quaesitor's new home, the character is left with a dilemma, for no "mortal man" could possibly strike down his newest foes, "the powers of the weather and ignorance." All but ready to give up, the hero instead embarks on a quest, guided by the "Spirit of Progress" to seek out "Alma Mater, daughter of Democracy," and bring her to his land.[43]

Needless to say, a committed and energetic scholar/teacher like Hattie Anderson found plenty of outlets for this kind of youthful energy and imagination. From the moment she arrived in Canyon, she began to plan for an organization that would capture the Panhandle's frontier history. Thanks to her own research, Anderson was all too familiar with the challenge of reconstructing the frontier past, so, with students, she set out to harvest the histories, memories, and material artifacts of the pioneers. As she understood it, the rapidity of "the kaleidoscopic changes" in the Panhandle's recent years presented students of history an unprecedented opportunity to hear and record firsthand the stories of the frontier from the men and women who had lived it.[44] Through the fall semester of 1920, she talked up the idea with faculty, administrators, and students. In February 1921, with the hearty endorsement of the college, she launched the Panhandle-Plains Historical Society (PPHS). The inaugural members included half a dozen faculty and thirty students. Lester Sheffy was its first president. Mody Boatright was the secretary.

Anderson never saw the PPHS as just a college group, but rather as a collaboration between the scholars of WT, the region's pioneer class, and the local cultural and economic elite, recognizing the obvious overlap between the latter two groups. All spring, Anderson and student reps from PPHS presented the Society and its goals to civic organizations and clubs all over the Panhandle. We can assume their appearances echoed Anderson's pitch for the new organization: "Because the frontier has disappeared, every attempt is being made throughout the United States to preserve an account of the experiences, the characteristics, and the ideas of these worthy ancestors," and with the Panhandle having "so recently emerged from the pioneer stage, we have an unusual opportunity here to collect historical material."[45]

Student enthusiasm was overwhelming. They fanned out everywhere, pestering old-timers for stories and permission to root around in sheds, attics, barns, and back rooms. They collected anything remotely associated with the old cowboy days and descended on the annual meetings of the Panhandle Old Settlers Association and cowboy reunions like a plague of question-peppering locusts. Their persistent enthusiasm was so great that even a level-headed old rancher like Charles Goodnight started to believe his own press and, for the first time, began to entertain scholars interested in hearing his remarkable story. No Anderson student was as energetic or persistent as J. Evetts Haley, who upon his graduation, became the field secretary of the PPHS and its first full-time employee.[46] A brilliant, pushy, and obsessed scholar of frontier history, Haley had an open-ended mission: travel the region, collect what historically significant items he could for a future museum, gather stories from the pioneers who had settled the region, and sell memberships at $2.50 a year. He got a small stipend and an old Ford. He journeyed everywhere, followed every lead, checked the veracity of every legend, recorded every story he could coax, and came back to Canyon only when the Ford couldn't hold any more stuff. With little money, he lived the old way, sleeping under the stars, making his coffee over a campfire, and taking advantage of the hospitality of the cow camps and chuck wagons. Raised in the ranch country of Midland, Haley had cowboyed since he was a kid and could fit in with the scrappiest of outfits. He collected everything—pool tables, animal oddities, weaponry.[47] His interviews, detailed and lengthy, are still among the most valuable primary sources regarding Texas ranching in any archive anywhere. (He even scored the entire set of records for the XIT Ranch.) Haley had a keen eye for detail and great ear for vernacular, especially the turns of phrase peculiar to cowboys, which he would later incorporate into the best and most literate books on the Texas frontier ever written. And he signed up seventy new PPHS members.[48]

And then there was the stuff that just showed up. Each week's mail contained all manner of historical ephemera, sent by someone or other who knew it was a valuable piece of history but had no idea what to do with it: random letters, pottery shards, account books, old newspapers and magazines, taxidermized animals, and other artifacts dug out of ancient chests and dragged out of barn lofts. Landowners donated battle sites. Ranchers donated saddles and bridles and pistols and rifles by the dozens. The JA Ranch donated its records. Six years after the Society's founding, it was making plans to build a museum, a testament to the pioneers.

III

By 1921, Turner's academic thesis had been folded into a larger cultural mythology that focused primarily on the cowboy and the cattle frontier. Through an explosion of mediums—painting, music, sculpture, literature, and film—the story had shifted away from tracing the wellspring of the American character and political economy toward celebrating the independence and individualism of cattle country. Its new hero was not the lonely plowman creating a garden from the wilderness but the dashing and freedom-loving cowpuncher drifting from adventure to adventure. For a big part of the twentieth century, the cowboy stood as the paragon of American masculinity and the repository of the nation's liberty. His toughness, honesty, individualism, and self-reliance were the frontier virtues that had made America great. While Turner had focused his scholarship on answering questions about the sources of American democracy and the processes that had created its seeming commitment to social equality, the cowboy myth rendered the frontier as a repository of a kind of crude libertarianism, one welcomed by a rising business class. As Mody Boatright would notice years later, businesspeople had to come to see the frontier as the place where America had learned to reject "social control [and] see in the cowboy, the last of the frontier types, a symbol of the American way."⁴⁹ While it's perhaps easy to see the cowboy conservatism that would come to dominate the political culture of many western spaces as performative—"putting on the hat," as the derogatory phrase goes—that would be a mistake. Seeing this brand of politics only as a style of speaking or clichéd costumes too heavily discounts how the values that folks associated with the cattle frontier helped them articulate their actual beliefs. The business class identified by Boatright did see the world through the kind of entrepreneurial, individualistic lens of the old ranchers. And through the PPHS, they would stamp that view directly on the official history of the region.

Before its first anniversary, the leaders of the Panhandle-Plains Historical Society decided that from then on, the presidency of the organization should be held by a prominent member of the local business community. This approach might insure buy-in from the corporate community and help secure the Society's financial health. It worked. By the end of the decade almost every single stakeholder in the organization was a member of the region's business elite: the usual assortment of banker/ranchers and lawyer/developers, along with oil tycoons, merchants, and railroad officials. The largest newspapers, law firms, banks, and civic institutions held institutional memberships. A 1928 fundraiser that sold life memberships yielded fifty-five new life members, almost every single one a member of the booster class. In its initial campaign to raise money for a museum, 90 percent of the donations were over $50, two weeks' pay for a workingman. The biggest came from chambers of commerce, law firms, newspapers, huge ranches, and banker associations.⁵⁰

The football team of West Texas State Teacher's College in 1922. J. Evetts Haley is seated second from the left.

The first of the business leader presidents was Thomas F. Turner, a frontier lawyer who had settled in Amarillo in 1889 and spent most of his career as the corporate counsel for local railroads and utilities. He was also a founding member of Amarillo's Lion's Club and its country club. In the new constitution and by-laws that he helped write, the Society's mission became clearer: to present the history of the Panhandle-Plains so that future generations would share "the desire to uphold, forever, the honor of the country [their] forefathers wrought out of the wilderness."[51] After a four-year term, Turner was followed by rancher Orville H. Nelson, a master cattle trader, ingenious breeder, and founding member of the Panhandle Stock Association, whose widespread business interests also included real estate, town building, packinghouses, and stockyards. Then it was Timothy Dwight Hobart, the real estate and ranching legend, who served six consecutive one-year terms. Other early presidents included H. E. Turner, pioneer merchant and land speculator turned railroad lawyer turned banker turned real estate developer, and superbooster Horace M. Russell, who ran one of the largest stationery companies in the country and, over the course of his career as a civic leader, served as president of Amarillo's Rotary Club, Chamber of Commerce, Red Cross, and Community Chest.

The Society's journal, which launched in 1928 under the editorial guidance of Evetts Haley, reflected its pro-business outlook. Almost half the articles that appeared in its first decade of publication focused on a particular industry, mostly ranching, but also retail, real estate, mining, and law. Among its first seventy articles was only one on agriculture.[52] Many of those early pieces were autobiographical accounts or reminiscences from the boosters themselves, literally writing their own history in the pages of the official historical journal of the region. Railroad lawyer Thomas F. Turner wrote on frontier lawyers; T. D. Hobart contributed articles on surveying and real estate development; oil consultant and geologist Charles Gould wrote about petroleum discoveries. C. W. "Mr. Helium" Seibel, who ran Amarillo's helium plant, wrote on helium production.

A second historical organization in the region, the West Texas Historical Association (WTHA), which formed in Abilene in 1924, was also dominated by business folk. It was founded by booster R. C. Crane, one of the loudest voices of West Texas nationalism, who envisioned the Association as the place for serious study of the Anglo conquest of Native Americans. Whereas the PPHS essentially celebrated the capitalist utopia of the frontier and ranching days, the WTHA was more focused on conflict, particularly the military campaigns that had subjugated the Comanche, Kiowa, and other Plains tribes. Although he founded the organization with two young historians from Abilene, Rupert Richardson and William Curry Holden, and recruited an impressive roster of local talent that included Carl Coke Rister (Hardin-Simmons), gifted local amateur scholar Jewel Davis Scarborough, and the presidents of both McMurry and Simmons colleges, the rest of the organization's leadership was drawn strictly from the booster class. (Crane would remain president of the organization for twenty-four years, stepping down only after he turned eighty-five.) They included frontier attorney and developer Fred Cockrell; politician, cattle breeder, and real estate magnate C. U. Connellee; the largest grocery wholesaler west of the Mississippi, J. M. Radford; frontier rancher, town founder, and developer C. A. Broome; Spade Ranch manager and founder of the Colorado City Bank, D. N. Arnett. And Clifford B. Jones.

The first books on the history of West Texas made it clear: the region was part of the larger American West, rather than the South, as was the case with Texas history in general in those years. Among the earliest was Carl Coke Rister's *The Southwestern Frontier* (1928), a history of western Texas and Oklahoma and the eastern halves of New Mexico and Colorado. J. Evetts Haley's history of the biggest ranch in Texas, *The XIT Ranch and the Early Days of the Llano Estacado* (1929), based on extensive research in ranch records and interviews with former employees, not only was one the very best books on ranching ever written but also had a distinct and intentional regional focus. (He would follow up the book with his masterful *Charles Goodnight: Cowman and Plainsman* [1936], which also stresses the distinctiveness of West Texas history.) No one made the argument for the distinctiveness of the region more forcefully than Walter Prescott Webb, who had also grown up on the Texas cattle frontier. In his monumental *The Great Plains*, one of the great environmental histories of the twentieth century, Webb not only cleaved Texas in two but let the history and environment of West Texas stand for the middle third of the entire continent. His narrative of the larger region was so powerful, and his argument so logically presented, that it even influenced New Deal land policies. As he summed up its argument: "The salient truth, the essential truth, is that the West cannot be understood as a mere extension of things eastern."[53]

IV

By 1927, the PPHS was ready to build a museum to display its already impressive collection of artifacts and present a living testament to the Panhandle frontier. The local economy was booming: wheat, cotton, oil, cattle, helium, carbon black, transportation. Fishing for a transformative gift, PPHS secretary Luella Reeves reminded the membership in her annual report of the "immense sums of money" held by many of the early settlers of the region. "Could any man," she asked, "better perpetuate his memory than to erect a building worthy of the pioneers of this region? Is there a better place in Texas than this in which to make a gift which will make a contribution to the culture, and ensure the perpetuation of those Americans ideals, for which the great Southwest is famed?"[54] Enthusiastic members agreed and began donating and raising money. The PPHS hired hotshot local architects Rittenberry and Carder to draw up plans. The firm came back with designs for a magnificent structure, a stunning and majestic example of prairie deco architecture.

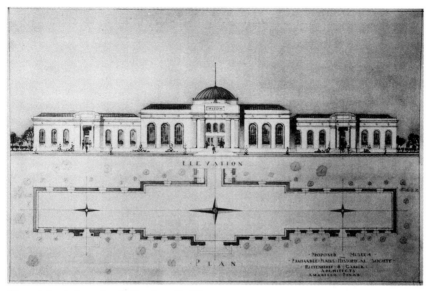

The original plans for the Panhandle-Plains Historical Museum. Only the wing on the left was completed.

The main building would be 60 feet high and 300 feet wide, with huge floor-to-ceiling windows and topped by a massive domed tower. On each side of the main building would be mirrored sandstone wings each 40 feet high and 160 feet wide.[55]

Construction on the west wing was set to begin in fall 1930. The Society had planned to accelerate its giving campaign to coincide with the ground-breaking ceremony. But that summer the bottom had fallen out of the local economy. Museum contributions dried up. With some creative budget requests for what was by then West Texas State College and a pledge to raise private money, PPHS leadership and politicians in Austin managed to get enough funding to build the first wing of the new museum. Construction began in November 1932. The wing, named Pioneer Hall, opened five months later. The rest of the planned structure, including its grand hall, was never built.[56]

The design and focus of Pioneer Hall told a specific story. Constructed from large blocks of gray-brown Texas Cordova limestone, the building calls to mind the sheer walls of Palo Duro Canyon bathed in bright sunshine. In the shallow alcove above the double doors are the words "Dedicated to the Pioneers." Above and along either side of the doors are bas relief carvings of the eighty brands of the earliest ranches

The Panhandle-Plains Historical Museum in 1936.

all surrounding the head of a longhorn steer. Facing each other across the alcove are more bas relief carvings of a cowboy and an "Indian brave." Other carvings under the building's front windows feature scenes of cowboys, army troops, and Comanche hunters tracking buffalo.

The museum claimed sixteen thousand visitors during its first four months—not bad for a facility that was only open four hours a day, three days a week. Laid out on display tables were the PPHS's treasures: "Indian" artifacts, cowboy tools and paraphernalia, and household items. There was a huge collection of guns, including a rifle that had supposedly been owned by Kit Carson and that Buffalo Bill had presented to Goodnight. There were spurs and saddles and brands. A century-old grandfather clock. Looking down on the guests from their perches on the walls were stuffed buffalo, antelope, and deer heads. A major attraction was a re-creation of a Comanche burial, complete with human skeleton. A modest art gallery occupied a small alcove on the east side of the main hall, and a matching room on the west side housed a small library and archive. Under the main floor was a basement work area where displays were prepared.[57]

Bas-relief carvings of the brands of pioneer ranches that frame the entrance of the Panhandle-Plains Historical Museum.

At the ribbon-cutting ceremony, WT regent J. O. Guleke, an attorney superbooster from Amarillo and intellectual leader of the budding conservative movement in West Texas, made it clear what the museum meant: "The cultural advancement of our people has been the greatest achievement in these forty years of plenty. . . . [W]hen we preserve the early traditions of the people of the Panhandle and extol the virtue of rugged honesty for its priceless work, we shall have profited and succeeded in greater abundance than had we discovered mountains of gold."[58]

5
BOOSTER POLITICS ASCENDANT

God is a politician; so is the devil.

CARRIE NATION, 1908

In 1887, Texans went to the polls to decide whether or not to amend the state constitution and forbid the manufacture, sale, and distribution of alcohol. The urge to ban "intoxicating spirits" was part of a larger political movement arising along the farmers' frontier, then decamped along the western edges of the Cross Timbers. Led mostly by farmer/preachers, many of whom were also active in the Farmer's Alliance, the Prohibition Party spearheaded the fight for statewide prohibition. (It also took up proto-Populist positions like banning commodity trading and demanding land and currency reform.) The amendment would replace Texas's local-option statutes, which had been in place since 1843, back when it was still its own country. Under those laws, each community would decide for itself whether or not to permit alcohol. As the Texas frontier expanded in the post-Reconstruction years, an obvious schism was revealed across the state: in almost every single local-option election, farmers pushing into new lands voted their communities dry.

As one might expect, prohibitionists made plenty of moral and religious arguments for banning alcohol; most southern denominations preached abstinence for their congregations. However, there were other arguments—including those of boosters. Prominent prohibitionist S. A. Hayden, editor of the state's largest Baptist newspaper, made this promise: "Give us prohibition in Texas and half a million of the best people in the older states will make our prairies bloom next year, and the prices of lands will double in less than five years."[1]

The amendment failed. But it enjoyed its greatest success in the western half of the state, passing in thirty-one counties and coming very close in another eighteen, almost all of them on the edges of the farming frontier. The zeal for prohibition was strongest in the newest communities. Over the next twenty years, as the agricultural frontier moved west, almost every single county voted itself dry. By 1907, nine out ten Texans lived in a dry county. Among the last holdouts was Amarillo.

The city had been founded the same year the Prohibition Amendment had failed, 1887. A group of Colorado City, Texas, speculators liked the site's chances of becoming a critical stop on the new railroad connecting Denver and Fort Worth, so, as the railroad was being laid out in the first months of the year, they platted and staked out a town on a section of school lands near the southern border of Potter County. The future city sat alongside a decent-sized if shallow playa that folks generously called a lake. The boundaries of several large ranches intersected near the site as well, including the Frying Pan, LX, and LS. Even after it was chosen as the county seat (thanks to heavy voting by cowboys at the LX), "Amarillo" was little more than a campground of canvas saloons and fly-by-night establishments tending to the lusty needs of cowboys and railroad workers. After heavy rains flooded the playa, it moved a mile east and to higher ground in 1889. Within months of the railroad's arrival, it became one of Texas's most important cattle markets.[2]

Within five years, it was the busiest cattle market in the world. Every year, 100,000 head passed through the city. Corrals and cattle pens lined the railroad for miles. Cowboys loaded steers onto cattle cars from one side, and lumpers lugged barbed wire rolls and barrels full of staples off the other. Other railroads arrived, connecting the city to Albuquerque, Kansas City, and Chicago. Amarillo was a cow town, pure and simple, as one visitor decried, with "no sidewalks, no trees, no nothing, and no conversation except cattle, cattle, cattle."[3]

And it had a lot of saloons. The ornate and well-stocked bar at the Amarillo Hotel was the unofficial headquarters of the Panhandle's ranching class, where the bourbon and branch water flowed and where the big deals got done. But the city had watering holes to fit every taste and every pocketbook: decent saloons, beer halls, and an uncountable number of no-name blind pigs, shebeens, and other seedy joints that came and went and came and went. Night and day, lonely and thirsty young men poured in with pocket-burning dollars and hours to kill.

Prospects arrive in Amarillo, 1908.

Prostitution and gambling thrived: there were high-end dance halls, fancy brothels, and elegant gambling dens with faro and poker. But there were also sex workers operating out of straw stalls in back alleys where the rougher dice games flourished. As the city grew, it channeled most of its vice into an unofficial red-light district everyone called the Bowery. Located directly opposite the Union Station were five square blocks of seedy hotels, greasy spoons, and almost twenty saloons. It was rough. A place where they said men would "slug you for a quarter and kill you for a dollar." Robberies, muggings, knife fights, and brawls were nightly occurrences, and drunken killings were common enough. Local law enforcement tended to ignore all but the most vicious of crimes.[4]

But Amarillo was changing. Developers like T. D. Hobart, C. W. Post, and William P. Soash were selling off the old ranch lands and bringing in new folks—farming families who were more interested in churches and schools than the carnal offerings of a place like the Bowery. By 1905, the city was no longer just a place for cowboys and railroad workers but the transportation nexus of the Agricultural Wonderland as well as its retail, legal, and financial center. By 1910, it had grown to ten thousand residents. Cattle, as a percentage of railroad traffic (which was growing exponentially), dropped from 60 percent to 6 percent.[5] It's not that cattle numbers dropped; they didn't. Amarillo was still the largest cattle market in the West. But farmers were coming that fast. Two thousand railroad cars a year arrived stuffed with their belongings. More warehouses went up: lumber, nails, pipe, windows, bricks, tractors, plows, automobiles, farm implements, and thousands of different products to fill the shelves of hundreds of new retail outlets across the Panhandle. The shopkeepers came, and so did the barbers and the preachers and the lawyers and the teachers, and multitudes who thought the city held their future. Neighborhoods sprawled and stately brick buildings reached to the heavens.

The Bowery was becoming a problem. Five blocks of sin sitting directly opposite the train station where the newcomers and prospects arrived in the Wonderland was not a good look. Unlike the choreographed first entrance to real estate towns like Pampa or Canyon with dawn arrivals and fake water features, Amarillo arrivals stepped straight into the dark chaos of one of the most dangerous neighborhoods in the West. Developers were promising a region of progress, an upstanding and moral society, built to accommodate a white, Christian middle class, supposedly far beyond the dangers and depravities of the old frontier. The Bowery had to go.

I

The grisly murder of a teenage boy spurred the community to action. Early in the morning of October 4, 1906, the body of a small young male was discovered next to the railroad tracks just beyond the Bowery. The boy, miraculously still alive, was naked, covered in dried blood and dirt, and unrecognizable because of "a dozen ghastly wounds" across his head and face. Police suspected a hatchet had been used, and the fetid condition of his wounds led them to conclude that the boy had been attacked the previous evening or very early that morning. The victim clung to life for two days, dropping in and out of consciousness. The severity of his injuries had made his feeble attempts at communication impossible.[6] Acting on a tip, police found the boy's clothes and the hatchet used by his attackers just a few blocks from where his body had been found, sunk to the bottom of a railroad water tank car. The clothes were new, a cheap knock-off of a trendy style readily available in mining and railroad commissaries. Police dressed the body in the clothes and took photographs, which they made available to press and law enforcement across the Southwest. A local mortuary laid the body in state for two weeks to give people a chance to try to identify the young man. Thousands filed by, paying respects, and hoping for clues. The boy's identity and the murder were the biggest mysteries in Texas, with media reporting a new theory seemingly every day. Amarillo businessmen raised $10,000 as a reward for information. Dread-filled parents of missing children trudged to Amarillo. It was his father who finally identified the body, traveling from Oklahoma on a tip from a relative. The boy's name was Foster Earl Dockray, and he had left his family's farm a few weeks earlier, hoping to make a little money working on the railroad. He was on his way home with a tidy bankroll when he was killed.

Given the public outcry over the crime, Dockray's funeral service was held at the Filmore Street Presbyterian Church, one of Amarillo's largest. City businesses closed for the day. The church's high-powered and thundering new minister, L. C. Kirkes, delivered the eulogy to a packed house. He laid the blame for the boy's murder at the feet of the city for its tolerance for a depraved place like the Bowery. "There ought to be from this crime a great upheaval of the public conscience," he roared. "Let the citizenship of this town make it a safe thing for men and women to go about in any part of town at any time, instead of tolerating a condition which makes certain sections of this city positively unsafe."[7]

The Republic of Texas had pioneered the regulation of alcoholic beverages when it established a policy of local option back in 1843.[8] Local option permits individual communities to decide for themselves whether to allow the sale and consumption of alcohol. It remains in place to this day. By shifting the responsibility to regulate liquor from the state to local jurisdictions, the issue of whether or not to ban alcohol was very often the first serious political question answered by frontier communities. In those years, voting in a "dry" community was evidence that a place had moved beyond its frontier days, an important last step of development.

Everywhere, the push for prohibition was led by clergymen like L. C. Kirkes. The young and ambitious minister, like many of his generational stripe, felt obligated to speak directly to issues of public morality even if it meant venturing into the political realm. As hard as it might be to believe now, traditionally, southern Protestant clergy had practiced a strict adherence to the separation of church and state. Texas, in particular, was known for its radical anticlericalism. But alcohol changed the equation. The largest Protestant churches in Texas held that drinking was a sin, but also that it was one's personal responsibility to conquer temptation. A new attitude among some ministers had emerged over the issue, whereby they believed that part of their responsibility to their congregations and communities was to work toward local moral improvement. Prohibition became their crusade, the most obvious example of a new publicly engaged and muscular Christianity.[9]

Fitting squarely within a forward-moving narrative of how frontier towns were supposed to develop, prohibition was also central to the booster vision. Upright, saloon-free communities were integral to their marketing of a white Christian homeland. Skipping over the rougher stages of development extended beyond guarantees of plow-ready fields and accessible transportation networks. "No saloons" was a promise and proclamation of developer marketing, right alongside the descriptions of soil, weather, and crop production. "There is not a saloon in the county," Lubbock promoters vowed. "The nearest is over a hundred miles away. There is not so much as a billiard or pool room in the town of Lubbock. . . . You will see that we are not living in a heathen land."[10] The Texas Land and Development Company of Plainview assured that "there has never been a saloon or den of vice of any description in Hale County, and Plainview is recognized as one the cleanest and most moral towns in the state."[11] Developers' efforts to recruit citizens interested in living in dry communities made West Texas *the* hotbed of prohibition statewide and lashed the alcohol question to boosterism.

In early November 1906, police arrested two men for the murder of Earl Dockray. They nabbed Frank Ellsworth and Joseph Burk at the Santa Fe depot in Wichita, Kansas, in a sting operation in which they lured the two men to claim a bright-green valise that had belonged to Dockray. Ellsworth was a knockabout tough guy who drifted around the Panhandle and the Southwest, sometimes working on the railroad and sometimes as a Bowery bouncer. His "countenance," as one newspaper described it, "shows one who has habitually and knowingly indulged himself in dissipation."[12] Detectives concluded that Dockray had flashed a wad of cash at a Hereford café just before boarding the train for Amarillo and drew the attention of Ellsworth, who followed him onto the train. That night, they posited, Ellsworth killed and robbed Dockray and dumped the body by the railroad tracks, stripping the boy, hacking up his face to prevent identification, and then stashing the clothes and the murder weapon in the nearby water tank car. Then, Ellsworth and his buddy Burk headed into the Bowery, where they blew through Dockray's 150 bucks in just a few hours. The following morning, the two men lit out on a train to Ochiltree County. There, they punched cattle and waited for the heat to die down. It was stories of Ellsworth's constant campfire brags about witnessing a murder that drew the attention of the police. Although evidence was mostly circumstantial, a jury quickly convicted Ellsworth and sentenced him to a life in prison.[13]

Militant prohibitionists—called drys—used the uproar over the case to launch a crusade to close the Bowery and ban alcohol in Amarillo. At issue, as Texas historian Lewis Gould has suggested, was "the nature and direction of their society."[14] Amarillo drys started their own newspaper to promote their cause. The Women's Christian Temperance Union (WCTU) and the Anti-Saloon League, both popular in the city, regularly staged rallies and marched through the Bowery. Carrie Nation was a popular visitor in Amarillo and the hottest book in town was *The 450 Mile Street of Hell*, a screeching prohibitionist tract. For Amarillo Methodists, the saloon was "the direst enemy of sober manhood, of pure womanhood, and prattling childhood" and "the arch-enemy of the home, the foe of the university and the iconoclast of the age." Baptists cried that "the vastest evil, the deadliest evil, the greatest overshadowing upas tree of the whole world is the organized liquor traffic."[15] (This kind of conspiratorial antimonopolism had been prominent in earlier agrarian movements.)

For some Amarillo boosters, prohibition was more than a moral issue; it made solid business sense. The city's rough reputation was, they concluded, slowing growth and costing them money. They attributed the selection of nearby Canyon as the site of the new teachers' college over Amarillo to the fact that the smaller city was dry.[16] Amarillo's richest banker, its most powerful attorney, and some of its wealthier retailers joined the movement. They and ministers like L. C. Kirkes (who with his wife moved fluidly within the booster universe) called for "constant pressure for righteousness and a cleaner and better city." Kirkes was a solid ally regularly speaking on the importance of church and business collaboration to improve private *and* public morality and create a community that lay between the "anarchist's idea of extreme individualism" and the collective fantasy of "all government."[17]

This is not to say that every booster was a prohibitionist; that was not the case, and in fact, the business community split over the issue. Judge James D. Hamlin, who led the "wets," believed that most businessmen were secretly against prohibition but refused to go public out of fear or conformity. The *Herald*, Amarillo's established newspaper, came out against prohibition: "Our forefathers came to this country to escape the iron hand of the exacting laws of Old England. They came here for the privileges later guaranteed them in the constitution which they formulated and fought to make eternal, guaranteeing to every citizen the right to life, liberty, and the pursuit of happiness."[18] While the owner and manager of the Amarillo Hotel was a prohibitionist, his manager and owner of the establishment's popular saloon and restaurant was obviously a wet. The wets themselves fell into different camps. There were those like the *Herald* editor and rancher/attorney James Hamlin, who hated the idea of a nanny government trying to "legislate" morality into existence. (Hamlin was as big a booster as anyone: he served in leadership roles in most civic organizations and a term as president of the West Texas Chamber of Commerce.) And there were those whose opposition stemmed from a fear that a government powerful enough to prevent the sale and consumption of alcohol would be powerful enough to dismantle segregation and threaten white supremacy.[19]

In December 1907, just weeks after the conviction of Earl Dockray's murderer, Amarillo held a local option vote on whether to ban alcohol. It passed by fifteen votes. Election day was an ugly affair, tainted by dark accusations of voter intimidation (including one very public arrest), ballot box stuffing, changing votes, and other charges. Local election judges, sympathetic to prohibition, ignored all the charges. (The wets took their case to the state courts, and after two years, a more objective judge heard the evidence, threw out the election results, and ordered a new vote.)

But those two years of Dry Amarillo were a violent and bloody catastrophe. Yes, the saloons closed, but they just reopened as pool halls, theaters, or bowling alleys and served alcohol under the counter. Dozens of blind pigs and password-protected places with secret passages and reinforced doors proliferated. With little interest in enforcing laws they felt were ineffective and culturally inappropriate, Amarillo police turned a blind eye to operators who could keep a low profile and their customers under control. Driven to apoplexy by this laissez-faire attitude, drys convinced the governor to send in the Texas Rangers to enforce prohibition. That's when all hell broke loose. The Rangers moved into the city and acted with the impunity and violence of an occupying army. They bullied citizens and fought local cops in the streets. They arrested dozens on the flimsiest of pretexts and without proper warrants. People reported the Rangers for confiscating personal property and demanding free admission into venues. Apparently, they went around bopping people on the head with the butt of their revolvers for laughs. They were accused of selling confiscated whiskey, shaking down suspects, demanding bribes, and spending their free time in brothels. It was so bad that Amarillo's mayor begged the governor to withdraw the squad and threatened to draft every adult male in the city into a special police force if the governor refused his request.[20]

Then, on the fifth day of 1909, Jim Keeton, Potter County jailer and part-time deputy, shot Texas Ranger "Doc" Thomas in the head during a quarrel in the office of the Potter County Attorney. The bullet struck Thomas just above the right eye and passed straight through his skull. The Ranger, even with a gaping bleeding hole in his head, lived for another hour. The immediate cause of their argument was a sketchy prisoner transfer, but Thomas and the local police had been beefing for weeks. Keeton claimed self-defense, claiming that Thomas, who had threatened him before, had set an ambush and was reaching for a gun when he shot him. The position of the body, however, offered no evidence to support Keeton's claim. Many viewed the killing as an assassination. Keeton's trial, held in Vernon, Texas, was a circus. Prohibitionists called for swift justice and tried to turn Doc Thomas, by most accounts not a very nice man, into a martyr. The WCTU maintained a vigil for the dead Ranger outside Keeton's jail cell for the duration of the trial. Keeton got five years and was pardoned by governor O. B. Colquitt two years later.[21]

The Bowery briefly reopened a few months after Thomas's death, but it was short-lived. The drys arranged another local-option election in 1911, and this time the results weren't even close. Amarillo went dry.

The whole state went dry eight years later, a year before the Eighteenth Amendment banned liquor nationwide. When prohibition was repealed in 1933, Texas went back to local option. Amarillo was one of the first places to allow alcohol again, but only in certain parts of town.

As late as 1980, there were still 74 completely dry counties in Texas, most of them in its western half. As of 2024, there are only five completely dry counties in all of Texas, all in the west. Amarillo still isn't completely wet.[22]

II

As with prohibition, it's useful to see the fight to extend the vote to women as an expression of West Texas's booster politics. Suffrage, many had come to believe, represented a logical next step in the expansion of democracy and American development. Here on the last frontier, they thought, bright and modern communities of West Texas women could forge the political future and infuse morality into public life. Booster women led the way, launching suffrage movements from civic clubs and church groups. Typically lumped together under the name "women's clubs," these organizations served an array of interests and purposes, from sewing circles and literary societies (often the first social organization of any type in a new community) to sororities and auxiliaries of civic organizations or political parties. While not as overt in their fixation on growth, these were important organizations for boosting towns and communities. Booster women tended to practice the soft power of the business class on behalf of progressive reforms to improve sanitation, increase access to recreation, and promote public education. They gladly accepted a role as the hosts of large community events and running local charity efforts. At the heart of their messaging and efforts was infusing a gendered morality into the public sphere.[23]

In the towns and cities, women's clubs drew their membership from the wives and daughters of the petty producers and professionals of the booster class—bankers, lawyers, merchants, and entrepreneurs—and saw theirs as a moral mission of uplift and progress. Out in the country, the new commercial form of farming meant that rural women laid claim to the same petty capitalist values and had the time to engage in club work. They too expressed a moral vision and a commitment to growth. By the mid-1910s, there were close to a hundred separate women's clubs scattered across West Texas, in the cities of course but also in villages as small as Aspermont.[24] In Amarillo there was the Pierian Club, the city's oldest and most prestigious, but also the Women's Club, the TPM, the

Criterion, the J.U.G. Club, the Friday 500, the Shadows, the Parajito, the Beau-Not, the Costura, and others. There were also clubs associated with churches and with schools and clubs for every hobby and interest. Politics, especially suffrage, became an issue for many.

Late-nineteenth-century efforts to win the vote for women had gone nowhere in Texas. Thanks to the movement's pre–Civil War association with abolitionism, white Texans, like most white southerners, cast a leery eye toward woman suffrage. Efforts to extend the franchise at the 1868 and 1875 constitutional conventions flopped. Alliances with other popular movements like prohibition failed to move the needle. In those years, suffragists framed their arguments around the ideals of equality and fairness. How was it logical to deny half the population *the* fundamental right in a democracy? they asked. For a century, opponents had the same reply: the nation's moral and democratic health depended on women serving society as pure and moral arbiters far removed from the vulgar world of politics. Or, as one Texas report on suffrage from 1868 put it, women "by keeping themselves in their appropriate spheres, and by exhibiting all those gentle qualities directly opposed to the rougher sex in their capacities as wives and mothers, [exercise] an influence mightier, far, than that of the elective franchise."[25]

Judo-style, a new generation of suffragists turned the power of that argument to their advantage and, as the twentieth century arrived, tied gaining the ballot directly to the moral and progressive vision of boosters and the narrative of frontier development.[26] No one did it better than Claude, Texas, newspaper columnist Phebe Kerrick Warner, the "Little Brown Wren of Texas." Originally from Illinois, Warner had moved to a small farm in Armstrong County on the edges of the old JA Ranch in 1898. A gifted writer with a keen scientific mind, Warner, who had graduated from Illinois Wesleyan (where she was Phi Kappa Phi) and who had once been hired by Illinois Female College to build its science department, turned to women's clubs for companionship and intellectual stimulation.[27] In 1903, she helped found the Wednesday Afternoon Club, a study group for local farm and town women. Members read and discussed history, economics, agricultural science, and politics, among other subjects, and were responsible for preparing reports and delivering lectures. Warner organized similar clubs across Armstrong and Potter counties. In 1913, to break down the "social clothesline" between rural and town women, she organized the Armstrong County Federation of

Women's Clubs, the first county-wide federation in the country. "Bringing the county woman and the city woman together" was important to Warner. In both her local work and as a statewide leader in the women's club movement, she was adamant about the clubs providing an outlet for and expression of the needs and values of rural women.[28] Her town-*and-country* philosophy also guided the formation of other regional booster organizations, such as the Panhandle Bankers Association and the Panhandle-Plains Press Association, which included representatives from the smallest and most rural of institutions.

While more outspoken woman suffrage activists like Minnie Fisher Cunningham grabbed the headlines and lobbied the political networks, Phebe Warner focused on consciousness raising, particularly among rural women.[29] She was, thanks to her regular column in the *Fort Worth Star-Telegram*, the most popular woman writer in Texas. Warner spoke to and for Texas farm women and never tired of extolling the virtues of women's clubs. In hundreds of columns (syndicated across the state) and speeches, she articulated a farm wife feminism: demanding greater inclusion of farm women in policy and public decision making and evangelizing for the economic and social value of farm women to the state and nation. (Warner once actually calculated the exact dollar value of farm women to the U.S. economy.) On suffrage, knowing that many rural women opposed it, Warner took an understated approach, pushing for a broader form of inclusion. "What can a woman do?" even without the ballot, she once asked. Well, she answered, women could obviously take care of home and family but also, when called upon, could "see to the needs of her hometown as well as her own home. She can see the needs of her community as well as her family. She can see the conditions around her children at school as well as at home. And she can make a way to improve them." Rather than simply prescribe woman suffrage as the most logical way to improve those conditions, Warner laid the foundation for political participation through what contemporaries and scholars have called the *municipal housekeeping* argument.[30] Characterizing women as "moral and different" made a good case for their inclusion as an antidote to corruption and immorality in public life. Municipal housekeeping was so prominent in suffrage arguments that Warner never had to make an explicit appeal for suffrage; the case was obvious. As she once queried readers, if a small group of club women could beautify a town or close a saloon, what could a "million Texas women do?"[31]

Integrating rural women into the projects of municipal housekeeping was Warner's greatest mission. She continually promoted the idea of county-wide organizations to bridge the interests of town and country. Warner promoted this integration not just for women's clubs but also county school districts, stronger and modern county systems of government, and county fundraising and civic projects.[32] By placing farm women at the center of public life, Warner was making the subtle but potent argument for their inclusion in the public sphere and politics. She made appeals to educators to include agricultural science and home economics in the public schools and to take into consideration the calendar and clock challenges of farm families. She continually reminded her city readers of what life was like beyond the city limits. Her presentations of women's shared history of suffering and sacrificing to build America's agricultural economy gave her arguments great moral force. The needs of farm women were the needs of Texas: an easily accessed, excellent system of public education, good roads and reliable cars, better travel accommodations (like public restrooms), child care, advances in agricultural science, and public investment.

Thanks to Warner and the region's women's clubs, West Texas, particularly the Panhandle, was a hotbed of woman suffrage. In Amarillo, rallies and speeches drew hundreds. Biweekly meetings of the Potter County Equal Suffrage Association drew fifty or more members. In nearby Canyon, a woman suffrage club was one of the first organizations on the West Texas Normal campus. It even had its own theme song.[33] When the Texas Democratic Party finally allowed women the right to vote in the state primary, Amarillo women registered at a rate twice that of the rest of Texas; a third of eligible women voters registered in the first two weeks.[34]

Just as with prohibition, it was becoming clear that the political ideas of West Texans were different than those in the rest of the state. These were modern ideas—closely tied to the national Progressive Movement—but expressed within a regional identity dependent on a progressive narrative and founded on establishing morality at the center of public life. While the virtues of individualism and self-sufficiency were still foundational to the culture of West Texas, new expectations for conformity and a fidelity to these moral crusades were becoming essential to booster politics.

III

It was Texas women who also led the fight *against* suffrage. Chief among them was Ida M. Darden, at the dawn of what would become a fifty-year career as a right-wing propagandist and activist. When tapped to become the primary publicist for the Texas Association Opposed to Woman Suffrage (TAOWS), Darden was a thirty-year-old lobbyist for the Texas Business Men's Association, an organization violently opposed to suffrage, organized labor, and prohibition. Over the course of that campaign, she founded what would become her political ideology—a fierce anticommunism, white supremacy, antistatism, and a passionate pro-business stance—based on her understanding of white southern womanhood. For Darden and most antisuffrage women, the Cult of True Womanhood was a form of inequality that *benefited* women. Suffrage, she warned, would upset traditional structures of gender and allow men rather than women the right to define and dictate equality. Darden also believed that women were neither intellectually nor psychologically suited to public life and held that if women received the right to vote they would let their emotions get the best of them and elect to end segregation. Also, she was prone to blaming secret communist plots for any unwanted change in American life.[35]

Darden, who had worked the Texas Business Men's Association for many years by that point, was well connected. In addition to her contacts from that community, her brother, Vance Muse, ran the Fort Worth Chamber of Commerce. She also enjoyed the patronage of three very powerful men: lobbyist J. A. Arnold, timber baron John H. Kirby, and Senator Joseph W. Bailey, essential figures in the formation of the radical right in Texas. Darden also grew up, it should be noted, in a conservative household that defined its politics primarily through its opposition to the liberal wing of the Democratic Party led by James Hogg. By the mid-1910s, she had a deserved reputation as a go-to political writer.

As the suffrage movement picked up momentum in 1916 and 1917, Darden launched her campaign. The TAOWS mostly avoided the rallies and parades preferred by the suffrage groups, in favor of targeted print mailers sent to rural women. In just two years, Darden produced more than 100,000 pieces of material. In addition to those that praised a system that allowed women to enjoy special rights, Darden also pushed the idea that woman suffrage was part of a communist-inspired plot that would "destroy individual responsibility and substitute governmental control and regulation of private conduct."[36] Others declared that public life was the antithesis of southern white womanhood, which obligated women to defend white supremacy against any potential threat, including other women.[37]

Despite the work of Warner and local women's clubs, Darden's calls to protect True Womanhood resonated in West Texas, where the new commercial farming economy had finally elevated farmwives into the middle class. For the first time, a generation of farm women could taste the fruits of privilege and "conform more closely to the role of the full-time 'homemaker.'"[38] Why would they risk losing that position to enter the sordid and corrupt world of politics? Also running deep through American rural culture was a belief that the "domestic sphere" for women was both the logical and positive result of America's unique democracy and the key to preserving it.[39] To give women the right to vote would mean nothing less than the fundamental reordering of gender. While the Wonderland they were creating was meant to be a modern and moral world, there were plenty of women and men who were not keen on unleashing such a major disruption in the operation of the political system.

Suffrage was offered to Texas voters in May 1919, in a special election that would amend the state constitution to allow women to vote in state elections. It passed easily in West Texas, carried by urban votes. Statewide, however, the race remained too close to call for several days. Ida Darden saw a conspiracy. With the U.S. Congress on the verge of passing a national amendment that would give women the ballot, Darden mused that cowardly Texas politicians were deliberately dragging out vote counting as part of a plot to overturn the will of the voters. (Through some complicated math, Darden had somehow determined that only one out of every eight Texans actually supported the state amendment but that an "unseen hand" had been clapped over the mouth of Texas voters.) When the votes revealed that the suffrage amendment had failed, losing 168,893 to 141,773, she celebrated: "All conscientious objectors to the amalgamation of home, church and state and who understand and respect the rights of people and property will rejoice that woman suffrage had been defeated."[40]

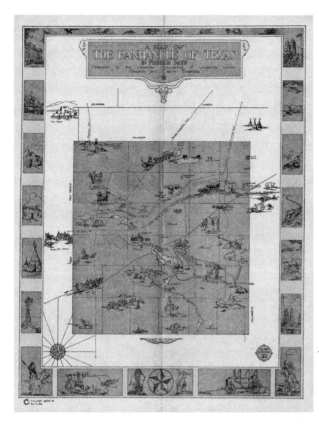

Map of the early Panhandle prepared for the Canyon-Amarillo chapter of the American Association of University Women.

Two weeks after the referendum, however, Congress passed the Nineteenth Amendment, with strong support from the Texas delegation. When the amendment went to the states for ratification, the Texas legislature, as Darden predicted, ignored the recent statewide vote, went into immediate session, and approved the national amendment.[41] Texas was the ninth state in the country and the first in the South to pass it.[42] "At last the time has come," Phebe K. Warner wrote, when women could "enlist for the greatest service to our state that has ever presented itself." Whatever opinion women might have held about suffrage before that point was moot, she declared. "It is here. You have it. It is now a part of your life's duty to your country. The state of Texas believes in it. Almost two-thirds of our politicians have believed in it and stood for it for several years. Our governor believes in it. Our President believes in it. Our nation believes in it."[43]

IV

The 1928 presidential election should have sent Texas onto a completely different political path. For the first time in its history, a majority of Texas voters supported a Republican, Herbert Hoover. The key to Hoover's victory? West Texas, where he ran up the score. Hoover took 70 percent of Abilene's votes and took three out of four in Snyder, Pampa, Levelland, Post, and Clarendon. He took 60 percent of the Amarillo and Lubbock vote. No Republican had enjoyed those kinds of numbers in those places—ever. Hoover won all but eleven West Texas counties. He won in cattle country and in the cotton counties and rolled in the wheatlands. He won huge majorities with women and prohibitionists. It was concrete evidence of a new kind of politics in West Texas, where loyalty to the Democratic Party was not as solid as in the rest of the state. As the Goldwater movement would do thirty-six years later, Hoover's candidacy showed the state GOP a path to permanence and perhaps even statewide power. A Republican Party led by women, preachers, and the western booster class could fundamentally change the algorithms that ordered Texas politics. It also showed a brand of political conformity that we see in the region now. Booster conservatism stood on the cusp of greatness. Nature and the national economy would have other plans.

Born in 1874 on a small Iowa farm to a blacksmith father and a Quaker mother, "Bertie" Hoover was only ten when he was orphaned. Living with various local relatives for a few months, he was finally packed up on a train and shipped off to a doctor uncle in another Quaker frontier community in Oregon's Willamette Valley. The uncle, who had gone to Oregon with plans to start a Quaker school, had instead settled on real estate development. His plan, like those of many Wonderland developers, was to reinvent local agriculture and transform the local landscape, in this case buying up thousands of worn-out wheat farms and turning them into turnkey orchard operations. He put young Bertie to work as the company's office manager. The boy thrived. He maintained company correspondence, wrote ad copy, and arranged housing and transportation for prospective buyers. He took business classes at night. At seventeen, Hoover left Oregon to attend Stanford University as a member of its "pioneer class." Stanford was to be a new type of college, one where the traditional liberal arts would be taught, but so would engineering, technology, and business.[44]

Hoover studied geology and prepared for a career in mining. A decent geologist (his wife was more talented), Hoover was a very good businessman and manager. Over two decades, he thrived as a mining executive and dealmaker. He had an industry-wide reputation as a turnaround specialist for played-out or troubled mining operations. In demand all over the world, he probably logged more travel miles than any other American of his day, working in Australia, Asia, and Latin America, mostly for European companies. He made his first million before he was forty.

He was semi-retired and living the life of a wealthy global mining mogul in London when the First World War broke out. Thousands of Americans were stranded in England when passenger ships canceled their voyages home. Hoover organized a vast and complicated effort to get each of them back to the States. He stayed in England, where he became an international hero as the creator and manager of an enormous and enormously intricate food relief program for Belgians trapped between German lines and the British blockade. His creation, the Commission for Relief in Belgium, was among the largest relief organizations in the history of the world. Hoover directed the logistics, diplomacy, and bureaucracy of transporting and distributing millions of tons of food across the Atlantic Ocean and onto Belgian kitchen tables. He also raised the money to pay the organization's $11 million monthly budget. When the United States entered the war in 1917, President Woodrow Wilson called Hoover home and named him the nation's food czar, responsible for feeding the country and its soldiers. Among Hoover's first acts was to recruit mothers and homemakers into his campaign to limit food consumption at the family table; "ninety-percent of American food production passes through the hands of our women," he explained.[45] He leaned on women's clubs to help him promote voluntary programs like Wheatless Wednesdays, Meatless Tuesdays, and the "gospel of the clean plate." He asked the nation's 30 million women to pledge to save food. Phebe Warner saw Hoover's invitation as "one of the greatest opportunities that has ever come to the women of Texas and the nation. A chance for us all to work together, in a cause that comes close to our hearts and our homes."[46]

In 1920, his name was bandied about by both parties as the thinking man's candidate for president. He demurred.

The victor in that year's presidential election, Republican Warren G. Harding, named Hoover his secretary of commerce. In 1921, the Department of Commerce was less than a decade old, with a vague mission, little power, and less money. It was responsible for keeping the nation's coastal maps up to date, inspecting steamboats and lighthouses, and maintaining fisheries. As one former commerce secretary put it, his job was "to put the fish to bed at night and turn on the lights around the coasts." Hoover, however, had different plans. He saw Commerce as nothing less than the steward of the modern economy. His goal, as one keen historian has noted, was to fuse his "corporatist and technocratic visions on to a base of nineteenth-century individualism, to build a superior socioeconomic order."[47] Hoover, the dealmaking businessman with the disciplined mind of an engineer, imagined the Commerce Department as the primary vehicle of an "associative state," which would bring together business, finance, labor, agriculture, and government to map out an efficient and harmonious program for equitable growth. In eight years, Hoover initiated three thousand different confabs among various (often competing) economic interests. An antistatist at heart, Hoover wanted a government that stood "behind" business rather than acted as its overseer or rival. Government, he believed, should tend to the economy like a gardener. A thoroughly modern man, he recognized the value of emerging industries like radio and aeronautics and created new agencies to nurture them. He wasn't shy about appropriating existing bureaucracies he deemed essential to the expansion of commerce, including the Bureau of Mines and the Patent Office. The economy roared, growing by 40 percent. The United States was responsible for *half* of the world's economic output. Per capita GDP increased by a quarter. Wages rose and prices dropped. And many credited Hoover.

Early in his tenure as Secretary of Commerce, Hoover published a book outlining his political and economic philosophy. He titled it *American Individualism*. Dismayed by the explosion of isms unleashed by the Great War—socialism, anarchism, communism, syndicalism—and worried about an alienation and malaise among the American people, Hoover made the case for individualism as the best ism for a nation committed to growth and an equitable society. It was individual achievement that made America work, he said. Progress, both individual and societal, depended on maximizing individualism and insuring equality of opportunity within the boundaries of responsibility to community and nation. It was, in short, a manifesto of the booster class. "No doubt," he wrote, individualism run amok would lead to "a long category of inequalities, of tyrannies, dominations, and injustices."[48] But, he promised that, "*while we build our society upon the attainment of the individual, we shall safeguard to every individual an equality of opportunity to take that position in the community to which his intelligence, character, ability, and ambition entitle him; that we keep the social solution free from frozen strata of classes; that we shall stimulate effort of each individual to achievement; that through an enlarging sense of responsibility and understanding we shall assist him to this attainment; while he in turn must stand up to the emery wheel of competition.*"[49] He left no doubt as to the origins of his thinking. Like Frederick Jackson Turner, Hoover believed that the "Pioneer Spirit" was the source of American exceptionalism.[50] "Our American individualism has received much of its character from our contacts with the forces of nature on a new continent. It evolved government without official emissaries to show the way; it plowed and sowed two score of great states; it built bridges, railways, cities; it carried forward every attribute of high civilization over a continent. The days of the pioneer are not over. There are continents of human welfare of which we have penetrated only the coastal plain."[51] No member of the West Texas Chamber of Commerce could have said it better.

Most political observers in 1927 assumed that President Calvin Coolidge—who had assumed office in 1923 after Harding's sudden death and had won on his own the following year—would stand for reelection. They were wrong; one morning in August 1927, while vacationing in South Dakota's Black Hills, Coolidge drove into Rapid City, gathered the press corps into a single-file line, and then handed each of them a piece of paper that read, "I do not choose to run for president in nineteen twenty-eight." He then remarked that there would be nothing else that day and drove back to his vacation lodge. Herbert Hoover became the instant front-runner for the GOP nomination. While many old guard Republicans distrusted Hoover, and many of the remaining progressives in the party despised him, Hoover won the nomination on the first ballot. His biggest sources of support were women, prohibitionists, and businessmen.

He was so popular in Texas that the state GOP chair endorsed Hoover without even consulting other party leaders. The state party used Hoover's campaign to launch an all-out organizational effort, particularly in West Texas, where there were actual pockets of Republicans, mostly Midwest expats in the wheat counties and urban professionals in cities like Amarillo, Abilene, and Wichita Falls. The campaign found great success in organizing entire industrial and associative groups to endorse and support Hoover: there were Saddle Makers for Hoover, Engineers for Hoover, Attorneys for Hoover, and so on. The Texas GOP had access to a huge trove of slick marketing materials created by the Madison Avenue wunderkinds at BBDO. Maybe the most powerful piece was the campaign film "Master of Emergencies," a hagiographic reminder of Hoover's successes feeding Belgium during the war and organizing the American food supply as the U.S. food czar. The film closed with some never-before-seen footage of Hoover and his efforts to bring rescue, relief, and recovery to the 700,000 people left homeless by the 1927 Mississippi River flood. It's said that the devasting pictures of hungry children and hollow-eyed parents brought tears to the eyes of audiences.

For many of his supporters, Hoover transcended politics. He was, as the editor of the *Canyon News* (a loyal Democrat) concluded, "more American than he is a Republican . . . a brainy engineer and business-man—more brilliant in these lines than he is a politician."[52] Will Rogers quipped that when a person got sick, they called a doctor, but when the country got sick, it called for Hoover.[53]

Women voters were the key to the campaign. As suffrage supporters had promised before the Nineteenth Amendment was ratified, Texas women were going to be more independent voters. The League of Women Voters, born from the Equal Suffrage Association, insisted on nonpartisanship. "It's better to be right than regular," it declared. Through the 1920s, Republicans had found respectful and informed audiences among women's clubs. In local and state elections, women had demon-strated their savvy in "leveraging" their votes for "specific policy goals."[54] With Hoover's candidacy, club women instantly formed "Women for Hoover" organizations. In tiny Idalou, eighteen women showed up to the first meeting. Lubbock's group was one of the largest in Texas, run by powerful club woman Minta Ellis Maedgen. Eight hundred women signed the Abilene Women for Hoover statement, which read in part: "Every woman should feel the deepest pride that her vote can help elect this great man the leader of our country."[55]

For many West Texas club women, Lou Hoover was the attraction.

By 1928 Herbert's wife was a feminist icon. Like her husband, she had been born on the Iowa frontier, but her family moved to the West Coast when she was quite young. Her childhood was filled with outdoor adventures and sports. She was an ace archer, a good baseball player, and a star player on Stanford's basketball team. She was the first woman in the country to get a degree in geology and published scholarly articles on mining. Legend had it that when in China during the Boxer Rebellion, she strapped a revolver to her hip as she delivered supplies to soldiers on her bicycle. Thanks to her insistence on accompanying Herbert to his various mining duties, she was probably the best-traveled American woman of her day. An earnest supporter of women's clubs, Lou Hoover sponsored more than a few in Washington. She led the women's division of the National Amateur Athletic Association and was president of the Girl Scouts of America. West Texas women adored her.[56]

Prohibition was the most pressing issue of the campaign in West Texas, by then a decade dry and happy. Hoover was the clear choice. The Democratic nominee, four-time governor of New York Alfred E. Smith, was obnoxiously forthright in his opposition to prohibition. He was, as *The Nation* pointed out, "personally, ecclesiastically, aggressively, irreconcilably wet."[57] And he was Catholic and part of a Tammany political machine that had come to stand in the popular imagination as the essence of political corruption. Smith was so unpopular in Texas that even the Texas delegation to the Democratic National Convention, held in Houston no less, refused to support him, reserving their votes for a favorite son candidate in both ballots. "Old" Cone Johnson, a delegate and white supremacist violently opposed to Smith and deeply disturbed by his selection as the Democratic nominee, attended the convention and wondered aloud what had happened to his Democratic Party: "While the parade passed following Smith's nomination, the faces I saw in the mile-long procession were not American faces. I wondered where were the Americans?"[58] Sixty thousand Texans in 249 counties joined "Democrats for Hoover" clubs.

Church leaders led the fight against the Democratic nominee. E. K. Salked, head of the First Christian Church of Abilene, described Hoover as a "great humanitarian" and Smith as a "creature" of the corrupt cities whose only support came from "bootleggers and most of their victims, the great crowds of Tammany corruptionists, the prostitutes, the grafters, the great army of aliens from New York and the north and east, of their Latin mentalities and foreign ideals and religion."[59] The president of McMurry College in Abilene, J. W. Hunt, was even more blunt, calling Smith a "dirty, drunken bum." The state Methodist Church painted a Smith presidency as a moral danger. Some ministers became deranged when speaking of Smith, spinning out wild conspiracy theories about a papal coup of America and the looming prospect of the Catholic Church moving its headquarters to Washington, D.C. There were stories about how modern immigration was part of a plot hatched in Rome to replace white American stock with loyal voters from Catholic countries. The *Baptist Standard* published paranoid stories about the secret "Black Pope" and his plan to destroy Protestantism.[60]

State Democrats could only plead for party loyalty, paint Hoover as a closet integrationist, and threaten retribution for defecting Hoovercrats.[61] But when the apostates included such prominent Democrats as governor O. B. Colquitt, national Democratic honcho Cato Sells, insurance magnate Carr P. Collins, and former San Antonio mayor Marshall Hicks, it was tough to make a traitor label stick. Most West Texas (and Texas) newspaper editors endorsed Smith.

Hoover won almost 105,000 votes in West Texas, 60 percent of his Texas totals. It was four times what Coolidge had captured just four years earlier. After the election, *Amarillo Globe* editor Gene Howe, who had endorsed Smith, acknowledged Hoover's talents: "Hoover is a man who has demonstrated extraordinary ability and the chances are that he will make a cool, cautious, careful president. If times remain good it will be most difficult to defeat him for a second term." But, he cautioned, "I have a hunch that within a year we're going to have some black days in this country. It's been years and years since business . . . has had much of a set-back. Folks in general have been so accustomed to prosperity, that they wouldn't know how to act if real hard times came along."[62]

Howe had no idea.

BOOK TWO

THE RIGHT-WING FRONTIER

That community whose troublemakers were always running off to the frontier where there was much work and no government was indeed happy. Democracy could function under such conditions, even an extreme democracy, not because it solved problems, but because it seldom had to meet them.

WALTER PRESCOTT WEBB, 1936

6

RUIN

The wind was the cause of it all. The sand, too, had a share in it, and human beings were involved, but the wind was the primal force, and but for it the whole series of events would not have happened.

DOROTHY SCARBOROUGH, *THE WIND*, 1920

He wanted to plow up land that should have been left to grass. We're just now learning that we can rob from nature the same way we can rob from an individual.

WILL ROGERS, RADIO BROADCAST APRIL 14, 1935
(BLACK SUNDAY)

Movie mogul Hickman Price wanted to reinvent farming, converting agriculture into, as he explained to *Popular Mechanics* in 1930, a "factory" that ran continuously. By scaling wheat production, he could lower his per bushel cost to the point that he would still profit "from prices that would embarrass" most farmers. Price was so confident in his "superfarming" that he quit his cushy $50,000-a-year job in Hollywood to start a 30,000-acre wheat factory in the Texas Panhandle. He adopted the integrative approach to agriculture popularized by the United Fruit Company in which speed, scale, and specialization were key. Price ran a fleet of top-of-the-line tractors that could plow and seed seventy square miles in the 23.5 hours they ran a day. At harvest he ran twenty-five combines at a time, day and night. Massive light trucks illuminated the hours between dusk and dawn. Specialized squads of men were ferried from field to field on private trains that also served as mobile housing. Motorcycle couriers shuttled messages around the farm. The day of the individual producer was over, Price declared: "Only through large-scale, collective, group, specialized, departmentalized activity has modern prosperity, with the accompanying high standards of living, become possible."[1] Price figured he could get his production cost to around 6 bucks an acre, or around 10 cents a bushel, an amount that would withstand even the most volatile of markets and the lowest of yields. In 1930, Price, the would-be disrupter, in his first year of full production, brought in half a million bushels of wheat on just over twenty thousand acres, a massive haul. It took a hundred trucks to ship the harvest to market. He was immediately America's single largest wheat farmer, the king of industrial farming. A year later he was broke.[2]

It was the end of a golden decade for Panhandle farmers, during which it looked as if, finally, someone had cracked the centuries-old riddle of how to farm an area with great sun and soil but limited rain. An agribusiness prophet like Price was just the flashiest and most famous of the hundreds of thousands who were enjoying incredible returns after terraforming the ancient grasslands into wheat and cotton fields. Over those ten years, West Texas farmers plowed up more than 5 million acres of grass and planted them mostly in wheat, cotton, and forage. One would-be corn king even broke out nine thousand acres on the old XIT lands, trying to scale the notoriously tricky crop. Loose credit, high commodity prices, cheap technology, cheaper land, and better-than-average rainfall made the project almost too easy.

|

The key to the whole enterprise was new agricultural technology, especially the tractor, and no one adopted these new machines with greater enthusiasm than the cotton and wheat farmers of West Texas. Every year tractors got faster, cheaper, and more powerful. A man with his own rig could make a living working other people's land. Hickman Price paid his drivers a $90-a-month salary and a bonus of a dime an hour while they were on the machine. One could find a Ford, John Deere, or International Harvester dealership, or all three, in every town of any size. Other transformative tech appeared with amazing regularity. The one-way disc plow, for example, designed specifically to slice through the thick root systems of prairie grasses, made it possible for a single farmer atop a John Deere or Ford to break out a half a section in just a few days. The number of man-hours it took to bring in a wheat crop dropped from 4.6 an acre to .75. Tractors, in addition to being more efficient, more versatile, and more powerful than animal power, also didn't require a farmer to put aside forage acreage for draft animals. More land for wheat or cotton, more profit. Even the USDA said that tractors were overall cheaper than mules or horses. By the end of the 1920s, there were over eight thousand tractors in the Panhandle.[3] The grasslands never had a chance.

If new technology made what became known as the Great Plow-Up possible, the mindset of the West Texas farmer made it inevitable. Two generations of pioneer agrarians pushing into America's "new" spaces after the Civil War had produced a different kind of farmer, more entrepreneurially inclined and more attached to markets than homesteads. They saw land as a commodity, its value linked almost exclusively to production or price per acre. These were the exact sort of buyers that developers like W. P. Soash and T. D. Hobart had recruited: farmers who saw themselves as businessmen running small companies and who viewed expansion and improved production as the keys to wealth. And over the course of the 1920s, the limitless tablelands of West Texas were so plow-ready, and wheat and cotton prices were so high, and rain so abnormally abundant, that their gamble paid off. A "capitalist ethos" had superseded the old Jeffersonian commitment to home, historian Donald Worster has noted, and "all-out dedication to cash . . . replaced a rural economy aimed at sufficiency with one driving toward unlimited wealth."[4] By the mid-1920s, West Texas was the hottest agricultural market in the country.

New prairie-specific farming techniques blended the machines, the economics, and the environment. Most important among them was "dry farming," an idea promoted as a water conservation system perfect for plains soils. Its biggest proponent was Hardy Webster Campbell, founder of the Dry Farming Congress and author of dozens of tracts on the subject. Dependent on tractor farming and special implements, including a subsoil packer designed by Campbell, the idea was to manipulate soil beds to absorb and retain the maximum moisture provided by the limited and seasonal rainfall on the Great Plains. It worked best at scale and speed. It was a complicated process but, done right, Campbell promised, a can't-miss method. The first step was to completely strip the

Panhandle farmer breaking sod with a tractor and disc plow.

landscape of any remnant of the grasses that had defined the region's ecology for millennia. Pulling their disc plows across the land, farmers turned the root systems of the grasses to the sun, where they dried out and crumbled. Then, using different plows set to different depths, farmers ran back and forth over their fields, pulverizing the dried clay and crumbly roots, folding them into the rich, loamy soil. They next ran a soil packer over the land, harrowed it, seeded it using a seed drill, harrowed the land again, and kept it weeded through interrow harrowing. Finally, a farmer was supposed to keep a shallow (two- to three-inch) layer of fine dirt and dust atop each field, harrowing whenever it began to crust up or especially after a rain. The idea was that this dust layer would serve as a barrier to the evaporation of subsurface water moisture.[5] From Texas to Alberta, brown, dust-covered farms were seen as a "a sign of good husbandry."[6] Campbell's media empire pushed the system in regular scientific reports, books, magazine articles, and newspaper stories. His acolytes could be found in all the major ag schools and in statehouses, Congress, and the USDA.[7] Western railroads, eager to sell off their millions of land grant acres, hyped Campbell and his method relentlessly. The XIT Ranch made him its farmer-in-residence. Aided by above-average and well-timed rainfall, the soil responded. Wheat and cotton yields increased; dryland farming was working.[8]

During the Great Plow-Up, even as production increased, wheat prices remained above $1 a bushel, and newly available government loans offered cheap credit for purchasing land or machines.[9] Tractor farmers, whose production costs ran about 70 cents a bushel, poured their returns into more land, more machines. The number of farms doubled. Even the poorest boll weevil refugee could often scrape together enough cash or get enough credit to put in a field of wheat or cotton, a chance to hit a crop and change their luck.[10] The game was so good and wheat farming so easy that even in-town professionals like lawyers and merchants hustled a little wheat on the side. By 1930, there were so many tenants and "suitcase farmers" that, even while the total number of farmers doubled, the number who actually lived on their own land was cut in half.

What made wheat farming so irresistible, besides the profit, was just how easy it was. The whole production was a few hard and fast weeks in the fall to prep the fields and plant the wheat and a few more to harvest it in late spring. The rest of the time was spent waiting around and fretting about the weather.[11] A lot of farming, folks joked, seemed to get done while chatting over coffee and eggs in small-town cafés.

Trouble started in summer 1929 when wheat prices grew volatile. American farmers had produced the largest crop in history, but domestic demand was down slightly and foreign markets had slowed. Prices per bushel dropped from $1.40 to less than $1. Undaunted, farmers plowed up more grass, planted more wheat. In January 1930, rumors of another record harvest spooked commodity brokers. Futures opened low and markets sagged all summer. By August, bushel prices sat at around 70 cents, right at the cost of production. That fall, Panhandle farmers responded by breaking out 2 million more acres in wheat. The weather was perfect and the rains timely. In May 1931, the greatest wheat harvest in human history began to hit the market—350 million bushels. The Texas Panhandle produced 10 percent of that total.[12] Prices plunged: 60 cents, 40 cents, 30, finally 20 cents, where the price hovered all summer. It wasn't just wheat; commodity prices collapsed across the board: cotton lint fell 63 percent, sorghum 61 percent, and cattle 59 percent. Fixed costs for the commercial family farms—mortgages, bank loans, taxes, tractor and implement payments—remained the same while farm income fell by more than half. Tax delinquency hit 50 percent. The Randall County farm agent reported in 1932 that area farmers were living in "a condition of near poverty."[13]

Then the drought started. Production and income collapsed. Of the

Abandoned farm near Dalhart, Texas.

109,000 acres Dallam County farmers planted in fall 1931, 106,000 failed to produce a single bushel of wheat. Cotton was the same. In Hall County, production dropped from 100,000 bales to 12,000. Cattle prices had been in freefall since the beginning of the Great Depression, and now, thanks to overgrazing and the drought, the grasses dried up and cows were starving. Desperate ranchers fed their cattle tumbleweeds with the thorns burned off. Even the oil business, which had boomed across West Texas in the 1920s, collapsed. Prices per barrel dropped from $1.19 to $0.15, half of production costs. Drilling slowed, rents plummeted, offices closed, employees fired. In just two years, Midland lost an eighth of its population.[14] The Agricultural Wonderland had become a desperate hellscape.

II

It was a catastrophe of their making, to be sure, but still, the Dust Bowl was a ceaseless nightmare of hunger, death, dust, and destruction. Many came to believe that they were being personally and collectively punished or tested by God. And why not? The drought was biblical in scope, dragging on for a decade, the worst in a millennium.[15] Annual precipitation fell to 40 percent of average and down two-thirds from the wet years of the 1920s. Even when it did rain, the precipitation did little good, coming down too hard and at the wrong time of the year. Wheat, cotton, and grass benefit from regular moist days during the first third of the year and long slow rains intermittently during the late spring and summer. But the rainstorms of the Dirty Thirties were violent, fast-moving things that dumped rain and moved on quickly. What moisture they left ran off or evaporated before penetrating the soil.[16] Heat waves defined the summer months. Day after day of hundred-degree heat. Fields baked, streams dried up, and asphalt melted. Stripped of its protective native grasses, the tractored soil, exposed to the heat and wind, blew away by the millions of tons, leaving dunes and hummocks of brown dust and sand that buried the windward side of homes, schools, and barns.

Dizzying dust storms transformed reality. Twenty-, thirty-, forty-mile-an-hour winds picked up dirt and dust and drove it miles into the air and across the land. The sky turned black or brown or even yellow depending on the soil composition of the storm's original source. Run-of-the-mill storms could reduce visibility to fifty feet; the really bad ones turned the world black. Confused chickens took to roost, and city managers turned the streetlights on in the middle of the day. People got lost during storms between the barn and the house, on paths they had taken thousands of times. Crashing particles of dust turned the air electric, creating such powerful static electricity that a shock could knock a man down. Roaring dust stripped the paint from cars and homes. The storms could go on for hours; terrified families huddled in dark houses with the wind screaming outside like some primordial creature from an ancient folk tale. They were the worst in the spring. In 1933, Amarillo averaged three storms a week. Over one three-year period, the city had 263 days of dust storms. Even with the windows and doors shut tight, the dust crept in, leaving a thick layer on every surface.[17] Sweeping up became a two-to-three-times-a-day chore. Dishes, glasses, and cups were stored upside-down. Parents draped cribs with wet sheets to catch the dust and keep it out of babies' lungs. Dust pneumonia, the all-purpose description for lungs filling with dust, killed the very old, the very young, and the very weak. Months of grazing on dust-covered grass ground cow's teeth down to the gums, and they starved to death when they could no longer chew, or the bellies of some got so full of dust that they no longer ate. A year into the Dust Bowl, the *Dalhart Texan* painted the grim picture: "cattle dying," "not a blade of wheat," "ninety percent of the poultry dead," "humans suffering from dust fever," "milk cows going dry," a third of the population "on charity or relief work."[18]

Dust Storm overwhelming Stratford, Texas.

III

On October 29, 1929, Black Tuesday, by a strange coincidence, Gene Howe, editor of the *Amarillo Globe*, happened to be in Manhattan to witness the "fog of gloom" that fell on New York City. He described the event for the folks back home, using the voice of his country-boy alter ego Erasmus Tack, one of the most popular media characters in the Great Plains. Tack explained that the crash meant the "collapse of the Hoover high prices in the New York Sock Market."[19] He sympathized with all those rich folks who suddenly couldn't afford to finish their tours of Europe. It would be good for Texas, Tack mulled; the "demand for fancy, high-priced beef" was bound to decline and Texas cattle might be all that the "sock market gamblers and speculators" could afford. Howe's morally superior tsk-tsking was a response common in Texas. So was his belief that the Crash was the inevitable conclusion to a decade of reckless gambling in the financial markets and a needed corrective to the nation's economic priorities.[20]

Back in Amarillo, the economy was still humming in late 1929, and Howe and other boosters saw that fact as clear evidence of the superiority of the moral and modern Agricultural Wonderland. Slight turbulence in that summer's wheat prices aside, harvests were great. Cities and towns were growing. A West Texas oil boom was creating thousands of jobs and spawning dozens of related industries. Amarillo had become the nation's chief producer of helium and carbon black. Regional railroad expansion, already leading the nation, continued apace. When Amarillo's newest skyscraper, the fourteen-story Gothic Revival headquarters of the Santa Fe Railroad, opened in January of 1930, it was the tallest building between Fort Worth and Denver. The U.S. Chamber of Commerce lauded the Panhandle as an economic haven in the post-Crash storm. Roger Babson's Survey, that era's *Mad Money*, named Amarillo the strongest city economy in America.[21]

But then the wheat market collapsed, then cotton, and beef and oil. The regional economy buckled. When the farms failed, they took the whole integrated system with them: first the gins, grain elevators, and stockyards, then the banks and the dealerships, then the insurance and real estate agencies. Then came the hotels and the barbers and the cafés and the stores and the gas stations. By fall, the economy verged on complete ruin. Then it stopped raining.

Local governments, led by a booster class still laser focused on development, were ill-prepared philosophically and logistically to deal with unemployment, farm foreclosures, bank failures, poverty, and a transient population, let alone an environmental catastrophe. In one of the newest places in the country and one that, up to this point, had been solidly middle-class, there were no long-standing charity organizations to address the crisis.[22] Infrastructure aside, institutional charity, as a concept, was an alien idea to the frontier mind. Traditionally, folks who faced personal catastrophe had relied on the helping hands of their neighbors, church, or family and, even then, only as a last resort. This ethos of self-reliance was so ingrained in the culture that city leaders couldn't even imagine what direct relief might look like. A year into the breakdown of his city's economy, Amarillo mayor Ernest O. Thompson, normally one of the more astute politicians of his time, still believed that relief was nothing more than "charity" better left to "private agencies."[23]

But those private agencies buckled under crushing demand. In a single month early in 1931, the Dickens County Red Cross served over 12 percent of the county's population. By 1932, Amarillo's Community Chest had $50,000 in the bank and nine thousand relief applications.[24] In Midland, the wives of the local Rotary Club had to convert their annual clothing drive into an all-purpose welfare agency, distributing food, taking care of Christmas presents, and helping people out with utility and medical bills.[25]

When city and county governments finally stepped in, they provided only a bare minimum of services and limited participation to those desperate enough to jump through deliberately difficult and humiliating hoops. Most of the programs were ad hoc, public-private, and restricted to "bona fide" members of the community. Transients were denied access and, more often than not, run out of town by the cops. With assistance from the state, thousands of Mexican nationals were rounded up and repatriated. Work relief, the only kind available, was temporary and physically demanding. Newspaper editors and politicians were insisting that people take greater responsibility for themselves, family, and neighbors. They called for cuts in government spending and insisted that citizens shun charity.[26] The greatest fear among the booster and political classes was that governments might overreact to the economic downturn and create permanent welfare programs and a class of citizens dependent on the "dole." Any government kept in power by the redistribution of wealth, they prophesized, was doomed to become paternalistic and corrupt.[27]

Before he finally started a city jobs program, Amarillo mayor Thompson first tried to privatize the effort. He turned to the city's American Legion post to help jobless men find work.[28] Its plan was a hopelessly complicated scheme to try to match thousands of job seekers to the tens of thousands of tiny tasks scribbled on honey-do lists tacked to kitchen bulletin boards all over the city. Legionnaires canvassed Amarillo's three thousand households to build their job bank. *Globe* editor and publisher Gene Howe took the same approach, turning over his sprawling column to pitch the cases of job seekers and list job openings. His personal staff ran what had become an ad hoc temp agency from the newspaper office.[29] The letters were heartbreaking:

> Dear Tack: I want a job on a ranch and I am writing to you for help. If anyone is in need of a man and his wife who knows how to handle cattle or sheep, I would like for them to give me a trial for I was raised in a saddle and worked cattle and sheep all of my life. There is no one to go but my wife and I. We are 30 years old and very settled, care nothing about any kind of life but ranch

life. Wish some ranchman that needs a man who would do his work right would read this and give me a trial. Thank you Tack for your kindness. You can find me by calling at the Bungalow Tourist Camp in person or by phoning and asking for the man who wants work. Thanking you again I am a man in need of work. F. C.[30]

Food distribution programs were constructed to avoid even the whiff of welfare. When the *Globe* opened a soup kitchen in 1933, Howe insisted that he was just being a good neighbor. Soup, restricted to "bona fide citizens of Amarillo," was served to go: "If you don't feel like accepting it free, make a note of it," he urged, then "sometime if you get back on your feet you can pay it back at the rate of 10 cents a gallon. We'll give it to you or trust you for it."[31] Lubbock and Midland city officials ran primitive food charities by sponsoring frontier-style rabbit hunts and donating the meat to the hungry. Neither could keep rabbit meat in stock. Cities planted community vegetable gardens, mostly turnips and potatoes.[32] A Dalhart doctor, with funding provided on the down-low by a local booster, turned his sanitarium into a massive soup kitchen serving up gallons of beans, potatoes, and coffee to as many as two hundred hungry people a day.[33]

Work relief was for locals only and mostly consisted of brutal, back-breaking labor: repairing railroad bridges, building parks, cleaning up fairgrounds, parks, and cemeteries. Using grain shovels, men on work relief in Dalhart were paid a dollar a day to fight back the dust. Each was allowed to work only three days in a week.[34] Officials were careful to make applying for relief as demanding as possible; the worthy and needy, the logic went, wouldn't mind the extra effort because the reward of a job was worth it, but the class of "professionals" who milked charities would move on. "The way of the panhandler," the *Amarillo Globe* reported, "will be made so hard he will be easily persuaded to make some effort to help himself and his family or leave town."[35] To get work relief in Midland meant starting out with a city cleaning crew and keeping up with its assignments. The "names of loafers who refuse to work are being kept on file," the agency assured citizens, and "if they appeal for aid this winter, they will go hungry as the absolute law is laid down that people must work or starve in Midland."[36] In Pampa, drifters were rounded up and given a choice—leave town or work in the local cotton fields. Those

West Texas farm smothered in dust.

expecting charity were reminded of 2 Thessalonians 3:10: "Those who eat shall also work."[37]

There were, of course, countless acts of private charity. This too was part of a frontier tradition that stressed a responsibility to family, neighbors, customers, and employees. Neighbors "shared" milk cows, eggs, cheese and cream, and slaughtered livestock. Merchants and bankers extended credit and relaxed collection; those who didn't became local villains. Storekeepers cashed vouchers that insolvent school districts had used to pay teachers long after the scrip was worthless. Every town had a story about a storekeeper or café owner who went out of business because their generosity would not allow them to turn away the hungry and desperate.[38] Local gas companies extended credit even operating at a loss. "We would have never made it if we hadn't had a man that delivered oil to us," one woman remembered. "He told us not to worry about how much we owed. As long as he had oil, we had oil, and we could pay him when we could pay him. We had a banker that was the same way. He helped us all he could help us. He told us when we could pay, pay and don't worry about it . . . without them, we never would have existed because we wouldn't have had a chance and I guess they knew it."[39]

Despite the misery, West Texans maintained an optimism that bordered on the delusional. In 1935, Robert Geiger, early in his long career with the Associated Press, wrote one of the most widely read accounts of life in what he named the Dust Bowl. His reporting was an impressive account of the hopefulness and even humor of the region's people. "If it rains," Geiger noticed, was the prefatory remark that opened any number of expectant stories. There was never a question that the country would come back; it always had before. Geiger couldn't find a single farmer who planned on leaving the region or who had hesitated to put in a crop, despite the dust and drought. "It takes grit to live out here," one farmer told him, adding, "Let her blow."[40]

No one projected optimism like Gene Howe, who seemingly took it upon himself to keep the entire Panhandle upbeat. His Tack persona looked on the bright side of everything, even praising the benefits of "Vitamin K," which Tack figured was a special mineral born of and borne by the blowing dust and the reason that West Texans were the smartest and best-looking and hardest-working people in the world.[41] Tack figured that someone could get rich by opening a resort where wealthy folks could soak up its benefits.[42]

Up in Dalhart, the epicenter of the Dust Bowl, the fiery editor of the *Dalhart Texan*, John McCarty, praised the dust storms in a tribute that offered both a regional mea culpa and an expression of faith:

> Let us humbly and in shame admit our part in the rapacity our land has suffered at our hands, but vow, with the raging winds of the prairies, that we will with God's help carpet our lands once again with grass and vegetation and with our heads unbowed, our spirit undaunted, view the majestic splendor and beauty of one of the great spectacles of nature gone rampant—a Panhandle sandstorm—and smile even though we may be choking and our throats and nostrils so laden with dust that we cannot give voice to our feelings. Let us realize that the force and the God capable of such gigantic and destructive demonstrations of nature can be just as calm and tender as the hushed quiet before the storm or the bright day which follows.[43]

This optimism reached its apex with Henry Ansley's slender volume *I Like the Depression*, a minor publishing sensation in 1932. One of Gene Howe's stable of young journalists, Ansley created the book from talks he had been giving at meetings of small-town civic groups, organized around short, goofy reminders of all the "good" things to come out of the Depression—sort of collective silver-lining therapy sessions. The book's larger theme was that the Depression represented a temporary cultural corrective that would reorient a population that had gotten too big for its britches. Rough times, he reminded, were teaching Americans what really mattered: family, faith, and community. And maybe, with life slowed to a more neighborly pace, people might once again better appreciate the wisdom of a good sermon or revel in the simple beauty of a pleasant day. Maybe the drought had finally convinced farmers that they were not businessmen, and businessmen that they weren't farmers. Maybe people were learning to reject consumerism and better live within their means. Ansley told readers that he and his wife had, for example, given up their "fancy twin beds" and now kept each other warm at night just like they did "before Hoover was elected." Wink, wink.[44]

Church attendance rose, especially in the smaller communities. New denominations and rustic sects like the Church of the Nazarene and Pentecostal Holiness congregations grew the fastest. Preachers delivered sermons about the necessity of suffering before God, the value of redemption, and the glories of the afterlife.[45] The faithful often understood the drought as God's punishment for past transgressions, including (ironically enough) plowing up the grasslands. The Dust Bowl was a test of the faithful—as an angry God demanded suffering as a precondition to eternal salvation, the onset of the seven-year tribulation that immediately presaged the return of Jesus Christ and his thousand-year reign of peace. The message resonated among the devout, besieged, and broke.[46]

IV

West Texans' flirtation with the Republican Party ended. "The Hoover Party" was, as the *Odessa American*, described it,

> a menace to the continuance of a Free and Democratic Government. It represents both in theory and in practice only the industrial oligarchy of wealth. It is interested, not in the economic well-being of the man who must work to live, but in the man who works for the sole purpose of making large and regular additions from the public purse, to his already accumulated millions. America now knows it has been duped, that it has been the victim of selfish exploitations on the part of men who con-

trol the money and the Hoover Party—the invisible government of Wall Street bankers and their hirelings.[47]

But there Herbert Hoover was in 1932, back on the campaign trail, still pushing "rugged individualism," still telling people that government shouldn't "solve every difficult economic problem." The president viewed the Depression as just a major economic downturn and believed that greater public optimism in the financial system would go a long way to ending it. He still distrusted government power and, even while interfering with the political economy more than any other president had ever attempted in peacetime, was still reluctant to introduce too many new and possibly permanent changes to the nation's governing structure. He still believed in self-reliance, efficient government, and the free market and private property. He still thought that private enterprise and private charities should lead the way in relief programs. He stood by prohibition and maintained his faith in industrial and community cooperation. But all his plans failed. Industrial cooperation had not stabilized employment, prices, or markets. His efforts to juice credit markets and spur economic activity flopped. His tax hikes hadn't eliminated budget deficits. A public works bill in summer 1932 was too little too late.[48] West Texans held him personally responsible for their suffering; John McCarty, as he thought back to the 1932 election, remembered "more hatred for Hoover and the Republican Party . . . [than] there's ever been against any man, any President, or any party."[49]

Democrats had nominated New York governor Franklin Roosevelt, who had replaced Al Smith as governor of New York in 1929. The youngish, charming, and empathetic Roosevelt had proven an effective and responsive leader during the Depression, winning accolades for his administration's unemployment, agricultural, and relief programs. He even took on Tammany Hall. He was the leading candidate for the Democratic presidential nomination from the get-go, brushing off challenges from Al Smith, who had grown to despise Roosevelt, and Texas's John Nance Garner, a longtime congressman who had been elected Speaker of the House just two years earlier.

Roosevelt promised creativity, compassion, and conservative economics. His farm policy, meant to win back the West and South, was a solid mix of tax cuts, commodity credits, and mortgage refinancing served with huge helpings of agrarian fundamentalism and frontier mythology. He could "speak the language of the farm," as one Abilene reporter gushed after hearing FDR's first major farm address.[50] Evetts Haley, who would build a political career on his hatred of Roosevelt and the New Deal, called it "one of the finest platforms that you've ever read . . . a conservative platform—concise, honest, and straight-forward."[51]

Roosevelt could speak more than just the language of farmers; he was also fluent in frontier-speak. When it came to the political economy, the candidate endorsed the progressive conclusions of Frederick Jackson Turner. For Roosevelt, there was no question that pioneering was the wellspring of American democracy and that the frontier molded the American character. After all, Roosevelt's college history course at Harvard had been taught by Frederick Jackson Turner.[52] In Roosevelt's most famous campaign speech, given before the Commonwealth Club of San Francisco, he linked the Depression directly to the absence of an American frontier:

> On the Western frontier, land was substantially free. No one, who did not shirk the task of earning a living, was entirely without opportunity to do so. Depressions could, and did, come and go; but they could not alter the fundamental fact that most of the people lived partly by selling their labor and partly by extracting their livelihood from the soil, so that starvation and dislocation were practically impossible. At the very worst there was always the possibility of climbing into a covered wagon and moving west where the untilled prairies afforded a haven for men to whom the East did not provide a place.

Scanning the contemporary world, he continued, it was obvious that "equality of opportunity" had disappeared with the frontier.[53]

Nine out of ten West Texans voted for Roosevelt. He won every single county.

V

Less than a week before Inauguration Day, the Texas banking system went into freefall, another domino in a nationwide crisis. Governor Miriam Ferguson (who had won back the office a few months earlier and had just started her second term) ordered state banks closed for a week. Before they were scheduled to reopen, FDR, in his second full day in office, ordered a national bank holiday. It was Tuesday. He promised Americans that federal bank examiners would spend the rest of the week evaluating the health of the nation's banks. That Sunday, March 12, the president gave his first "Fireside Chat," describing the efforts his administration had taken to shore up the banking system. Response was positive and immediate.[54] Texas banks opened the next day. In Amarillo, they were overrun with customers who waited in lines around the block to *deposit* money—that day alone, close to $1.5 million. In Lubbock, it was almost a million and in Abilene a half million. At Pampa's biggest bank, there were so many deposits that a bookkeeper set up in the lobby with a basket and an adding machine, like Uncle Billy at the end of *It's a Wonderful Life*.[55]

The booster class put great trust in the new president. When FDR announced the National Recovery Administration (NRA) in June, a federal effort to regulate commerce through voluntary acceptance of various industrial codes regarding prices, wages, and hours, local chambers of commerce launched 100 percent fulfillment campaigns. In San Angelo, where just about every business joined the NRA, the local newspaper credited the program for slashing unemployment and pumping close to a quarter of a million dollars into the city economy.[56] In Canyon, led by newspaper editor and chamber of commerce president Clyde Warwick, shopkeepers, feed store operators, barbers, and others signed up for the NRA in record numbers. Canyon's mayor warned against any action "contrary to the dignity that should accompany such an exalted movement."[57] In Abilene, Mayor C. L. Johnson believed Roosevelt's NRA would "mean a job for everyone at decent living wages." In Amarillo, there weren't enough Blue Eagle signs (the store window symbol of participation in the NRA) to meet demand. On Blue Eagle Days, merchants gave away special prizes, including good seats to home games of the Amarillo High Sandies football team, the best in the state.[58]

Federal relief for the jobless and hungry was available almost immediately, with full-blown programs up and running by May. New Deal agencies pumped millions into the economy and helped tens of thousands of families. With great imagination and a seemingly bottomless budget, various New Deal agencies operated across the region, hiring anyone willing to work. Even the unskilled could earn a living wage by working just twenty-five hours a week. Skilled laborers could make up to $80 a month. The work was gendered—women sewed, took care of children, assisted families, and did office work. Men built and fixed things, usually out of doors. New Deal agencies were everywhere making clothes; building roads, schools, hospitals, bridges; planting trees, terraforming farms, and canning vegetables. A Civilian Conservation Corps brigade turned Palo Duro Canyon into a national tourist destination; the Works Progress Administration (WPA) erected a new federal building in Amarillo, financed an archaeological dig at Antelope Creek, built the Castro and Palo Pinto county courthouses, and constructed a preservation laboratory for the Panhandle-Plains Historical Museum; the Public Works Administration fixed the sewer in Wheeler, built a post office in Dalhart and courthouses in Jack and Childress counties, and erected a modern grade school in Crosbyton. New post offices went up in Dalhart, Borger, Pampa, Shamrock, Wellington, Littlefield, Seymour, Electra, Quanah, Odessa, Anson, and Lamesa. In just four years, the WPA district headquartered in Amarillo paid almost $3 million in wages and salaries.[59] Other New Deal agencies distributed beef, pork, fruit, beans, corn, cheese, cabbage, flour, onions, powdered milk, cornmeal, and other foodstuffs directly to hungry people. In one year alone, various New Deal agencies gave away close to $200,000 worth of food and almost $100,000 worth of clothing.[60]

VI

Initial enthusiasm and obvious need aside, West Texans remained wary of New Deal programming. Many—if not most—viewed "dependence upon the federal government as an unthinkable alternative . . . a fate worse than death." Abilene congressman Tom Blanton thought relief was a needless giveaway to those "too lazy" to work. Baptist firebrand J. Frank Norris warned from the pulpit of Texas's largest church that federal relief programs would doom democracy.[61] Those ranchers and farmers who depended on seasonal and migratory (i.e., cheap) labor despised the interference in the economy, seeing it as a mortal threat to a wage system in which the pay for hired help hadn't gone up in a half century. Evetts Haley, running his family's Midland ranch and still paying 1880s wages, complained that relief programs were making it "almost impossible to get cow hands."[62] In a 1938 survey conducted in Wheeler County, almost every single respondent said that they would accept a lower-wage private sector job than go to work for a federal relief project.[63] "I don't and cannot believe that any person that has the backbone to do it," one suggested, "can't buckle down to labor of some kind and make a go of it without the aid of the government." Even while acknowledging that government aid had helped her keep her farm, one widow believed that federal aid lowered "the national standards of the individual." A local schoolteacher declared the New Deal an "expensive failure," and the wife of the school principal believed it would produce a "generation of shiftless perverse people."[64]

Representing the 18th Congressional District, which included twenty-eight counties of the Panhandle, was Marvin Jones.[65] It's no exaggeration to say that Jones, who chaired the House Agriculture Committee, was the most important New Dealer in Congress when it came to farm policy. The son of a frontier farmer, he had spent enough days under a white-hot North Texas sun, staring through sweat-filled eyes at the south end of a north-bound mule to know he wanted off the farm. Charming and energetic, he worked his way through Southwestern University and UT Law School as a door-to-door salesman. He was smart and a successful attorney and, at twenty-six, had hung his shingle at a downtown office in Amarillo, the fastest-growing city in Texas. He was a popular lawyer (town founder Henry Sanborn was a client) and rose to the top of the booster class, organizing charity baseball games (lawyers versus doctors) and serving as president of the Young Men's Civic League.

In 1916, Jones, only thirty-four years old, went into politics, taking on a popular ten-term member of Congress to represent the Texas 18th.[66] The incumbent, John Hall Stephens, was an old populist and frontier lawyer, pushing seventy.[67] There was no way he could keep up with the relentless energy of Jones, whose district-wide "handshake campaign" gave him great recognition. Everywhere he went, Jones told a story about how, when he was a boy, he heard Stephens give a stump speech in which he promised that when the time came, he would gladly step aside for a younger generation. And Jones, the story would conclude, was of that generation, a new, modern Democrat, a just-folks Wilsonian progressive: a supporter of business, free trade, women's suffrage, and cheap farm loans and an opponent of alcohol, foreign entanglements, and communism.[68] The "Panhandle Kid," as the papers took to calling him, won in a landslide. The nickname, much to his pleasure, we can be sure, didn't stick.

During Jones's first few terms in Congress, farm policy was a major issue. While farmers and ranchers in the Agricultural Wonderland prospered, across the rest of the country, they suffered: falling commodity prices, overproduction, shrinking overseas markets, collapsing land values, staggering debt, and rural bank failures dogged farmers across the South and Middle West.[69] A boll weevil infestation relentlessly, almost methodically marched through the South, destroying cotton crops and local economies. Farmers demanded action. Blue-ribbon panels produced blue-ribbon studies with an assortment of ideas: co-ops, banking reform, government warehouses, trade expansion, cheaper credit—Granger wine in new bottles. A boisterous farm bloc pushed what became known as McNary-Haugenism: policy prescriptions to guarantee parity pricing through a government takeover of commodity markets. Jones had little use for such radical ideas. As much an agrarian as anyone, Jones considered farmers the country's "most important" citizens, yet he felt a government takeover of the farm economy would be disastrous.[70]

Jones's approach, not surprisingly, reflected the needs and philosophy of the Agricultural Wonderland: individualistic, producerist, community-focused, and entrepreneurial-cooperative. Rather than federal guarantees of "parity"—which he compared to trying to dam the Mississippi with toothpicks—Jones sought federal assistance in ensuring greater efficiency in the processing and distribution of farm goods. A cheaper and better trade infrastructure that connected farmers to consumers (and overseas markets) would allow American farmers to increase production and dominate global commodity markets.[71] To create these conditions, he suggested that the federal government lower tariffs on agricultural goods and offer American farmers cheaper credit. These two policy changes, he believed, would allow the final step in farming's shift toward a profit-centered, commercial model. It might even, he hoped, lure entrepreneurial-minded young people back to the farms and reestablish independent farmers as the foundation of a moral democracy.[72] Jones's idea, which he pushed in one form or another over most of his legislative career, was called the Export-Debenture Plan.[73] It worked like this: For every unit of a particular commodity (think bushel of wheat or bale of cotton) that went overseas, a farmer would receive a chit for a predetermined sum of money. Farmers could borrow against those chits at a low rate or cash them in with the money coming directly from tariff receipts. With a "minimum of administrative machinery," the tariff could be tweaked to work toward greater parity for farmers, who would retain their independence and limit direct government involvement in the commodities markets.[74] Jones saw the plan as a corrective to a generation of Republican policies that had favored industry over agriculture and a chance to restore farmers to the center of commodity markets. The farmer, he told colleagues in a 1935 speech, "has been hedged about by organized groups on every side. Had there been no legislation on behalf of these groups, had there been no regulations of commerce, had there been no trade barriers and no monopolies, the farmer would have needed no legislation. Standing on dead level with every other citizen, the farmer could have fought his own battles, protected his own interests, and carved his own niche in the affairs of our common country."[75]

When Democrats took back the House in 1930, the Speaker, fellow Texan John Nance Garner, named Jones as chair of the House Agriculture Committee. When Roosevelt took office, Jones became the point man for federal ag policy in the House. Over the next few years, he would, sometimes in concert, sometimes in conflict with New Deal reformers, hammer out the policies that revolutionized American farming. At heart a Jeffersonian agrarian, deeply invested in the individualism of the farmer and the sanctity of the market, Jones usually refused to go along with some of the more radical proposals coming from certain New Dealers, but he was also a patient and creative legislator who consistently bent policy toward his business-minded approach. He established his independence and his talents from the start: publicly objecting to certain parts of Roosevelt's first major farm bill, the Agricultural Adjustment Act, he wrung important concessions from the White House on the bill. And, despite his misgivings, it was Jones who introduced the bill on the House floor and urged its passage. "We are at war," he reminded many of his conservative colleagues, "and war is the grimmest business that ever engaged the attention of mankind. While this war is on, I am going to follow the man at the other end of the Avenue who has the flag in his hand."[76] He would bite his lip several more times in those first hundred days and quietly begin to prepare for alternative legislation that fit more squarely into his agrarian philosophy.

First came the Agricultural Adjustment Act (AAA) and Agricultural

Adjustment Administration. Run out of the USDA, the AAA gave the secretary of agriculture wide latitude in reducing the production of seven commodities, including wheat and cotton. Among the options available to Secretary Henry Wallace were paying farmers directly for reducing acreage (even plowing under planted fields), regulating commodities markets, and setting fee rates for processors. The program was voluntary for farmers and paid for by taxing commodities processors—for example, by charging millers 30 cents for every bushel of wheat they turned into flour.[77]

In West Texas, entering its second year of the drought, overproduction was no longer an issue. Bankruptcy, starving cattle, collapsed credit markets, barren fields, and hungry families were. The way the AAA worked in West Texas was that farmers received an "allotment" payment that covered a little over half of their average production in the years between 1928 and 1932. It was a massive, unprecedented, and expensive undertaking. County agents met with interested farmers and helped them calculate their allotment according to a complicated rubric; in exchange for a 15 percent reduction in acreage (not a problem in the Dust Bowl), wheat farmers received 27 cents per allotted bushel, in two payments. The plan was immensely popular. At a 1935 renewal vote, Randall County farmers voted to continue participating 809 to 31.[78] Cotton farmers received between $7 and $20 an acre left unplanted. In Donley County alone, farmers plowed under a third of the 1932 cotton crop. When the cotton checks started in September 1933, farmers, as one newspaper put it, suddenly "felt like wearing their hat brims turned up . . . in the fashion of the pioneers who did so when they had corn in the crib, hogs in the pen, and money in their pockets."[79] Wheat allotment checks were literally front-page news when they arrived in December. The *Canyon News* blared "WHEAT CHECKS BRING MONEY TO COUNTY."[80] By the end of the year, West Texas farmers had cashed $5 million worth of AAA checks. In 1934, participation in most counties reached over 90 percent. In four years, The AAA spent almost $55 million in West Texas.[81]

When the U.S. Supreme Court declared the AAA unconstitutional in 1936, Marvin Jones helped create the Soil Conservation and Domestic Allotment Act, which essentially did the same thing—paying farmers not to grow crops—but this time, the law was predicated on protecting soil.[82] It was particularly effective and appreciated in West Texas, then entering the fifth year of the drought, and administered locally through farmers' associations. In Randall County, 91 percent of farmers participated. By that point, most of the tenants and suitcase farmers had been driven out of the fields and only the landowning class remained. They liked the Soil Conservation Service (SCS), not just because of the program's local control aspect but also because it was grounded in a larger project of finding new ways to get the soil to produce more wheat, cotton, or forage. West Texans were, after all, as a regional SCS director once claimed, very willing to "face new problems with new methods."[83]

Which was true. As we've seen, the agriculturalists and business folk of West Texas were nothing if not adaptable. Flexibility, industrial cooperation, and acceptance of new techniques and ideas were all deep-seated in the region's culture. They just folded New Deal farm programs and money into their business plans as additional sources of income or credit. In 1935, for example, southern plains farmers spent $1 million of their AAA money buying new tractors.

But soon enough, New Dealers started asking different questions: What if the plains and prairies weren't suitable for farming? What if the government had been wrong to allow settlement on these semiarid lands? Who should be blamed for the Dust Bowl? Had Americans' frontier experience led to failure? That's when things got weird.

7
NEW DEAL AGONISTES

Bureaucracy is ever desirous of spreading its influence and
its power. You cannot extend the mastery of the government over the daily working life of a people without at the
same time making it the master of the people's souls and
thoughts.

HERBERT HOOVER, 1928

His name was Rexford Guy Tugwell, and he was an economist and a
good one. A star student at the Wharton School of Business, he was
a full professor at Columbia University before he was forty. One of
the nation's leading public intellectuals, a respected and prolific scholar
with a wide range of interests, Tugwell published in the nation's leading
academic journals and wrote for popular magazines like the *Saturday
Review* and the *New Republic*. He was witty and smart, devilishly handsome and charming, and a snappy dresser. He moved easily in political
circles and was a valuable adviser to the New York and national Democratic Party organizations. In 1928 he wrote Al Smith's positions on agricultural economics, and four years later FDR tapped him to serve in the
original "Brains Trust." He was, by then, the nation's foremost advocate
of the planned economy, believing that anarchic markets had damaged
the overall economic health of the country and that greater government
regulation would benefit more Americans. After taking office, Roosevelt
named Tugwell second-in-command at the Department of Agriculture.
Two years later, the president rearranged whole segments of the federal
bureaucracy to give Tugwell his own massive new agency, the Resettlement Administration (RA), tasked with ending rural poverty and fixing
the Dust Bowl. Within eighteen months, Tugwell—by then one of the

most hated men in America—was out of government, the Resettlement Administration smashed, and the shards of his agency stashed across the governmental world like horcruxes.

In West Texas, debates over Rexford Tugwell turned on whether he was a ruthless communist who had wormed his way into Roosevelt's inner circle as part of a plot to sovietize American agriculture, or just an out-of-touch eggheaded dilettante who was exploiting the tragedy of the Dust Bowl to test a bunch of impractical economic theories. A kinder impression was that the economist was just an obvious and embarrassing example of a liberal bureaucracy gone haywire. Conspiracy theories about Tugwell abounded; among the most widespread was that he was launching a secret plan to depopulate the plains and move farmers into the cities. One Panhandle congressman promised to sock Tugwell in the nose. The RA's publicity director in Amarillo quit his job to protest Tugwell's leadership and urged every "newspaper, chamber of commerce and public spirited citizen living on the Plains" to do what was necessary "to bring about the resignation of Dr. Rexford G. Tugwell, Resettlement Administrator."[1] For someone looking for the moment when West Texans began to distrust and fear the federal government, Tugwell's Dust Bowl years might be a good place to start.

I

A thing to understand, maybe *the* thing to understand, about West Texas history is the fact that the Dust Bowl and the New Deal changed everything. The glorious, rapid, almost magical advance of progress across the Agricultural Wonderland stopped. First people stopped coming and then people started leaving. A quarter of the counties in what would become the country's most reliably Republican congressional district lost a quarter of their population (this following a decade of 50 percent growth). The exodus continued. By 1970, two-thirds of these counties had smaller populations than they did in 1930.[2] County seats survived, but villages collapsed. Amarillo grew, as did Lubbock, Abilene, Midland, and a few other places, but mostly at the expense of smaller nearby towns. There was very little in-migration. Booster politics, founded on growth, shifted inward and became more focused on protecting populations, economies, and increasingly, culture.

The West Texas economy would recover once the rains returned. The remaining farmers and ranchers adopted new technologies (especially irrigation and fertilizers) and new techniques (like stockyards and diversification) that permitted even larger economies of scale that produced higher yields and needed fewer farmers and ranchers (and fewer banks, feed stores, implement dealers, and cafés). A major partner in creating and sustaining this new economy would be the federal government, a relationship that began in the 1930s and with projects first tasked to Rexford Tugwell.

In 1935, when Tugwell launched the Resettlement Administration, the ecology of West Texas was on the verge of collapse. One hundred million acres were in danger of permanent desertification. Summer brought a domestic refugee crisis, with tens of thousands of blown-out farmers and families hitting the road.[3] Towns emptied. Emergency relief funds were the only thing keeping many people alive. Livestock starved; fields lay barren. Tugwell was responsible for fixing all of it (along with rural poverty in general). Drawing whole agencies and divisions from other parts of the federal government and appropriating whatever state agencies he thought might help, Tugwell created the largest, most complicated, and most expensive bureaucracy in the federal government.

One of the nation's leading agricultural economists, Tugwell had long believed that the nation's history of frontier farming—which he labeled "riotous"—lay at the root of rural poverty. A chaotic land system that had, over a century and half, pushed the nation's poor and desperate out beyond the limits of established agricultural areas onto a frontier that itself beckoned reckless capital and risk-takers had created a modern reality of a hypertransient farming population, out-of-whack land prices, and terrible soil management. A place of ruin. America's frontier heritage, as Tugwell saw it, was no triumph but rather an embarrassing arrangement where generations of farmers had pushed onto barely farmable lands and gone broke, but not before destroying the soil, the ecosystem, and the local economy. The Dust Bowl was Exhibit A.[4]

Broadly, the Resettlement Administration was supposed to relocate poor and destitute farm families to new homes and on new land; restore the nation's soil, streams, coasts, and forests; and protect them from future floods, droughts, and natural disasters. Further, it was to provide American farmers the resources and programming they needed to rehabilitate their ravaged acres. Although the RA operated hundreds of projects across the country, the Dust Bowl presented its greatest challenge, and nothing less than the future of the Great Plains and American agriculture was at stake. Tugwell ran his Dust Bowl project out of the RA's District 12, a specifically designated region tasked with addressing the problems of drought and dust in Texas, Oklahoma, western Kansas, and eastern Colorado. The office took up 18,000 square feet of office space in downtown Amarillo's most prestigious business address. Using the federal government's biggest and most productive publicity department, Tugwell first sought to rewrite the history of settlement on the Great Plains. The Dust Bowl was the story's penultimate chapter, and the villains were greedy and shortsighted farmers guilty of committing the greatest ecological crime in history. The last chapter introduced the story's ultimate heroes, government planners who would strictly regulate space, people, and markets and usher in a new golden age.[5] It didn't play well in the Agricultural Wonderland.

II

It was October 1935, and the RA was just five months old, when rookie filmmaker Pare Lorentz and his small crew showed up in Dalhart to wrap up principal shooting for the Resettlement Administration's first major media venture, a documentary about the Dust Bowl. It was one of the strangest productions in film history. Lorentz and his camera and sound men had spent the previous six weeks traveling south from Montana, just shooting whatever random scenes caught the director's eye. There was no script, no story board, not even a treatment. But Lorentz had a $6,000 budget, some cool new special cameras, a tricked-out pickup, and a steadfast belief that if he captured enough dusty images of the Great Plains deathscape, he could stitch together his story of disaster. He was even lucky enough to score footage of a massive dust storm as it smothered Amarillo. Over his month and half filming the American interior, Lorentz found his movie: close-ups of plows scraping hardpan, wrecked fences, miles of dunes, lean, sunburned men staring into rainless skies, farm machinery buried in dust, broken-down and loaded family trucks lurching west, broken women shoveling dust out front doors. His most powerful images were from his last week in the Texas Panhandle. What he couldn't find, he staged.

Lorentz was an interesting choice as the nation's first-ever government documentarian. Before going to work for the RA, he was known mostly as a clever and caustic movie critic.[6] His witty and keen reviews appeared in magazines like *Judge*, *The New Yorker*, *Vanity Fair*, *McCall's*, and *Town and Country*. He was the youngest film critic in the country with his own byline. Lorentz was, as they say, a "director's critic," interested in the entirety of a film. He saw movies as more than just acting, script, and story; they were lighting, set design, music, camera work, and much else. Even in his most scathing reviews—and there were plenty—Lorentz was quick to offer praise for quality work by a set designer or sound engineer, often naming the person and taking the time to explain their work. It was an approach steeped in his profound appreciation of film as art. He had no patience for much of the drivel that he believed a profit-driven system served up to an unwitting public. In 1930 he coauthored one of the earliest and most in-depth critiques of movies and the industry. *Censored: The Private Life of the Movies* was a survey of the most egregious examples of Hollywood studios altering a film's source material to avoid controversy or appeal to mass audiences. "At its worst," Lorentz said, American film "is illiterate and childish. At its best, it's America's greatest contribution to art. Yet, at its best, it is unable to escape the unlearned and stupid hecklings of the censor."[7]

Lorentz leveraged his reputation as a film critic into a larger role as an observer of American culture and politics in essays for *Newsweek* and a regular column of D.C. snark for the Hearst newspapers.[8] He tried to get a documentary on Roosevelt's first year in office produced but couldn't get the funding. Instead, he used the images he had collected and published a coffee table book for Funk and Wagnall's, *The Roosevelt Year*.[9] That book earned Lorentz the attention of Henry Wallace, the secretary of agriculture, who called the critic and writer to his office in Washington. At their first meeting, Lorentz pitched a movie that would document the USDA's efforts to save the American farmer. Wallace demurred and passed him along to Tugwell. The new RA director grew so excited about movies that he started babbling to Lorentz about producing ten, fifteen, eighteen new films. Lorentz talked him down to one—about the Dust Bowl.

The novice filmmaker imagined a first-class, serious film playing to packed audiences in every movie house in America. State-sponsored films were all the rage in Europe, especially in England and Germany, but in the United States, government films had until then been restricted to short instructional reels for small, targeted audiences. But this was a chance to create important art, make a significant statement, and do real good. "We used the film," as he later told Congress, "as a graphic medium to reach millions of people, city people, who never had seen the Panhandle of Texas; who never saw the western plains; who had no idea about conditions." He believed that for the millions of Americans who had never set eyes on the Great Plains, "only the camera" could capture its size and grandeur.[10]

Lorentz, to the frustration of the professional Hollywood camera crew he used to do that capturing, had only a vague sense of how he planned to put his movie together.[11] He wanted to tell his story through historical vignettes in which the land itself would be both subject and setting. The film was to be a visual experience, without any need for narration, or so Lorentz thought. He planned to create his movie in the editing bay, stitching together the images he and his crew had filmed into a logical and linear narrative about the Dust Bowl. He had plenty of footage of languid cattle and dust-covered farms, forlorn farmers, abandoned land and worn-out machines, and sand stretching across horizons. Lots of symbols of death and dying. When hit with inspiration while on his filming tour, Lorentz would improvise whole scenes and hire locals as actors and rent whatever equipment he needed to bring his visions to life. For one important scene in the movie in which a brigade of tractors crests a hill in formation he had to purchase gas for the machines that had been dormant for years. He filled out his movie with supplementary images culled from studio stock footage.[12]

As he stitched together his movie, he began to interview composers to score the film. Music was the only thing for Lorentz that was as important as the images. He hired the brilliant young Virgil Thomson, an innovative musician whose first opera, *Four Saints in Three Acts*, had opened on Broadway the year before. It featured a libretto written by Gertrude Stein and had an all-Black cast. Lorentz had enjoyed the opera and was captivated by Thomson's use of contrasting music types and his willingness to take risks. Although Thomson had never scored a film before, he and Lorentz were in sync as to style and inspiration. The composer drew on traditional folk music, especially cowboy songs and church hymns, as he wrote the score while watching footage and looking at stills. He and Lorentz worked closely, with the director even editing the movie in many cases to fit the soundtrack, and with Thomson arranging softer spaces (mostly woodwinds) in his score where narration could be added if needed. The final score was recorded by the twenty first chairs of the New York Philharmonic Orchestra under the direction of Alexander Smallens. It is widely considered one of the finest examples of midcentury American music and among the most effective soundtracks in the history of film.[13]

Eventually deciding to include narration, Lorentz kept it to a minimum—just seven hundred words—and hired Thomas Chalmers, a baritone former opera singer, actor, and aspiring director, to narrate the movie. Chalmers, who hated narration almost as much as Lorentz, nevertheless offered a knowing and powerful interpretation of the script imbuing the different repetitions required—there are, for example, four different versions of the phrase "country of high winds, and sun and of little rain"—with great meaning and capturing the script's tonal shifts and perspective changes with grace and brio.[14]

The final product was one of the most powerful documentaries of the first half of the twentieth century. *The Plow That Broke the Plains* screened at the White House in March 1936. Roosevelt loved it. Tugwell couldn't wait to get it into movie theaters.

Then the trouble started. First it was Hollywood; studio heads were incredibly wary about the government getting into the movie business. And over the course of his career, Lorentz had made his share of enemies among studio elites.[15] When the film was ready for distribution, the studios, which then owned almost all the nation's theaters, simply refused to book it. Most claimed that its twenty-eight-minute running time made for awkward showtimes, and a few squawked about not wanting to broadcast government propaganda—one unnamed producer said, "We would not release [the] picture even if it were Ben Hur."[16] Independent theaters picked up the movie: "Dare to See the Movie that Others Won't Show." It got very positive reviews: the *Boston Globe* called it a "valuable addition to modern pictures [that] illustrates what uncharted territory the commercial pictures have yet to discover."[17] It went into wide distribution by June. One scholar has estimated that the film was screened seven thousand times over the next three years.[18]

The message of *The Plow That Broke the Plains* is as subtle as a brick to the face. Arranged in ten linear vignettes, the movie spreads across three acts. Act I tells the story of the grasslands from their days as a cattlemen's paradise to the beginning of the Dust Bowl. Act II focuses on the tragic and sad story of the people and land on the contemporary plains. A short third act describes the current efforts being made by the federal government to help people and restore the land. The film makes a simple and powerful indictment of plains farmers. This "country of high winds, and sun and of little rain" was never meant to be plowed. The federal government and national media had been tiptoeing around naming the actual causes of the Dust Bowl since 1931, focusing instead on the drought as a natural disaster and an indomitable people toughing it out on the last frontier, but *Plow* takes a hard stand: greedy boosters and gullible farmers had brought farming to a land historically, ridiculously unsuited for agriculture. The Dust Bowl, *Plow* made perfectly clear, was a man-made disaster, the unfortunate but logical consequence of an acquisitive, restless, and individualistic mentality that had no place in the modern world.

The grass is the star of the movie. After its expository title sequence, *Plow*'s first two minutes are little more than loving and lingering shots of grass; medium shots of grass, close-ups of grass, long shots of cowboys on horses riding up grassy slopes. The plains were, as Chalmers intones, a "cattleman's paradise" and "an uncharted ocean of grass." But, in the first of the jarring shifts that define the film, as Chalmers declares the "plowman followed the herder and the pioneer came to the plains," the screen fills with chaos: abrupt, nonlinear jump cuts of wagons, dust, and terrified cattle accompanied by Thomson's spastic arrangements of bugles and banjos along with weird mash-ups of hymns and folk songs.

The title's villain makes its first appearance around a quarter of the way into the film, a close-up shot of a moldboard plow slicing prairie sod. The narrator warns: "Settler plow at your peril." From there, Lorentz presents a juddering chronicle of agricultural technology and expansion, the rise of wheat markets, and the proclivity for drought on the plains. A master of visual storytelling, Lorentz marches toward the inevitable destruction of the prairies and an indictment of all Americans for their role in the Great Plow-Up. Particularly powerful is his treatment of the expansion of wheat markets during the Great War when, in a fit of Eisensteinian frenzy, Lorentz merges the mechanical destruction of plains grasses by tractors with the mechanical destruction of the Belgian wheat lands by tanks. With Thomson's militaristic score overlaying the minute-long section, Lorentz moves back and forth between tractors and tanks, including the shot of his battalion of tractors moving in formation. Moving seamlessly from the wartime demand for wheat into his history of the Bonanza years of the 1920s, Lorentz lays out his case against the farmers and speculators. Thomson's score shifts from his breezy interpretations of American folk tunes to his only original composition, a funereal take on Dixieland jazz. Over rapid cuts that move between various ads for wheat lands, stock tickers, headlines on wheat prices, smokestacks, tractors, combines, and, for some reason, a jazz drummer, Chalmers narrates, noticeably switching to first-person plural:

> Then we reaped the golden harvest
> then we really plowed the plains
> we turned over millions of new acres for war
> we had the man-power
> we invented new machinery
> the world was our market
> By 1933 the old grass lands had become the new wheat lands
> a hundred million acres
> two hundred million acres
> More wheat!

A stock ticker falls from its perch.
[FADE TO BLACK]
[FADE IN: DAY: CLOSE ON COW SKULL IN DRIED CREEK BED]

The second act is pure disaster porn, a catalog of catastrophe clocking in at just under six minutes. Broken, abandoned machinery smothered by dust, cracked creek beds, sand dunes. There's a fifteen-second, 180-degree tracking shot of a desert outside Dalhart. Dejected peasants trudge along dusty paths. Blowing dust. Abandoned homesteads. Chalmers narrates, "The rains held off and the sun baked the earth." A dust storm is accompanied by a soaring Thomson score that crashes into melancholy. The second act concludes with shots of families digging out their homes with grain shovels and piling their meager belongings into the bed of a barely running truck, abandoning their homes, and heading west. Chalmers chants:

Rexford Tugwell and local farmer inspect a piece of barbed-wire bird's nest made famous in The Plow That Broke the Plains.

Blown out—baked out—and broke . . .
nothing to stay for . . . nothing to hope for . . .
homeless, penniless, and bewildered
they joined the great army of the highways.

All they wanted, he assures us, was a chance to start anew. In the film's "last" shot, the camera moves across the desert one last time to slowly zoom in on a bird's nest constructed of barbed-wire perched in the crook of a long dead tree.[19]

The Resettlement Administration shows up in Act III. The shortest part of the film, it's a clunky, preachy, and stat-filled description of the agency's work over government B-roll. Even Chalmers seems bored. Lorentz was not really involved in the production of this third act and didn't care for it. He liked his bird nest ending.[20]

On June 2, the film made its glitzy Panhandle premier at Amarillo's most prestigious movie house, the Paramount Theater. There were fancy dresses and red carpets and searchlights, a little taste of Hollywood in Potter County. The day before, at what the Amarillo newspapers called a "business man's theater party," local Jaycees screened the film for 1,400 area boosters. The Jaycees had sent a telegram to Rexford Tugwell a couple of weeks early, demanding a local screen; they were nervous about how the region might be depicted.[21]

Once boosters saw the movie, they were not happy. Calling for the government to yank the film from distribution and toss Tugwell from office, boosters, politicians, and editors objected to almost every aspect of *The Plow That Broke the Plains*. What they found most galling was not the historical narrative, which cast Panhandle farmers as the perpetuators of the greatest environmental crime in history, but the section of the film that focused on the contemporary conditions in the Dust Bowl. Boosters worried that the film cast the region in an unflattering light. It was OK, as the regional director of the RA suggested, to show the film to Congress so that its members might be "frightened" into coughing up more money for relief, but the film should not be meant for broad consumption. The Amarillo Chamber of Commerce launched a fundraising drive to "effectively combat" the film's negative publicity. The *Globe-News* called the movie "thinly disguised" propaganda and predicted that "theater goers are going to rebel." The paper's official review of the film criticized it for its "low and cheap propaganda" and for its "innuendo, misrepresentations and plain untruths." It called it a "vicious and damaging document, produced by taxpayers' money," and warned that "the agricultural population of the country will look with suspicion upon any program offered by Mr. Tugwell to the detriment of all concerned."[22] The West Texas Chamber of Commerce sent out a carefully worded press release, urging the RA to screen the film only in the Dust Bowl so as not to scare potential settlement or investment. (It also praised federal efforts in "water and soil conservation.")[23] One Amarillo man urged his neighbors to "form a united front with solidarity of purpose and unanimity of thought to stop this malicious portrayal (or betrayal) of our territory." If it must be shown, he said, only show it to Congress and "ONLY in order to obtain increased appropriates for our territory."[24] John McCarty, ever boosting, called *Plow* a "tool of the government, designed to drive people from the land," that was ultimately "bound to do more damage to our credit and our agriculture."[25] The *Pampa Daily News* called the movie "The Libel on the Plains" and urged the "Federal EXPERTS who judge the plains" to remember the proverb "Más sabe el loco en su casa que el cuerdo en la ajena" (A fool understands his own home better than a wise man can understand a stranger's).[26] Fiery young Shamrock politician Eugene Worley (who would replace Marvin Jones in Congress) threatened to punch out Rexford Tugwell if the film wasn't pulled immediately. The Texas Panhandle, he proclaimed, "is far from being a desert. It is a rich agricultural region, and home of the nation's finest, most hospitable, and courageous people."[27]

Ralph Bray, the publicity director for the Resettlement Administration's District 12, not only quit his job over the film but published an open letter in the *Amarillo Globe-News* explaining why: "I am resigning in protest against a lot of pedantic principles by Tugwell's academy of bubble blowers, dilettantes and doctrinaires whose carnival of blundering and squandering of public funds the past year is making doubly difficult the reconstruction of agriculture." It was time, he said, to shed the government's "radical philosophies" and for West Texans to reclaim control of their land. "I sincerely believe that I could take a group of dirt farmers, prominent county officials and public-spirited citizens and, with a small part of the expense incurred, show some material program in correcting misuse of lands throughout this section that have caused wind erosion and dust storms."[28] He demanded Tugwell's immediate resignation and called on the RA to put an end to its propaganda. "The people on the Plains don't want charity and they don't want a lot of Communistic philosophies foisted upon them, and they don't want their country, which is one of the finest on earth, . . . maligned and pictured as an American Sahara by a bunch of Tugwellian sophists."[29]

III

At one point the Spade Ranch was one of the largest and most modern cattle operations in the American West. Originally conceived as a showcase for barbed wire, it was the brainchild of longtime pioneer rancher John "Spade" Evans and the Superior Wire Company. A quarter of a million acres were divided into pastures by tight, arrow-straight, six-string fences. Each pasture had a windmill and water tank and was connected to the others by telephone and caliche roads. Cowboys were still on horseback, but management drove automobiles. Once the Santa Fe Railroad finally arrived in 1924, the Spade pivoted to farm sales. In those land-hungry years, Ellwood Farms (the name of the Spade's real estate division) sold close to 100,000 acres, fetching great prices, upward of $35 an acre. The typical buyer either purchased a half-section plot and tractor farmed cotton or bought a two-section family ranch.[30]

Starting in 1931, the drought brought land sales to exactly zero. Worse, farmers failed to make their payments and went into tax default. And Ellwood Farms still had a hundred thousand acres to sell. As the drought dragged on, Lubbock boosters grew nervous. It wasn't just Ellwood Farms; the entire real estate business had bottomed out and cotton markets and production were in the tank.

In 1934, a semidesperate Lubbock Chamber of Commerce applied to join a new government program designed to persuade city folks to move back to the country where they would run subsistence farms. It was a pet project of Roosevelt, a true zealot of agrarian fundamentalism, who believed deeply that self-sufficient family homesteads played a key role in American life. (Tugwell harbored no such feelings.) Part of a suite of programming in the first months of the New Deal, the Subsistence Homestead division was set up to settle the urban poor on small government-owned farms where they could grow their own food, market a few commodities, work for wages a few hours a week in some nearby factory or mill, enjoy a healthier life, and build strong, frontier-like communities. It was run out the Department of the Interior by the hopeless romantic agrarian M. L. Wilson. In addition to providing prebuilt homes and ready-to-go farms, the new homesteading program would also organize work programs and other government assistance. Lubbock boosters, facing high unemployment and an agricultural economy in tatters, loved the idea of a government-sponsored back-to-the-land movement.[31]

The Lubbock Chamber proposed an "Industrial Farm," consisting of small truck farms each of forty to sixty acres, ringing the city and providing Lubbockites with fresh produce and cotton mills with industrial labor. Once the operation was in place, boosters assumed "private capital" would step in and run the operation. With the one-time startup cost borne by the government, yet another new style of farming might replace or serve the cotton kingdom. If successful, the Chamber reasoned, the model could be adopted by local land developers to sell off more of the old ranch lands. As a special bonus, the Industrial Farm might "rehabilitate" tenant farmers and sharecroppers "instead of dropping them on the dole."[32] The Chamber wrote up a proposal full of rosy projections about yields (based on the output of a single irrigated farm nearby, even though it had no intention of irrigating the Industrial Farm) and sent it off in January 1935.

It was approved a few weeks later. With no other agency in place to facilitate the project's funding, the Federal Emergency Relief Administration (FERA) bought four thousand acres from Ellwood Farms, whose manager had sat on the committee that wrote the original proposal. The government paid $25 an acre, two and a half times the going rate for undeveloped ranch property.[33] Just as the project was about to launch, the Resettlement Administration absorbed FERA and took over the planning for the Industrial Farm.

Director Tugwell had little patience for nostalgic fantasies of poor folk making good in the country with vegetable gardens, industrial piecework, fresh air, and old-time pioneer spirit. This was 1935, not 1866. What Tugwell wanted was data to help him solve the riddle of rural poverty. So he turned the Subsistence Homestead program into an "experiment" as to the feasibility of rural farm life on the plains.[34] Was it even possible, under optimum conditions and with adequate help and expertise from the government, for a family to make it on a small southern plains farm? That's what Ropesville—the project's new name—was designed to find out. Given the cyclical nature of the region's ecology, the RA sought to plot a solution to the boom-and-bust cycles that had plagued the American prairies for three quarters of a century. It considered every variable it could think of—crops, credit, equipment, farm size, personal food production, outside income, quality of farmer—as it designed the Ropesville experiment.

The RA carved up its four thousand acres into thirty-three farms, each around 130 acres: big for a family farm, but too small to tractor. (Tugwell never even considered the Chamber's proposed farmers market–mill worker model.) It also arranged with Ellwood to bring forty-four more units online over the next couple of years. With the government holding the title and promising credit and other benefits, the RA was able to convince farmers to experiment with crops and agree to gather appropriate data on finances, food, production, and use of technology. While grinding out a living on a hundred acres of government scrubland in Hockley County and filling out regular reports for eager bureaucrats was nobody's idea of the American Dream, the RA still received a thousand applications for the first thirty-three slots.

Seeking applicants familiar with the country, the RA recruited exclusively among locals. There were four criteria: "If you were a good farmer, if you were stable, if you paid your debts, and if you were broke," as one former resident described them.[35] The lucky few who made the cut stepped onto some of the best-thought-out farming units ever devised. The RA had no interest in replicating frontier conditions, allowing

Ropesville farmhouse. Notice the windmills, water tanks, shrubs, and drapes.

residents to live in holes in the ground, or forcing them to build out their farms piece by piece. To eliminate variables, the land had already been terraced and fenced, and there was an easily marketed crop in the ground or ready for planting. Every farm had a windmill, water well, small barn, and corral. Each had a cute little four-room farmhouse with lots of windows, front porches, trellises, running water, and a water pressure system.[36] Every resident was provided access to low-cost loans that allowed them to purchase equipment, furniture and household goods, and supplies. An onsite manager provided advice on farming techniques, home finance, and planning. There were regular community meetings, events, and programming. Farm experts from the USDA and Texas Tech held exclusive seminars and provided one-on-one tutorials for residents. There were regular visits by specialists in home economics and rural health. A large community center included a commercial-style kitchen and plenty of space for dances or quilting bees. Ropesville even had its own baseball team.

The plan was designed to answer a simple question: Given every logical advantage, could the average American farm family work its way out of poverty and become "become successful, contributing citizens"?[37] To answer that question, the RA needed to gather information. To get more accurate production capabilities, the agency would not allow sharecropping (which encouraged overproduction), but instead insisted on cash rents (to gain a more accurate assessment of crop and land values). Every family was required to keep and regularly share a detailed record book. Each year, the household had to submit a lengthy and complicated action plan for its farm and home. The plan had to be approved by the local manager, who also gave families "accomplishment" slips that they had to fill out and return. Personal family economics were shared publicly at annual meetings. Any larger-than-usual expense meant another round of application and approval. Farm women had to track their canning, garden production, and household expenses and were subject to visits by the project manager. Families even had to file reports on how much food they ate. What residents resented as useless red tape and embarrassing intrusions into their personal lives the RA saw as necessary data. No fewer than four separate RA agencies leaned on the community's manager for more information, more reports. Ropesville's first manager quit in frustration over the demands.[38]

Lubbock boosters hated Ropesville. The government, it seemed, had completely abandoned the frontier model of settlement that they believed to be the foundation of the region's character. The RA, rather than insisting on hard work, had instead rewarded poor and lazy farmers with a new utopia. Keep in mind that the original Industrial Farm plan, concocted by the Lubbock Chamber of Commerce, was to take advantage of a government program to help them find a new way to market the millions of acres in the area that had not yet been developed. They were not expecting luxurious turnkey farms subsidized by the American taxpayer. Their biggest gripe seemed to center on the fact that the government had not forced its residents to undergo the rugged rigors of frontier life. "I know a little about this country," one of them claimed. "You go out there and see people living in dugouts" on $200 farms and "go back in three or four years, and they have a nice house. There is something beautiful about it."[39] Acting as if modern necessities would somehow spoil the poor, they halted efforts to have Ropesville houses plumbed and electrified. Texas Tech president Bradford Knapp, a huge supporter of Ropesville, nevertheless boasted that he had grown up without indoor plumbing (he was born in 1870) and was willing to bet "that nine-tenths of the people in that country don't have them [bathrooms]." Another booster added that if the project was to furnish residents with "bathtubs, electric lights and a lot of other things they are not used to, they will never be able to pull out [of poverty]."[40]

While Lubbock businessmen might view years of using an outhouse as an important life experience, New Dealers saw it as a reckless and stupid attachment to an archaic way of life. While the sixty-six-year-old

Knapp might wax nostalgic about latrines and burning buffalo chips for heat, RA officials asked, Why, in 1935, should anyone live in a house without electricity or plumbing? This "work up from nothing on virgin soil" frontier thinking was, Tugwell thought, exactly what had created the Dust Bowl and every other farming catastrophe scattered across American history. And as a trained (and gifted) economist, he, of course, took no truck with the attitude, common in rural America, that the poor were somehow solely responsible for their fate and that only by publicly demonstrating their worth—through the sod house–to–tidy farm experience—should they be allowed to live like modern folk. Nor did he agree with the notion that rural "poverty was the result of shiftlessness and incompetence" or individual "faults of character." It was that kind of regressive thinking, he would come to believe, that explained the lack of support in rural America for the Resettlement Administration.[41]

By all accounts, Ropesville was a success. It grew to seventy-nine units and was taken over by the Farm Security Administration (FSA) in 1937. The FSA completely changed the way the project worked. It eliminated most of the reporting requirements and permitted sharecropping arrangements with tenants. The program was phased out starting in 1941 when its lands were sold off (mostly to residents) under the Bankhead-Jones Farm Tenant Act.[42] The farms sold out in two years. A careful and detailed study by the FSA based on the data that it had collected during its five-year experiment at Ropesville, however, revealed an important truth: there was simply no way a family could live on a subsistence homestead on the southern plains; the annual "cash outlay for family living is less than the actual earned income."[43]

IV

Rexford Tugwell visited Amarillo in August 1936. He was a member of a research delegation sent by President Roosevelt to investigate conditions in the Dust Bowl. He looked characteristically crisp in his white linen suit and carefully blocked Panama hat as he stepped off the train on a blazingly hot, sunny Monday morning. The other members of the Great Plains Drought Area Committee followed him onto the platform and across the street to the Herring Hotel ballroom, where they would breakfast with the Amarillo Chamber of Commerce. Along the

Morris L. Cooke, from the Great Plains Drought Area Committee, speaking with a Dust Bowl farmer.

way they jostled with reporters and joked about the weather and long train ride from D.C. Marvin Jones was there and photographer Arthur Rothstein. The committee chair, Rural Electrification Administration (REA) head Morris Cooke, chatted with reporters, as did Tugwell. They spoke about the committee's plans for the next few days and the need to craft a long-term plan for the region. But first, as Tugwell put it, the men needed to "rub shoulders" with the Dust Bowl.[44]

The stakes could not have been higher in August 1936. The essential questions were whether the federal government could or should save the Great Plains, and at what cost. Many in and out of government, including Tugwell, had determined that the Dust Bowl had moved beyond the disaster stage and now represented an existential threat to the nation. Three years, a half billion dollars, and hundreds of different programs had done no noticeable good. Every recent study on the economic and environmental health of the region came to the same bleak conclusion: that bankruptcies would continue, as would foreclosures, tax delinquency, bank failures, and the collapse of local governments. Experts predicted crop losses in the hundreds of millions of dollars in 1936. Scientific predictions were even more dire. Without immediate action, Paul Sears, America's most respected ecologist, warned (in his *Deserts on the March*) that the entire middle third of the nation was in danger of becoming an uninhabitable wasteland, the American equivalent of the Sahara Desert. And it was an election year. On July 22, President Roosevelt announced the formation of the Great Plains Drought Area Committee. Hand-picked experts from a variety of government agencies would conduct an intensive study of the region and produce a report before the end of the year. The committee's eight members included agricultural economists, engineers, and experts in soil, hydrology, and management. The project manager was L. C. Gray, Tugwell's right-hand man at Resettlement. There would be no need to spend time examining the possible causes of the Dust Bowl, as the president himself had baked the answer to that question right into the committee's charge: "In this area of relatively little rain, practices brought from the more humid parts of the country are not most suitable under the prevailing natural conditions."[45]

From the jump, the committee was ambushed by conspiracy theories. A few days before launching its research tour, an Oklahoma climatologist had published a report which concluded that the Great Plains was overpopulated and overfarmed and urged that the government work out a program to reduce the number of people living and farming in the region. The national media got hold of the story, and soon paranoid delusions about the committee's *real* purpose swirled across the plains.[46] It started with the breakfast meeting with the Amarillo Chamber. "Foolishness," Tugwell called the idea that he was in the Panhandle to figure out how to get people to leave. "If there's one agency interested in keeping this area from being depopulated, it is ours," adding, "We don't want to depopulate the country; we want to fortify it to withstand drouth." The delegation was there, Cooke said, only to develop a plan to conserve soil and water for farmers and ranchers.[47] "We are out to prove this is permanent country." The afternoon paper carried the fifty-point headline "No Depopulation."[48]

Even so, boosters were not dissuaded and insisted on delivering a six-point resolution that various city chambers of commerce had cooked up over the weekend. As an example of the kind of thinking that characterized the booster class during the Dust Bowl, it's worth quoting at length:

1. The people of the Panhandle want to stay where they are, even if they go broke and have to start over.
2. Farmers want some form of a government financial program to aid the man not yet detached from his land because of the drouth and not now a client of any federal relief agency, but unable to get aid from banks.

3. Help for stockmen who are seeking to keep their foundation herd intact.
4. The committee endorses the federal plans for small dams and checks to prevent rain runoff.
5. Financial assistance in pumping water for irrigation.
6. More adequate aid in financing diversified farming.[49]

A universal declaration that the people of the region were going to stick it out, even if they went broke, was followed immediately by five separate demands for government aid.

That afternoon, the committee enjoyed good news from the Soil Conservation Service as it toured a demonstration project outside Dalhart. Members saw firsthand the remarkable work of local director H. H. Finnell, who had, in just a year, begun to turn back the desert through a careful program of terracing land, planting native grasses, and contour plowing. In the same spot where Pare Lorentz had filmed sand dunes, there was now once again grassland. As they walked across one of the projects, Peden Farm, Finnell showed them the soil restoration process at work. He sent them away with armloads of reports. On the way back to Amarillo, committee members made a quick detour to snap some photos of that barbed-wire bird's nest featured so prominently in *The Plow That Broke the Plains*. That night, while most committee members whiled away the hours over bourbon and branch water, Tugwell caught an early movie and went to bed. It was going to be a long trip.[50]

For ten days and three thousand miles, the committee drove north in a kitted-out army convoy, touring more sites, meeting with more suspicious farmers, hearing from more agricultural and soil experts, reassuring more booster groups and agricultural organizations, linking up with more local New Deal agents and agencies, and gathering up more reports. At the end of the line, the committee had a big summit with President Roosevelt in South Dakota. There it submitted its initial report, most of which had been written before their tour even began. It was grim. If something could not be done to stop the desertification of the Great Plains, the nation would not survive. The agricultural economy would collapse completely, Americans across the country would go hungry, local governments would lie in ruin, and the nation would face a refugee crisis that it simply could not withstand. The report knocked

*Members of the Great Plains
Drought Area Committee
scale a sand dune just outside
Dalhart, Texas.*

down several optimistic theories floating around: that the environment
on the plains was changing, that farmers could use gimmicks to overcome the lack of rain, and that the Dust Bowl was simply the result of
drought. "The problem of the Great Plains is not the product of a single
act of nature, of a single year or even of a series of exceptionally bad
years." It had been, the committee made clear, misguided governmental
policies combined with a foolhardy and speculative economic system
that had been imported into an environment whose basic ecology could
not withstand the stress of commercial agriculture. Luring farmers onto
the plains through the Homestead Act and private settlement schemes
forced settlers into "almost an obligatory vow of poverty."[51] It was now
time for the government to take responsibility for its mistakes and step
in to establish a new form of agricultural economy more in line with
"natural conditions." The committee proposed many different specific
policies, but the entire preliminary report, stamped "personal and confidential," was predicated on the reclassification of much of the land in
the Great Plains as submarginal and then limiting its use to govern-
ment-approved activities like pastures, if not retired altogether.[52] Roosevelt won reelection easily. He cut Tugwell loose two weeks later.

The final report, the most important document the federal government created on the Dust Bowl, *The Future of the Great Plains*, dropped
at the end of the year. Tugwell acolyte L. C. Gray wrote much of the
text and put the whole thing together. At over 150 pages, *The Future
of the Great Plains* laid out a plan for the region and had plenty to say
about its past and present. Capturing the government's new, techno-

cratic approach to farming, the report also included another seventy
pages of appendixes and maps. The root cause of rural poverty, Gray (like
Tugwell) believed, was that too many farmers were working submarginal land. In good years, they contributed to overproduction and drove
prices down, and in bad years, they defaulted on loans, went into tax
delinquency, and took down local economies. There was no romance in
turning a desert into a garden; disaster was never more than a few years
away. And, without fail, the report demonstrated, in the years between
catastrophes, people fell into the same destructive patterns of land speculation, boosting, and settling more submarginal land. Irony is the great
theme of the document; through repeating the same mistakes over and
over, frontier farmers kept bringing about their own demise. The report
chronicled the sorry destruction of a once majestic landscape and the
downfall of a once proud people. It was a complete rebuke of the foundational mythology of West Texas and an unqualified rejection of its
economy and culture.

The numbers were worse. Gray, who had spent months poring over
the data that the committee had gathered, presented a "disquieting picture": 24,000 farms covering 15 million acres were incapable of producing anything. Ninety-five percent of all rangelands were overgrazed.
Even the land's forage value had plummeted in recent years. Tenancy
had risen to 50 percent and was climbing. Whole communities were
emptying, and local governments were going broke. Farm income was
still falling, five years after wheat prices had collapsed. Entire harvests
were being used just to pay taxes. Credit markets had gone bust. Abandoned farms were scattered across every community. Dust Bowl relief
and recovery programs had grown so expensive, they threatened to break
the federal budget. Depending on the county, somewhere between 10
and 20 percent of families were on direct relief. The federal government
was spending an average of $200 for every person on the Great Plains.[53]

The heart of the report was a lengthy section spelling out all the misguided ideas held by prairie folk that would have to change before the
region could be saved. It read in part:

> The Plainsman cannot assume that whatever is for his immedi-
> ate good is also good for everybody—only of his long-run good
> is this true, and in the short run there must often be sacrifices;
> he cannot assume the right always to do with his property as he

likes—he may ruin another man's property if he does; he cannot assume that the individual action he can take on his own land will be sufficient, even for the conservation and best use of that land. He must realize that he cannot "conquer Nature"—he must live with her on her own terms, making use of and conserving resources which can no longer be considered inexhaustible.[54]

It was time, Gray wrote, to let go of those "inherited assumptions which had become ingrained through generations of pioneering experience" and accept a new world of production regulation, government planning, and land classification. Only through new cooperative arrangements and governmental policies would plains farmers be able to enjoy "a mode of life that gives sustenance and great satisfactions to generations."[55]

While never going into great detail, the committee's recommendations start with the premise that the federal government would play a much larger role in the lives of individual farmers. Not to the level of Ropesville, to be sure; but in the view of the average Panhandle wheat or cotton farmer, who saw themselves as the absolute lord of their domain and the independent commercial farmer as the bedrock of society, the report's recommendations must have read like dystopian fiction. It suggested an overhaul of credit and capital systems and significant changes to tax, property, and water laws that would generate greater cooperation among farmers, local banks, and government.[56] It recommended conservation be introduced into public education. Other "Lines of Action" included government-led, multiyear scientific, economic, and demographic surveys that would collect and collate data on soil, productivity, population, topography, water, grass, and markets. It suggested that the government immediately step in and purchase 24 million acres of submarginal land and either retire it or offer it as grazing land. (This measure rekindled paranoia about the government forcibly removing people from the plains.) Inexpensive federal loans for farmers would be tied to restrictions on land use and production. There were detailed plans for land rehabilitation and sketches of "scientifically selected" farms where the land would be reconfigured with terraced farms, new crops and new streams, orchards, and lakes. Working with federal agencies, individual states and counties would survey land, build roads, launch irrigation projects, create erosion and grazing districts, reorganize local government, and reform the tax code. Independent grazing and wind erosion districts would also work with government agencies on behalf of local farmers and ranchers.

Roosevelt introduced the report during a January 1937 Fireside Chat. He lauded its conclusions and reflected on his own recent tour of the Dust Bowl. He made it clear he didn't believe that the people of the region could survive another winter without immediate reform. Relief alone, he promised, would not be enough to save the "courageous and energetic people who have been stricken by several years of drought." He urged members of Congress to immediately take up its recommendations. They didn't. And *The Future of the Great Plains* went nowhere. Partly due to the fevered opposition among politicians from the Great Plains, but mostly because, thanks to a controversial plan of the president to revamp the nation's judiciary and expand the size of the Supreme Court, FDR no longer had the political capital to force through any significant change.

Tugwell was gone by then, chased from government by a coalition of Democrats and Republicans from agricultural states who had been clamoring for his head for months, threatening hearings and investigations into the Resettlement Administration, and writing legislation that would curb its authority.[57] Few in West Texas were sorry to see him go. The *Lubbock Avalanche*, responding to the news that the nation's "eminent sidewalk agriculturist, Dr. Rexford Guy Tugwell, has resigned his official position to enter private business," had this to say:

> To the man on the street—no matter how much he may like the administration and admire the President—Doctor Tugwell is "one of them smartelick professors" and that's all there is to it. The chief trouble with Professor Tugwell is that he finds the nation, its traditions and the general views of its people entirely out of step with him. He wants to remake everything to set up a little Utopia, regardless of the cost or whether people want it. As an early day active Socialist, he continues to be a dreamer in a world faced with practicalities and as such is, we think, entirely unsuited to any public post of power or importance.[58]

The rains came back in 1941, just as wartime demand drove the prices for wheat, cotton, cattle, and oil to their highest levels in more than a decade. Government agriculture and other programs, however, remained in place, binding West Texas farmers and ranchers to the federal government. Discomfort over this unprecedented relationship and the continuation of programs that were, in agriculturalists' minds, never meant to be permanent, was, for most, offset by the protection offered against disaster that these programs provided. Nevertheless, the nascent antistatism that fueled ranchers' fights in Austin back in the nineteenth century and led boosters to talk of secession in the 1910s now had a new expression—a distrust of government bureaucrats and federal meddling in local markets. And it would be one of their own who would come to articulate the most powerful arguments against the New Deal and federal intervention in the economy.

8

THE ORIGINS OF THE TEXAS RIGHT

It is the pride of kings which throws mankind into confusion.

THOMAS PAINE, *COMMON SENSE*

Dwarfed by the surrounding fifty-story-plus, mirrored abominations that define the downtown Houston skyline, the Kirby Building, at 917 Main Street, is easy to miss—another mixed-use, mid-rise full of hip lofts for cool downtown types. But back in 1926, the shiny new Kirby Building was the center of Houston's economic universe, home to the Kirby Lumber Company, the biggest company in Texas, a dominant player in land, oil, and timber. Its founder and president was John Henry Kirby, Texas's most important industrialist and its biggest employer. The fifth floor of the Kirby Building was set aside for his political projects, the home and headquarters of a dizzying array of organizations meant to protect the power and assets of the wealthy, to promote white supremacy, to fight organized labor, to lower taxes and raise tariffs, and to warn the nation about the dangers of communism. They included the Southern Committee to Uphold the Constitution, the Texas Tax Relief Committee, the Texas Taxpayers League, the Citizens Committee on Constitutional Amendments, the Constitutional Democrats of Texas, the Jeffersonian Democrats of Texas, and the protofascist Order of American Patriots and Sentinels of the Republic. Anyone looking to place a historical marker noting the birthplace of the radical right in Texas might consider 917 Main Street in Houston.

It's an address far from West Texas, to be sure, but in order to better understand the origins of the Texas radical right, we need to shift our geographic focus for a bit; while the ideas that would animate ultraconservatism would come straight out of the state's prairies and deserts, the money and initial infrastructure came out of the malarial forests and grimy oil fields of East Texas, where John Henry Kirby ruled as "Prince of the Pines."

Kirby was a wholly familiar Texas archetype. Born hardscrabble in Tyler County in 1860, the future industrialist grew up on a thousand-acre farm in the Great Piney Woods. The Kirbys were small-time slaveholders, and the paterfamilias supplemented the family income as county sheriff. In the years when the community could get up a school, Kirby went; when it couldn't, he worked the farm and was homeschooled. At seventeen, he started college at Southwestern in Georgetown. While a student, he turned a part-time position assisting an ambitious Texas politician into a gig as the calendar clerk of the state senate. Admitted to the bar at twenty-four, Kirby worked at timber lease deals and, within three years, was widely recognized as the biggest timber hustler in Texas. Using eastern capital to fund his ventures, he formed companies by the dozens, buying or leasing hundreds of thousands of acres of virgin pine still trapped in the wild thickets and steamy swamps of Texas and Louisiana. He grew richer by the year. By thirty-six he was building a railroad.[1] At forty, he consolidated his massive and scattered holdings into the Kirby Lumber Company (KLC), instantly making it the biggest business in Texas. When combined with its interlocking partner, the Houston Oil Company (HOC), a complicated and creative business structure that brought together several combinations of real estate speculation, oil production, and the timber-lumber business, the Kirby Lumber Company was valued at $40 million ($1 billion today).[2] The undisputed lumber baron of the South, Kirby had twelve lumber mills that produced a million and a half board feet a day. Beaumont, the eighth-largest city in Texas in 1910, was practically a company town. In his dozens of timber camps and lumber towns scattered across the Piney Woods, Kirby enjoyed the power of a medieval baron.

He was a trusted adviser to presidents and a titan of industry. Kirby served five terms as president of the Southern Pine Association and two as head of the National Lumber Manufacturers Association.[3] He spent lavishly; like any high-ranking Gilded Age industrialist, he kept a vacation home in the Adirondacks and maintained a suite at the Waldorf Astoria in New York City. He entertained often at his well-appointed Houston mansion—the city's largest—hosting lavish events in his gardens, Houston's loveliest and most expensive. He prized his reputation as a civic-minded philanthropist and gave away millions. He served on countless boards and even did two stints in the Texas legislature.

The Prince of the Pines considered himself a benevolent employer and a great philosopher on the motivations of the workingman. A paternalist, Kirby paid his employees more and required fewer hours than most timber companies. Each camp and town had a doctor on staff, and he provided (mandatory) accident and medical insurance. Every Fourth of July, he threw a massive company picnic. He spent months planning and tens of thousands of dollars on the company's annual Christmas party, where Santa himself presented gifts to each of the children of Kirby Lumber Company employees.[4]

Most of his subjects lived and worked in communities completely controlled by Kirby. This was the golden age of the company town. From sooty mining villages in West Virginia to aspiring utopias like Pullman, American industrialists were reconfiguring the domestic spaces and lives of their employees. Companies constructed entire communities for their workers, laying out the streets and building the homes. They controlled the stores, the local media, and even houses of worship. Paternalistic, the ultimate project of most of these communities was to socially engineer the lives of employees and instill certain values among them, often with an ulterior effort to maximize production capabilities. In his timber camps and lumber towns, Kirby was in absolute control; he owned every building and employed every person, all the way down to the ministers in his churches and the editors of his newspapers. He not only set wages but also issued his own form of currency by paying his employees in scrip redeemable only in company stores.[5] One of his vassals described life in Kirby's kingdom: "He is born in a Company house, wrapped in Company swaddling clothes, rocked in a Company cradle. At sixteen he goes to work in the Company mill. At twenty-one he gets married in a Company Church. At forty, he sickens with Company malaria, lies down on a Company bed, is attended by a Company doctor who doses him with Company drugs, and then he loses his last Company breath, while the undertaker is paid by the widow in Company scrip for the Company coffin in which he is buried on Company ground."[6] It was as if, as one journalist pointed out, "time had rolled back to the days of Ivanhoe" and notions of freedom, equality, and democracy were only rumors.[7]

The real power of the Kirby towns, however, was that they made it infinitely easier for him to keep labor unions out of his business. Like so many of his contemporary industrialists, Kirby was relentlessly and ruthlessly opposed to organized labor. The dawn of the twentieth century had witnessed an upsurge in union organizing, especially in the lumber business. It was, after all, violent, dirty, and dangerous work. One industry study counted 80,000 accidents and 10,000 deaths in a single year. Men were sliced, crushed, boiled, burned, and smashed to death. Promising that collective action could mean safer working conditions, labor organizers, led by the Brotherhood of Timber Workers, began trying to organize lumber and timber employees into unions in 1911. Kirby saw these efforts as a mortal danger to free enterprise and democracy and as an irreversible step toward communism and anarchy. He responded with violence and vehemence. He created a company spy agency that kept watch over every employee and visitor. He planted moles in the camps and cultivated confidential informants. He had a squad of thugs that roughed up and ran suspected union sympathizers out of his camps and counties. He built a blacklist and shared it freely with other lumbermen. Freedom of speech, assembly, and the press were suspended. Even sermons were screened.

Like C. W. Post, Kirby joined the now radicalized National Association of Manufactures. He also organized and led regional groups devoted to crushing unions in Texas and the lumber business including the Southern Lumber Operators Association and the Southwestern Open Shop Association (later the Texas Employers Association). His "Beaumont Plan" to keep unions out of individual cities was a Texas version of C. W. Post's open shop associations, founded on the pledges of local business owners to refuse to allow their employees to organize and to cooperate with one another to stamp out unions in their town. He pitched the idea to booster groups all over the state.

II

In 1906, Kirby helped create the Texas Business Men's Association (TBMA), ostensibly a booster group, but one whose antilabor and pro-business lobbying efforts were so blatant that it drew an investigation by the state attorney general. Its attitude toward government regulation was captured in its motto: "Fewer laws and better laws." The State of Texas, Kirby believed, had no right to "declaim against capital or impose burdens" on business. To do so, he warned, was to "strike at the very root of your industry and blow upon it the mildew of ultimate failure." Every tax, every regulatory policy was a burden to business that would ultimately chase industry from the state. What Texas needed, according to Kirby and the TBMA, was greater "encouragement" to business and to abstain from "Socialistic attacks and meddlesome supervision."[8]

When reform-minded governor Thomas Campbell pushed through a few mild measures meant to give Texas greater regulatory power over the state's railroads, Kirby saw it as nothing less than an attempt to subvert "the divine economy of God." With this kind of government threat to the elysian future envisioned by Kirby and a growing industrial class, the TBMA began assembling a blatantly pro-business faction within the Democratic Party to install a more corporate-enlightened politician in the governor's office.[9] It also opened an office in Austin, where it would lobby for tax reductions and against regulation and labor. It was also a powerful opponent of both woman suffrage and prohibition.[10]

An indispensable offshoot of the TBMA in its fight against unions (and in the emergence of the far right), was the Texas Commercial Secretaries Association, a group made up of the folks who ran the day-to-day operations of all the booster organizations in Texas. A Kirby fixer named J. A. Arnold organized and ran the thing. Kirby had discovered Arnold in Beaumont, where the former railroad clerk had developed a reputation as a cranky critic of labor, suffrage, business regulation, and prohibition. Kirby hired him to run the Beaumont Chamber of Commerce.[11] As head of the new commercial secretaries group, Arnold set up shop down the hall from the TBMA offices in Austin and hired the sister-and-brother propaganda team of Ida M. Darden and Vance Muse to handle marketing and media. Through the Commercial Secretaries

Association, Arnold, Muse, and Darden injected their radical brand of pro-business and antilabor thinking, along with their ideas of white supremacy, county seat conservatism, anticommunism, and unfettered capitalism, directly into the infrastructure of Texas's booster class.[12]

Soon, Kirby took Arnold nationwide, setting him up in a D.C. office and coming up with different organizations for him to run. There was the Southern Tariff Association, which sought higher tariffs to protect the domestic timber industry.[13] The keynote speaker at its first significant meeting was Vice-President Calvin Coolidge. Then there was the American Bankers League, which became the American Taxpayers League, which lobbied for tax cuts for the wealthy and was instrumental in pushing through the 1926 Mellon Tax Bill, which lowered the marginal income tax rate for the wealthiest Americans from 46 percent to 20 percent, halved the estate tax, and eliminated the gift tax. It was the largest set of tax cuts in U.S. history to that point. Kirby also established the National Council of State Legislators, which lobbied for tax cuts at the state level. Arnold ran that too.

By 1929, J. A. Arnold, thanks to Kirby, was America's highest-paid lobbyist. His multimillion-dollar empire of influence operated from a suite of offices in the Munsey Building on E Street, just a block from the White House. That was when Arnold caught the attention of a fiery and idealistic senator from Arkansas named Thaddeus Horatius Caraway, who categorically hated lobbyists. Caraway launched an investigation into Arnold and, over a series of public hearings excitedly covered by the national media, exposed the former railroad clerk as an unprincipled huckster right out of a Christopher Buckley novel. For two weeks, Senator Caraway grilled Arnold, John Kirby, Vance Muse, and Ida Darden on their intricate and interlocking organizations, their finances, their strategies, and their supporters. The hearings revealed shocking levels of contributions by an astonishing array of well-known companies like Kellogg's, Colt firearms, Maytag, Wrigley, Hoover vacuums, Armour meats, Hamms beer, and Florsheim shoes, as well as staggering sums from lesser-known energy companies, mills, foundries, banks, and merchants. In just one three-year period, Arnold had raised a million dollars, which, Caraway delighted in reporting, hadn't seemed to produce any results. All his groups, fundraising appeals and campaigns, and marketing materials existed, as far as the chair could tell, only "for the purpose of making a living for [Arnold] and a small group associated with him." He concluded his report with an admission: "How business men of ordinary sagacity can be induced to contribute to Arnold's purposes is entirely inexplicable to your committee."[14]

III

The Great Depression wiped out John Henry Kirby. With the national collapse of the housing market in the late twenties, the demand for lumber dried up. By the end of 1929, Kirby only had three mills operating and was running skeleton crews in the timber camps. Oil collapsed in 1930. After Daisy Bradford no. 3 led to the discovery of the East Texas Oil Field, the flood of cheap Texas crude drove the price per barrel from $1.10 down to $0.13. A risky timber venture on the West Coast failed. Kirby stayed afloat for a few years by shuffling his debt around, but by 1933, even his considerable financial talents could not save him. He declared personal bankruptcy in May. The Kirby Lumber Company followed suit a month later. Thanks to wealthy and influential friends, Kirby kept his house, his position at Kirby Lumber, and his Main Street office. That was when the bored and bitter timber man launched his political vendetta against Franklin Roosevelt and the New Deal (which he blamed for his troubles) from the Kirby Building's fifth floor.

He put together a team. Vance Muse, J. A. Arnold's right-hand propagandist, took the lead. Ida Darden and her magical typewriter were always on call when they needed a few thousand words on some subject or other. Filling out the squad was Lewis Ulrey, a paranoic anti-Semite (on loan from oil baron Maco Stewart) who believed that an international conspiracy of Jews and communists had already taken over America's churches and were in the final stages of a plan to secretly overthrow the federal government.

By 1933, Muse had been lobbying for Kirby and the bigwigs of Texas business for more than twenty years, fighting against child labor laws and the eight-hour day and promoting tax cuts and tariffs. He was a familiar face in the legislative halls in Austin and the boardrooms of Dallas and Houston. A big man at six feet, five inches and built like an eighties-era power forward, Muse was a cunning and charming back-slapper, quick with a joke and able to handle his liquor. A long and jagged scar stretching across a sallow right cheek gave even his warm grins a hint of menace. He knew how to count votes, who to tap for money, and whose palm to grease. Loud and eloquent, he could hold forth in any crowd. If the depths of his convictions were sometimes called into question, his capacity for going low remained unplumbed. Up to this point, however, Kirby had used Muse only as a media and marketing developer or for retail political influence, one-on-one in small, smoky rooms.[15] But taking on Roosevelt was going to be a different enterprise altogether.

To tear down Roosevelt in Texas and the South, where the president was wildly popular, Muse launched a campaign to paint FDR as the tool of a secret, integrationist-inclined, communist-inspired plot to take over the country. To get there, Kirby and Muse formed a slew of new organizations, all headquartered on the fifth floor of the Kirby Building. There was the Election Managers Association of Texas, a coalition of county election officials, lawyers, and industrialists tasked with limiting the African American vote. (The idea that President Roosevelt was going to use southern Black votes as the foundation of the unbeatable political machine that would usher in the communist takeover was canon in the Kirby Building.) The Texas Tax Relief Committee, on the other hand, was devoted mostly to fundraising, tapping wealthy donors by warning of a secret White House plan to eliminate private property. The Citizens Committee on Constitutional Amendments was a catchall lobbying center promoting a sales tax and fighting the various relief and reform amendments to the Texas constitution prompted by the Great Depression. Muse also headed two clandestine fascist societies, the Order of American Patriots and Sentinels of the Republic.

Until 1935, Muse and Kirby ran a quiet crusade: the occasional pamphlet, a few fundraising campaigns, strategic alliances with other anti-Roosevelt groups. Sometimes Muse would purchase some radio time to rebut one of FDR's Fireside Chats and spell out for listeners the broader details of Roosevelt's alleged communist plot. But as the 1936 election approached, Kirby and Muse cranked up a new campaign, an audaciously racist scheme to deny Roosevelt the Democratic nomination for president. They formed yet another organization to implement their plan—the Southern Committee to Uphold the Constitution (SCUC).

The idea was to mount a southern challenge to Roosevelt by finding a well-liked southern Democrat to run against the president. A southern challenger, accompanied by a campaign that would paint President

Roosevelt as a secret integrationist and a willing participant in a communist plot to destroy the country, could, Kirby's thinking went, deny FDR his party's nomination. There were plenty of sympathetic southern ears for this message, particularly among the men who controlled the Democratic Party at the local level; many among the county seat elite had come to see federal agricultural programs as an existential danger to their hold on the local economy and a Roosevelt-controlled party as a threat to their power.[16] The Southern Committee to Uphold the Constitution was launched in August 1935 with an aggressive articulation of "constitutional nationalism," a political philosophy which maintains that the Constitution holds the nation's fundamental values and provides the instruments needed to protect Americans' rights.[17] Roosevelt and his New Deal, Kirby charged, were determined to "ruthlessly change beyond recognition [this] supreme law of the land."[18]

Claiming widespread membership across the South (Muse boasted fifty thousand members, surely an exaggeration), the SCUC attracted mostly businessmen, including some of the wealthiest and most powerful men in Texas, figures like cotton broker Lamar Fleming, millionaire oilman Hugh Roy Cullen, corporate attorney Clarence Wharton, rancher/oilman James Marion "Big Jim" West, and rancher/lawyer H. E. Hoover (then serving as president of the Panhandle-Plains Historical Society), along with right-wing firebrands like George B. Terrell, whose anti–New Deal antics while serving as an at-large congressmen were legendary. There were a few influential out-of-state politicians attached to the movement, including Georgia governor Gene Talmadge, U.S. senator from Oklahoma John Harreld, and former New Mexico governor James Hinkle.[19] The SCUC claimed to stand for states' rights, individual rights, separation of powers, and limited government and to oppose "usurpation of power," taxes, and a "government of boards, bureaus, commissions and administrations."[20] Muse worked the scheme he and J. A. Arnold had perfected over the previous two decades; setting up commissioned agents in regional territories who beat the bushes for contributions among the business classes of the South and Middle West. Muse, dropping Kirby's name, worked Wall Street, securing large donations from industrialists and Liberty Leaguers like Irénée du Pont and John J. Raskob. In just a few months, it had raised $40,000. The agent working C. W. Post's old stomping grounds of Battle Creek, Michigan, raised $260 in a single day.[21]

The plan was to recruit Huey Long, the second-most popular politician in the country, to challenge Roosevelt for the Democratic nomination. Over the previous year and a half, Long, who had clear eyes on the presidency, had been building a movement to serve as a political base. He called it "Share Our Wealth," and it offered a simple but revolutionary economic plan for the nation. Raising the income tax rates on the very wealthy would, Long promised, enable the country to guarantee all Americans a basic income, a free college education, free health care, subsidies for vocational training and farmers, and pensions for everyone over sixty-five. The plan, as one might guess in the middle of the Great Depression, was very popular; Share Our Wealth had an estimated 27,000 chapters and 7 million members. While Huey Long and John Kirby might appear strange bedfellows—after all, Long's plan was a pretty radical set of proposals, far more liberal than anything Roosevelt had yet proposed—Long was also an unrestrained ideologue for individualism, local sovereignty, and segregation—the foundations of Kirby's politics. And Texas oil men loved Long, seeing him as a powerful ally in their fight against Standard Oil.[22]

The man who actually ran the Share Our Wealth organization and the major reason for its explosive growth was one of the strangest figures in twentieth-century American politics, the fire-breathing Disciple of Christ minister and Nazi sympathizer Gerald L. K. Smith.[23] The preacher had caught Long's attention shortly after he launched a radio ministry in Shreveport in 1928, where he led the city's largest Christian congregation. Smith was perhaps the greatest stump speaker of his age. H. L. Mencken thought so, declaring that Smith was better than William Jennings Bryan, better than Clarence Darrow, better than Billy Sunday (and Mencken had seen them all), and not just best by "an inch or a yard or a mile, but the greatest by two light years." Smith, the Sage of Baltimore said, "begins where the next best leaves off." Mencken wasn't done: "He is the master of masters, the champion boob-bumper of all epochs, the Aristotle and Johann Sebastian Bach of all known earsplitters, dead or alive."[24] Smith's sermons and radio addresses, pitched to the poor farmer and oil worker, took on the fat cats and the utilities and the corrupt politicians. Long was impressed, once calling Smith the second-best "rabble rouser" in the country (Long considered himself number one) and hired him in April 1934 to organize Share Our Wealth clubs. Smith hit the road, promising every American "a real job, not a little old sow-belly, black-eyed pea job but a real spending money, beef-steak and gravy, Chevrolet, Ford in the garage, new suit, Thomas Jefferson, Jesus Christ, red, white, and blue job."[25] After every Smith speech, as Hodding Carter reported, "five hundred gaunt, grinning farmers and small-town ne'er-do-wells will file beside the sound truck and sign the cards that automatically make them members of the National Share Our Wealth Society."[26] In just four weeks, 207,000 cards were collected. By the time Kirby and Muse cranked up the SCUC, Smith was adding 20,000 Huey Long disciples to the rolls every week. But then Long went and got himself murdered in the hallway of the Louisiana State Capitol, gunned down by the son-in-law of a state judge whose position Long had gerrymandered out of existence just moments earlier.

Gerald L. K. Smith tried and failed to take over as head of Share Our Wealth but was excommunicated after he lost a power struggle with other members of Long's inner circle. Angry and dejected, Smith turned to Kirby and Muse and helped them come up with a plan B for the SCUC. They decided to try to rally southern Democrats around Georgia governor Eugene Talmadge, the Wild Man from Sugar Creek. For a decade, Talmadge had crashed through Georgia politics, building a powerful organization from among the state's poor white farmers. In the most recent gubernatorial election, Talmadge had won all but three of the state's 159 counties. "Ole Gene" ruled the state as a despot—never hesitating to declare martial law or disband elected commissions to get his way. Claiming to speak directly for the people, he used executive orders to establish policy and ignored the state legislature when it went against him. Not only was he a fiery and outspoken critic of Franklin Roosevelt, but he also knotted his individualistic and laissez-faire agrarian fundamentalism with violent racist demagoguery. The New Deal, he claimed, would bring about the end of Jim Crow and dismantle the instruments of southern white supremacy. Talmadge had been quietly nursing presidential ambitions for a while and came to think that launching a southern white-supremacist challenge to the incumbent might be his route to the nomination.[27] The SCUC hoped to help make that happen.

Seeking to recruit Talmadge, Kirby and Muse convened the inaugural meeting of the SCUC in Macon, Georgia, in January 1936 and invited the governor to give the keynote speech. Their best-case scenario would be to nominate Talmadge right there and then. Kirby, who had convinced himself that the poor white farmers who were depending on federal programs to survive somehow hated the New Deal as much as he did, expected a crowd of 10,000 white farmers who would "start the ball rolling" toward an eventual Talmadge victory over the "socialist" Roosevelt.[28] Gracing the convention's stage was a cavalcade of white supremacists that even included Thomas Dixon, one of the nation's best-known racists, author of *The Clansman: A Historical Romance of the Ku Klux Klan*, who, like Kirby and Talmadge, was convinced that the New Deal was part of a communist plot to take over the government and end segregation.[29]

Only 2,400 people showed up to the convention, mostly Talmadge acolytes eager to hear Ole Gene rip and roar and announce a presidential run. They went away disappointed. Despite two furious days of cajoling by Muse and Kirby and agitated press speculation that he would announce, Talmadge had decided not to run. The convention then devolved into a two-day orgy of Roosevelt bashing. It passed a resolution that read the president out of the Democratic Party. Dixon spun out an elaborate description of Eleanor Roosevelt's plot (launched with the NAACP—the "rottenest communist organization in the United States") to turn Black southerners into communists and take over the United States. Smith, though, stole the show. He ranted. "Roosevelt is rapidly becoming the most despised President in American history." He raved. The "AAA Army alone contained 40,000 more men than the standing army of the United States." He name-called. Eleanor Roosevelt was a "female Rasputin," and Franklin Roosevelt was a communist, an atheist, and a cripple. Talmadge bombed. Normally, Talmadge could gallus thump, podium slap, and flop sweat with the best of them, but whether because he was disappointed in the size of the crowd, or because he had to follow Mencken's "champion boob-bumper of all epochs," or maybe just feeling deflated from his decision not to run for president, Talmadge gave a short and mostly listless address that focused on tax cuts and deficit spending.[30] Closing the convention, Kirby got in a few more digs as the Talmadge crowd quietly slipped out: the New Deal was a "slavish, contemptible, all oppressing bureaucracy," and Roosevelt's ultimate plan was the destruction of "private initiative and enterprise" and instilling "hatred of the poor for the rich."[31]

A racist stunt by Muse at the meeting landed him and Kirby in front of another Senate committee. As delegates streamed into the Macon City Auditorium on the first day of the SCUC meeting, they found in their chairs a special edition of *Georgia Woman's World*, a segregationist tabloid put out by the Talmadge machine. On its front page was a photograph of Eleanor Roosevelt flanked by two African American ROTC officers, students from Howard University. (The photo had been taken during the First Lady's recent tour of the school in Washington, D.C.) On its pages, readers found stories that claimed the Roosevelts regularly entertained Black guests at the White House, some even spending the night. The stories and photo caused an immediate scandal. No one claimed credit for the paper's publication or its appearance at the convention. Alabama senator Hugo Black, an FDR supporter who knew what that kind of story could do to Roosevelt's popularity in the South, dragged Kirby and Muse before a Senate committee to explain the photos and, while they were at it, tell the committee about who exactly was supporting the SCUC financially. At the hearing, Muse was defiant, parrying with Senator Black on every question. That is, save one. When asked to describe the photos, Muse replied, "It was a picture of Mrs. Roosevelt going to some n—— meeting with two escorts, n—— on each arm."[32] Although denying that he was the source of the photo, Muse had for several weeks been distributing the image through the Election Managers Association of Texas as part of a fundraising campaign "to keep the Democratic Party white."[33]

While Muse's testimony made the national news, the blockbuster of the hearings was the revelation that the SCUC was mostly financed by the Du Ponts and the other wealthy industrialists who had founded the Liberty League, an organization so transparently devoted to the interests of America's 1 percent that one joke went that it should be called the American Cellophane League because it was made by the Du Ponts and you could see right through it. A quarter of the cost of the meeting had been paid by John J. Raskob and Pierre S. du Pont, two of the wealthiest men in the country. Seen as just another tool of rich Roosevelt haters, the SCUC collapsed soon thereafter.[34]

IV

Enter the Jeffersonian Democrats of Texas (JDT), *the* first significant organization of the Texas Right. Too often written off as little more than a hayseed Liberty League by political observers then and by historians since, the JDT brought together most of the characteristics that would animate right-wing conservativism in Texas for the next few decades: a conspiratorial, dualistic world of communists and conservatives, a violently pro-business and vigorously racist agenda, an organizational ethos steeped in a bellicose white Christianity, and a rural nationalism dependent on Lost Cause and frontier mythology and agrarian fundamentalism.[35] The Jeffersonian Democrats were going to be a much different political project than anything Kirby had launched before. This wasn't about lobbying or fundraising, but instead deliberate movement building, true grassroots politicking. And the man he tapped to lead it was a political newcomer, J. Evetts Haley, a shy, awkward intellectual who preferred the company of horses and cattle to people. When Kirby recruited Haley into his world, the historian was working at the University of Texas, gathering artifacts and helping plan exhibits for the Texas Centennial Exposition. Unlike Muse and Arnold, Haley was no backslapping lobbyist or booster insider; he was a purist, an ideologue, and a conspiracy theorist who had become convinced that it was his duty as a scholar and citizen to alert Texans to the dangers of Roosevelt and the New Deal.

When we last saw Evetts Haley, he was working for the Panhandle-Plains Historical Society, collecting relics, conducting interviews, and signing up members. Since those days he had emerged as one of Texas's most promising young historians. He earned a master's degree from the University of Texas, where he produced a four-hundred-page thesis on cattle drives. The XIT Ranch had commissioned him to write the official history of the company, and the Texas and Southwestern Cattle Raisers Association named him its official historian. He had helped launch the *Panhandle-Plains Historical Review* and served as it first editor. A prolific and deeply engaging writer with a unique, almost Victorian voice, Haley's histories were widely sought, and he published regularly across a spectrum of publications, from his hometown newspaper to *Nature* magazine. By the mid-1930s, he was, along with Walter Prescott Webb and J. Frank Dobie, one of the young guns of Texas letters.

Haley had proudly voted for Roosevelt in 1932 and, for decades afterward, proclaimed the 1932 Democratic platform the finest the party had ever produced. But Roosevelt's New Deal was a complete rejection of every plank on that platform. He saw the sudden appearance of federal aid programs as clear evidence that the president had abandoned the traditional Democratic values of self-reliance and small government and had embraced something foreign, dangerous. As a historian, he believed that frontier hardship had created the American character and that individualism had to be protected and promoted. As a Turnerian, Haley was among those who saw the cattle frontier as the actual pinnacle of Americanism. Turner's town and farm stage of development was the lame epilogue to the main story. The real pioneers, the best models of American egalitarianism and independency were those men who tamed the dangerous frontier and made it safe for a weaker breed of American.[36] When cattle companies, including the Haley Ranch, were forced into a federal cattle-killing program, it shook him.

When the AAA began in 1933, western ranchers rejected the opportunity to include cattle. Solving the crises of drought and depression, the head of the National Livestock Association scoffed, was "a job for God, not the New Deal."[37] Farmers readily jumping on the AAA bandwagon only confirmed what ranchers had long known—that stockmen were purer economic creatures than those clodhoppers who so readily ceded their independence in exchange for a few dollars of government relief. All ranchers wanted from Roosevelt were the same things they had been demanding since the 1890s: better regulation of railroads and meat packers and higher tariffs on foreign beef.[38]

But the drought dragged on into a fourth year and spread to Utah, California, and Wisconsin. Cattle prices dropped month to month, week to week. In the Dust Bowl, cattle were falling dead from starvation or thirst. Wheeler-dealer cattleman Dolph Briscoe, head of the Texas and Southwestern Cattle Raisers Association (and father of the future governor), asked Secretary of Agriculture Henry Wallace for help early in 1934. While no permanent arrangement was made, the federal government set up a temporary feed subsidy program and arranged for rail transportation to get cattle to market at a reduced rate. In the fall, with no break in the drought and beef prices in freefall, Briscoe worked out a plan with the Drought Relief Service (DRS) whereby the government bought up cattle, slaughtered them, canned the beef, and distributed it through food programs. Cattle too sick or skinny were just killed and buried in mass graves. Each animal brought in a few dollars, and the program arranged for part of every payment to go into a special account off-limits to creditors.[39]

By all accounts the program was a success. Ranchers complained about the below-market prices, but the animals they brought in were in rough shape, more like the cannibalistic skeletons that haunted the dreams of pharaohs than a product ready for market.[40] The DRS bought 2 million head of cattle that produced millions of pounds of canned beef. Hundreds of thousands of other cattle, however, were herded in pits, shot with high-powered rifles, and covered in dirt by steam shovels and bulldozers. Ranchers kept permanent regulation off the table and came out of the program "untainted by the requirements of government controls."[41] Still, the psychological costs of the mass slaughter of so many cattle were immeasurable. Tales of industrial-scale viciousness were told in hushed horror in the cow camps for years. The Haley family was not immune. Haley took a brief leave from the University of Texas to drive home and help his family drive their cattle to the local slaughter site. Haley himself shot their starving cattle. Everything he thought he knew about West Texas, its people, and its values lay buried, rotting under a few feet of dust and dirt. The very premise of the cattle-killing program violated every natural law that Haley believed ruled the universe. It was if the New Deal had reversed gravity.

Taking to his typewriter, he aired his exasperation in the pages of America's most beloved magazine, the *Saturday Evening Post*.[42] Haley's "Cow Business and Monkey Business," which appeared in the December 8, 1934, issue, was a witty and outrageous condemnation of the cattle-killing program. Full of folksy nostalgia and reverence for traditional rural notions about the political economy, the piece vaulted him to national prominence as a New Deal critic. The authenticity of Haley's voice gave his argument great weight; when a genuine cowman who understood the realities of the cattle business and who was also a nationally recognized and well-respected historian of the cattle frontier spoke to the issue, people listened. The twin pillars of working cowpuncher and respected scholar would be vital to Haley's brand for the rest of his political career. His cowboy-scholar style was particularly suited for *Saturday Evening Post* readers, a generation raised on pulp Westerns. Using the language of the range and the lessons of history, Haley laid out his case against the New Deal with an antistatist logic borrowed from Edmund Burke, heaps of historical evidence, a keen understanding of modern cattle markets, and an alarmist dash of slippery-slope paranoia. Modern ranchers, he claimed, were the philosophic heirs to the old-timers like Charles Goodnight—hardworking, honest, and frugal men forging a life on the hard lands of the arid West. They asked no quarter and gave none. But the federal government had, through misguided, scattershot, and half-thought-out policies disrupted natural markets to such a degree that ranchers had been forced into the cattle-killing program. In one critical example, Haley explained that the AAA's artificial reduction in corn production had put premium prices on the grain, making it impossible for ranchers to use it as supplemental feed during the dry months. If corn production had been allowed to continue at its pre-1933 levels, the ranchers, he argued, could have made it through '34 without resorting to killing cattle.[43]

"We are in the cow business," Haley declared, men and women from that part of the country where the "rendezvous of individualism and independence" had fulfilled the American democratic promise, where "the inside of each man's range was inviolate," and where before "the Brain Trust, no one would have had the temerity to suggest how a cowman would manage his personal affairs." In the hard lands of cattle country, people still believed in the profit system and accepted the reality of a business in which the rate of "financial mortality" was high. Ranchers understood that "poor managers and poor cowmen" would not last long and certainly didn't expect the government "to keep the inefficient and prodigal in business."[44]

Federal work relief projects, Haley claimed, were also wreaking havoc on the labor system that had served ranchers for half a century. Even after the shift toward pasture ranching, ranchers—even small outfits like the Haley Ranch—still hired seasonal labor to help with spring branding and fall market seasons. For room and board and forty bucks a month, a working cowboy could string together a few months of work. But New Deal work jobs were more regular and paid better, making it "almost impossible to get cow hands." Worse, according to Haley, hopefully tongue in cheek, cowboys were getting spoiled by programs that provided a "balanced ration [of] butter, cured meats, canned vegetables, and milk, sugar, syrup and so on."[45]

After "Cow Business and Monkey Business" came out, Haley found himself fielding requests to give public talks on contemporary politics. His maiden political speech was to the Alpha Chi Honor Society at UT, where he offered some "casual comments on current trends." Speaking to the students, Haley laid into the New Deal's "soft, sophisticated, supercilious mediocrities" and its economic philosophies, which had set the nation adrift on "uncertain seas of political chicanery." He claimed that FDR aspired to totalitarianism and planned to confiscate private property. Laying into the UT faculty, Haley criticized them for their embarrassing willingness to prostrate themselves before New Deal agencies and parrot New Deal talking points. Haley closed his speech by dissing his audience, telling the honor students that their degrees would be meaningless, mere tokens of appreciation for "passing four frivolous years in college."[46]

Soon, Haley was a regular guest columnist for the Hearst-owned *San Antonio Express*. Every few weeks, he would launch into Roosevelt and the New Deal—"plain bungling, disturbance, . . . disruption"—and passing along every rumor of a government gone mad.[47] He even tried his hand at poetry:

> Destroy the potato and the humble tomato
> So justice may prevail
> The diminutive pig and everything "big"
> For the cause of the New Deal.[48]

In July 1936, Haley took his case against the New Deal straight to the West Texas booster class in the lead article of that month's *West Texas Today*, the official publication of the West Texas Chamber of Commerce. In "Texas Control of Texas Soil," he reminded his lawyer, rancher, developer, merchant, banker, and oilman readers that "still beating in our hearts is the optimism of the frontier, the strong belief in the excellence of our domain, and the aggressive assertion of our own rights" and that, despite proclamations of eggheaded social scientists to the contrary, "there are still vestiges of independence left in Texas." Calling up the region's long-standing apprehension over faraway, centralized power, he urged the West Texas business class to recommit itself to the "pioneer's love of independence, impatience with governmental restraint, and suspicion of governmental bureaus and agents."[49]

A month later, he was working for Kirby.

Haley received an invitation to a meeting of concerned "patriots" to be held at the Adolphus Hotel in Dallas on the first day of August. Thirty-seven people showed. Leading the meeting was W. P. Hamblen, a corporate lawyer and antilabor activist from Houston. Also in attendance were heavy hitters like Texaco Oil founder and former president of the Houston Chamber of Commerce J. S. Cullinan and rancher/oil and timber man/media magnate Big Jim West. A rising star in the conservative galaxy, "Little Joe" Bailey, was there. Son of the Lost Cause fossil and hardened Democrat Joseph Weldon Bailey, Little Joe ran his law office out of the Kirby Building and had won an at-large seat in Congress by running a hard-edged states' rights campaign that would have made his daddy proud. Lewis Ulrey was there, ready to bring his trove of anti-Semitic conspiracy theories to whatever project the men might launch. Rounding out the attendees was a gaggle of various business folk, with an oversampling of corporate attorneys, cotton millers and ginners, and oil men.

Taking over the hotel's stunning beaux arts ballroom, the men spent the day carping and moaning about the unfairness of federal programs and spinning lurid conspiracy theories about the foundations of Roosevelt's policies. Haley, who had spent eighteen straight months as the loudest, barmiest, and most vicious New Deal critic in Texas, was the star of the show. Always an indefatigable researcher with a keen memory for facts and figures and a man who loved nothing more than showing off his command of language, literature, and history, Haley held forth his views with such verve that at one point, after a particularly impassioned soliloquy, when the historian stepped away to relieve himself, he came back to discover that the group had elected him as their chair. For the rest of his life, he would jokingly warn of the dangers of using the restroom at meetings that had not yet elected officers. They decided to call themselves the Constitutional Democrats of Texas. Working with a couple of the lawyers, Haley drafted the group's first statement, a declaration of principles that sought to reaffirm the values that he believed had guided the Democratic Party since the days of Jefferson and Jackson: white supremacy, states' rights, strict constitutionalism, and Christian and agrarian fundamentalism. The group then endorsed Republican

Alf Landon for president. They hadn't left the Democratic Party, Haley said in a lot of words; the Democratic Party had left them.[50]

Before he knew it, Haley, along with John Kirby and Little Joe Bailey, was on a train bound for Detroit to attend the inaugural national convention of a group calling itself the Jeffersonian Democrats. The meeting had been called by James Reed, an old racist and xenophobe who had once represented Missouri in the U.S. Senate and who was enjoying a political renaissance as a Democratic enemy of Roosevelt. Most of the attendees were little more than political has-beens and never-would-bes affiliated with assorted anti-Roosevelt and Liberty League front groups. Reed was a full-blown anticommunist paranoiac by that point, who had come to believe that the president was a secret communist who was confiscating private property, spying on Americans, and having his enemies murdered. Hiding behind the "poisonous doctrines" of the New Deal were, he said, "the red garments of bolshevism, communism, socialism, and fascism."[51] The new group's second-in-command was St. Louis attorney Sterling Edmunds, who had headed Kirby's Southern Committee to Uphold the Constitution in Missouri and who was active in the Sentinels of the Republic.[52]

The national group went nowhere. The national press mocked it as nothing more than a Hail Mary tossed by desperate Liberty Leaguers (a charge difficult to deny when John J. Raskob himself covered the meeting's $50,000 bill). The national Jeffersonian Democrats couldn't even agree to endorse Republican Alf Landon. Little Joe Bailey enjoyed a few days of national press by grabbing any reporter who would listen and explaining his innate southern apprehension about voting Republican. Other delegates mumbled vague plans about convincing Democrats that the New Deal was really a communist plot and they should vote Republican. Quipsters boiled the meeting's outcome down to the notion that the Jeffersonian Democrats had managed to convince themselves that Republican Alf Landon was a better Democrat than Franklin Roosevelt.

Haley, however, came out of the meeting jazzed. He even got to write the organization's official platform, a catalog of the Sins of Roosevelt: the lust for power, the disrespect for constitutions and courts, and the abandonment of party and principle. Haley criticized FDR's "wanton waste" and reliance on "theories and hidden designs." Left unchecked, the JD platform declared, the New Deal would bring about the immediate collapse of civilization. In the statement's money line, Haley accused Roosevelt of "exerting in every conceivable way to strike down the beneficent structure of Democratic government and to substitute for it a collectivist state, replacing the doctrines of democracy with the tenets and teaching of a blended communism and socialism."[53] Subtlety would not prove to be Haley's strongest rhetorical device.

Back in Texas, Kirby and Haley put together the Jeffersonian Democrats of Texas at a statewide convention in mid-August; it was the first full-fledged right-wing political organization in the state. The JDT was backed mostly by wealthy cotton brokers, ranchers, oilmen, and lawyers. Big Jim West and oil tycoon Hugh Roy Cullen were its biggest financial supporters. Haley, determined to take his case directly to the people of Texas, launched a multifaceted statewide marketing campaign anchored by a six-issue newspaper pitched to the class of middling Texas farmers that Jim Ferguson had so carefully cultivated two decades earlier. For Haley, the campaign's key to success was voter education. Once Texans knew the facts about Roosevelt and the New Deal, they would be compelled to support Republican Alf Landon, despite their understandable discomfort in voting Republican. As election day drew near, the JDT even shifted its marketing focus to teach voters *how* to vote a split ticket. It was that rare.

The group launched weekly radio addresses on the state's largest networks and printed and mailed hundreds of thousands of copies of its newspaper, the *Jeffersonian Democrat* (which Haley edited) to every rural mailbox in Texas. Haley himself wrote most of the paper's long-form essays and then had them reprinted and distributed as pamphlets. These included racist screeds like "The New Deal and the Negro Vote," in which Haley asked if Texas was to remain a "white man's country" or "be sunk [to] the cultural level of the negro, and have the purity of its blood corrupted with mulatto strains." And his anti-Catholic rant "Did Jim Farley Romanize the American Post Office System?" in which Haley claimed a Catholic takeover of America's civil service was part of a plan to "wipe out Protestantism."[54] He pounded out dozens of cold-call letters a day: "I have been advised that you are in harmony with our conviction that the New Deal is undemocratic and extremely dangerous, and that it should not be continued," he wrote as he sought donations and support. (He would build on and mine this mailing list of the like-minded for decades.)[55] Haley targeted mailings for different professions: for doctors, he included information about the New Deal and socialized medicine and for retailers, messages about taxes and the administration's encouragement of consumer cooperatives. One of the campaign's more expensive endeavors, though funded by one of its more zealous patrons, was a mass mailing of Elizabeth Dilling's lurid and anti-Semitic book *Roosevelt's Red Record*.

Haley proved to be a natural when it came to publicity. Among his first acts as state director of the Jeffersonian Democrats was to call a press conference and tell reporters about how he had been fired from the University of Texas for "exposing the fallacious, devious and dangerous policies of the Roosevelt regime and its impending dangers of national bankruptcy, general demoralization and communism."[56] Portraying himself as an innocent victim of President Roosevelt's unquenchable thirst for power, Haley declared, "We are today a country ruled by fear." The truth was, Haley had not been fired. When he became head of the JDT, he asked for a leave of absence from UT and was denied. But the denial had nothing to do with his new position. Rather, the grant money that had been paying for his position had run out. A patient UT president H. Y. Benedict explained this to the historian in a private meeting and had assured Haley that he planned on putting a formal request to the Board of Regents to continue funding Haley's project and position. Caught off guard by Haley's press conference, Benedict put out a press release to set the record straight and publicly thank Haley for the "crackerjack job" he had done for the university.[57] For the rest of his life Haley would repeat the claim that he had been fired for his politics.[58]

Across the fall campaign, the JDT pushed its conspiracy-laden message of paranoia and fear. Red radicals had taken over government, hellbent on destroying the nation in the name of communism. The only issue of the election, as Haley summed the matter up, was "Democracy vs. Communism." The future under a second Roosevelt term would be the completion of "a communistic state" where individuals would no longer have rights and instead would be mere servants to the state.[59] In the world of the Jeffersonian Democrats, Rexford Tugwell was "as red or redder than Stalin," the New Deal had been lifted from the Communist Party's 1932 platform, deficit spending was a plan to bankrupt the nation, and agricultural programs were designed to hasten Americans' acceptance of communism.[60]

As the election drew closer, Haley grew convinced that he had turned the tide and began to predict a Landon victory in Texas. One West Texas ally figured the Republican would win seven out of every eight votes in his county. (It went nine to one for Roosevelt.) Haley privately and publicly sent out his breathless analysis of a *Publisher's Weekly* poll indicating that Landon had a chance.[61] (Every other poll showed Roosevelt winning in a cake walk.)

Roosevelt won 87 percent of the votes in Texas. He took three out of every four votes in all but nineteen counties. He took nine out of ten in more than half. He lost only two German counties in the Hill Country.

Looking back, Haley claimed some pride in his "campaign of education." As he confessed to a friend, he might be guilty of "stupid politics" but not "dirty politics," boasting that under his leadership, the Jeffersonian Democrats had not spent any money lobbying, "not one cent upon a cigar or a bottle of liquor."[62] He did, however, establish himself as the leading ultraconservative intellectual in Texas. He now had a five thousand-person mailing list of like-minded allies across Texas and coterie of wealthy patrons. And he was just getting started.

9
THE RIGHT-WING POPULISM OF PAPPY O'DANIEL

Let anyone speak long enough, he will get believers.

ROBERT LOUIS STEVENSON

I

It started, supposedly, as a means to raise brand awareness for a flour company. It ended eight years later in disgrace. But in the years between 1938 and 1946, the political career of W. Lee "Pass the Biscuits Pappy" O'Daniel altered Texas politics forever. The state's first honest-to-god right-wing populist, O'Daniel moved Texas's fork-of-the-creek farmers to the right, reinvented political media, turned the Establishment's political ideology into practice and policy, normalized paranoia and conspiracy theories, and introduced antilabor and anticommunism politics to the masses. Too often dismissed as a joke or a quirk of Texas politics, his quick evolution as a candidate and politician marked a critical stage in the development of the Texas Right.

Even for Texas, the O'Daniel years were bizarre. A political novice before his first campaign—O'Daniel wasn't even registered to vote in the first contest he won—the flour salesman won four statewide elections in less than five years, racking up record numbers of votes. While running as a straight-up man of the people, a "common citizen" candidate, he governed as a tool of the state's business interests. Making it up as he went along, O'Daniel, along with his western swing band, the Hillbilly Boys, reinvented campaigning, bringing a spectacle and showmanship that could have made P. T. Barnum blush. On the trail he abandoned policy along with political stratagems and reduced his campaign to Texas nationalism, hymns and scripture, vague assurances of economic expansion, and odes to Momma. When cornered, he laid out his platform as the Golden Rule, the Ten Commandments, no sales tax, and pensions for Texans over sixty-five. His campaign song, which he wrote, was "Thirty Bucks for Momma." Once elected, he abandoned protocol and continued to air his daily radio show as well as push his business interests. His was a populism for the radio, a honeyed dulcet voice as reassuring as a minister's. "How do you do, ladies and gentlemen, and hello there, boys and girls. This is W. Lee O'Daniel speaking." Eschewing the mechanisms of party, O'Daniel took his message directly to Texans, never burdening them with facts, figures, or details, but rather depending on a relationship that he built on the road and on the airwaves. Perhaps strangest of all was O'Daniel's political mutation from bland prophet of chamber of commerce–style boosterism to raving anticommunist paranoic.[1]

His biography spoke for itself: a real-life Horatio Alger story of a poor and honest farm boy who leveraged pluck and hard work into fortune and fame. Raised on a Kansas dirt ranch, O'Daniel had an entrepreneurial streak a mile wide. At sixteen, seeking to raise tuition for business school, he opened his own pop-up restaurant. At the Salt City Business College in Hutchinson, Kansas, O'Daniel earned his walking-around money by throwing papers and waiting tables. A good student, he graduated early and took a job as a stenographer and bookkeeper at a small flour mill. Within a few months he had taken his boss's job, director of sales. Only three years out of college, O'Daniel had saved enough money to buy his own small mill; he then poured all his profits into buying up other mills. When he went bust thanks to an ill-conceived flour brokerage scheme, O'Daniel brushed himself off and started over, working as a sales agent for Burrus Mills in Fort Worth, one of the biggest in the Southwest. Within a decade he was running the company.

While clearly a great salesman, O'Daniel's real talent lay in marketing, especially branding. At Burrus, through constant repetition and a brilliant advertising campaign, he managed to establish—in Texas anyway—the idea that Texas wheat was a superior product to that of Kansas, which had for many years enjoyed a better, if not necessarily deserved, reputation for its grains. His efforts forever won him the love of Texas wheat farmers, especially in the Panhandle. The key to the campaign was his radio show, which he built from a barely-there broadcast out of a closet at the mill to the most popular show in Texas and, in the process, made Burrus Mills Light Crust Texans' favorite flour. Music was an important part of the show; early on, O'Daniel hired an out-of-work western swing band, which he named the Light Crust Doughboys, to play fun and upbeat songs and provide dramatic background music to the show's mixture of scripture, stories, and plugs for Light Crust Flour. Early incarnations of the band featured future western swing legends Milton Brown and Bob Wills. Anyone who ever heard *Prairie Home Companion* back in the Garrison Keillor days would recognize the format. The show grew so popular that O'Daniel built out the Texas Quality Network of radio stations to broadcast it across the state, for years afterward Texas's most powerful and influential network.[2]

O'Daniel was too ambitious to remain the head of someone else's company for long, and in 1935 he struck out on his own, forming the W. Lee O'Daniel Flour Company, which produced Hillbilly Flour. He had long known that the flour business was basically marketing. Flour was flour. Hillbilly didn't even mill its own product; O'Daniel just bought flour from other mills and packaged it under his brand. The company was little more than bags, music, a supercool logo, and a radio show. He charged a little more per sack, but each was bright and colorful printed cotton that could be cut into patterns and used as material for children's clothing, an important consideration during the Great Depression. Women's magazines at the time had even taken to printing patterns for flour sacks in each issue. The back side of each bag had patterns for cut-out dolls of the Hillbilly Boys—the new name of the show's western swing band. Unlike the Light Crust Doughboys, the Hillbilly Boys were marketed as something of a cartoon band (think Gorillaz), with outsized personalities and names like Mickey Wickey, Patty-Boy, Klondike, and Texas Rose.

O'Daniel understood three essential things about the radio: who was listening, when they were listening, and what they wanted to hear. While most advertisers paid a premium to run ads in the early evening when they assumed the breadwinner of a household was likely listening, O'Daniel sought out time in the cheaper hours of the middle of the day, when Texas's wives and mothers were home tending to their countless household chores. He pitched his entire show to these women with daily lessons from the Bible, poetry (often his own), heroic tales from the past, and musical numbers (which he also wrote) devoted to mothers: "The Boy Who Never Grew Too Old to Comb His Mother's Hair" and "Marvelous Mother of Mine" were listener favorites. Every episode was about family and the respect a boy owed his mother. The show was overtly if generically Christian, delivered in a comforting conversational style, more like a pleasant afternoon spent drinking iced tea with the parson on the good sofa than a sermon. But O'Daniel also included a little profane to go with the sacred. Scattered through each episode of the Hillbilly Flour show were upbeat western swing numbers by the Hillbilly Boys, a tight dance band defined by its jazzy fiddle, ripping guitar riffs, and 4/4 tempos. It was music that would make anybody want to dance around the kitchen. When it came time to slow it down, the band would drop to the background, playing softly while O'Daniel's voice filled the room once again. Understanding "that a microphone is an ear and not an auditorium," he cooed and coaxed, his voice soft enough that listeners could hear it catch and quaver as he described his own mother or read a particularly beautiful psalm.[3] It was all an act, but a good one; the most popular radio show in Texas reached over a million listeners per broadcast. Every day at 12:30 time stopped: "This is W. Lee O'Daniel speaking." They said you could walk down any street in Texas ten minutes into the show and hear every word and every note through open kitchen windows. Even the farm and ranch wives in barely populated West Texas could catch the show thanks to Pappy's border radio station, XEPN in Piedras Negras, one of the most powerful stations in the world, boasting 100,000 watts and a directional antenna pointed straight north that broadcast O'Daniel's voice for hundreds of miles across the prairies.[4]

In 1938, Pappy decided to run for governor. Win or lose, Hillbilly Flour would enjoy unprecedented publicity. As was natural for such a popular figure, O'Daniel had received the occasional telegram encouraging him to consider public office, but he had always ignored them; he had a business to run. But '38 was different: there was a discernible distaste for professional politicians that year. The Depression had been dragging on for close to a decade, and the drought for almost that long. New Deal programs helped, no doubt, but compliance was confusing, and relief was demeaning. O'Daniel thought the time might be right for a businessman to run for governor. Floating a trial balloon in a

W. Lee O'Daniel and the Hillbilly Boys.

Mother's Day broadcast (of course), he asked his loyal listeners if he should throw his hat in the ring. Fifty-seven thousand telegrams and letters poured into the offices of Hillbilly Flour. All but four answered yes. And those four said no only because they didn't want Pappy to be sullied by public life.

Two weeks later, during his show, O'Daniel announced his candidacy:

> From the Texas plains and hills and valleys came a little breeze wafting on its crest more than 57,000 voices of one accord—we want W. Lee O'Daniel for governor of Texas. Why that avalanche of mail? Surely each and every one of you 57,000 folks could not have known that W. Lee O'Daniel is an only living son of one of those tired, forlorn, disappointed, and destitute mothers—a son who had played at that widowed mother's skirts, while during each day and way into the darkness of the nights she washed the dirt and grime from the clothes of the wealthy on an old, worn-out washboard—for the paltry pittance of twenty-five cents per day—and that by that honest drudgery

provided corn bread and beans for her children which she had brought back with her from the Valley of the Shadow of Death.[5]

He would run for governor for his sainted Momma.

II

The front-runner in the race was Amarillo's competent and capable former mayor Ernest O. Thompson, an undisputed leader of the West Texas booster class. As a boy he had turned his newspaper delivery route into a distribution empire by hiring other lads and organizing their routes. While still in high school, he started a Pope-Toledo automobile dealership and ran a side hustle renting out his cars to real estate developers with prospects in town. He entered World War I as a private and left as a lieutenant colonel, famous for his heroism and tactical ideas about machine gun placements. After the war, he got a law degree, married a world-class opera singer, and helped found the American Legion. He bought and ran the Amarillo Hotel and was elected mayor of the city just a month after his thirty-seventh birthday. He was appointed to the Texas Railroad Commission in 1932 and was widely praised for his fairness and balance in bringing order to the chaotic oil industry. In 1938, he ran for governor on a well-considered platform of protecting Social Security, lowering taxes and spending, and reducing utility rates, along with a pro-labor, investment-seeking approach to the economy that blended practical Texas economic nationalism with small-*p* populism. He was, in short, the sort of candidate one would expect Amarillo to produce back then—the booster ideal in candidate form. And in any other election. . . . Also in the race was state attorney general William McGraw, who ran on a platform similar to Thompson's. The men were friendly rivals who even campaigned together on occasion.

The conservative in the race was perennial candidate Tom Hunter, an oilman from Wichita Falls whose previous campaigns had seemed designed primarily to troll the Fergusons. Rounding out the field was a menagerie of also-rans, idealists, and opportunists. Most observers placed O'Daniel's campaign firmly in the last group. It was such an obvious stunt to sell flour, no one took it seriously.[6] Not a single major newspaper in Texas endorsed Pappy.

Five weeks before the Democratic primary, O'Daniel hit the road, opening his campaign with a massive rally in Waco. No one had seen anything like it. The crowd was huge, somewhere between eight and nine thousand people, making it the largest political campaign event in Texas history. It stretched for blocks. Over half were women, with their children. O'Daniel's "speech" was "informal, extemporaneous and wandering, with chaotic politics and nebulous economics," according to one veteran news reporter. When the band broke into "Beautiful Texas," the crowd sang along. One Waco reporter said of the event: "This isn't politics, it's a revolution."[7] The O'Daniel bandwagon only grew from there. While Thompson and McGraw spoke earnestly to small crowds and bought up radio time to explain their studied positions, O'Daniel created a road show more concert tour than campaign rally. O'Daniel would pull into town in a tricked-out bright-white Desoto flatbed that the campaign used as a portable stage. On either side of the bed were huge loudspeakers, and a bright banner stretched across the length of the truck, "W. Lee O'Daniel for Governor." In just four weeks, he traveled over twenty thousand miles, speaking to enormous crowds: 8,000 in San Angelo, 3,000 in Colorado City, 40,000 in Austin. When he showed up in Lubbock, 4,000 people came to see him, including farmers, mechanics, "women with their babies," and as one reporter quipped, "apparently babies without their mothers." The crowd took to the trees and stood atop cars. Kids perched on their fathers' shoulders.[8] The rallies were basically live versions of the radio show with plenty of plugs for Hillbilly Flour: Pappy dispensed anecdotes, recited scripture, and shared pearls of common wisdom as the Hillbilly Boys crooned and played softly in the background. It was Jesus, Momma, Texas, country music, and the Constitution.[9] What politics showed up in Pappy's speeches mostly consisted of harangues against the "professional politicians" along with promises to give elderly Texans pensions. Whenever O'Daniel's energy flagged, the Hillbilly Boys broke into songs like, "I Want to Be a Cowboy's Sweetheart" or "The Old Rugged Cross." As each rally closed, O'Daniel's children took up the collection, the crowd tossing coins in miniature flour barrels as the Hillbilly Boys played the Offertory, a new tune, "The Hillbillies Are All Politicians Now."

While the popular portrayals of O'Daniel's platform tend to focus on his famous slogan "Less Johnson grass and politicians, more smokestacks and businessmen," Pappy did have slightly more to offer. His sig-

W. Lee O'Daniel gubernatorial campaign rally in Lubbock, 1940.

nature issue was a pension—$30 a month for anyone over sixty-five—it was incredibly popular. Just three years earlier, more than 80 percent of Texans had supported a constitutional amendment that would establish state pensions, the largest margin for any amendment in state history. O'Daniel tapped into the anxiety felt by the older Texans who, after a decade of economic and environmental disaster, wondered how they might survive when and if they became too old to work. He gently pushed some other generic populist proposals: lowering taxes, reducing the cost of state government, and abolishing the poll tax and death penalty, but specific policy prescriptions were not his strong suit. He also promised an aggressive campaign to lure industry (and jobs) to the state, spoke out against a sales tax, and pretended to be a friend to organized labor. To the surprise of absolutely everyone, O'Daniel walked away from the July primary with a clear majority; he was the first candidate to win without a runoff since Pat Neff's reelection campaign in 1922. O'Daniel, a man with no political experience and so little interest in politics, he had not even paid his poll tax that year, was the new governor of Texas.[10] During the campaign, sales of Hillbilly Flour had doubled.

Political observers then and since have pondered the O'Daniel phenomenon. Was it unalloyed populist anger directed at the professional
political class, a testament to the power of mass media to put one over
on the rubes, a return to the blatant religiosity of the temperance years,
or all or some of the above?[11] The nation's most astute political scientist
at the time, V. O. Key, saw it as the logical consequence of the collapse of
Fergusonism; in a one-party system that had no "factional cliques," there
was no mechanism in place to stop an "outsider" candidate or a situation
where "attention-getting antics substituted for an organized politics."
O'Daniel, according to Key, had just cashed in during a change year.[12]
Key might have been right. On election day, William Deloach, a southern plains cotton farmer wrote in his diary: "I do not know that he is the
man to put in, but it will be a change."[13] The overwhelming consensus
was that O'Daniel was not a complete unknown; rather, after years of
hearing him on the radio, Texans felt that they had elected a good Christian man to the office. Historian Seth McKay has clearly demonstrated
the direct correlation between geographic sources of O'Daniel support
and the broadcast range of his show. Although usually associated with
rural voters, O'Daniel won every major Texas city except Thompson's
hometown of Amarillo. All those cities had powerful stations that were
part of the Texas Quality Network.[14] Although disgusted by the reali-
zation, Evetts Haley came to the same conclusion as McKay. In one of
the more sarcastic things he ever wrote, "Harmonizing O'Daniel," Haley
dismissed those who saw O'Daniel as a man of the people. Instead, the
historian argued, what they were witnessing was a debasing of politics
wherein an obvious charlatan had substituted spectacle for principle and
country music for policy. It was, he warned, the "most significant and
dangerous political development of all time."[15]

But neither Haley nor the others knew the whole story. Behind the
music and the rallies and the homespun rhetoric was a sophisticated
operation run and paid for by powerful and wealthy businessmen who
hated the New Deal. Prominent among them were zealots like insurance mogul and patent medicine salesman Carr P. Collins and oil baron
Maco Stewart.[16] O'Daniel's political persona was partly the creation
of his longtime friend and public relations expert Phil Fox, who just
a few years earlier had run the publicity department of the Ku Klux
Klan.[17] O'Daniel was also coached regularly by his "spiritual advisor"
J. Leslie Finnell, the pastor of the Magnolia Street Christian Church

in Fort Worth. Blending the pro-business elements of his platform (the creation of a businessman's committee for example) with his common-citizen message and his generic Christian populism allowed voters to see what they wanted to see. O'Daniel never tried to hide his pro-business agenda. In fact, he campaigned on the idea, suggesting that only a man who had to meet a budget and a payroll would be able to find the "screws loose at Austin."[18] And despite the folksy radio personality, O'Daniel was a ranking member of the Fort Worth business elite who had a net worth of more than a half million dollars. He had even served two terms as president of the city's Chamber of Commerce. In 1938, he had been smart enough to keep his anti–New Deal sentiments to himself and his right-wing advisers off the stage.

The national conservative press ate up O'Daniel's populist appeal and image. The Hearst newspapers called him a "typical, big, good-natured, plain American male who sings in his shower bath—loves roast beef n' brown gravy but no dessert—is still in love with the same girl—and haw haws over Donald Duck."[19] A real man of the people, he would appeal, Hearst columnist Damon Runyon opined a few days before the election, to those folks who never "have the opportunity of making their voices heard over the land." He might not be the savior that they hope for, but "they accept him as at least the chance to express themselves . . . who gives them a form of articulateness."[20] Radio priest Charles Coughlin called O'Daniel's victory a great day for "social justice" and hoped that "O'Danielism will spread throughout every other State in the Union."[21]

Pappy's record-breaking inauguration ceremony was held at the filled-to-capacity War Memorial Stadium on the UT campus and was followed by the "noisiest, largest, and most hilarious series of inaugural receptions that the capital of Texas has ever seen."[22] The Hillbilly Boys killed it at a street dance that stretched six blocks. Fireworks and airplanes filled the sky.

But it was soon obvious that this political knave with no experience in government or governing, no allies in the Texas legislature, and no natural constituency was out of his depth. O'Daniel managed to alienate the Democratic Establishment even before taking office by interjecting himself into primary races and embarrassing himself at the state convention. O'Daniel found Austin a lonely place. His "Thirty Dollars for Momma" pension proposal went nowhere; awash in debt, the state just didn't have the money. Able to read a balance sheet as well as anyone, O'Daniel knew this fact going in, but pushed the plan anyway. He blamed the legislature for its failure.[23] Once the pension idea burned out, O'Daniel revealed his ultimate plan, a highly regressive "transactions" tax of 1.6 percent on any goods bought or sold. No matter its name, it was a painfully obvious sales tax (which O'Daniel had campaigned against). The idea came straight out of the Texas Industrial Conference, an off-shoot of the open shop movement created by John Kirby two decades earlier and was designed to create budgetary space for tax breaks for Texas corporations. Legislators were having none of it; state senator W. C. Graves described the proposal as a "tax on poverty." Undaunted, O'Daniel pushed for a constitutional amendment to enact the tax. It also went nowhere. Pappy's pleas on the radio fell on deaf ears. He called out the legislature, especially the "Gang of 56," who had banded together to stop his transaction tax. They, in turn, called the governor a tool of the wealthy, put in office to "save the poor man's soul and the rich man's money," a "Sabbath Caesar," a "political charlatan," and the "crooning corporal" of the "panoplied forces of financial marauders." A vindictive O'Daniel froze the taxes on oil and gas and took a Bowie knife to the state budget, slashing funds for schools and insane asylums.[24]

His appointments were even worse. O'Daniel nominated a host of barely qualified right-wingers, fans, and cronies to seemingly every position. He named Dallas oilman, antilabor zealot, and ultraconservative E. B. Germany as head of the state Democratic Party. Without even meeting with state labor leaders, he nominated for state labor commissioner a twenty-nine-year-old desk jockey from Southwestern Bell Telephone whose only qualification seemed to be the fact that he had written a fan letter to O'Daniel. For adjutant general, over the objections of the American Legion, he appointed one of Texas's largest grocery distributors (and Hillbilly Flour's biggest customer), a man with limited military experience. His failed appointments to the position of Texas highway commissioner are the stuff of Texas legend. First O'Daniel tried to appoint benefactor and anti-Roosevelt extremist Carr Collins; the state senate, afraid that it might mean losing New Deal highway money, rejected him. The governor then turned to West Texas oilman and banker J. C. Hunter, who also faced fierce resistance and withdrew before he was voted down. Undeterred, O'Daniel tried to name the apostate Jeffersonian Democrat Big Jim West to the post. The senate said no again. He tried to appoint militant prohibitionists (including the president of the WCTU) to head the state liquor control board and named his personal secretary as state life insurance commissioner.[25] He put right-wing reactionaries like lawyer, oilman, and railroad magnate Orville Bullington and oilman/rancher Dan J. Harrison on the UT Board of Regents. Later, he even tried to name J. Evetts Haley as livestock sanitary commissioner, but he too was rejected for his Jeffersonian Democrat ties. Frustrated over the parade of zealots, hacks, and hangers-on, one solon complained: "What the governor has done has shown a reckless disregard for everything political, everything precedential and everything traditional . . . everything reasonable." He further warned that if "the legislature is not careful, if the people are not careful, more crimes may be committed under the guise of protecting the common people than this state every dreamed of."[26]

By any measure, O'Daniel's first term was a dismal failure. There was no pension, no transaction tax, and his appointments were nonstarters. O'Daniel sulked and blamed the legislature. "Every time I stick my head in an office in Austin to see how they're spending your money," he complained loudly, "they slam the door in my face." He took to the radio: these "professional politicians," this "little bunch of pin-headed legislators" refused to accept the will of the electorate. As *Collier's* magazine's snarkiest reporter put it: "Greater administrators than Pappy have been slapped down by better legislatures when they've advocated alterations in hundred-pocket government overalls."[27] O'Daniel lashed out at the state press (which seemed to take great delight in exposing the governor's foibles and failures).[28] "No recent governor, he complained, "has been so unfairly dealt with as the press has dealt with me." He canceled news conferences and took to the radio to take his message—unfiltered—directly to the voters. Taking a cue from the Fergusons and the Jeffersonian Democrats, he started his own newspaper, the *W. Lee O'Daniel News*; he had to, he said, because Texas newspapers were too full of "deception, propaganda, and unreliable dissemination." His paper, on the other hand, would "keep the masses of citizens of Texas properly and reliable informed."[29]

Despite a fruitless two years in office, Texas voters reelected the governor in 1940. He had run on the same basic platform—pensions and the Ten Commandments—but with a couple of new twists: a no-new-taxes pledge to counter his disastrous transaction tax, and dire warnings about the threat of communists and Nazis in Texas. Long before Joe

McCarthy shambled onto the national scene, Pappy launched his own Red Scare. At one point, he even claimed to be working directly with President Roosevelt to root out commies in Texas. (People flooded the governor's office with reports of the suspicious behavior of their neighbors.) The race again came down to O'Daniel and Amarillo's Ernest Thompson (who engaged in a little Red-baiting of his own), but O'Daniel won easily, with 54 percent in the first primary election.[30] Our Lubbock County cotton farmer described his vote for Pappy: "I do not think he is too hot for the Governor, but the way these hi [*sic*] birds in politics have slung mud, I am glad he beat the whole field."[31]

O'Daniel's popularity in those years is tough to categorize as he was popular everywhere and among every class. In the 1940 race, he won 77 percent of farmers' votes and 71 percent among rural folk in general. He took 74 percent of old folks' votes and 68 percent of twenty-somethings. The poor: 68 percent. The rich: 58 percent. He did well across West Texas, only failing to win in the counties near and around Ernest Thompson's Amarillo. Despite a general unease about O'Daniel among labor leaders, most workingmen liked Pappy.[32] We should note two things: neither African Americans nor Latinos were allowed to participate in the Democratic primary in those years; and O'Daniel, unlike most of his contemporaries, never resorted to race-baiting. Trying to explain Pappy's appeal, the director of the most important polling service in Texas was at a loss: "Most of the people are for O'Daniel just because he is a good Christian man."[33]

With his second term assured, O'Daniel went after organized labor. Until then, he had kept his antilabor attitudes well hidden. But suddenly, the governor started talking constantly about "labor leader racketeers" out to destroy democracy and American tranquility. He even called the legislature into session and demanded that it pass the O'Daniel Anti-Violence Acts, a collection of embarrassingly unconstitutional laws designed to wipe out organized labor in Texas. Under the pretense of protecting Texas's war production capabilities from disruptive strikes, O'Daniel sought to strip all power from labor unions. The package called for a sixty-day "cooling-off" period between a labor dispute and a labor stoppage. Another part of his suite of antilabor laws made it a felony, with mandatory prison time, for even threatening violence during a strike. Yet another outlawed picketing. Freedom of assembly was forbidden in a place experiencing labor strife. After a watered-down version of his proposals passed, O'Daniel started advertising Texas as a place where employers would enjoy near autonomy over their workers. Texas, he promised, would be the state where rabble-rousers and union organizers would find themselves picking cotton on a chain gang if they dared start any trouble. This was O'Daniel's version of a pro-business climate.[34]

O'Daniel framed labor unions and labor leaders as unpatriotic, even treasonous, a new tack for Texas conservatives. With a possible war looming, the approach had great power and gave business conservatives a chance to win over new audiences. Their efforts were spurred by new threats from an invigorated Congress of Industrial Organizations (CIO) determined to make inroads into the South and a Roosevelt Administration clearly sympathetic to labor unions. Promoting his plan, O'Daniel began to liberally sprinkle his radio addresses with references to the "communistic, radical, wild-eyed, labor leader racketeers"—a phrase he used in various combinations up to a dozen times per speech. He warned that the radicals would not stop until they had taken over Texas.[35] He even blamed wartime strikes (though there had not been one in Texas) for forcing the Allied surrender at Bataan.[36]

And just like that, Vance Muse oozed back into public life. He'd gone semidark after the debacle of the SCUC and losing his place as the mouthpiece of the Texas Right to Evetts Haley. He and Lewis Ulrey had kept busy running an organization they called the Christian Americans, a just-folks media outlet that produced "Christian American literature of a nonpartisan and nonsectarian nature for the promotion of Americanism, religion, and righteousness and to conduct a program of education and organization to combat Communism, Fascism, Nazism, Socialism, atheism, and other alien 'isms' designed to destroy faith in God and Jesus Christ, the church, the home, and the American system of one's own conscience."[37] In actuality, the Christian Americans was little more than a channel for Ulrey (by this point an outright admirer of Adolph Hitler) to spew his out-there conspiratorial delusions about African Americans, Jews, unions, and the New Deal, and a paycheck for Muse, who collected a $4,000 annual salary.[38] But when Muse saw O'Daniel veer into his lane, he found a powerful new ally and a new purpose for the Christian Americans as the marketing and lobbying branch of Pappy's antilabor politics. And, even more appealing, Pappy was on his way to the U.S. Senate.

It was a strange season in Texas politics. Just a few weeks after O'Daniel's second inauguration, longtime Texas senator Morris Sheppard died unexpectedly. The governor saw a chance to go nationwide. (Many suspected he had presidential ambitions by this point.) O'Daniel met with patrons Collins, Stewart, and West and came up with a plan. Texas law demanded that the governor immediately name a suitable person to the Senate seat and set a date for a special election to fill the remainder of Sheppard's term. Many thought O'Daniel would and should name himself to the position and enter the special election as the incumbent. Mark Kersey, a legislator from Lubbock, even introduced a ten-paragraph resolution that the "best beloved and most popular governor this state has known since the immortal James Stephen Hogg" should immediately resign and accept the post. It passed by a rising vote. (There was plenty of speculation that many in the legislature saw the measure as a way to get O'Daniel the hell out of Texas.) Instead, O'Daniel pulled out a deep cut, appointing the septuagenarian son of Texas legend Sam Houston to the post, on San Jacinto Day no less. It was a great move. In terrible health, Andrew Jackson Houston would not be able to make a run in the special election, and naming him to the Senate made Pappy look as "Texas" as Stephen F. Austin. Although his family begged him not to, the eighty-two-year-old Houston took the long trip to Washington. He was sworn in, attended a single committee meeting, fell ill, was hospitalized, and died two months into his term.

O'Daniel busily prepared for the special election. It was a huge field, twenty-nine candidates. There were four heavy hitters, including O'Daniel: the crusading anticommunist congressman Martin Dies; the New Dealer's New Dealer Lyndon B. Johnson, who practically wore FDR's endorsement around his neck; and the popular state attorney general, former SMU football star Gerald Mann. O'Daniel pulled out the stops—running on his recent Anti-Violence Act and promising to take his fight to Washington: "Everybody knows that the radical wild-eyed labor leaders of the AFL and CIO and the communists are fighting me and supporting the other candidates."[39] Pappy claimed to march in lockstep with FDR and the New Deal and had the Hillbilly Boys play a song he had written, "On to Victory Mr. Roosevelt," at every campaign stop. He saved his contempt for those other "professional politicians" in Washington. "What DC politicians feared most," he said, "was a good, capable, honest common citizen up there who would not be one of the gang, and [who] might find out the truth about what is going on in this circle of petty politicians and get right up on the radio at Washington and tell the common citizens back home all about their tricks."[40] The race was tight: O'Daniel defeated Johnson by just over a thousand votes, with some curious late ballots securing him the victory.[41]

O'Daniel was miserable in the Senate. It was even lonelier than Austin. The hillbilly schtick didn't fly. Neither did his constant hunger for attention. On his first day in town, he demanded a meeting with Roosevelt. (Declined.) On his first day in the Senate, he introduced a new version of his antiviolence strike bill. (He would introduce it three more times.) On his second day, he gave a self-serving speech promising not to be a "'yes man' or 'rubber stamp'" for Roosevelt. He took dumb stands on dumb things just to stand out. He was the only southern senator and the only member of the Texas delegation to speak against an extension of the Selective Service Act and gave a twenty-three-minute speech as to why. It was an isolationist address that could have come out of the 1940 Ohio Republican Party platform.[42] The running joke was that O'Daniel was the first Republican senator from Texas since Reconstruction. He pushed and pushed his antilabor platform, introducing legislation that would end overtime pay and the forty-hour week, ban draft deferments for labor leaders, and outlaw picketing. He warned that labor leaders were secret socialists who planned to use the war to destroy American democracy at home while we were fighting to preserve it abroad. Weeks before the Japanese attack on Pearl Harbor, he declared that "the most serious problem confronting the nation" was the "powerful, dominating labor-union leader racketeers."[43]

Once the United States entered the war, Pappy proudly presented his eleven-point plan to win it. Other than twice-daily prayer, civil defense, outlawing alcohol on military bases, and taxing war profiteers to oblivion, his plan was unfiltered anti–New Deal business conservatism: cut spending, remove restrictions on agricultural production, outlaw violence in labor disputes, eliminate price controls on big business, send labor leaders to war, open the public lands to resource extraction, and guarantee the open shop. Around Washington, he gained a reputation as an enemy to the war effort. The *New Republic*, in a special issue dedicated to electing a "Congress to Win the War," called him an "obstructionist" and urged Texans to elect a new senator.[44]

The summer 1942 primary was a tough one for O'Daniel. He faced two popular ex-governors, Dan Moody and James Allred. Most of the state newspapers came out strongly against Pappy. By that point, he had developed a national reputation as a rabid isolationist, a hindrance to the war effort, and an unhinged Roosevelt hater. In Texas, many thought he was a secret Republican. Allred (who faced O'Daniel in the second primary) summed up this view: "I don't say that everyone who votes for my opponent is a Republican, but I do say that every Republican who enters the Democratic primary will vote against me. I don't say that everyone who votes for my opponent is a Roosevelt-hater, but I do say that everyone who hates Roosevelt first and Hitler second will vote against Jimmy Allred. I don't say that everyone who votes for my opponent is a Nazi sympathizer, but I do say that every Nazi sympathizer in Texas will vote against Jimmy Allred."[45]

O'Daniel ran a primal right-wing populist campaign, Texas's first. He pulled the old Desoto flatbed out of the garage and cranked up the *W. Lee O'Daniel News* again. This time there were no warm bromides or calming hymns; this was O'Daniel as the only man standing between Texans and a secret communist plot to take over the country. "Labor racketeers" working in concert with New Deal Democrats had laid the groundwork for an immediate socialist takeover and were waiting until after the 1942 elections to launch the last stages of a vast conspiracy. To ensure victory, he claimed, the communists had created a special slush fund and committed a million dollars to defeat him in the election. The primary recipients of the cash were the "gold dust twins"—Moody and Allred. The plot went deeper than that; he told voters that "the professional politicians, the politically controlled newspapers, and the Communistic labor leader racketeers have joined forces" in the "dirtiest campaign of misrepresentation in the history of Texas."[46]

Truth be told, O'Daniel was desperate. In his four years as a public servant, he hadn't really accomplished much. His only signature achievement, his slate of antilabor laws, was being dismantled in the courts. As governor, he had not produced pensions or implemented a sales tax. In the Senate he seemed to spend most of his time railing against organized labor, which was still very weak in Texas. He had little to offer voters. And politics in the Lone Star State at the time, despite the oversized personalities, was still largely transactional. Public questions about O'Daniel's church membership and choice not to fight in World War I dogged him at campaign stops. Allred hammered him day after day about his ineffectiveness in the Senate and his lack of support for Roosevelt. Texas newspapers published long editorials outlining his deficiencies. (O'Daniel responded by claiming that newspapers had been bought off "with the filthy gold of Communistic labor leader racketeers.") In the second primary, O'Daniel squeaked by with 51 percent of the votes. He lost every urban county. His support in West Texas slipped significantly. Common wisdom held that there were still plenty of folks who simply refused to believe the nice Christian man whom they knew so well stood against the war and President Roosevelt.[47] O'Daniel escaped with one last victory.

For the next six years, he served, essentially, as a Republican.[48] And not just any kind of Republican, but a Robert A. Taft Republican: isolationist, conservative, and violently anti–New Deal. He expanded his diatribes against the labor racketeers who "plundered, waxed wealthy and become politically powerful" to include the government in general and FDR in particular. "We are fast vesting the power to control every line of business in the hands of boards and bureaus in Washington." The "theorists and star-gazers," he warned, "wish completely to regiment every line of business in this country and . . . force their ideas of government reform upon the people of this nation." He actively campaigned against the president in 1943, telling national audiences that if the Republicans nominated "the right man," Roosevelt could be defeated. Texans, he told a California audience, "are disappointed with the New Deal." Leaving Washington for days at time, he went on tour with the Christian Americans, speaking to state legislatures and urging them to adopt antilabor bills: North Dakota, Oklahoma, Tennessee, Iowa, Missouri, North Carolina. "Pappy O'Daniel–Christian American" laws, as they came to be known, passed in Colorado, Kansas, Florida, Alabama, Mississippi, and Arkansas.[49]

In 1944, Pappy hit the campaign trail once more, as an unofficial spokesperson of the Texas Regulars, the latest and most complicated concoction of wealthy right-wingers to stop Roosevelt. John Henry Kirby was dead by then, and leadership of the Texas Right (especially among the money men) had passed to oil baron Hugh Roy Cullen, the "King of the Wildcatters" and one of the wealthiest people in the world. A fifth-grade dropout with a knack for finding oil in places others ignored, Cullen was also driven by an obsession with obtaining wealth and power. Raised in poverty by a South Carolinian mother who spoke lovingly of the antebellum South, Cullen wanted nothing less than to live the life of a plantation aristocrat. And enough of his hunches and educated guesses in the oil business had been right to make that a reality. His best buddies were Kirby, Big Jim West, and Maco Stewart. Like them, he contributed heavily and regularly to right-wing causes and, like them, was one of the guiding lights of the Jeffersonian Democrats. He despised Roosevelt and the New Deal not only for its economic liberalism but also for the president's views on race. Cullen himself believed that the president was a closeted communist whose New Deal relief and recovery programs were part of a larger, secret plan to create a totalitarian communist state. The 1944 election, he believed, might be the last chance to save the nation.[50]

The first step, he believed, was to take back the state's Democratic Party and purge it of New Deal collaborators. In that effort, "regular" Democrats, drawn from lists of conservatives that men like Cullen and Haley had been collecting since 1936, were recruited to overwhelm local party conventions that selected delegates to the state nominating convention in May. At that meeting, when the Democratic Party would elect its delegates to the national party convention in Chicago, Cullen's "regular" Democrats laid out the state party platform. It looked innocuous enough: a promise to return the two-thirds rule to the national nomination process, denouncing the Supreme Court's decision in *Smith v. Allwright* (which outlawed the white primary), demanding the federal government condemn strikes, criticizing a growing bureaucracy, and ending federal power grabs.[51] But once the delegates to the national convention were named, it became obvious that the state party was about to send an entire delegation of anti–New Deal conservatives to Chicago. Three hundred pro-FDR state delegates marched out of the convention hall in protest, singing "The Eyes of Texas Are upon You." In a rump convention, they nominated their own delegates committed to supporting the president and his platform. At the national convention that summer, the party sat both delegations, effectively diffusing the power of the Regulars and nominating Roosevelt easily.

Undeterred, Cullen and the money men changed their plans and launched a new political project—the Texas Regulars. The idea behind the gambit was to take control of Texas's members of the Electoral College. Perhaps a short refresher in how the College works might be in order. When American voters cast their ballots for president and vice-president every four years, they are not choosing the candidates but rather selecting state delegates who will take part in an exclusive presidential election to be held a few weeks later. Voting for the Democratic candidate actually means choosing a set of electors who are allied with the Democratic Party and who are pledged to vote for their party's nominee in that private election. Ditto for the Republicans, the Greens, the Libertarians. Of the 531 people who would vote in the 1944 electoral college, twenty-three would be from Texas. If President Roosevelt won Texas, its delegates to the Electoral College would cast all twenty-three of their votes for the president. This is where the Texas Regulars came in: they promised a slate of electors who would *not* be pledged to Roosevelt, but would, rather, be free to support any candidate in the Electoral College vote.[52] Through some fantastical and wishful mathematics, the Texas Regulars believed that if enough Texans gave their support to the Regular set of electors they could create a situation where Roosevelt would fall five votes short of the necessary electoral votes to win.[53] The election would then go to the House of Representatives, where southern conservatives would determine the outcome.[54]

The Regulars were less an actual political party than a pet project of the state's wealthy oilmen and their lobbyists, bankers, and lawyers, who had become deluded into thinking that most Texans believed as they did and hated the New Deal as much as they did. They assumed voters just needed a non-Republican, non-FDR ticket to punch, and so they gave it to them; Texas Democrats could remain Democrats and still "vote the New Deal OUT!"[55]

With Cullen and his fellow oilmen paying the bills, the Regulars blitzed the state's newspapers, taking out quarter-page ads, sometimes two per issue, along with constant radio spots and prime-time speeches. They schlepped O'Daniel and his fellow conservative Martin Dies to rallies all over the state and bankrolled the resurrection and mass distribution of the *W. Lee O'Daniel News*. So as to slip around state election finance laws, a front group called the Common Citizens Radio Committee ran the media campaign. Besides precise descriptions of how to vote for the Regular electors and an otherwise straight Democratic ticket, the rest of the messaging was unfiltered right-wing paranoia and promises to restore the southern way of life. The Regulars pledged a "return of state rights which have been destroyed by the communist-controlled New Deal"; "restoration of the supremacy of the white race, which has been destroyed by the Communist-controlled New Deal"; a "restoration of government by laws instead of government by bureaus"; an end to federal efforts to "mix negroes and whites in the South"; protection from "foreign-born racketeers"; and so on. O'Daniel, on the radio and in person (and in print copies of those addresses distributed by the Common Citizens Radio Committee), warned that FDR was more dangerous than Hitler.[56] In one interesting twist, the Regulars offered nice-sized cash incentives to small-town newspaper editors brave enough to write editorials explaining why they would be voting against the New Deal.[57]

The Regulars also invented and introduced two new villains to Texas politics: CIO activist Sidney Hillman and American communist Earl Browder. To hear the Texas Regulars tell it, these two communist agents were secretly running the country in 1944. In reality, Browder was just a figurehead of a tiny and powerless group of American communists and an uninfluential mouthpiece for Joseph Stalin. Hillman, on the other hand, rightly terrified business conservatives. He was a smart, smooth, and tough up-from-the-ranks union man committed to turning the CIO into a powerful political force. An adviser to FDR who worked closely with Labor Secretary Frances Perkins, Hillman believed (correctly, it turned out) that he could leverage union votes into a position of power within the Democratic Party. Forming and leading the CIO's political action committee, the first PAC in the nation, he had millions to spend and a well-organized army of voters and volunteers. Businessmen saw the danger a Democratic-Labor coalition could mean to wages, regulations, and taxes. Southern business leaders feared him even more; Hillman was dedicated to organizing southern workers, Black and white. They saw the CIO as "a fearsome hydra, threatening not only moral corruption and political subversion but the near-unspeakable prospect of race-mixing." Hatred of Hillman within the Party of the Fathers turned the campaign, in the words of historian Stephen Fraser, "into a cathartic outpouring of rage" over every way that the New Deal "offended the pieties and prejudices of Middle America: its gaudy cosmopolitanism, its 'Jewishness,' its flirtations with radicalism, its bureaucratic collectivism, its elevation of the new immigrant, its statism, its intellectual arrogance, and its racial egalitarianism."[58] Accompanying the vitriol was a large dose of anti-Semitism. For his part, Earl Browder, America's best-known communist, was a stand-in for a host of nebulous and half-articulated fears of a poorly understood communist threat and a refusal to distinguish communism from socialism from liberalism.[59]

The campaign intensified over the fall. It was a rare event—in one-party Texas most campaign drama was over after the late spring primaries. But that year the novelty and intensity of the Texas Regulars' campaign, along with the unprecedented attempt by Roosevelt to win a fourth term, lent the campaign great excitement. This was also the first election since the Supreme Court had outlawed the white primary in *Smith v. Allwright*, which injected ugly and overt racism into the campaign.

Pappy was on tour for five weeks, attacking the "communistic and racketeering elements who control the Democratic Party" and claiming that Roosevelt had turned the Democratic Party "into nothing more than a political machine to pass out patronage and perpetuate the New Deal in power." He hoped aloud that southern electors would "not allow Russian-born Sidney Hillman, ex-convict Browder, . . . and the other communistic and racketeering elements who control the Democratic party, to trade off everything the South holds dear for a few CIO votes and a few negro votes in the northern states."[60] The crowds this time, however, were smaller and now sprinkled heavily with hecklers and gawkers. A riot broke out at an O'Daniel rally in Houston a few days before the election, and the senator was chased from the stage and pelted with tomatoes and eggs. (O'Daniel claimed they were communist plants and demanded police protection for the rest of the tour.)

The Texas Regulars lost, of course, but their campaign marked an important step in the development of the right wing in Texas. Almost one in eight voters bought into the idea of trying to throw the election into the House of Representatives. The Republican nominee, Thomas Dewey, scored 17 percent statewide.[61] All in all, almost a third of Texas voters chose someone other than the incumbent president in an election held in wartime. A formidable political force was gathering against Roosevelt's New Deal: wealthy and powerful businesspeople, antilabor zealots, white supremacists, paranoid anticommunists, and conservative ideologues were finding one another and founding a movement.

As for Pappy O'Daniel, his political career was over. By 1948, his standing with voters had plummeted. Even Texas's primitive polling showed he had no chance for reelection that year, so he chose not to run. Lyndon Johnson would go on to defeat the conservative former governor Coke Stevenson in one of the closest and wildest elections in Texas history. Twice more Pappy tried to catch the lightning, running for governor in 1956 and 1958 on the Hell No! segregationist platform that was de rigueur in the South in those years. He finished third both times. During his last campaign, Willie Morris, the hotshot young reporter from the *Texas Observer*, accompanied the candidate on a few campaign stops. One afternoon on the road, O'Daniel entered a café full of cowboys and proudly and loudly introduced himself. One of the cowboys drawled over his coffee cup: "Pappy O'Daniel? I thought he was dead."[62]

IO
RANCHER/SCHOLAR/ REACTIONARY

Then a voice came to him and said, "Why are you here, Elijah?"

He said, "I have been very zealous for the Lord, the God of Armies, but the people of Israel have abandoned your covenant. They have torn down your altars and killed your prophets with the sword. I alone am left, and they are seeking to take my life."

I KINGS 19:13–14

As promised, J. Evetts Haley went back to "punching cows" after the 1936 election. Exiled by academia, the historian headed back into the subhumid prairies where he started a second career as a rancher and ranch manager. He spent a modest advance for a biography of George W. Littlefield on a small spread on the Canadian River near Spearman. He called it the JH. He also got a job managing the Zeebar Ranch in northern Arizona, six hundred miles away. He built stables and herds and spent days in the saddle and nights under the stars and wore out tires and trucks. After he got the Zeebar running right, he was poached by Big Jim West, who put Haley in charge of his massive cattle operations, which stretched from Houston to New Mexico. Haley was a good rancher: thrifty, hardworking, honest, and simple. Into his late fifties, he could still cowboy with men half his age, going days in the saddle on a diet of beans, biscuits, beefsteak, and coffee. He still rode fence, strung wire, and dug postholes. He knew cattle and weather and grass and took enormous pride in the fact that he never took a dime in government subsidies (though he was eligible) and never let his cattle graze on federal grass. In his spare time, Haley researched and wrote two biographies: one of rancher/banker George W. Littlefield and the other on Texas Ranger Jeff Milton.[1]

In 1938, Haley got into the newspaper business with a Spearman ranch neighbor, S. B. Whittenburg, grandson of pioneer rancher J. A. Whittenburg and heir to a massive oil fortune. They bought the *Amarillo Times* and Haley ran the editorial page. For Whittenburg, an ambitious twenty-something, the purchase was his first acquisition of what would become a publishing and broadcasting empire. From the beginning, the *Times* took on a conservative slant; it came out against an antilynching bill in Congress, took on Panhandle congressman Marvin Jones (who Haley thought was walking hand-in-hand down the left side of the road with Rexford Tugwell), railed about the CIO and the liberal Supreme Court, and antagonized the silk-stocking crowd of the Amarillo Establishment. Haley took particular pleasure in mocking Carl Hinton, the puffed-up and publicity-hungry secretary of the Amarillo Chamber of Commerce.[2] The paper's political stance, Haley promised, was "rooted deep" in the region's soil and steadfast in its "devotion to its pioneer traditions of freedom, self-reliance and resourcefulness [and] its ideas of courage, integrity and thrift."[3]

Spending most of his time ranching, Haley drifted in and out of the newspaper for a few months a year, penning the occasional editorial. One of the best was a four-part exposé of the boondoggle of a 1935 Confederate soldier reunion held in Amarillo.[4] But in 1940, when the Board of Regents at the University of Texas sacked its president for refusing to go along with the board's plans to fire faculty for their political beliefs, eliminate tenure, and institute mandatory loyalty oaths for university employees, Haley sprang into action—to defend the regents.

Thanks to appointments by Pappy O'Daniel and his conservative successor Coke Stevenson, by 1940 the UT Board of Regents was dominated by ultraconservative businessmen who were convinced that UT had become a necrotic mass oozing and spewing dangerous and communistic ideas. The regents included Republican Orville Bullington, who thought the university was chock-full of "gutter reds and parlor pinks," and oilman Dan Harrison, who feared the influence of its "unscrupulous, designing, subversive professors." There was Kerrville rancher Scott

Schreiner (long suspected of being one of the forces behind the Texas Regulars) and Judge D. F. Strickland, a corporate attorney and a lobbyist for Texas's biggest antilabor zealot, Dallas movie theater mogul Karl Hoblitzelle.[5] The makeup of this particular board had not happened by chance; rather it was the culmination of a plan hatched years earlier by powerful right-wingers to place conservative businessmen in charge of higher education in Texas with the goal of ridding the state's universities of New Deal sympathizers, liberals, and integrationists.[6]

I

When he accepted the offer to become the university's eighth president in 1939, Homer Rainey must have seemed a godsend. He was a native Texan, an ordained Baptist minister, an alumnus of Austin College, a veteran, and a former star baseball player. He was also considered the most able young higher education administrator in the country. Rainey was only thirty-one when he became president of Franklin College, the youngest college president in the country. Four years later, he was named the president of Bucknell University. He was an innovative administrator who specialized in management and finance and had written important texts on the subject. A staunch faculty advocate, Rainey believed that quality professors were the best measure of the strength of a college. And those were dark times at UT: the school was having a hard time recruiting academic talent, the war had drastically reduced the student population, and the football team was terrible.[7]

UT's regents had specific plans for Rainey. At its first meeting, the board handed its new president a list of faculty to fire. Shocked, Rainey refused. The relationship went downhill from there. For the next five years the regents tortured Rainey with half-thought-out and unreasonable demands largely predicated on their conviction that UT had become a safe harbor for communists: They wanted to dismiss professors for their political beliefs and get rid of tenure. They launched petty assaults and spiteful intrusions—demoting Rainey's staff, refusing outside funding, meddling in committees, and hauling professors before them to explain why certain books were on course reading lists.[8] The board invited Texas congressman Martin Dies, the head of the House Committee on Un-American Activities to investigate rumors of one thousand communists on campus (he found nothing) and the Texas Department of Public Safety to look into a possible ring of homosexuals on campus (it found nothing). Demands to remove certain faculty regularly appeared in Rainey's in-box for such apostasy as challenging the wisdom of the sales tax, ruling in a committee that nineteen-year-olds couldn't play high school football, or supporting the forty-hour work week.

By 1943, the regents' outrageous behavior had drawn the ire of J. Frank Dobie, Texas's most beloved academic, who had, until then, supported the board. He warned that this group of "millionaires and corporation lawyers, Roosevelt-haters and new-style fascists" were leading UT "to the status of fascist controlled institutions of learning and farther away from the democratic ideal of free and inquiring minds."[9] If the regents continued their behavior, he wrote in a widely reprinted editorial, UT would no longer produce free thinkers and go-getters, but only "belly-crawling imitations of men."[10]

Rainey's patience finally ran out in 1944 when he was forced to fend off board-inspired rumors that he was a secret integrationist and that his nineteen-year-old daughter was clandestinely living with a Black communist. He called the faculty to a special meeting and presented a report that charged the Board of Regents with sixteen counts of interfering with academic freedom. The professors gave Rainey a ten-minute ovation and their unanimous support.[11] Two weeks later, the Regents, with a single dissenting vote, fired the president. Students revolted; eight thousand marched in silence to the Governor's Mansion, where they held a funeral for academic freedom. Then they went on strike. Damage done, three Regents resigned.

Rainey's firing was national page-one news. The *Washington Post* called it a "symptom of a dangerous tendency . . . to make teaching conform to the prejudices and narrow purposes of the economically dominant elements in our society."[12] *Harper's* mocked the regents for their ridiculous conspiracy theories. The Association of American Colleges demanded that Governor Coke Stevenson dismiss the regents. The Southern Association of Colleges and Secondary Schools put UT on probation. The American Association of University Professors (AAUP) demanded Rainey's immediate reinstatement. With headshaking disbelief, the organization could not understand how the regents of a major university could think that their role was that of a "private employer" without "any moral restrictions" from foisting their own prejudices and political views on education and from using their power "to gratify their private antipathies and resentments."[13]

The regents couldn't understand the fuss. In the real world, there were bosses and there were employees, and bosses had the right to fire any employee, particularly one guilty of gross public insubordination. They scoffed at the threat of an AAUP blacklist (which would mean no serious scholar would take a job at UT) and bragged that they would field a first-class faculty with homegrown, Texas-proud scholars. Academic freedom meant nothing. If an economics professor, one regent suggested, "did not think that the sit down strike the most damnable thing in American life, he didn't deserve a place on the University's faculty."[14] When their employer-employee argument failed to quell the uproar, regents hinted that something more sinister was behind Rainey's dismissal. Bullington said the president had been fired for protecting "a nest of homosexuals" guilty of an "unspeakable and unmentionable social crime."[15]

Evetts Haley ran to their defense in an eight-part series that appeared in newspapers across Texas. (He would bundle the editorials together in a pamphlet, *The University of Texas and the Issue*.) It was an important piece of writing for Haley, the first of a significant set of documents he would produce over the next fifteen years that helped define the cowboy conservatism of West Texas.[16] First, he suggested that the proper governing structure of a university should mirror that of a corporation, with a president serving to execute the will and wisdom of the Board of Regents. Second, he argued that the mission of higher education should be one of indoctrination (particularly to American and Texas values) and functionality. Third, in his exoneration of UT's regents for their decision to fire Rainey, Haley put forth a unique theory about their role in the Texas political structure. Since the regents were named by the governor and approved by the state senate, they were—by law, tradition, and logic—public servants faithfully tending to the will of Texans. And, as their employee, Rainey served at their pleasure. The firing was a nonissue. The regents were just fulfilling their duty. It was a logical-sounding premise and one that would appear (slightly amended) a few years later in William F. Buckley's *God and Man at Yale*, the book that launched his long-running career as the dean of conservative intellectuals.[17]

But, in strange quirks that appear in Haley's writings in these years—and that would become commonplace in right-wing rhetoric—

we see the historian-turned-activist push past straightforward inter-pretations and explanations into the realm of the ridiculous, vicious, and paranoid. Consider for example his logic-defying counter to one of the more serious (and true) charges lodged against the regents, that they had met secretly in 1940 and plotted to rein in Rainey and bring all state universities under tighter control—a meeting that one regent had already admitted to having attended. Haley concluded that since he could find no direct evidence of the meeting and since there were conflicting stories about it, the meeting must not have happened. And there's the constant character assassination. With careful use of passive voice and other clever linguistic techniques, Haley barely skirts libel as he portrays Rainey as an unscrupulous, power-mad liar and autocrat heading an organized and well-financed conspiracy to take over the University of Texas on behalf of a cabal of liberal professors and outside agitators.[18]

The big takeaway of Haley's defense of the regents is his elucida-tion of the purpose of education, especially higher education, an inter-pretation that would become a centerpiece of his right-wing ideology. For Haley, a school's first obligation is to instill patriotic American and Texas values in young people. Any educator teaching ideas that stood in opposition to those values should be fired. Since public schools, includ-ing universities, were paid for by the people of Texas, those schools had a public duty to teach only what Texans wanted their children to learn. Academic freedom, for Haley, represented an existential threat to a moral democracy. And tenure, particularly when used to protect faculty from reprisals for the expression or exploration of alternative ideas, was an affront, impossible for the "average Texan, who has a tradition and an almost congenital conviction that each man should be able to fight his battles alone," to understand. Tenure's only purpose was to shield eggheaded intellectuals who lacked the "aggressive, the individualistic, and the independent nature of man." The perversions of tenure and aca-demic freedom, he argued, had led the state's flagship university into an impractical boondoggle where the "narrow interest[s]" of faculty could thrive "lustily in the cloistered pursuit of a literary ideal or the obser-vance of the antics of the atom."[19] The whole system, he concluded, was a sham.

II

In 1950, the Harte-Hanks newspapers, a conservative outlet with major papers around the state, invited Haley to become a syndicated columnist. He lasted a year. But in those columns, which he called *Texas Tory Talk*, he further articulated his cowboy conservatism and began to attract a following. As had become his calling card by then, Haley drew on his career punching cattle *and* his historical expertise on the Texas frontier to lay out a political ideology framed by frontier mythology and Texas history.

In his introductory column, he established his bona fides: "I am a cowpuncher. And while I may have taken my degree from a man-made institution, my elementary training and my post-graduate work in what constitutes the enduring lessons of life were taken from nature—on the ranges of grass—where no creature man or beast, can escape the effects of his folly."[20] He wasn't just "putting on the hat" as the expression would later go. Haley's reputation as a rancher preceded him: he was one of the best in Texas. And let's not forget the cultural power and authority that cowboys enjoyed in the 1950s, when Westerns dominated the movie theaters and the drugstore bookshelves. Tough, authentic, straight-shooting cowboys like Haley were the protagonists of almost all of them.

Haley looked and dressed the part. His dark and sun-creased face often broke into a wide, white grin. He was lean and muscular and moved with grace. He stood five feet, eleven inches, or a little taller in his cowboy boots, which he always wore (along with a Stetson). It was boots, jeans, and a cotton snap-button shirt when he was working, and nicer boots, a suit, and tie when doing business or giving talks. He had a habit of tipping his hat way back on his head, making him look friendly and open. With his resonant and deep West Texas drawl, when Haley spoke about self-reliance, honesty, thrift, and courage, he looked and sounded like a character in a John Ford Western.

He was among the best-known historians in the state and *the* authority on the West Texas cattle frontier. His books on Charles Goodnight, the XIT Ranch, Jeff Milton, and George Littlefield sold tens of thousands of copies. No Texana library is complete without them. He wrote scores of historical articles for both academic and popular audiences and was a regular contributor to the *Southwest Review* and the *Southwestern Historical Quarterly*. He was the editor of and a prolific essayist in the *Panhandle-Plains Historical Review*. He had three entries in the prestigious *Dictionary of American Biography*. He produced over two dozen articles for the *Cattleman*, the official magazine of Texas's largest stock-raising organization and published work on brands, trails, and cowboys for Haliburton's company magazine, the *Cementer*. He was the house historian for the Shamrock Oil and Gas Company, and his annual Christmas story was the highlight of its corporate magazine. He spoke regularly to all manner of civic organizations and study groups. A gifted raconteur, he could keep a crowd spellbound for hours. When Haley claimed to speak for frontier Texans and on behalf of their values, people listened.

It was clear that Texans were ready to hear his message. These were years of a full-blown Red Scare in the state. In Houston, the local Minutewomen group turned every PTA election and school board election into a fight to save the country from the clutches of communism, the city school system rejected federal aid that would have helped feed the city's poorest children, and city government refused to enact zoning laws because they saw them as part of the larger communist conspiracy. These were the years when a Texas governor sent a bill to the Dome that would make being a member of the Communist Party a capital offense. (The final bill just made it a felony punishable by a twenty-year stretch.) These were the years when the legislature passed some of the strictest antilabor legislation in the country, much of written by Vance Muse. Anticommunism became the lingua franca of Texas's booster class, especially when it came to taxes, regulation, and labor.[21] The "Big Rich," whose remarkable fortunes were built on oil, considered any threat to the 27.5 percent oil depletion allowance, the greatest tax break in the history of American finance, as a communist plot against the country's energy producers. They were joined by the "Little Rich," who, "swept by their emotions of fear and insecurity see in every school board contest, in every independent candidate who repudiates their leadership, the hand of Moscow or the CIO bent on destroying Texas institutions."[22] The national leader of the 1950s Red Scare, Senator Joe McCarthy, was a state hero who spent so much time being feted over and ferried about (in private planes) by Texas oilmen that he was called Texas's third senator.[23]

During his year with Harte-Hanks, Evetts Haley laid out the right wing's take on the contemporary political scene.[24] Picking right up from

J. Evetts Haley.

his days as a propagandist for the Jeffersonian Democrats, he held that the New Deal had dealt an almost mortal blow to democracy and free enterprise and that the nation's only chance at survival was an immediate return to a pre-1933 world order: small and locally focused government devoted to protecting individual freedom. White supremacy was the basis of society. Isolationism the foundation of foreign policy. And free enterprise the natural state of the economy. Politicians were not to be trusted. Education must focus on the basics: reading, writing, arithmetic, and instilling love of country. Modern art, income taxes, regulation, and liberalism were aberrations and likely stalking horses for communism. His tenor was apocalyptic, and his preferred format was the jeremiad. Adopting a tone that the far right has since embraced with zeal, Haley found room in every essay, no matter the form, for snarky and snide asides on contemporary issues or taunts of public officials. Paranoia and conspiratorial thinking were a constant.

What had made the New Deal so damaging to American society, Haley believed, was that it had embraced unproven and unrealistic theories of governance espoused by foolish eggheads who had completely rejected natural law. Usually associated with Thomas Aquinas, natural law advances the idea that God imbued humanity with a set of standards and values that made humans rational creatures, set apart from animals. Humans could, through study and observation, learn the laws that governed nature and build their world accordingly. Since natural law was eternal and divined by God, any "positive law" created by man, political or otherwise, that ran counter to its strictures and structures was counterfeit, irrational, and immoral. A sin. And for Haley, America was very much in violation of natural law. "The catalogue of our transgressions against the moral nature of man should move us to eternal penance," he said in a Christmas column, and "the rectification of certain major ones are absolutely essential to our survival."[25]

For Haley, devastating tragedies like the Great Depression or Dust Bowl were no excuse to change the structure and purpose of government, because they were part of the natural order, part of God's "chastening and cleansing process."[26] Irrigating the dry plains, rather than a miracle technology, violated a natural world in which God determines where and when rain falls. Programs meant to help struggling farmers ran "counter to the all-pervasive laws of nature."[27] Any attempt to regulate a market, an industry, or an economy was a direct violation of the primacy of supply and demand, the only moral economic system. Any American who still retained "a speaking acquaintance with natural law," Haley promised, could speak to the dangers of economic controls.[28] The "standard for all men" was the pioneer ranchers, the priests and prophets of natural law, men whose daily lives were governed by the strictures of a stingy western landscape, men who dealt in seasons and beasts and distance and death.[29]

Although raised a Methodist, Haley's religious beliefs were more regional than denominational. His was a folk religion, one that had been practiced on the Texas frontier for a century and on the southern frontier for two centuries before that. It was a form of Christian humanism practically defined by its rabid individualism. For Haley, Jesus Christ was a maverick, and the Sea of Galilee the place where the "tenets of individual freedom" sprang to life "to brighten the whole world with the concept that every man was possessed of an inviolable personal nature— that he was, in truth, the master of his own soul." It was on the Texas frontier, another harsh and bitter desert culture, where, Haley believed, this Christian philosophy had reached its apogee. Only on a landscape this cruel and sparse (and unsaid but certainly implied, without the arti-

fice of organized religion) could Christians understand the demands of
Old Testament God and the promise of New Testament Jesus.[30]

The discovery of the law of supply and demand was, for Haley, one
of mankind's greatest applications of natural law because it eliminated
the need for man-made systems to govern markets: "When this natural flow of forces usually known as the law of supply and demand has
relatively free sway, and genuinely patriotic men intent on serving the
country are in power, there is little need for government except in the
role of an impartial umpire going by the rules of fair play." Only self-
ish miscreants would have the temerity to interfere with such a perfect
system.[31] Everywhere he glanced in the modern economy, he saw the
work of these degenerates: inflation, cheap credit and price controls;
aberrations endorsed by fools and ne'er-do-wells.[32] Governmental planning and farm programs were foolhardy gambits, the tools of totalitarian
regimes and wannabe despots to create machines to keep them in power.
He railed against farm programs, child labor laws, civil rights, college
professors, credit manipulation, commodity regulation, progressive education, social science, and one-worldism, and the list went on.

The natural state of foreign affairs, Haley explained, was isolationism. While clearly fearful of an aggressive Soviet Union, the historian/
philosopher had no use for the nation's growing entanglements around
the world. He constantly criticized the Marshall Plan, the North Atlantic
Treaty Organization (NATO), the United Nations ("it is time to pitch
this diplomatic travesty into the East River"), and the war in Korea.[33]
He viewed U.S. involvement in the two world wars as "tragic" and likely
avoidable "fatuous crusades for 'peace and democracy.'"[34] He was convinced that the United States was losing the Cold War and would continue to do so as long as Harry S. Truman and his Secretary of State,
Dean Acheson, were running things.[35] If he had his way, Haley would
place General Douglas MacArthur in charge of both American foreign
policy and the military and rid government of the "mental aberration
known as one world."[36] Instead, he urged an American hemispheric
retreat, along with a massive buildup of defensive power, particularly air
power. Let the rest of the world fend for itself. The last "Texas Tory Talk"
ran in July 1951.

Fifteen years after leaving the University of Texas and going to work
for John Kirby and the Jeffersonian Democrats, J. Evetts Haley was the
most important conservative voice in Texas, "the Thomas Paine of the

Southwest." His audiences were eager to hear his thoughts on politics and not just about the Old Ways. In fall 1951, he gave one of his most important talks, the keynote address at the regional meeting of the American Natural Gas Association. Speaking to four hundred oil and gas executives at Amarillo's Herring Hotel Ballroom, Haley titled his speech "Patriotism in Our Hour of Decision." For over eighty minutes, to near-constant ovations, Haley blasted the "perverted Supreme Court," excoriated foreign aid and inflationary monetary policies, warned of the "avaricious, creeping power of government," and pushed for his form of Cold War isolationism. He saved his most biting criticism for a public education system that no longer instilled a love of country or inspired students "with the tales of men of honor and of derring-do, who, in peaceful service and mortal conflict, went down with the poignant regret that they had but one life to offer to their country."[37] A few weeks later, Haley was offered a chance to launch his own think tank at Texas Tech—the Institute of Americanism.

III

The Institute was the idea of an ultraconservative Lubbock banker named Charles E. Maedgen.[38] Almost seventy, Maedgen was one of the most powerful and wealthy men in West Texas. His Lubbock National Bank, which he had founded in 1917, had grown with the city and was now one of the largest banks in the state. Lubbock's leading booster and developer, Maedgen had also founded the city's chamber of commerce, its Kiwanis Club, its symphony orchestra, and its country club. He built its first skyscraper. He was a Methodist and a Mason and sat on the committees that brought Texas Tech, the Fort Worth and Denver Railway, and paved roads to the city. Turning over the day-to-day operations of his banking and real estate (and cotton and oil) empire over to his son in 1951, Maedgen set out to devote his retirement to philanthropy. The Institute of Americanism was going to be his first big project—a way for him to inculcate Americanism and American values into students and the community. The old banker was quite clear as to what those values were: property rights, moral government, freedom of religion, constitutionalism, thrift, and individualism.[39]

Helping Maedgen bring his vision to life was his old friend and fellow ultraconservative Clifford B. Jones, "West Texas's #1 Citizen," the man as responsible as anyone for Texas Tech's existence and who, over the years, had grown convinced that the communist takeover of the country was imminent. Also lending a hand was the chair of Tech's history department and director of its historical museum, W. C. Holden, who believed the shocking lack of understanding of American history among young people was responsible for permitting the "traditional American way of life to be destroyed by socialistic forces."[40]

Maedgen was highly influenced by the work of George S. Benson, an instrumental figure of the radical right in those years. As president of tiny Harding College in Searcy, Arkansas, Benson had created the school's National Education Program (NEP), the most productive and prolific distributor of right-wing (particularly pro-business) propaganda in the country. Along with its wildly popular Disney-quality animated shorts that cheered unrestrained capitalism, the NEP also sponsored regular speaking events and forums, sent out a monthly newsletter to almost fifty thousand subscribers, contributed a Benson-penned column to four thousand newspapers, and produced dozens of serious-looking black-and-white filmstrips where solemn men in dark suits and somber haircuts sat on desks and talked straight about the dangers of communism. As he was thinking about his plans, Maedgen, along with Tech president Dossie Wiggins, took the train to Searcy and spent a day with Benson and the NEP's executive director. Beyond impressed, they came back to Lubbock excited to do it all: a film and speakers bureau, an endowed professorship, maybe a new academic department. Eventually, they decided that they would first build an institute, financed by Maedgen but located on campus.[41] Maedgen set up a $20,000 annual budget in a special account at his bank. He and his cofounders sent out a few feelers for a director.[42] By May they had settled on Evetts Haley; the job description, after all, read: "Distinguished Professor, well-recognized for his complete loyalty to the United States of America and to the concepts of government and individual rectitude."[43] Evetts Haley was going back into academia.

The rancher/philosopher/historian had lots of ideas on how to spend Maedgen's money and promote his politics: new radio and television programs, a publishing house and speakers bureau, regular forums on campus. His keystone project, however, was going to be changing Tech's curricular requirements so that every student would have to take two

Haley-designed American history courses—classes that would promote the "Jeffersonian tradition, the development of free enterprise, individual initiative and the American tradition, respect for the Constitution."[44]

Of course, on his first day on campus, Haley called a press conference. Like a cowboy Cincinnatus, he told reporters that he was still just a rancher but agreed to come back into the world of higher education so that he could serve the young people of West Texas by teaching them American values before they were exposed to "subversive influences."[45] When asked if the Institute of Americanism was not little more than a propaganda center for the extreme right wing, Haley exploded: "If expounding principles of Americanism is propaganda, then this is propaganda."[46] Haley's $10,000-a-year salary was more than that of any other professor on campus. He had $7,000 in an Institute bank account, a suite of offices, and a full-time secretary.[47]

Over the next several weeks Haley promoted the Institute in speeches to every civic club that would put him on its schedule: the Lubbock Exchange Club ("our confusion results from the loss of faith in our institutions and ideals"), the Kiwanis Club, the Real Estate Board, the Daughters of the American Revolution, the League of Women Voters, the American Association of University Women, the Cottonseed Crushers, the Lubbock Optimist Club ("no amount of legislation can make the system of paying to cut production morally right"), the American Business Club, Tech sororities, the Junior League, and the Lubbock Women's Clubhouse.[48]

The highlight of his fall promotional tour was the keynote address at the annual meeting of the West Texas Chamber of Commerce: "Americanism without Apology." By the early 1950s, the WTCC was the largest organization of its kind in the country. It was Texas's most powerful lobbying organization, representing the state's biggest industries: oil and gas, cattle, carbon black, media, helium, wheat, banking, cotton, and railroads, as well as the merchant/professional classes of half a dozen of Texas's fastest-growing cities and hundreds of thriving small towns. Its efforts toward railroad regulation, reclamation projects, public investment in irrigation and roads (especially farm-to-market roads), and the privatization of Texas's remaining public lands, along with its work against oil taxes and utility regulation, were instrumental in the remarkable transformation of postwar West Texas.

As they gathered in Wichita Falls in mid-October, the region's boosters were in crisis mode. West Texas was suffering from its worst drought since the 1930s. Two themes dominated the weekend's discussions: conserving water and preventing another round of federal intervention.[49] Across committee meetings and speeches, business leaders spoke of the need for Texans to solve their own problems and avoid another New Deal. Vivid nightmarish descriptions of federal control contrasted with heartwarming stories about how places like Big Spring had tackled the drought with box lunch fundraisers and community elbow grease.[50] Los Angeles minister James W. Fifield Jr., the "Apostle to Millionaires," opened for Haley.[51] The founder of the prosperity gospel and an emerging figure on the religious right, Fifield stalked the stage and thundered from the lectern. The United Nations was an "instrument of evil." Democrats were destroying American morals. The nation was on the brink of collectivization and would soon be "Sovietized." The crowd loved it, leaping to its feet in spontaneous applause throughout the sermon and giving Fifield a lasting and standing ovation at its close.

Then came Haley. More than three hundred West Texas businessmen pressed closer to the stage in the Kemp Hotel Ballroom on an unseasonably warm afternoon to hear him. He was the historian they loved, the political philosopher they read, and a personality they knew. Everyone in the room had heard him speak at least once. He was there on a mission: "Americanism without Apology." Eighteen months of weekly political commentary had sharpened his message, and the new Institute of Americanism gave him a cause. Haley was there, he told the men who ran West Texas, to lay out an uncomfortable truth: the greatest danger to the United States was neither China nor the Soviet Union but American liberals. Internal subversion, he warned, was rotting America from the inside. By this point in his ideological development, Haley functioned in a binary world; his brand of aggressive Americanism was one option and everything else was just some form of communism. A fuzzy-minded liberal was just as big a problem as a devoted apostle of Karl Marx. The hour was late, he told them: everywhere you could hear the loud and "dangerous pulse of a bankrupt, hopeless and near chaotic world." There was but one solution, a national recommitment to rugged individualism and the immediate recognition of a few incontrovertible facts: liberalism was evil and would end in communism; government power always came only at the expense of individual freedom; the current government was corrupt and stayed in power only through propaganda and bribery; taxation was robbery; and government bureaucracy was eroding moral character.[52] It was one of Haley's shorter speeches, about twenty minutes, a focused and disciplined paragraph-by-paragraph outline of his right-wing vision and the dangers he saw confronting the nation. The boosters loved it; a pamphlet reprint of the speech can be found in archives and file cabinets across West Texas. They would rely on Haley's arguments and points for years.[53]

Showing remarkable self-discipline, Haley managed to wait until his second semester at Tech before he started tossing bombs across campus. By spring commencement, though, he had alienated Tech's new president E. N. Jones and most of the faculty, who saw him, as W. C. Holden remembered, as "sort of a fascist or a Nazi or something."[54] Haley didn't care. He wanted nothing to do with the bureaucracy of Tech; when Jones suggested a faculty advisory committee to help guide the work of the Institute, Haley rejected the notion out of hand; committees, he suggested, were antithetical to the Institute's entire philosophy. Haley's obvious isolation at Tech began to worry Maedgen, who had envisioned a much closer relationship. But it was Haley's survey of administrative and programming bloat at Tech that drove the first major wedge between the director and the administration.

Shortly after the start of the spring semester, Haley, convinced that higher education was rife with academic overlap, mission drift, and boondoggling, drafted a five-question survey requesting faculty's "frank appraisal" of redundancies and overextended departments or programs and mailed it to every faculty mailbox in Texas. The header, in sixteen-point boldface italics, read: "At the request of the Governor of Texas." (There was no request.) Haley asked the state's university faculty for their suggestions as to which programs or departments in their institution could be eliminated without harming the educational mission. He also solicited opinions on academic trends that might be a deviation from "sound educational policy."[55] Haley hadn't told anyone at Tech about the survey. Not even the new president, E. N. Jones, who spent weeks fielding angry and confused phone calls, telegrams, and letters from Tech faculty and college administrators from across Texas, asking just what the hell was the Institute for Americanism and why was it sending out such a "loaded" survey.[56] Jones, furious with Haley, ordered him to personally write to every college president and explain that his survey did not have the approval of Texas Tech. Haley complied and skipped town before commencement.[57] A confused Maedgen demanded to know what was happening with his Institute of Americanism. Jones told him that Haley seemed not to be interested in establishing a "cooperative working relationship" with Tech.[58] The next year, it got worse.

Laid up with a bum knee for several weeks in fall 1953, Haley launched his next big project, a weekly speakers series in which the Institute invited wealthy businessmen/history buffs to give public talks on their area of expertise or interest. The presentations were mostly a heady blend of right-wing politics and skewed historical interpretations. The speakers, as Haley promised in his introduction to the first event, "are being drawn from the top ranks of American life . . . men of large affairs and heavy responsibilities [who] are saddled with the intricate problems that these troublous and dangerous days ruthlessly impose upon those who carry the burdens of management, of property and of business."[59] Palmer Bradley, an oil lawyer and airline executive, went first and spoke on the horrors of federal control in Reconstruction Texas. Jeffersonian Democrat founder and cotton mogul Lamar Fleming gave a history of the cotton business and concluded his remarks with hope that future entrepreneurs could live in a world where the fruits of their labor weren't stripped from them to "finance political extravagance or egalitarian theories designed to reduce the industrious and frugal to the levels of the indolent and improvident."[60] WTCC president and railroad executive Wright Armstrong finished off a searingly dull history of track gauge and locomotive technology with a rant against the federal government, the trucking industry, and the expanded highway system.[61] Edgar E. Townes, the oil lawyer, vice-president of Humble Oil (now Exxon), and founder of the ultraconservative Americans for Constitutional Government, spoke on the chilling threats to individual freedom that had defined the Progressive Movement. Haley, noticeably, kept politics out of his informed, interesting, and restrained history of cattle drives.

At the series' halfway mark, audiences got a break from the cavalcade of right-wing millionaires spinning out their versions of the American past when Pulitzer Prize–winning historian Allan Nevins took the stage to preview his forthcoming book on the early days of the Ford Motor Company.[62] Nevins was followed by former women's suffrage leader and nationally syndicated columnist Lucia Loomis (Mrs. Walter) Ferguson, whose appearance was cosponsored by the Panhellenic Council. To an audience made up primarily of Tech sorority members, Loomis, with great wit, veered, from topic to topic: America's "committee civilization," fad diets, communists on college campuses, women who spend too much time at the beauty salon, misbehaving children, permissive parents, materialism, unseemly doting grandparents, divorce (a woman's responsibility to prevent), and the power and responsibility of the press. She also offered her opinion on what modern women really needed: "a masterful person around, one who puts his fist down and says: 'This is the way things should be.'" The evening was dedicated to Julia Evetts Haley (Evetts's mother), a former member (and an excellent one by all accounts) of the Tech Board of Directors.[63]

Then came the big guns: General Bonner Fellers, Frazier Hunt, and Clarence Manion. Reflective of Haley's growing stature in the conservative movement, these were three of the most important right-wing activists in the country whom Haley hoped to bundle together in a three-day saturnalia of ultraconservatism—something he called "The Grass Roots of Liberty Forum." Fellers, a lifelong military intelligence specialist officer whose specialty was psychological warfare, had been Douglas MacArthur's right-hand man and was as responsible as anyone for the emerging right-wing narrative on Asia. Frazier Hunt was a longtime *Chicago Tribune* reporter who also wrote popular histories of the American West. He had just finished a conspiracy-laden, anticommunist bluster of a biography of MacArthur, *The Untold Story of Douglas MacArthur*, a text that would become part of the far-right canon.[64] Rounding out the forum would be Clarence Manion, former dean of the University of Notre Dame law school, who had made national headlines earlier in the year when he was fired from his position as head of the Intergovernmental Relations Committee by President Eisenhower for his outspoken support of the anti-internationalist Bricker Amendment. He and Robert Wood, the former head of Sears, Roebuck and publisher of the *Chicago Tribune*, were in the late stages of founding the Manion Forum, America's first nationally syndicated right-wing radio program, and a new national political organization, For America, that promised "enlightened nationalism."[65]

By the time the Liberty Forum rolled into Lubbock, interest in the series among faculty and students, never strong to begin with, had dropped to zero. The Institute moved the program to the Slaton Jr. High Auditorium a couple of miles south of campus. It was all locals who heard Manion lay out his fanciful vision of America's doomed future when Washington would seize private land and property and liberal Democrats would install a dictatorship to manage the affairs of government. He left his audience with a new definition of communism—'concentrated, unlimited governmental power."[66] Frazier Hunt cataloged U.S. Cold War foreign policy failures—Alger Hiss's betrayal at Yalta, the loss of China and Korea, joining the United Nations—as parts of a grand plan to create a one-world government. He heaped praise on Douglas MacArthur and claimed that the general had been removed by "internationalists in the State Department" who were more loyal to the UN than the USA. He accused FDR of trapping Japan into attacking Pearl Harbor and described the late 1930s as a "low and dastardly page of American history." There could be hope for the future, Hunt said, only if we "re-Americanize our country and make its freedom real again."[67] Bonner Fellers closed out the event the following week with two addresses, focusing on American foreign policy failures and advocating a brand of Cold War isolationism dependent on a massively superior air power (another fixation of the right in those years): "If we wish to win without slaughter of our youth, we must have an Air Force that can provide supremacy and security." He warned that an essential part of Soviet strategy was to weaken the United States by luring it into expensive and unwinnable proxy wars in Asia.[68]

The Grass Roots of Liberty Forum was the Institute of Americanism's one and only success. An attempt to create a six-semester-hour requirement of Haley-designed Americanism classes got diluted over the summer of 1954 into a two-course requirement in "American Heritage" that would draw on courses already taught by the history and government departments and with a curriculum guided by a committee.[69] Although named to the committee, Haley never attended a single meeting. Instead, he took a leave of absence and tended to his ranches. The Institute of Americanism became little more than a sign on a door, empty offices, a bored secretary, and boxes of "Americanism without Apology" pamphlets. Haley resigned at the end of January 1955.[70] Maedgen pulled his funding from Tech the next month, set up a new Institute of Americanism at McMurry College (where he was a trustee), but spent most of his attention and fortune on his latest enterprise, the Texas Bureau of Economic Understanding, which created programming to teach Americanism in the public schools. Those programs lasted well into the 1990s.[71]

J. Evetts Haley takes Clarence Manion shopping for cowboy boots at Lubbock's famous Lusk's Boot Shop.

IV

Two weeks to the day after Haley resigned as director of the Institute of Americanism, Governor Allan Shivers named him to Texas Tech's Board of Directors. President E. N. Jones now reported to Haley. Shivers also appointed ultraconservatives Tom Lineberry, a wealthy rancher/oilman from Kermit, and Douglas Orme, who ran the massive Cosden oil refinery in Big Spring. The board, already dominated by right-wing businessmen, became easily the most reactionary group of trustees of any college or university in the country.[72] With Haley as the exception, not a single member had any experience in higher education administration. Within three years of Haley's joining the board, Texas Tech faced censure by the American Association of University Professors and was in danger of losing its accreditation.

To a man, this new board understood the structure of higher education administration and management exactly as Haley had laid it out a decade earlier in his *University of Texas and the Issue*. The Board of Directors ran Texas Tech on behalf of the people of Texas and its administration, and faculty worked for the board. They did not believe in academic freedom or tenure, which they considered alien, probably socialistic notions.[73] Once on the board, Haley pushed it to get involved at a more granular level of supervision, particularly in efforts to protect the school from integration and communism. Soon the board was secretly investigating and building files on individual faculty. Haley feuded publicly with President Jones and privately undermined his authority.

Everything blew up in July 1957. At that summer's board meeting, the directors went into executive session, ushered President Jones from the room, and a short while later announced that they had voted to fire two professors (one of whom was tenured) and terminate the adult education program run by a third. There had been no warning. Asked to explain the firings, Haley offered only that the professors "do not measure up to the high intellectual and academic standards" of Texas Tech.[74]

Herbert Greenberg, a psychology professor recently recommended for a promotion and salary increase, was an expert in segregation. Blind, Greenberg had built his academic career by studying the psychological dangers of segregating the sighted from the visually impaired. He had recently expanded his intellectual interests to include studies of racial segregation. At the time, he was conducting research into Texas high schoolers' attitudes toward integration (work cited later in this book). He also publicly supported the Supreme Court's decision in *Brown v. Board of Education*.[75] Per Stensland ran Tech's adult education program with funding from the Ford Foundation. Offering up educational opportunities for adults in small towns, it was a national model for university outreach. Haley called it "plush, academic boondoggling." Byron R. Abernethy, a tenured professor of government who had been at Tech for fifteen years, was a well-known advocate for organized labor and a recognized leader of the Democrats of Texas, the liberal wing of the state party.[76] He had also once spoken favorably of *Brown* in a classroom lecture.

The dismissals were national news. Everyone in Texas assumed the men had been fired for their political views. Haley didn't care: "As both a former college faculty member [which he never really was] and as a broken-down cowhand [he was a successful rancher] I'm for academic freedom. I'm also for the academic freedom of the board of regents to hire and fire. The right to fire is just as fundamental a freedom as to hire.

If the board is denied the right to fire, who is going to run the school? As far as I'm concerned, those three men are fired—and that's that."[77]

Abernethy and Greenberg found out they had been fired when newspaper reporters showed up on their doorsteps asking for a reaction. One was hosting a dinner party. Neither could believe it. The state's press, even conservative outlets like the *Dallas Morning News* and the *Fort Worth Star Telegram*, condemned the firings. In Tulia, the renowned liberal newspaperman H. M. Baggarly jeered Tech. Haley, a noted "political crackpot," he said, had no business "on the Board of Regents of any college."[78] Tech students rallied around the fired faculty and passed around petitions. The Faculty Advisory Committee denounced the board's secrecy and its denial of "basic American principles of justice." More than three hundred faculty members met and unanimously passed a resolution that condemned the board for "destroying" the morale of the students and professors, violating "freedom of thought," and putting Tech's accreditation in jeopardy. Abernethy and Greenberg pleaded for a hearing. The board, by a vote of 8–1 refused. Haley was the lone dissenter: "I think the Board should see these men."[79]

Board chair Winfield D. "Windy" Watkins, a cotton oil executive from Abilene, met with Abernethy and Greenberg in private and accidentally revealed that the board had files on each of the men, including, somehow, Abernethy's income tax returns. Defending the firings, Watkins simply read letters of support for the board like the one from a Tech alum who demanded that the college reject all federal grants and monies, kick the Ford Foundation off campus, and fire President Jones because he had once spoken in favor of the United Nations to an integrated audience.[80] Herbert Greenberg left his meeting gobsmacked, telling the press, "I am prepared to swear under oath that at no time during the meeting was I given one single charge against me. . . . I walked out of the meeting as completely in the dark as to the reasons for my firing as I was when the meeting began."[81]

Under pressure, the board at its next meeting buckled and began measures to implement new policies regarding tenure and executive sessions. Haley threw a fit and demanded that the state legislature meet and decide once and for all "whether or not any college employee has a vested right in a job" and whether the state's great universities were going to become nothing more than "sounding boards for radical elements everywhere."[82] His motion did not receive a second. From there, his influence waned, until he and Lineberry became little more than a two-person voting bloc, wanly voting "no" until they cycled off the board in 1961, the year Tech integrated its campus.

After leaving Texas Tech, Byron Abernethy went on to a brilliant career as an arbitrator and helped found the National Association of Arbitrators. Per Stensland became one of the world's great experts in adult education, consulting for the World Health Organization, the World Bank, and the Kellogg Foundation. He became the president of the Milbank Fund in 1967. Herbert Greenberg landed a job at Rutgers after leaving Texas Tech and eventually founded Caliper, a global management consulting firm that offered companies psychological assessment programs to evaluate potential employees. He wrote several massively influential books on corporate hiring. In 2015, McGraw-Hill published a biography of Greenberg that focused on his eighteen principles of business.

V

In 1956, Haley decided to run for governor. On a plane back to Texas after a weekend schmoozing with national right-wing luminaries at the inaugural "For America" rally at Carnegie Hall, where he had been named head of the Texas branch of the organization, he sketched out a platform. Like a lot of southern politicians that year, he planned to run on a white-supremacy platform and make the Supreme Court and its *Brown v. Board of Education* decision his main issue. He would be the candidate for those who wanted to save school segregation and prevent the "spiritual degradation" and "biological decline" of white Texas.[83] Over a half-hour layover in Austin while he waited for the train to Canyon, Haley dialed up newspapers and read a press release announcing his run. They were the first to hear it. He had made no mention of running for governor to his political allies, to the members of the Randall County Democratic Party, or even to Governor Allan Shivers, his longtime political benefactor, who had not yet announced whether he would seek another term. Haley hadn't even told his wife. News spread fast. By the time he disembarked in Canyon, friends met him at the platform sporting "Haley for Governor" buttons.

He founded his campaign on Interposition, a previously obscure constitutional interpretation most often associated with John C. Calhoun and the slaveocracy and usually studied only by history students cramming for an exam. But a segregationist newspaper editor in Virginia had recently resurrected the idea, making high-sounding arguments about how states still held the power to ignore any federal law or court decision that they held unconstitutional. The idea took off that spring with state legislatures passing Interposition resolutions and politicians like Haley latching onto it as a campaign issue. In Texas, Allan Shivers, mired in scandal, put an Interposition referendum on the primary ballot. Haley, who fancied himself a political philosopher, thought he might ride the idea to the governor's chair.[84] Of course, he also promised that if high-minded intellectual arguments on constitutional principles didn't work, he could always send the Texas Rangers where they were needed to prevent school integration.

The rest of Haley's campaign was a cowboy conservative spectacle, replete with chuckwagons, cattle sales, threats of frontier violence, and speeches laced with colorful cowboy metaphors. It was also a vulgar, racist, regressive, antilabor, conspiratorial, anticommunist, and antistatist expression of his peculiar expression of extremism that few, save for the 88,000-some-odd Texans who voted for him, took seriously.[85]

The year 1956 was a strange one in southern politics, the first election season since the *Brown* II decision, a season of massive resistance. The original *Brown* decision had come down in May 1954, but the case that would determine the timing of its implementation, *Brown* II, was not decided until a year later. Most white southerners assumed (and were assured by the local political media elite) that it would be years, perhaps decades before desegregation would begin. But in May 1955, the court ordered schools desegregated "with all deliberate speed." When state legislatures next convened (sometimes in special sessions), massive resistance laws were passed by the hundreds. In Georgia, the state government built in a doomsday option whereby, if a single school was integrated by a single Black student, the state would have no choice but to disband and defund its entire public education system. Entire southern delegations in Congress signed the "Southern Manifesto," which condemned the *Brown* decision as a "clear abuse of judicial power" whereby the justices (it was a unanimous decision) had substituted their "personal political and social ideas for the established law of the land." Texas senator Price Daniel and Panhandle representative Walter Rogers signed the manifesto.[86] Shivers was prominent among the massive resisters, pioneering the stunt of "standing in the schoolhouse door" when he used the Texas Rangers to prevent school desegregation in Mansfield.[87]

Haley was hardly the only segregationist in the race. Price Daniel, who had dramatically resigned his Senate seat to run for governor, not only signed the Southern Manifesto but also reminded audiences that it had been he who had argued to protect segregation in Texas in its biggest case before the Supreme Court.[88] Pappy O'Daniel ran as a rabid white supremacist. Even Ralph Yarborough, who led the left wing of Texas's Democrats, ran on a segregationist platform.[89]

Haley never really campaigned seriously. Although the occasional rumor of a favorable poll or a batch of fawning positive letters might lead him into brief flights of fancy about a possible victory, he readily portrayed his candidacy as a vehicle to promote Interposition. He had managed to convince himself that the concept had never really been tested (it had) and when it had, Interposition "had never failed."[90] (It had. Repeatedly.) All that was needed for success—and a brand-new era of political independence for states—was a governor with the intellect to understand how Interposition worked and the will to wield it. As he explained it in one of the less tortuous metaphors of his campaign, the Constitution was like a breakfast order in a café.[91] If a customer ordered ham and eggs and the café instead brought them brussels sprouts, the customer would obviously have the right to refuse to pay for the brussels sprouts, and it would be ridiculous and immoral for the café to insist that they do so.[92] He stuck mostly to friendly audiences, segregationist groups like the white citizens' councils or ranching organizations. Other than Interposition, his campaign messaging was mostly devoted to explaining his theories on how *Brown* fit into the communist plot against America:

> The communist conspiracy is determined to desegregate the south. Why are they out to do this? The fighting power of this country, the chief refuge of freedom on the face of the earth, is the South. There, primarily do people have the character and courage to stand up and fight. Therefore, the communist international cannot conquer this country until they destroy the pride, the fighting pride, and the racial pride of the South.[93]

Of course, he played the cowpuncher. He once hosted a press conference at an Austin city park, arriving in an old-fashioned chuck wagon and serving up beefsteaks, biscuits, and beans to an enthusiastic crowd. The interest in the event was, by most accounts, largely because Haley was, like his mother, a great cook. To pay his $1,200 filing fee, Haley made great press by very publicly selling off a bunch of yearling calves: "a small fee to pay for public discussion of our way of life when our liberties are being liquidated."[94] He wore boots and a Stetson at every public appearance. Describing his policy regarding organized labor, Haley said: "If on my ranch a bunch of my hands quit and you fellows come up there trying to interfere with the people I then hire to flank a bunch of yearlings on my land, I'll meet you at the fence with a .32, and, if necessary, I'll draw a bead on you and rim a shell and leave you lying on the fence line."[95]

One juicy rumor about his campaign was that it was being secretly financed by H. L. Hunt, the ultraconservative oil mogul. Reputed to be the richest man in the world, Hunt was a longtime, huge financial supporter of right-wing extremism. There was no question that for two decades Haley had been a loyal, articulate, and outspoken defender of the interests of Texas oil barons. In his campaign he also explained how, in addition to preventing school integration, Interposition could be used to protect the state's oil and gas industries from "perverted judicial authority" and "ambitious executive veto."[96]

Always seen as just an extremist candidate courting the votes of the state's most violent racists and reactionaries, Haley finished a distant fourth. The Interposition referendum passed by a four-to-one margin. Summing up Haley's candidacy, Ronnie Dugger, the sharp-tongued editor of the *Texas Observer*, concluded: "J. Evetts Haley had made his case for rebellion, autocracy, and reaction cogently and consistently."[97] And yet, almost ninety thousand Texans went to the polls to support this candidate of rebellion and autocracy and reaction. Haley was building a following.

II

BRAINWASHED

If both the past and the external world exist only in the
mind, and if the mind itself is controllable—what then?

GEORGE ORWELL

t was an unseasonably warm January day in 1962 when J. Frank Dobie,
the most respected man of letters in Texas, strode into the chamber of
the old Texas Supreme Court building. Still spry and feisty at seventy-
two, Dobie was in unusually high spirits; he was there to raise hell and
to call out his old friend J. Evetts Haley over recent efforts to censor
schoolbooks. That morning was the latest hearing of a textbook committee that Haley and his army of right-wingers had been terrorizing
for weeks. It was Haley's latest crusade, a statewide effort to expose an
evil communist plot to brainwash Texas children through subtle and
subliminal techniques buried in schoolbooks. Calling themselves Texans for America (TFA), they were a loosely affiliated offshoot of For
America, a national organization formed in 1954 by Clarence Manion.
Starting in 1961, Haley and the TFA began harassing those responsible for choosing the textbooks that would be available for adoption in
Texas public schools. By fall, the Texas State Legislature had appointed
a special textbook committee to investigate potential subversion in educational materials, and the committee held public hearings across the
state. With testimony dominated by the "Haleyites"—as the press took
to calling them—the hearings were mostly a cavalcade of way-out-there
conspiracy theories spun by earnest stay-at-home Bircher moms. While
certainly entertaining to intellectuals like Dobie, who had a grounded
sense of humor and a keen sense of irony, they were also terrifying. He
was there to represent the Texas Institute of Letters, the state's most
prestigious literary group, and speak out against censorship.

Dobie and Haley had been friends for thirty years, since the day Haley arrived at UT, fresh from his gig with the PPHS, full of juice to start his academic career. Dobie's biographer suggests that the older folklorist might have seen a kindred spirit in Haley, "a younger version of himself," someone carved "out of the old rock." Dobie had even line-edited Haley's first book with the blunt advice of a true friend: "You will never make a historian until you learn to write."[1] The Rainey Affair had pulled them apart. As Haley moved right, Dobie moved left. They remained cordial and called on each other on occasion. But Dobie, who regularly poked fun at the ridiculousness of Texas conservatives in his newspaper column, had grown incensed by the textbook hearings and the silliness of much of the testimony. It was time, Dobie thought, to inject reason into what had become ceaseless one-sided monologues from TFA lackeys parroting the same old lines about communism and textbooks.

I

Beginning in summer 1960, just around the time, noncoincidentally enough, that the John Birch Society (JBS) was forming in the state, Texans for America launched an investigation into potential subversion lurking in the pages of schoolbooks. Brainwashing and textbooks were *the* right-wing obsessions that season. A book, *Brainwashing in the High Schools* by E. Merrill Root, had them convinced that communists were using textbooks to indoctrinate schoolchildren.[2] A key argument for Root was that the nonpatriotic content and mushy structure of history books was ultimately responsible for the seeming ease that the communist Chinese had enjoyed in "brainwashing" American troops during the Korean War. A generation of Americans had proven too mentally weak and not patriotic enough to withstand the pressure. A respected poet, Root was no random eccentric but a bona fide star of the hyperliterate right, who had helped found *National Review* and contributed regularly to *Human Events*. But over the back half of the 1950s, he had drifted further into the conspiratorial wing of the conservative movement, publishing out-there pieces about multidecade communist plots to use the education system to brainwash Americans into accepting communism.[3] By the time he published *Brainwashing in High Schools*, his "exposé" of eleven American history books, Root was on his way out of *National Review* (over its editorial criticism of Ayn Rand and Robert Welch) and on the verge of becoming a propagandist for the John Birch Society.

Textbook investigations were a big project for the right that year. In addition to the Texans for America, the Daughters of the American Revolution, the American Legion, and plenty of homegrown groups were launching programs to investigate potential subversion in children's schoolbooks. The Texans for America approach was to comb through the index of a particular book (very often history) looking for any reference to any person or thing that had also shown up on the House Committee on Un-American Activities (HUAC) Cumulative Index of possible subversives. A single match to the HUAC list was enough to condemn a book. The method was highly popular. The DAR, for example, found 170 separate, objectionable textbooks using the HUAC-communist cross-index method.[4]

The sheer size and power of the state's textbook market made the textbook hearings important events in Texas. Unlike most states, Texas buys every book for every child in every public school. It was the largest single textbook buyer in the world. Having a book approved by Texas, a deal that usually lasted six years or so, could make a publishing company. Rejection could doom a book. To choose, Texas had established a special committee of educators representing a variety of subjects and grades that would review potential books and make recommendations. Each year, the committee would select two to five texts for each subject and grade, purchase copies, and store them. Each district would choose which text it would use across its schools, and the state would ship them the books. The lists of approved books were public. In fall 1960, Texans for America requested to appear before the textbook committee.[5]

II

Haley launched Texans for America in 1957.[6] Over the spring and summer of that year, he built a mailing list, rented eleventh-floor office space in Fort Worth's Texas and Pacific Building, and organized a few chapters. A petition drive to impeach Supreme Court justices added new names to the mailing list. (Haley spent the summer dealing with the blowback from the Texas Tech firings). TFA was to be the state chapter of the national organization For America, founded by Clarence Manion a couple of years earlier. The principal cause of the national organization was repealing the income tax; its president, former Utah governor Bracken Lee, was absolutely nuts about the subject. But Haley's Texans for America were less focused on the income tax than they were about protecting "states' rights, competitive enterprise, private property and individual liberty" and defending against "internationalism, socialism, communism, and collectivism." Haley launched the group at a two-day convention in September 1957. Bracken Lee and Bonner Fellers gave major addresses. Dan Smoot was the master of ceremonies. Haley ran the organizational meetings. All of America's issues, he said, boiled down to "Christian morality versus illegitimate authority."[7] The first official act of Texans for America was to condemn the *Brown v. Board of Education* decision. It called the recent desegregation of Little Rock, Arkansas, schools "the beginning of the destruction of all the rights of all the citizens."[8] Over its first two years, the organization sputtered about, conducting sporadic petition drives, sponsoring right-wing programming, publishing an irregularly timed newsletter, hosting the occasional speaker.

Over those years Haley built TFA's membership, expanding his circle of the like-minded: political supporters, friends, campaign contributors, and well-wishers. It was most popular (no surprise here) in West Texas, particularly in Haley's hometown of Midland, itself becoming a far-right stronghold. Like a lot of Haley's schemes, he had big plans for the TFA, hoping to build it into a voting bloc large enough to change Texas's political algorithms. But like anything he ran, the TFA's opportunities for growth were always going to be limited by the reality of Haley's extremist views and his demands for dogmatic purity. Put simply, he was ideologically and temperamentally incapable of building coalitions. Like a lot of ideologues, Haley sought not power but purification. Dealing only in absolutes, his stridency and intolerance for anyone who deviated from pure orthodoxy would always limit the boundaries of his circle of support to the far, far right. But that didn't mean they couldn't make a lot of noise and be an incredible nuisance.

The first TFA project that really landed was a series of coordinated letter-writing campaigns focused on newspaper editors and political figures across Texas. Drawing on the mythology of the nation's founding, TFA groups they called Committees of Correspondence would, under

Haley's direction and using his talking points, write dozens of letters on subjects of concern to the organization. The committees sent out hundreds of letters to newspaper editors, radio station managers, and politicians from city council members to U.S. senators. Letter writers spoke to their distrust of Lyndon Johnson, decried raises for schoolteachers, and called for greater financial responsibility in government and education. There were letters that criticized farmers for using chemical fertilizers ("dope"), those that opposed Khrushchev's visit to the United States, still others that detailed how mental health programs, water fluoridation, or school guidance counselors were part of a communist brainwashing conspiracy. Some opposed taxes, bond issues, and federal support for education and public housing. Others praised the poll tax, balanced budgets, or the John Birch Society. Letter writers criticized the Forand Bill (an early Medicare program) for "communizing medical treatment" and condemned UNESCO and foreign aid. They loved the Connally Reservation and hated the World Court, a "communistic-atheistic monster."[9] Committee members also combed their local newspapers for letters written by like-minded potential new members. Those letters would be clipped and sent along to Haley, who would then extend a personal invitation to the newly identified "Patriot" to join Texans for America, along with a copy of the latest TFA newsletter.[10]

Texans for America News looked a lot like the *Jeffersonian Democrat* from twenty years earlier. Stories and editorials ran a strange gamut of political observation and commentary. Speculation about mid-level political races and swipes at LBJ shared the page with tirades over the communist infiltration of the National Council of Churches and the NAACP. There was lots of sniping at federal agricultural programs and calls for various impeachments. Harangues over integration accompanied the sorts of biblical endorsements of segregation popular among white supremacists. Serious-looking charts, created from misleading and cherry-picked data from FBI reports, were placed alongside reports of Black criminality and violence. New mental health laws were hyped as steps toward left-wing totalitarianism: "You may now be arrested without complaint and without a warrant, and thrown into an insane asylum by any 'health or peace officer' who simply 'believes' that you're mentally ill."[11] The *Texas Observer*, which observed Haley more closely than most media outlets in those years, ran an entire article on the cacophony of right-wing sputtering one could find in just one issue. "Amuricca for

(Texas) Amuriccans," penned by Lyman Jones, perfectly captured the sense of the whole thing. The TFA, Jones concluded, was "way out in right field—so say that everything to the left of Lynn Landrum, or perhaps Bill Blakley, glows with a faint, but unmistakably crimson—that is to say, Red—tinge." (He was partly right; later that year, when William Blakley refused to come out four-square against the income tax, the TFA endorsed Pappy O'Daniel for governor.)[12]

And then came textbooks.

It was only natural for Haley to turn the TFA into a watchdog over public education. He had been involved in education in one way or another his entire adult life. And he had become convinced that communists were using public education to indoctrinate American schoolchildren. Texans for America started taking over school board meetings and school boards, monitoring library books, and placing right-wing materials in schools and libraries. In 1959, the TFA hosted Myers Lowman, the founder and head of the Circuit Riders, communist hunter, compiler of lists, and segregationist detective known for his attempts to root out the dangerous doings in the nation's schools and churches. That year, he was pushing a two-volume reference book on communists in the educational establishment that he was about to publish: *6000 Educators*.[13] This "Compilation of Public Records" and other material collated by Lowman would become an important part of the TFA's reference library.

One textbook and one author became an obsession of Haley and the TFA: Southern Methodist University (SMU) history professor Paul F. Boller, who wrote *This Is Our Nation*, a high school history text. Boller was a brilliant, funny, logical, and incisive and accurate critic of the world around him. Nothing seemed to delight him more than to punch holes in some of the sillier (but foundational) ideas of the far right. He was in Dallas only a few weeks (having come from Yale) before he published a piece in SMU's *Daily Campus* newspaper that defended Truman's firing of Douglas MacArthur. (It was dogma on the right that the firing was clear evidence of the communists' influence in the Truman White House.) He also wrote a fiercely critical review of William F. Buckley and Brent Bozell's *McCarthy and His Enemies*, the official right-wing account of the rise and fall of Joseph McCarthy, in which the senator was the hero of the story of America's awakening to the dangers of communism. In several other books and articles, Boller demonstrated that George Washington and the Founding Fathers had not been fundamentalist Christians but rather deists and explained how many of them had been wary of organized religion. Boller insisted that FDR's recognition of the Soviet Union in 1933 was not clear evidence that Roosevelt and his Brains Trust were soft on communism, but rather a popular and logical response to the realpolitik of the time. In a particularly devasting shot at the *Dallas Morning News*, which throughout the 1950s had been pushing the recognition-as-betrayal line, Boller wrote a piece about the enthusiasm the *News* had demonstrated in 1933 when it endorsed recognition. In class, the professor calmly and carefully explained that the United States had not "lost China" in 1949 and had positive things to say about the New Deal.[14] And he regularly and rightfully explained that the Communist Party posed no threat to the United States. He lived exclusively and proudly in the world of reality. He drove Haley nuts.

And not just him. Right-wingers across the country began to call out SMU as a den of leftists and communist sympathizers.[15] The *American Mercury*, by then near the bottom of its slide from smart and biting Menckenian wit to unhinged fascist bombast, warned of the university's pampering of leftists and one-worlders and called it a "theater for radicalism."[16] Dan Smoot, Texas's most important right-wing media figure, with his own television and radio shows and monthly magazine, called out Boller regularly. The TFA bundled up the *American Mercury* article and one of Smoot's more malicious pieces into a brochure and mailed it to eight thousand SMU alumni, students, and parents. Boller's biggest crime in the eyes of Texans for America was his refusal to take seriously the internal threat of communism. As he remembered, nothing in those years "damaged me more with the Paranoid Right in Texas than my insistence the CP, USA was a negligible force in American life. To minimize American Communism was, in those days, like taking the Wicked Witch out of the *Wizard of Oz* or Captain Hook out of *Peter Pan*, or the wolf out of the Little Red Riding Hood story. What is a fairy tale, after all, without witches, wizards, and goblins?" As Boller figured, the "reactionaries needed the Communist Party far more than I did."[17]

Then Boller's *This is Our Nation* came before the Texas state textbook committee.

By that point, Haley had turned the TFA into one of the most aggressive, best-organized textbook watchdog groups in the country. Armed with all the textbooks up for adoption, Haley delegated responsibility to local TFA committees all over Texas. The Midland group alone had forty-five members. Three or four people were usually assigned to every book, and they read each line by line. They harassed and bullied teachers and principals for copies of books under consideration by their district. Haley himself believed that local boards of education were secretly plotting to keep potential "books from the hands of alert Americans."[18]

Conroe High School Latin teacher Ilanon Moon wrote the TFA's "Textbook Criteria for Young Americans," a handy rubric and guide for textbook evaluations. She was perfect for the job: witty, flamboyant, clever, and convinced that the world had started down the road to Hell the day William McKinley was murdered. She was well known in Texas as a demanding and excellent teacher who ran one of the state's best glee clubs. She was a nationally recognized classics scholar with an MA in history from UT. She was also a go-to wedding organist. But her main passion was English and, to be specific, English grammar. She saw grammar on a plane with higher mathematics, a complex subject worthy of lifelong study and commitment. She also believed that most of her students were numbskulls, the entire education establishment a sad joke, that communists had taken over the National Education Association, and that modern educational practices and philosophies (such as deemphasizing grammar) were part of a plot to create a nation of muddleheaded losers. As one of Moon's favorite witticisms had it, "The only way to save the American educational system is to crucify the N.E.A., hang the American professors, and burn the teachers' colleges." She once confided to a sympathetic Haley, "We do not have a shortage of schools. What we have is an excess of morons filling up the seats in our buildings." And no one in America was more convinced that communists had laced brainwashing messaging into American textbooks than Ilanon Moon.[19]

In "Textbook Criteria for Young Americans," Moon made TFA's educational objectives clear. The "general criteria by which the education of American youth should be measured" should be how well it celebrated patriotism, individualism, the "Christian Nation," the Constitution, and free enterprise. Pedagogically, textbook reviewers should be looking for a return to the old ways of instilling discipline and teaching the three R's. She even suggested reinstating *McGuffey Readers*. Schools should teach the "ethical concepts and moral principles" of Christianity. Students should learn that "the Constitution of the United States is the greatest political document ever conceived by the mind of man and a sacred possession of every American"; that under its protection the nation is a government of laws; and that the only alternative to strict constitutionalism is "dictatorship and slavery." The "words 'capitalism,' 'free enterprise,' 'personal initiative,' and 'profits' should unabashedly be brought back into the classroom vocabulary and given the honor they deserve." Instead of encouraging students to "distrust our capitalistic system," schools should teach that changing any part of the free enterprise system would spell the end of democracy and the establishment of a tyrannical police state where patriots would be enslaved. Blatant nationalism was the only way to train "the immature mind."[20] The stakes were too high to bother with teaching critical thinking: "Until they are old enough to understand both sides of a question, they should be taught only the *American* side."[21]

This philosophy as the guiding principle of the TFA's textbook auditors is important to keep in mind. It wasn't just references to potential subversive individuals, groups, or movements that could disqualify a book; any seeming deficiency in pushing the TFA political interpretation of America or American history could as well. Only those books that unequivocally and forcefully trumpeted the *American* and capitalist "side" were acceptable. Still, the TFA enumerated plenty of subversive characters whom its members should be looking out for: Pearl S. Buck, Sinclair Lewis, Lincoln Steffens, James Thurber, Carl Sandburg, James Weldon Johnson, Christopher Morley, Maurice R. Robinson, William Saroyan, and William Allen White, all of whom had appeared in the index of the hearings and meetings and reports of the House Committee on Un-American Activities. A single appearance by someone in that index or any of the other lists used by the TFA, even if only in a further-reading section or bibliography, was taken as evidence of potential subversion.[22] The argument, which perhaps gave schoolchildren unwarranted credit for their curiosity and research skills, went like this: even a single mention of a suspected communist in a Texas schoolbook could send inquisitive young scholars down a path of exploration that could go from chuckling over a James Thurber cartoon, to reading communist-inspired literature, to joining the communist cause. Or, with Langston Hughes, the TFA proposed this scenario: "A youngster will read about the Negro poet, Langston Hughes, . . . in his textbook. Then he'll ask himself: 'Why isn't Hughes' poem Goodbye Christ all right for me to read?' The poem is strictly antireligious and pro-Communist. But the fact that Hughes or any other writer of this sort of thing is included in the textbook makes it all right in the minds of young students."[23] As they gained experience, TFA researchers were soon digging deeper into potential secret meanings in the narratives and interpretations, and here, even calculus texts and songbooks were found wanting.

The TFA rejected *The Stockman's Handbook*, used in high school agriculture classes, because its coverage of "agricultural welfare programs" lacked any accompanying "mention of the moral ramifications" of those programs. An economics text was rejected for including an 1833 political cartoon that featured bankers in a negative light (though the whole point of the cartoon was to show Andrew Jackson's disparaging views of bankers). The TFA saw it as antibanker propaganda and criticized the text for not including an explanation that destroying the bank was an "economic blunder" and that "government meddling with the economy benefits no one in the long run." Haley wasn't above demanding that history books, especially books on Texas history, conform to his own historiographical interpretation; he crossed off Lynn Perrigo's *Texas and Our Spanish Southwest* for its "false historical premise and thesis."[24]

The TFA demanded that books be rigorous and instill moral lessons. Any book that "does not contribute directly and definitely to training the mind of youth in clear, systemized and organized thinking which leads him to master facts and put them together into reasoned conclusions which he can express in concise and cogent language" was subversive. Any new pedagogical approach was seen as potentially serving the communist conspiracy. The New Math, for example, was "not immune from problems which indicate poor ethics, dubious morality, or fallacious political and economic thought." Indeed, its focus on abstract concepts could, some argued, destroy an individual's belief in absolutes and threaten democracy and Christianity.[25] TFA watchdogs scrutinized songbooks for new music, especially folk songs or newer religious music. Any book with "He's Got the Whole World in His Hands" was rejected for "one-worldism," as were any books that had songs from different countries, because it was apparently "possible to turn the mind of the American child toward one-worldism by teaching him the folk tunes of other countries and neglecting those of his own." They found fault in typing books. World history was a hoax. How would it possible, as Moon asked, for a third-grader not to confuse the rest of the world for their country? This kind of befuddlement was clearly "not conducive to patriotism."[26]

All through summer 1961, the Committees of Correspondence did their research and filled out their reports, hundreds of them. Then Haley approached the state textbook selection committee and demanded that he and his colleagues be allowed to appear before its fall meetings. What had been for decades a watching-paint-dry boring event run by and for educational professionals became a circus. In the center ring was Haley. Each week, twenty or so Texans for America would show up for a hearing, and as they waited to testify, they studied their mimeographed sheets of notes and scanned their underlined textbooks. On the stand, they read their reports of the communist subversion that they had uncovered. Most were women, mothers of high school or college students who dressed in their Sunday best and seemed slightly embarrassed to be the center of attention. Not Haley, though. He directed everything from the wings, steering testimony and crafting arguments, taking the stand when he felt it was needed, which was usually at least two or three times a day.

The very serious mothers of the TFA explained how a book with positive mentions of Albert Schweitzer should be banned because the scientist had once rejected the scientific possibility of the Virgin Birth. Books with the famous proverb of the Prophet Muhammad "Trust in God but tie your camel" should not be allowed in Texas classrooms because Mohammad was not the "one true prophet." What about books that mention the Abominable Snowman? "Take this missing link out of the curriculum." Storybooks that contained tales of fictional rich housewives failing to pay fictional boys who mow their fictional lawns enough fictional money? "Injecting class conflict." What about dictionaries that failed to include "anti-communism" in their examples of how to use the prefix "anti-"? Ban them.[27]

Paul Boller's *This Is Our Nation* was a popular point of testimony, a classic example of left-wing subtlety, according to Haley, riddled with subversion that was tough to see by any but the most practiced eye. It had, he testified, "the usual left-wing obsession with democracy . . . and it reiterates the matter of class and caste in keeping with the communist dialectics and semantics." TFA members took to the stand to call attention to the book's shortcomings and dangerous messaging: its friendliness toward the United Nations and apparent "affinity for Roosevelt" and the way it exaggerated and overemphasized Native American history, the "morbid" Salem witch trials, slavery, and the contributions of minorities. Some even told the committee about how including an 1867 political cartoon about the U.S. purchase of Alaska that labeled the new territory "Russian America" was placed in the book to prepare schoolchildren for an eventual communist takeover.[28]

Hotshot *Texas Observer* journalist Robert Sherrill, who attended every hearing, was transfixed by the "Haleyites" as

> they made clear their bitter opposition to any favorable textbook mention of the federal income tax, social security, federal subsi- dies to farmers and schools and TVA, John Dewey, the United Nations, the memory of the League of Nations, every aspect of UNESCO, disarmament, racial integration, the memory of General George Marshall, the Supreme Court, use of the word democracy when describing this country, any one of a number of famous writers and artists (who either ran afoul of the House Un-American Activities Committee or the Texans for Ameri- ca's own investigation into supposedly subversive activities), and anything remotely connected with the political Deals, New and Fair especially.[29]

Horrified novelist John Howard Griffin observed: "TFA demand the truth be truncated wherever it reveals an incidence of weakness or error in our national past. In effect, they require the historian to abandon the science of history and become an amateur therapist, or at least a pro- pagandist to pump into the young a spurious and hard patriotism; and what is more, a patriotism that never wavers from the narrow harmonies of extreme conservatism."[30]

But it worked. The hearings were statewide news, and Haley and his band of would-be censors gained incredible publicity. The TFA forged strong ties to other conservative organizations that were also looking into textbooks, like the Daughters of the American Revolution, the American Legion, and the new-to-Texas John Birch Society. The Tex- ans for America even convinced the committee to request publishers to change certain texts. And the committee yanked some books from consideration altogether. But not Boller's *This Is Our Nation*. That's when Haley demanded to appear before the committee with a new charge: that the publisher of *This Is Our Nation* had been involved in a project meant to brainwash American troops with communist propaganda. He was referring to a series of pamphlets about life in the USSR that had been commissioned by the U.S. military in 1942 to help American soldiers and sailors better understand their Soviet allies.[31]

When Dobie heard about the committee's decision to give in to the Haleyites—as they were by then being called—and ban certain texts, he grew apoplectic, calling it "one of the worst things that has happened to Texas education in my lifetime." Speaking at a gathering of Texas writers, he called for a stand against censorship. When Haley heard what his old friend was up to, he turned his acolytes on Texas's most beloved folklorist. TFA witnesses started objecting to books in which Dobie was mentioned in a positive light. Complaining about a Dobie book's appearance in a popular history text's further-reading section, one "witness" said that Dobie should not be allowed to "mold the minds of our youth." His crime, she explained, was to be among the signatories of a letter to the *New York Times* fourteen years before that had called for protecting the democratic rights of the then-legal Communist Party.[32] In fact, although Dobie didn't know it at the time, Haley had already compiled a dossier on him and made a list of fourteen possible connections between his old friend and suspect organizations.[33]

In December, the politicians got involved. House Speaker Jimmy Turman, who held a PhD in education, named a five-person panel to investigate the charges of "subversive" textbooks. Concerned primarily with history texts, the Textbook Investigation Committee (TIC) was charged with finding and recommending books that highlight "our glowing and throbbing history of hearts and souls inspired by wonderful American principles and traditions." Bob Bass, who wrote the bill that created the TIC, believed that textbooks should "contain the teachings of good Americanism."[34] W. T. Dungan, an obvious TFA ally, was named the panel's chair. A graduate of West Texas State, Dungan had recently sponsored a bill that would have public school teachers swear an oath that they believed in God. The TIC's first public hearing, in January 1962, was a zoo. Gone was the disciplined parade of TFA members stepping to the mic and making their case to a committee of fifteen; now every Bircher, preacher, and homemaker angry about schools and books flooded into the old Supreme Court building. The throng waiting to speak made for a raucous audience of the like-minded. There was much gnashing and rending and wailing over MacKinley Kantor, George Orwell, Ernest Hemingway, John Steinbeck, and others. One Midland woman, part of a large contingent from the city, asked her preacher to read aloud some of the "filth" contained in Kantor's *Andersonville*, one of the books under question. As he read the dirty words aloud, a fellow minister (from Amarillo) clapped the back of his hand to his forehead and cried out: "Preacher, that's enough!" There were plenty of expositions on communist plots and moral laxity in textbooks. It seemed that everyone had their own pet notion: one woman explained how personality tests were designed by the Reds to "drive a wedge between students and parents." A Kerrville attorney warned about the impending destruction of Christianity. A local TFA chairman told how he feared books more than bombs. A Huntsville Bircher came out against public education completely, believing it was creating a "generation of brainwashed people." Still others complained about the committee, the board of education, and television.[35]

By the time J. Frank Dobie testified, the textbook subversion hearings were the biggest story in Texas. Attending against his doctor's orders, the old folklorist arrived in a good mood, waving to reporters and joking with friends. As he entered, he sought out Haley and offered a warm and sincere handshake. The two men sat side by side throughout the day, often sharing a joke or friendly aside. In his initial testimony, Haley limited his remarks to Boller and *This Is Our Nation*. Looking out at the obvious Dobie-friendly crowd of UT students and professors, Haley couldn't resist the opportunity to complain once again about his firing from the university a quarter century earlier—dismissed, he claimed, for "telling the truth." Pointing accusingly at the crowd, he asked, "Where were the liberal, the bleeding hearts when I was fired?" (Haley conveniently left out the fact that Dobie had vigorously and publicly defended Haley in 1936 and had worked privately to help his friend keep his job.)

Dobie, who at this stage in his life, bore a striking resemblance to the Spencer Tracy of *It's a Mad, Mad, Mad, Mad World*, took the stand. "Mr. Texas" charmed, mugged for the cameras, joked, flopped his red tie around, and continually swept his unruly white hair back from his eyes. The crowd ate it up as he laid into the textbook committee: "Censorship is never to let people know but always to keep them in ignorance; never to bring light but always to darken. It is and for thousands of years has been a main force used by dictators and all manner of tyrannical governments, from Nero to Khrushchev." He described censors as the utensils of the ignorant: "Not one censor of history is respected by enlightened men of any nation." Any man, he roared, looking directly at Haley, "who imagines he has a corner on the definition or conception of Americanism and wants to suppress all conceptions to the contrary is a bigot and an enemy of the free world." He tore into the textbook publishers who caved to the ridiculous demands of the foolishly misguided, and called the committee "politically minded" dopes who read only chamber of commerce brochures and "*Reader's Digest* waterings." Calming down, he assured the crowd that "school kids aren't fools. They aren't going to be fooled by some dull tail-twisting and flag-waving propaganda." The crowd cheered. Committee chair Dungan tried, in vain, to gavel them to silence. Haley sulked.[36]

The committee broke for dinner, and Dobie headed to the house. In his absence, Haley climbed to the stand once again, specifically to rebut his friend. He lashed out at the crowd, calling them "supercilious" "left-wingers" and "long-haired, super-intellectuals, and super-sophisticates." Then he publicly accused J. Frank Dobie of being part of the movement to destroy America. Hearing about Haley's testimony the next day, Dobie could only shake his head. "He hates, hates, hates."[37]

When the legislature convened a few days later, it was hammered with requests for more hearings, so it renewed the TIC's mandate and gave it a budget. The committee took its act on the road. Its first stop was the most ultraconservative city in America, Amarillo. Birchers had recently elected one of their own to the mayor's office and had hosted the National Indignation Convention. They had just won a campaign to have certain books removed from the high schools, the local libraries, and even Amarillo College. Textbooks had been a major local issue for months. The Amarillo Conservative Club hosted a special night on the subject, featuring appearances by M. G. Lowman and Mrs. Harry Artz Alexander, a DAR member and professional textbook watchdog from Mississippi. The Panhandle organization of school boards had been studying the liberal bias of American history books. Louise Evans all but turned her "Politicus" column into a forum on textbooks.

The *Globe* welcomed the committee in a front-page editorial. Both Amarillo papers printed an application form for anyone interested in appearing before the committee. They also included a helpful primer on how history textbooks had changed over the years, offering side-by-side coverage comparisons of historical figures and events. Nathan Hale, lauded as a great hero and patriot in older texts, had disappeared. So had coverage of Patrick Henry's cry of "Give me Liberty or give me Death." Students no longer read about Fort McHenry, and Paul Revere's famous ride had been reduced to a single sentence.[38] These were textbooks not likely to pass the TIC's "glowing and throbbing history of hearts and souls" test.

Haleyites and Birchers milled through the crowd on the morning of the hearing, passing out Billy James Hargis pamphlets on communism, the UN, and schoolbook brainwashing. Mildred Shively, a local junior high school teacher and chair of the Amarillo Conservative Club's textbook committee, spoke first. She not only demanded local control of textbook selection but even suggested that individual parents should decide which books their children might use and that textbook companies might do well to peddle their wares door-to-door. Like many who would speak that day, she longed wistfully for the patriotism and historical accuracy of the texts from long ago and squirmed uncomfortably as she described the embarrassing "spiritual emphasis" in modern textbooks. Only by recommitting to the values of the old ways and reestablishing a love of country could America win the Cold War, because, as she concluded (to much applause), "our real battle is not so much of bullets but of wills, not of space but of spirit."[39]

The next eight hours saw more of the same: long-drawled monologues on preschool books that taught children to take advantage of their parents, history books whose coverage of the New Deal was part of a communist plot, the claim that the Civil War was really about states' rights and not slavery, and complaints about language, people, movements, places, images, authors, interpretations, and much, much more—all connected in some way to a grand scheme to undermine the patriotism and intelligence of schoolchildren.[40]

It was exhausting. The two members of the TIC who were not sympathetic to the TFA cause began quizzing witnesses about their relationship with the John Birch Society and peppering them with requests to accurately describe and define things like socialism and democracy. When a witness defined socialism as "government help," John Alaniz, the poker-faced representative from San Antonio, asked her if she thought that federal protection of bank deposits or Social Security was socialistic, driving the witness stammering from the stand. A practicing Catholic, he also tussled with Mrs. Harold Boots, who complained about the "Catholic propaganda" in Texas history books. When committee member Ronald E. Roberts, a schoolteacher from Hillsboro who had also let his frustration with the direction of the hearings become clear, left for the restroom during her testimony, Boots grumbled that she was sorry he left before she had the chance to ask Roberts "how long he had been a card-carrying Communist."[41] By the dinner break, Alaniz and Roberts had decided that they had heard enough and took the last plane out of town for Austin.[42]

Alaniz later calculated that three out of every four of the "repetitious" witnesses the committee heard over its run received most of their information from publications associated with the John Birch Society. "Anyone who differed with their position or even questioned their ideals, was, they thought, against them and by inference, Communistic."[43] He and Roberts told reporters that the hearings had devolved into little more than "a forum for right wing views."[44]

The committee had two more hearings: a raucous affair in San Antonio that opened with a screening of a short movie titled *The Ultimate Weapon*, narrated and hosted by Ronald Reagan, which described the dangers of brainwashing. It had been produced with money from the Volker fund, then in the full throes of its transfiguration from legitimate libertarian think tank to fascist propaganda mill. When the projectionist had difficulty getting the film started, people in the crowd began yelling "sabotage." It got worse from there. The last event, in Dallas, which had been called by the committee chair, also the only member to show up, was little more than an "Edwin Walker for Governor" campaign event. Over the objection of the chair, the committee voted itself out of existence in summer 1962.

By that point, Texans for America was no longer the largest and loudest right-wing organization in Texas. That distinction would go to the John Birch Society, which swept across the state in 1961 and 1962 and almost immediately became the political force that Haley had imagined for the TFA.

As for Dobie, his last word on the subject appeared in his regular column a couple of weeks after his appearance in Austin. "Sheep Instinct Often Strange" was a very thinly disguised attack on the Haleyites. "The bleating of sheep can become almost as tiresome as the wagging of some human tongues," it opened. Sheep, however, he explained, at least "show individual variations—if only in stupidity."[45]

And Boller? The state textbook committee would approve *This Is Our*

Nation as one of five American history texts approved for adoption. But the controversy and testimony over the book had its effect—only one school district chose the text. There would be no second edition. The publisher went out of business shortly thereafter. Boller left SMU for UMass, Boston, where he began building a career as one of the nation's best and most beloved historians. He returned to Texas in the late 1970s as the Lyndon Johnson Chair of American History at Texas Christian University. His books on presidential anecdotes, inaugurations, Hollywood, fake quotes, political myths, and the First Ladies have sold tens of thousands of copies.

BOOK THREE

COWBOY CONSERVATISM

We are in contention with a movement which evidently
visualizes only two alternatives for its future: as a fundamentalist oligarchy dedicated to the suppression of off-
color drama and the pornographic novel or a kind of West
Texas Viet Cong. To regard them as Neanderthals roaming the plains with their knuckles dragging in the buffalo
grass only increases the possibility of their defection from
our traditions of civil procedure.

DAVE HICKEY IN THE Texas Observer, 1964

12

BIRCHTOWN

Because a Bircher is more than just that: he can be a father, an employer, a doctor, he usually has children and he worries about the kind of world they'll grow up in, he's certainly not sluggish and almost always articulate, and more often than not he's financially and socially secure. Yet he pays his dues, faithfully attends his cell meetings, and there's no telling what else he might do if he thought—or was convinced—that the need was dire enough.

HUNTER S. THOMPSON, 1961

The joke went: "Amarillo politicians join the John Birch Society to win the middle-of-the-road vote." Dallas and Houston had (deserved) national reputations as Bircher strongholds to be sure. And the Society was popular all across West Texas, in big cities like Lubbock and Abilene and small cities like Borger and Pampa (where Birchers stretched an "Impeach Earl Warren" banner across Main Street).[1] One could find small cells or unaffiliated members in the smallest villages. But it was in Amarillo where Birchers tore the city into pieces and stitched it back together as the most right-wing city in America.

A 1964 investigative report on the rise of the far right opened with a description of the political climate of Amarillo in spring 1961: "A shadow of fear and suspicion moved in across the city . . . pitting people against people, and setting off a wave of antics so bizarre it appeared that some outlandish circus had encamped in town."[2] The city was the home of the first JBS chapter in the Panhandle, organized by the editor of Amarillo's biggest newspaper.

Over the 1960s, voters elected two Birchers to the mayor's office (one

an admitted member, the other assumed). Amarillo Birchers ripped the
city's most prestigious and largest church in two. They weaponized the
Chamber of Commerce and the civic clubs, took over the PTA and
the Girl Scouts, ran the local medical establishment, and tried to create
their own auxiliary police force. Amarillo is still widely recognized as the
most conservative city in the nation.

The call to join the Society came in an unsigned above-the-fold editorial in an early August edition of the 1960 Sunday *News-Globe*, the most
widely read newspaper in Amarillo (and West Texas). Likely penned
by editor Wes Izzard, the thousand-word promotional piece excitedly
lauded the Society: "A Most Amazing Organization Leaves Members
Latitude of Individuality." Much of the piece was lifted from the *Blue
Book*, the Society's organizational manual. It described the martyrdom
of John Birch, the group's namesake, a Baptist missionary who had been
murdered by the Communist Chinese at the close of World War II and
whose death, the JBS believed, had been covered up by pro-Chinese
members of the U.S. government. It described the Society as a new organization for American patriots eager to help educate their fellow Americans about the dangers of communist subversion. Izzard, or whoever
wrote the piece, stressed the JBS's commitment to individualism and the
autonomy of each chapter. It lauded its founder and lodestar, the former
industrialist Robert Welch.[3]

A week after the piece appeared, Wes Izzard, the most powerful
media figure in West Texas, hosted an organizational meeting at Amarillo's YMCA. The meeting was led by C. O. "Buck" Mann, the John Birch
Society's regional coordinator, along with General Jerry Lee, a recently
retired air force general. There was a brief presentation, a short Q&A,
and the screening of a two-and-a-half-hour film in which founder Robert Welch explained the basics of the communist plot against America
and laid out the Society's philosophy and structure. Membership was
secret. Fourteen people signed up that night.[4]

I

The movie screened that evening was a distillation of a pitch Welch had
been making for a year and a half by that point. The live version took
two full days. Something about Welch's message was clicking because

the JBS was the hottest thing going in the right-wing universe that year. It was different from groups like the Texans for America or the various anticommunist training academies. First, it was well ordered, with a clear top-down structure and organizational chart (based, ironically, on communist "cells"); it was made up of white-collar professionals; and it avoided the overt racism and anti-Semitism of other right-wing groups. It was held together by one unimpeachable dogma: that the communists had already all but taken over the country's most important institutions (churches, schools, government, media, entertainment) and had placed in important positions of power figures who were devoted to or at least sympathetic to their cause. The communist plot was everywhere you looked, Welch promised—*if* you knew where to look. And he promised to show people where to look and what to look for.

Welch himself was an interesting guy. He was by all accounts a legit intellectual prodigy, reading at three years old and graduating from the University of North Carolina at seventeen. He went to both Harvard Law School and the U.S. Naval Academy. He found his true calling in sales, spending his career in the cutthroat world of the candy business, most of it working for his brother's company, which made Junior Mints and Sugar Daddys. He was a major player in the National Association of Manufacturers—even occupying C. W. Post's old position as head of its educational programming. As much as anyone, he was responsible for the NAM's brutal lurch in the 1950s from a straight-ahead antilabor group to the far reaches of the paranoid anticommunist right.[5] His work at the NAM led Welch to the conclusion that a vast, evil, and all-powerful communist conspiracy, launched by Lenin himself three decades earlier, was responsible for certain curious and unwanted changes in American life. Welch grew so obsessed with uncovering the plot that he took early retirement to conduct his own research.

He was, by then, well known within conservative circles as a reliable money guy at election time and a staunch defender of Joseph McCarthy and Douglas MacArthur. He even published a book with conservative publisher Regnery. (To the regular world, he was mostly known for a classic book on business, *The Road to Salesmanship*.) It was 1958 when conservatives around the country started getting bizarrely long "letters" from Welch, reports from his findings about the communist conspiracy. That December, he called eleven "superpatriots" to Indianapolis for a meeting, where he explained the plot and outlined his plan to fight the communist takeover. For two straight days. Breaks for coffee and meals only. The self-assured and gifted salesman held their attention. By weekend's end all but one of his guests had agreed to join the John Birch Society's National Council.[6] For the next year, Welch held similar meetings in midsize cities all over America. Most of his guests were from the executive class of mid-level manufacturing, the world of the NAM. One of the earliest members was the oil and gas man Fred Koch, originally from Quanah in the Texas Panhandle, where his father was the editor and publisher of the local paper. Just as he might set up a new business, Welch hired regional coordinators to establish new "branches" and recruit among America's booster class.[7]

In those years there was no shortage of wannabe right-wing leaders: low-wattage radio demagogues, bulk-mail mimeographers, silver-tongued preachers and healers, anticommunist seminar hosts. And there were plenty of ultraconservative groups, from Texans for America to the Daughters of the American Revolution to the American Legion to the Farm Bureau. Three things set the John Birch Society apart. First was the Society's strident urgency: Welch terrified members with calculations of the exact date of the final communist takeover and percentages of communists already in place within the leadership of American institutions. Their fear helped Birchers rationalize completely absurd behavior like persecuting their neighbors and harassing public officials, business owners, and others. In the Birchers' world, anyone could be a communist agent: sales managers, schoolteachers, deacons, Little League coaches. No one was above suspicion. Not even the President of the United States.[8] Welch's estimations varied, but the communist takeover was anywhere between 60 and 80 percent complete. It was a silent campaign—one day Americans would simply wake up to find themselves slaves in a totalitarian state. The only hope was to expose the plot before it was too late. Of course, demanding members buy into such a fantasy was always going to limit membership to a small subset of those on the right. Not everyone was ready to believe that the nice young minister who had taught Johnny how to throw a curve ball was a communist just because he once gave a sermon about Jesus and the money changers. Most contemporary observers estimated that the Society never topped more than 100,000 members nationwide. But those 100,000 raised holy hell in their local communities. Its fervency, importantly, drew into the JBS orbit ultraconservatives from across the spectrum of the paranoid right: white supremacists, antitax and antilabor zealots, Cold War hawks, extreme moralists, opponents of progressive education, modern art, and folk music, and others lurking on the fearful edges of American politics.

The JBS's second great strength went largely unrecognized then and has been overlooked since. On its surface, the Society looked and acted like an authoritarian, top-down, regimented organization. Robert Welch had no use for democracies or debates, and orders came from the top. Each month, Welch described the Society's projects and priorities in a *Bulletin* mailed directly to members who were to report their monthly activities directly to headquarters. (They were called Members Monthly Memos, or MMMs.) But how a Bircher might fulfill their monthly obligations (less than 50 percent fulfillment of duties could lead to expulsion) was largely up to members. There were plenty of ways to participate: writing letters, viewing films, gathering signatures on petitions, attending school board or city council meetings, reading books and magazines. Every month, it seemed, Welch uncovered different aspects of the conspiracy and added new potential projects for members. This sprawling catalog of participatory possibilities lent the individual Society member or chapter (limited to twenty people) greater autonomy than the authoritarian model outlined in the *Blue Book* might suggest. There was a constantly expanding set of subjects for letters to the editor: praising a new martyr to the cause, pointing out the dangers of a possible piece of legislation, calling attention to some secret meaning of a news item. There was the always reliable cry to "Get US out of the UN." Every month there were books to read, films to screen, articles to clip and mail, front groups to establish, library books to protest, establishments to boycott, textbooks to examine, political figures to support, dirty tricks to play, organizations to take over. With a conspiratorial "octopus so large that its tentacles" could reach from the labor hall to "the majority of religious gatherings" to Yale Law School, as Welch put it, there were literally infinite locations and approaches for defeating the Reds.[9] It really was as the *Sunday News-Globe* had promised, an organization for the individual.

Lastly, there was the *southernness* of the John Birch Society. Welch was a North Carolinian, a scion of the landowning class, and he infused the organization he built with his views on race and religion. While nondenominational, and even, as Welch liked to boast, open to Catholics and Jews, the John Birch Society membership across the country,

and particularly in Texas, was still overtly and overwhelmingly fundamentalist Christian—mostly Baptist, Methodist, and Church of Christ,
the folk religions that dominated the southern frontier in Texas. Short
on doctrine, long on fervor and faith. The Society's white supremacy
was that of the courthouse elite, incredulous to the very idea that Black
southerners were unhappy with the social status quo. Welch himself
refused to consider the possibility that the Civil Rights Movement arose
in response to the treatment of African Americans in a Jim Crow world,
a world where segregation was enforced by mortal violence and economic intimidation. Instead, he recast a timeworn story of outside agitators stirring up trouble, turning the movement for civil rights into part
of a diabolical communist plot to overturn the social order and carve
out a Black republic in the American South. Civil rights as communism
played well among the segregationists in Texas.

II

As contemporary social scientists crunched the numbers on the sixties
radical right, they uncovered the stats of the typical Society member.
They were white. They were white-collar professionals, college educated,
and solidly middle-class. Most had attended second-tier state schools
and majored in the liberal arts. They considered themselves conservative
and, depending on where they lived, Republican. They all loved Barry
Goldwater and were mostly fundamentalist Protestants. What separated
the Birchers from all the other managers and history majors and Methodists was the remarkable fact that nine out of ten believed that the
biggest danger to the country was a secret communist plot to destroy
America from within. Nine in ten believed that colleges and universities had become communist training grounds. Half thought that communists secretly set Democratic Party policy. Most saw the UN as a
communist organization.[10] Birchers also tended to live in similar types
of places, mostly towns and cities experiencing astonishing population
and economic growth, places where the established political and social
organizational infrastructure had not kept pace with population. Places
where this rapid growth had created a participation and leadership
opportunity vacuum that newcomers (or the previously shut out) could
fill with right-wing groups like the TFA or the JBS. And, in Texas, as

we will soon see, the Republican Party. The Society, the studies revealed, tended to thrive in low-density cities like Amarillo where "the illusion of local independence and individual responsibility" dominated and where the population looked to the past as the best model on which to build their new society.[11]

This was not demography as destiny, however; Amarillo was already primed for Welch's right-wing ideology. An organization that combined a muscular and active pro-capitalist message with overt religiosity, white supremacy, and hyperindividualism was sure to be popular. Believing in the existence of a massive internal communist conspiracy was perhaps not much of a stretch in a place that had held a deep distrust of outside sources of power since the days of the Cattle Kingdom. And, though not yet recognized as such, Amarillo might have already been the most right-wing city in America by the time Welch's regional coordinators showed up looking to form chapters. Ultraconservatives dominated local and regional media. The Whittenburg brothers, S. B. and Roy, controlled not only the *Amarillo Daily News* (which S. B. had purchased with Evetts Haley back in 1938) but also the local NBC television station and KGNC, the most powerful radio station around.[12] They also held major interests in the *Lubbock Avalanche-Journal* and the *Borger News-Herald*, the latter edited by J. C. Phillips, maybe the loudest and looniest right-wing voice in America. Wes Izzard, the editor in chief of the *Daily News*, set the tone of the empire's editorial policy. Nicknamed the "Izzard of Was" by *Tulia Herald* editor H. M Baggarly, Izzard was as responsible as anyone, other than Evetts Haley, for defining and articulating the political ideology of the Panhandle. While more aggressively pro-business and booster-oriented than the historian, Izzard was nevertheless his equal when it came to sermonizing the values of self-reliance, individualism, and ultraconservative dogma. He was, according to the nationally syndicated conservative columnist George Dixon, a "veritable Sir Galahad" among conservative newspapermen, never "besmirched by even the breath of liberalism."[13]

Izzard's front-page column "From A to Izzard" was as much a part of an Amarillo businessman's morning routine as coffee. Coming up under the tutelage of Gene Howe, Izzard was an unabashed booster, framing his columns around two basic premises: Amarillo was the center of the universe, and its values were the foundation of American democracy.[14] His columns were a strange brew of local musings, colorful anecdotes, and blatantly right-wing messaging about "communist infiltration" and "soft thinking."[15] Many of his columns were just setups for reprints of articles written by ultraconservative reactionaries like George S. Benson and Dan Smoot. He had, as columnist Bill Cox called it, a "cult following" among the Panhandle's politically active and aware.[16]

Izzard was everywhere. In addition to his five-day-a-week column and his twice-daily radio broadcasts, he was a regular speaker before civic clubs. His forty-five-minute long-form addresses allowed him to go into great length on how "federal aid to education is a form of socialism" or how government planning "is making us more dependent on others, forcing us more and more into molds of conformity." Or to trumpet about how the nation had been built on the "shining idea" that "the individual is his own master and that according to his conscience he may work out his own destiny."[17]

In the great phrase coined by Izzard's nemesis H. M. Baggarly, the *Globe-News* empire draped a "newspaper curtain" around the Panhandle, where only a form of state-controlled media was allowed broadcast. "People living in Amarillo and vicinity," he wrote, "have crammed down their throats three times a day via newspaper, radio and television, almost every ultra-rightist of any note who writes a column or has a radio or television commentary." Baggarly wasn't exaggerating. Wire service stories were given headlines that skewed their context in a conservative light. Ultraconservative books like J. Edgar Hoover's *Masters of Deceit* were serialized in the daily papers. The local NBC television affiliate even censored national news. It famously preempted a special Chet Huntley broadcast on the farm problem in the United States. (Farmers were leaving the business in droves, and small towns across the country, dependent on agriculture, were suffering.) In place of the program, KGNC broadcast a recent Ronald Reagan speech to the Amarillo Chamber of Commerce, "How We Are Losing Our Freedom in Installments."[18] The editorial page of the *Globe-Times* and *Daily News* regularly featured columns by a pantheon of ultraconservative writers: George S. Benson, Billy James Hargis, Fulton Lewis, Tom Anderson, John T. Flynn, J. Edgar Hoover, Barry Goldwater, Westbrook Pegler, Ida C. Darden, Holmes Alexander, and others. Editorial page editor Louise Evans's "Politicus" was, along with Izzard's, one of the most conservative columns in the state. *The Dan Smoot Report* was broadcast on KGNC every Saturday night at 10:30. *Life Line* was on every night after the late news on ABC. *The Manion Forum* ran across multiple radio stations for years, and Fulton Lewis and Billy James Hargis were on the radio twice a day. It wasn't much different outside Amarillo; the editorial content of the *Pampa Daily News*, the *Odessa American*, and the nearby *Clovis (New Mexico) News Journal* was all controlled by ultraconservative newspaper publisher R. C. Hoiles (owner of the *Santa Ana (California) Register*) and his Freedom Newspaper chain.

Beyond the media, in schools, churches, clubs, civic organizations, and other social groups, speakers and educational committees focused on the threat of communism more than any other topic. They held film screenings and gave members reading assignments. For important events, larger groups scored big-name speakers like Tom Anderson or J. Bracken Lee or Ronald Reagan. For its Golden Anniversary, the Amarillo Chamber of Commerce invited right-wing propagandist and president of Harding College George S. Benson to speak. He told them that America was raising a generation of "soft, spoiled youngsters" and that only the business community could save the nation and "private enterprise and freedom of the individual."[19] For every Benson, there were half a dozen presentations by club members who stuttered through their presentations on the communist threat from material they had gathered from *The Dan Smoot Report*, *Life Line*, *Human Events*, or an Izzard column. As one Texas journalist noted: "No after-dinner speaker in Amarillo has done his duty until he has referred to one of the Kennedy clan in a derogatory manner and has said that 'the way to get Washington is to go to Harvard, then turn left.'" Failing to respond to the Harvard joke with anything other than a "deep belly laugh powered by full inhalation of pure high plains air is, of course, suspected of that highest of crimes short of mayhem: liberalism."[20] And there were the films, many of them produced by Benson's National Education Program: forty-five-minute filmstrips, the perfect length for a lunch meeting: *The Truth about Communism*, *Communist Encirclement*, *Communism on the Map*, or *Operation Abolition*. A typical Amarillo businessman could quote them from memory.[21]

Plenty of homegrown organizations popped up too. In Abilene, there was the Abilene Anti-Communism Educational League, a study group that met at the Baptist church. High school students formed the Abilene High School Freedom Fighters, "young people wanting to defeat communism." The local Jaycees put on an annual Anti-Communism

Seminar and so did the public schools. The latter brought in W. Cleon Skousen to speak, a man who was so far right that he would get kicked out of the John Birch Society.[22] But it wasn't just Abilene or Amarillo; these groups and activities were in every West Texas town and city. Around the same time, long-standing national organizations popular in the region, including the Daughters of the American Revolution, American Legion, and Farm Bureau, were all taking up extreme positions on the far right. Suffice it to say, West Texas was rich soil to plant JBS chapters.

The JBS's celebration of old-time religion, self-reliance, moral rectitude, states' rights, and individualism meshed seamlessly with the local culture. And let's not forget that by this point in West Texas, frontier mythology was seamlessly meshed with pro-business conservatism. And Welch was unequivocal on the subject: protecting pioneer values was the only sure antidote to the disease of collectivism. As he wrote in the *Blue Book*, "It is perfectly visible and incontrovertible that the rugged pioneer settlers of a new land want as little government as possible; that as the new society becomes more settled, as population grows, as commerce and/or industry increase, as the society grows older, more and more government creeps in."[23] Standing opposed to government overreach was seen as an essential frontier virtue, a foundational idea of cowboy conservatism.[24] (Senator Gale McGee, recognizing this trend in his home state of Wyoming—the "Cowboy State," no less—once warned President Kennedy that the devotion to this brand of "rugged individualism" in the West made the entire region susceptible to right-wing extremism.[25])

III

Buck Mann was an exceptional regional coordinator. A native of West Texas and a rock-solid member of the Midland-Odessa booster class, he moved effortlessly through the white-collar professional world where the JBS drew its membership.[26] His first career was in sales (insurance), but he found his calling in the oil game (transportation). He was a statewide player in both the Jaycees and the Oil Field Haulers Association. He coached Little League. He chaired the Ector County Democratic Party at thirty-four. He was a founding member of Texans for America and created and chaired the Americanism subcommittee of the Texas Jaycees. When he joined the John Birch Society, he resigned from the Democratic Party with a flourish, saying in a statement that Democrats were "no longer interested in personal liberty" and were refusing to rec-ognize "limitations on the power of government."[27]

The job of regional coordinator for the JBS was like that of a regional sales director. It certainly played to Mann's strengths: local knowl-edge, connections, organization, hard work, and people skills.[28] He was constantly on the move. First there was recruiting—organizing meet-ings, giving talks, screening films, and setting up chapters. And there was directing chapter projects, especially letter-writing campaigns and grooming new leaders. Membership was secret, so discretion was a strength. Mann's efforts to keep the organization on the down-low for as long as possible were successful. By the time the national media started poking around the Society and cranking out unflattering stories in early 1961, Mann had already set up a huge network all over the state. There were fifteen chapters in Amarillo alone. (He was also successful in organizing eastern New Mexico, with active chapters in Portales and Clovis.) Covert letter-writing campaigns had shifted political conver-sations, and screenings of JBS-approved films were on the rise. Front groups pitched local projects on behalf of the Society. Amarillo was the great success story: piggybacking on the city's textbook fight, the Society grew quickly through personal connections and word of mouth. It qui-etly launched dozens of different projects in autumn 1960.[29]

The Society remained mostly a rumor for most folks until March 1961, when Amarillo coordinator General Jerry Lee went off the rails. Out of nowhere, the former head of the Amarillo Air Force Base started lobbing accusations that the National Council of Churches was part of a communist conspiracy and guesstimating that that there were at least five thousand communists living and plotting in West Texas. He was widely believed to have been the source of a list of purported communist agents in Amarillo that included a prominent minister and a candidate for the city commission. Amarillo now had its own Red Scare.

Lee was a native of West Texas who, thanks to a career in the air force, had lived all over the world. His last post, as the commander of the Amarillo Air Force Base, capped off a brilliant military career. He was a good pilot and great flight instructor. He had taught Dwight Eisen-hower to fly and built the Philippine Air Force from scratch. Lee was smart, sincere, curious, hardworking, loyal, and a good administrator. He also had a reputation as a hothead—not necessarily dangerous, but certainly someone to be treated with caution. They called him the "toughest guy in the Air Force." Despite his wide travels and experiences, he was proud to be hopelessly old-fashioned and believed that only a return to bedrock American values—West Texas values—offered any hope in the fight against communism.[30]

Military officers like Lee were widespread across the far right. Thanks to a National Security Council project launched to educate soldiers and the stateside public to the "menace of communism," the military often in those years found itself relying on supposed "experts" on communism to run their programs. Too often, those authorities were right-wing extremists like George S. Benson, Fred Schwarz, or Billy James Hargis, whose programs for the military pushed radical-right narratives about internal subversion and communist conspiracies. They featured regular screenings of NEP films like *Communism on the Map* and *Operation Abolition*. The textbooks of these "freedom schools," as they were often called, had been written by right-wingers like Cleon Skousen and Dan Smoot. The central theme of most of the schools was that "the primary, if not exclusive danger to this country is internal communist infiltration." Before the whole thing got shut down in early 1961, soldiers, sailors, airmen, and marines were learning that the domestic goals of the Kennedy administration were "steps toward communism."[31]

At Lackland Air Force Base near San Antonio, where Lee had learned to fly, the head of the communist education project distributed a manual to recruits and reserves which claimed that "Communists and Communist fellow-travelers have successfully infiltrated our churches" and accused San Antonio pastors of being "card-carrying communists." The manual's author was a low-level technical writer named Homer Hyde, already half-convinced that the threat of internal subversion was real. As he was preparing the document, and on the advice of his own pastor, the head of San Antonio's Grace Temple Baptist Church, Hyde reached out to Billy James Hargis for research information. The fire-breathing Tulsa minister and professional anticommunist happily responded by sending Hyde half a dozen of his pamphlets, including "The National Council of Churches Indicts Itself on 50 Counts of Treason to God and Country" and "Apostate Clergymen Battle for God-Hating Communist China." Hyde relied heavily on Hargis's material. When the head of the

National Council of Churches got a hold of the manual, he complained to the Secretary of Defense, the handbook was yanked, and the whole education project canceled.[32]

That the National Council of Churches (NCC) was infested with communists was dogma within far-right circles, particularly the John Birch Society. Welch himself loved to repeat the claim that there were seven thousand communist or communist-sympathizing ministers in the United States. We'll soon get to the ways that Welch's brain worked, but for now, here's how he came to his conclusions about the NCC: There was a massive communist conspiracy at work in America. For that plot to succeed, the communists would have to take over the nation's religious infrastructure, and since the NCC was the nation's largest religious organization, it had to be part of that plot. Simple. As for where the seven thousand number came from, it was probably cooked up in Welch's head. His only "evidence" for the NCC's communist sympathies were the facts that the NCC praised the *Brown v. Board of Education* decision, called for the admission of China to the United Nations, and publicly supported several social justice causes. In early 1961, he launched his—and the Society's—attacks on the NCC after the organization publicly questioned the motives and arguments of an anticommunist film produced by the House Committee on Un-American Activities.

The movie was called *Operation Abolition*, and it was a huge recruiting tool for the John Birch Society; regional and local coordinators showed it several times a week at civic group meetings and even at schools. The message of the film was that communists had been behind recent student protests against HUAC in San Francisco. By 1960 HUAC had fallen on hard times; the committee was seen by most as the place where party leaders could stash their more embarrassingly far-right members, where they could do the least damage. Its hearings, ignored by almost everyone, resembled show trials, and its reports, also ignored by almost everyone, read like conspiratorial fan fiction. Far-right supporters conjured up the movie *Operation Abolition* as a publicity tool to rescue HUAC's reputation after a particularly disastrous set of committee hearings in the Bay Area. Purportedly investigating possible communist infiltration in the local public schools, the hearings drew massive protests, especially among college students from Berkeley. The nightly news ran footage and reported on an overreactive police force that arrested students by the dozens and dragged them out of the building and down staircases.

Americans were horrified. HUAC subpoenaed the news footage and spliced it together into a forty-five-minute film portraying the protests as part of a communist plot to disrupt the committee's work. It tapped ultraconservative activist Fulton Lewis III to narrate the film. HUAC made hundreds of copies of *Operation Abolition* (the name of the plot, or so the committee claimed) and distributed them to right-wing groups across the country, including the Society.[33]

It was the constant barrage of demands to screen the movie in churches and to church groups that forced the NCC to get involved.[34] Members kept writing headquarters for advice. The NCC's official response was that the film should be shown only if there were people on hand to offer context and balance. The council also put together a pamphlet, "Some Facts and Some Comments," about the film, the controversy, HUAC, and the protest. For Welch, who believed the film was doing a great service in exposing the depth and reach of the communist plot, the NCC's response was clear evidence of its support of a communist agenda. Included in that spring's monthly bulletins were directions to members to demand their churches withdraw from the NCC.[35]

Jerry Lee, the "toughest guy in the Air Force," took up the fight in Amarillo. From his position as local JBS leader, he encouraged members to observe their ministers more carefully. Soon Birchers were analyzing every sermon for evidence of communist sympathies. Lee publicly claimed that the Society had "documented proof" that the NCC was harboring communists and that, once local clergy listened to reason, they would scramble to cut their ties to the group and "the issue would be settled."[36] Instead, however, Amarillo's ministers released a statement demanding that Lee put up or shut up. If the JBS had actual evidence that NCC was infiltrated by communists, it should immediately turn that evidence over to the FBI. They reminded Lee that the NCC had already unequivocally denied the charges of communist infiltration and censured the general for resorting to "conviction by accusation and defamation of character by rumor."[37]

Faced with such a public rebuke from every major religious figure in the community, perhaps the prudent approach might have been to lay low and quietly seek some common ground. Not Lee. He wanted a fight. Hackles up, the general banged out a 2,300-word manifesto laying out his case against the National Council of Churches. His "irrefutable proof" turned out to be nothing more than a case study of Bircher logic where barely-there connections assume the strength of suspension bridge cables. It went, in part, like this: Back in the 1930s, J. Edgar Hoover warned that American communists had gained some access to the "mainstream of American life," coming into regular contact with those "influential in melding public opinion." And, since preachers were influential, it was a safe conclusion, Lee assumed, that many of these ministers had been "DUPED" into promoting the communist agenda and "STIFLING ANTI-Communist views."[38] *Quod erat demonstrandum.* He called the NCC's very public denials of communist influence an "insult upon the intelligence of all who support this pseudo-religious political organization." Communists, he explained, were too smart to "neglect as important a field in our national life as the churches" and must have infiltrated the NCC, as it was the most important religious organization in the country. Therefore, it was up to the churches and the NCC to prove they had *not* been secretly infiltrated: "The burden of proof still rests upon the ministers." And, he warned, if they didn't get with the program, they "will be left preaching to near empty pews served by the remaining left-wing and pinko deacons or the idol worshippers of the ministers."[39]

And he meant it. Amarillo Birchers began a passive-aggressive and largely silent campaign in their churches. Collection plates grew lighter by the week, and annual campaign goals grew harder to reach. Preachers received unsigned notes and anonymous late-night phone calls complaining about collectivism in sermons. One local minister lucky enough to buy a new car got a nasty letter demanding to know why he had chosen a red automobile. Suspect connotations or references in church bulletins and Sunday School programs were underlined and circled and shoved under church office doors. Birchers worked to move into leadership positions in their churches and began demanding adherence to Society dogma. Amarillo novelist Al Dewlen, who made a nice literary career out of skewering the more ridiculous elements of Amarillo society, made the Society takeover of a church the main plot point in his *Servants of Corruption.*[40]

The basis of the novel was the real-life breakup of the Polk Street Methodist Church, the city's oldest and most prestigious house of worship. An estimated five hundred Birchers and sympathizers in the congregation split from Polk Street and organized the First Congregational Methodist Church of Amarillo. That church, easily the most politically conservative in West Texas, soon attracted like-minded parishioners from other denominations who abandoned their own churches in favor of one that hewed more closely to their political ideology.[41] As one befuddled preacher confided: "I can't understand what is happening. Do you know that I've never actually seen a communist, not even a member of one of those fringe things, yet the town is all worked up about this 'internal communist menace.'" Another added: "I felt Amarillo was the national capital of the John Birch Society."[42]

Of course, denominational weakness had been a constant in religious life in West Texas since the frontier days. Churches across the Christian fundamentalist spectrum had always preached individualism and treasured their independence. And the kind of uncompromising, independent, antistatist, and pro–free market philosophy of the JBS was integral to what historian Darren Dochuk has called "Texas Theology."[43] If anything, large, well-heeled, and nationally connected churches like Polk Street Methodist were the exception to the average religious organization in the region. (It's also no coincidence that new, independent and nondenominational churches exploded in the region as its population grew.)[44] As one Minnesota-born Lutheran minister observed, "The interpretive tool by which [the members of his Amarillo congregation] interpret the Scriptures is highly privatistic, individualized, I would call it hyper individuality."[45]

We should see the establishment of a Bircher church as a logical extension of both local religious culture *and* the message of the Society. Birchers, after all, considered Welch the "greatest of all Christian Freedom Fighters" and the JBS as a Christian organization.[46] Bent as many folk denominations were toward a form of biblical dispensationalism, they viewed the Cold War as the last stage in the eternal battle between God and Satan for control of humanity—an interpretation encouraged across the political spectrum—and saw Satan himself pulling the levers of the plot against the United States, the only Christian nation strong enough to thwart his plan.[47] The Society, as one Amarillo man understood it, was "the spark of fire God could fan into a flame," America's best chance at survival.[48]

IV

Robert Welch hit town in April 1961, the first stop on a Texas speaking tour. The Founder was on edge. Over the previous month the national news media had been putting out a steady stream of negative press on Welch and the Society. They focused on its authoritarian structure, its secrecy, and its philosophy. Reporters peppered their stories with juicy out-there quotes from Welch, like the one about Dwight Eisenhower being an active communist agent. Many delighted in pointing out that JBS tactics such as establishing front groups and working from secret cells were the same sort of approaches employed by the communists. They revealed to the world the conspiratorial mind of Robert Welch, portraying him as the paranoid, authoritarian mastermind of a movement that threatened to destroy American democracy.[49] There was no shortage of Hitler comparisons.[50] Locally, Ben Ezzell, editor and publisher of the *Canadian Record* and usually a reliable conservative, published his own report on a Society meeting he attended. This one, also hosted by Wes Izzard, was actually held at the offices of the *Amarillo Globe-News*. There, sitting among Amarillo's "most prominent citizens," were a people who "were absolutely seditious." He titled one of his many pieces that spring "The John Birch Society: A Threat to America?"[51]

The editorial pages of the Amarillo papers, however, breathed nervous excitement about Welch's visit. The day before he was to appear, *Globe Times* editorial page editor Louise Evans penned a front-page story refuting all the charges against Welch and the Society. JBS chapters and front organizations took out quarter-page ads inviting one and all to "see and hear undistorted documented truths from one of the greatest of all Christian freedom fighters."[52]

On the night of Welch's appearance, Amarillo police dispatched ten officers to the city auditorium just in case the event turned unruly.[53] They need not have feared; it was a polite, well-dressed, not-quite-capacity crowd of eighteen hundred. The founder was introduced by J. C. Phillips, the editor of the most reactionary right-wing paper in the nation, the *Borger News-Herald*. Over the course of his ninety-five-minute address, Welch, one of the least dynamic speakers in the history of public life (one local editor called him a "restrained haranguer") was, nevertheless, interrupted by wild applause eighteen times.[54] For the faithful in the crowd, those gripping their dog-eared and marked-up *Blue Books* and who faithfully mailed their MMMs to Belmont each month, the talk was a soothing medley of hits: well-placed communists had denied Robert Taft the presidential nomination; the New Deal was "foreign, phony, and a failure"; the Supreme Court was an instrument of communism; Joe McCarthy was a true American hero; and time was short. And, yes, there were seven thousand communist ministers preaching in the United States. In one of the stranger moments of the evening, Welch, responding to a cough from the audience, reprimanded the crowd, telling them—with full seriousness—that coughing was a form of heckling and heckling was part of a larger communist conspiracy to discredit the JBS.

The highlight of the speech was Welch's discourse on the "Principle of Reversal," the key to unraveling the communist conspiracy. It went like this: The communist conspiracy was so layered, so widespread, and so dense that it warped reality. Nothing, Welch warned, was as it seemed. Unless, of course, it was exactly as it seemed because the communists were using the principle of reversal. Only Welch, apparently, thanks to his long study of the enemy, could recognize the truth.[55]

In the cheering crowd that night was Amarillo's new mayor-elect, Jack Seale, a member of the John Birch Society. Just a few days earlier, Seale, a relatively minor local political figure, had staged a massive upset in the mayoral election, defeating a powerful and comfortable incumbent. (The new mayor of Odessa, another Society stronghold, was also an admitted Bircher.) Seale had not openly run as a Society member; in fact, he revealed that fact only after the election. But it became obvious that he owed his victory to bloc voting among the JBS cells in the city. He had announced his campaign just six weeks before the election, surprising everyone. Until that day he had been quietly serving a nondescript first term on the Amarillo City Commission. In February, however, Seale had suddenly cast a lone dissenting vote that would have allowed the city's public library to host the Great Decisions program. An annual set of public discussions hosted in cities across the country on topics of great import and sponsored by the Foreign Policy Association (FPA), Great Decisions had never attracted much attention. But that winter, the FPA had become the latest of Welch's obsessions, and letters began pouring into city editors and officials, grousing about Amarillo hosting a propaganda event for one-worlders.[56] Some suggested instead of Great Decisions the library should screen *Communism on the Map* instead. Two weeks after voting against Great Decisions, Seale threw his hat into the ring for mayor.[57]

Candidate Seale ran a straight-ahead good government campaign, playing up the business acumen and relative youth of "the thinking young man for mayor." There was no hint of his Bircher ties. He was the only candidate running for city office in that election to win without a runoff.[58] After taking office, Seale started translating Society ideology into city policy. He pushed for incentive-based pay for city employees. He refused to sign a declaration by the nation's mayors in support of American aid to foreign countries. In a statement also signed by city commissioners, the mayor disagreed with the notion that foreign aid "contributes materially to either peace or solidarity."[59] In August, Amarillo gained national notoriety when the city turned down a $250,000 federal grant that would have paid for a desperately needed new sewage treatment plant.[60] Seale said that the city would not "seek nor will it accept . . . financial aid from the government of the United States for the purpose of solving local problems that can and should be solved at the local level."[61] The "nation's strength" was not in federal programs, a resolution coming out of the mayor's office read, but instead "is found in its individuals and communities."[62] Local folks praised the decision. "Somewhere along the line, the people of this nation must begin to turn back the onslaught of the welfare state, and we can think of no better place to start than right here in our own city," wrote one supporter of the mayor.[63]

Mayor Seale extended the city's official welcome to a pantheon of Bircher superstars, often serving as master of ceremonies at the events. When General Edwin Walker came to town, Seale declared it "American Patriots Day." Official welcomes also accompanied visits by Billy James Hargis, Clarence Manion, Dan Smoot, Tom Anderson, John Tower, Barry Goldwater (who campaigned for Seale), and others. Seale canceled Amarillo's official United Nations Day activities and instead proclaimed it "United States Day." And the mayor was the official host of a National Indignation Convention rally held in the city in December 1961.[64]

The following year, Seale sought to take his talents to the U.S. Congress and challenged long-term incumbent representative Walter Rogers. Running as a Republican, one of eighteen campaigning for

Congress in Texas that year, Seale hoped to ride a wave of enthusiasm for right-wing politicians set off by conservative John Tower's successful run for the Senate the previous year. Tower had taken 62 percent of the district's vote, and Seale hoped to utilize the local party infrastructure that conservatives had built for that campaign.[65] Seale faced a basic problem, however: Rogers was a popular, rock-ribbed conservative, one of the few Texans to sign the Southern Manifesto.[66] Rogers made Seale's JBS membership a centerpiece of his campaign, accusing the mayor of being a plaything for Robert Welch and not independent enough to represent the people of the Panhandle. He challenged the former mayor to publicly denounce Robert Welch and the JBS. Seale refused. Rogers ran ads that claimed "a vote for Seale is a vote for the dictatorial John Birch Society" and urged voters not to "vote for a secret society—vote for a man."[67] The Amarillo Establishment rejected Seale, recognizing in Rogers a solid, stable conservative who tended to the region's interest in banking, oil, cattle, and wheat. It seemed that most of Seale's support came from "the professional middle class in the cities—doctors, dentists, a few lawyers, white-collar salaried people, large numbers of rather severely distressed middle-class ladies."[68] Seale won only five counties and ran well behind GOP gubernatorial candidate Jack Cox. Rogers took 60 percent of the overall vote. Seale even lost Potter and Randall counties, JBS strongholds.[69] Out of office, Seale went back to selling real estate and, two years after the election, replaced Buck Mann as JBS's Texas coordinator.[70]

Following Seale as Amarillo mayor was Shamrock Oil and Gas executive F. V. Wallace. For four years, the city enjoyed relative calm. But in 1967, Amarillo voters put another right-wing activist in the mayor's office. This time, it was J. Ernest Stroud, whose JBS membership was the worst-kept secret in town. Stroud was so widely known as a Bircher that his campaign ads had to contain the tagline "not paid for by the John Birch Society." But everyone knew he had been a prominent and public leader of several far-right causes since the early 1960s. Stroud had fronted the Amarillo delegation to the inaugural National Indignation Convention in Dallas back in 1961, a protest movement against the United States training Yugoslavian pilots and trading with Eastern Bloc Countries. The convention featured a cavalcade of right-wingers, including Evetts Haley, who enjoyed a few days of national notoriety when he joked that the moderates who had preceded him to the stage wanted only to impeach Chief Justice Earl Warren. "I'm for hanging him," he cracked.[71] The convention's main attraction was General Edwin Walker, who had just been kicked out of the army for distributing John Birch Society materials to his soldiers. An FBI investigation into the convention concluded that the whole thing was a front for the John Birch Society. In 1963, Stroud gained national fame with his "Millions of Americans for Goldwater," a campaign finance scheme meant to raise money for a potential Goldwater presidential campaign and to show the GOP Establishment the fervency of Goldwater's grassroots supporters. Stroud served on the advisory board of the local Young Americans for Freedom chapter and was known to take out full-page ads to broadcast his various right-wing views.[72]

Stroud had also been instrumental in turning the Randall County Republican Party into a vehicle for ultraconservatism, helping write its 1964 platform, a document that would have made Robert Welch blush. Besides unanimously and "harmoniously" endorsing the candidacy of Barry Goldwater, the platform recommended that the federal government "encourage an armed citizenry," loudly restate the Monroe Doctrine, and "vigorously" prosecute communists. It opposed an early draft of Medicare, deficit spending, foreign aid, federal aid to education, international courts, the 1964 Civil Rights Act, and federal farm programs. And it demanded that religion play a greater part in the daily lives of Americans.[73]

Stroud's 1967 mayoral platform pushed an all-purpose frugal, good-government, save-downtown-businesses campaign. Against an overconfident F. V. Wallace, who barely campaigned, Stroud, like Seale, won without a runoff. He took his victory to be a mandate for his politics. He started a weekly radio address in which he took his hatred of bureaucracy out on city employees whom he accused of being lazy and incompetent. He badmouthed and berated the city manager and made no secret of the fact that he wanted him fired. He accused city telephone operators of listening in on his calls. His idea of frugal city government included selling off the city's buses, even those used to transport children to and from school. He wanted to eliminate public transportation and parking meters. He wanted to cut city taxes and end city contracts with utility providers.[74] He proposed a return to well water to get out of the city's water and sewer obligations. His temper and vindictiveness were legendary. He stormed out in the middle of meetings with no explanation; he scheduled important votes when his opposition was absent. He constantly complained of being undermined by the powers that be. Thanks to Stroud's antics, Amarillo became a laughingstock. Native son Buck Ramsey, writing for the *Texas Observer*, asked the question that many pondered when he titled an article on the Stroud administration, "Is Amarillo Ready for Self-Government?"[75]

The most frightening element of Stroud's early mayoralty was an attempt to start an "auxiliary police force" for the city. In light of 1967's national summer of riots, Stroud proposed that a special police squad of men "interested in protecting the public welfare" might prove necessary. Trained in riot control, the force would be purely "precautionary." Black Amarilloans were mortified. Leaders from the North Heights Council of Community Organizations warned against the measure, calling it "drastic" and "emotional." It was widely suspected that the whole thing was a radical offshoot of a new John Birch Society project, "Support Your Local Police," founded on Welch's paranoid belief that the federal government was going to use urban riots as a pretext for the federalization of the nation's police departments. Stroud would head off that plan with his own private army of patriots. Within hours of floating the idea, he had already compiled a list of 212 volunteers and named a local police officer, known to have Bircher and white-supremacist sympathies, as head of the special squad. A *Globe-Times* beat reporter did a little snooping around and found the list of "volunteers." It seems that it had been prepared weeks earlier and was basically a "who's who of the male right-wing in Amarillo." Once word about the list and its membership became public, the city council quickly scotched the whole thing.[76]

By the time Stroud came up for reelection, Amarillo's dysfunctional government was the main issue. The two candidates were Stroud and his nemesis on the city commission L. O'Brien Thompson, who had support of the Chamber of Commerce crowd. It was, as one voter put it, a clear choice between "the John Birchers or the Establishment."[77] Stroud won easily.

13
THE WEST TEXAS CROWD

I was also fortunate that I was raised in a part of the world, West Texas, where individualism is strong. Where people can dream big dreams and achieve them.

GEORGE W. BUSH

For most of the twentieth century, to be a Republican in Texas was a matter of faith, an illogical yet conscious choice of political irrelevancy in service to a lost cause. It meant becoming an object of curiosity, if not perfidy, in one's community. There were pockets of Republicanism in the German Hill Country. Some of the rectangular counties in the far northern Panhandle, settled by midwestern wheat farmers, had Republicans. African Americans voted Republican when given the opportunity, which wasn't often. To be white and Texan meant allegiance to the Democratic Party, as essential to one's identity as home, family, or faith. Which left the Republican Party in the hands of the iconoclasts, the ideologues, and the opportunists. In terms of functionality, the GOP existed primarily to distribute federal jobs when Republicans occupied the White House—a post office appointment, a harbor or health inspector, a judgeship. To run the state party was literally a one-man job.[1] There was no infrastructure to maintain, no district or county or precinct captains to wrangle, no committees to organize. Every four years, the loyal few earned a trip to the national Republican Convention to hand one lucky candidate the state's votes. Like other southern Republican parties, "lily white" Republicans had purged African Americans from leadership positions by the early twentieth century and spent the next three decades squabbling over personal grievances and patronage. The New Deal changed all that.

Passionate opposition to Roosevelt's policies drew into the party a new breed of political actors. They rejected Roosevelt and his activist federal government, loathed organized labor, and embraced white supremacy. So many of these new Republicans were from the western half of the state that they became known as "the West Texas Crowd." The faction was led by Orville Bullington, a Wichita Falls oilman/banker/rancher/railroad lawyer and product of the Cross Timbers frontier.[2] The son of a farmer/preacher/teacher, Bullington found his calling in the law and in 1909 moved to Wichita Falls, where he grew a profitable practice and moved in the city's best circles, even marrying the daughter of a prominent railroad baron/banker/mill owner.

Bullington thrived in the go-go town of Wichita Falls: Real Estate. Banking. Oil. Railroads. Hotels. Cattle. Radio. He boosted with the best of them: Rotarian. Chamber of Commerce. President of the American National Bank. He was also president of the Texas Exes, one of the most powerful alumni organizations in the country. He jumped into electoral politics in 1922, running as an independent (though everyone knew he was a Republican) in a special election to represent Texas's 13th Congressional District, then the northernmost counties of the Cross Timbers. His platform was a hodgepodge of white supremacy, tariff support, farmer's cooperatives, limited and cheap government, immigration restriction, and distribution of the public lands as homesteads. He finished a distant third but ran strong enough to attract the attention of GOP higher-ups.[3]

By 1924, he was serving as temporary state chairman and the acknowledged leader of the party's lily-white faction. His opposition to the income tax and free trade had drawn him into the orbit of John Henry Kirby and the emerging far right in Texas. Bullington was pro-business and pro-prohibition and anti-Klan and anti-Ferguson. He was the Republican candidate for Texas governor in 1932, challenging Miriam "Ma" Ferguson and pinning his hopes on a wave of defections by anti-Ferguson Democrats to the GOP. He did receive endorsements from some prominent Democrats, and Roosevelt-Bullington clubs popped up around the state. (Keep in mind, however, that FDR's 1932 platform was so conservative that Barry Goldwater once claimed that he would have felt comfortable running on it.) Bullington campaigned heavily in West Texas and ran well there, winning twenty-five counties outright, including most of the urban counties of Midland, Ector, Randall, Potter, and Tom Green, and barely losing Taylor. He ran well in both the wheat and the ranching counties. He received more votes than any other Republican gubernatorial candidate in history—five times that of 1930's standard bearer.[4]

In the mid-1930s, Bullington, one of the loudest anti-Roosevelt voices in Texas, started running with the Jeffersonian Democrat crowd— Big Jim West, Evetts Haley, John Kirby, Vance Muse. In his keynote at the 1936 Republican state convention, he denounced the president as a "demagogue" whose administration was overrun with communists, and the leader of the "costliest and most corrupt political machine" in history.[5] He supported the Texas Regulars and was one of the regents who fired UT president Homer Rainey. A Taft Republican, Bullington attended eight straight national GOP conventions where he worked to eliminate or weaken any civil rights planks the party might consider. Under his leadership, which lasted from the 1920s to the mid-1950s, the West Texas wing of the GOP became the noisiest antiliberal, anti-Roosevelt, antilabor, anti–civil rights, anti–New Deal wing of any political party in the country, an ideologically pure vehicle for the expression of the ultraconservative id. At the height of his influence, Bullington took on an apprentice—John Tower, a brilliant, dapper, and diminutive young political science professor who had just married Bullington's cousin.

I

Perhaps it's ironic that John Tower, the first national figure produced by the West Texas Crowd, could not have looked more out of place in the region. He wasn't tall or lanky or weathered. He didn't wear boots, jeans, or a Stetson, and he didn't drawl any homespun political philosophy born of lessons from the range. He was a short, hyperarticulate scholar who wore his hair slicked straight back and smoked imported cigarettes. He favored Savile Row suits, highly polished oxfords, and rep ties. He spoke in full paragraphs that would have included footnotes if possible. But Tower was still Texas through and through. The son and grandson of East Texas Methodist ministers, Tower had grown up in timber camps and oil patch towns. He graduated from Beaumont High School in 1942 and like a lot of Texas boys, joined the navy during World War II. He washed out as a pilot and spent the war swabbing the decks of various gunboats. Once discharged, he enrolled at Southwestern University and studied political science. An excellent scholar, he received an MA from SMU, where, after conducting research at the London School of Economics, he wrote his thesis on working-class support for Britain's Conservative Party.[6]

He was hired by Midwestern University in Wichita Falls and began to move through the city's professional circles.[7] He met and fell in love with the organist at his church, Lou Bullington, Orville's cousin. Tower had become a Republican while in college, having come to his conservatism through his scholarship, and was particularly devoted to the ideas of Edmund Burke and Thomas Jefferson. Like other conservatives of his time, his political ideology was firmly planted in eighteenth-century conceptions of the political economy. He saw deficit spending, inflation, and government interference as violations of natural law and believed governments were formed and societies functioned to protect individual freedom and private property.[8] Tower believed that neither liberty nor freedom nor happiness nor even equality were possible under a government that failed to recognize private property as anything less than absolute.[9]

Orville Bullington took his new cousin-in-law under his wing and put him to work developing policy for the West Texas Crowd of the Texas GOP. The professor thrived; ever a good student, Tower soon mastered the details of Texas politics: the stories, the players, the data, and the written and unwritten rules of the game. By age thirty, Tower was running the state party's education and research programs. He was its intellectual Young Turk, convinced that he could help create an honest-to-god two-party system in Texas by developing an honest-to-god conservative party.

He attended his first Republican National Convention in 1956 and was named a sergeant at arms. Two years later, he chaired the Texas GOP's platform committee and wrote its statement of principles, warning of the "creeping socialism" of farm programs, federal regulations, and foreign spending and calling for more defense spending and standing up to Soviet aggression. By the time he attended his second convention in 1960, the professor not only sat on the national platform committee but was considered the intellectual leader of the southern Republican Party.

In that role, he took on the task of redefining the GOP's position on civil rights. A new breed of Republicans, led by Texan Peter O'Donnell, believed that the future of the party lay in the South, and the key to the South was to make the GOP an unequivocal defender of states' rights and the racial status quo. Tower crafted a pro-segregation position, but one that stopped short of the southern fire-breathers ranting about blood in the streets and shuttering the schools. Tower called for prudence and caution, even recognizing the frustration within Black communities. Slow and local was the way to go. He criticized his own party and the Eisenhower administration for its seeming recklessness: "We don't want the segregation issue shoved down our throats."[10] That's what passed for "moderate" in those days in Texas. But that moderation was exactly what many in the booster-professional class were looking for. The state party's 1958 platform, largely written by Tower, operated on the "respectable" edges of massive resistance, condemning the *Brown* decision and denouncing federal enforcement of desegregation. In 1960, after soon-to-be Republican nominee Richard Nixon met with liberal party leader Nelson Rockefeller and agreed to a pro–civil rights plank in the 1960 Republican platform, southern delegates were ready to bolt. The West Texas Crowd, which distrusted Nixon anyway, were ready to lead the walkout. Tower stepped in and reworked the civil rights plank into a meaningless catalog of Republican accomplishments under the Eisenhower administration and vague pledges to make "best efforts" going forward. Southern delegates stayed in line. Tower's reputation grew.[11]

He was soon defining the Texas GOP's other positions. Tower believed that since coexistence with the Soviet Union was impossible U.S. foreign policy should be predicated on the eradication of communism. The Soviet Union, the mortal enemy of the United States, must be defeated and soon. Even at the cost of war. It was a simplistic approach to be sure, but it had a logic that appealed to many, especially those frustrated with the Cold War, deep into its second decade. An aggressive anti-Soviet stance was infinitely better, as Tower put it, than the "defeatist, passive half-measures, designed only to hold the status quo, to appease the enemy, to retreat with dignity and good humor."[12] He was antilabor and echoed the same burly right-to-work philosophy that had animated the Texas Right since the days of John Henry Kirby. Stripping away the paranoiac and white-supremacist foundations of his predecessors, however, Tower instead painted the modern labor movement and its leader Walter Reuther as dangerous radicals who posed a mortal threat to democracy. Powerful national unions had restrained trade, limited competition, and hurt consumers through artificially high prices. He recommended new legislation that would place organized labor under the same antitrust laws that governed businesses and trade associations.[13]

In 1960, mostly because no one else wanted to do it, new state chairman Peter O'Donnell asked Tower to be the party's Republican candidate for the U.S. Senate, taking on Lyndon Johnson. It was the kind of quixotic campaign that only a young and hyperactive true believer might relish; six years earlier, LBJ had dispatched his Republican opponent with 85 percent of the vote and hadn't even bothered to campaign. Tower, "too young and idealistic to know better" (his words), couldn't wait. He saw himself as the "quarterback for a scrappy, underdog football team," taking on the district juggernaut, like Odessa High taking on Permian.[14]

Sports metaphors aside, Tower understood that Texas had changed a lot in the six years since Johnson had rolled to victory. Conservatism was on the move. Groups like Haley's Texans for America had generated an energetic army of activists desperate for a conservative challenger to LBJ. A new generation of professionals had been steadily moving into the GOP, eager to organize a legitimate campaign. A twenty-six-year-old data whiz named Richard Viguerie, for example, managed Tower's campaign in Houston.[15] Volunteers were everywhere. The editorial pages of some of the state's most important newspapers were ready with endorsements: the *Amarillo News-Globe*, *Midland Telegraph*, *Lubbock Avalanche*, and *Dallas Morning News*.

Running Tower's statewide campaign was the brilliant and equally energetic Peter O'Donnell, a brainiac out of the Wharton School whose technocratic approach to finance had made him rich. Applying his algorithmic zeal to politics had transformed the Dallas GOP into the most effective Republican organization in the South. O'Donnell's strategy was simple: recruit, organize, and mobilize the ultraconservatives who populated Texas's white-collar, suburban class into Republican functionaries. With enough urban and suburban votes, he could circumvent the power of the county courthouse gangs and counter the votes of rural Texans who still couldn't get their head around voting for a Republican. It was a particularly effective strategy in West Texas, where most of the population lived in the cities and big towns and where ultraconservatism was flourishing.[16]

Tower flat out rejected the "modern Republicanism" of the Eisenhower years, a governing philosophy that acknowledged the continuing viability of government programs. Instead, he pushed what was quickly becoming known as Goldwaterism, a new articulation of conservative thought that, while at times veering into the extremist lane, was for the most part a positive, even forward-thinking articulation of the antistatist, hawkish, and pro-business attitudes that had been rousing the right since the 1930s. What spurred Tower and others in that election year was a remarkable little book "written" by the Arizona senator that dropped in February. By that point, the blunt, funny, and charming Goldwater had been in the U.S. Senate for eight years and had become his party's most popular speaker. And, after the death of Robert Taft in 1953, he had taken the mantle as the national political leader of the conservative movement. Prompted by *National Review* editor and publisher William F. Buckley, Goldwater agreed to have a book published outlining his views—*The Conscience of a Conservative*. While Goldwater had little to do with the actual writing of the text—that was handled by Buckley's cousin and fellow conservative Brent Bozell—the book was an accurate account of his views.[17]

The Conscience of a Conservative, which would become a publishing phenomenon, distilled the more widely held ideas on the right to ten short topical chapters with titles like "Freedom for the Farmer," "The Welfare State," and "The Soviet Menace." It sold millions of copies and quickly became the bible for right-wing Republicans. It detached the word "conservative" from its association with gray-suited, monocled bankers and industrialists and bestowed it on the sunbaked and smiling sons and daughters of the Southwest. It rejected Yankee claims of tradition in favor of bringing frontier values into politics. It was even, as historian Rick Perlstein put it, "idealistic."[18] Its main premise, stated right on page one, should sound familiar: America "is fundamentally a conservative nation." Everything that had happened since 1933 had been an aberration, a (hopefully temporary) rejection of the principles that made America great. Goldwater-Bozell proclaimed that the nation could get back on track only if it returned to fundamentals: cut the federal budget, reestablish the sovereignty of state power over the federal government, end federal farm subsidies, affirm right-to-work laws, create a flat income tax, eliminate federal interference in civil rights and education, and defeat the "Soviet Menace" once and for all.[19]

The book, published and packaged by an obscure printer in Kentucky created solely for that purpose, wholesaled for a dollar (but could be bought for much less in bulk) and retailed for three bucks. It climbed the best-seller list all year—ironically enough, right along with John Kenneth Galbraith's *The Liberal Hour*. It was a huge hit in West Texas, the subject of countless study groups and book clubs. It was reviewed (favorably) in local newspapers and gushed over by all the national syndicated columnists: Westbrook Pegler, George S. Benson, Holmes Alexander. One reviewer called it "timely" as well as "short and pungent, yet quite readable."[20] Randall County GOP organizer Richard Brooks called it "a rallying point," praising its ability to demonstrate that conservatives "should be concerned about the welfare of other people; to help make life better for them in any way possible, but a strong central government with a Socialist approach was not the right answer."[21]

The Conscience of a Conservative came out just as John Tower was launching his campaign. It was a perfect distillation of the Texan's own philosophy and linked the professor's run at the Senate to a larger national movement. Tower wasn't just a Republican but a "Goldwater Republican," a phrase that suddenly had great meaning. Goldwater himself helped the campaign with plenty of appearances with Tower, even piloting his personal plane to escort the candidate to rallies and meetings. It made for quite a sight in Texas towns, the dashing Arizona senator and the snappy Texas candidate, zipping onto some small runway for a quick campaign stop on the tarmac. The campaign was a critical moment in the development of the Texas Right, an expression of a new and vibrant style of antiliberal politics that carried neither the excess paranoia of Texas Birchers nor the ugly demagoguery of hardcore segregationists. When Tower came out against farm programs or foreign aid, it wasn't because they were part of a plot to Sovietize the nation but because they were bad policy. For Tower, states' rights were not paramount to protecting white supremacy, but rather a timeworn and effective means of governance. He was against taxes and government regulation because history had shown the free market to be the most efficient and equitable means of managing the economy.

Still, ideological enthusiasm alone wasn't going to get a Republican elected to the U.S. Senate from Texas. (Not yet, anyway.) And in a cash-strapped campaign, the Tower strategy was to get out there and meet and mobilize the like-minded, tap into a growing interest in the new conservativism, and build a legitimate grassroots movement. That meant constant public appearances—retail politics. And besides, Tower couldn't afford to purchase splashy media buys in Texas's multiple markets.[22] The professor proved a tireless and talented campaigner. No event was too small—in one five-week period, he made a hundred speeches. He once estimated that he covered 100,000 miles in airplane seats and thousands in more in the backs of cars.[23] At each appearance, Tower would build out the campaign's volunteer network and help direct on-the-ground programming. O'Donnell, with plenty of help from the national party, ran the campaign, one of the most professional and efficient in Texas history.[24] Volunteers working from carefully calibrated lists knocked on doors all day every day and made phone calls deep into the night. They were an impressive bunch, young, well dressed, articulate, and attractive. Most had gone to college, and many if not most had joined fraternities and sororities; they knew how to network and how to socialize. Women outnumbered men.[25] The kernel of most local organizations consisted of those already predisposed to a conservative message. For almost all of them, the Tower campaign was their first foray into the world of electoral politics. They found building a party and working toward an election a heady brew.[26]

On the trail, Tower hammered on LBJ all day, every day, portraying him as a duplicitous and vainglorious professional politician who long ago had traded principles for power. (A common opinion of Johnson on the right and the left in those years.) The "cunning and powerful" LBJ had "sold out the people of Texas."[27] He was a "Judas goat" responsible for leading faithful westerners and southerners "blindly into the Democratic fold."[28] Tower laid into LBJ for running for two offices at once. (Worried that his national ambitions might cost him his Senate seat, Johnson had rammed a bill through the Texas legislature that allowed him to run for his Senate seat and the vice-presidency in the same election.) Borrowing an earworm jingle from Wrigley's, Tower urged Texans to "double their pleasure, double their fun, scratch Lyndon twice."[29]

To the shock of everyone except maybe Tower and O'Donnell, the neophyte political science professor won a little over 40 percent of the vote; 926,653 Texans voted for him, ten times the number of votes cast for Johnson's previous Republican challenger. Tower did very well in West Texas. He won Midland, Canyon, Pampa, and Odessa easily and came within a hair's breadth of taking Potter County. He also did quite well in Houston and Dallas. Keep in mind, this was a performance against an incumbent Democrat who was the Senate majority leader and had made a career of bringing jobs and money back to Texas.

But Tower's run was just getting started. Johnson, of course, won the vice-presidency. Which left an open Senate seat. A special election to fill it was set for April. Energized by Tower's performance, the Texas GOP, better and more widely organized than at any time in its history, kicked it into high gear. The "incumbent" in the race was William "Dollar Bill" Blakley, temporarily appointed to the post by Governor Price Daniel. Blakley was a banker/lawyer/rancher/real estate mogul, one of the wealthiest men in Texas and a serious power broker in Democratic circles.[30] Most saw Blakley as a seat warmer for former governor Allan Shivers, whom they expected to run for and win the seat. But Shivers declined and the race became a free-for-all. Blakley announced, as did a handful of second-tier contenders. With a pittance for a filing fee, the race attracted dozens and dozens of candidates who had zero chance of winning but who wanted a laugh or maybe to get their name in the paper and on the ballot. Tower was the lone Republican. Special elections in Texas were nonpartisan, low-turnout affairs, giving Tower some hope. More important, he still had a campaign infrastructure in place: precinct captains, phone banks, literature, a corps of volunteers in every major town and city, *and* as the only Republican in the country running for election that spring, the full support and resources of the national party.[31]

First came the general primary, with seventy-one candidates, the largest field in Texas history. In a candid appraisal of the serious candidates for the *Texas Observer*, Tower, the astute scholar, laid it out: Blakley was such an obvious second-rate cog in the Rayburn and Johnson machine that he would generate little enthusiasm, but his ego would give him a foolish and misplaced confidence. Tower described the self-styled moderate Will Wilson's campaign as an exercise in vanity, appealing mostly to country club bankers. Jim Wright, he predicted, would be too frightened to run as an authentic liberal and would instead straddle the fence to a fourth- or fifth-place finish. Tower wanted to run against the actual liberal in the race, Maury Maverick: "People will then have the chance to make a clear ideological choice." He also predicted (correctly) that Texas liberals would split their vote between Maverick and the San Antonio firebrand Henry Gonzales.[32]

In the first part of the campaign, Tower didn't bother to run against Blakley or Maverick or Wilson. (The leading Democrats in the race, however, spent plenty of time sniping about one another.) Instead, Tower ran against the new president and his New Frontier, deeply unpopular in Texas. Kennedy had proposed to increase welfare benefits, raise the minimum wage, and develop urban areas and improve slums. He wanted to expand Social Security benefits and increase the power and budget of the Department of Education. To Texas conservatives, Republican and Democrat, it looked like the last stages before the United States would finally succumb to collectivism. Tower excoriated the "creeping socialism" of the nation and predicted that if any of his Democratic opponents were to win, Texans could expect to see their lives controlled "by the coercive force of the federal government."[33]

Tower played his Republicanism as a virtue, a chance for Texans to have an independent voice in Washington, to have a senator not obligated to follow the Democrats' dangerous new directions. He was, as he put it, the only "courageous conservative" in the race. In the first election that April, Tower cruised to a first-place finish with roughly a third of the vote. Blakley finished a distant second. A runoff was scheduled for late May.[34] That's when the national GOP set up shop in Texas. Barry Goldwater spent so much time campaigning for Tower in those weeks that wags started referring to him as Texas's third senator.[35] A Goldwater appearance, for Tower though, was like Aladdin's genie: "We asked for financial contributions—and the money rolled in; we asked for energetic campaign workers—and volunteers came in the droves."[36] The most powerful Republican in Washington, Senate minority leader Everett Dirkson, came down to campaign, as did Connecticut senator Prescott Bush, the latter at the request of his son George Bush, quickly becoming a player in the Texas GOP in his own right. Bush lent Tower the Establishment's blessing and, as Tower put it, "negated the allegation that I was some kind of right-wing kook [who] would be shunned and ineffective in the Senate." He also lent Tower his private airplane.[37] Tower even snagged a filmed endorsement from former president Dwight Eisenhower, which he quickly turned into a campaign ad.[38]

At the grass roots, the campaign went into hyperdrive: Amarillo Republicans organized their city block by block. Precinct and ward captains met regularly to map door-to-door campaigns and turnout strategies. The same went for Lubbock, Midland, Pampa, Borger, Odessa,

Barry Goldwater campaigning with John Tower, 1961.

and Hereford. The campaign worked symbiotically with local parties. As Lubbock's Nita Gibson explained: "When we would have John Tower here, we would invite people from all around. . . . You have them register. You know their names and their addresses. You know that they are interested in John Tower [and conservatism]. You keep a good record of these people. When you go into that county, you say 'hey, would you like to serve as county chair, or county vice-chair, or would you help us with the primary?"[39]

It worked. John Tower stunned the world. He won, barely. And Texas sent a Republican to the Senate for the first time since Reconstruction. More important, his victory established the validity of a second party devoted solely to right-wing conservatism. A Republican could win in Texas, a Goldwater Republican. The campaign proved O'Donnell right: mobilizing the young professionals and conservatives in the state's cities and big towns was the path to victory. Tower won every major urban county and ran up the score in West Texas counties: Midland (72 percent), Potter (70 percent), Randall (66 percent), Gray (67 percent), Ector (65 percent), and Lubbock (58 percent). No Republican outside a presidential election had ever done so well.[40] The GOP in Texas was suddenly a very real thing.

Republicans moved their state headquarters from Houston to Austin, taking up a suite of offices in the Littlefield Building. And just like that, Tower, as the only Republican senator from the South, became a major national player, second only to Barry Goldwater in the number of speaking requests he received from Republican groups. He was suddenly addressing crowds in the thousands.[41] He was thirty-six years old. The party gave him plum committee assignments and a seat on its policy committee. Tower was the highest-ranking Republican in the South. He was also recognized as a serious player in the national conservative movement—a political leader and an intellectual force. Within six months of his swearing in, Tower published a major book of conservative political policy, the *Program for Conservatives*, a 128-page policy primer meant to accompany Goldwater's *Conscience of a Conservative*.[42]

II

No one worked harder for John Tower across those two campaigns than Ed Foreman, a twenty-seven-year-old whirling dervish and oilman from Odessa, one of the ultraconservatives whom Peter O'Donnell had lured into the party. If John Tower was a *National Review* conservative, slicked back, articulate, blithely dropping quotes from Burke and Jefferson into everyday conversation, Foreman was a conservative born over a thousand lunch speeches on the perils of communism and the glories of free enterprise. An *Odessa American* editorial come to life. Basking in the glow of Tower's May election to the U.S. Senate, Foreman decided that he should run for Congress.[43]

A self-made man in the oil game, a tireless booster, and as much a conservative as any JBS chapter leader, Foreman was also the picture of a young man on the go. He was movie star handsome: golf course tan, chiseled jaw, bright blue eyes, dazzling smile. With a longish flattop and rock-solid build—six feet and a muscular 215—Foreman looked like the former college football player that he was. Charismatic and athletic with a sarcastic streak, Foreman moved confidently through the booster class of Odessa and among the roughnecks in the fields. (He later made a career as a motivational speaker.) He got into Republican Party politics early and was vice-chair of Ector County's GOP within just a few years of arriving in Odessa. He was also as well connected as anyone in town: state director and county chair of the American Heart Association, important posts within the United Fund (now the United Way). Three times he was tapped to organize and run the Permian Basin Oil Show, the most important trade show in the region. He was director of the Odessa Chamber of Commerce and ran its membership committee. He was a Rotarian and a steward at the Highland Methodist Church. He was a Mason, a Shriner, and a Jester. He was the Odessa Jaycees' Outstanding Young Man of the Year in 1960, and one of the Five Outstanding Men in Texas in 1963. The national Jaycees named him one of the Ten Outstanding Young Men in the country.[44]

He was intimately familiar with the brand of right-wing politics coming into view in those years across the Permian Basin. Foreman was originally from Portales, New Mexico, a ranching/farming/oil town just twenty miles west of the Texas state line, a place cultural geographers call "Little Texas." Portales (and Clovis, Hobbs, Melrose, Lovington, and Roswell) was all but indistinguishable from any town on the other side of the state line: the same economy (oil, cattle, wheat, cotton), the same demography (with a slightly higher percentage of Latinx people), the same history (Comanchería, ranching, railroads, stock farming, Dust Bowl, irrigation, oil). Most of its settlers in the twentieth century were from the American South and had brought their fundamentalist religion, their Democratic Party, and their devotion to white supremacy with them.[45] Portales was a railroad town, a cattle stop between Roswell and Amarillo. It was dry until the 1970s and a sundown town until the mid-1950s. It had one of the most active John Birch Societies in New Mexico.[46] A relatively small town of only around nine thousand in the 1950s, Portales was still able to host events for a number of right-wing celebrities: Fred Schwarz, Tom Anderson, Billy James Hargis, even Ronald Reagan. The region's biggest newspaper was part of the ultraconservative Hoiles chain.[47]

And the oil business where Foreman made his living was rife with reactionaries and ultraconservatives. Oil money had been funding the far right throughout the 1950s, from the founding of the *National Review* (Buckley's family had made its fortune in oil) to the multitude of causes and projects funded by millionaires like H. L. Hunt and Hugh Roy Cullen. Fears of federal regulation and a fierce antistatism trickled down to everyone in the oil game. And Foreman practically bled midcontinent crude. He had been in the business since his teens when he worked as a roughneck to save money for college. He majored in civil engineering at New Mexico State (where he graduated with honors) with every intention of getting into the oil business. After graduation he moved to Odessa, then the wildcatting capital of the world. Foreman was smart and observant and quick to seize opportunity. He started a company that bought up excess brine produced by oil refineries and sold it to downhole drillers, who liked the solution as a cooling and lubricating agent when punching through salt formations. Before long, Foreman was sinking his own brine wells to mine underground saltwater.[48] As business grew, so did Foreman's fleet of tank trucks. He started a second business, transporting oil and brine for smaller companies and providing onsite well service. He then formed a third company to manufacture specialty lubrication equipment. By twenty-six, this son of an eastern New Mexico peanut farmer was a wealthy man.

To attend a civic organization meeting like the Jaycees in those years meant hearing the same ideas again and again—that communism was an existential threat to humanity and that democracy depended on free enterprise. And Ed Foreman could express these thoughts better than most. A popular luncheon speaker, Foreman framed his anticommunism as the antithesis of the entrepreneurial culture of the oil business. His entire professional career was a living testament to the role of independent capitalists in correcting market inefficiencies. While his descriptions of drilling fluids and salt formations surely excited few beyond geologists and engineers, his defenses of the oil depletion allowance were eagerly embraced. He would explain how the allowance had produced 2,000 new wells, 4,800 jobs, and $150 million in West Texas alone.[49] Sometimes in his many invited talks, he opened by screening a slick fifteen-minute cartoon, "It Never Rains Oil," produced by John Sutherland Studio, the animation house of Harding College's National Education Program.[50]

As the Tower campaign drew him more directly into party politics, Foreman's talks grew more stridently conservative, with a focus on protecting the country from communism and liberalism. It was pure cowboy conservatism. The first form of community, he believed, was the frontier family forging a new life on the prairie. Even as neighbors filled in around them and local villages sprang up, along with schools and churches and business districts, the community at heart remained a grouping of independent families, banding together for mutual benefit. An expanding federal government determined to reinvent community and make families dependent on government, Foreman believed, posed a direct threat to communities like Portales and Odessa. Towns and cities like these, he promised his listeners, would always be "better and stronger . . . when they handle their own affairs."[51]

The issue that launched his political career was a direct expression of this ideal. Foreman was, strangely enough, completely incensed over an effort to make old Fort Davis, a well-preserved example of a frontier military post near Alpine, into a national historic site. The man behind the measure was J. T. Rutherford, who represented the area in Congress. In June 1961, Foreman went to D.C. to confront the congressman about such federal overreach. "Wouldn't it have been better," Foreman asked, to have the site "developed by a private individual who would have used his own money? . . . saving the government money and . . . making income for the government through taxes."[52] Foreman then told Rutherford that he was going to challenge him in the next election.

J. T. Rutherford was a worthy and hardworking representative for the 16th Congressional District. He kept his constituents informed with a regular column in the *El Paso Times* and had a standing office rule that every constituent letter be answered within one business day. He personally met with any constituent who came to Washington. In ten years, he missed only one floor vote. He served with distinction and on appropriate committees, bringing jobs and projects to the district. He was a conservative who voted his conscience and in his constituents' interests, in that order.[53]

During the 1962 campaign, what Foreman lacked in a district-specific platform he made up for in sheer energy, biography, and an intense devotion to Goldwater-Tower conservatism. Driving across one of the largest congressional districts in the country (at 42,000 square miles, the 16th was larger than Ohio) in a Model T Ford festooned with a sign that read, "Cars go out of style. Honesty in government never should," Foreman estimated that he shook fifty thousand hands during that campaign. Instead of aiming at Rutherford, the Republican mostly ran against Kennedy, criticizing the president for interfering with the steel industry, for his foreign policy, for his trade agreements. Urban renewal was "absurd" and a "gross waste of money"; the Peace Corps was a massive liberal boondoggle and part of a set of socialistic tendencies that were "ruining the moral fiber of Americans."[54] The president, he would say, was adding four new federal jobs every minute and spending a million dollars an hour.[55] It's hard to know if Foreman's straight-ahead conservatism would have been enough to knock off a five-term incumbent who was good at his job. But we'll never know, because six months before Election Day, the Billie Sol Estes scandal broke, rocking the politics of West Texas and dooming Rutherford, an innocent victim of the escalating Bircher politics of West Texas.

One of the all-time great wheeling-dealing con men, Billie Sol Estes was a big supporter of liberal causes and one of the best-connected Democrats in the state. He ruled over an agricultural empire worth, on paper, tens of millions of dollars. And he was brought down by the Bircher publisher of his hometown newspaper. It's a strange story worth recounting briefly as it shifted the state's political universe and gave the growing right-wing movement a powerful weapon to wield in its battles against Lyndon Johnson, Washington corruption, and critically, agricultural subsidies.

In short, Estes ran a multiangled con on the USDA, a whole bunch of banks, and a major supplier of chemical fertilizer. It started when Estes calculated that he could establish a monopoly on the sale of anhydrous ammonia in West Texas, one of the biggest markets for the fertilizer in the country. Liquified at cold temperatures, the gas was the main ingredient in the chemical fertilizers popular among the cotton farmers of the Agricultural Wonderland, who used them to increase yields and skirt federal production controls (which were based on acreage). They couldn't get enough of the stuff, and only a few companies produced anhydrous ammonia—few enough that Estes thought he could corner the market on distribution and sales. He tried to run the classic scheme, buy his way to dominance, and then chase off the stragglers by undercutting prices until they went out of business. But Estes was impatient. Before he had taken control of the market, he started underselling when there were still too many competitors. Anhydrous ammonia sold for around $90 a ton in those years, but Estes started to sell his for $70, $50, even $40 dollars a ton. He burned through cash and was hundreds of thousands in debt to his main supplier, Commercial Solvents, when it cut off his credit. That's when things got . . . complicated.

At this same time up in the Panhandle, the overproduction of wheat was so rampant that the USDA had to buy up surpluses just to keep prices from collapsing. It offered huge subsidies to anyone who would store the grain. Estes snapped up twenty-two silos and warehouses and milked the government for $8 million in just four years. He pumped all that grain storage money into his anhydrous ammonia monopoly scheme. And he still didn't have enough cash. That's when Estes started taking out bank loans on nonexistent ammonia tanks. He found plenty of small-town bankers eager to get in on the hottest thing in agricultural tech. Based on an earlier scam in which Estes sold fake mortgages on fertilizer pumps, the con was simple. Estes would approach a small farmer and strike a deal. The farmer would go to his local bank and apply for a loan to put an ammonia tank on his property. Estes then leased the tanks from the farmers for the amount of the payments along with a 10 percent bonus for the farmer for the use of his credit. Famous by that point for his outrageously opulent lifestyle—three Cadillacs, two airplanes, a pet monkey, swimming pools and tennis courts, a living room waterfall—Estes would explain that in his tax bracket and with his complicated deals, he was always looking for new partners. It was about the tax break, he said. He made a lot of deals. In Reeves County alone, $13 million worth of loans were made on 14,000 tanks, enough tanks that, if they existed, would mean one on every four-acre plot. A single Reeves farmer took out loans on 450 tanks. There were deals in Hale, Deaf Smith, Lamb, Dawes, and Lubbock counties. Estes established a company to make the tanks and another to sell them. A third bundled up the small bank loans into securities to sell to bigger banks. In the paperwork there were serial numbers, loan documentation, detailed maps, sales contracts, and refill schedules. But there were no actual tanks. And Estes *still* hadn't cornered the anhydrous ammonia market. By 1962, he was over $20 million in debt.

An organizational savant, Estes covered his tracks with financial transactions and agreements so complicated and intricate that no one else could understand them, let alone the small-town bankers or an overworked and understaffed USDA. Estes managed eighty bank accounts, controlled more than sixty-five separate companies, and had arranged so many thousands of deals that it took the accountants of Ernst and Ernst (now Ernst and Young) weeks just to find most of them: $100,000 in billable hours. A Senate committee would eventually have sixty different investigators working the Estes case. An FBI investigation was even bigger, with 452 agents in 46 separate offices. Unwinding Estes's books would become the most expensive congressional investigation in history.

The story first broke in Estes's hometown newspaper, the *Pecos Independent and Enterprise* (formerly the *Pecos News*). This is where the Birchers enter our tale. In the early 1960s, the old frontier semiweekly had been bought out by a group of local right-wingers led by a doctor named John Dunn, a friend and ally of Evetts Haley.[56] The investors wanted the paper to be more like the newspapers in Amarillo, Lubbock, and Midland. Soon enough, the *Independent and Enterprise* was carrying syndicated columns from Barry Goldwater, Tom Anderson, Paul Harvey, and David Lawrence and using its own editorial space to spin out Bircher fantasies about communist plots, the United Nations, Earl Warren, socialized medicine, and infiltration of churches, schools, and government. It pushed an overt Christianity and claimed that "the government's primary and paramount role is the protection of [individual] freedom." Its new owners left the day-to-day running of the paper to twenty-eight-year-old Oscar Griffin Jr., just two years out of J school.[57]

Griffin, who would win the Pulitzer Prize for his reporting on the Estes scandal, published his first story in February 1962. It was about the unusual number of ammonia tank mortgages in Reeves County. Without naming Estes, Griffin questioned why there were thousands of storage tanks in a county where just a few dozen would easily suffice. The story hinted darkly that all those tanks might not be real: "Reeves County may well be the anhydrous ammonia tank capital in the world—on paper that is."[58]

The exposé had been Dunn's idea; he had been trying to uncover Estes's scheme for over a year. The legend went something like this: Dunn or Griffin (in some stories, it's Dunn's mother) had overheard a group of farmers joking and jostling over a café breakfast about how some local rich guy was paying them thousands of dollars for doing nothing—"pennies from heaven." Suspicious, the hero of the story launched an investigation that would eventually lay bare the Estes fraud. The reality was more mundane. Around the same time that Dunn and his partners purchased the *Independent and Enterprise*, they also bought the Retail Merchants Association, a business research and index operation that published local financial and commercial data. Paging through its monthly publication, it was obvious that a lot of farmers were taking out an implausible number of loans for ammonia storage tanks. (Estes had once even approached the association and asked it to stop publishing the details of the loans, because, as he argued, it was hurting local farmers' credit.) Dunn sent researchers digging into county records for more details.[59] As he gathered intelligence, Dunn kept trying to get someone in government to investigate further. Through right-wing media personality and former FBI agent Dan Smoot, he tried to get the Bureau interested. He even sent a dossier to John Tower. Neither responded.

John Dunn hated Billie Sol Estes. And vice versa. Politically, the men stood at extreme ends of the political spectrum. While Dunn was a nationally recognized John Birch Society leader, Estes was one of the most liberal Democrats in Texas. He believed in integrated public schools, an expanded federal government, and farm programs and was an ardent supporter of the New Frontier. As a politically minded participant in more than a few agricultural ventures and always eager to expand his circle of friends, he worked hard to cultivate political relationships. He kept signed photos of Kennedy, Johnson, and Ralph Yarborough on the wall of his home office. He even got Kennedy to name him to the President's Cotton Council. He threw fundraisers and made big campaign contributions. Thinking about a future career in politics himself, Estes even ran for the Pecos school board in 1961 on a strange platform of liberalism and Church of Christ dogma (Estes was a lay minister): he came out for the National Education Association, school integration, and federal aid, and against dancing and short skirts. Running unopposed, he was a lock. That's when Dunn and his newspaper began publicly mocking his outdated ideas and launched a write-in campaign for an incumbent who had not planned on running for reelection. When Estes lost, he blamed Dunn and decided to put the *Independent and Enterprise* out of business. He launched a competing paper, the *Pecos Daily News*, and hired serious talent from papers in Amarillo, Odessa, and even the head of sales from the *Atlanta Constitution*. He started a rate war for advertising, cutting the prices for grocery stores (a local newspaper's biggest client) to well below what the *Independent* could offer. He called on his four hundred–plus employees to boycott any business that advertised in the competition.[60] The newspaper war was raging when the *Independent's* series on storage tanks started appearing. Every two weeks, readers learned of the millions of dollars in mortgages held in Reeves, Hale, Deaf Smith, and other counties. One Pecos farmer held almost $6 million in tank mortgages.

Bank presidents from the institutions holding the loans (or the bundled packages of loans) for the phantom tanks started getting news clippings in the morning mail. Panicked, they hired lawyers and investigators. In one all-out and coordinated effort, eighteen separate investigators descended unannounced upon dozens of farmers one morning to inventory the tanks; by the end of the day, it was obvious there were no tanks. (And as the hours passed, few farmers.) The attorneys, meanwhile, snooped around Estes's tank-manufacturing company and discovered that even if it ran three shifts and operated twenty-four hours a day every day, it could only produce a fraction of the tanks it supposedly sold each month. His bankers called a meeting with Estes in Lubbock in late February and told him that they simply wanted to know where the tanks were. That's when Estes confessed that there were no tanks. A month later, thirty-three bankers representing twenty-two companies holding Estes paper met at a fancy Dallas hotel and spent a frustrating two hours grilling a difficult and defiant Estes. The next evening at suppertime, the FBI arrested Billie Sol at his home in Pecos.

The scandal dominated headlines. Estes was indicted by Reeves County, the State of Texas, and the United States government. A few USDA officials lost their jobs or quit when it was revealed that they had received gifts from Estes in exchange for awarding him grain storage contracts, including—and it doesn't get much more 1960s Texas than this—shopping sprees at Neiman Marcus, where midlevel government functionaries were treated to fancy shirts, alligator shoes, and expensive suits. The wife of an assistant to a USDA assistant secretary was hired by Estes's newspaper as a Washington correspondent and paid $300 a month. Another official was caught using Estes's credit card to make long-distance phone calls. Then there was the curious death of the USDA investigator who was found with five bullet holes in his chest from a bolt-action rifle, which the local coroner ruled a suicide. The *Time* magazine issue with the story and Estes on the cover was the best-selling issue in the magazine's history. The story was so ubiquitous that one Lubbock radio station looked to juice ratings by offering an Estes-free week, and promised any sharp-eared listener who heard his name on the air would win a free transistor radio.[61]

It was late May when the story broke that Estes had once donated $1,500 to Rutherford's campaign. And the painfully honest, always reticent, always careful J. T. Rutherford had forgotten to report it.

And suddenly, Ed Foreman had an issue. He huffily demanded Rutherford's resignation. "We should expect no less from a congressman who has displayed such a flagrant disrespect for the public trust," Foreman said. If Rutherford was so irresponsible with his own campaign finances, Foreman asked, "how can we expect him to be any different with millions of our tax dollars?" He claimed that Rutherford's insistence that he forgot about the check was an insult to voter's intelligence.[62] Instead, Foreman hinted that the campaign contribution was quid pro quo for Rutherford's help in negotiating with the USDA over Estes's cotton allotment contracts.

The Estes scandal wrapped up a host of right-wing talking points into a nice campaign package. The villain was a liberal wheeler-dealer integrationist whose newspaper had once described the John Birch Society as "the Quixote of this age—galloping off frantically in four directions at once, while their obedient mental servants ride their donkeys into all the lunatic fringe movement of the ultra-right-wingers."[63] Estes's escapades showed the corruption and ineptitude of the USDA and revealed that the farm program was so poorly thought out that a devious con man with a high school education could scam it for a fortune. Worse, they said, was the fact that thirty years of farm programs had so corrupted the nation's farmers that they would get in bed with someone like Billie Sol Estes. They had learned that getting something for nothing was possible. It was a clear case for eliminating government from agricultural markets.

On the Sunday before the election, Foreman's campaign took out full-page ads in newspapers across the district that laid out a "case" against Rutherford. It was a slick piece of political advertising. Using carefully arranged facts prefaced by dripping innuendo; they accused Rutherford of "political favoritism" for the "free-spending Estes." The $1,500 could have been, they suggested, "a payment for special favors." Reproduced next to the text were copies of various letters from Rutherford to Estes, innocuous, standard-issue constituent mail that, in the light of the scandal, appeared more sinister than otherwise might have been the case.[64]

Rutherford never had a chance. Remaining in D.C. until mid-October (Congress was still in session), he scrambled as best he could in the last three weeks before Election Day but could never get out from under the Estes case. Foreman won with almost 54 percent of the vote.

He served a single term. Once in Washington, Foreman turned out to be an insufferable loudmouth all too willing to accuse other members of Congress of being pinkos. San Antonio representative Henry Gonzales once punched him out in the lobby of the Speaker's office after Foreman had accused him of being a communist sympathizer. The new congressman questioned the cost of every item on every bill that crossed his desk. He even led the fight against a $5 million program that would have helped clean up the Pecos River basin in his own district. As one source reported, Foreman "spent his time uncloaking the scoundrels and exposing them to the ever-watchful eyes of such vigilant organizations as the John Birch Society."[65] In 1964, Foreman was crushed in his bid for reelection by conservative Democrat Richard White, who would go on to serve the 16th Congressional District for nine terms.[66]

14
VIVA! OLÉ!

When he was done, they blew Dirksen down, the high screams of New Year's Eve went off, a din of screamers, rattles, and toots, a clash of bands, a dazzle of posters in phosphorescent yellow and orange and gold, the mad prance of the state standards, wild triumphant pokes and jiggles, war spears, crusader's lances, an animal growl of joy, rebel cries, eyes burning, a mad nut in each square jaw, *Viva-Olé, Viva-Olé*, bugle blasts and rallying cries, the call of heralds, and a fall from the rafters of a long golden rain, pieces of gold foil one inch square, hundreds of thousands of such pieces in an endless gentle shimmer of descent. . . . There was an unmistakable air of beauty, as if a rainbow had come to a field of war, or Goths around a fire saw visions in a cave. The heart of the beast had loosed a primitive call.

NORMAN MAILER, REPORTING FROM THE 1964
GOP CONVENTION

From one end of San Francisco's Cow Palace would come a yell, "Viva!" Those within earshot responded, "Olé!" Then louder, "Viva!" and louder still, "Olé!" It took no time for every Republican on the floor of their national convention to be lustily and loudly committed to either the call or the response. Or both, depending on one's state of mind. The cheer could go on for minutes and break out several times an hour. For four days and nights. On the night George Bush (then running for the U.S. Senate in Texas) spoke, the cheer went on for over five minutes. When

Odessa representative Ed Foreman spoke later that evening, the cheer went on even longer.[1] And on the last night of the convention, when Texas senator John Tower stood before fourteen thousand members of his party and seconded Barry Goldwater's nomination as the Republican candidate for president, the cheer reached its crescendo. The Texas delegation snaked through the convention floor, tears in their eyes, and screamed themselves hoarse.

That was the moment that West Texans launched their takeover of the Republican Party.

I

Better situated than anyone to make the call, Barry Goldwater believed that there "was no better place in the nation to study 1964 from the GOP grassroots level than the state of Texas."[2] The relationship between the Goldwater presidential campaign and the rise of Texas Republicanism was completely intertwined. Symbiotic. The Arizona senator was more popular in West Texas than he was in Arizona. The money men valued his uncompromising opposition to organized labor and big government. The far right loved his fierce anticommunism and militarism. He was related by marriage to Amarillo royalty. Even his highest-priced fundraising dinners in places like Amarillo or Lubbock sold out in just a couple of days. His weekly syndicated column was carried in newspapers across the region, and the editorial pages of the *Amarillo Globe-News* and the *Lubbock Avalanche-Journal* covered Goldwater as if he were president.

Starting in 1962, Peter O'Donnell, the newly appointed chair of the Texas GOP, hatched a plan to use a Goldwater presidential candidacy to build out the state party and the rest of the South. At that year's state convention, its largest ever, O'Donnell helped to write an official platform based on Goldwater's *Conscience of a Conservative*. There were planks that objected to farm subsidies and government spending and those that demanded lower taxes and "right to work" laws. It called for victory in the Cold War. And, importantly, the party resolved that "the election of Senator Goldwater to the office of the presidency of the United States would constitute the most effective step toward a return to conservative Constitutional principles."[3] It didn't take any complicated political wrangling to create such a platform; Goldwater polled 83 percent among delegates at the convention. For the new Texas GOP, as one insider mused, it was easier "to build a stronger party around Goldwater's impending candidacy than to sell abstract conservative principles."[4]

O'Donnell arranged splashy new events to build momentum for the party and show enthusiasm for Goldwater. The biggest were "Resignation Rallies," where groups of conservative Democrats full of "evangelical fervor" publicly denounced the Party of the Fathers and became Goldwater Republicans. The first rally, held in Littlefield, brought 126 into the fold; 700 crossed over in Fort Worth, including prominent Democrat Jack Cox, who had just wrapped up a strong gubernatorial campaign. Reporting from one rally, *Human Events* reported, "Texas Republicans bluntly label themselves 'Goldwater Republicans' to kill any doubts about their genuine conservatism."[5] That year, the *Texas Observer* posited that nine out of ten Texas Republicans were Goldwaterites.[6]

The quieter part of O'Donnell's "Texas Plan" was a massive canvassing effort across Texas's cities and large towns.[7] In what were called "Elephant Walks," after the Henry Mancini hit song, and organized down to the city block, a canvassing army of zealous Republicans went out every night after work and on weekends to gather household information about how people felt about Goldwater.[8] Those with positive views were incessantly recruited into the party; those with mixed feelings or no opinion were flooded with literature. O'Donnell hired six full-time researchers and media consultants, two statewide organizers, and two professional fundraisers. By the end of 1963, he had built one of the best-run and most efficient state parties in the country. In 1960 only 68 counties had a Republican Party capable of putting together a primary. Four years later, the Texas GOP held 252 separate county conventions that drew almost 134,000 voters.

The most important Republican activists were women. By this point, self-described "housewives" and "homemakers" had already proven to be the most active members of the so-called patriot organizations like Texans for America and the John Birch Society. Their "housewife populism," to borrow historian Michelle Nickerson's phrase, was founded on traditional ideas about gender and domesticity and was a politics framed around the customary concerns of republican motherhood—child-rearing, family, morality, and community values—that had, until now, largely manifested in protests over textbooks and curricular shifts in the public schools. Under O'Donnell, Republicans "invited conservative women to become political right where they were."[9] These were, for the most part, women with a college education who had been active in sororities and other college organizations. Many were now married to white-collar professionals or entrepreneurs and found themselves with time on their hands and energy and intellectual firepower to spare. And, as opposed to the hidebound good ol' boy network of the Democratic Party, Texas Republicans welcomed these women with genuine enthusiasm and plenty to do.

It had started with "Womenpower for Tower" a couple of years earlier. In that campaign, as Lubbock's Jane Anne Stinnett explains, "women did the legwork, put rallies together, did the conventions, built precinct organizations, and did the phoning. They did everything." (When Tower ran for reelection in 1966, the Texas Federation of Republican Women raised half his campaign cash.)[10] The very first door-to-door canvassing operation in Odessa's history was organized in 1962 by the Ector County Republican Women's Club on behalf of Ed Foreman. In Amarillo, the women who ran the phone banks and maintained the maps and mailing lists had more up-to-date information than the official city directory or local phone book. There were plenty of counties where there was an official Republican women's organization before there was a functioning county party.

The second-most important Republican organizer in the state was Barbara Man of Wichita Falls. The four-time "Baylor Beauty" from Van Horn, who had worked up quickly through the Tower organization, became the Texas conference chair at the national Republican women's conference and head of the Texas Federation of Republican Women (TFRW) in 1961. Man—smart, ambitious, brimming with ideas, and full of energy—crisscrossed Texas using enthusiasm for the Arizona conservative to build the TFRW a chapter at a time. By fall of 1964, she had tripled the number of chapters and led an organization of six thousand.[11] She and O'Donnell were cochairs of the "Draft Goldwater" campaign in Texas, and Man would become the regional director for Goldwater's official campaign.

II

What was it about Barry Goldwater that created such a fervor in Texas? The simple answer was that for a lot of Texans, especially West Texans, the Arizonan was one of them, a product of what pundits and social scientists called the Sunbelt. The term "Sunbelt" is, probably for most of us, some seventies throwback, like feathered hair or harvest gold appliances. Despite its later use to describe everything from lifestyle to housing to newer forms of regionalism, the term was first used in a 1969 book. In *The Emerging Republican Majority*, political prodigy and quant savant Kevin Phillips, after sifting through the granular data of the 1968 presidential race, declared that voting patterns revealed the existence of an ongoing regional shift in the South and the West toward the Republican Party. His research indicated that this Sunbelt Republicanism meant the dawn of "a new, conservative political era."[12]

The buckle of this political Sunbelt, which stretched across the lower third of the United States from South Carolina to Southern California, was West Texas. As Phillips put it: "Because of the rapid growth of agricultural, oil and commercial centers like Tulsa, Oklahoma City, Amarillo, Lubbock, Odessa and Midland, the political power of the Southern Plains is on the rise," and it wasn't a "coincidence that conservatism is strongest in [these] booming areas."[13] And, while plenty of Sunbelt scholarship (rightly) observes the impact of a restless generation of newcomers, those hundreds of thousands of midwestern or eastern college graduates who flocked to the fresh professional opportunities in Sunbelt boomtowns, we need to keep in mind the demographic reality that for every Ohio State grad who packed up the family in the new Buick and headed west, there were plenty of other newly minted professional suburbanites who had been born and raised within a hundred miles of Amarillo or Lubbock or Phoenix or Irvine. The Sunbelt GOP would draw on both populations.

Most Sunbelt cities in the Southwest shared a common history and culture: they had started as frontier towns built to service an extractive industry (mining, agriculture, ranching) and had, over the twentieth century, become core cities in regional economies. These were places run by a booster class still committed to growth. They were segregated cities that pushed their small African American and Latino populations to the other side of some transportation barrier like a railroad or one of the new interstate highways. And all over the Sunbelt, including Goldwater's Phoenix, Texans had dominated early settlement and still made up large portions of the population. In the years that Goldwater rose through local politics, 20 percent of the population of the Valley of the Sun were from Texas.[14]

III

Barry Goldwater was the embodiment of the new Sunbelt culture and politics—deeply appreciative of the West's past and its natural beauty, but just as enthusiastic about the modern world and its possibilities. This ruggedly handsome son of Arizona's most successful merchant family was just as comfortable camping in the desert as he was golfing at the country club. He flew airplanes, shot rapids, tinkered on his ham radio late into the evening, collected Native American art, and was a nationally acclaimed nature photographer. Goldwater was a natty dresser with a deep tan and a visible tattoo. His thick, black horn-rims were an essential part of his considerable style. He had grown up with the modern West: in 1909, the year of his birth, Arizona was still a territory and Phoenix wasn't even on the railroad.

He was only twenty-one when his father died and he had to take over the family business, the biggest department store in Phoenix. Goldwater, who never really enjoyed business, threw himself into the world of the small-city booster. He took over for his father as head of the Phoenix Chamber of Commerce and joined the Elks and the Shriners and the Masons. He won the Phoenix Country Club golf championship. In those years, Goldwater's politics were booster politics built around booster issues: growth and establishing a "friendly business climate," which translated to fierce opposition to organized labor, taxes on business, and government regulation. Goldwater himself was a good employer: he paid higher-than-average wages, solicited employee opinions, and offered health insurance, paid sick leave, retirement plans, and a profit-sharing program. He maintained a company farm for employees and ran a summer program for their kids.[15]

Like many businessmen, Goldwater moved to the right during the 1930s in direct response to federal intervention in the economy. He was, as a retailer, concerned about the long-term implications of man-dated wage and price controls. And the gains made by organized labor in the Roosevelt years scared him. He started speaking out against the president in the pages of his hometown newspaper "as a businessman and a citizen." He wanted to know what had happened to Roosevelt's promises of tax reductions and economy in government. His own taxes, he pointed out, had increased by 250 percent, and the government had spent more money during the New Deal than it had over the previous 150 years. He also wanted to know why more business leaders weren't speaking out against such wasteful spending. "If businessmen who pay the cost of government" didn't speak out, who would?[16]

He was, like so many Sunbelt suburbanites, a veteran, having served in the Ferry Division of the Army Air Corps, flying dangerous mis-sions across the Atlantic and Africa, including ferrying Douglas Sky-train cargo planes "over the hump," a treacherous supply route across the Himalayas that cost one thousand Americans their lives and that wrecked so many planes, pilots called it the Aluminum Trail. He came back from the war with an interest in politics.

A Republican thanks to his mother, a native of Illinois who brought her fierce devotion to the party with her to Arizona, Goldwater had always been a political outsider in the heavily Democratic state.[17] Like his outnumbered comrades in Texas, Goldwater's political philosophy developed as he responded to the political realities of the growth of mid-century liberalism and the Cold War. In his first political campaign, he helped orchestrate a businessmen's takeover of the Phoenix City Coun-cil, where they lowered corporate taxes and adopted antilabor policies. He was a major force behind a statewide referendum that made Ari-zona a right-to-work state. In 1950, after running a Republican friend's doomed gubernatorial race, Goldwater was hooked on electoral poli-tics. He became an essential voice for the Arizona Republican Party, outlining its pro-business, antilabor, and rigid anticommunist politics. He also demanded honest and effective government, supported federal reclamation and other development projects for Arizona, and made the case that low taxes were the key to city and regional growth. In 1952, Senate minority leader Everett Dirkson, recognizing a rising star in the party, asked Goldwater to challenge the popular two-term incumbent Arizona senator Ernest MacFarland for his seat. It was a fool's errand, but Goldwater didn't care. He wanted to run.

And he had a great time, putting on one of the most exciting races in state history. Goldwater, who loved to talk politics almost as much as he loved to fly airplanes, now had an excuse to zip all over the state (often flying solo), land at some tiny airstrip, meet local dignitaries, glad-hand for a bit, and then jump on a stage for a blistering attack on the outgoing Truman administration: Korea, MacArthur, corruption, taxes, inflation, a little Red baiting. If they sent him to Washington, Goldwater boomed to the crowd, out would go the "intellectual radicals and parlor pinks and the confused and the bumbling." Then, he'd hop back on his plane, crank up the propellers, and fly off to the next little city and do it all again. The national GOP sent down some heavy hitters like Robert Taft and Joseph McCarthy for bigger events. Texas oilmen provided half his campaign money. He won by 6,725 votes.[18]

Goldwater never made a secret of his disdain for governance. As far as he was concerned, Arizonans had sent him to Washington to vote "no." He thrived, however, as an evangelist for conservatism and as a fundraiser and campaigner for the Republican Party. The dashing and straight-talking pilot cowboy from the Wild West was one of America's most popular politicians. The media loved him. Goldwater was always good for a quote and an original take. Before it was a political brand, a "Goldwaterism" referred to his frequent outlandish statements. The GOP hustled him onto the Senate Republican Campaign Commit- tee as soon as he got to Washington and named him chair in 1955. Two hundred nights a year on the Republican pea-and-chicken circuit. But he got to fly all the time and arrange meetings on his ham radio (another of his many, many hobbies). Over those lunches and dinners and speeches he honed the modern conservative message. American democracy and freedom depended on individualism, religious faith, and private property, and those cherished values were under assault from an expansionist federal bureaucracy, labor unions, and an aggressive Soviet Union. Over seven years, he gave the speech more than two thousand times. No one in the country had shaken more Republican hands or eaten more Republican meals than Barry Goldwater.[19] A lot of those hands belonged to Texans, and a lot of those meals were Texas brisket.

By 1963, Peter O'Donnell was growing frustrated with Barry Gold- water's seeming lack of interest in running for president. It wasn't just Texas: the entire conservative wing of the Republican Party was primed for a Goldwater campaign, desperate even.[20] In truth, Barry Goldwater didn't really need to run for president; he had a pretty sweet life. He got to travel, fly planes (he would eventually learn to fly 250 different types of aircraft); he had a ham radio set up at his D.C. place, and everywhere he went, people waved "Goldwater for President" signs. He was the second-most sought-out speaker on college campuses. Besides, he wasn't sure he would win the nomination or if it was even worth the effort. When he heard rumors of a "Draft Goldwater" movement in early summer 1963, Goldwater was unmoved: "It's their time and money. But they are going to have to get along without me." That was when O'Donnell went public. He announced his position as the national spokesman for Draft Goldwater and opened a D.C. office.[21] He set up thirty-three state groups and cranked up the resignation rallies. In a stroke of genius that would set up the right wing of the Republican Party for years, O'Donnell launched a new type of petition drive to get Goldwater on the ballot: in addition to collecting the critical data—name, address, and phone number—petitioners also asked for a small donation, a little skin in the game, a way to separate the buyers from the spiers. Those lists would be the source of Goldwater's "vast volunteer army" in 1964 and the foundation of a donor-volunteer database that the GOP would mine and build for decades.[22]

O'Donnell scheduled a huge bash on July 4 and reserved one of the biggest spaces in Washington, D.C., the Armory Building, a venue so large that it had only filled its 6,500-person capacity twice: an Eisenhower inaugural ball and a Billy Graham Crusade. Goldwater—still not a candidate—wasn't even going to be there; he would be back home, riding in Prescott's annual rodeo parade, a family tradition. O'Donnell put together an all-star lineup with John Tower, the second-most popular Republican in the country, as the headliner. The undercard included John Ashbrook, the young firebrand conservative from Ohio, Governor Paul Fannin from Arizona, and Hollywood movie stars (and well-known conservatives) Efrem Zimbalist Jr., Chill Wills, and cinema legend Walter Brennan. Working from the lists he had gathered in his petition drives, O'Donnell sent out thousands of invitations. It was a huge gamble. No one had any idea whether anyone would even show up. Then, on the morning of the rally, the chartered buses started rolling into the parking lot. Goldwater fans by the hundreds poured out. The Texas delegation, subsidized by plenty of oil money, arrived in a fleet of private planes. Nine thousand screaming Goldwater fans jammed into the Armory and shouted themselves hoarse: "We Want Barry! We Want Barry!"[23]

Goldwater announced in January 1964. O'Donnell closed his Draft Goldwater offices in D.C. and headed back to Austin to run the Texas campaign. The party grew by the week. All over the state, but especially in West Texas, the prospect of a Goldwater presidency brought dozens of new volunteers to local headquarters every day. The state convention in May was gaga for Goldwater. He had the undying support of three-fourths of the delegates. (Six other candidates split the remainder evenly.) At a $100-a-plate fundraising dinner in the ballroom of Dallas's Statler Hilton the night before the convention, Goldwater gave the after-dinner address. The fifteen hundred people in the room interrupted his speech forty-five times with ovations.[24] The next day, eleven thousand delegates from everywhere in Texas crammed into the Dallas Municipal Auditorium. "Viva!" they would shout. "Olé!" they would respond. All day. When Tower finally introduced the candidate, the crowd stood for a six-minute ovation. The party platform was almost identical to the one they had passed two years earlier: right to work, support for school prayer, reducing oil and beef imports, a balanced budget, tax cuts, and cutting foreign aid and eliminating farm programs.[25] Texas's fifty-six delegates to the national convention left Dallas that day "irrevocably committed" to his candidacy.

IV

The next time you find yourself in a used bookstore in Texas (or anywhere, really), check out the politics, history, or biography section. Run your fingers along the LBJ books, keeping an eye out for a thin six-inch paperback with a white spine and a title in black all-caps: A TEXAN LOOKS AT LYNDON. The cover will be a faded periwinkle with a photograph of Johnson. He'll be wearing his Stetson Open Road and the collar of his khaki windbreaker will be popped. Hands jammed in his pockets, he'll be examining some metal wreckage. Up in the upper right-hand corner you'll see the author's headshot. Also wearing a Stetson, a Boss of the Plains, is J. Evetts Haley. The subtitle appears across the bottom: "A Study in Illegitimate Power." It was Haley's greatest publication success: dropping in early summer 1964, it sold 7 million copies in five months. The book vaulted the historian into the national political consciousness. But at a cost. *A Texan Looks at Lyndon* was such a vicious, unwarranted, and poorly argued book that it forever wrecked his scholarly reputation.[26]

Haley had nursed a grudge against Johnson for years, ever since the pushy young LBJ stole the 1948 senatorial election from Coke Stevenson, one of Haley's political heroes.[27] In Haley's eyes, Johnson embodied everything wrong in American public life—the President was ruthless, unprincipled, ambitious, and willing to destroy traditions and values in an unrelenting quest for power. An avid collector of stories, rumors, and news clippings, Haley already had an extensive file on Johnson when he was suddenly thrust into the presidency by the assassination of John F. Kennedy.[28] Haley decided sometime that winter to write a book that would expose the new president as the grasping and cruel mountebank that Texans knew. Obsessed, the sixty-two-year-old, now widowed Haley researched and wrote himself to exhaustion.[29] When he found his files had holes, Haley hopped in his truck or on the train to track down rumors and spend days poring over the files of his friends and allies (John Dunn gave Haley access to all his material on Billie Sol Estes, for example) and digging through newspaper morgues. He finished the book in just five months.[30]

As the manuscript came together, Haley mulled whether to serialize the book in the John Birch Society's monthly magazine *American Opinion* or publish it with an established right-wing press like Regnery. He eventually decided to self-publish the book, which would give him control over distribution and promise greater profits. (He would later claim that mainstream publishers wouldn't touch the book because they feared retribution from President Johnson.[31]) Haley set up the "Palo Duro Press" out of the garage of his house in Canyon and made a deal with an Ohio printer for a 20,000-copy run. He would charge a dollar a copy, promising a neat windfall.[32]

That first run came out in early June, and Haley debuted the book at the inaugural convention of the new Conservative Party of Texas (CPT). The CPT was a far-far-right group that had splintered from the far-right Texas Constitutional Party (the kind of dogmatic schism lampooned by the squabbles between the Judean People's Front and the People's Front of Judea featured in Monty Python's *Life of Brian*). The CPT was shopping around for a fringe candidate to back that year and had invited Alabama governor George Wallace, himself looking for organizational support for a potential third-party presidential bid, to keynote the convention. The CPT's first-ever platform included planks that demanded immediate U.S. withdrawal from the United Nations, the restoration of prayer in schools, and the abolishment of the income tax. It also came out against the 1964 Civil Rights Act, disarmament, and the registration of firearms. The new party was holding back on endorsing Barry Goldwater until it was sure that he wasn't just another tool of "the internationalists."[33] It was, in other words, the perfect place for Haley to launch the book.

Initially, distribution was handled by Timely Publications, a shabby right-wing pop-up out of Dallas, the gasping remnants—mailing lists, office equipment, and a couple of diehard staffers—of a couple of earlier right-wing flameouts: Bircher Robert Morris's failed 1964 Senate run and the National Indignation Convention. Those first 20,000 copies spread quietly but quickly. Conservative bookstores couldn't keep them in stock. By July, it was the featured book at the Freedom Information Center in Amarillo, the city's biggest right-wing bookstore. It was the subject of countless editorials and letters to the editor.[34] Haley had to find a second printer to keep up with demand, then a third, and a fourth. By early August, the book's phenomenal success was its own story, the self-published exposé of Johnson that was selling somewhere between 25,000 and 30,000 copies a day.[35] Haley, coyly playing the role of overwhelmed and humbled author, told stories about "enthusiastic" individuals buying up small lots of the book to share with their friends and the few big orders from "book and retail stores."[36]

That was nowhere near the truth. The overwhelming bulk of book sales came from right-wing organizations, especially the John Birch Society and the *Farm and Ranch* media empire run by Tom Anderson. (After the election, Anderson had 100,000 copies left in a warehouse.) In 1964, the vastness of the right-wing media universe was still largely unknown to the mainstream press, allowing Haley to aw-shucks his way through interviews. The reality was more mundane: then, as now, the right-wing media machine needs a steady stream of content, and keeping up with the latest arguments of the far right was an important part of most ultraconservatives' ongoing education. *A Texan Looks at Lyndon* was just the sort of book that dominated their scholarship. It was small enough to carry around and cheap enough that no one felt uncomfortable underlining passages in ink or scrawling notes in the margins. It was also full of lurid conspiracy theories and dressed up as an academic text with lots of footnotes and literary and historical references.[37]

Howard Jarvis, who headed Businessmen for Goldwater, bought 150,000 copies to mail to conservative Democrats. Birch leader and magazine publisher Tom Anderson ordered in 12,000-unit batches and sold the book through his *Farm and Ranch* magazines.[38] A Florida motel owner ordered them by the hundreds and gave them away free to guests like Gideon Bibles. The John Birch Society bought hundreds of thousands of copies that it distributed to members from warehouses in Belmont and Costa Mesa, California. Its two hundred American Opinion bookstores featured the book in their window displays. It was required reading for JBS members. New Orleans Birchers got supercreative and spent their days at the airport, wandering the terminal, giving the book to strangers, and pretending that they had just read it on their flight and couldn't wait to pass it on.

The book reads like a prosecutorial brief. Haley includes plenty of footnotes for information drawn from legitimate sources, including newspapers, national news magazines, court records, government publications, even the *Texas Observer*. But he has more than plenty citations from dubious far right outlets like the *Dan Smoot Report*, Ida Darden's *Southern Conservative*, and publications from the Christian Crusade. Woven through the narrative are true-enough stories and easily checked facts, but the bulk of Haley's "case" against Johnson is held together by rumor and innuendo and founded on paranoid and conspiratorial fantasies. It argues that Lyndon Johnson is a power-mad mastermind who ascended to the presidency on a ladder of shocking criminality: bribery, fraud, influence peddling, even murder. Over ten chapters, Haley details every scandalous scrap of gossip and recounts every negative rumor that had dogged LBJ's thirty-year political career. Carefully written, Haley prefaces every unfounded criminal accusation with phrases like "a persistent but completely unconfirmed story" before launching into his version of events, never directly accusing Johnson of anything. Most of his readers, however, eager for the dirt on Johnson, hardly recognized Haley's rhetorical subtleties as they devoured the historian's tales of the president's venal path to power.[39]

It was *the* campaign book in the year of the campaign book. Republican and allied organizations officially and unofficially made it part of their campaign materials.[40] It was passed out so widely and mailed so frequently it was easy for active right-wingers to end up with several copies. Despite a standing order from the national campaign against it, the book kept showing up at Republican campaign events and headquarters. Republican groups in Texas were among Haley's biggest customers.[41] Amarillo GOP official Mayetta Parr grew sick and tired of having to spend every morning going through and tossing copies of the book that volunteers kept sneaking into the party's distribution materials: "I got so I hated to go to headquarters in the morning because we were throwing stuff away. . . . We must have had 5,000 copies of *A Texan Looks at Lyndon* go into the trash because Goldwater said he did not want that in his headquarters."[42]

Just as the book was entering the mainstream consciousness, the first real book reviews started showing up. They were brutal. Texas reviewers, best able to provide context, were among the harshest. The legendary Robert Sherrill, by this time at the *Miami Herald*, described it as "a book in which normal actions, seen through a steaming mirage of hate, take on strange shapes."[43] In the *Dallas Times-Herald*, A. C. Greene called the book "so outrageously wrong it's almost impossible to isolate the heavy, thick aura of wrongness and define it." He suggested that a "more candid subtitle might be 'A Study in Unhospitalized Paranoia.'" Texas's *Baptist Standard* called it "distasteful" and had it removed from the state's forty-nine Baptist bookstores. Newspaper mogul Houston Harte, the man who had encouraged Haley's Texas Tory column years earlier, declared that Haley "can no longer be considered a serious historian."[44] The *Observer* called it "little more than a vicious personal attack," good only for those interested in the study of rhetorical devices that allow for "all logical connections, casual and sequential," to be eliminated so that every word can be "used for its most destructive emotional effect."[45] The most widely cited and distributed critique of the book came from the typewriter of Pulitzer Prize–winning journalist Jim Mathis, then writing for the *Houston Post*, who framed it as the "logical outgrowth of what Haley has been and is," a book "nurtured in an air of personal political defeat and frustration, harvested in a climate of unrestrained anger, . . . the festering climax of Haley's fantasies."[46]

Closer to home, Ben Ezzell of the *Canadian Record* called it "quite possibly the most vicious bit of character assassination ever to roll off a press." Haley, he concluded, was "beneath contempt." H. M. Baggarly, who had crossed swords with Haley more than once, shook his head over the popularity of a book he considered "crap" and "gutter talk" and wondered aloud what had "happened to America?" The *Shamrock Texan* said the book was "based on imagination and insinuations of such ridiculous magnitude that if ten per cent of the contents were true, President Johnson long since would have been indicted by a grand jury, tried, convicted and sentenced." At Dumas Junior High School, twelve-year-old Randy Porter, writing a book report on *A Texan Looks at Lyndon* for his seventh-grade English class concluded that "the book is interesting but not necessarily truthful. The arguments present are not supported by enough evidence."[47]

Forced on the defensive, Haley, accustomed to friendly crowds, resorted to the slippery and nonsensical. His go-to retort, which he would use for the rest of this life, was, if what he said wasn't true, why hadn't Johnson sued him for libel? He also liked to say that he had "merely cataloged the facts" and it was up to the reader to "decide the truth—he or she is the judge."[48] He even, in a spectacular use of circular logic, defended his reliance on rumor: since "people are denied the truth by [Johnson's] illegitimate power," the products of their imagination become evidence. "Rumor," as he explained, "is a psychological phenomenon in the public mind, the existence of which is a historical fact."[49]

The negative press caught up with Haley, and the market for the book dried up. On Election Day there were still some 2 million unsold copies stacked in warehouses and garages.

V

For most of the first half of the twentieth century, Haley's hometown of Midland had struggled to make a go of it. In its earliest days, it was a dusty speck of a railroad town—the literal midpoint between Dallas and El Paso. This was where the plains recede into desert, where grasses come in bunches rather than carpets. A land of draws, mesquite, and rarely more than a dozen inches of rain a year. Wet years brought some growth and prosperity; dry years misery and outmigration. A brief oil boom in the early 1930s was laid low by the discovery of the East Texas field. Wartime demand, however, lured a few adventurous wildcatters back to the Permian Basin, where, drilling deeper than ever, they discovered several new oil reservoirs. Trapped in massive pools across geologic basins that lie between the Matador Uplift in the north and Marathon Ouachita Fold Belt to the south was half the oil in Texas. Miles-wide lakes of oil lying below ancient underground hills of porous rock were just a mile below the surface of the worthless West Texas scrub. Wildcat crews and leasing outfits popped up everywhere, making deals and punching holes. A single hit could make a man rich. Midland became America's new oil center.

Midland was a different kind of Texas boomtown. It was dominated by young, white, middle-class professionals who flocked to the city to get in on the oil game—leases and legal matters, distribution and financing, engineering and equipment. The dirty end of the business, discovery, was run out of Odessa, a few miles down U.S. 80. In 1960, 70 percent of Midland's population was under thirty-five; half of those were under eighteen. Over the course of the 1950s, the number of babies born in Midland was larger than the total number of city residents in 1940. It was an entire city of young families. It also boasted the greatest percentage of college graduates of any city in America. And almost every single one of them was in the oil business.

Despite the oxford shirts, new buildings, and shiny Oldsmobiles, the basic values of the ranching class still dominated the city's culture. It was still a place that worshiped at the altar of entrepreneurial capitalism and whose citizens drank deeply of the myth of the frontier. And it was still a town founded and built by white southerners. (It named its second high school after Robert E. Lee when it opened in 1961.) Like the ranchers, the new oilmen embraced individualism, ambition, self-reliance, honesty, and risk-taking. They distrusted centralized political power and valued hard work and independence. The city was overwhelmingly native-born white and deeply segregated. The really big deals still went down in the Scharbauer Hotel, the ranching class's favorite haunt. As the business grew, plenty of ranchers got into oil and plenty of oilmen got into ranching. Cowboy boots were everyone's choice of footwear.

Among those ambitious young men on the make who made Midland their new home was a recent Yale grad named George Herbert Walker Bush. With his pedigree: Greenwich Country Day School. Phillips Academy. Yale. Skull and Bones. Deke president. Phi Beta Kappa. Starting first baseman in two College World Series. War hero. Bush was primed for a comfortable life among the nation's elite, a future mover and shaker in the Eastern Establishment. Most likely he'd go into finance; his degree (finished in only two and half years) was in economics, and a seat at Brown Brothers Harriman, the whitest of the white-shoe Wall Street brokerage firms, was waiting for him. His grandfather had put the firm together and his dad was its managing partner. But young Bush was looking for something different.[50]

With the help of a family friend, Bush got into the oil business. Just a couple of days after his college graduation, he and his wife, Barbara (whom he called "Bar"), loaded up their Studebaker, bundled up baby George, and drove from Connecticut to Odessa. It was 1948. Bush was twenty-four. First, he dealt in drilling equipment, and the Bushes moved around, a lot. Housing was boomtown tough in those years; the young family once shared an Odessa duplex with a mother-daughter prostitute team. After three years of talking up wildcatters and penning deals in the cabs of pickups, Bush struck out on his own. A low-key friends-and-family financing round set him up as an independent oil producer. He and a partner leased an office downtown. The Bushes bought a house in Midland's "Easter Egg" neighborhood.

An independent works two primary angles: They buy leases, which means digging through county records, tracking down rumors, fighting off competitors, making relationships, and striking deals. And they punch holes, which means poring over geologic data, working with the scientists and the drilling teams, and crossing fingers. It came down to fortune, brains, and hard work. And Bush was lucky, smart, and worked hard. A second company grew from the success of the first. Supposedly named after a hit movie playing in a local theater, the Zapata Petroleum Corporation focused on exploration. Bush ran its offshore subsidiary. Oil exploration in those years offered the superwealthy one of the greatest tax breaks around. Bush never lacked for investors. If he hit, which he often did, they made money; when he missed, they paid less in taxes.

The Bushes glided like royalty through the Midland booster class—a rather uniform group of young, well-educated, well-mannered, upwardly mobile couples, many from the East. George's father became a U.S. senator from Connecticut shortly after they moved to Midland full-time, and Bar was the daughter of publishing magnate Marvin Pierce.[51] She had attended the Ashley Hall preparatory school in Charleston, South Carolina, and was a member of Round Hill Country Club in Greenwich, Connecticut. She and George had met at the club's Christmas dance. In Midland, they were gracious and energetic socializers, playing golf and tennis at the club, enjoying horseshoes and hamburgers in the backyard, book clubs and cards in the evenings. It was a social world then, as hundreds of young families found themselves stranded in the desert hundreds of miles from anywhere and thousands of miles from home. George and Bar were active Jaycees; the organization named George one of its Outstanding Young Texans in 1956, and Barbara ran the Women's Auxiliary. They were also leading Republicans.

In 1959, Bush spun Zapata Offshore away from the main company and moved to Houston, America's fastest-growing city and the heart of the offshore world. In those days nearly every drop of oil produced within a thousand-mile radius ended up in Houston somehow. As did every dollar in the business. It was the home of thousands of mid-field players and all the Big Boys had offices downtown. George was ready to join them, moving Zapata into the seventeenth floor of the Houston Club Building, the hottest office space downtown and the last major building project of real estate legend Jesse Jones. George and Bar joined the Houston Country Club and played golf, tennis, and bridge. George got involved in politics and with the Harris County GOP, the largest Republican organization in Texas. Those were volatile years in the local GOP as a faction of homegrown crackpots fought to turn the party into a mechanism to push a rabid anticommunist, white-supremacist, and fundamentalist agenda.

In 1962, with a party chair position set to come open the following year, county leadership asked Bush to run. A decade in Midland had taught him how to get along with those who lived in the fevered dreamworld of the far right, and there was no one in the city more capable of moving within the Establishment. He spent a year working quietly and competently for the job, visiting every precinct, and consulting every major party player. Bar accompanied George to every meeting, every dinner, conspicuously tranquil as she worked her needlepoint. Bush won and became one of the most important Republicans in Texas.[52]

Peter O'Donnell had been watching Bush for a while. He admired his ability to weave between the racist reactionaries and buttoned-down business conservatives, and obviously, he had a stronger connection to the GOP Establishment than anyone in Texas. If the Texas GOP chair was to have any chance at building the Republican Party, he would need all these factions working together. A statewide Bush candidacy might do the trick. The new chair of the Harris County GOP was a pragmatic Cold War internationalist in the Eisenhower vein, but on domestic issues, particularly civil rights and the expansion of federal programs, Bush lined up squarely with the Goldwater-Tower states' rights and limited government crowd. His dashing good looks, charisma, pedigree, and oil and finance connections were certainly plusses. Even the *Observer* appreciated the logic; Bush had, it said, "Goldwater's policies and Kennedy's style."[53]

Goldwater and Bush at the top of a GOP ticket would play well in Texas. The party had enthusiastic volunteers, a growing organization, and exciting candidates like Ed Foreman (who was up for reelection), and up in the Panhandle, local war hero and young rancher Bob Price was making a play for Walter Roger's congressional seat. Statewide, the party was running more candidates for more offices than at any time in history. Dial in the right frequencies and anything was possible, maybe even, to borrow a useful anachronism, turn Texas red. A full year before the election, George Bush announced that he would run for the U.S. Senate. At a press conference in the Capitol Press Room in Austin, Bush called himself a "Goldwater man." He made a case for states' rights and another against Kennedy's civil rights bill. He promised he would get tough with Russia and take on the spendthrifts in government. Asked about the John Birch Society, Bush said he was not a member and that he was more "concerned about the left than the right."[54]

There were two main challengers in the primary, the biggest Republican field in state history. Both ran to the self-proclaimed "Goldwater man's" right. Jack Cox had been a conservative leader in the Democratic Party until he had joined the GOP at one of O'Donnell's Resignation Rallies. He had run for governor twice before. He had also once led Freedom in Action, a supersecret ultraconservative organization that served as an organizational and ideological forebear to the JBS.[55] To Cox's right was Robert Morris, former counsel to the Joseph McCarthy committee, Edwin Walker's personal attorney, and high-ranking Bircher, who had concluded that the Kennedy administration was actively implementing a plan to merge the United States and Soviet Union into a new communist world government.[56] A third ultraconservative, a little-known Dallas doctor, rounded out the field. Cox and Morris attacked Bush as a carpetbagger, an Eastern Establishment plant, and a secret liberal. Bush took first in the primary and easily dispatched Cox in a runoff, taking on,

George Bush posing with supporters from the Muleshoe and Lazbuddie Blue Bonnet Belles in 1964.

as he later recalled, "General Walker, the National Indignation Council and the rest of those people," adding, with understated posh, "It got most unpleasant, as you can imagine."[57]

Awaiting Bush in the general election was incumbent Ralph "Raff" Yarborough, the leader of the liberal wing of the Democratic Party and one of the most powerful politicians in the state. Raff, whose political slogan was "put the jam on the bottom shelf where the little people can reach it," had spent the 1940s and 1950s building a winning coalition of Texas liberals strong enough to challenge the reactionaries in his own party. After three memorable runs for governor, Yarborough won his Senate seat in a special election in 1957 and held it in 1958. The differences between Bush and Yarborough could not have been starker. Yarborough was a friend of labor, a supporter of civil rights, and a believer in the social safety net. Bush, running as an unabashed Goldwater acolyte, called his platform a "Freedom Package," a regular season-highlight reel of far-right positions: a balanced budget, a strong foreign policy predicated on American dominance, encouraging prayer in schools, pro-

George Bush eating brisket and beans at a campaign stop in Lubbock, 1964.

tecting the right to work, abolishing federal aid to education, slashing foreign aid, calling out the "failures" of the United Nations, curbing the power of the Supreme Court, and pushing a "free-market agricultural economy."[58] Bush was smoothly and skillfully ambiguous as he outlined these positions; a lot of Birchers assumed he was one of them, a reality that made his friends nervous. Yarborough was convinced, regularly calling Bush the "darling of the John Birch Society" and asking him why he, unlike Goldwater, had not repudiated the organization, but rather "clasped it to his bosom."[59] Bush, the Connecticut Yankee, replied with jeers about Yarborough's "desertion of the South" and reminders about Yarborough's deciding vote that enabled passage of the 1964 Civil Rights Act. Yarborough called Bush a carpetbagger, trying to buy a Texas Senate seat for his Wall Street pals. "His political well surfaces in Connecticut but he's trying to reach pay-dirt in Texas. He's trying to tap our governmental programs for agriculture and oil, REA, Social Security, and old age pensions into Connecticut and Wall Street surface tanks that would drain all of them." Bush, slipping into his version of a

Midland drawl, quipped that he had been born in Connecticut so that he could be close to his mother.[60]

Bush had a clever and simple campaign slogan: "Put more Texas in Washington and have less Washington in Texas." He plastered the highways with billboards and covered the airwaves with ads. When Yarborough refused to debate him, Bush bought time on seventeen different television stations and debated an empty chair. A moderator would ask a question, and Bush would play recordings of Yarborough's positions and then respond with his own take. He traveled all over the state and even got his own campaign band, the Black Mountain Boys, a bluegrass outfit from Abilene, to entertain the crowd.[61] (Critics liked to point out that bluegrass wasn't exactly Texas music.) On the stump, Bush kept to his message: Yarborough was a liberal out of step with Texas values, a tool of the liberal elite, a New Frontier stooge in the pocket of big labor. What Texas deserved, he would say, was a senator "who will stand up to [labor leader] Walter Reuther, not rubber stamp every radical program he sends to Capitol Hill."[62] In a Labor Day speech, Bush promised to protect the "rights of the individual" from the constant attacks from "left-wing labor leaders."[63] He further promised to "represent primarily the typical Texans, the man with family and an honest job and all the problems that beset a man in this day."[64] Bush wasn't above a little theater either. Late in the campaign, the candidate announced that his campaign was having its office checked for listening devices. He wasn't accusing Ralph Yarborough, mind you, but there were "leaks" that couldn't be explained any other way.[65]

On Election Day, George Bush, running for public office for the first time, won 1,134,337 votes, more than any other Republican in Texas history, more than Tower, more than Nixon, more than Eisenhower. Even Goldwater ran 180,000 votes behind Bush. Yarborough won easily with 56 percent of the total vote. But out in West Texas, a different story developed. Bush won every urban county, save Taylor (Abilene), where he lost by 56 votes. Bush tallied 68 percent in Midland, 61 percent in Ector, 57 percent in Potter, 66 percent in Randall, and 60 percent in Lubbock. He won nine of the ten wheat counties in the northernmost Panhandle along with smaller cities like Pampa, Hereford, Borger, Perryton, and Dumas. He had the endorsement of every West Texas newspaper except H. M. Baggarly's *Tulia Herald*. The election made it clear: West Texas was a Republican stronghold.

VI

The most notable event of the 1964 campaign in West Texas was probably a Barry Goldwater rally in Amarillo just a few weeks before the election. It was a busy day in friendly territory for Goldwater; he began his morning with a rally in Tulsa and ended it with a rally in Fort Worth. In between were events in Amarillo and Albuquerque and a quick appearance in Odessa—where he was entertained by four dancing elephants with gold toenails. The subject of the day's speeches was LBJ's disastrous foreign policy and American failures in Vietnam, a war that the president refused to declare. That day was also the Goldwaters' wedding anniversary and Amarillo wanted to treat them right. After all, he was family; the candidate's brother Bob had married local heiress Sally Harrington in Amarillo years earlier. Wes Izzard turned that morning's *Amarillo News* into an unofficial program for the event and hired a daredevil motorcyclist to deliver film in time for a special photo-heavy early edition of the afternoon's paper.

Goldwater's campaign plane banked across a perfect Panhandle sky late on a crisp autumn morning. Looking down, he could see a colossal "Welcome Barry" banner stretched across the tarmac. Five hundred well-wishers welcomed him and his wife as they stepped from the plane. There was still a bit of moisture from a light early-morning rain. Pampa's Bob Price, a hyperactive Goldwater clone running for Congress ("A Courageous Conservative for a Conservative District"), handled the official handshakes and introductions. Price's wife presented Peggy Goldwater an anniversary bouquet of roses. After photos and a few remarks, the official delegation stepped to a motorcade and began a slow drive into Amarillo. From the back of a red Eldorado convertible, at the head of an eighteen-car procession, the Goldwaters waved to twenty thousand Amarilloans lining downtown sidewalks and made their way to Gold Sox baseball stadium.[66]

Eleven thousand Goldwater fans packed into a stadium meant to hold five thousand. School buses littered the parking lot from local high schools that had brought students from Dumas, Pampa, Dalhart, and Dimmit. Along the left side of the stage stood a group of clean-cut teens in blue t-shirts and khakis holding a twenty-five-foot banner saying, "Amarillo Teen-Agers for Goldwater." Several of their friends, also in blue T-shirts and khakis, moved through the crowd, passing out six hundred Goldwater signs and two thousand hand-stenciled placards. One hundred Republican women, each in a white blouse, blue skirt, and red vest (with an elephant on the back) manned the merch tables, selling sweaters, jewelry, books, T-shirts, buttons. A lone vendor wandered the stands, hawking *A Texan Looks at Lyndon.* Joining Goldwater on the stage were congressional candidates Bob Price and Ed Foreman, former mayor J. Ernest Stroud, and GOP gubernatorial candidate Jack Crichton. Wes Izzard was the emcee. Goldwater—particularly dashing in a black suit, white shirt, and steel-gray tie—gave a great speech under a perfect sky and the crowd went nuts.

Six weeks later, Goldwater lost one of the most lopsided elections in history. He lost Texas, even Amarillo. Bush lost. Price lost. Foreman lost. Even Bruce Alger, a five-term incumbent Republican from Dallas, lost. Almost every single Republican in the Texas legislature (and there weren't many) lost. The chattering classes both in Texas and nationally wrote off Goldwater and cowboy conservatism.

They were so wrong.

15
UNINTENDED CONSEQUENCES
Civil Rights and West Texas Football

But West Texas where the sun
Shines like the evil one
Ain't no place
For a colored
Man to stay!

LANGSTON HUGHES, 1959

Before the Oakland Raiders of the 1970s there were the West Texas State Buffaloes of the 1960s: a football team made up of miscreants, philosophers, hell-raisers, misfits, maniacs, good ol' boys, street kids, rebels, and way-out-there castoffs. These were players who cut down campus trees for kicks and who held footraces along the roofs of cars lined up in front of nightclubs. These were teams that produced fifty-nine professional football players in eleven years, including NFL stars Eugene "Mercury" Morris, Duane Thomas, and Jerry Logan and some of the biggest superstars in professional wrestling—Terry Funk, Dory Funk Jr., Bruiser Brody, Stan Hansen, Dusty Rhodes. Teams that week after week rolled up the most impressive offensive numbers in football—400 and 500 yards a game. Teams no big program would schedule because they feared getting beat at home by a no-name team from a nowhere school. Teams whose assistant coaches spent months on the road scouring for talent that everyone else had missed, neglected, or feared. The most racially integrated football team in the South. Teams "known throughout the land for a bellicose coach and a bunch of guys who may not have been the greatest athletes in the world and whose dipstick didn't touch the oil but who played the game from the inside out and left it on the field after the game."[1] Teams coached by Joe Kerbel—brilliant, self-aware, fearless, fair, and perhaps the most explosively volatile coach in the history of sport. And teams that brought civil rights protest to West Texas.

For thousands of years, it was its stark isolation that had defined the Despoblado. Little changed when it became the heart of Comanchería or the Cattle Kingdom or the Agricultural Wonderland. As the twentieth century unfolded, the region's economic and demographic conformity, combined with a still-primitive national media apparatus, kept the region more or less sequestered from most of the political, cultural, and social upheavals that characterized the immediate post–World War II era. While the region basked in unprecedented economic expansion and its cities grew, it was still largely provincial, still inwardly focused. Still white. Still middle-class. Still fervently if blandly patriotic. It still clung to a frontier mythology that explained history and defined the characteristics of the ideal American. But homegrown protests, like the sort that erupted at WT, would bring "the Sixties" to West Texas and forever change its politics.

I

In May 1960, Canyon, Texas, was a bona fide, used-to-have-the-city-limits-sign sundown town. It had six thousand residents, and not a single one of them was African American. In Randall County, Black residents made up only 0.0016 percent of the population. West Texas State College (WT) was still segregated, still mostly a finishing school for aspiring teachers, and still a college that drew its student body from lily-white Panhandle towns. And the school was under a court order to desegregate.

Desegregating WT was always going to be a very different cultural experience than in other parts of Texas or the larger South. For the overwhelming percentage of its students, having regular encounters with a single African American would be a novel experience. The population of West Texas in 1960 was still 98 percent white and native-born. A third of West Texas's 107 counties had a total Black population of less than 1 percent. Even in the handful of counties where the Black population approached 10 percent, strict residential segregation kept the populations separate.[2] It was this homochromatic demography that contributed to the fact that many West Texas public school systems were among the first in the state to desegregate after the *Brown v. Board of Education* decision. Places like Friona, the very first school district in Texas to integrate, were relieved to be free of the financial and organizational burden of maintaining a separate school system for six students.[3]

In the six years since the Supreme Court's decision in *Brown*, WT's strategy had been to ignore or turn down without comment applications from African American students. But in February 1960, when Amarillo High School and Amarillo College graduate John Matthew Shipp Jr. sued for admission to West Texas State, with the backing of the local NAACP, school administrators had to act. Admitting that Shipp had been turned down because of his race, WT's lawyers offered up the "salt and pepper" argument for retaining segregation. The tactic, making the rounds of southern lawyers seeking to prevent the integration of schools that season, argued that since Texas already had some desegregated schools, there was no need to integrate the rest. In May, a federal judge rejected WT's argument and ordered the school to admit Shipp.[4] Although Shipp had by then given up and moved to Houston, the order held, and three African Americans enrolled for the fall semester. Among them was Helen Neal, an Amarillo elementary school teacher who earned her last few degree credits at WT and became its first African American graduate in 1962.[5]

What happened next was one of the stranger stories in the history of Texas sports. Somehow, WT's administrators arrived at the conclusion that they could perhaps offset the discomfort that parents, locals, and students felt about integration by recruiting talented Black athletes and building a winning football program. Which sort of makes sense in football-mad Texas. A 1957 study on attitudes among West Texas high school students toward integration revealed that 95 percent of white high school seniors believed that Black students should be allowed to play sports.[6]

WT administrators found an eager accomplice in new head coach Joe Kerbel. A barrel-shaped, three hundred–pound offensive genius, Kerbel was already a Texas high school coaching legend and an assistant coach at Texas Tech when WT hired him in 1960. Born in Dallas and raised in an oil-boom town in Oklahoma, Kerbel was the star center and play caller for his high school football team. In college, he bounced back and forth between the University of Tulsa and the University of Oklahoma (where he played on Bud Wilkinson's "B" team) for two seasons before joining the Marine Corps in 1943. He spent two years in the Pacific Theater, attaining a captain's rank, and, when the war was over, returned to Oklahoma to finish his degree and work as an assistant coach.[7] Upon graduation he went into high school coaching, first in the oil town of Bartlesville and then fifty miles down the road in Cleveland, where during the 1950 and 1951 seasons, his first two as a head coach, he went 20-3. That's when he was recruited to take over the head coaching job of the Buckaroos at Breckenridge High School, one of the most storied programs in Texas. In three years, Kerbel went 29-6-1 and won two state championships. That's when Amarillo High, hoping to return the Sandies to the glory years of the 1930s, hired Kerbel away. It was a good move. In just two years, he built the program back into a power-house; in 1957, the team ran through district like a mule through the stalks. Going into the state semifinal, the Sandies were undefeated and ranked number one in the state, but ran into Abilene, on the verge of winning its third straight state championship.

Over eight seasons as a high school head coach, Kerbel racked up a record of 74-17-1. He had five district titles and two state football championships (along with two more in track). He'd made the state finals four times. There were two simple reasons for his success: his teams (including track) were among the toughest, most disciplined, well prepared, and physically fit in Texas. And Kerbel was an offensive mastermind. He was the man who brought the Split-T to high school football and who drilled its countless permutations into his players during legendary six-hour practices.[8] As one of his standout high school players later attested, "Everything I've done in my life—playing at Oklahoma, working in the oil business—has been easier than playing football for Joe Kerbel."[9]

After two years helping run the offense at Texas Tech, Kerbel was hired by WT in 1960 to be its new head football coach. He was a very popular choice. The local press loved him (since the beginning, Kerbel had always kept a good relationship with the media)—he was honest, funny, and quotable. WT football boosters loved him; many were Amarillo High grads grateful to him for resurrecting the program. And WT had gone 1-9 its last two seasons. Kerbel surrounded himself with some of the best high school assistant coaches in West Texas, young and hungry men. That first year, Kerbel inherited only sixteen lettermen and a recruiting class less than enthusiastic about his style. Still, he managed a 3-7 season. That's when the recruiting blitz started and Black players started showing up in Canyon. He focused on recruiting junior college athletes, good football players looking to play big-time ball. He signed fullback Ollie Ross and end Bobby Drake out of California and the blazingly fast Pete Pedro from Trinidad College in Colorado. When the 1961 season opened, he had the fastest running back in the country.[10]

The Buffaloes went 6-4 that season, defeating Brigham Young University and handing the 8-1-1 Arizona Wildcats their only loss. Pedro was an immediate sensation; he led the NCAA in scoring, finished second in rushing yards, and averaged 7.1 yards a carry. Kerbel demanded that Pedro and the other Black players be treated with nothing less than equality and respect. And he ordered all his players to be responsible for one another, Black or white. Still, Black players were obvious novelties in an all-white school and town and were subject to drive-by epithets and discrimination in town. The local press and boosters insisted that Pedro was Puerto Rican, for example, not African American. For the most part, however, the players were accepted on campus and embraced by the team.[11]

Kerbel recruited even more Black athletes and sent his assistants all over the country. He particularly liked California and Pennsylvania (Joe Namath's high school center ended up at WT) and drew from the junior college ranks when he could. But he also enjoyed a pipeline of Black high school talent in Texas who were still not allowed to play in the Southwest Conference, along with white players in the state considered too raw or wild to be a Longhorn or an Aggie or a Horned Frog. He promised, "If black players will win for us, we're gonna keep recruiting 'em."[12] By 1967, almost every Black man on campus was a football player.

Recognizing the nature of Kerbel's racial broad-mindedness is important. There was no larger social project at play here, nor was his use of Black players steeped in some transactional cynicism. It was simpler than that. Joe Kerbel was consumed by winning. Black players helped him win games. So he recruited Black players. For the first time in his coaching career, he was in control of choosing his players, and he took full advantage. He pushed West Texas State's athletic budget and the administration's patience to every limit. His spending was out of control; he ran up enormous long-distance phone bills and put coaches on planes to recruit rumors. His assistants spent weeks on the road recruiting, living out of motels, eating at drive-ins, and constantly wiring for more cash. And he took good care of his players once they were on the team. When they were on the road, players enjoyed first-class treatment, staying in nice hotels and eating good meals. They took airplanes to away games, and Kerbel always scheduled at least one game a year far out of state—Ohio, Tennessee, California, Michigan, Montana, North Carolina, Illinois. (For most of his players it was the first time they had flown on a plane and, for many, their first time out of Texas.) He insisted that his players use the same equipment as professional teams.

That treatment came at a price. His practices were brutal hours-long exercises in working toward perfection and building an endurance few teams could match. Former WT running back Mercury Morris compared the program to the Marine Corps's Parris Island (where Kerbel had done his basic training). Offensive and defensive backs could expect to put in more mileage in the fall than during track season. He roamed the field, watching his teams through his ever present blacked-out Wayfarers, yelling at players ("Hey, stupid, if you put your brains in a gnat's ass it would fly backwards"), punching them in the chest, pulling their ears. A go-to Kerbel move was to angrily waddle onto the field, kicking players in the butt as he went. Fifty years later, Texas football coaches still swap Kerbel stories. One of the best is the player who showed up in the training room with bruises all over the back of his legs, and when asked how he got them, the player explained that Kerbel was trying to kick his ass but couldn't reach. There were curfews and mandatory meetings and study halls. Players could not miss class or church on Sunday. Most of his players were convinced they hated him.

On Game Day Kerbel would get so worked up, he could barely function. It started with the pregame prayer, which he always led. It would begin, appropriately enough: Kerbel quietly appreciating the opportunity to play and requesting that players be safe from harm. As the prayer went on, he got louder and angrier. "By the end of it," as one player remembered, "he was asking for the strength to go out there on the field and beat the hell out of those sunuvabitches from the other school . . . screaming at the top of his voice and swinging his fists in the air."[13] He got worse during the game; roaming the sidelines like a madman, firing assistant coaches, screaming at players and officials, punching people. One time he grabbed a campus cop, demanding that he go on the field and arrest a player who had missed an assignment. If a player fumbled the ball, he was forbidden from speaking. When his lunacy reached a fever pitch, the backup quarterback on the sidelines and quarterback coach sitting in the press box stepped in and took over the play calling. Kerbel was self-aware enough to know his own tendencies and planned for this exact contingency by spending several evenings a week with his quarterbacks and coaches, going over every single situation and forcing them to memorize four or five of the options for each. In order. They actually practiced taking over for Kerbel during the week. Perhaps it's no surprise that in addition to his success in producing NFL players, Kerbel also produced dozens of great high school and college coaches. As NFL legend Jerry Logan put it: "If you could survive Joe Kerbel, you could survive anywhere."[14]

By mid-decade, the Buffs were one of the most feared teams in the country. With the collapse of the Border Conference in 1962, West Texas State became an independent program, and Kerbel scheduled home and away games with schools like Memphis State, Bowling Green, Pacific, Northern Illinois, East Carolina, and Montana State and big programs in the Southwest like Arizona State, Utah State, and Colorado State. Kerbel's teams were high-scoring, high-yardage juggernauts. He ran a pro-style Split-T no-huddle offense, and over three seasons the Buffs averaged almost thirty points and 400 offensive yards a game. Hank Washington, a rangy six-feet, four-inch signal caller with a bullet arm, was one of the few Black quarterbacks playing Division I football in 1966 when he led the nation in scoring, completing 261 passes for over 2,000 yards and 17 touchdowns. (Many predicted he would be the first Black quarterback to start in the NFL.) When Mercury Morris arrived on campus, Kerbel switched up the offense to use more sweeps and take advantage of the speed, agility, strength, and acumen of one of the best running backs in college football. In 1967, Morris battled O. J. Simpson all season for the rushing title. He lost (by less than 100 yards), but with 254 yards receiving, Morris won the overall yardage title. Morris averaged almost 7 yards every time he ran the ball and scored 17 touchdowns. He was even better the following year, again battling Simpson for the rushing title and even appearing on a few Heisman lists. At one point he broke the NCAA's single-game rushing record (Simpson eclipsed it the next week) when he ran up 340 yards and had touchdown runs of 20, 54, 66, and 89 yards.[15]

WT had a reputation for more than just big offensive numbers. It was an "outlaw" program, one of the most unusual teams in college football, "a home for those who just didn't fit anywhere else."[16] Forty percent of the team was Black, an unheard-of number for a college football team in Texas. It was the most integrated institution anywhere in West Texas. When on the road, Kerbel assigned rooms by position and had Black and white teammates room together, an unheard-of gesture in 1960s Texas. A Black player who demonstrated a talent for public relations or a flair for words would soon find himself roaring down some highway with Kerbel at the wheel on the way to mingle with one booster group or another. To the shock of some parents, Kerbel had both Black and white players helping him with his summer high school clinics. The players, both the good ol' boys from Texas and the Black players from across the country, got along. The team reveled in its reputation for being tough and a little crazy. And Kerbel's sole focus on winning gave his players the freedom to exercise a degree of individuality that few college coaches in those years could possibly comprehend. It's perhaps one of the reasons that WT was considered not only a pipeline to the NFL—at one point in the early 1970s, more than fifty former Kerbel players were in professional football, rivaling the numbers of the big schools like Ohio State and Alabama—but also a wellspring of professional wrestling. Across the 1970s and 1980s, the top bills of wrestling cards were chock-full of ex-Buffalo football players. So many pro wrestlers showed up at the spring alumni game one year that they were able to sneak Dick Murdoch (Dusty Rhodes's tag-team partner) into uniform. Legend has it he even scored a touchdown.[17]

Kerbel was untouchable. He once told star running back Duane Thomas, "As long as I keep winning these sons of bitches can't say anything to me."[18] He was wrong.

II

In spring 1968 the racial climate at WT began to change. That semester, Black students, led by football players, stood up to challenge the mechanisms, symbols, and practices of white supremacy on campus and in the community. While most Black men at WT were on athletic scholarships, the African American student population had grown beyond just athletes. There were plenty of other students of color, who had been attracted to the school's business and education programs. Two Black fraternities had been chartered, Omega Psi Phi and Kappa Alpha Psi.

The African American community grew close over that year, drawn together by the countless micro and macro aggressions its members faced each day. WT administrators' scheme to change the local racial climate with a winning football team had largely failed. Canyon was still very much an unwelcoming environment for Black students. Local rednecks screamed racial slurs as they drove through campus. Black students were not welcome at local restaurants and were barely tolerated in stores. The drugstore kept its "black" makeup under lock and key. The only larger African American community nearby was in Amarillo, and sometimes WT students were not welcome there either.

The assassination of Martin Luther King Jr. was the catalyst for change. As Mercury Morris remembered: "We raised our fists. And for the first time, Whites began to fear us . . . and listen."[19] There was no official recognition of King's murder in either Amarillo or Canyon, where the flags still flew at full mast. As native son Buck Ramsey reported, "When news came to the Panhandle that Dr. King had been assassinated, the general reaction seemed to be one of rejoicing and celebration, a feeling of relief and, undoubtedly, of vicarious vengeance."[20] But it was different at WT, where local ministers and faculty, including a sociology professor who had gone to graduate school with King at Boston College, organized an informal march from the Presbyterian Church to the Episcopalian Student Center. It began with twenty parishioners from the Presbyterian Church and grew as it passed other churches: First Christian, First United Methodist, First Baptist, St. Paul Lutheran; congregants from some of the smaller chancels off 4th Avenue joined. Canyon police had denied a permit request to use the street and warned of arrests, so marchers kept to the sidewalks. Local police watched the procession carefully, as did military intelligence and the FBI, whose agents took photos of every participant. A dozen Black WT students joined, each wearing a black armband. The march ended on the lawn of the Episcopal Student Center, where a short tribute service to King was held.[21]

Mourning and angry, WT's African American community met informally and with great frequency over the next few weeks to talk about how race worked at WT and in Canyon. It was all ad hoc: there was no Black Student Alliance, no NAACP chapter on campus or even in

Canyon, few obvious allies among the faculty or administration. Other than the athletes, most Black students didn't even live on campus. There was, however, one solid bloc of students interested in forcing change at WT: football players, including several white players. One of the consequences of creating a team out of misfits was populating campus with free thinkers willing to challenge authority. As ironic as it might seem, Kerbel's draconian and dictatorial approach to football built not only a sense of solidarity among his players but also a willingness among them to confront the coach when they thought he was wrong or stepped over a line.[22] And Kerbel was confident enough and honest enough that— once he had cooled down—he could admit when he was wrong. He taught them, whether intentionally or not, the importance of standing up for themselves and one another and to call out unreasonable behavior.

The big issue that spring was West Texas State's official participation in "Old South Day," an annual celebration of the Confederacy put on by the Kappa Alpha fraternity. The Kappa Alpha Order, founded immediately after the Civil War by a former Confederate soldier, was among the most important Lost Cause organizations in the South. Through its rituals, publications, and celebrations it pushed a narrative of southern history that painted the antebellum South and plantation slavery in a positive light and portrayed the Civil War as a fight for the noble and glorious cause of states' rights, Reconstruction as a corrupt failure, and Ku Klux Klan terrorists as heroes who restored white supremacy to the South. Unlike most of the rest of Texas, its western half had largely avoided organizing its history around the Lost Cause, preferring, as we have seen, to emphasize its own frontier mythology as a narrative structure and ideological framework.[23] The first Confederate monument in West Texas didn't go up until 1931 (in Amarillo's Ellwood Park), and while there were plenty of counties named for Confederate officers, those counties had been named long before white settlers moved to the region. There were no schools named for Confederates until after World War II. The United Daughters of the Confederacy and Sons of Confederate Veterans were unusually weak in the region.

But that began to change in the 1950s. In direct response to the Civil Rights Movement, Lost Cause mythology surged again; this time it reached West Texas. New schools were named for Robert E. Lee and other Confederate heroes. New monuments to Confederate dead appeared in front of county courthouses in towns that hadn't existed in 1865. When all-white Tascosa High School in Amarillo opened in 1958, it adopted the "Rebel" as its mascot. A student dressed as a Confederate general roamed its sidelines at football games and took center court at basketball games. He slashed the air with his saber, leading students in a Rebel Yell as they waved the Stars and Bars. The school's choir called themselves the "Dixieland Singers," and "Dixie" was its fight song. The cutest and most popular girl in school was named "Southern Belle."[24] It was also in 1958 that the Kappa Alpha Order organized at West Texas State.

Prior to that year, WT, like so many other colleges, had forbidden national fraternities and sororities. Once the ban was lifted, however, Kappa Alpha was among the first four fraternities chartered on campus. As an organization, Kappa Alpha was unabashedly southern. As the official history of its founding put it in 1891, "By a true instinct—happily almost universal—its members have readily perceived that in the South, and in the South alone, can it find a congenial home."[25] Among its most famous members was racist and pro-Klan author Thomas Dixon Jr., whose work was the basis of D. W. Griffith's *Birth of a Nation*.[26] Old South Day was started in 1949 at the University of Alabama as a celebration of the Confederacy. It kicked off every year with the fraternity "seceding" from the university and parading in confederate uniforms through campus. After that came the white-supremacist cosplay dance balls with hoop skirts and elaborate Confederate regalia. The event was, as historian Anthony James described it, a place where white male students "performed the drama [of the horrors of the Civil War and Reconstruction] from a position of dominance. They could glory in past defeat because, ultimately, they emerged victorious. White supremacy, albeit in a different form, was restored."[27]

The WT Kappa Alphas (KAs) started celebrating Old South Day in 1961. Each year, in late spring, members on horseback would ride to the President's House, recent pledges on foot behind them, to present a formal notice of secession. Students and townspeople lined the route, waving the Confederate flag and singing "Dixie." That night would be a fancy dinner dance at some upscale Amarillo venue, where the men wore their dress-up uniforms and the women their hoop skirts.

Led by football players, the first Old South Day Protest began in May 1968. A meeting on May 2 created a petition demanding that the administration refuse to participate in a grotesque celebration of the Slave South. The meeting also produced special committees that would articulate other grievances and plan demonstrations. Gary Puckrein, a freshman football player from New York, emerged as the group's spokesman. He appeared before a student court and not only demanded that the Administration not take part in Old South Day but also called attention to the "Whites Only" signs at fraternity lodges, the fact that there were no faculty of color at WT, and that WT did not offer courses in either African or African American history. "Black people need to know about their history," he said, and summed up the attitudes of the administration this way: "They don't care about the Negroes; they are racists." As he lodged his complaint about the parade, he said: "It's about time white America wakes up that they are hurting the Negro. What if a little Negro boy sees it on TV, a gay festivity out of his slavery." He concluded his remarks by comparing the Confederate flag to the swastika and promised the court that he would burn it if he saw the flag flown on campus.[28]

The administration ignored the demand for an injunction, and student petitions gained more signatures. The Kappa Alphas kept preparing for their big weekend and seemed genuinely confused about the uproar (even though other chapters had discontinued Old South Day after facing similar protests). Fraternity president Dick Flynn promised that the Kappa Alphas meant no offense and tried to reassure the campus community by saying that the fraternity had no interest in the "revival of slavery." The Thursday of the parade was warm and humid; a huge rainstorm had pelted Canyon the night before and light rain continued to fall intermittently throughout the day. As the hour of the parade approached, a nervous tension gripped campus. Canyon police had placed sharpshooters on rooftops and brought in State Department of Public Safety officers to help them secure the route. Campus administrators feared a riot. Protesters lined the streets, waving signs: "The war is over—You Lost!" and "To Hell with the Old South." But they were peaceful. The Kappa Alphas nervously made their way to President Cornette's door, where Dick Flynn read a greatly abbreviated version of his speech. Cornette snatched the order of secession and quickly shut the door. Flynn looked at the closed door for a moment before remounting his horse and leading the KAs away from campus. WT's official involve-

*Kappa Alpha member flying
the Confederate flag during
the Old South Day parade in
Canyon, May 11, 1968.*

ment in Old South Day ended there. Mercury Morris recalled the event as the day the fraternity exercised "its constitutional right to make a fool of itself" and he and his teammates exercised "their constitutional right to protest their tasteless, not-so-hidden message."[29]

Local conservatives freaked. The Randall County Republican Party, led by Evetts Haley, who had played football for WT half a century earlier, prepared a special resolution for the upcoming county convention. Among its various WHEREASes were scattered complaints about Kerbel and his players. The party decried his "indiscriminate recruitment of Negro athletes" and "the moral principles involved." The very presence of Black players, the resolution insisted, had "accentuated" social unrest, placed an undue burden on local police, and had offended the "moral sense of this community." The Republicans labeled the Old South Day protests as "communistically-oriented agitation and anarchy" and an affront to "the exercise of a traditional wholesome rite on the West

Texas State University campus." They demanded that WT administrators recognize that the continued threat of "violence and bloodshed" was more important "than the winning of ball games."[30]

III

Franklin Thomas was older than most of the other African American students on campus and one of the few Black men not on scholarship. The older brother of star running back Duane Thomas, Franklin had come to WT after a stint in the army and paid his own tuition. (Their younger brother, Bertrand, also attended WT and was the football team manager.) The brothers had been raised on Baldwin Street in South Dallas, one of the roughest neighborhoods in Texas. Their father was a hardworking, taciturn man who owned a house-painting business. Their mother was an educated woman who worked as a domestic. Those were violent years in South Dallas, as African Americans moved into formerly white neighborhoods and were met with dynamite. In one five-month period while Franklin was in elementary school, six Black-owned homes in his neighborhood were blown up.[31] But by the time Thomas graduated from high school, South Dallas from Haskell Avenue to Lamar Street was all African American. A city within a city, the area had neat, one-story 1920s cottages with porches and yards, and tarpaper shacks with no running water on muddy lanes. The pride of South Dallas was Lincoln High School. Built in the 1930s, it was one of the largest and most modern school buildings in the state, a striking and bold architectural statement in the International Style. It had good programs in music and science and a majority-Black faculty. And on Thursday nights in the fall, the Mighty Tigers played football.[32]

Franklin Thomas had been an all-city and all-district offensive and defensive guard at Lincoln, lightning fast and strong. He was also an all-state hurdler on the track team. Graduating high school in 1964, he moved to California to play football and run track for Los Angeles City College (LACC). (He hoped to make the U.S. Olympic team in the high hurdles.) That's where he first ran into Joe Kerbel, a regular at LACC practices. Franklin stayed at LACC for a few semesters but dropped out in 1966 and was drafted into the army. Developing a life-threatening case of strep throat during basic training, Franklin spent close to a year in the hospital fighting kidney failure. When he finally got healthy, he was discharged from the army and had to figure out what to do with his life. It was early 1968. Duane was in Canyon, playing football for Joe Kerbel. He convinced his coach to offer Franklin a chance to play at WT. Kerbel gave Franklin a shot.

Within weeks of arriving in Canyon, however, Franklin's kidney troubles flared up and he spent months in the hospital. His football career was over. He was finally discharged and got back to campus just in time to attend the Old South Day Protest. It was an important moment for Thomas. Always a deep thinker, interested particularly in race in modern America, he found the event confusing and the WT administration's participation doubly so. "If you lost, what are you celebrating? Are you celebrating your defiance to your country?" He found the whole thing "absurd." As he watched the Kappa Alphas parade down the street in their Confederate getup and waving the Stars and Bars, he thought to himself how "nothing fit." "Kerbel didn't fit. The football players didn't fit." He felt like he was at Ole Miss or Alabama. WT was actively recruiting Black football players and desegregating their campus, but still allowed this neo-Confederate celebration. Taking advantage of his GI bill benefits, Thomas decided to stay at WT, where his financial freedom gave him an advantage for speaking out that most Black students lacked.[33]

"You have to understand," he later told *Los Angeles Times* sportswriter Paul Zimmerman, "West Texas State was still a primitive place when I got there. Advanced athletically, yes, thanks to Kerbel, but primitive socially, with heavy racist overtones."[34] When students returned in the fall of 1968, WT had changed. There were more students of color who were not scholarship athletes. Thomas and a few football players had chartered the school's first Black fraternity (Omega Psi Phi) and were hungry for change. When Franklin Thomas faced harassment by the administration for dating white women—"he became a regular in Dean Carruth's office"—it galvanized what was becoming a larger community. African American students rallied around Thomas.[35] They found willing allies not just among the football players but also from a growing number of left-leaning students, including members of the school's Students for a Democratic Society chapter.

In November, Black students and white supporters nominated Claudia Stewart, a Black sophomore from Dallas, for homecoming queen. To the shock of the community, she finished second in the voting, becoming the first attendant of the Homecoming Court. When halftime announcers tried to announce the court in alphabetical order instead of the traditional introductions by numbers of votes, which would have put Stewart last, she refused to take the field. The folks in the press box reversed their decision and announced Stewart second. African American students cheered and beamed. But the next day, when the *Canyon News* published its images of the homecoming parade, Stewart could not be seen in the photo, her face hidden behind the beehive hairdo of another attendant. The Student Senate was outraged. Two students marched down to the *Canyon News* office to complain. The next week, editor Troy Martin printed a nonapology apology. ("We had no thought of discrimination, racial or otherwise. We simply used the best picture as any editor worth his salt would do.")[36]

At home basketball games, fistfights devolved into near riots when Kappa Alphas insisted on waving Confederate flags. Rumors flew that white female students dating Black students were having their financial aid threatened. (The head of the financial aid office denied the rumors, but added, "If a white girl owes me some money and is married to a Negro, she has less chance of getting a job and paying us back.")[37] Students began reporting discrimination in local housing and from local merchants. The administration responded by forming the Committee to Reduce Interracial Tension, whose first few meetings erupted into shouting matches. The Kappa Alphas accused Gary Puckrein of being a tool of the Students for a Democratic Society, the ACLU, and the communists and cried that they were the victims of a "created political issue."[38] Administrators accused Black students of exaggerating the level of discrimination they faced in town and on campus. And Gary Puckrein resorted to yelling as he tried to explain why African Americans found the Confederate flag offensive.[39]

Black students then formed the Afro-American Society and planned counterprogramming to Old South Day. Most of the society's male members were current football players or former ones. Star defensive back Hardy Williams explained in the student paper that Black students were simply demanding respect, explaining that "respect means being able to move into a white neighborhood and live next door to a white man if I want to." He talked of his embrace of Malcolm X and Black Power and warned that "next year there could possibly be a few new Negro students who won't be content to wait for broken promises of the administration to be patched up and put into operation—there could be trouble."[40] At the opening event of WT's first Afro-American Week, Williams demanded Black faculty and Black history courses. He told the crowd, "The black man has been denied the greatest contribution of his cultural heritage—how to know himself as a man."[41] The Committee to Reduce Interracial Tension fell apart as it took up issues like the administration's response to interracial dating or the discrimination by landlords in town or Franklin Thomas's suggestion that the committee investigate the "exploitation" of Black and white athletes.[42]

If Williams was the fiery radical (a photo in the school newspaper featured him reading Black Panther Eldridge Cleaver's *Soul on Ice*), Thomas was the militant philosopher. When the Amarillo NAACP suggested that Black and white students cooperate in putting together the events for Afro-American Week, Thomas rejected the notion. "How can we celebrate our heritage by including the white student?" he asked. "Would they include us in the Old South celebration?"[43] In one of his speeches that week, Thomas described his memories of the 1965 Watts Riot. The Black men with guns on rooftops, he told the crowd, were not snipers, as the national news had reported, but rather frustrated Los Angelenos who "just wanted to see the white man run." And that's what he wanted, he told his audience, to see white people run, but to run "back to the history books, the Bible, and other sources of learning until he finds the Declaration of Independence and the Constitution."[44]

IV

In 1969, Duane Thomas had an amazing senior season, racking up 1,000 yards and scoring ten touchdowns. He was probably the most complete running back in the 1970 draft; he could block, catch, go outside or up the middle, and was all but uncatchable in an open field. Scouts compared him to Jim Brown. Even with 4.6 speed, Thomas didn't so much run as glide through defenses, practicing an almost judo running style, perfectly paced and directed to use a defense's energy against it. He slid and twisted and bolted away from multiple tacklers with grace and precision. (He likened his approach to playing jazz.) He could move laterally better than anyone else in the game; his legs and upper body seemed detached at times. He could change gears like Lewis Hamilton. And at

Duane Thomas speaking with a reporter at a West Texas State home game, November 25, 1969.

six feet, one inch and a rock-solid 220, he could and did just run over people. The Dallas Cowboys took him in the first round.

Even as he chafed under the strict and strangely arbitrary rules of the Cowboys and Coach Tom Landry, he shone in his rookie year, gaining 800 yards despite not starting until the fifth game of the season. He led the league in rushing average. He was a rock star on special teams. In the 1970 playoffs, Thomas added another 300 yards to his season and took Dallas to the Super Bowl, where the Cowboys lost to the Baltimore Colts. *Sporting News* named Thomas its offensive Rookie of the Year. But the racial climate in the Cowboy organization bothered Thomas. The Cowboys always talked like they were family, but it was a much more segregated organization than Joe Kerbel's Buffaloes. And the Cowboys had a reputation as one of the more racially divided teams in the NFL. Coach Landry was rumored to have a quota of how many Black players he would allow on the team. Most of the white players had grown up in the segregated South, a fact that Thomas (and others) believed was deliberate.[45] When Thomas arrived, it had only been two years since the team had rescinded a rule that forbade Black and white athletes to room together on the road.

After his award-winning rookie season, Thomas demanded a raise from Tex Schramm, maybe the cheapest general manager in the NFL. When Schramm refused, Thomas threatened to retire and do social work.[46] He left Dallas and moved to California where he roomed with former football star and Black activist Jim Brown. On the day he was to report to training camp in nearby Thousand Oaks, Thomas called a press conference and explained why he wasn't there. He told reporters that he wouldn't play until the Cowboys began to treat him with respect. He called Schramm "sick and demented" and Landry a "plastic man, no man at all." And he laid into the larger race issue in professional football: "The problem is I'm black. If I was white, it would have been totally different. They would have done me justice. A revolution is coming in pro football. Players like me are tired of being on our knees all the time. I want equality. I've stated my position and they know what I want."[47]

Duane and Franklin spoke regularly. His big brother stripped the issue to its essentials: the Dallas Cowboys were a business, and Duane was a big part of the product they were selling and should be compensated accordingly. When Thomas finally showed up to camp, he was wearing a dashiki and sandals and was accompanied by a Black Muslim friend. Thomas demanded a tryout for his friend and that they room together on the road. Dallas refused. Thomas asked to be traded, got his wish, didn't get along with his new coach, and was back with Dallas in less than a week. The press crucified him. Thomas sat out the first three games of the season, and when he finally joined the team, he took an oath of silence. His refusal to speak to the press or his teammates was *the* story of the Cowboys that season.

But the story should have been Thomas's work. Despite missing the first three games, he still ran for almost 800 yards, scored 11 touchdowns (leading the league), and took the team back to the Super Bowl. Even Landry admitted that although Thomas never spoke up or answered questions in team meetings or when reviewing film, the running back knew not only his every assignment for every play but also those of everyone else on the field. The Cowboys came to rely on him more and more as the season progressed. In the last regular season game, he scored four touchdowns. As Hunter S. Thompson described it: "All he did was take the ball and run every time they called his number—which came to be more and more often." At that year's Super Bowl, "Thomas was the whole show."[48] His 95 yards rushing, 17 yards receiving, and 1 touchdown don't begin to describe his dominance of the game. Dallas quarterback Roger Staubach couldn't find open receivers, so Landry switched to a running game. In their two crucial scoring drives, Thomas carried or caught the ball on half the plays. He should have been Super Bowl MVP; even Staubach, who got the award, thought so. Rumors flew that Thomas wasn't chosen because the sponsor feared he wouldn't show up to receive the award. That day would prove to be the highlight of his career. Dallas traded Thomas to San Diego almost immediately after the season, but Thomas suited up for only one game with the Chargers. He bounced around the NFL and the short-lived World Football League for a bit and was out of football five years after being drafted.

Meanwhile, Franklin was taking on the WT administration and the city of Canyon. He spoke out against financial aid, describing it as a tool to create a "dependency" among students. He was constantly calling out instances of racial discrimination on campus and in town. He was a supporter of an ongoing lawsuit against landlords who refused to rent apartments to Black students.[49] He wanted to show WT and Canyon what could happen "when you have people actually standing up and articulating realities that you have suppressed." He told Black students that there were three alternatives to changing the racial dynamic on campus: "God can come down and intervene, or he can give man the perceptiveness to realize the problem and work toward eliminating it, or man can resort to physical violence. The last one is not going to be very pretty."[50]

West Texas, he believed, simply was not prepared for African Americans willing to challenge unspoken social mores. Other than on the football team, WT's white students did not have extended opportunities for meaningful interaction with African Americans. They were never going to understand that Black students "have the same basic characteristics, drives, and incentives." Thomas blamed an administration that had, he believed, deliberately made such interactions difficult by refusing to incorporate Black students or African American culture into the curriculum or social life. With no Black counselors, faculty, administrators, or coaches, Black students had no one within the governing structure of the university who understood or could appreciate the issues that they faced in the overwhelmingly white community and school.[51]

Afro-American Week took on a decidedly militant tone in 1970. "There are two radical groups in this country," Franklin Thomas announced as he opened the festivities: "One is the whites. They call for abolishing the entire system. The other is the blacks. They want to sustain the system and infiltrate the system." There were screenings of movies about Africa, an exhibit of African art, and a demonstration of African dances. The president of the Texas NAACP pushed for greater economic and educational opportunities for African Americans. The head of Upward Bound told his audience that the "black man . . . asks for what is his as an American citizen." He added, "It's a hard thing to take when you have to pay for something which is already yours."[52]

Three weeks later, the Kappa Alphas held Old South Day. Black athletes led the protests, which began with picketing the administration building at 10 a.m. Bertrand Thomas was dressed in the typical "uniform" of the Black Panthers: dark beret, dark sunglasses, dark turtleneck, and dark trousers. He stood near the steps with a sign asking administrators, "DO YOU SANCTION THE CELEBRATION OF OPPRESSION AND TREASON?" He told a reporter: "The war has been over 110 years. I'm not against this fraternity or anything. I'm against the celebration of oppression of the black man." Football player Bruce Latimer added, "When you celebrate Old South Day you still celebrate slavery and everything else that went with the Old South." The protesters remained in front of the building most of the day, gathering dozens and then hundreds of supporters until finally lining the streets of the parade route. Franklin Thomas demanded that the president lower the flags to half-mast to protest the parade. Cornette refused. As the KAs marched down the street, one side of the street was full of white students cheering them on. The other side was full of Black and white students protesting the parade. That night, someone threw Molotov cocktails made of 7-Up bottles and bed sheets through the back door of the Randall County Abstract Company, starting a small fire. Police suspected that it was an attempt to firebomb the KA lounge, which was next door. No one was ever charged.

▼

On Tuesday, November 2, 1971, Canyon police raided Franklin Thomas's apartment. They found marijuana and arrested him on possession charges. The *Canyon News* just happened to have a photographer on hand when he was being arraigned. It described him as a "vocal black leader" on campus. Two months later Duane and Bertrand, driving through Greenville, Texas—where for decades a huge sign downtown announced "Welcome to Greenville, The Blackest Land, the Whitest People" (it had only come down in 1965)—were pulled over and arrested by local police, also for possession of marijuana. Thomas believed he had been set up. Franklin imagined it this way:

> Are you making any headway with Thomas?
> Not really.
> We need to break him a little bit more under the hammer.
> Well, what are his habits?
> Let's see if we can do something to whip that boy into line.[53]

After its most successful decade in football history, early in 1971, the WT Board of Regents declined to renew Joe Kerbel's contract. By all accounts, the 1970 season had been successful. The Buffaloes had gone 7-3, and star running back Rocky Thompson had been drafted in the first round by the New York Giants, making it two years in a row that a WT player had gone in the first round. The team had just joined the Missouri Valley Conference, largely thanks to the efforts of Kerbel. But there were grumblings about the coach and his players. Despite the winning records, bowl appearances, and professional successes, locals wanted more West Texas kids on the team, fewer transfers from faraway places. There was no question that many didn't like the large numbers of Black players recruited to Canyon and that many feared interracial relationships between Black players and local white girls. The activism of the players angered local conservatives.[54]

When informed of the decision, Kerbel resigned on the spot. Every single one of his assistant coaches followed suit. He was replaced by high school coach Gene Mayfield, a straight-laced Tom Landry replicant who had grown up in the Panhandle and played quarterback for WT in the 1950s. A successful coach to be sure, over the previous six years, Mayfield, the "Father of Mojo," had led Odessa Permian to the state finals three times, winning once and compiling a 62-10-2 record.[55] In his first year at WT, despite inheriting perhaps Kerbel's best recruiting class, he went 2-9. In six years, he had a single winning season (6-5 in 1974). In fact, over the next twenty years, the Buffs would post winning seasons only five times, never better than 7-4. In 1991, WT even suspended football for a season.[56]

A little over two years after being fired, Joe Kerbel died of a heart attack. He was fifty-one years old. After drifting away from football, Duane Thomas all but disappeared, only to make the occasional and unexpected appearance on a sports program or at a Cowboys event. Franklin took over his father's house-painting business in Dallas and turned it into a home energy company. He died in 2005 of kidney disease. In 2020, less than 5 percent of the student body at WT was African American; in Canyon the Black population was less than 3 percent. Kappa Alpha banned Old South celebrations in 2016.

16
RIGHT-WING REPUBLICANISM

In Texas, conservative Democrat means Republican, while
Republican means Bircher.

H. M. BAGGARLY, 1963

In the 1960s, there was no better political writer in Texas than Herbert
Milton Baggarly Jr., editor and publisher of the *Tulia Herald*. With
great wit and even empathy, West Texas's lone liberal newspaper editor tracked the rise of cowboy conservatism. His weekly column, "The
Country Editor," probably the most-read small-town column in the
country, sprawled over a third of every front page and took up as much
of page four as Baggarly thought he needed. It was the highlight of an
excellent newspaper, one of the best in the nation. In the thirty years that
Baggarly helmed the *Herald* it won every editorial and publishing award
in Texas, along with a slew of regional and national awards. In 1961,
it was named one of the three best newspapers in the country by the
National Editorial Association.[1] Fearless and honest, Baggarly provided
a weekly dose of counterprogramming to the right-wing media that
dominated West Texas. To be clear, Baggarly was no iconoclastic outsider raging against his neighbors but an absolute pillar of Tulia society:
a Jaycee, the organist at the Presbyterian Church, a member of Kiwanis,
and the man who organized the town's local summer concert series. And
he was a Panhandle boy, born and raised, a West Texas State alum, a man
who, other than the years he was in the service, had spent his entire life
along one fifty-mile stretch of Highway 87.

For two decades, with an incredulity that ranged from eye-rolling to tearing-his-hair-out-by-the-roots, Baggarly took on the radical right of West Texas. He didn't waste his time discriminating between the dizzying array of right-wing denominations that had descended on West Texas; he just called them all "Birchers" or sometimes "Haleyites."[2] When the muse descended, which seemed to happen a couple of times a year, Baggarly would devote an entire long-form column to cataloging the hypocrisy, tortured logic, and plain wrongheadedness of *Amarillo Daily News* editor Wes Izzard.[3] No one in Texas was better at taking the wind out of the sails of Evetts Haley, whom Baggarly often used as a shorthand example of every loudmouth fanatic and reckless bigot in Texas. (Haley was convinced that Baggarly was an unredeemable social-ist.) Baggarly called Haley "a blue-jeaned and booted spinner of Texas tall tales," "a radical fool," a "fanatic," and a "reprobate historian." He mocked Haley's run for governor as the act of a "precocious little boy" who paid the $1,500 filing fee just to see his name on the ballot. Publicly musing about a governor's race with only Haley and Satan as candidates, Baggarly admitted that "it wouldn't be an easy decision."[4]

But nothing prepared Baggarly for 1968. J. Evetts Haley was run-ning the Randall County Republican Party as a Bircher front group. Wes Izzard had turned his vast media empire over to promoting an out-there presidential candidate most people knew from the Late Late Show. The most prominent Democratic politician in the Panhandle was speaking on behalf of a doomed Republican presidential candidate at a $100-a-plate fundraising dinner before his own party had even named its nominee. A third-party candidate running a blatant segregationist cam-paign was polling well ahead of the Democratic presidential candidate. Every civic group and church organization in the region was offering weekly doses of right-wing paranoiac speakers or screening movies that spun various conspiracy theories. Just a month of attending one's basic social obligations—Monday Rotary luncheon, Wednesday PTA, weekly Bible study—meant hearing stories about how rock-and-roll music was part of a communist brainwashing plot, that the Civil Rights Movement was being run from Moscow, that Black Power terrorists were preparing for a violent overthrow of the government, that college students had rejected all morality and decency, that brain-altering drugs were turning kids into zombies, that Washington was preparing to confiscate private guns and to build a federal police force. It was relentless. Where were the "rugged individuals who thought for themselves?" Baggarly asked.

How had West Texans become "so frustrated and irrational"? Who had robbed them of their "reason and sanity"?[5]

I

The answer to his question was hiding in plain sight. It was the John Birch Society, then enjoying its greatest period of growth and influence. By the late 1960s, the Society had expanded its messaging and was working a lot of new angles. Finding great success with various front groups and taking advantage of an ever expanding right-wing media universe, the JBS nimbly responded to an emerging set of cultural fears manifested in the white middle class: riots, drug use, pornography, student unrest, Black Power, feminism. By the 1968 election season, West Texas Birchers were well positioned in local Republican groups and were running George Wallace's presidential campaign in Texas. It is ironic, given the vast attention paid to the "radical right" in the lead-up to the Goldwater campaign, that most contemporary political observers missed the Birchers' growing influence as the decade wore on. Perhaps the temptation of a narrative arc that concluded with the far right's defeat at the 1964 election proved too strong. It is true that the GOP and the gatekeepers of the respectable right wrote the extremists out of the party and the movement. Even Goldwater and Tower came out against the JBS. And anyone relying on the editorials in the *National Review* or Republican National Committee memoranda could conclude that the radicals had slunk away, embarrassed by what they had done to the party and the conservative cause.[6] But Birchers hadn't gone anywhere. In fact, their membership and influence were growing.

The late-sixties Birchaissance was possible thanks to Robert Welch's manic attention to any cultural shift that could be linked to the larger communist conspiracy. Rock and roll, feminism, drugs, pornography, student unrest, antiwar protests, Black Power, television programming, hippies. As the Society took interest in the subjects that had come to dominate the nightly national news, it attracted new members. It also helped that JBS front groups like Support Your Local Police (SYLP), the Movement to Restore Decency (MOTOREDE), and Truth About Civil Turmoil (TACT) kept the more outrageous communist plot stuff out of most of their publications, saving that material for more private encounters. While the Society never completely abandoned its quests to impeach Supreme Court justices or to expose the National Council of Churches as a den of communists, its more forward-facing work centered on issues like urban rioting, campus unrest, and sex education in schools. Make no mistake, every aspect of Bircher philosophy was still animated by anticommunist paranoia, but these new issues simply had greater relevance to most West Texans than worries over whether or not sixth-grade music books were being used to brainwash kids into embracing communism.

In early 1965, just weeks after Goldwater's defeat, the Society made its first big messaging shift. In a series of directives over the first half of the year, Robert Welch announced that the Society's main priority would be to "fully expose the civil rights fraud" and "break the back of the communist conspiracy."[7] He made his case in a sixteen-page pamphlet called "Two Revolutions at Once," wherein he declared that Martin Luther King Jr. was a dupe and a "troublemaker" and that the Civil Rights Movement "is Communist-plotted, Communist-controlled, and . . . serves only Communist purposes." He had half a million copies of the document printed and mailed to Birch chapters across the country. He then tasked Alan Stang, one of the most dependable writers in the Birch stable, to write a book-length version of the argument.[8] *It's Very Simple: The True Story of Civil Rights* dropped in summer 1965.[9] Stang claimed that the Civil Rights Movement represented the penultimate stage of a plot hatched by Lenin back in the 1920s. Like most Birch arguments, it depended on long-discredited evidence, imaginary documents, unreliable testimony, and Carl Lewis–worthy leaps of logic. Welch prepared one more version of the argument later that summer, a 2,300-word broadside titled "What's Wrong with Civil Rights?" which Birchers could run in their local papers. Which they did. It appeared in almost every single newspaper in the country, sometimes several times a year, well into the 1970s.[10]

The civil-rights-as-communist-plot messaging allowed Welch to tap into a growing unease about the Civil Rights Movement in the wake of urban rioting and the emergence of Black Power advocates. Outside the South—and here I would include West Texas—it allowed a criticism of the movement not necessarily based on any overt racist ideology. Delinking race from what was still an effort to protect white supremacy, the new JBS approach also moved the defense of segregation away from hidebound constitutional posturing and toward a more emotional and immediate white terror of riots, ghettos, and radicals.

Films were a big part of Bircher programming. Two movies in particular, *Anarchy USA: In the Name of Civil Rights* and *Civil Riots, USA: The Watts Story*, pushed the civil-rights-as-communism message hard. *Anarchy USA* was a "documentary" created by Bircher and rabid conspiracy theorist G. Edward Griffin that came out in 1965. For most of the film, a narrator reads a script version of Welch's message over film clips of angry civil rights activists and protests. The film's postcredits scene advertised other sources in the Bircher Cinematic Universe where viewers could learn more about the "conspirators' plans to subjugate the United States." The *Civil Riots, USA* film, directed by Bircher and politician Bill Richardson, who had been assigned by the Society to cover the Watts Riots, not only linked that event to the communist conspiracy but also called the entire concept of police brutality a "communist lie."[11]

Civil Riots, USA and *Anarchy USA* were shown everywhere in West Texas in the mid-1960s—schools, American Legion meetings, gun clubs, women's reading groups, and all the civic organizations. Bircher and real estate mogul W. W. Carruth III sponsored screenings of *Civil Riots, USA* in Dallas schools. When parents complained about Bircher propaganda, it made national headlines.[12] That sort of negative publicity was rare in the western half of the state. In Odessa, five days after the murder of Martin Luther King Jr., the city's TACT chapter sponsored two days' worth of continuous free screenings of *Anarchy USA* at the Rio Theater. Ads promoting the event promised that the film would provide "the TRUTH about MARTIN LUTHER KING."[13] In Abilene, TACT bought weekly radio time to broadcast the audio version of the film. The typical pattern for film distribution was to have a copy in one town for a week or so and saturate the market. In just one week in Childress, for example, *Revolution Underway*, George Benson and the NEP's version of the "civil rights as communist conspiracy" narrative, was shown for the first time at the Tuesday lunch meeting of the Lion's Club. The next day, the Rotarians saw it and the Jaycees the day after that. It was screened at the Thursday night meeting of the American Legion and at the Burlington (social) Club on Saturday.[14]

It wasn't just movies; JBS front groups TACT and SYLP regularly sponsored local appearances by speakers from the Society's speakers bureau. One of the most popular was an African American woman,

Julia C. Brown. A bona fide former undercover FBI informant (who had a code name and everything) who had spent most of the 1950s spying on the communist party in Cleveland, Ohio, Julia Brown was among the brightest stars in the Bircher media galaxy. A spellbinding speaker, Brown was very popular in Texas, where audiences couldn't get enough of her daring tales of adventure as a secret agent reporting on America's domestic enemies. And what was her takeaway message from the decade she spent observing the communists at close hand? That the communists were covertly guiding the Civil Rights Movement as part of their diabolical plot to overthrow America. It was a lucrative message; Brown pulled down $18,000 in speaking fees in 1968 alone, over twice the national median income. And that didn't include book sales.[15]

It had been a strange road for the sixty-two-year-old Brown. One of ten children born to a bank messenger and stay-at-home mom in Atlanta, Brown dropped out of high school in tenth grade, got married, and moved to Chicago. After a couple of failed marriages, she settled down with James "Curly" Brown and built a nice life in Cleveland; James ran his own truck hauling business, and Julia tended to the couple's real estate interests. Moving into a mostly white neighborhood, Brown began to get involved in Democratic Party politics. A zealous advocate for civil rights, she caught the attention of local leaders of the communist party, who wooed her into joining the organization. She lasted less than year, frustrated over the party's inattention to actual civil rights causes and its constant talk of overthrowing the government. A few weeks after quitting the organization, Brown later took her story and concerns to the local FBI field office, but apparently the agent she met wasn't interested. That was in 1948.

Three years later, three years deeper into the Red Scare, the Cleveland FBI office reached out to Brown. Would she be willing to serve her country, rejoin the Communist Party, and work as an FBI informant? They would pay expenses and provide a small stipend. Brown agreed. For nine demanding years, she led an exhausting double life. To keep her cover and gather the information the Bureau needed, she threw herself into party work: she was treasurer for five different front groups and attended hours-long meetings almost every night of the week. She handed out leaflets in the rain and heat and snow and tended the telephones and the teletype. Then, there were the clandestine debriefs in out-of-the-way parking lots. Brown had to memorize every name, face, and conversation. Openly known as a communist, she was ostracized by friends and neighbors. "I was just something that smelled to them." Only her husband knew her secret. In 1958, some party members began to question her loyalty and a few openly accused her of being an informant. (Not much of a stretch: by that point the FBI had recruited so many informants that the odds of any one attendant at a meeting being a mole were around three to one.) She was tailed home after meetings. Finally, in 1960, an exhausted and stressed-out Brown left Cleveland for California. And started writing her memoir.[16]

In March 1961, she told her remarkable story to *Ebony* magazine. "I Was a Spy for the FBI" was a three thousand–word spread with over a dozen photos—including staged recreations of events. It was an instant sensation. The next year, over five days in June, the "housewife-turned-spy" was the star witness in a House Committee on Un-American Activities hearing about communists in the Cleveland area. That was about the time she caught the attention of the John Birch Society. They paired her up with Carleton Young, a longtime character actor, who helped her craft her public appearances and who ghostwrote her memoir.[17] By 1963, Brown was appearing in front of various conservative organizations and Bircher front groups. Once Brown joined the Bircher media machine, her descriptions of the relationship between communism and civil rights underwent a significant transformation. For example, during her years as an informant, she consistently reported her frustration with the communists' efforts to undermine the NAACP and other African American civil rights groups. In her *Ebony* story she was adamant that the NAACP had purged itself of communist influences. But by the time the JBS published her memoir *I Testify* in 1966, Brown was claiming that communists had not only infiltrated all the civil rights organizations but were directing the entire movement through Moscow.[18]

Brown toured Texas most years, with her local appearances sometimes sponsored by SYLP, sometimes by TACT, and occasionally by other Society offshoots like Amarillo's Fact Finders. She would hit town, do a couple of sit-down interviews with sympathetic news outlets, promote the event, and then speak to full houses packed into high school auditoriums. In Amarillo, Wes Izzard's KGNC often broadcast her talks live. At a dollar a ticket, Brown's speeches helped keep local JBS chapters flush and brought in plenty of new members. She told audiences what they wanted to hear; that the Civil Rights Movement was "phony" and government programs just created a "'gimme' attitude among the Negroes." She called the Southern Christian Leadership Conference and Congress of Racial Equality communist fronts and claimed most television programming was controlled by communists.[19] The title of her 1968 Texas tour was "America Blackmailed by Threats of Violence," and it promised to reveal "how the communists are using the Civil Rights Movement to take over America."[20]

II

Despite Robert Welch's near-constant pronouncements that the John Birch Society was only an educational organization and was in no way partisan or political, the fact is, Birchers were drawn to politics. Thanks to Barry Goldwater, they had flooded into the GOP in 1964, where they were universally praised for their work ethic and enthusiasm. In the aftermath of his historic defeat, as national party leaders sifted through the wreckage, they concluded that it had been extremism that cost them the White House, so they purged the Birchers and the Bircher-adjacent from positions of power. But in Texas, especially West Texas, where Birchers had built the party from scratch, the extremists remained in control. In Randall County, home of the rapidly growing Amarillo suburbs, the party elected J. Evetts Haley as county chair in 1967. They set out to make the Republican Party more like the John Birch Society, not less.

Before 1960, the Randall County Republican Party (RCRP) was barely a rumor. In 1958, it held its county convention in the chair's living room. With only five people, they didn't even have to rearrange the furniture. The fervor of John Tower's run at the Senate changed all that. Across those two campaign seasons, Tower brought a massive surge of new members and an incredible new energy into the local GOP. The RCRP even opened a new headquarters (with the Potter County Republicans) in the Santa Fe Building in downtown Amarillo. J. C. Phillips, the fire-breathing editor of the *Borger News-Herald*, whose politics were further right than Robert Welch, gave the ribbon-cutting speech.[21] Within just months, the RCRP was hosting $50-a-plate fundraising dinners at the Amarillo County Club and landing Goldwater as a speaker. By 1962, the party was running its own candidates for county office.[22]

To the surprise of exactly no one, in its first official act of 1964, the RCRP unanimously and enthusiastically endorsed Barry Goldwater for president. In that spring's state convention primaries, one in three Randall County voters requested a Republican ballot. At that year's county convention, J. Evetts Haley held the floor as he directed the creation of the RCRP's pro-Birch platform. It opposed Medicare and gun registration, demanded the restatement of the Monroe Doctrine (the Bircher solution to Castro's Cuba), repudiated international courts, and urged a rejection of federal aid to education and agriculture. It opposed the Civil Rights Bill and wanted to end foreign aid. A resolution to cut diplomatic ties with the USSR was narrowly defeated. It demanded a congressional investigation of the communist infiltration of the State Department and an end to deficit spending. It reaffirmed the sanctity of the free enterprise system and called for a "crackdown on the communist conspiracy." And of course, it included the long-standing Bircher demand of U.S. withdrawal from the United Nations.[23]

The politics in West Texas began to reflect the growing power of this right-wing GOP. John Tower won reelection in 1966 and almost swept West Texas. He received 70 percent of the Randall County vote. Bob Price, the Goldwater Bioroid from Pampa making his second run to be the Panhandle's U.S. representative, had grown so popular that eight-term incumbent Walter Rogers bailed on his reelection campaign just six weeks before Election Day. His last-minute replacement, a nice-enough young Amarillo lawyer, never had a chance.[24] That year, the platform of the Randall County GOP included "Support Your Local Police" planks like opposition to gun registration and any measure that might "be restrictive on *local* law enforcement." Other planks reflected the Society's fixations that year: official recognition of Rhodesia, demanding a statement from the White House of an intent to "win the Vietnam War," and the reinstatement of JBS martyr-of-the-month Otto Otepka, a State Department employee recently fired by the White House.[25]

In 1967, Evetts Haley and his Bircher allies took control of the RCRP. Without "indulging in hyperbole," Haley promised as he accepted the position, "the stakes for the civilized world are the highest in history. For if we fail, Almighty God may well decree that we have had our last chance."[26] That was the Bircher Republican mindset going into 1968.

III

Among the most unoriginal observations one could make about Ronald Reagan would be that he was particularly suited for the modern media landscape. More political actor than politician, he had a great image and a fantastic delivery. He knew his lines and hit his marks. But more important for our story is to understand Reagan as a star in the right-wing universe long before he entered electoral politics.

Reagan had always been more movie star type than actual movie star. Coming up in a studio system where brands of actors were plugged into particular roles, Reagan enjoyed a modest Hollywood career as a good-looking, generic aw-shucks nice guy. When he was younger, he specialized in playing the mischievous best friend of the lead whose main contributions were sly comic retorts and a let's-get-serious third-act pep talk. As he got older, he specialized in put-upon professor types in light-hearted comedies, but he also got the occasional chance to mix it up with some B-movie men-of-action roles. Although appearing in more than a half-dozen movies a year, Reagan rarely enjoyed anything higher than third or fourth billing. In the mid-1950s, Reagan was showing up on the late show on television more than in movie theaters, and his career looked to be on the decline. That's when he landed the gig that would make him one of the most recognizable and trusted men in America.

He went to work for General Electric as the host of *General Electric Theater* at the start of its second season in 1954. Airing on Sunday nights on CBS, right after Ed Sullivan, the show became a massive hit. Part of its success was surely its interesting format, one that Americans, just getting used to television, appreciated. Each week, the show would present a half-hour version of a play, short story, or novel—like a *Reader's Digest* story but dramatized. There were mysteries, Westerns and other adventure stories, romance, comedy, and drama. Another reason was the star power. As one of the best-liked actors in Hollywood (elected president of the Screen Actors Guild six times), Reagan was instrumental in landing guest stars like Joan Crawford, Henry Fonda, Jack Benny, Rita Moreno, Myrna Loy, Lee Marvin, Fred Astaire, Judy Garland, Lon Chaney Jr., James Dean, Jimmy Stewart, Greer Garson, Tony Curtis, even the Marx Brothers. In addition to introducing each episode, Reagan acted in three or four stories a season.[27] For a decade, the show consistently won its time slot on the biggest night on television. By the end of Reagan's *GE Theater* run, he had an audience of over 50 million households. He and Sullivan owned Sunday nights in West Texas, where CBS all but monopolized the major markets, Amarillo, Midland, Abilene, Lubbock, and San Angelo.[28]

If his hosting duties had been limited to brief introductions and the occasional appearance, Reagan's career might have taken a different trajectory. But, as it was, GE executives had plans to use *GE Theater* to build its corporate image around professional nice guy Ronald Reagan and his strikingly photogenic family. Each episode opened with the corporate motto: "In Research, in Engineering, in Manufacturing Skill, at General Electric, Progress is Our Most Important Product." Fade in on Reagan, looking effortlessly middle-class cool and modern-dad dapper: "Good evening, I'm Ronald Reagan speaking on behalf of General Electric." Instead of commercial breaks, the show featured a three-minute intermission in the middle of the half hour, with a short film promoting GE products or the GE brand. Several times a season, those spots were reserved for slice-of-life moments shot in the Reagan family home—the "All Electric House" that GE had built for the Reagans in Pacific Palisades—where the family would ooh and ahh over their GE lighting, heating and cooling system, lawn sprinklers, and appliances, which they called "electric servants." In one long-form ad, Ronnie and Nancy play a naming game with toddler Patty as she calls out all the appliances in the kitchen: "That's a clock," "That's Mommy's iron." The home, as much studio as house, would remain the Reagan's primary residence until they moved to Washington in 1981.[29] It was one of the most successful branding exercises in American advertising history. The Reagans became the nation's first reality television stars.[30]

Reagan honed his political ideology and message as he fulfilled the other part of his GE spokesman role, touring GE plants and facilities all over the country. Several times a year, the company would send him on short tours where he polished his man-of-the-people routine over thousands of grip-and-grins with line workers, typing pools, and office drones. After a morning of tours, jokes with the boys, and harmless flirtations with the ladies, Reagan would give a lunchtime address. Speaking in auditoriums and large lunchrooms, Reagan delivered a stem-winder on the sanctity of free enterprise, the dangers of communism, and the wisdom and benevolence of General Electric. He was good at it. Soon,

GE started adding talks to local civic and business clubs to his schedule. With the ease of a practiced politician, Reagan listened closely during those tours, picking up on issues and themes that he would work into "The Speech," a constantly evolving thing chock-full of curious particulars, unusual statistics, and apocryphal stories. He had been leaning right for a while by that time, particularly worried about communist influence in Hollywood, but these tours hardened his position. Afraid of flying, Reagan spent a lot of time on trains, conversing with GE executives, especially Lemuel Boulware, who ran the company's public image and labor relations departments and who schooled the actor on business conservatism. He also consumed a steady diet of conservative literature, from the *National Review* to the *Dan Smoot Report*.[31]

By the late 1950s, "The Speech," or at least the version he gave in Texas, had veered hard right into Bircher territory. In 1959, he told the Abilene Chamber of Commerce that communists were trying to infiltrate "colleges, churches, even the PTA."[32] A 1962 tour of Texas cemented his place as a popular speaker for the right wing. Seventy-five hundred people braved freezing temperatures to hear him give the keynote at the Dallas Freedom Forum: "What Price Freedom?"[33] When he spoke to the Amarillo Chamber of Commerce a few days later (where he was introduced by Wes Izzard), local television and radio broadcast his remarks live. The speech hit all the Bircher talking points: liberalism, socialism, and communism were just shades of the same corrupt philosophy; communists were actively infiltrating American institutions; federal spending was out of control; the income tax, invented by Karl Marx, was a drag on the economy; labor unions were corrupt; Social Security and compulsory health insurance would destroy the rights, welfare, and liberty of Americans.[34] Over the next several weeks, the speech was rebroadcast on television and radio and serialized in newspapers throughout Texas.[35] In 1963, Reagan, the guest of honor at Mexia's enormous Americanism Day celebration, told the crowd that among the communists' active programs was a plan to discredit "anti-communists as crackpots." He defended the John Birch Society. And, perhaps for the first time, uttered one of his most famous phrases. He reminded the crowd that like most of them, he had been a lifelong Democrat, but he had recently joined the Republican Party. But, he explained, "I didn't leave the Democratic Party, it left me."[36] Texans were already talking about Reagan for president.[37]

Around this time, Reagan began to appear as host or narrator of right-wing films. There was *The Ultimate Weapon*, a film dramatization about how the Communist Chinese brainwashed American POWs in Korea.[38] And there was 1962's full-length NEP film *The Truth about Communism*, which laid out the previous three decades of history as the unfolding of a communist plot. The latter was not only shown to conservative groups everywhere but was also chopped into four chapters and shown in thirty-minute blocks on television. *The Welfare State*, "an expose of the drive to substitute Welfareism for the traditional system of Individual Liberty and Local Rule," made the rounds in 1964 and 1965.[39] It was the final entry at a 1964 film festival sponsored by the Austin Anti-Communism League, the American Freedom Bookstore, and the Austin Patrons.[40]

A vigorous, nationally televised pitch for Goldwater in the days running up to the 1964 election cemented Reagan's place as the country's most eloquent and forceful right-wing personality. The speech, "A Time for Choosing," was so powerful that the Texas Cattlemen for Goldwater had it printed in its entirety and published it as a full-page ad in newspapers across the state.[41] As the money poured into the Goldwater campaign in the hours and days after Reagan's speech, a group of California moneymen determined that Reagan could become much more than just the earnest narrator of right-wing movies and a popular after-dinner speaker. Under their tutelage and with their capital, they thought they could get this commonsense conservative candidate elected governor.

In 1966, Reagan, running as a "citizen-politician," challenged the popular incumbent, Pat Brown, who mostly dismissed the actor as a play-acting amateur and a blunt instrument of the cranks who had infiltrated the California GOP. But Reagan ran a disciplined and smart campaign, one influenced heavily by the new fixations of the far right: student protests and urban riots. Put simply, being a conservative in 1966 was different than just two years earlier, for this wasn't about communism; this was about, as Reagan presented it, taking "control of a society in chaos."[42] The JBS had recently made the same pivot, a fact not lost on Reagan's critics. His biggest issue of the campaign was student protest at UC Berkeley, California's flagship university. As the legend goes, Reagan's handlers warned him against making Berkeley an issue, saying it would open him up to charges of anti-intellectualism. But the citizen-candidate saw what the professionals missed: regular people hungry for someone to do something about what they saw as an out-of-control student body. It didn't matter where he was campaigning, as Reagan said later: "In the mountains, the desert, the biggest cities of the state, the first question is: 'What are you going to do about Berkeley?'" What the lore leaves out is that in 1966, Berkeley was also the latest obsession of the John Birch Society. Welch and the Society had been preoccupied with Berkeley since the *Operation Abolition* days, and recent events like the Free Speech Movement and antiwar protests only confirmed suspicions that the school was a proof-of-concept exercise for a communist plot to take over colleges and brainwash America's young people. That year, Bircher Bill Richardson put together a new film, *The Berkeley Revolution*, which told of the "communists' seduction of American youth." The movie screened at TACT and SYLP events in California and elsewhere all year. Communists, it warned, were "working openly on our college campuses, . . . leading young Americans into a miasma of rebellion, civil disobedience and perversion."[43]

Reagan's campaign echoed the film's themes, particularly its more prurient aspects. In one major campaign address, "The Morality Gap at Berkeley," Reagan, while toning down the communist indoctrination angle, still echoed the far right's obsessions over permissive administrators, spoiled students, and moral and sexual deviancy at a public state university. There was a simple solution, Reagan said: "Obey the rules or get out!"—a phrase that would be repeated in letters to editors and in luncheon speeches for the next decade.[44] He promised to restore order at Berkeley, throw out the rabble-rousers by the "scruff of the neck," launch an investigation into the communism and sexual deviancy on campus, and implement a code of moral conduct for faculty.[45] When Reagan won the election that November, his victory was front-page news in both Amarillo newspapers.

IV

Reagan had barely been sworn in before West Texas Birchers began plotting his presidential campaign. No one was more committed than Evetts Haley. From the moment he took office as RCRP chair, the old right-winger, now in his fourth decade as an activist, spun up the Rolodex and hit the phones. Every Bircher stronghold in West Texas had a major

Reagan faction in its Republican Party: Midland-Odessa, Lubbock, Wichita Falls, Pampa, Borger, Amarillo, and Abilene. Haley directed an effort to put Reagan supporters in key positions in the Texas Federation of Republican Women, even questioning the credentials of anyone he didn't feel was totally committed to his brand of Reagan-facing Americanism. Joan Paxton, an indispensable founder of the modern GOP in Midland, was, he feared, too "Establishment." The "biographical record" of another long-standing member "suggests liberal leanings." Just having worked on the 1964 Bush campaign was cause for suspicion. Haley also orchestrated a behind-the-scenes effort to install county chairs for a statewide Texans for Reagan organization.[46]

These kinds of backroom shenanigans were driving Peter O'Donnell nuts.[47] Thanks to their strong positions in the southern wing of the party, he and John Tower had survived the post-1964 purges of Goldwaterites and, by 1968, were full-blown Establishment, committed to winning the South for Nixon. They had little patience for another right-wing Hail Mary. Besides, Nixon was a lock for the nomination. Since his back-to-back defeats for president and California governor in 1960 and 1962, Nixon had rebuilt his position in the party over six years of tireless work on behalf of Republicans everywhere. That spring he had cruised through the primaries, basically running unopposed. The vice-presidency, however, was up for grabs, and O'Donnell and Tower thought that having the Texas senator as the number two might be a key to victory against the Democrats in the general election. In the Texas county conventions that year, O'Donnell instructed Texas Republicans to support favorite-son candidate Tower so they could go to the national convention with fifty-six delegates to dangle before the Nixon forces. The hitch in the plan was Reagan. Put simply, Texas Republicans liked him better than Nixon or Tower, especially in West Texas, where "Reagan for President" bumper stickers were suddenly everywhere in the summer of 1968.[48]

The Texas GOP split: The Two-Party crowd, as they came to be known, followed O'Donnell, Tower, and the party line, accepted the inevitability of Nixon's candidacy, and worked the Tower favorite-son gambit. These folks, many of whom actually preferred Reagan, were playing a long game; no single election was more important than building a powerful state GOP. Then there were the Birchers, the Dead-Enders for Reagan. For them a strong GOP was hardly an end but the immediate tool to help thwart an impending communist takeover. Nursed on decades of apocalyptic visions that predicted an end to the Republic, they had a fervent urgency in their politics. Reagan himself regularly echoed the old Bircher chestnut that "by 1970, the world will be all slave or all free." The Dead-Enders were fine with a Tower favorite-son strategy, but for very different reasons. They had no interest in wresting concessions from the Nixon campaign; they wanted to deny him a first-ballot victory and open the convention for a Reagan candidacy.

The split even reached into the Randall County Republican Party. All spring, while Haley schemed for Reagan, a group of Two-Partiers launched a quiet trap for Haley and many of the more outrageous Birchers who sought to serve as precinct chairs at the county convention. Haley preened in huge newspaper ads: "Never in the history of the Randall County Republican Party have so many PRECINCT CHAIRMEN (his fellow workers who know him best), endorsed an incumbent County Chairman as are presently endorsing J. EVETTS HALEY." Dick Brooks, meanwhile, worked the phones and lined up votes of Randall County Republicans tired (and a little scared) of Haley.[49] At the precinct conventions everything looked to be going Haley's way; every Bircher plank for the county platform passed with lusty and unanimous vigor. But when it came to time to elect precinct chairs and delegates to the county convention, Brooks sprang his trap. In a coordinated effort across almost every precinct, the Two-Partiers would, at the last minute, put in a new name, an "unknown" to challenge the Haleyites who had already announced their desire to be delegates. The unknowns mumbled platitudes about the importance of free elections and assured their fellow precinct members they were just running so that everyone would have a choice. Then, voting as a bloc, the Two-Partiers swept the newly announced candidates to victory. By the time the Haleyites realized they were facing a coordinated effort, it was too late. In a county-wide election of delegates held a couple of weeks later, Brooks defeated Haley by twenty-three votes.[50]

Haley didn't take the loss well. Still chair at the county convention in May (Brooks wouldn't take office until June), he presided over a day of fighting and screaming matches and rammed through a platform so reactionary that almost none of it survived the district caucus a few weeks later. This, the same platform that condemned the West Texas State football program, also included planks decrying "rioting and civil

order," "murder and looting," and "mobs and anarchists." It produced separate resolutions denouncing the Supreme Court for coddling criminals,
taking God out of the classroom, and "supporting the communists." It
remained obstinately committed to Reagan and only Reagan.[51] At the
state convention, Haley led a walkout and a demonstration for Reagan—
and lost his election to be a delegate to the national convention in Miami.

V

Two weeks before that convention, Ronald Reagan came to Amarillo.
Ostensibly, he was in town to drum up support for GOP candidates and
hold confabs before a big meeting of the nation's governors. In reality,
he was delegate hunting as part of a stealth campaign to win the nomination.[52] It was the biggest political event in the city since Goldwater's
Gold Sox Stadium rally four years earlier. Advertised weeks in advance,
"An Evening with Ronald Reagan" was officially a $100-a-plate barbe-
cue feast to raise money for Bob Price's reelection campaign. When he
arrived that afternoon, Reagan huddled with seventy or so Republican
delegates from Texas, New Mexico, Colorado, and Oklahoma, the most
blatant evidence of his actual candidacy to date. Reagan outlined his
plan. He could not and would not announce an official candidacy until
his name was put into nomination at the convention, but after that he
would "run like hell" to win. He absolutely refused to consider the second spot on the ticket. The delegates came away impressed, and maybe
a little starstruck. Given his "dynamic personality" and their enthusiasm, they began to fantasize about the possibility of a Reagan candidacy.
Maybe even a third-ballot victory.[53]

That night, 600 Republicans filled the floor of the Amarillo Municipal Auditorium and dined on dried-out brisket, too-sweet coleslaw, sour
potato salad, and soggy corn on the cob.[54] But the atmosphere was light
and fun; swing music and laughter filled the air. Once the plates were
cleared, the doors opened and 3,000 more people, who had paid between
$5 and $40 for their seats, filled the arena. As they settled in, Wes Izzard,
the master of ceremonies, surprised the crowd. He told them that it
would not be Bob Price introducing Reagan, as their programs read,
but rather Grady Hazelwood, Amarillo's powerful state senator, who,
up to that moment, had been nothing but the most loyal of Democrats.

Stunned initially when they heard his name, the Republicans broke out into wave after wave of applause as he approached the dais. The Old Gray Fox, as Hazelwood was known, was now one of them.

Grady Hazelwood was old-school Texas. Born in 1902 near Sweetwater and raised on a farm south of Canyon, he had built a career as a no-nonsense, tough-on-crime lawyer and politician. In his years as Amarillo's district attorney, there was no prosecutor in Texas more supportive of the police. In Austin, he supported mandatory minimum sentencing and once introduced legislation that would try ten-year-olds as adults on felony charges. He was also something of a prude, obsessed with enforcing a strict moral code—in the 1950s, he pushed a bill that would forbid carhops from wearing hot pants and halter tops. He wanted higher taxes on beer, greater enforcement of blue laws, and restrictions on gambling.[55] Mostly, though, he was a good politician who did good things for Texas and West Texas. He cosponsored the nation's first version of a GI bill, promising tuition-free college for World War II veterans, and helped found one of the nation's best-run student-loan programs. A lifetime member, he was also a tireless supporter of the Panhandle-Plains Historical Society and constantly worked to increase its funding.[56] He helped create the Canadian River Compact and Lake Meredith, a recreational lake that also provides water for eleven Panhandle counties. He worked for funding and resources for Palo Duro State Park and West Texas State. He was instrumental in gaining the latter its own Board of Regents, which he later served on. His most significant accomplishment was probably the expansion of Texas's farm-to-market road system into the largest secondary road program in the country. At 41,000 miles, it connected rural Texas in a way theretofore unimaginable. The longest stretch, 140 miles, extends from Umbarger to the old New Deal Project at Ropesville and doesn't go through a single community larger than a village.

The "sixties" turned Hazelwood's world upside down. Like many of his constituents, he found the America of 1968 a confounding, corrupt, and wicked place. The man who had fought against hot pants and beer sales suddenly confronted a world where college students wore their hair long, took drugs, and made questioning authority a badge of honor. He introduced legislation against psychedelic drugs because he was convinced thousands of UT students were regularly dropping acid. He launched a crusade against a campus organization—the Student League for Responsible Sexual Freedom—that had demanded an end to sodomy laws, birth control for UT students, and lowering the age of consent to sixteen. He promised the Texas Police Association that he would "never vote for another appropriation of the University as long as that group of queer-minded social misfits remains officially approved to operate on the university campus, using public facilities to wage a campaign to abolish our criminal laws prohibiting sodomy, homosexuality, fornication and adultery."[57]

His constituents cheered. Like Hazelwood, like Reagan, they too saw college campuses as the modern root of chaos and moral degradation. As one wrote to his local paper: "It's time those we elect, like Grady Hazelwood, do something . . . to stop the traffic in pornography, smut, [and] sex offenses" on Texas's "tax supported college campuses."[58] In one fan letter to the state senator, a woman praised Hazelwood: "On campuses in years gone by there was always that teeny minority—but we both ignored them and ridiculed them and that was the last we heard of them. But that was before our Federal Supreme Court said: All must be heard—Freedom of speech for all—regardless of the annoyance and moral taste of the majority." Another supporter commended Hazelwood for his "recent stand on the sexual freedom baloney."[59] Hazelwood had clearly found a kindred spirit in Reagan, the man who had taken on Berkeley.[60] He wrote to the governor: "You are the only candidate whom 'independent Democrats' like myself and others could ever vote for with any enthusiasm."[61]

So, just a few weeks before his own party would nominate its candidate for president, Hazelwood found himself at the Reagan dinner about to endorse a Republican for president. In his speech, which he was still rewriting up to the minute he stepped on stage, Hazelwood summed up how he—and many others—had come to support Reagan. There were none of the paranoid and conspiracy-driven anticommunist rants that had fueled the West Texas Right for decades, just the carefully prepared summation of facts and conclusions from a lifelong attorney. A closing argument in his case against modern liberalism, which had enabled criminality, protected law breakers, instigated riots, and encouraged moral decline. Under Democratic leadership, America "seethed in anarchy, political insanity, and near bankruptcy." As he moved into the meat of his remarks, Hazelwood painted a vivid picture of modern America: "We live in a nation . . . where riots are in full swing" and "where pro-communist students . . . beatniks, and draft card burners have taken over our universities." A nation, Hazelwood continued, "where a black militant minority flaunts the law, murders, and burns," where the Supreme Court has "torn the Constitution . . . to threads and pitched it in the garbage can," where "illegitimacy and venereal disease are at an all-time high; general morality at an all-time low," and where "our national debt is at an all-time high." The crowd erupted.[62]

Reagan basked. He stepped to the mic and promised that once he returned to California, he would introduce legislation to protect "old gray foxes." In his speech, Reagan hit his applause lines like the pro that he was—America was "divided at home, despised abroad, and standing in the shadow of economic chaos"—and nailed his jokes about ten bureaucrats for every problem, and LBJ's crime program consisted of making "money so cheap it isn't worth stealing." There was a blur of statistics and a lot of great stories. But there were no policy proposals or even underlying governing philosophy—it was boilerplate small-government, law and order, "get tough with the Soviets." In the audience that night was Barbara Bush, who had been listening to Republican speeches for well over a decade by then. She struggled to understand Reagan's appeal. "He has all the poise in the world [and] great timing," she admitted to her diary, but that was all. He "didn't say much. . . . 'We must show the world where we stand in Vietnam' [got] a standing ovation"? she wondered. Regardless, though, she noted: "They loved him."[63]

The next morning, Hazelwood joined Evetts Haley for breakfast, and the two old friends rehashed the evening and planned a trip to the Republican convention in Miami. Hazelwood was to be a special guest of the Texas GOP, and Haley was able to scare up some credentials somehow. Despite his forty years in politics, it was Hazelwood's first national convention.

And it was wild. The Texas delegation and various hangers-on, a force five hundred strong, took over the Barcelona, a faded jewel of a hotel right on the Strip. Like a conquering army, they redecorated the hotel lobby with banners: Reagan for President, John Tower for Vice President, Bob Price for Congress. They flew the Texas flag from the hotel flagpole and raised hell at the hotel pool. When Reagan showed up at the hotel to pitch the delegation, he was mobbed.[64]

Mathematics won out. Reagan's scrambling was for naught. Nixon won on the first ballot. Hazelwood and Haley flew back to Amarillo crestfallen. There was a bright spot for Haley, however, at a banquet held in Reagan's honor; he met Rosalind Kress, a delegate from Savannah and heir to the S. H. Kress dime store fortune. They fell in love and married two years later.

VI

The day after Richard Nixon won the Republican nomination, Republicans swarmed the George Wallace campaign headquarters in Amarillo, cleaning out its inventory of "Wallace for President" bumper stickers. Some couldn't wait until they got home and slapped the stickers right on top of their Reagan '68 stickers. The Potter County American Party chair was delighted but not surprised; with Reagan out of the race, "the common class of people are now looking to him [Wallace] for a change."[65] People like Marguerite Terrell, who just a week earlier had told Grady Hazelwood that "if Reagan is not nominated next week, I am going to have to support Wallace . . . this is the only protest we have in this unusual year for Politics."[66]

Ronald Reagan and George Wallace were obviously very different kinds of politicians: one the smooth and popular two-time governor of the nation's coolest state, the handsome and glamorous former movie star, and the best-looking and most charming conservative in America; the other the sweaty, pugnacious, and ambitious "fighting governor" of Alabama, the most famous segregationist in the country. Wallace had first gained national notoriety for his blunt white-supremacist run for governor in 1962, which he capped off with an over-the-top inauguration speech, written by one of the state's most violent and villainous Klansmen, Asa "Ace" Carter. Standing on the exact spot where Jefferson Davis took the oath of office as the first president of the Confederate States of America 102 years earlier, Wallace made his politics clear: "Let us rise to the call of freedom-loving blood that is in us and send our answer to the tyranny that clanks its chains upon the South." Wallace's voice rose: "In the name of the greatest people that have ever trod this earth, I draw the line in the dust and toss the gauntlet before the feet of tyranny and I say segregation now, segregation tomorrow, segregation forever." Wallace and the speech were national news. He started pondering a run at the presidency soon after.

Where Reagan was smiling and western, Wallace was scowling and unabashedly southern. His only high-minded principle was the traditional call for states' rights. Other than that, he was pure neopopulist—promising to stand up for the little guy, "the taxi driver, little businessman, beautician or barber or farmer," and protect them and the nation from the greedy millionaires, the bumbling bureaucrats, the liberal elite, and "pointy-headed professors" who "couldn't park their bicycles straight." Spending his four years as governor on creating news events to burnish his tough-guy, anti-Washington image, appearing on the Sunday morning news shows to lay out his case for states' rights and segregation, and holding rallies in northern industrial cities, he was a national figure by 1967. That was the year he formed the American Independent Party (everyone just called it the American Party) to make a third-party run for the presidency.

There wasn't a "dime's worth of difference between the Democratic and Republican parties," he said, and he pitched himself as the only real conservative in the race. His version of conservatism certainly reflected the direction of the right wing since 1964: get tough on crime, win or get out of Vietnam, make the hippies take a bath and get a job, stop the protests and the rioting and the anarchy. He was going to rein in government, straighten out the Supreme Court, and put the "intellectual snobs," the "hypocrites who send your kids half-way across town while they have their chauffeur drop their children off at private schools," and the "briefcase-carrying bureaucrats" firmly in their place. He was going to end busing, lower taxes, and put prayer back in schools. His rallies were seething, electric things. In New York he told a cheering, adoring crowd gathered in Madison Square Garden that there were no riots in Alabama: "They start a riot down here, first one of 'em to pick up a brick gets a bullet in the brain, that's all. And then you walk over to the next one and say, 'All right, pick up a brick. We just want to see you pick up one of them bricks, now!'"[67] His biggest appeal was among white, working-class men between eighteen and thirty-five.

While Ronald Reagan and George Wallace might have been very different types of conservatives, when it came to their support in West Texas, they were drilling into the same pool of discontent. Wallace built his first potential-donor campaign lists from the rolls of the John Birch Society and the citizen's councils and courted Texas oil money. His Texas campaign was run by vets of the far-right-wing Constitutional Party, including its former head Bard Logan, a proud member of the John Birch Society. A third of the signatures he needed to get on the ballot came from just fourteen West Texas counties. The first county-wide American Party in the state was formed in Randall and was led by Amarillo mayor J. Ernest Stroud. Its spring conventions drew nine hundred delegates.[68] In Midland, Wallace's county chair was Dr. Dorothy Wyvell, the Constitution Party's candidate for Congress in 1960 (she finished second) and a local leader of Tax Reform Immediately (TRIM), a JBS front group.[69] In Borger, the party was led by an ally of the raving neo-Nazi Gerald L. K. Smith.[70] Prominent among American Party members in Texas were Bircher stalwarts like Edwin Walker and Dan Smoot. Wallace's main Texas spokesman was right-wing extremist Glenn Young, leader of the Congress of Freedom and publisher of the *American Adviser*, a far-far-right-wing publication.[71]

Once Reagan was out of the picture, Bircher Republicans overran the American Party. By August, they were purging non-Society members. The turmoil was national news. American Party state chair (and Society leader) Bard Logan told the *New York Times*, "It's not the Birch people that are causing trouble. It's the anti-Birch people."[72] In Randall County, Dick Brooks, having just wrested control of the county GOP from Evetts Haley, couldn't keep his party together; ten of his eighteen precinct chairs quit to join the Wallace crusade. As he lamented in a master class of mixed mythology metaphors: "They seem to have succumbed to the siren-song of George Wallace, and overlooking the Pandora's Box a third-party uprising can open to plague our Republic." How could so many of his allies, friends, and neighbors, he wondered, believe that "our country is about to be taken over by black power groups, mobs, gangsters, communists, or other sinister and vicious enemies"?[73]

The Wallace campaign failed to meet expectations. He had polled even with Nixon in West Texas well into October, yet, on Election Day, he won less than 20 percent of the region's vote. Nixon dominated West Texas. Humphrey narrowly took the state and lost the election. A young political scientist who had spent the election season gathering data on Humphrey, Nixon, and Wallace voters in the Panhandle concluded that unlike his supporters in other parts of the country, including the eastern half of Texas, West Texas Wallace supporters were in the midst of a political metamorphosis, triggered by abstract national issues and events (urban rioting, the Vietnam War, civil rights, the counterculture) *and* local challenges to the status quo. They were angry, disaffected, oriented toward the extreme right wing, anti-intellectual, and antielite, but still committed to the democratic process. Compared to the typical Wallace voter, they were older, wealthier, better educated, and more stable. And much, much more right wing. Almost 70 percent of them believed that there was a "definite blueprint and time schedule" for a communist take-over of the world, and even more believed that urban rioting had been planned and plotted by the communists. Almost three in four believed that there were communists in high-ranking federal positions.[74]

Four years later, Nixon romped through West Texas, winning three out of every four votes—the most dominant performance in the region since Roosevelt had swept to victory in 1936. In Lubbock and Randall counties, homes of the region's two largest colleges, Nixon took 75 percent and 84 percent of the votes. In Canyon, he even won the campus precinct. The Randall County Republican Party won every single county election but one.[75] West Texas was again a one-party state.

REAGAN COUNTRY

There are no liberals in this party. There are no moderates
in this party. We are all conservatives.

CHET UPHAM, CHAIR, TEXAS REPUBLICAN PARTY, 1983

At seventy-five years old, still full of vim and vigor, J. Evetts Haley was
finally selected as a delegate to a national party convention. Active
in Texas politics for forty years, he had always been the outsider, the
knight errant of the far right, the protector of frontier values, dueling liberals and courting conservatives. Staking out the movement's *pas d'armes*
over textbooks and rebellious football coaches and farm policy. And, yes,
tilting at windmills.[1] But now, in 1976, here he was, a full-blown member of the court, invited to Kansas City to help the Republican Party
choose its next president. As he boarded the plane that August, he was
accompanied by what was surely the most conservative state delegation
ever sent to a Republican Party convention. An emotional man. It's easy
to assume his blue eyes welled up more than once on that plane ride. A
man who relished a good fight. Surely he must have been excited by the
fact that this would be the first contested convention since 1948. He
and the rest of the Texas delegation were all-in, one hundred percent
committed to the underdog in the race, the leader of the Republican
Party's right wing, Ronald Reagan. The former California governor was
heading into Kansas City trailing President Gerald Ford by a little over
a hundred delegates. The Texas delegation meant to fight for every one
of them. Haley must have been smiling through the tears.

Haley was now living in a political world that he had helped create.

Forty years after he had boarded a train to attend his first national political gathering, the inaugural meeting of the Jeffersonian Democrats, and twenty years after he had attended the founding of For America, here he was, an official delegate of the Texas Republican Party going to the national convention to support a candidate who shared his long-standing political views.

Just a few weeks earlier, on May 1, Texas had held its very first presidential primary. The GOP shattered records. Almost a half million voters took part, three times more than even the loftiest of expectations. Even with an oddly complicated setup that favored Ford, Reagan crushed the president. He won almost every single county, most by 2:1 or 3:1 margins. In West Texas, it was rarely that close—in some counties, Reagan ran up margins of 8:1 or even 10:1. What was once the howling frontier of American politics, where ideologues like Haley had created the politics of cowboy conservatism, was now all but fully settled. The Texas GOP, which Haley had helped build, was now easily among the most conservative organizations in the nation. What had been the conservative frontier was now Reagan Country.

And here, in this striking moment, is where our story ends. This was a tale of pioneering and settlement, a saga of the "unsettled" lands of American politics: the story of the *origins* of the "New Right."

The New Right would be the next stage in the political development of ultraconservative politics. It was, to be sure, born from the right-wing frontier of West Texas and shared the cowboy conservative devotion to individualism, militarism, and the free market. And the New Right was also animated by anticommunism and prone to paranoid fantasies. White supremacy and adherence to traditional gender roles were still central to its politics. And, especially in Texas and the West, the New Right still traded in the language and symbols and costumes of cowboy conservatives. Plenty of buckles and boots and Western movie clichés.

But it was different. The New Right, which would dominate the Republican Party from 1980 until 2016, was more professional and tech savvy than the operatives on the old conservative frontier. If cowboy conservatism was Haley's typewriter, telephone, Rolodex, and filing cabinets overstuffed with news clippings, the New Right was the offices of RAVCO, the direct-mail fundraising empire of fellow Texan Richard Viguerie, with its millions of carefully tabulated punch cards, room-sized computers, slick and tailored fundraising letters, and tens of millions of dollars raised a year. If the frontier was Texans for America dashing off letters to the editors of their local newspapers and offering heartfelt testimony to schoolbook committees, the New Right was the hundreds of policy papers streaming out of the Heritage Foundation every year. Republicans on the conservative frontier met in fiery conventions where they drafted county platforms that addressed immediate and long-standing outrages; New Right Republicans hammered out disciplined messaging within the Republican Study Committee in the U.S. Congress. The leaders of the frontier movement counted on conservatives to work hard: to canvass neighborhoods, make calls, screen movies, read and talk about books, and attend meetings, so many meetings. All that the pros of the New Right wanted from conservatives was their money and votes and to keep their radio dials on the right station and their televisions tuned to the right network.

The location shifted as well. If Texas (and the rest of the West) was the place where cowboy conservatism emerged and thrived, the New Right was rightfully more associated with the South.[2] Across Dixie, just as their predecessors had in West Texas, a hungry and disgruntled generation of conservatives set up shop in the empty shells of their local Republican Party and transformed them into vehicles to spread their brand of far-right politics. After the Democratic Party nationally began to focus its efforts on civil rights and social justice, those white southerners irritated over these challenges to white supremacy moved into the Republican Party. This new southern GOP, would, over the course of the rest of the century, come to dominate the politics of the South and rise to positions of considerable power in the U.S. Congress and the federal courts. As it grew in those years, it attracted ambitious and aggressive young activists determined to recalibrate the basic organization of American politics. By the mid-aughts most of the white South was as devoted to the Republican Party as any part of West Texas.[3]

That right-wing takeover of the southern Republican Party was central to Reagan's calculations in 1976.[4] It was an unusual set of circumstances that led him to challenge an incumbent Republican for the presidency. The first and most obvious was the strange way that Gerald Ford had become president. In 1972, President Richard Nixon and Vice-President Spiro Agnew had won reelection in a historic landslide. Republicans with national aspirations like Reagan had been looking toward 1976, when there would be no incumbent to challenge for the nomination. But in 1973–1974 as the scandals that surrounded the Nixon White House took out first the vice-president and then the president, the political world of the Republican Party was in chaos. When Agnew resigned in October 1973, Nixon appointed Gerald Ford to serve out the rest of the vice-president's term. But then, when Nixon resigned less than a year later, Ford was suddenly the incumbent. But the "accidental president" had no natural national constituency. Before 1973, Ford had seemed perfectly content to represent the good folks of Grand Rapids and the rest of the Michigan 5th Congressional District for the near future. But there he was, at the start of the 1976 primary season, now President Ford, who had had an office in the White House for only twenty-six months and who had been president for less than a year and a half, having run as an incumbent. Republican apparatchiks were split over Ford's candidacy. Some hoped that the American people were ready to put Watergate behind them and to support Ford, and believed that the scandals of the Nixon administration had so damaged the Republican brand that only a fresh face like Reagan's offered any shot at the White House.

Unlike Ford, Reagan *did* have a national constituency. In Texas, especially, cattlemen's associations had been talking about Reagan for president as far back as 1962. Across the 1960s and the first half of the 1970s, thanks to his uncompromising stances against hippies and radicals and Black Panthers and the other goblins that haunted the dreams of Birchers, Texans had grown to admire him even more. In the year before he launched his 1976 presidential campaign, Reagan spoke to huge and adoring Texas crowds a half-dozen times. Giving a speech that *Newsweek* called "pure counter-revolutionary rage," Reagan brought the house down as the keynote at the Texas Manufacturers' Association, the San Antonio Chamber of Commerce, the National Soft Drink Association, the Southern Republicans, National Republican Women, and the Texas Society of CPAs. His fundraising speech on behalf of the Women's Forum of Wichita Falls brought in $25,000—eight times expectations.

On the surface, Ford and Reagan looked evenly matched in Texas. On the eve of the primary, the *New York Times* said the race was too close to call. In defense of the paper, no one could have really known what might happen. The Texas GOP was growing so big and so fast that predictions were a fool's errand. One variable was just the sheer volume of newcomers to the state. These were years of double-digit population growth. Hundreds of thousands of newcomers a year. Many of them were Republicans from the Northeast and Midwest, and it was tough to know where their loyalties might lie. And, just as they had been doing since the Goldwater days, Democrats were changing parties in massive numbers. Making it even more complicated was the fact that the primary was open to anyone regardless of party registration.

The two most powerful men in the Texas GOP, John Tower and Peter O'Donnell, backed Ford. Whether or not they were just that removed from the reality of the sources of party growth, or whether they had calculated that there were enough newcomers who would remain loyal to Ford, or whether they had determined that the far-right Reagan posed an existential risk to all that they had built, or some combination—they went all-in for the president, placing the infrastructure and leadership of the Texas GOP at his disposal.

There was also a weird setup for Texas's first presidential primary. Originally designed to benefit Democratic Senator Lloyd Bentsen's presidential campaign, the state legislature had put in rules and regulations for that year's primary that called for twenty-four separate elections, one in each of the state's congressional districts.[5] Rather than vote for the actual presidential candidates on primary day, voters would instead choose four delegates from each district in a winner-take-all contest. Just scoring a plurality in a district would win a candidate all four delegates. Bentsen had figured that in a wide-open campaign, he could recruit a popular slate of Democrats in each district and possibly sweep Texas.[6] O'Donnell and Tower pursued the same strategy, lining up reliable Republican activists to serve as Ford delegates in each district. A respectable who's who of Texas Republicanism. It would prove an embarrassing miscalculation.[7]

Too few understood just how popular Reagan had become by 1976. Over his two terms as California's governor, he had demonstrated an unexpected talent for governing, pushing conservative policy prescriptions in the state legislature with demonstrable results. The citizen-politician schtick he had parlayed into the governor's mansion still played. He was perhaps the most popular Republican within the national party. Once he left office in early 1975, his staff set him up as a media figure, offering the conservative take on contemporary issues. His daily five-minute radio program, *Viewpoints* (which Reagan usually wrote himself) broadcast on 230 stations, including every major Texas market. And his weekly newspaper column was carried by 226 newspapers. Throughout 1975, Reagan used these new outlets to lay out his opposition to federal monetary policy, the minimum wage, welfare, taxes, the New Left, gun control, bureaucracy, government regulation, and socialized medicine. And to speak in favor of small government, cold beer, the free market, law and order, Herbert Hoover, a strong work ethic, faith in God, computers, and nuclear power.[8] He also hit the speaking circuit, giving long-form talks on the right to work, balancing the federal budget, the American withdrawal from Vietnam, détente, ending farm commodity sales to China, the Soviet menace. He went on *The Tonight Show* and talked politics with Johnny Carson.[9]

When it came to Texas, his campaign knew exactly who should be running the team—energetic right-wingers who had been working the grass roots for years, the "Reagan crazies" as some took to calling them.[10] There were three statewide campaign cochairs. Ray Barnhart was a loud, uncompromising, and rough-around-the-edges ditch-digging entrepreneur from Pasadena. He had gotten into politics in 1964 to support Barry Goldwater and had recently been elected to the Texas House, one of a baker's dozen of Republicans. Ernest Angelo was a petroleum engineer and mayor of Midland. Coming of political age at the same time and in the same circles as Ed Foreman, Angelo had been president of Midland's Young Republican group and headed the Midland branch of the John Birch Society. (He once griped to Robert Welch about how the Society's campaign to impeach Chief Justice Earl Warren was going nowhere.)[11] Rounding out the squad was Barbara Staff, an activist Republican from Irving. Staff, as a forty-five-year-old empty nester, once audited a political science class at a nearby university and was so dismayed by her professor's liberalism that she converted from a New Deal Democrat to a rock-ribbed conservative seemingly overnight. She was also an active member of W. A. Criswell's ultraconservative First Baptist Church of Dallas, a key institution in the development of the New Right. Signing on to Reagan early, she believed his candidacy was "the last gasp of democracy."[12]

The punditocracy also missed the issues that drove many Republican voters to the polls that May. Following the coverage of the campaign, one might have thought that the main issue was whether the United

States should turn the Panama Canal over to the nation of Panama. But that might have been because Reagan had such a strong stance and a great soundbite: "We paid for it, we built it, it's ours, and we are going to keep it." Brought 'em to their feet every time. Or was the race a referendum on Henry Kissinger? Or was it about Ford's decision to bail out New York City? Or the president's snub of Soviet dissident Aleksandr Solzhenitsyn? All were regularly reported as the big issues of the campaign. And Reagan's direct attacks on the president over Panama and Kissinger and the rest made the campaign spicy. But a Reagan speech, especially a campaign speech, was rarely the same thing more than once. It was more like a jazz combo than a symphony. There was always room for improvisation. Depending on the crowd or Reagan's mood, there were plenty of riffs on classic right-wing issues: moral degeneracy, law and order, bureaucratic disasters, or the evils of communism, socialism, liberalism and ground beats about entrepreneurial genius, small government, and the sanctity of free markets. The variations were endless. But in 1976, Reagan added new refrains: coming out against gun control and accusing the Supreme Court of coddling criminals. Opposition to the Equal Rights Amendment. Scorn for busing. Calling for a return to school prayer. And, at the start of a movement that would sustain the Republican Party for decades, insisting on a constitutional amendment against abortion on demand.

This newer set of beliefs, talking points, and ideas didn't have a name yet, but it was clear that Reagan was looking for support from a new type of voter, one more attuned to a politics of morality than to issues of economy or foreign policy. Believing that their freedom and faith were under direct threat from overreaching governments and courts and from a generation of young people committed to overturning the moral order, Christian conservatives began to rally around what they would come to describe as "family values." Reagan was speaking directly to these voters when he called for a "spiritual revival" and promised to find ways "to get God back in the classroom."[13] The classroom line typically drew the largest applause in any of his speeches, even more than his witty riposte about the Panama Canal.

In yet another preview of the politics of the New Right, the Reagan campaign took able advantage of new regulations on campaign spending. The new laws permitted individuals or groups to raise and spend unlimited amounts of money on behalf of a candidate as long as they did not coordinate their efforts with that candidate's official campaign. While miniscule compared to today's campaign spending, this was the first election that demonstrated the power of this third-party support. The American Conservative Union, which would lay out $180,000 in the campaign that year, spent half of that money in Texas for Reagan. A report from the Federal Election Commission revealed that a third of the top-twenty biggest campaign spenders that year were on behalf of Reagan in Texas. Fifth on the list was "Texas Friends of Reagan," led by J. Evetts Haley.[14]

The Republican primary drew 456,822 Texan voters—a massive turnout, four times what counted for normal. Statewide, Reagan won two-thirds of those votes. He won every district and took all ninety-six delegates. He won all but three of Texas's 254 counties.[15] The most common estimate was that 300,000 registered Democrats crossed over to vote for Reagan. Most would not remain Democrats for much longer. The blowout was exceptional in West Texas. Across the region, local election officials ran out of ballots. Many by noon. Desperate precinct offices scrambled, rounding up election judges to make temporary rulings that would allow them to print and use mimeographed ballots or record votes on legal pads. Working through the night, they were still counting votes by Sunday breakfast. Reagan won Roberts County by a margin of 18:1. In Castro it was 14:1, Andrews 9:1, Briscoe and Bailey 10:1; in Cottle, Floyd, and Swisher it was 6:1. Reagan racked up massive numbers of votes in Amarillo, Midland, Lubbock, and Abilene. In Randall County, where just sixteen years earlier the local Republican convention had been held in the chair's living room, the Reagan-Ford primary drew 25,000 voters, more than the Democratic contest. Describing Reagan supporters, the county Democratic chair was flabbergasted: "They've gone wild."[16]

The landslide obliterated the infrastructure of the Texas GOP. At the state convention, two-thirds of the 1,672 delegates were Reagan supporters. And they were in a mood. After months of being ignored or dismissed by the Ford regulars, they set out to put the Texas GOP firmly on the Reagan path. They named Ernest Angelo state chair. Instead of naming Senator John Tower as an at-large delegate to the convention, they chose J. Evetts Haley. Fort Worth political reporter Larry Neal offered his thoughts: "Just how conservative the Texas Republican party is may be exemplified by the state convention's decision Saturday to

J. Evetts Haley and Ronald Reagan in 1978.

name J. Evetts Haley of Canyon an at-large delegate to the National Republican Convention in Kansas City."[17] But if one wanted even more exemplification as to how conservative the Texas GOP had become, one need only read its 1976 platform. It came out against abortion on demand, the Equal Rights Amendment, gun control, amnesty for Vietnam War draft dodgers and deserters, busing, and revenue sharing. It sought to abolish OSHA, the EPA, and the Federal Energy Administration (soon to be the Department of Energy). It supported mandatory prison sentencing, restoring the oil depletion allowance, curbing foreign aid, welfare reform, and subjecting labor unions to antitrust laws.[18]

Haley reveled in the moment.[19] "Young people, working people, farmers and ranchers are fed up with big government and look to Reagan to stop increasing bureaucratic intervention in Americans' Lives. These farmers are disillusioned with Washington. They've been on the sugar tit too long, they've been kept men, and there is a great disillusionment with Washington as a solution to our problem. The encouraging thing is the number of young men and women getting involved. . . . There's something stirring at the grass roots, and there's going to be a changing of the guard."[20]

When the Texas delegation, "souls grafted to Ronald Reagan's," got to Kansas City, it found itself relegated to a far corner in the Kemper Arena and stuck in a hotel ten miles away. When things did not go their way, the delegates sulked and they booed. They tried to chant Ford supporters down in hotel bars. The hundred votes Reagan would need for the nomination proved elusive. Texas delegates cajoled behind the scenes and picked fights in public. They refused to stand when First Lady Betty Ford took the stage. They waved signs and covered themselves with Reagan buttons and wore plastic Reagan cowboy hats. Their demonstrations of fealty failed to move the needle. The convention broke for Ford. On the night of the nomination vote, defeated, the Texans pulled one more trick, "out of pure orneriness," as Ernest Angelo later remembered. For hours, they refused to come to order and instead disrupted the convention with snake dances, camera muggings, kazoo concerts, and yelling themselves hoarse, until after the moment had passed when President Ford could have been nominated during prime-time television. When Reagan's name was placed in nomination, they forced the vote and went nuts when his name was called. For forty-five straight minutes they—along with the California delegation across the arena—screamed their call and response: "Viva!" "Olé!"[21]

I moved to West Texas in 1976. I was a kid, just a few weeks removed from the greatest moment of my life—playing King Arthur in the Chandler, Oklahoma, Bicentennial Parade, at every stop and a few times a block using my aluminum foil and cardboard sword to battle the balsa-wood-chicken-wire-crepe-paper dragon that my classmates were carrying down Manvel Avenue. My brother and I left our family's Oklahoma farm where my grandfather, in retirement, ran a tiny cow-calf operation and arrived in a new suburban tract on Amarillo's south side. We went to Canyon schools. No more swimming in the pond; we had a community pool. By 1980, my first year of high school, we were living in Canyon, just a few blocks from J. Evetts Haley's house. Although I never would have known him, I probably waited on Haley in my various jobs in town: pumping gas at Kerr-McGee, sacking groceries at Taylor and Sons, working the register at McDonalds or at the Pak-A-Sak. That year, Canyon High held a mock presidential election. I didn't follow politics. At all. The fact that Jimmy Carter was the president was probably the only political fact I knew at the time. I knew we were Democrats because of

Franklin Roosevelt and the New Deal. We had kept our Oklahoma farm thanks to Roosevelt. And the only thing I think I knew about Reagan was that he was once in a movie with a monkey. I can't remember a single conversation about that mock election beforehand—or after it for that matter. I voted for Carter. I gave it zero thought. The next week, the school paper came out. Out of something like five hundred votes, only seven people had voted for Carter. That moment stuck with me.

ACKNOWLEDGMENTS

Over the course of bringing this book to press, I've accumulated more debts than I could ever hope to repay. A public thanks is a good place to start.

My editor and friend Robert Devens saw the potential of this project back when it was little more than a colossal heap of words pumped out by an overconfident and hyperenthusiastic mid-career scholar. His patience and incredible counsel (*Boomtown*) finally helped me get my head around this thing. Thank you, Robert! The entire production team at the University of Texas Press was incredible to work with. Special shout-out to freelance copyeditor Steven Baker. Thank you, UT Press!

To all the teachers, professors, and scholars who helped me become a better historian and a better writer, especially John Matthews, Cliff Kuhn, Howard Rabinowitz, and Ferenc Szasz, thank you. David Farber, who has forgotten more about how to research and write history than I will ever learn, was a valued mentor and comrade who directed this work back when it was a dissertation. His craftmanship and work ethic have formed a guiding star in my own approach not only to writing and interpreting history but also to teaching and advising my own students.

My deepest gratitude goes out to the lifelong friends who've helped make this book a reality thanks to their patience, support, critiques, edits, and suggestions: James, Catherine, Amy, Rex, Michelle, Ben, John, Andy, Madonna, Greg, Katie—you know who you are and, I hope, know how much you mean to me.

I am forever thankful for the year I spent putting this book together as a visiting scholar at the Center for the American West, where Patty Limerick and Kurt Gutjahr provided unbelievable guidance, encouragement, and the coolest and quietest place to work anywhere at the University of Colorado.

I've spent many, many hours in the archives of the Panhandle-Plains Historical Museum, the Southwest Collection at Texas Tech, the Bentley Historical Library at the University of Michigan, and the Haley Library in Midland. The archivists in those places were so incredibly kind, helpful, and understanding—very special thanks to Betty Bustos, Warren Stricker, and Cathy Smith.

Since 2001 I have had the privilege and pleasure of teaching at the College of Wooster in Wooster, Ohio. It has provided financial assistance, research leaves, and amazing opportunities to share and develop this work with students and fellow scholars. My colleagues in the history department and beyond are a constant source of inspiration.

I cannot possibly conjure how many students over these years have helped me fashion the arguments and narrative of this project. In classes, seminars, and tutorials and in my own role as adviser, I have tried out endless permutations of pretty much every part of this text on countless unwitting volunteers. Thank you all for your understanding and suggestions.

Lastly, none of this is possible without the love of my family. My mother, Sheila, and stepfather, Doug, have been sounding boards and editors and cheerleaders since I was an undergraduate. They've read and reread chapters. My brother Chris, who has his own book coming out soon, has also provided his invaluable editorial assistance and advice. My grandparents Ina Earle and Chris Martin established a love of history and reading that has steered me since I was ten years old.

My son, Christopher, has lived with this book literally his entire life; going back through some of the oral histories I recorded when the project began, I could hear him, just weeks old, softly cooing in the background as he swung back and forth in his Neglectomatic 2000 (our nickname for his baby swing). Cathy, my wife and partner, with a patience one normally finds only in fables, has read and heard every iteration of every word, sentence, and paragraph of this book. Most of them more than once. More truthfully, a lot more than that. They have both been unrelenting in their encouragement and enthusiasm and patience.

Thank you, and much love to you all.

NOTES

For full listing of sources, please consult jeffroche.net.

ABBREVIATIONS

AAS	Austin American-Statesman
AC	Atlanta Constitution
ADN	Amarillo Daily News
AG	Amarillo Globe
AGN	Amarillo Globe-News
AGT	Amarillo Globe-Times
AH	Agricultural History
AMN	Abilene Morning News
ARN	Abilene Record-News
AT	Amarillo Times
ATLAL	J. Evetts Haley, *A Texan Looks at Lyndon: A Study in Illegitimate Power* (Canyon, TX: Palo Duro Press, 1964)
BH	Brownsville (TX) Herald
BHR	Business History Review
BNH	Borger (TX) News Herald
BSH	Big Spring (TX) Herald
CN	Canyon (TX) News
DMN	Dallas Morning News
EPHP	El Paso Herald Post
EPN	El Paso News
EPT	El Paso Times
ETHJ	East Texas Historical Journal
FWST	Fort Worth Star Telegram
GPQ	Great Plains Quarterly
JAH	Journal of American History
JEH	Journal of Economic History
LA	Lubbock Avalanche
LAJ	Lubbock Avalanche Journal
LEJ	Lubbock Evening Journal
MNM	Marshall (TX) News Messenger
NMHR	New Mexico Historical Review
NYT	New York Times
OA	Odessa American

PDN   *Pampa Daily News*
PN   *Paris (TX) News*
PPHM   Panhandle-Plains Historical Museum, Canyon, TX
PPHR   *Panhandle-Plains Historical Review*
PSQ   *Political Science Quarterly*
SAEN   *San Antonio Evening News*
SAST   *San Angelo Standard-Times*
SWC   Southwest Collection, Texas Tech University
SWHQ   *Southwestern Historical Quarterly*
SWSSQ   *Southwestern Social Science Quarterly*
TH   *Tulia (TX) Herald*
TO   *Texas Observer*
WDT   *Wichita Daily Times*
WFT   *Wichita Falls Times*
WTHAY   *West Texas Historical Association Yearbook*
WHQ   *Western Historical Quarterly*
WP   *Washington Post*

INTRODUCTION

1. The Crowdpac study was widely covered in the national and local press. See *Salon*, December 17, 2015, and the *Washington Post*, December 14, 2015. Chris Tausanovitch and Christopher Warshaw, "Representation in Municipal Government," *American Political Science Review* (August 2014); Derek Miller, "The Best Places to Be a Liberal and the Best Place to Be a Conservative," *Smart Asset*, September 7, 2016.

2. The CPAC ratings are produced by the American Conservative Union (ACU), the oldest conservative lobby group in the country. It began rating politicians in 1971 according to how legislators voted on key pieces of legislation that the ACU determined would indicate conservative positions. Anyone with a score over 80 percent receives the ACU's "conservative" stamp. Since the early days, West Texas congressional representatives were CPAC all-stars: Bob Price (13th Congressional District) had a lifetime ACU rating of 90 percent. San Angelo Democratic representative Ovie Fisher's lifetime rating was 93 percent. Over his thirty years in Congress, Omar Burleson's rating was 89 percent. In his two terms representing the 13th back in the 1980s, Beau Boulter nabbed an overall rating of 95 percent. In almost twenty years as Lubbock's representative, Larry Combest had a lifetime rating of 95 percent.

3. I remember a particularly tense job interview from a couple of decades ago where I tried to explain to one of the country's leading presidential scholars why I thought it was more fruitful to understand the career of a state senator than a U.S. president. I believed it then and I believe it now. I didn't get the job.

4. The great exception to this rule is the demand for access to Texas's public lands that animated the Farmers' Alliance in the western Cross Timbers in the mid-1880s. New land laws passed under the Hogg administration in the late 1880s and early 1890s relieved much of that tension. Alliance activists then turned to issues of more interest to the state's cotton farmers—like the subtreasury and expansion of the nation's money supply.

5. Amarillo and Phoenix, for example, had roughly the same size populations in 1930.

6. The biggest difference in how folks tend to define the boundaries of the region is usually whether to include the Trans-Pecos. I do not, largely because I agree with those

cultural geographers and historians who think that history, culture, demography, and geography set the Trans-Pecos apart. Where to draw its eastern border is the other big question.

7. Political geographer Daniel J. Elazar in 1980 pointed out the uniformity of the region's politics, in "Political Culture on the Plains," *WHQ* (July 1980).

8. The Oklahoma 3rd was rated as R+26, and the Kansas 1st and the Nebraska 3rd were R+23. With 50 percent representing a baseline, a district that is R+26 is one where the GOP candidate regularly polls 76 percent of the vote in that district. Not only is the Canadian province of Alberta widely recognized as the most conservative in the country, but its brand of conservatism is very similar to that of West Texas.

9. For a great example of "putting on the hat," see the deliberately ironic dust jacket of Rick Perlstein's *Before the Storm: Barry Goldwater and the Unmaking of the American Consensus* (Hill and Wang, 2001). There's Barry Goldwater in a distressed leather jacket, denim shirt, jeans, and holding a rifle. Look behind the rifle and you'll see his modern patio furniture. In his defense, Goldwater himself thought the whole photo shoot was silly.

10. Jedediah Morse, *The American Geography; or, A View of the Present Situation of the United States of America* (Shepard Kollock, 1789), 253. A couple of centuries later, American cultural geographer Wilbur Zelinsky gave Morse's thesis a cool new name, "The Doctrine of First Effective Settlement," a foundational study in the field. Zelinsky extrapolated on his predecessor's idea: "Whenever an empty territory undergoes settlement, or an earlier population is dislodged by invaders, the specific characteristics of the first group able to effect a viable, self-perpetuating society are of crucial significance for the later social and cultural geography of the area, no matter how tiny the initial band of settlers might have been. . . . Thus in terms of lasting impact, the activities of a few hundred or even a few score, initial colonizers can mean much more for the cultural geography of a place than the contributions of tens of thousands of new immigrants a few generations later." Wilbur Zelinsky, *The Cultural Geography of the United States* (Prentice-Hall, 1973), 13–14.

11. In the late 1960s, a sociologist conducted a study of the "value clusters" of the Panhandle and concluded that the lasting influence of the frontier era contributed greatly to the region's traits of individualism, mistrust of centralized authority, and entrepreneurialism and that its small-town provincialism and lack of in-migration had also created a culture characterized by conformity, fundamentalism, puritanism, and 'babbitry.'" Benjamin Gorman, "Fundamentalism and the Frontier: Value Clusters in the Texas Panhandle," PhD diss., Tulane University, 1965, 147–149.

EXPOSITION

The Despoblado

1. Albert Pike, "Narrative of a Journey in the Prairie," *Publications of the Arkansas Historical Association* 4 (1917): 72–73; Walter Lee Brown, *A Life of Albert Pike* (University of Arkansas Press, 1997), 13–28.

2. Edmund Burke, *A Philosophical Enquiry into the Origin of Our Ideas of the Sublime and Beautiful* (1757; reprint, D. Buchanan, 1803), 57.

3. For excellent physical descriptions of West Texas, see Fred Rathjen, "The Physiography of the Texas Panhandle," *SWHQ* (1961); and Paul Howard Carlson, *Deep Time and the Texas High Plains: History and Geology* (Texas Tech University Press, 2005).

4. This is not to say that there are no significant archaeological sites in West Texas—nothing could be further from the truth. It is to say that most sites reveal a community that lasted only a short time and often, as in the case of the Alibates Flint site (one of the best in the West), was arranged around the exploitation of a particular resource. See James B. Shaeffer, "The Alibates Flint Quarry, Texas," *American Antiquity* (1958).

5. Pedro Castañeda, *The Journey of Coronado*, March of America Facsimile Series, Ann Arbor, Michigan, 364.

6. John Miller Morris, the region's best geographer, calls the Llano "an irrational landscape, a strange world full of deception . . . [where] the sheer enormity of the sky and the plain left so many observers feeling insignificant and very much alone." Where the "monotonous lack of perspective left a sojourner virtually *landsick*: disoriented, paranoid . . . a land of illusion and subjectivity." Morris, *El Llano Estacado: Exploration and Imagination on the High Plains of Texas and New Mexico, 1536–1860* (Texas State Historical Association, 2003), 119.

7. The description appears in the middle of a frontispiece map of the western United States, just to the west of the Salt Fork of the Brazos and just north of present Post, Texas. John Russell Bartlett, *Personal Narrative of Explorations and Incidents in Texas, New Mexico, California, Sonora, and Chihuahua* (D. Appleton and Company, 1854).

8. Edwin James, *Account of an Expedition from Pittsburgh to the Rocky Mountains*, vol. 3 (Longman, Hurst, Rees, Orme, and Brown, 1823), 236, 237.

9. See Pekka Hämäläinen's amazing book *The Comanche Empire* (Yale University Press, 2009), which has completely upended how scholars consider the histories of the Southwest in the eighteenth and nineteenth centuries.

10. An interesting alternative interpretation can be found in Daniel J. Gelo, "Comanche Land and Ever Has Been: A Native Geography of the Nineteenth-Century Comanchería," *SWHQ* (January 2000).

BOOK ONE. WONDERLAND

1. The Rise and Fall of the Cattle Kingdom

1. Harley True Burton, "History of the JA I," *SWHQ* (October 1927): 105–107; quotes on 105. A terrific version of the story is recounted in part one of Harley True Burton's four-part history of Goodnight's JA Ranch, which was serialized in four successive issues of *SWHQ* in 1927–1928.

2. Goodnight estimated that he drove ten thousand buffalo out of the canyon.

3. In the years to come, Quanah frequented the ranch often. He and Goodnight became friends and business associates. In 1916, Goodnight even invited a few Comanche warriors to return to the canyon to act in a movie he was directing. In the film they hunted buffalo in the old way from a herd Goodnight had built over the years, one of the nation's largest. The rare two-reeler, titled *Old Texas*, can be viewed online at the Texas Archive of the Moving Image.

4. Frederick Jackson Turner was an American scholar who famously organized the history of the American frontier into a recognizable linear set of stages. Among them is the moment when Native Americans give way to stock raisers. More about him later.

5. Nineteenth-century economist Johann Heinrich von Thünen was the first to articulate this "spatial land-rent" theory in his 1826 work *Der Isolirte Staat*.

6. Novelist Larry McMurtry believes that Goodnight had more influence on the ethos and philosophy of West Texas than any other man. McMurtry, *In a Narrow Grave* (Simon and Schuster, 1968), 5.

7. The herd had been built and maintained by Charles Goodnight's wife, Molly, in one of her many business ventures.

8. Now the National Cowboy and Western Heritage Museum in Oklahoma City. The other four inaugural members were Theodore Roosevelt, Charlie Russell, Will Rogers, and rodeo legend Jake McClure.

9. The standard biography is still J. Evetts Haley's *Charles Goodnight: Cowman and*

Plainsman (Houghton Mifflin, 1936). A more modern—and less hagiographic—take is Willian T. Hagan's *Charles Goodnight: Father of the Texas Panhandle* (University of Oklahoma Press, 2007). A very good pictorial biography is B. Byron Price and Wyman Meinzer, *Charles Goodnight: A Man for the Ages* (Badlands Design, 2012).

10. Quoted in Haley, *Charles Goodnight*, 273.

11. Liam Dolan, *Land War and Eviction in Derryveagh* (Annaverna Press, 1960); W. E. Vaughan, *Sin, Sheep, and Scotsmen: John George Adair and the Derryveagh Evictions, 1861* (Apple Tree, 1983).

12. Castrated bulls, known as steers, gain weight faster and were the primary "crop" in early ranching.

13. There is no shortage of scholarship on the range business, but don't miss Clara M. Love, "History of the Cattle Industry in the Southwest" *SWHQ* (1916); and Edward Everett Dale, *The Range Cattle Industry: Ranching on the Great Plains from 1865 to 1925* (University of Oklahoma Press, 1960).

14. In total, the state gave away over 30 million acres, mostly to railroad companies.

15. Goodnight quotes from Burton, "The History of the JA Ranch II," *SWHQ* (January 1928): 230.

16. This mutually beneficial approach to dealmaking would also characterize the early days of the West Texas oil industry. Visitors to cattle country regularly commented on its about dealmaking culture. Robert G. Athearn, *Westward the Briton* (Scribner, 1953), 79–115.

17. Across cattle country, stock associations (particularly in Wyoming) were able to write much of the code into state or territorial law, and the values associated with the code are still foundational to its culture.

18. A great contemporary description, "The Cow-Boy at Home," can be found in the September 1886 issue of *Cornhill Magazine*. The code has been the subject of some good scholarship as well. See Dale, *The Range Cattle Industry*; and Joseph Kinsey Howard, *Montana: High, Wide, and Handsome* (Yale University Press, 1943), both of which describe the code and its implementation. For the specific rules on violence, see Eugene Manlove Rhodes's description of what he called the "barbarous code of the fighting man" in *West Is West* (Grosset and Dunlap, 1917), 20–21; and for its deeper social and cultural meaning, see Richard Maxwell Brown, "Western Violence: Structure, Values, Myth," *WHQ* (1993).

19. No one viewed cattle country as a utopia more than Owen Wister (except for maybe his buddy Teddy Roosevelt). In fact, one may easily read Wister's 1902 novel *The Virginian*—an account of Wyoming's Johnson County War, where a stranger to the land is constantly being taught the ways of Wyoming's unique cultural norms and practices—as a utopian novel.

20. The code, thanks in large part to the spread of the popularity of the Western genre, became central to the American identity in the twentieth century. Two of its earliest popular expressions were created by novelist Zane Grey (explicitly in his *The Code of the West* [1924]) and movie star Gene Autry. Both stressed honesty, friendliness, courage, kindness, and being respectful toward and protective of women, children, and the elderly. Grey is a bit more specific about the rules governing violence. Holly George-Warren, *Public Cowboy No. 1: The Life and Times of Gene Autry* (Oxford University Press, 2007), 256–257. For a recent exploration, see James P. Owen, *Cowboy Ethics: What Wall Street Can Learn from the Code of the West* (Stoecklein, 2005).

21. Almost every British and eastern observer commented on how little men talked in cattle country.

22. "And it is worthy of note," he added, "that no better standard has ever been kept with such faith." Rhodes, *West Is West*, 13.

23. Mody C. Boatright, "The Myth of Frontier Individualism," *SWSSQ* (1941): 25–26.

24. Karen R. Jones and John Wills, "The Trailblazer and the Homesteader," in *The American West: Competing Visions* (Edinburgh University Press, 2009), 133; Jacqueline S. Reiner, "Concepts of Domesticity on the Southern Plains Agricultural Frontier, 1870–1920"; James Fenton, "Critters, Sourdough, and Dugouts: Women and Imitation Theory on the Staked Plains, 1875–1910," in *At Home on the Range*, ed. John R. Wunder (Greenwood Press, 1985).

25. Phebe Kerrick Warner, "The Wife of a Pioneer Ranchman," *Cattleman* (March 1921); Michaele Thurgood Haynes, "Mary Ann (Molly) Dyer Goodnight," in *Texas Women on the Cattle Trails*, ed. Sara R. Massey (Texas A&M University Press, 2006), 135.

26. Terry G. Jordan, *North American Cattle-Ranching Frontiers* (University of New Mexico Press, 1993), 214–215.

27. Most Black cowboys describe winning that respect only by performing the toughest and most dangerous jobs often and well.

28. Ron W. Wilhelm, "Jim Perry," in *Black Cowboys in Texas*, ed. Sara R. Massey (Texas A&M University Press, 2000), 211. See also Ana Carolina Castillo Crimm, "Mathew 'Bones' Hooks," 226; and Michael N. Searles, "Addison Jones," both ibid.

29. Suspicion worsened when the wannabe rancher's chosen brand could be reverse engineered to reveal an LS or Long S brand as part of the design.

30. Quoted in Burton, "History of the JA III," *SWHQ* (April 1928): 346. As B. Byron Price notes in his "Community of Individualists" the PSA, while open to anyone, was still dominated by larger ranchers. Price, "Community of Individualists: The Panhandle Stock Association, 1879–1889," in *At Home on the Range*.

31. Zelinsky, *The Cultural Geography of the United States*, 13–14.

32. Walter Prescott Webb, *The Great Plains* (Ginn and Company, 1931; reprint, University of Nebraska Press, 1981), 206.

33. W. B. von Richtofen, *Cattle-Raising on the Plains* (D. Appleton and Co., 1885), 91.

34. W. G. Kerr, "Scottish Investment and Enterprise in Texas," in *Studies in Scottish Business History*, ed. Peter Lester Payne (Cass, 1967), 369.

35. The 2024 number is derived by employing economy cost, the relative share of the investment as a percentage of total national economic output—a formula commonly used to measure the historical value of large-scale investment. Across the West, British capital promoted thirty-seven different large-scale cattle operations with initial capital investments of $34 million.

36. Although almost every one of these ranches has at least one full-length history, a great overview of the period is Laura V. Hamner's *Short Grass and Longhorns* (University of Oklahoma Press, 1943).

37. One apocryphal story out of Wyoming tells of a bunch of ranchers trapped in a saloon during a blizzard lamenting their possible losses from the storm when the bartender set up a round on the house and reminded them that no matter the weather, "the books don't freeze."

38. There's no shortage of scholarship on the British cattle syndicates and their various adventures in the American West. A good overview is Peter Pagnamenta, *Prairie Fever: British Aristocrats in the American West, 1830–1890* (W. W. Norton, 2012). Particularly helpful for West Texas is Herbert O. Brayer, "The Influence of British Capital on the Western Range-Cattle Industry," *JEH* (1949); Richard Graham, "The Investment Boom in British-Texan Cattle Companies 1880–1885," *BHR* (1960); and J. Fred Rippy, "British Investments in Texas Lands and Livestock," *SWHQ* (1955).

39. Most helpful in understanding the cowboy strike is Ruth Allen, "A Cowboy Strike," in her *Chapter in the History of Organized Labor in Texas* (University of Texas, 1941), 33–42;

and Elmer Kelton's magnificent novel *The Day the Cowboys Quit* (Doubleday, 1971). A more recent take is Mark Lause, *The Great Cowboy Strike: Bullets, Ballots, and Class Conflicts in the American West* (Verso, 2017).

40. Steven Hahn, *A Nation without Borders: The United States and Its World in an Age of Civil Wars, 1830–1910* (Penguin, 2016), 42.

41. The group was named for the Grange, or Patrons of Husbandry, a popular farmers' organization that would remain a force in state politics through the 1930s.

42. Goodnight himself, whom many assumed to be British, was named on the floor of the legislature as one of the "hobgoblins" and "unrestrained monsters" who sought to expand his fortune using the children's grass. *AAS*, March 3, 1887.

43. General Laws of Texas, Acts 1883, 18th R.S., chapter 88, 85–89.

44. The terms did set off a rampage of fraud and con artistry. The writer O. Henry, who as a young man worked at the Texas Land Office, suggested that "volumes could be filled with accounts of the knavery, the double-dealing, the cross purposes, the perjury, the lies, the bribery, the alteration and erasing, the suppressing and destroying of papers, the various schemes and plots that for the sake of the almighty dollar have left their stains upon the records of the General Land Office." O. Henry, "Bexar Scrip 2692" (1894) in O. Henry, "Stories of the Old Land Office" (pamphlet, Daughters of the Republic of Texas, 1964), 6.

45. For example, it cost about $100 a mile to put up a five-strand stretch of fence. To fence in a massive rectangular pasture of 64,000 acres (100 sections and 130 miles of fence) would have totaled about $13,000, or 2 cents an acre. But to enclose a 160-acre farm would cost $100 or 62.5 cents an acre.

46. It's likely that the checkerboard pattern also worked against the TLB plan; fencing in massive pastures was the goal all along, rather than access to strange sections far from the home range.

47. The grass lease fight is a famous story in the history of the Texas cattle business. No one tells it better than J. Evetts Haley, "The Grass Lease Fight and Attempted Impeachment of the First Panhandle Judge," *SWHQ* (1934). In Haley's eyes, the fight was a great example of commonsense, well-intentioned business folk getting the runaround by nincompoop politicians who didn't understand what they were doing. It would become a major theme in his scholarship and his politics.

48. Quoted in Rippy, "British Investments in Texas Lands and Livestock," 334, 335.

49. Hagan, *Charles Goodnight*, 86.

50. Goodnight was convinced the entire trial was punishment for his refusal to endorse Templeman's man for judge. Haley, "Grass Lease Fight," 4–5.

51. Templeton would, as Texas attorney general, bring impeachment charges against Willis, claiming collusion with the defendants. The Texas House of Representatives, dominated by the Granger Bloc, impeached Willis, but the judge avoided conviction in the senate by delivering a stem-winder (sadly, lost to history) in his defense. He would go on to become the corporate attorney for the Panhandle and Santa Fe Railroad. The prosecutor in the case, the newly elected attorney general James Hogg, would go on to become one of the greatest governors in Texas history.

52. Haley, "Grass Lease Fight," 8.

53. Some date the beginning of the end of the cattle bubble to fall 1885. Many ranchers who believed it was too late to get the cattle to northern ranges and who feared West Texas could not support any more cattle began to dump steers on the market. Cattle prices dropped through the fall and into the winter.

54. For a remarkably prescient article about the dangers of winter storms following droughty seasons, see Frank Wilkeson, "Cattle-Raising on the Plains," *Harper's* (December 1885).

55. Unlike other animals, in particular bison, cattle will walk in front of a storm rather than into it.

56. David L. Wheeler, "The Blizzard of 1886 and Its Effect on the Range Cattle Industry in the Southern Plains," *SWHQ* (1991).

57. Some of the losses reported were surely a convenient way to bring the books back into balance.

58. A series of equally horrible blizzards hit the cattle ranches of the northern plains the very next winter with the same results. That disaster, sometimes called the Hard Winter, also came to be known as the Great Die-Up. And there are those who insist on treating the two together under the name Great Die-Up. To avoid confusion, I'll just call the Texas disaster the Die-Up. For a good treatment of what happened in Montana and the Dakotas, see Ray H. Mattison, "The Hard Winter and the Range Cattle Business," *Montana Magazine of History* (1951).

59. The song was based on a poem written by Hermann Hagedorn, "Medora Nights," *The Outlook* (1921): 26.

60. John S. Spratt, *Road to Spindletop: Economic Change in Texas, 1875-1901* (Southern Methodist University Press, 1955), 95–96; United States Department of Agriculture, *Annual Report, 1889*, 67–68.

61. A 1902 Texas Supreme Court decision that ended perpetual leasing of the school lands certainly helped in this decision making.

2. Agricultural Wonderland

1. Most of the biographical information about Hobart may be found in Lester Fields Sheffy, *The Life and Times of Timothy Dwight Hobart* (Panhandle-Plains Historical Society, 1950). Despite the florid language, drearily romantic framework, and blatant hagiography, this book is a remarkable source of West Texas history with more than its fair share of keen insights. Sheffy's analysis and understanding of Texas land law rivals that of Walter Prescott Webb.

2. The land was the remaining asset of two bankrupt Texas railroad companies. Hobart's cousin, a Republican carpetbagger who had hoped to strike it rich in the railroad business, had created the NY&TLC to sell off or lease the land that the company had been awarded by the state.

3. Growing in the shadow of Fort Elliot, Mobeetie was the legal center of the entire region. Consequently, it was the center of operations for the land men and the lawyers.

4. *Texas Livestock Journal*, December 6, 1895.

5. Plemons was an Amarillo lawyer–real estate developer. The act would be amended ten years later to allow for 5,000-acre homesteads in the Trans-Pecos.

6. J. Evetts Haley and William C. Holden, *The Flamboyant Judge, James D. Hamlin* (Palo Duro Press, 1972), 12. See also Leland Kent Turner, "Grassland Frontiers: Beef Cattle Agriculture in Queensland and Texas, 1870s-1970s," PhD diss., Texas Tech University, 2008, 129–131.

7. Terry G. Jordan, "Windmills in Texas," *AH* (1963).

8. Cowboys who learned to fix windmills became highly skilled and well-paid members of a ranch's workforce. Most of them hated the task.

9. The joke went that the water came out so slowly that someone could die of thirst while drinking from a windmill pipe.

10. Sheffy, *Life and Times of Timothy Dwight Hobart*, 124–125; and Sheffy, *The Francklyn Land and Cattle Company: A Panhandle Enterprise, 1882–1957* (University of Texas Press, 1963), 45–58, 249–257.

11. Quoted in Sheffy, *Life and Times of Timothy Dwight Hobart*, 104.

12. *Fort Worth Gazette*, February 7, 1887. W. E. Hughes was a serial entrepreneur. He had been a sheep raiser, schoolteacher, lawyer, banker, real estate broker, and saltworks owner before he got into ranching. By the time of his speech, ranchers' place in the settlement order was thoroughly baked into American understanding of the frontier process. Hughes was giving his speech in the wake of the Great Die-Up.

13. "The Texas 'Pan-Handle' As It Is: The Texas 'Pan-Handle' As It Was," Colonizing Agency Southwestern Lines, Texas Promotional Materials, Baylor University Libraries Digital Collections.

14. Farm size numbers from 1890 and 1910 U.S. Department of Agriculture (USDA) censuses.

15. David B. Gracy, "Selling the Future: A Biography of William Pulver Soash," *PPHR* 50 (1977): 1–76. Don't miss the fantastic online exhibit of Soash's Texas real estate career: "The Rise and Fall of the Soash Empire: A West Texas Hard Luck Story," posted by Eric Ames, November 15, 2012, Baylor Digital Collections Blog, https://blogs.baylor.edu /digitalcollections/2012/11/15/the-rise-and-fall-of-the-soash-empire-a-west-texas-hard -luck-story/.

16. The total cost of the building was a little over $3.7 million. A century later the 3 million acres of the former XIT tract would be valued at $7 billion. Robert C. Cotner, *The Texas State Capitol* (Pemberton, 1968).

17. The entire XIT story is best told by J. Evetts Haley, in his *XIT Ranch in Texas: and the Early Days of the Llano Estacado* (1929; reprint, University of Oklahoma Press, 1953). For a more granular account of the XIT's corporate operations, see Michael M. Miller, *XIT: A Story of Land, Cattle, and Capital in Texas and Montana* (University of Oklahoma Press, 2020).

18. W. P. Soash Company, "The Big Springs Country of Texas," 1909, 9, Texas Promotional Materials, Baylor University Libraries Digital Collections.

19. Versions of this idea regularly showed up in full-page ads. See *Fort Wayne Journal Gazette*, October 1, 1908.

20. Although the term has fallen out of use in recent years, the "Middle West," also sometimes called the "Old Middle West," was a recognized region of the United States for most of the last third of the nineteenth and first third of the twentieth centuries. The region, made up almost exclusively of farms and small towns, extended across the eastern half of the Great Plains and also included the rural counties of Iowa, Illinois, Indiana, and Ohio. It was, in the minds of many contemporaries, the "epitome of [American] virtue," a region whose citizens and culture were defined by "morality, independence, and egalitarianism." James R. Shortridge, *The Middle West: Its Meaning in American Culture* (University Press of Kansas, 1989), 30, 8.

21. One ad read: "A man may own 1,000 acres in Texas for the price of one quarter section in the older settled country. The farmer can sell his old farm from the proceeds of the sale, realize enough money to purchase a large Texas farm for each of his grown sons, a home in town for himself, and then he has fulfilled [h]is duty both to himself and his family. Fifteen years from today Texas land will be worth as much as land in the older states today, and the young generations prefer to go to the new country and grow with it." *Des Moines Register*, August 27, 1908.

22. From a full-page spread in the *Des Moines Register*, October 1, 1908. See also Vance Johnson, "Saga of Soash" in *Amarillo Sunday News and Globe*, Special Golden Anniversary Edition, August 14, 1938.

23. W. P. Soash Company, "The Big Springs Country of Texas," 44; See *Des Moines Tribune*, August 23, 1907; *Des Moines Register*, September 25 and October 9, 1907.

24. Charles Moreau Harger, "The Land Movement and Western Finance," *North American Review* 192, no. 661 (December 1910): 747. Harger, a Kansas journalist, was probably the best contemporary analyst of the rural economics of the Great Plains.

25. In a situation eerily similar to the 2008 financial crisis, crappy loans on investment real estate almost brought down the entire economy in 1907. The land bubble that accompanied the new century was so pervasive that it, too, posed a systemic risk. Seeking steady and decent returns on their investments, life insurance companies bought up many of the loans made to farmers in the places where land values were rising quickly. (Eastern investment banks also fell in love with the product.) These insurance companies got themselves in deep, often with tens of millions of dollars tied up in loans on plains farmland. Although the farm loans themselves were relatively long-term notes, usually around five years, with rapidly rising prices, banks needed ever more capital to make additional loans, which the insurance companies sent, automatically it seems. No one had an inkling exactly how much the insurance companies were exposed to what was by then an almost purely speculative market. When auditors discovered the vulnerability of the industry's position, insurance company executives convinced eastern bankers to ease the bubble by reducing the money supply and restricting credit. When it looked like credit would soon become tighter and more expensive, small banks everywhere, most of which were struggling to make their capital reserves in the bubble economy, scrambled and bought as much commercial paper as they could from larger eastern institutions. The size and extent of these purchases massively disrupted normal credit markets. The subsequent mad dash for credit and capital pulverized the already weak prairie town banks and the larger regional systems. Their failure was as much responsible for taking down the Knickerbocker Bank (which kicked off the Panic of 1907) as the run on copper by the United Copper Company, normally credited with precipitating the crisis. In its aftermath, as the nation's bankers began rehabilitating the banking system, they put the kibosh on land speculation on the prairies. Harger, "The Land Movement and Western Finance."

26. Don't miss Jan Blodgett's *Land of Bright Promise: Advertising the Texas Panhandle and South Plains, 1870–1917* (University of Texas Press, 1988). For an even larger view, see David M. Emmons, *Garden in the Grassland: Boomer Literature of the Central Great Plains* (University of Nebraska Press, 1971). The collection of land promotional materials at Texas Tech's Southwest Collection is an invaluable resource and many of its materials are available online.

27. "Description of Shackelford County" (brochure), Land Promotionals Collection, SWC.

28. Johnson, "Saga of Soash."

29. W. P. Soash Company, "Big Springs Country of Texas," 44.

30. Gracy, "Selling the Future," 11–12.

31. A great description of the general Soash sales experience in West Texas is related by an Iowa reporter and reprinted in Johnson, "Saga of Soash."

32. Johnson, "Saga of Soash."

33. O. G. Lloyd, "Studies of Land Values in Iowa," *Journal of Farm Economics* 2, no. 3 (July 1920): 136.

34. W. P. Soash Company, "Big Springs Country of Texas," 30.

35. Quotes from "Three Stages of Crosby County Texas," (brochure) Land Promotionals Collection, SWC.

36. For more on this phenomenon across the twentieth century, see David M. Wrobel, *Promised Lands: Promotion, Memory, and the Creation of the American West* (University Press of Kansas, 2002); Robert L. Dorman, *Revolt of the Provinces: The Regionalist Movement in*

America, 1920–1945 (University of North Carolina Press, 1993); and John M. Findlay, *Magic Lands: Western Cityscapes and American Culture after 1940* (University of California Press, 1992).

37. *Austin Democratic Statesman*, May 18, 1875. The *Galveston News*, which enjoyed the largest circulation in Texas in those years, consistently spun a tale of Texas immigration motivated by white southerners seeking to escape the Reconstruction South. It declared that Texas was "a white man's country and will remain a white man's country." *Galveston Daily News*, April 29 and September 25, 1874. These are only a couple of examples. The idea that Texas was a "white man's country" appeared throughout the Texas press in the five decades following the Civil War. See Jason Pierce, *Making the White Man's West: Whiteness and the Creation of the American West* (University Press of Colorado, 2016).

38. This approach was in no way limited to Texas. As historians William Deverell and Doug Flamming have revealed, Los Angeles boosters, perhaps the most successful in all the American West, "inevitably mediated regional racial attitudes, stereotypes, and commitment to hierarchies, and they did so through influential and powerful media. 'Boosterspeak' often meant 'racespeak,' albeit in encoded or symbolic language." Deverell and Flamming, "Race, Rhetoric, and Regional Identity," in *Power and Place in the North American West*, ed. Richard White and John M. Findlay (University of Washington Press, 1999), 117.

39. The ad ran all over the Middle West in 1909. See, for example, *South Bend Tribune*, March 31, 1909.

40. *Fort Worth Daily Gazette*, February 7, 1893.

41. *Franklin (MA) Sentinel*, August 13, 1909.

42. North Texas Land Company, "The Panhandle Country of North Texas," n.d. (probably 1906), Land Promotionals Collection, SWC.

43. Quoted in Blodgett, *Land of Bright Promise*, 97.

44. "The Panhandle vs. Black Land," *Hereford Brand*, April 7, 1909.

45. See *Canyon News*, November 20, 1908.

46. Dillard-Powell Land Company, "Buy Texas Land," Land Promotionals Collection, SWC. As Jason E. Pierce points out, this message was spread across the entire western settlement project. See Pierce, *Making the White Man's West*.

47. W. P. Soash Company, "The Big Springs Country of Texas," 17.

48. Spur Ranch, "The Spur Lands," Land Promotionals Collection, SWC.

49. Lubbock Chamber of Commerce, "Lubbock, Land of Opportunities," Land Promotionals Collection, SWC.

50. Texas Land and Development Company, "60,000 Acres of Irrigated Farms," n.d., Land Promotionals Collection, SWC.

51. Soash quoted in Johnson, "Saga of Soash."

52. "Why You Should Invest in the New Town: Soash Texas," in Ames, "The Rise and Fall of the Soash Empire."

53. When he found out that the spur heading south out of Lubbock would go through Lamesa, Soash tried to buy out the town and force the Santa Fe to change its route.

54. A few years after his Big Springs Country development went under, Soash ended up working for the Littlefield Lands Company.

55. For an excellent analysis of Littlefield and the larger settlement project in West Texas, see David B. Gracy, *Littlefield Lands: Colonization on the Texas Plains, 1912–1920* (University of Texas Press, 1968).

56. I include this unusual geometric/geographic town layout information to emphasize that not even the cold logic of urban planning could dislodge the commitment to the accepted town design in West Texas.

57. The spatial cloning of American towns in this era was widely observed. As London journalist Edward Dicey complained in 1862, "Every town is built on the same system, has the same series of more or less lengthy rectangular streets, the same large spacious stores, the same snug unpicturesque rows of villas, . . . the same somber churches, . . . the same nomenclature of streets—the invariable Walnut, Chestnut, Front, and Main Streets—crossed by the same perpendicular streets, numbered First, Second and so on to any number you like, according to the size of the town." The difference in West Texas was of course the new foundational transportation mode—a railroad rather than a river or an ocean—that served as the access and commercial focal point. Dicey quoted in D. A. Hamer, *New Towns in the New World: Images and Perceptions of the Nineteenth-Century Urban Frontier* (Columbia University Press, 1990), 45.

58. Open any map program and zoom into any town on the Great Plains and you'll see the pattern. It is particularly acute in the towns built in the first decade of the twentieth century, when a consensus had seemingly been reached about the ideal house, lot, and street size; when new homes were built within a planned water, electric, trash, and phone system infrastructure; and when the automobile was becoming commonplace.

59. John Miller Morris, "When Corporations Rule the Llano Estacado," in *The Future of the Southern Plains*, ed. Sherry L. Smith (University of Oklahoma Press, 2003), 51.

60. The standard text is John C. Hudson, *Plains Country Towns* (University of Minnesota Press, 1985).

61. Sociologist Harvey Molotch famously described this phenomenon in "The City as a Growth Machine: Toward a Political Economy of Place," *American Journal of Sociology* (1976).

62. "Buy Texas Land," Lubbock: Lubbock County, Land Promotionals Collection, SWC.

63. Amarillo, Abilene, Big Spring, Lubbock, Pampa, San Angelo, and Sweetwater.

64. The dean of West Texas agricultural history is Garry L. Nall. Among his body of excellent work, I found the following the most helpful in my understanding of the development of farming in West Texas: "The Farmers' Frontier in the Texas Panhandle," *PPHR* (1972); "Agricultural History of the Texas Panhandle, 1880–1965," PhD diss., University of Oklahoma, 1972; "Panhandle Farming in the 'Golden Era' of American Agriculture," *PPHR* (1973); and "Specialization and Expansion: Panhandle Farming in the 1920s," *PPHR* (1974).

65. Texas Agricultural Experiment Stations, *Twenty-Fifth Annual Report* (1913), 113.

66. University of Illinois, "Mechanical Harvesting of Cotton as Affected by Varietal Characteristics and Other Factors" (1939), 46–47; James H. Street, "Mechanizing the Cotton Harvest," *AH* (January 1957).

67. All mid-1920s agricultural statistics from the 1925 USDA Census of Agriculture.

68. Raper quoted in James W. Loewen, *Sundown Towns: A Hidden Dimension of American Racism* (New Press, 2005), 230.

69. While not as prominent as other parts of the American West, there were a handful of ethnic and religious colonies scattered across the region, even some that emigrated directly from Europe.

70. Sheffy, *Life and Times of Timothy Dwight Hobart*, 293.

3. Capitalist Utopia

1. *Kalamazoo Enquirer*, March 15, 1906.

2. Post had taken to wearing western garb several years earlier. His white Stetson was something of a trademark by this point.

3. It's difficult to measure Post's influence in today's terms, but suffice it to say, the press,

even much of the national press, doted on him. Recognizing the limitations of historical comparisons, but with the reminder of the narrowness of media outlets and Post's position as one of the most famous and outspoken men in the United States, and the fact that he commanded the largest single advertising budget in the country, most of which was spent on newspapers, I would liken his place in the public imagination to the attention we have recently awarded to men like Jeff Bezos or Steve Jobs.

4. For an official biography approved and written with the cooperation of the Post estate, see Nettie Leitch Major, *C. W. Post: The Hour and the Man* (Judd and Detwiler, 1963). A more objective take is Peyton Paxson, "Charles William Post: The Mass Marketing of Health and Welfare," PhD diss., Boston University, 1993.

5. Nineteenth-century boosterism is the subject of several good works, including Carl Abbott, *Boosters and Businessmen* (Greenwood Press, 1981); Don Harrison Doyle in *The Social Order of a Frontier Community: Jacksonville, Illinois, 1825–70* (University of Illinois Press, 1978); Stephen V. Ward, *Selling Places: The Marketing and Promotion of Towns and Cities, 1850-2000* (Routledge, 1998); Timothy R. Mahoney, "'A Common Band of Brotherhood': Male Subcultures, the Booster Ethos, and the Origins of Urban Social Order in the Midwest of the 1840s," *Journal of Urban History* (1999); and Jocelyn Wills, *Boosters, Hustlers, and Speculators: Entrepreneurial Culture and the Rise of Minneapolis and St. Paul, 1849-1883* (Minnesota Historical Society Press, 2005).

6. Most of the stories from these years play up the villainy of the man who took over Post's company. The reality was a little more complicated and the conflict played out over several years.

7. Post, usually accompanied by other Springfield investors, had spent the fall visiting potential new sites for investment opportunities mostly in Texas and Kansas. He was advertising in the Springfield newspapers looking for investors in Fort Worth real estate as early as September 1887. He promised returns between 25 and 50 percent.

8. Post, interview with *Fort Worth Gazette*, September 24, 1887.

9. It's now the Riverside neighborhood of Fort Worth.

10. For a general economic history of the city, see Harold Rich, *Fort Worth: Outpost, Cowtown, Boomtown* (University of Oklahoma Press, 2014).

11. I constructed much of Post's years in Fort Worth from the documents in "Financial Matters, 1882–1887" in Box 2, Post Family Papers, Bentley Historical Library, Ann Arbor; and from *Fort Worth Gazette*, especially May 27, 1887; June 15, 1888; February 26 and 29, June 13, December 31, 1889, April 8, May 4 and 11, September 15, October 8, 1890.

12. Originally founded by the Seventh Day Adventist Church in 1866, it was called the Western Health Reform Institute. When John Harvey Kellogg took over the institution a decade later, he renamed it the Medical and Surgical Sanitarium, but most folks called it the Battle Creek Sanitarium or just the "San."

13. Among the most famous guests were Amelia Earhart, Mary Todd Lincoln, Eugene Debs, Henry Ford, Sojourner Truth, and Warren G. Harding.

14. For scholarly accounts of Kellogg's and the San's contributions to the history of America diet and exercise, see Nicholas Bauch, *A Geography of Digestion: Biotechnology and the Kellogg Cereal Enterprise* (University of California Press, 2017); and Brian C. Wilson, *Dr. John Harvey Kellogg and the Religion of Biologic Living* (Indiana University Press, 2014) But nothing beats T. C. Boyle's outrageously funny novel *The Road to Wellville* (Viking, 1993) for capturing the nuttiness of the whole Battle Creek vibe.

15. The San's failure to cure Post is the opening act in the Post-Kellogg feud, one of the greatest in American business history.

16. Like much of the biography of his pre-Postum fame, the story of Post-Kellogg-Gregory and his miraculous recovery suggests some exaggeration. Overcoming weakness

and sickness through his own power was a central moment in the biography of Post the man and essential to the marketing of Post the business. The Posts, while never joining the church, were large financial supporters of Christian Science for several years, even donating money for the construction of its church in Battle Creek. Post himself, not surprisingly, developed his own views on religion.

17. Post's partner, Jacob Beilhart, had been fired from the San for practicing faith healing. He would go on to form the Spirit Fruit Society, one of America's longest-lasting communes.

18. He was happy, however, to allow rumors to circulate that he had spent time in France and Bavaria studying alternative medicine.

19. He hawked the book in various forms over the years, including pocket-sized condensed versions that came packaged in boxes of Grape-Nuts. Quote from the full treatment, C. W. Post, *I Am Well!* (La Vita Inn Company, 1894), 4. Post advertised the book heavily in the mid-1890s in journals associated with New Thought and Mind Cure movements, including *Now: A Journal of Affirmation, To-Day, The Globe* and others.

20. Ads, placed in a growing number of slick magazines, promised that the "unseen scientific suspenders" were perfect for "summer wear, full dress, professional men, well-dressed men, businessmen, athletes" and the "world at large."

21. Post always claimed that he got the idea for Postum from his days in West Texas where plains women, far from markets, had created a coffee substitute by grinding up a mixture of baked grains and molasses. His product was, nevertheless, remarkably similar in style and taste to the coffee substitute available at the San. Marketing the product was the second act in his feud with the Kelloggs.

22. Post borrowed many of his techniques from patent medicine advertising.

23. Robert Collier, *The $50,000 Verdict* (P. F. Collier and Son, 1911). The federal government would not begin demanding truth in advertising until the 1930s. That said, even today, Grape-Nuts regularly appears on lists of healthiest breakfast cereals.

24. Gerald Carson, *Cornflake Crusade* (Rinehart, 1957), 165; Paxson, "Charles William Post," 91.

25. *A Trip through Postumville* (Postum Cereal Company, 1920).

26. Post was a genius at free advertising. One of his great efforts was how he spread the story of his home-building benevolence through Homer Cray's "The Girl Who Bought a Home on Nine Dollars a Week" that appeared in *Leslie's Weekly* in November 1912 and, thanks to his marketing department, was reprinted in newspapers across the country.

27. C. W. Post, "A Peaceful Industrial Family" (reprinted speech), *Square Deal* (July 1913): 498.

28. The open shop movement has been the subject of excellent scholarship. See John D. Hibbard, "The Necessity of an Open Shop—An Employer's View," *Publications of the American Economic Association* (1905), and in the same issue, John Graham Brooks, "The Issue between the Open and Closed Shop." The *North American Review* that year also featured famed diplomat Henry White's views on the subject, "The Issue of the Open and Closed Shop." Historical analyses include Richard W. Gable, "Birth of an Employers' Association," *BHR* (1959); Allen M. Wakstein, "The Origins of the Open-Shop Movement, 1919–1920," *JAH* (1964); Doris B. McLaughlin, "The Second Battle of Battle Creek—The Open Shop Movement in the Early Twentieth Century," *Labor History* (1973); and Rosemary Feurer and Chad Pearson, *Against Labor: How U.S. Employers Organized to Defeat Union Activism* (University of Illinois Press, 2017).

29. Samuel Grafton, "Propaganda from the Right," *American Mercury* (March 1935): 264.

30. For more on the NAM, see Clarence E. Bonnett, *Employers' Associations in the*

United States (Macmillan Company, 1922); Albert Kleckner Steigerwalt's sympathetic account *The National Association of Manufacturers, 1895–1914* (Graduate School of Business Administration, University of Michigan, 1964); and the more recent and thorough Jennifer A. Delton, *The Industrialists: How the National Association of Manufacturers Shaped American Capitalism* (Princeton University Press, 2020).

31. *NYT*, December 13, 1904.

32. Creel would go on to great notoriety for the effectiveness of his propaganda campaign during World War I, when he headed up President Woodrow Wilson's Committee on Public Information.

33. Open shop advocates saw themselves as patriotic progressives. Also in 1909, the CIAA morphed into the National Council for Industrial Defense.

34. One barely veiled threat went: "Your attention is invited to the enclosed from Mr. Post. He has in the past withheld some heavy display advertisements from papers too much under the domination of the labor trusts to print his announcement seeking the emancipation of the people. Experience proves that mediums which cater most to the relatively small number of labor union readers are not sought by the great buying public, and therefore not profitable for the advertisers of high grade goods." Grandin Advertising Agency to Publishers, July 7, 1905, Box 1, Advertisements [1–5], Post Family Papers, Bentley Historical Library, University of Michigan.

35. "Don't Weep at the Ice House," *Buffalo Enquirer*, January 4, 1910. This article appeared everywhere.

36. Quotes from a story about the founding of Post City that appeared in newspapers across the country on its ten-year anniversary. *Sioux Falls Argus Leader*, June 2, 1917; *Jackson Daily News*, June 2, 1917.

37. Zach Moore, "Making Dreams Come True," *Pearson's Magazine* (October 1909): 316.

38. *FWST*, January 26, 1908.

39. Charles Dudley Eaves and C. Alan Hutchinson, *Post City, Texas: C. W. Post's Colonizing Activities in West Texas* (Texas State Historical Association, 1952).

40. The story ran nationwide. For one example, see *Raleigh Times*, December 24, 1907.

41. *Marysville (KY) Public Ledger*, April 6, 1908. See also *Los Angeles Times*, November 16, 1908.

42. *Abilene Daily Reporter*, November 28, 1908.

43. See, for example, *Los Angeles Times*, November 16, 1908.

44. *Detroit Free Press*, April 19, 1908.

45. "How C. W. Post Solved the Problem of Providing Cheap Homes for His Workmen," *Fort Wayne Daily News*, June 14, 1913, and C. W. Post, "A Step Forward," *The Square Deal*, April 4, 1909.

46. "He Dreamed of Homes for Others," in *C. W. Post: A Memorial*, ed. Edward Branson (n.p., 1914), 13.

47. Eaves and Hutchinson, *Post City, Texas*, 53–60.

48. Quoted in Eaves and Hutchinson, *Post City, Texas*, 113.

49. One of Post's stranger ideas was that he could solve rural loneliness by placing farmhouses at the corners where four farm properties meet. He assumed that having homes close together might foster community. The first thing most farm families did after purchasing a Post City farm was to move the home to the center of their property, far from their neighbors.

50. Eaves and Hutchinson, *Post City, Texas*, 50, 122, 147–153 (Post quote on 113); Blodgett, *Land of Bright Promise*, 80; *Sioux Falls Argus Leader*, June 29, 1917.

51. Quoted in Eaves and Hutchinson, *Post City, Texas*, 117–118.

52. C. W. Post, "Making Rain While the Sun Shines," *Harper's Weekly*, February 27, 1912; Eaves, "Charles William Post, Rainmaker" *SWHQ* (1940); Michael Whitaker, "Making War on Jupiter Pluvius," *GPQ* (2013).

53. *Hardware Dealers' Magazine* (July 1910); *National Druggist* (December 1908).

54. Eaves and Hutchinson, *Post City, Texas*, 84.

55. *Appeal to Reason*, June 17, July 22, and August 5, 1911.

56. Strangely, Post hated the idea of using slick brochures to sell land; he much preferred a more direct approach. All queries, which went straight to Wilbur Hawk, were to be answered personally by letter. Post wanted prospects to visit the land; he wasn't interested in selling to folks who were impressed by "flashy literature." When he finally broke down and produced "A Chance to Own a Fine Farm," it had no photos. Instead, Post planned on sending out agents with large photograph books and later even motion pictures to show the land and the town. Blodgett, *Land of Great Promise*, 79.

57. The pitch opens with the story of two cowboys wondering what Post was going to do with his Texas lands: "Well, I'll tell y'u Jake, y'u know I heard it confidential, he's goin' to plant it all out to Grape-Nuts." *Nebraska Farm Journal*, October 25, 1913.

58. Post quoted in Eaves and Hutchinson, *Post City, Texas*, 147.

59. This would be the 2025 equivalent of almost $11 billion.

60. Post City Proclamation on the Death of C. W. Post, Box 9, Tributes, Post Family Papers.

61. It had dropped "City" from its name shortly after Post's death.

62. The event was widely covered in the local press. See, for example, *LA*, September 14, 1917; *Waco News-Tribune*, September 17, 1957.

63. The storm was bad enough to leave many of the other celebrities, like Jack Benny, cowering in the Hotel Algerita.

64. Audiotape of dedication ceremonies, Box 48, Post Family Papers.

4. West Texas Nationalism

1. Keep in mind, though this was disputed, in 1845, the Republic claimed a size half again as large as the state's current borders: half of present-day New Mexico, a quarter of Colorado, the southwestern corner of Kansas, and even part of Wyoming. Its current state borders were determined as part of the Compromise of 1850.

2. Celebrity statistician Nate Silver gave it a shot in "Messing With Texas," *FiveThirtyEight*, April 9, 2009; as did the editorial staff of *Texas Monthly* in its early years: Griffin Smith Jr., "Divide and Conquer," *Texas Monthly* (January 1975).

3. This was a particular interest of John Nance Garner in the early 1930s and more recently of Republican strategists.

4. See the magnificent Golden Anniversary issue of the *Amarillo Sunday News and Globe*, August 14, 1938: hundreds of pages of short remembrances and testimonials that celebrate the pioneer days.

5. Clyde A. Milner II, "The View from Wisdom: Four Layers of History and Regional Identity," in *Under an Open Sky*, ed. William Cronon, George A. Miles, and Todd Gitlin (W. W. Norton, 1992).

6. Western historian David Wrobel has produced some excellent work on this subject. See, in particular, "The Politics of Western Memory," in *The Political Culture of the New West*, ed. Jeff Roche (University of Kansas Press, 2008).

7. William Curry Holden, *The Espuela Land and Cattle Company: A Study of a Foreign-Owned Ranch in Texas* (Texas State Historical Association, 1970).

8. Not yet forty, Jones had also punched cattle, owned a newspaper in Colorado, and managed the Kansas City Waterworks.

9. See Charles A. Jones's short memoir on this time in West Texas that appeared in the June 1934 issue of the *Atlantic Monthly* titled "On the Last Frontier."

10. Connor, "Clifford B. Jones," in *Builders of the Southwest (1959)*, 102–106.

11. *AAS*, January 30, 1915.

12. Weston Joseph McConnell, *Social Cleavages in Texas: A Study of the Proposed Division of the State* (Columbia University, 1925), 176–177.

13. *Fort Worth Record*, January 29, 1915.

14. R. M. Chitwood quoted in *Bryan Daily Eagle*, April 9, 1921.

15. There might have been upward of 200,000 college-age young people in West Texas by 1920, according to some rough estimates.

16. Jane Gilmore Rushing and Kline A. Nall, *Evolution of a University: Texas Tech's First Fifty Years* (Madrona, 1975), 1. See also Robert Rutland, "The Beginnings of Texas Technological College," *SWHQ* (1951).

17. *FWST*, October 5, 1916.

18. The Fort Worth chamber also lent the new West Texas Chamber of Commerce the talents of its up-and-coming marketing and lobbying whiz Vance Muse. William Curry Holden, *Alkali Trails* (Southwest Press, 1930), 126.

19. Norman D. Brown, *Hood, Bonnet, and Little Brown Jug: Texas Politics, 1921-1928* (Texas A&M University Press, 1984), 96.

20. This should not be confused with the present West Texas A&M University in Canyon, which at that time was known as West Texas Normal College. It would become West Texas Teachers' College in 1923, West Texas College in 1949, West Texas State University in 1963, and West Texas A&M three years after it joined the larger Texas A&M system in 1990.

21. Three older sources tell the story well: Cortez A. M. Ewing, "The Impeachment of James E. Ferguson," *PSQ* (1933); John A. Lomax, "Governor Ferguson and the University of Texas," *Southwest Review* (1942); Ralph W. Steen, "The Ferguson War on the University of Texas," *SWSSQ* (1955); Bruce Rutherford, *The Impeachment of Jim Ferguson* (Eakin Press, 1983). For more modern takes and a useful collection of primary documents, see Jessica Brannon-Wranosky and Bruce A. Glasrud, eds., *Impeached: The Removal of Texas Governor James E. Ferguson* (Texas A&M University Press, 2017).

22. In a special election, W. A. Johnson, author of the State of Jefferson bill from 1915, became lieutenant governor.

23. Neff had practically swept the region in the election the year before, running against former senator and noted "wet" Joseph W. Bailey.

24. Quoted in the *Bryan (TX) Eagle*, August 14, 1921.

25. *Bryan (TX) Eagle*, April 4, 9, 1921.

26. Chitwood quoted in *El Paso Herald*, April 13, 1921. Nineteen separate speeches were given in four hours. *FWST*, April 7, 1921. Not surprisingly, the *Bryan Eagle* covered in depth the story of a potential second ag school in the state. See April 6, 9, 14, 1921; see also *AAS*, April 6, 1921, for a generous selection of responses from West Texas newspapers. See also R. C. Crane's version of the story in "The West Texas Agricultural and Mechanical College Movement," *WTHAY* (1931): 20–21; and Ernest Wallace, *The Howling of the Coyotes: Reconstruction Efforts to Divide Texas* (Texas A&M University Press, 1979), 14.

27. *Bryan Eagle*, April 4, 1921; Crane, "The West Texas Agricultural and Mechanical College Movement," *WTHAY* (1932): 24–28.

28. And only after pulling a great prank on Homer Dale Wade, the man as responsible as anyone for the new college bill. The evening that the bill was delivered to the governor, Neff was attending a banquet for newsmen in Austin. Called on by the toastmaster to

give some impromptu remarks on the future of the state, Neff opened by saying he was disappointed by the specificity of his given subject for, given his choice, he would rather have spoken to the reason that he planned on vetoing the West Texas A&M bill. As the air went out of the room, every eye turned to Homer Wade to see the blood drain from his face. Without further comment, Neff made some generic remarks about Texas's bright future. First thing the next morning, Wade was in the governor's office. Neff let him cool his heels in the lobby for an hour before finally admitting the irate West Texan into his office and letting him in on the joke. Of course, he was going to sign the bill. Wade recalls the story in *The Growth of an Idea: Establishment of Texas Technological College* (Texas Tech University Press, 1956), 91–93.

29. The application binders are housed in the Southwest Collection at Texas Tech. Post's was particularly impressive, lined with cotton sheets from the local mill.

30. *LA*, August 28, 1923.

31. Even in history, subfields had become gendered with women mostly scattered among ancient, medieval, and English history. See the remarkably informative and detailed National Science Foundation Report, *U.S. Doctorates in the 20th Century* (October 2006). That 15 percent number held until 1979.

32. As previously noted, what would become West Texas A&M went by many names over the years, but like most folks in that part of the world, I'll just call it WT most of the time.

33. In 1921, when Texas passed a law requiring public school teachers to have a college degree, WT became one the state's first (and most important) teacher colleges.

34. Historian Robert Dorman argues that it was schools like WT that helped foster regional identity. See Dorman, *Revolt of the Provinces*, 40–45.

35. A good item for any western U.S. history starter kit should include the three essays included in Frederick Jackson Turner, *History, Frontier, and Section: Three Essays*, and the accompanying essay by Martin Ridge (University of New Mexico Press, 1993).

36. Richard White, "Frederick Jackson Turner and Buffalo Bill," in *The Frontier in American Culture*, ed. James R. Grossman (University of California Press, 1994).

37. Beard quoted in Richard Hofstadter, "Turner and the Frontier Myth," *American Scholar* (1949): 433. Hofstadter, in the same essay, complained that Turner's Thesis in the hands of most scholars was "less a working hypothesis than an incantation" (435).

38. West Texas State Normal College, Prospectus (1910), 16.

39. Cousins, among the best school administrators in the history of Texas (he had resigned as state school superintendent to take the West Texas State position), enjoyed a long career organizing and running frontier schools.

40. Robert Bartow Cousins and James Abner Hill, *American History for Schools* (D. C. Heath, 1913), 333–334.

41. Sheffy, *Life and Times of Timothy Dwight Hobart*, 12–13. Throughout the book, Sheffy's unrelenting focus on the early frontier period can be incredibly frustrating in its lack of attention to the last several decades of Hobart's life, including his work developing Pampa and the White Deer Lands.

42. Another Sheffy hire was Ima C. Barlow, a European diplomatic historian and author of a still-referenced book on the Agadir Crisis, and who while at WT penned Texas history books geared to high school students.

43. Mody C. Boatright, "Alma Mater the Immortal: An Allegorical Representation of the History and Growth of West Texas State Normal College" (1920).

44. Hattie Anderson, "The Plains Historical Society," *Missouri Valley Historical Review* (1923).

45. Anderson to W. R. Bledsoe, April 18, 1923, quoted in Duane F. Guy, "The Panhandle-Plains Historical Society: The Formative Years, 1921–1940," *PPHR* (1996): 5–6.

46. J. Evetts Haley's legendary efforts to get Goodnight to talk are wonderfully recounted in B. Byron Price, *Crafting a Southwestern Masterpiece: J. Evetts Haley and Charles Goodnight: Cowman and Plainsman* (Nita Stuart Haley Memorial Library, 1986). See also J. Evetts Haley, "Charles Goodnight—Pioneer," *PPHR* (1930).

47. His first major trip produced thirty interviews and filled his tricked-out Model A with paraphernalia. Among the highlights were a leg of a billiard table from a long-abandoned saloon, the remains of a two-headed calf, the skull of an "Indian," and a collection of arrows supposedly taken from the last Indian killed on the Panhandle. For examples of his work with the PPHS, see Haley to Hattie Anderson, November 1, 1925, and February 24, 1927, File 7, Box 1, Hattie M. Anderson Collection, PPHM.

48. For more on those early days, see Horace M. Russell, "Some Leaves from the Minute Book," *PPHR* (1930): 115–124; and Guy, "Panhandle-Plains Historical Society."

49. After graduating from West Texas State, Boatright went on to receive MA and PhD degrees from the University of Texas. He was one of Texas's two greatest folklorists, the other being J. Frank Dobie. His first major critique of the misinterpretation of frontier life came in 1941 with his essay "The Myth of Frontier Individualism," which appeared in the *Southwestern Social Science Quarterly* that June.

50. "Life Memberships 1928–1946," PPHS Papers, PPHM; Sheffy, *Life and Times of Timothy Dwight Hobart*, 286.

51. PPHS charter, quoted in Guy, "Panhandle-Plains Historical Society," 5.

52. Walter Prescott Webb tested out in its pages some of the more interesting ideas that would appear in his magisterial *The Great Plains* (1931). And Angie Debo wrote some of her first excellent Native American history for the journal. There were also solid contributions from many of the best historians of the region, including William C. Holden, J. Evetts Haley, Rupert N. Richardson, and Carl Coke Rister.

53. Webb, *Great Plains*, 507.

54. Quoted in Guy, "Panhandle-Plains Historical Society," 12.

55. Museum Plans, PPHS Papers, PPHM; L. F. Sheffy, "The Museum Building," *PPHR* (1933): 8–9; Guy, "The Panhandle-Plains Historical Society," 16–17.

56. Sheffy, "The Museum Building"; Guy, "Panhandle-Plains Historical Society," 16–17.

57. *CN*, October 27, 1932; April 16, September 21, and November 10, 1933; Sheffy, "The Museum Building," 8–11; Guy, "Panhandle-Plains Historical Society," 16–17.

58. Quoted in Sheffy, *Life and Times of Timothy Dwight Hobart*, 285.

5. Booster Politics Ascendant

1. Quoted in James D. Ivy, *No Saloon in the Valley: The Southern Strategy of Texas Prohibitionists in the 1880s* (Baylor University Press, 2003), 56.

2. Henry Sanborn, who ran the Frying Pan, was the biggest instigator and beneficiary of the move. The stories of the early days are captured well in Willie Newbury Lewis, *Between Sun and Sod: An Informal History of the Texas Panhandle* (1938; reprint, Texas A&M University Press, 1976), 133–135. The original site of the city is still prone to flooding during heavy rains.

3. Mary Turner quoted in David G. McComb, *The City in Texas: A History* (University of Texas Press, 2015), 135.

4. Marty Kuhlman, "The Wild Side of Amarillo," Caprock Chronicles, *AGN*, December 21, 2018.

5. "The Panhandle Country and Its Metropolis," *Texas Magazine* (July 1910): 53.

6. *AAS*, October 6, 1906; *Amarillo Twice-a-Week Herald*, October 9, 1906.

7. Kirkes's sermon was reprinted in full in local newspapers. See, for example, *Amarillo Daily Panhandle*, October 20, 1906.

8. It also tried to ban saloons in 1845, but that law went nowhere.

9. Joseph L. Locke, *Making the Bible Belt: Texas Prohibitionists and the Politicization of Southern Religion* (Oxford University Press, 2017). For Texas religion and politics during this period, the place to start is Robert Wuthnow, *Rough Country: How Texas Became America's Most Powerful Bible-Belt State* (Princeton University Press, 2014), 51–153. Historian George Norris Green once quipped that the easiest way to sum up Texas politics was that it was "cotton and religion until the Civil War, cattle and religion until the end of the century, and by oil and religion since then." *The Establishment in Texas Politics: The Primitive Years, 1938–1957* (Greenwood Press, 1979), 24.

10. Dillard-Powell Land Company (Lubbock), "Buy Texas Land," Land Promotionals Collection, SWC.

11. Texas Land and Development Company, "60,000 Acres of Irrigated Farms."

12. *Amarillo Weekly Herald*, June 6, 1907.

13. *Amarillo Weekly Herald*, June 13, 1907. Ellsworth's attorneys managed to get him a retrial in Donley County, which he lost. He lost his final appeal in 1908. Burk spent two and a half years in the Amarillo jail, and charges against him were dropped in 1909.

14. Lewis L. Gould, *Progressives and Prohibitionists: Texas Democrats in the Wilson Era* (University of Texas Press, 1973), 54–55.

15. The upas tree was said to let off fumes so poisonous that no man could touch its trunk before dying. Quote from Joseph Locke, "Conquering Salem: The Triumph of the Christian Vision in Turn-of-the-Twentieth-Century Texas," *SWHQ* (2012), 255.

16. And was, as a personal note, still dry when I arrived on campus in fall 1981.

17. *Amarillo Daily Panhandle*, October 20, 1906.

18. *Amarillo Herald*, August 15, 1907.

19. Haley and Holden, *Flamboyant Judge*, 202–203.

20. The mayor's proclamation read in part: "I denounce that part of the Ranger service in Amarillo that has been so prominent for the past few months where insults have been given to the aged, helpless and to women, where abuse has been promiscuous and profuse, residences and business houses broken open, doors kicked open, without the proper warrants . . . slapping law-abiding citizens, or any other class of citizens at their own will and desire, striking men over the head with six-shooters and with other dangerous weapons, causing bloodshed and bodily injury and suffering; arresting men and incarcerating them in jail without complaint and warrant, arresting, assessing and collecting fines without a court present, to receive the plea of guilty or hear and determine the defense, refusing to answer questions before a grand jury of this count when accused of committing violence upon citizens." Reprinted in *Houston Post*, October 31, 1909.

21. *Randall County News*, January 8, 1909; *Texas Criminal Reports*, volume 59, 316–333; Robert M. Utley, *Lone Star Justice: The First Century of the Texas Rangers* (Oxford University Press, 2002), 283–294.

22. *Texas Almanac*, 1982, 2015, 2021. For a recent list of dry communities in Texas, see "Dry Counties in Texas: Still a Thing," Texas Law Changes, accessed March 13, 2025, https://texaslawchanges.com/dry-counties-in-texas/.

23. See, especially, Jessica Brannon-Wranosky, "Southern Promise and Necessity: Texas Regional Identity and the National Woman Suffrage Movement, 1868–1920," PhD diss., University of North Texas, 2010.

24. *Official Register and Directory of Women's Clubs in America* (1913).

25. "Committee Minority Report against Woman Suffrage," Journal of the Reconstruction Convention, December 7, 1868, reprinted in *Citizens at Last: The Woman Suffrage Movement in Texas*, ed. Ellen C. Temple, Ruthe Wincgartcn, and Judith N. McArthur (Texas A&M University Press, 2015), 137.

26. Elizabeth A. Taylor, "The Woman Suffrage Movement in Texas," *JSH* (1951); Stella L. Christian, *The History of the Texas Federation of Women's Clubs* (1919; reprint, 2019); Elna C. Green, *Southern Strategies: Southern Women and the Woman Suffrage Question* (University of North Carolina Press, 2000).

27. Most biographical sketches of Warner mistakenly refer to the institution as Illinois Woman's University. The Female College was a different place; it was founded as a Methodist school for girls in 1846 and went through several name changes. Its last iteration was MacMurray College, a coeducational institution that closed in 2020.

28. Quote from profile in *FWST*, February 6, 1921. A collection of Warner's editorials was published in 1964 by the Naylor Company under the title *Selected Editorials*.

29. Cunningham was a brilliant strategist, persuasive lobbyist, and able organizer who built up the Texas Equal Suffrage Association (of which Warner was a member) into a political force 10,000 members strong and organized in each of Texas's thirty-one state senatorial districts. Judith N. McArthur and Harold L. Smith, *Minnie Fisher Cunningham: A Suffragist's Life in Politics* (Oxford University Press, 2003).

30. Although the concept of municipal housekeeping had been a motivation for woman suffrage since the 1880s, the idea emerged as a powerful force in the growing Progressive movement of the first couple of decades of the twentieth century. As Mildred Chadsey explained in her influential article on the subject: "Housekeeping is the art of making the home clean, healthy, comfortable and attractive. Municipal housekeeping is the science of making the city clean, healthy, comfortable and attractive." Chadsey, "Municipal Housekeeping," *Journal of Home Economics* (February 1915). See also Jane Addams's 1910 broadside *Women and Public Housekeeping*. Addams had been using the term since at least 1906.

31. *FWST*, January 2 and February 8, 1917.

32. Warner, "A Few Big Things," 1918 editorial reprinted in Warner, *Selected Editorials*, 88.

33.

Equal suffrage, we beg for thee
May we hide our wrongs in thee.
May the ballot men have stole
From their soiled hands be removed;
If polluted, here's the cure;
Equal suffrage'll make it pure.
"Vote for women" is our cry;
We will scream it till we die.
When we pass this earthly pale,
We may go to heaven or—well,
Matters not our lot maybe—
Equal suffrage makes us free.
Poem of the West Texas State Normal College Equal Suffrage League, quoted in Marty Kuhlman, "Women's Suffrage in the Texas Panhandle, *PPHR* (2020), 13.

34. Marty Kuhlman, *DMN*, August 18, 2020.

35. Elna C. Green, "From Antisuffragism to Anti-Communism: The Conservative Career of Ida M. Darden," *JSH* (1999).

36. "Statement of the Texas Association opposed to Woman Suffrage," *Grosbeck (TX) Journal*, May 11, 1916.

37. For more on suffrage outside the cities in Texas, see Kevin C. Motl, "A Time for Reform: The Woman Suffrage Campaign in Rural Texas, 1914-1919," PhD diss., Texas A&M University, 2006.

38. Katherine Jellison, *Entitled to Power: Farm Women and Technology, 1913–1963* (University of North Carolina Press, 1993), xii. Jellison argues that women in established farm communities worked to retain their role as essential members of the farm economy.

39. Jane Jerome Camhi, *Women against Women: American Anti-suffragism, 1880-1920* (Carlson, 1994); Thomas J. Jablonsky, *The Home, Heaven, and Mother Party: Female Anti-suffragists in the United States, 1868-1920* (Carlson, 1994); Susan E. Marshall, *Splintered Sisterhood: Gender and Class in the Campaign against Woman Suffrage* (University of Wisconsin Press, 1997); Anne Myra Benjamin, *Women against Equality: A History of the Anti-suffrage Movement in the United States* (Edwin Mellen Press, 1991).

40. *FWST*, May 27, 1919.

41. The vote in the Texas House was 96–21 in favor.

42. It was also the second state in the West. Kansas—where boosters' support for suffrage (and prohibition) was also a major factor—was first by twelve days. Beverly Beeton, *Women Vote in the West: The Woman Suffrage Movement, 1869–1896* (Garland, 1986).

43. *Quanah (TX) Tribune-Chief*, July 4, 1918.

44. There's no shortage of books on Hoover. I found the following most helpful: Glen Jeansonne, *Herbert Hoover: A Life* (New American Library, 2016); Joan Hoff, *Herbert Hoover: Forgotten Progressive* (Little, Brown, 1975); Kenneth Whyte, *Hoover: An Extraordinary Life in Extraordinary Times* (Alfred A. Knopf, 2017).

45. Jeansonne, *Herbert Hoover*, 113.

46. *FWST*, July 9, 1917.

47. Ellis Hawley, "Herbert Hoover, the Commerce Secretariat, and the Vision of an 'Associative State,' 1921–1928," *JAH* (1974): 117.

48. Herbert Hoover, *American Individualism* (Doubleday, Page and Company, 1922), 8–9.

49. Hoover, *American Individualism*, 9–10 (italics in original).

50. Mody C. Boatright, in "The Myth of Frontier Individualism," went so far as to describe the myth as the "Turner-Hoover interpretation of frontier democracy." *SWSSQ* (1941).

51. Hoover, *American Individualism*, 63–64.

52. *CN*, August 30, 1928.

53. Quoted in Whyte, *Herbert Hoover*, 329.

54. Lorraine Gates Schuyler, *The Weight of Their Votes: Southern Women and Political Leverage in the 1920s* (University of North Carolina Press, 2006), 193.

55. *ARN*, October 28, 1928.

56. Annette Dunlap, *A Woman of Adventure: The Life and Times of First Lady Lou Henry Hoover* (University of Nebraska Press, 2022). See also Allene Sumner's adoring profile of Lou Hoover in the *El Paso Evening Post*, May 24, 1928, or that in *CN*, November 8, 1928.

57. James M. Cannon Jr., "Al Smith—Catholic, Tammany, Wet," *The Nation*, July 4, 1928.

58. Quoted in Brown, *Hood, Bonnet, and Little Brown Jug*, 400.

59. Salkeld made his remarks in Lubbock at the request of the local Hoover club. *LAJ*, October 27, 1928.

60. *Baptist Standard*, February 28, 1928; *LAJ*, September 25, 1928.

61. For a thorough summary of these arguments, see Wade Shaffer and Reed Welch, "The Texas Panhandle Press and the Presidential Election of 1928," *PPHR* (2023).

62. *AGT*, November 7, 1928.

BOOK TWO. THE RIGHT-WING FRONTIER

6. Ruin

1. Price quoted in Vance Johnson, *Heaven's Tableland: The Dust Bowl Story* (Farrar, Strauss, 1947), xx.

2. "Super-Farm Runs Day and Night," *Popular Mechanics* (October 1930): 555–557; "Holds That Farmer Can Make Profit on Fifty Cent Wheat," *Chicago Tribune*, August 31, 1931; *AAS*, December 27, 1930.

3. "Mechanization of Agriculture as a Factor in Labor Displacement," *Monthly Labor Review* (October 1931). Figures from Garry L. Nall, "Specialization and Expansion: Panhandle Farming in the 1920s," *PPHR* (1974).

4. Donald Worster, *Dust Bowl: The Southern Plains in the 1930s* (Oxford University Press, 1979), 96–97.

5. Mary W. M. Hargreaves is the best scholar on the subject. See her "Dry Farming Alias Scientific Farming" (1948) and "The Dry-Farming Movement in Retrospect" (1977), both in *Agricultural History;* as well as her *Dry Farming in the Northern Great Plains: Years of Adjustment* (University of Kansas Press, 1993).

6. Margaret A. Bickers, *Red Water, Black Gold: The Canadian River in Western Texas, 1920–1999* (Texas State Historical Association, 2014), 47.

7. Mary W. M. Hargreaves, "Hardy Webster Campbell," *Agricultural History* (1958).

8. Farmers failed, however, to appreciate the symbiotic relationship between prairie grasses and the soil. Primarily calcareous, the soil was held together in flocculated particles, moist globules clustered like microscopic grapes. Perched atop a hard layer of caliche, the colloided soil worked in tandem with the deep-rooted grasses to hold and distribute moisture in every direction. Once the grasses had been turned, the soil aggregates (the globs) dried out in the sun, becoming dust particles a thousand times finer than a grain of beach sand. This was the dust that farmers used to cover their fields, a dust with the consistency of flour. Which, once the rain stopped, became more than a just a layer covering the soil. It was the soil.

9. Sarah M. Gregg, "From Breadbasket to Dust Bowl: Rural Credit, the World War I Plow-Up, and the Transformation of American Agriculture," *GPQ* (2015).

10. Many of these folks were part of a migratory community of farmers who roamed across the Southwest in these years. For descriptions, see Sheila Manes, "Pioneers and Survivors: Oklahoma's Landless Farmers," in *Oklahoma: New Views of the Forty-Sixth State*, ed. Anne Hodges Morgan and H. Wayne Morgan (University of Oklahoma Press, 1982); and Harry C. McDean, "The 'Okie' Migration as a Socio-economic Necessity in Oklahoma," *Red River Valley Historical Review* (1978).

11. Leslie Hewes, *The Suitcase Farming Frontier* (University of Nebraska Press, 1973).

12. *Taylor Daily Press*, June 9, 1931. The story of the harvest was national news. James C. Young, "Stricken Empire of Wheat," *NYT*, August 9, 1931.

13. Quoted in Garry L. Nall, "Dust Bowl Days," *PPHR* (1975): 44.

14. Marion Martin Nordeman, "Midland," in *Texas Cities in the Great Depression*, ed. Robert Crawford Cotner (Texas Memorial Museum, 1973), 92.

15. It was actually a series of droughts. The worst, in 1934, was named by NASA scientists as the worst North American drought of the past thousand years. Benjamin I. Cook, Richard Seager, and Jason E. Smerdon, "The Worst North American Drought Year of the Last Millennium," *Geophysical Research Letters* (October 2014): 7298–7305.

16. *AG*, April 21, 1936.

17. Amarillo had twenty-three dust storms in March 1936 alone. The following March the city suffered through twenty-five. Soil Conservation Service, "Dust Storm Report," 1938, Soil Conservation Service Records, Records of Regional Offices, National Archives and Records Administration, Record Group 114.10.6, Fort Worth. Much of the information about life during the Dust Bowl was culled from the dozens of oral history interviews conducted by students at West Texas State A&M and collected at the Panhandle Plains Historical Museum. It's a treasure trove.

18. *Dalhart Texan*, June 20, 1933.

19. This kind of word play ("sock" for "stock") was typical of Howe's schtick as Tack. Through 1929, as the market rose to unprecedented heights, Tack grew particularly fond of "sock brokers" and the "New York Sock Exchange." For more on Tack and Howe, see Jack Alexander, "Panhandle Puck," *Saturday Evening Post*, January 1, 1944.

20. Tactless Texan, *AG*, November 11, 1929. Other West Texas papers also pushed the comeuppance narrative for Wall Street gamblers. See *EPH*, October 3, 1929; *CN*, October 17 and 31, 1929; *Vernon Daily Record*, October 31, 1929. Arthur Brisbane, a national columnist for the Hearst paper chain, promoted it as loudly as anyone.

21. Frank Greene, "A Bright Dawn for 1930," *Nation's Business* (January 1930), 34; *AG* March 10, April 7, June 16, and August 15, 1930.

22. Of course, a modern and progressive Amarillo had a branch of the Community Chest, but it was small, understaffed, and barely funded.

23. Ernest O. Thompson to Robert La Follette, November 30, 1931, reprinted in 75 Cong. Rec. S3236 (February 2, 1931).

24. Louise Evans, "Live on 5.50 a Year," *AG*, November 16, 1932.

25. Nordeman, "Midland," 95–98.

26. R. Reynolds McKay, "Texas Mexican Repatriations during the Great Depression," PhD diss., University of Oklahoma, 1982, 39.

27. Donald W. Whisenhunt, *The Depression in Texas* (Kennikat Press, 1980) 149–150; and Whisenhunt, "The Texas Attitude toward Relief, 1929–1933," *PPHR* (1973).

28. Thompson was one of the founders of the national organization.

29. It's difficult to overestimate the power of the small city newspaper editor in the years before television. And Howe's influence was unmatched anywhere else in the country.

30. *AG*, January 6, 1931. A "tourist camp" was a primitive campground run for profit.

31. Howe quoted in David Nail, *One Short Sleep Past: A Profile of Amarillo in the 1930s* (Staked Plains Press, 1974), 50–51.

32. Nordeman, "Midland," 96, 98.

33. Timothy Egan, The *Worst Hard Time: The Untold Story of Those Who Survived the Great American Dust Bowl* (Mariner Books, 2005), 189–190.

34. John C. Lawson, *High Plains Yesterdays: From XIT Days through Drought and Depression* (Eakin Press, 1985), 240; Nail, *One Short Sleep Past*, 37–38, 46–47.

35. *AG*, November 16, 1932.

36. Midland Community Welfare Association quoted in Nordeman, "Midland," 96.

37. Nail, *One Short Sleep Past*, 37–38; Evans, "Live on 5.50 a Year"; *Pampa News-Post*, October 4, 1931.

38. This is a recurring theme in Egan, *The Worst Hard Time*.

39. Robert M. Sanford, interview with Christopher Sanford, April 15, 1977; Edith Steddum, interview with Dennis J. Hataway, March 22, 1990; Eleanor Hudspeth, interview with Diane Skelton, May 1, 1973; Ethel Faust, interview with Regina Hillier, November 17, 1976; Gordon Ruthardt, interview with Darren G. Ruthardt, April 18, 1990, all in PPHM; Ruby Winona Adams, "Social Behavior in a Drought-Stricken Texas Panhandle Community," MA thesis, University of Texas, 1939. Quote from Grace Vera Raymond Evans, interview with Sharon Diana Evans, October 31, 1981, PPHM.

40. The stories appeared across the nation in mid-April 1935. See, for example, *PN*, April 15, 1935.

41. *AG*, February 27, 1935.

42. "Tack" hit the Vitamin K routine especially hard after bad dust storms. For more on those days when s he was "particularly charged" up, thanks to its wonderful properties, see *AG*, March 27, 1935, March 3, 1936, February 16, 1937, and March 6, 1935.

43. McCarty, "A Tribute to Our Sandstorms," *Dalhart Texan*, February 22, 1935; draft, Last Man's Club File, John L. McCarty Papers, Amarillo Public Library. See also McCarty, "Grab a Root and Growl," *Dalhart Texan*, April 11, 1935.

44. Henry Ansley, *I Like the Depression* (Bobbs-Merrill, 1932). See also the condensed version of the book that appeared in the April 1932 issue of *West Texas Today*, the official publication of the West Texas Chamber of Commerce. Ansley did not have the chance to enjoy his newfound fame; he was killed in an automobile accident just a few weeks after his book was published.

45. This turn to religion countered national trends toward greater secularism and a struggle among churches to maintain finances and membership. Martin E. Marty, *Modern American Religion*, vol. 2 (University of Chicago Press, 1997), 250–257.

46. Brad Lookingbill, "A God-Forsaken Place: Folk Eschatology and the Dust Bowl," *GPQ*, (Fall 1994), 275–278; Charles E. Ritchie, interview with Kathryn Ritchie, April 22, 1933, transcript; Seth Coyett McFather, interview with Bobbye Hobdy, June 26, 1991, transcript, both PPHM.

47. *OA*, November 4, 1932.

48. David Hamilton, "War on a Thousand Fronts: Herbert Hoover and the Great Depression," in *Uncommon Americans: The Lives and Legacies of Herbert and Lou Hoover*, ed. Timothy Walch (Praeger, 2003).

49. John L. McCarty, interview with Don Green, July 26, 1968, SWC.

50. *AMN*, September 15 and 17, 1932; *NYT*, September 15, 1932. Not every listener was impressed; the reporter from the *Iola (KS) Register* challenged its readers to comb through the speech for any evidence of the governor's "plan for farm relief." Historian Martin Fausold called the speech "superficial" and "merrily flexible." Fausold, "President Hoover's Farm Policies, 1929–1933," *AH* (1977): 374.

51. Adding that FDR, once in office, "just threw it overboard." J. Evetts Haley, interview with Bill Modisett, June 2, 1989, Sub Series J, Interviews, Series IV, Literary Productions, J. Evetts Haley Collection, Haley Memorial Library, Midland, Texas.

52. Roosevelt was not apparently a particularly attentive student in those years, however. Enrolled in Turner's American history class in 1900, when the historian was at Harvard, Roosevelt skipped the first six weeks of lectures. Karl Helicher, "The Education of Franklin D. Roosevelt," *Presidential Studies Quarterly* (1982): 50–53.

53. Franklin Delano Roosevelt, Commonwealth Club Address, September 23, 1932, reprinted in *American Political Rhetoric: Essential Speeches and Writings*, 7th ed., ed. Peter Augustine Lawler and Robert Martin Schaefer (Rowman and Littlefield, 2016), 181–182.

54. Will Rogers quipped that the speech was so good, even the bankers understood it.

55. Nail, *One Short Sleep Past*, 70; "More than $800,000 Flows into Lubbock Banks," *LA*, March 16, 1933; "Bank Deposits Here Gain Half Million," *AMN*, March 16, 1933; "Bank Reopens; Cash Flows," *PDN*, March 16, 1932; "Crosbyton Bank Deposits Increase," *LAJ*, March 19, 1933.

56. Robert F. Colwell, "San Angelo, 1933–1936: Drought, Flood, Depression," in *Texas Cities in the Great Depression*, 178.

57. *CN*, August 3 and 10, 1933, January 18, 1934, December 19, 1935.

58. *AMN*, June 27, 1933; Nail, *One Short Sleep Past*, 84–92, 128–134. Amarillo High School won 140 football games in the 1930s with only five losses and one tie. The team won the state championship in 1934, 1935, 1936, and 1940. See also Frances Powell, interview by Laurie Groman, July 24, 1987, transcript, PPHM.

59. *AG*, February 9 and 26, 1936. These statistics come from dozens of different documents contained in the Works Progress Administration Collection at PPHM. I would like to thank accountant extraordinaire Cathy Roche for her help in compiling these figures from WPA expenditure reports from individual counties.

60. "Surplus Commodities Distributed, 1939," WPA Collection, PPHM.

61. Whisenhunt, "Texas Attitude toward Relief," 95, 98 (Blanton quote).

62. Haley, "Cow Business and Monkey Business," *Saturday Evening Post*, December 8, 1934. More on this article later.

63. Considering the economy of Wheeler County, this was purely an academic exercise, for there was no private sector work. It was so bad that the county suffered one of the greatest population losses in West Texas, 20 percent over the decade. Adams, "Social Behavior."

64. Quoted in Adams, "Social Behavior," 62, 64, 66, 79.

65. The southern half of West Texas (then the 16th Congressional District) was represented in the 1930s by R. Ewing Thomason, a capable and well-connected attorney and former mayor of El Paso.

66. From 1918 to 1932, the district included the fifty-three counties of the Panhandle and southern plains. It stretched from Haskell County to Dallas County and from Lipscomb to Gaines.

67. In his first few terms as representative, Stephens's district included most of the western half of Texas.

68. See *Wise County Messenger*, January 14, 1916, August 11, 1916; *Houston Post*, August 8, 1916; *AAS*, July 7, 1916; Marvin Jones, with Joseph Ray, *Memoirs* (Texas Western Press, 1973).

69. Much debt was the result of heavy borrowing to expand production during World War I. When prices dropped off after the war, farmers were stuck with loans. Gregg, "From Breadbasket to Dust Bowl."

70. 55 Cong. Rec. 5751 (Jones speech, August 3, 1917).

71. Irvin May, "Marvin Jones: Agrarian and Politician," *AH* (1977): 423. See also May's book-length treatment, *Marvin Jones: The Public Life of an Agrarian Advocate* (Texas A&M University Press, 1980).

72. David E. Hamilton, "Building the Associative State: The Department of Agriculture and American State-Building," *AH* (1990): 207–218. Although he despised Herbert Hoover, Jones's approach mirrored many of Hoover's basic ideas.

73. Texas senator Tom Connally also supported this idea. Jones, *Memoirs*, 77–78.

74. Theodore Rosenof points out that expanding exports was an idea favored by many of those who desired to raise purchasing power but were still wedded to a producerist philosophy. Rosenof, *Dogma, Depression, and the New Deal: The Debate of Political Leaders*

over Economic Recovery (Kennikat Press, 1975), 43–47 (quote from 153). Jones finally got a chance to try out his plan when he slipped an amendment into a must-pass bill to amend the AAA that guaranteed 30 percent of tariff receipts be used to distribute surplus farm goods. It became the basis of the school lunch program. May, "Marvin Jones," 431–432; Jones, *Memoirs*, 112–114.

75. 79 Cong. Rec. 14785.

76. 77 Cong. Rec. 674.

77. Keith J. Volanto, "Burying White Gold: The AAA Cotton Plow-Up Campaign in Texas," *SWHQ* (January 2000); Volanto, *Texas, Cotton, and the New Deal* (Texas A&M University Press, 2005).

78. *CN*, May 30, 1935.

79. *PDN*, September 24, 1933.

80. *CN*, December 28, 1933. Randall County farmers received almost $200,000 that month.

81. Nall, "Dust Bowl Days," 42–49. The twenty-six counties of the Panhandle represented almost half that amount. *Texas Almanac* (1936), 251–252. See also R. Douglas Hurt, *The Dust Bowl: An Agricultural and Social History* (Nelson-Hall, 1981), 93–94.

82. For more on the criticism of the AAA from both the left and the right, see Rosenof, *Dogma, Depression, and the New Deal*, 62–71.

83. H. H. Finnell, "Prevention and Control of Wind Erosion of High Plains Soils in the Panhandle Area," the first paper ever produced by the USDA on wind erosion (Washington, DC: USDA, 1935). For more on the history of the SCS, see Douglas Helms, "Conserving the Plains: The Soil Conservation Service in the Great Plains," *AH* (Spring 1990).

7. New Deal Agonistes

1. *AG*, May 19, 1936. Ralph Bray resigned over the Resettlement Administration movie *The Plow That Broke the Plains* and accused Tugwell of using the film to "pry more money out of Congress and the White House to continue his Communistic experiments."

2. Region-wide between 1930 and 1970, the population of West Texas grew by just 3 percent. Just for comparison, in those same years the U.S. population increased by 65 percent and Texas's population doubled.

3. They were joined by thousands more migrants from places like eastern Oklahoma and Arkansas where the sharecropper economies had failed.

4. Tugwell laid out this argument in an essay just as the Resettlement Administration was launching. Rexford G. Tugwell, "No More Frontiers," *Today*, June 22, 1935. See also an earlier Tugwell essay, "The Problem of Agriculture," *PSQ* (December 1924).

5. Bernard Sternsher, *Rexford Tugwell and the New Deal* (Rutgers University Press, 1964).

6. In his review of the biggest movie of 1933, Noel Coward's *Cavalcade*, which won three Academy Awards, including Best Picture and Best Director, and which the *New York Times* called "affecting and impressive," and *Variety* described as a "big, brave and beautiful picture," Lorentz dismissed the film as a "superlative newsreel" and "very cheap theatrical observation from the choleric old empire-builder, Mr. Coward." *Vanity Fair*, March 1933, 48. In a testament to his indefatigable energy and the catholic nature of his reviews, in the same issue, he reviewed the "latest boo epic," *The Wax Museum*; Mae West's *She Done Him Wrong*, "good fun" and "surprisingly good"; *Hot Pepper*, "just a hundred percent wrong"; *State Fair*, directed by Henry King and starring Will Rogers ("good-humored"); the Irene Dunne vehicle *The Secret of Madame Blanche* ("the re-write of all the re-writes of *Madame X*"); and *Parachute Jumper* (a "wry attempt to turn Fairbanks Jr. into Fairbanks Sr."). He

also threw in some random comments on *The Vampire Bat, Hard to Handle, Hello Everybody* ("a movie in which Kate Smith sings"), *Tonight Is Ours,* and *42nd Street.*

7. Morris L. Ernst and Pare Lorentz, *Censored: The Private Life of the Movie* (Jonathan Cape, 1930), 13.

8. Hearst fired him when he wrote a complimentary story about Franklin Roosevelt's Secretary of Agriculture, Henry Wallace.

9. Pare Lorentz, *FDR's Moviemaker: Memoirs and Scripts* (University of Nevada Press, 1992), 17–36; Pare Lorentz, *The Roosevelt Year: A Photographic Record* (Funk and Wagnalls, 1934).

10. U.S. Senate Appropriations Committee, *Hearings on Department of Labor—Federal Security Agency Appropriations Bill, 1941,* 76th Cong., 248.

11. They were also not completely down with the idea of a movie about land; committed leftists, they wanted to focus on capitalism as the destructive force that brought farmers to ruin.

12. Daniel J. Leab, "Pare Lorentz and American Government Film Production," *Midcontinent American Studies Journal* (Spring 1965): 41–45; Robert L. Snyder, *Pare Lorentz and the Documentary Film* (University of Nebraska Press, 1994), 30–40.

13. Jason M. Hartz, "*The Plow That Broke the Plains*: An Application of Functional Americanism in Music," PhD diss., Ohio University, 2010.

14. The script is included in Lorentz, *FDR's Moviemaker,* 45–50. Jason Hartz included a transcript of the epilogue in his dissertation.

15. When he was putting his movie together, studio heads refused to allow Lorentz access to the stock footage he needed to finish, and he had to rely on his good friend the director King Vidor to sneak him the film he needed.

16. "Dust-Storm Film," *Literary Digest,* May 16, 1936.

17. *NYT,* May 24, 1936; *Boston Globe,* July 16, 1936.

18. Leab, "Pare Lorentz and American Government Film Production," 46.

19. John E. O'Connor, "Case Study: *The Plow That Broke the Plains,*" in *Image as Artifact: The Historical Analysis of Film and Television,* ed. John E. O'Connor (Robert E. Krieger, 1990), 286–288; Hartz, "Plow That Broke the Plains," 77–88, 191–202.

20. Apparently competing versions of the film were in distribution simultaneously over the next couple of years. The epilogue version was pulled from distribution sometime in 1937. Many speculate that because of its specificity in solutions, the epilogue was too easily read as "socialist." Removing *Plow's* overt "political" message, the reasoning went, strengthened its cultural and historical importance.

21. *AG,* May 28, 21, 1936.

22. *AGN,* May 31, June 1 and 2, 1936.

23. *AGN,* June 5, 1936.

24. Joe Jacobson, Letters to Tack, *AG,* June 3, 1936.

25. Quoted in Egan, *The Worst Hard Time,* 261. In another article, reprinted in several newspapers across the nation, McCarty pointed to recent rains and predicted (incorrectly) that "bumper crops and prosperity are bound to follow the bountiful rain . . . corn and small grain production may be so great as to upset the market places of the world." *AGN,* June 1, 1936.

26. *PDN,* May 31, 1936.

27. *NYT,* June 10, 1936; *Wellington (TX) Leader,* June 25, 1936.

28. See *AGN,* May 19, 1936. The letter was reprinted across Texas. See, for example, *Rio Grande Farmer* (Harlingen), May 22, 1936; *PDN,* May 19, 1936; *LA,* May 19, 1936.

29. Anticommunism as an essential part of criticisms of government programming,

which emerged with greater clarity in the 1950s, showed up often in critiques of *The Plow That Broke the Plains.* When it played in New York City as part of a series of documentaries from around the world, local wags wryly commented that it was no coincidence that the film shared the marquee with two Soviet films. *AG*, May 26, 1936; Hurt, *Dust Bowl*, 62–63.

30. Mayme Carol Ludeman, "The Land Phase of the Colonization of the Spade Ranch," MA thesis, Texas Tech University, 1938.

31. Russell Lord and Paul H. Johnstone, eds., *A Place on Earth: A Critical Appraisal of Subsistence Homesteads* (U.S. Department of Agriculture, 1942); Paul K. Conkin, "The Subsistence Homesteads Program," in *Tomorrow a New World: The New Deal Community Program* (Cornell University Press, 1959); David B. Danbom, "Romantic Agrarianism in Twentieth-Century America," *AH* (1991).

32. William Clayson, "The Lubbock Chamber of Commerce, the New Deal, and the Ropesville Resettlement Project," *GPQ* (Winter 1998), quote on 5.

33. USDA, Census of Agriculture, 1935, vol. 1, no. 37, Texas, 751.

34. Rural sociologist Paul Jehlnik summarized the plan for Ropesville in a report prepared by the Bureau of Agricultural Economics (BAE) of the USDA in 1941: "The project is admittedly an experiment. The people, coming from diverse areas, had little in common except the common feeling which may have grown out of their former individual experiences in the disheartening struggle against the overwhelming forces of drought and depression. Many of them were most familiar with the simple cash-crop system. In their new environment they must learn a new system if they are to make a living. To inaugurate the diversified system requires considerable capital resources, which they do not have. The Farm Security Administration [which replaced the RA] is loaning them the needed capital, giving them technical guidance, and supplementing incomes with grants." Paul J. Jehlnik, "Level of Living on the Ropesville Project," USDA BAE (1941), 2.

35. Quoted in William R. Johnson, "Rural Rehabilitation in the New Deal: The Ropesville Project," *SWHQ* (1976), 284.

36. Marion Clawson, "Resettlement Experience on Nine Selected Resettlement Projects," *AH* (January 1978): 39–44. For images of the homes, see the Winston Reeves Photograph Collection, SWC.

37. Johnson, "Rural Rehabilitation," 286.

38. Jehlnik, "Level of Living on the Ropesville Project," 3.

39. Quoted in Clayson, "Lubbock Chamber of Commerce," 16.

40. Clayson, "Lubbock Chamber of Commerce," 15, 16.

41. Rexford G. Tugwell, "The Resettlement Idea," *AH* (Fall 1959): 162. See also Brian Q. Cannon, *Remaking the Agrarian Dream: New Deal Rural Resettlement in the Mountain West* (University of New Mexico Press, 1996).

42. Sponsored by Marvin Jones and Senator John Bankhead from Alabama, the Bankhead-Jones Farm Tenant Act of 1937 provided low-cost, long-term, and flexible loans to sharecroppers and tenants to purchase land or machinery and offered special incentives to adapt worn-out farms for new uses.

43. Jehlnik, "Level of Living on the Ropesville Project," 7.

44. *AGT*, August 17, 1936.

45. Great Plains Drought Area Committee, "Report" (August 1936), 2–3.

46. The study, led by C. Warren Thornthwaite, of the economy and population of the Great Plains was part of a larger two-year project by the University of Pennsylvania's Wharton School (with a grant from the Rockefeller Foundation), to investigate possible relationships between poverty and population distribution. Basing his conclusions on

long-term studies of climate and twenty years of economic data, Thornthwaite suggested that wheat farming was a losing bet. "The farmers who are hoping to get rich by raising wheat in the Great Plains are unable or unwilling to consider realistically, the odds against them." At best, the report concluded, the region could support a population of 1.3 million people, and 59,000 people should be resettled outside the region as a necessary first step. C. W. Thornthwaite, "The Great Plains," in *Migration and Economic Opportunity* (University of Pennsylvania, 1936).

47. *AG*, August 17, 1936. It should be said that in 1936 Soil Conservation Service efforts in the Panhandle were yielding promising results. See Garry L. Nall, "The Struggle to Save the Land: The Soil Conservation Effort in the Dust Bowl," in *The Depression in the Southwest*, ed. Donald W. Whisenhunt (Kennikat Press, 1980).

48. *AG*, August 17, 1936.

49. *AG*, August 17, 1936.

50. *AG*, August 18, 1936.

51. The committee was impressed with the historical land policy of Texas, where the state, as we have seen, responded to the different environmental conditions on its western lands by creating homesteads sixteen times larger than those offered by the federal government.

52. Report of the Great Plains Drought Area Committee, August 1936, (Washington, DC, 1936).

53. *The Future of the Great Plains*: Report of the Great Plains Committee (Washington, DC: Government Printing Office, 1936), 5–6.

54. *Future of the Great Plains*, 6.

55. *Future of the Great Plains*, 66–67.

56. An outline near the end of the document lists the fifty-six separate departments and agencies that "exercise functions of varying importance in relation to the readjustment of the economy of the Great Plains Region." And this list didn't even include the "state county, and municipal and numerous types of districts (conservation irrigation, grazing, etc.) which will have been or will be formed under the provisions of state laws." Great Plains Drought Area Committee, *Future of the Great Plains*, 87.

57. The coalition continued to hammer on the RA's successor, the Farm Security Administration, until they drove it out of existence in 1944.

58. *LAJ*, November 19, 1936.

8. The Origins of the Texas Right

1. After just five years, he sold his short line, built mostly to serve the East Texas lumber industry, to the Santa Fe Railroad for an enormous profit.

2. It was such an innovative enterprise, the KLC-HOC became the subject of its own business monograph, John O. King's *The Early History of the Houston Oil Company of Texas, 1901–1908* (Texas Gulf Coast Historical Association, 1959).

3. Kirby is often miscredited as a former president of the National Association of Manufacturers (NAM). But it was another John Kirby, president of the Dayton Manufacturing Company (and ally of C. W. Post), that served as NAM's president from 1909 to 1912.

4. George Creel, "The Feudal Towns of Texas," *Harper's*, January 23, 1915, 76–77. Most of what's been written about Kirby has been in conjunction with his antilabor activities. Good examples include George T. Morgan Jr., "No Compromise—No Recognition: John Henry Kirby, the Southern Lumber Operators' Association, and Unionism in the Piney Woods, 1906–1916," *Labor History* (Spring 1969); and George T. Morgan Jr., "The Gospel of Wealth Goes South: John Henry Kirby and Labor's Struggle for Self-Determination,

1901–1916," *SWHQ* (October 1971). A more business-forward treatment can be found in Robert L. Bradley Jr., "The Prince of Bankruptcy: John Henry Kirby," in *Edison to Enron: Energy Markets and Political Strategies* (John Wiley and Sons, 2011), 373–400.

5. For Kirby, the company stores became important profit centers. Thanks to his bulk purchases and efficient transportation and distribution networks, his wholesale prices were usually much lower than at other stores, but he still charged employees a premium greater than average local retail prices.

6. *The Rebel* (Hallettsville, TX), February 17, 1912.

7. Creel, "Feudal of Towns of Texas," 76. This was the same George Creel who, a decade earlier, had worked on the marketing team of C. W. Post's CIAA and its *Square Deal*.

8. *Fort Worth Record*, August 27, 1907; Kevin C. Motl, "Under the Influence: The Texas Business Men's Association and the Campaign against Reform, 1906–1915," *SWHQ* (2006).

9. Quoted in Bradley, *Edison to Enron*, 376.

10. The only evidence of typical booster activity in the TBMA was the Five Million Club, a Kirby-led effort to increase Texas's population to 5 million people by 1910, a number that would not be reached until the mid-1920s.

11. Gould, *Progressives and Prohibitionists*, 24–25.

12. Arnold's most successful campaign was his alliance with the Texas Farmers' Union, in which he and his team cranked out pro-business, antiprohibition, and antisuffrage articles and bribed Farmers' Union officials to submit them under their own names to farmer-friendly newspapers across the state. Most of the money came from brewers like Anheuser-Busch. Christopher Loomis, "The Politics of Uncertainty: Lobbyists and Propaganda in Early-Twentieth-Century America" *Journal of Policy History* (2009): 190–191. See also the exposé of the TBMA's antisuffrage efforts in "Brewing Propaganda," *New Republic*, August 21, 1915, 62–64; and Arnold's testimony in *Brewing and Liquor Interests and German and Bolshevik Propaganda: Hearings Before a Subcommittee of the Senate Committee on the Judiciary*, 65th Cong., 2:2524-2611 (1919).

13. Southern farmers, particularly cotton growers, were net exporters and (correctly) feared that a tariff on agricultural goods might close off markets.

14. "He [Arnold] has had no training or experience either," Caraway added, "as an economist, a statistician, or a tax expert that would fit him to be of service in any capacity in connection to revenue legislation. He is on terms of intimacy with no Member of Congress so far as your committee has been able to learn. He has contributed nothing toward the preparation of briefs to be presented to committees of either House, nor has he been a witness before any such, yet he gets the money." 72 Cong. Rec., Supplemental Report on J. A. Arnold, Caraway Committee, 993–996 (quote on 994).

15. For more on Muse, see Vance Muse III, "Making Peace with Grandfather," *Texas Monthly* (February 1986); and Michael Pierce, "The Origins of Right-to-Work: Vance Muse, Anti-Semitism, and the Maintenance of Jim Crow Labor Relations," Labor and Working-Class History Association, January 12, 2017, https://lawcha.org/2017/01/12/origins-right-work-vance-muse-anti-semitism-maintenance-jim-crow-labor-relations/.

16. For more on the emergence of the "banker-merchant-farmer-lawyer-doctor governing class" see George Brown Tindall, *Emergence of the New South, 1913–1945* (Louisiana State University Press, 1967); and an earlier version of the idea in Jasper Berry Shannon, *Toward a New Politics in the South* (University of Tennessee Press, 1949).

17. Jared A. Goldstein, "The American Liberty League and the Rise of Constitutional Nationalism," *Temple Law Review* 86 (2014): 289.

18. *FWST*, September 22, 1935.

19. The SCUC received national press coverage—not all of it good—upon Kirby's announcement. See *Philadelphia Inquirer*, August 4, 1935; *Indianapolis News*, August 5, 1935; *Atlanta Constitution*, August 7, 1935.

20. *FWST*, August 4, 1935. Political reporter and columnist Albert L. Warner outlined Kirby's plan in an editorial in the *New York Herald-Tribune*, September 14, 1935.

21. *Hearings Before a Special Committee to Investigate Lobbying Activities, U.S. Senate*, part 4, 74th Cong., 2nd sess., 1995–2014 (March 2–6, 1936) (testimony of John Henry Kirby and Vance Muse). For more on general operating procedures, see ibid., 1985–1994. For the $40,000 figure, see Elna C. Green, "From Antisuffragism to Anticommunism: The Conservative Career of Ida Darden," *JSH* (May 1999): 303.

22. The best account of the popularity of the Long movement is in Alan Brinkley, *Voices of Protest: Huey Long, Father Coughlin, and the Great Depression* (Alfred A. Knopf, 1982). Also important is Glen Jeansonne, "Huey Long and Racism," *Louisiana History* (Summer 1992). The standard biography of Long remains T. Harry Williams, *Huey Long* (Alfred A. Knopf, 1970).

23. Both his father and grandfather were also Disciples of Christ ministers, mostly on the frontiers of the old Middle West, where they preached on Sunday and hustled a living on a farm or in town during the week. The best work on Smith is Glen Jeansonne, *Gerald L. K. Smith, Minister of Hate* (Yale University Press, 1988). Jeansonne also published several articles on Smith across a variety of scholarly fields.

24. Mencken quoted in Jeansonne, *Gerald L. K. Smith*, 2.

25. Jeansonne, *Gerald L. K. Smith*, 37.

26. Hodding Carter, "How Come Huey Long?" *New Republic*, February 13, 1935, 11.

27. Jason Morgan Ward, *Defending White Supremacy: The Making of a Segregationist Movement and the Remaking of Racial Politics, 1936–1965* (University of North Carolina Press, 2011), 10.

28. *AC*, January 19, 1936.

29. The son of a slaveowner and nephew of one of North Carolina's most powerful Klan leaders, Thomas Dixon Jr. built a literary career on racist books and plays that celebrated white supremacy and the Ku Klux Klan. Two of his first novels, *The Leopard's Spots* (1902) and *The Clansman* (1905), were the basis of D. W. Griffith's *Birth of a Nation* (1915), a pro-Klan film that is credited with the revival of the Hooded Empire in the 1910s. Obsessed with Roosevelt and communism, Dixon published his last novel in 1939. He thought of it as an alternative history of the nation since 1900 whose third act described a race war–revolution instigated by W. E. B. Du Bois that ended with the formation of a white guerilla army out to overthrow the Soviet Republic of the United States.

30. William Anderson, *The Wild Man from Sugar Creek: The Political Career of Eugene Talmadge* (Louisiana State University Press, 1975), 137–138; *AC*, January 19 and 30, 1936.

31. *AC*, January 30, 1936.

32. *Kingsville (TX) Record*, November 6, 1935.

33. When the head of the Election Managers Association of Texas, a militant Democrat from Houston, was asked why he was against African Americans attending the 1936 Democratic Convention, he replied: "Science of today teaches us that the white race cannot absorb the black race; there are two bloods, the blood of the white man and the blood of the black man, and that they will not mingle to the betterment of either, and that the efforts of designing politicians such as now inhabit the White House and probably some of our Legislative Halls, are but futile attempts to defy the will of God in their scheme of social equality." *Quanah (TX) Tribune-Chief*, November 15, 1935.

34. The story was national news. See *NYT*, April 16, 1936; Bryan Burrough, *The Big*

Rich: The Rise and Fall of the Greatest Texas Oil Fortunes (Penguin, 2010), 142–145; Ward, *Defending White Supremacy*, 12–13.

35. The short list of scholars who have recognized the importance of the JDT would include John S. Huntington, "'The Voice of Many Hatreds': J. Evetts Haley and Texas Ultraconservatism," *WHQ* (December 2017); and a couple of fine MA theses, M. Scott Sosebee, "The Split in the Texas Democratic Party, 1936–1956," Texas Tech University, 2000; and Stacey Sprague, "James Evetts Haley and the New Deal: Laying the Foundations for the Modern Republican Party in Texas," University of North Texas, 2004.

36. In this interpretation, Haley lined up with the more popular versions of the frontier myth that dominated Western films and novels.

37. Charles Collins quoted in Worster, *Dust Bowl*, 113.

38. For Haley, the entire concept of the government giving away money for killing animals or plowing under crops was an obvious "false economy" and a sin. See J. Evetts Haley, interview with Bill Modisett, June 13, 1989, Series IV, Subseries J, Literary Productions; and J. Evetts Haley and John McCarty, "Dust Bowl Album and Diary," Photo Collection, both in the Haley Library.

39. The banking lobby much favored the program; many small stockmen's banks believed it was the only way they would see any of the money owed by ranchers. See C. Roger Lambert's essays on the subject, "The Drought Cattle Purchase, 1934–1935: Problems and Complaints," *AH* (1971); and "Texas Cattlemen and the AAA, 1933–1935," *Arizona and the West* (1972).

40. "And, behold, there came up out of the river seven kine, fatfleshed and well favoured; and they fed in a meadow: And, behold, seven other kine came up after them, poor and very ill favoured and leanfleshed, such as I never saw in all the land of Egypt for badness: And the lean and the ill favoured kine did eat up the first seven fat kine." Genesis, 41:2–4.

41. Lambert, "Texas Cattlemen and the AAA," 142.

42. The *Saturday Evening Post* had a well-deserved reputation by then as an anti–New Deal publication. Richard Hofstadter called it "an unimpeachable source of anti-intellectualism" where one could find anti–New Deal writing on almost every page. Hofstadter, *Anti-Intellectualism in American Life* (Vintage Books, 1963), 218.

43. Haley, "Cow Business and Monkey Business," *Saturday Evening Post*, December 8, 1934, 26, 94. See also the Haley interview by Modisett, in which he bitterly reflects on the cattle-killing program, and the Haley-McCarty Dust Bowl photograph collection at the Haley Library. It includes several photos of the cattle dying on the Haley ranch outside Midland. A few months after Haley's piece appeared, journalist Alva Johnston would make similar claims, calling the cattle-killing program "propaganda to convince the cattleman that he should let Washington handle his affairs." Johnston, "The Hamburger Bonanza," *Saturday Evening Post*, May 4, 1935, 18–19, 99–104.

44. Haley, "Cow Business and Monkey Business," 26, 94. It wasn't just Haley; the cattle-killing program shook the worldviews of many West Texans for decades. The following interviews from the Oral History Collection at the Panhandle-Plains Historical Museum describe the psychic impact of the program: Gordon Ruthardt, interview by Darren G. Ruthardt, April 18, 1990; H. M. (Flip) Breedlove, interview by Garry Lynn Nall, March 16, 1972; Thurman Joel Richardson, interview by Gary Richardson, April 8, 1978; Wade Daugherty, interview by Paul Bell, November 15, 1985; Fritz Gerdtsen, interview by James Flugel, April 12, 1987; James William Witherspoon, interview by Tommy C. Reiter, June 30, 1991.

45. Haley, "Cow Business and Monkey Business."

46. Haley, "Casual Comments on Current Trends," pamphlet, Haley File, Clifford B. Jones Papers, 1814-1975 and undated, Southwest Collection/Special Collections Library,

Texas Tech University, hereafter cited as Haley File, Jones Papers, SWC. Sometime after my initial research into this collection, the Clifford B. Jones Papers were reprocessed with different box and file numbers.

47. Haley, "A New Deal in Culture," *San Antonio Express*, November 10, 1935.

48. Haley, "Cows in the Cotton Patch," *San Antonio Express*, October 13, 1935.

49. Haley, "Texas Control of Texas Soil," *West Texas Today* (July 1936).

50. The statement appeared in most of the state newspapers. See, for example, *DMN*, August 2, 1936.

51. He also accused government agencies of meeting in secret to "concoct" regulations that stood as law. The Liberty League reprinted Reed's address as a pamphlet (he was a member of its lawyer's group) titled "Shall We Have Constitutional Liberty or Dictatorship?" Address Before the Lawyers' Association of Kansas City, Pamphlet, American Liberty League Pamphlets 120, Jouette Shouse Collection, University of Kentucky Special Collections.

52. Edmunds, former editor in chief of the *St. Louis Chronicle* and an expert in international law, was also a delusionary when it came to the potential of federal power and the author of *The Federal Octopus: A Survey of the Destruction of Constitutional Government and of Civil and Economic Liberty in the United States and the Rise of an All-Embracing Federal Bureaucratic Despotism* (Michie Company, 1932).

53. "The Jeffersonian Party Platform," *Chicago Tribune*, August 9, 1936. Ostensibly a national organization, the Jeffersonian Democrats was little more than a shell outside Texas and, even there, most likely had no more than five thousand members. David Farber, *The Rise and Fall of Modern American Conservatism: A Short History* (Princeton University Press, 2010), 23. For Texas numbers, see Keith Volanto, "The Far Right in Texas Politics during the Roosevelt Era," in *The Texas Right: The Radical Roots of Lone Star Conservatism*, ed. David O'Donald Cullen and Kyle Grant Wilkison (Texas A&M University Press 2014), 74.

54. Jeffersonian Democrats, "The New Deal and the Negro Vote" and "Did Jim Farley Romanize the American Post Office System?" Box 4, Wallet 23, Sub-Series A, Jeffersonian Democrats, Series 3, Political Interests, Haley Papers.

55. The JDT amassed almost an entire archival box of mailing lists organized by county and cross-listed in various ways.

56. Haley quoted in *Corsicana (TX) Sun*, September 12, 1936.

57. Benedict's statement was widely reported. See, for example, *AAS*, September 13, 1936. Moreover, as Haley confessed to his friend J. Frank Dobie, he had "been looking for an excuse to leave the University." He was afraid that the liberal, pseudointellectual climate there might drive him to violence. Steven L. Davis, *J. Frank Dobie: A Liberated Mind* (University of Texas Press 2009), 120.

58. Few were sorry to see him go. Stubborn, loud, and outspoken, Haley liked to talk politics, and his angry and intractable take on the New Deal rubbed plenty of people the wrong way. Over the previous few months, the library—preparing the UT exhibits for the Centennial—was in a warzone as Haley was constantly fighting with the head archivist and the rare-books curator. The story is well told in Don E. Carlton, "Communism, Fruit Flies, and Academic Freedom," in *The Texas Book Two*, ed. David Detmer (University of Texas Press, 2012), 81–82.

59. "The Issue: Democracy vs. Communism" appeared everywhere, including the inaugural issue of the *Jeffersonian Democrat*, September 26, 1936.

60. "Jeffersonian Democrats Declare Stand" (statement), Box 4, Subseries B, Texans for America, Series 3, Political Interests, Haley Papers.

61. The poll was conducted by phoning those who had recently completed an auto-

mobile registration, skewing its results to those who could still afford cars and telephones during the Great Depression.

62. J. Evetts Haley to W. P. Hamblen, November 2, 1936, Box 2, Wallet XI, Subseries A, Jeffersonian Democrats, Series 3, Political Interests, Haley Papers.

9. The Right-Wing Populism of Pappy O'Daniel

1. The place to start with O'Daniel is Seth Shepard McKay, *W. Lee O'Daniel and Texas Politics, 1938–1942* (Texas Tech University Press, 1944).

2. O'Daniel forced band members to work at the mill when they weren't playing. Brown left the band first and was followed by Wills a couple of years later. Pappy had them replaced.

3. J. P. McEvoy, "I've Got That Million Dollar Smile," *American Mercury* (October 1938).

4. Gene Fowler and Bill Crawford, "Please Pass the Tamales Pappy," in *Border Radio: Quacks, Yodelers, Pitchmen, Psychics, and Other Amazing Broadcasters of the American Airwaves* (University of Texas Press, 1987), 159–198.

5. Quoted in McEvoy, "I've Got That Million Dollar Smile."

6. They were curious, however. The O'Daniel phenomenon, in the days before he actually began campaigning, was the main topic of conversation at a meeting of small-town newspapers in early June. *Waco News Tribune*, June 13, 1938.

7. *Waco News Tribune*, June 14, 1938.

8. McEvoy, "I've Got That Million-Dollar Smile"; *Lubbock Morning Avalanche*, June 17, 1938.

9. Wayne Gard, "The Texas Kingfish," *New Republic*, June 23, 1941, 848.

10. Well into the 1970s, winning the Democratic primary in Texas (and the rest of the South) was tantamount to winning the election. In the 1938 general election, O'Daniel took 97 percent of the vote. Robert Caro's coverage of the election in *The Years of Lyndon Johnson: The Path to Power* (Alfred A. Knopf, 1982) is excellent, especially his analysis of the pension as a campaign issue (695–703). See also George N. Green, *The Establishment in Texas Politics: The Primitive Years, 1938–1957* (Greenwood Press, 1979), 22–25; and Bill Crawford, *Pass the Biscuits Pappy: Pictures of Governor W. Lee "Pappy" O'Daniel* (University of Texas Press, 2004), 28–36.

11. John C. Granbery, "Political Revolution in Texas," *Christian Century*, August 10, 1938, 963–964.

12. V. O. Key, *Southern Politics in State and Nation* (Vintage Books, 1949), 266–267.

13. William G. Deloach, *Plains Farmer: The Diary of William G. Deloach, 1914–1964* (Texas A&M University Press, 1991), 187.

14. Key, *Southern Politics*, 266–267; McKay, *W. Lee O'Daniel and Texas Politics;* McKay, "O'Daniel, Roosevelt, and the Texas Republican Counties," *SWSSQ* (June 1945).

15. Haley, "Harmonizing O'Daniel," July 1938, Subseries I, Misc. MSS, Series IV, Literary Productions, Haley Papers.

16. Carr P. Collins was also a radio pioneer and sponsor of a popular radio program called *The Crazy Gang*, which he used to advertise his "Crazy Crystals," a laxative made by hydrating crystals from Mineral Wells, Texas. He joined the camp of the New Deal haters after Rexford Tugwell (before his tenure with the Resettlement Administration) cracked down on patent medicine advertising. Tugwell, then still with the Department of Agriculture (where the FDA was then housed), pointed to Crazy Crystals as one of the great scams of the time. Tom Peeler, "Nostalgia Healing Waters," *D Magazine* (November 1983); Pamela Grundy, "'We Always Tried to Be Good People': Respectability, Crazy Water Crystals, and Hillbilly Music on the Air, 1933–1935," *JAH* (March 1995).

17. *Texas Monthly* (October 1982): 206; Patricia Bernstein, *Ten Dollars to Hate: The Texas Man Who Fought the Klan* (Texas A&M University Press, 2017), 123.

18. *Waco News Tribune,* June 14, 1938.

19. *San Francisco Examiner,* August 21, 1938.

20. Damon Runyon, "The Brighter Side," *Chillicothe (OH) Gazette,* July 29, 1938.

21. Coughlin quoted in Jesse Walker, "Before Trump, There Was Pappy," *Reason,* May 1, 2016.

22. *AAS,* January 18, 1939.

23. Crawford, *Pass the Biscuits Pappy,* 37.

24. Green, *Establishment in Texas Politics,* 25–27. For a blow-by-blow account of O'Daniel's interactions with the legislature, see McKay, *W. Lee O'Daniel,* 166–197. The fight was widely covered in the state's newspapers. Quotes in *Amarillo Globe,* June 8, 1939; and *Marshall (TX) Messenger,* June 2, 1939.

25. These appointments, from his second term, went over about as well as those in his first term. O'Daniel also got all the Hillbilly Boys state government jobs. For more on his appointments, see Green, *Establishment in Texas Politics,* 30.

26. McKay, *W. Lee O'Daniel,* 146–166, 358–360, 397–399 (quote on 160).

27. Walter Davenport, "Where's Them Biscuits Pappy?" *Collier's Weekly,* January 6, 1940.

28. Among O'Daniel's fiercest critics was conservative Lynn Landrum, who used his front-page column in the *Dallas Morning News* to mercilessly ridicule O'Daniel's hillbilly government. He called the governor "inchworm" because O'Daniel's crooked explanations for his policies were "as involved and tenuous as an inchworm on a corkscrew." O'Daniel, on the other hand, called the *Dallas Morning News* "the great grandcadoodle of the corporation press." William Murchison, "Lynn Landrum vs. the Modern World," *D Magazine* (September 1987); Fowler and Crawford, *Border Radio,* 184.

29. McKay, *W. Lee O'Daniel,* 268–269, 307; Fowler and Crawford, *Border Radio,* 177, 181–182.

30. Green, *Establishment in Texas Politics,* 29.

31. Three months earlier, DeLoach had written that he liked the way the governor "hit those capital rats hard." Deloach, *Plains Farmer,* July 28, 1940, 198, 201.

32. Percentages from McKay, *W. Lee O'Daniel,* 345–346.

33. Joe Belden, "Texas Surveys of Public Opinion," *AAS,* October 13, 1940.

34. Willson Whitman, "Keep Them Out!" *The Nation,* July 18, 1942; Booton Herndon, "Pappy's Dixie Fascists," *New Republic,* July 20, 1942; George N. Green, "Establishing the Far Right in Texas," in *The Texas Right,* 88.

35. The phrase "labor leader racketeers," widely used by conservatives across the country, had remarkable resonance as it allowed them to lay claim to protecting the workingman from the evil extortionists. David Witwer, "The Racketeer Menace and Antiunionism in the Mid-Twentieth Century US," *International Labor and Working-Class History* (Fall 2008).

36. Green, *Establishment in Texas Politics,* 31–32; Thomas Brewer, "State Anti-labor Legislation: Texas—A Case Study," *Labor History* (January 1970), 67; Haley to O'Daniel, April 20, 1941, Alphabetical Files, Series V, Correspondence, Haley Papers.

37. Quoted in Darren E. Grem, *The Blessings of Business: How Corporations Shaped Conservative Christianity* (Oxford University Press, 2016), 28. See also Helen Fuller, "The Christian American Cabal," *New Republic,* January 25, 1943, 116; and Muse, "Making Peace with Grandfather."

38. Ulrey was in those years a regular contributor to American Nazi sympathizer Gerald Winrod's *The Defender.*

39. *AAS*, June 5, 1941.

40. Roland Young, "Lone Star Razzle Dazzle," *The Nation*, June 21, 1941, 722–724.

41. The election was legendary in Texas, with plenty of rumors of chicanery by both the O'Daniel and the Johnson camps. One of the juiciest—and one broadcast nationally by columnists Walter Winchell and Drew Pearson—was that the state's liquor interests did everything they thought necessary to get O'Daniel, who had threatened to end beer sales around military bases, out of the state. The best account is Caro, *The Years of Lyndon Johnson: The Path to Power*, 675–740.

42. McKay, *W. Lee O'Daniel*, 502–505; Whitman, "Keep Them Out!"

43. Quoted in McKay, *W. Lee O'Daniel*, 506; and Whitman, "Keep them Out."

44. *New Republic*, May 18, 1942, 710.

45. Allred added to his list of those who would vote against him: whoever "loved his money more than his country," whoever "would like to deprive labor of its rights," and "isolationists." *FWST*, August 18, 1942.

46. *DMN*, July 23, 1942; McKay, *W. Lee O'Daniel*, 569–571.

47. O'Daniel needed 100,000 crossover Republican votes to win.

48. The Republican Party in Texas in these years, as you will soon see, supported Senator Robert A. Taft and was moving to the far-right edges of the GOP.

49. Quote from an O'Daniel speech against the Office of Price Administration. The speech was reprinted with commentary and placed as a half-page advertisement, "made possible by friends of Senator W. Lee O'Daniel," in newspapers across Texas in fall of 1943. *Freeport (TX) Facts*, August 19, 1943. The second quote is from the *San Francisco Examiner*, October 5, 1943.

50. Burrough, *The Big Rich*, 23, 142–144.

51. The Texas Regulars regularly traded in racist and conspiratorial language; one of the group's ads, titled "How We Can Lick the New Deal in Texas," which ran in newspapers across the state in fall 1944, read: "The Texas Regulars are against the Communistic, anti-Christian doctrines of the New Deal. Against attempts of the federal enforcement to mix negroes and whites in the South." See, for example, *LAJ*, October 22, 1944.

52. The best account of the Texas Regulars is Green, *Establishment in Texas Politics*, 45–57. See also Keith Volanto, "Far Right in Texas during the Roosevelt Era"; and Judge Paul Pressler, *The Texas Regulars: The Beginning of the Move to the Republican Party in the South* (Hannibal Books, 2001), a reprint of his 1951, Princeton University dissertation.

53. Roosevelt would win 432 electoral votes to Dewey's 99.

54. The details of the plan appeared in many of the Texas Regulars' advertisements. See, for example, *BH*, October 22, 1944; and *Mexia (TX) Herald*, November 3, 1944.

55. "Texans, Mark It Like This!" appeared across Texas in the weeks leading up to the election. See, for example, *LAJ*, October 29, 1944; and *SAEN*, November 7, 1944.

56. *BH*, October 22, 1944.

57. The ads appeared in almost every newspaper. See, for example, *BSH*, November 6, 1944; and *CN*, November 2, 1944.

58. Steve Fraser, *Labor Will Rule: Sidney Hillman and the Rise of American Labor* (Free Press, 1991), 525, 526.

59. James G. Ryan, *Earl Browder: The Failure of American Communism* (University Alabama Press, 2005), especially 244.

60. When an investigation into the lobbying activities and supporters of the *W. Lee O'Daniel News* began in late October, O'Daniel would often go off script and attack the "gestapo court tactics" of the administration. *LAJ*, October 27, 1944.

61. West Texas voters ran slightly under these numbers with 15 percent for Dewey and 10 percent for the Texas Regulars.

62. Willie Morris, *North toward Home* (Houghton Mifflin, 1967), 265.

10. Rancher/Scholar/Reactionary

1. Haley's anti–New Deal politics come through clearly in both books.

2. *AT*, February 5, 1938. The editorials also appear in "Unsigned Editorials," *Amarillo Times*, Subseries D, Newspaper Articles and Editorials, Series IV, Literary Productions (hereafter cited as "Unsigned Editorials"), Haley Papers.

3. *AT*, May 21, 1938.

4. Haley, "How a Convention Is Planned," "How a Convention Is Financed," "How the Money Was Handled," "As a Matter of Policy," *AT*, May 17, 18, 19, 20 1938, "Unsigned Editorials," Haley Papers.

5. Three other ultraconservatives, corporate attorney for Southwestern Bell John H. Bickett, lumber baron Lutcher Stark, and oilman Hilmer Weinert, were also on the board.

6. John Moretta, "Governors, Regents, and New Deal Liberalism: Student Activism at the University of Texas at Austin, 1917–1945," *SWHQ* (July 2022); "The Battle for the Texas Mind," *Houston History Magazine* (February 2010), 41.

7. The Longhorns had gone 1–9 the year before, with the only bright spot a victory against Texas A&M to close the season. They went 8–2 in Rainey's first year.

8. The regents, for example, were obsessed with John Dos Passos's *The Big Money* (Harcourt, Brace and Company, 1936), the third book in his *USA* trilogy. They found it filthy and pro-communist. While no faculty had assigned the text, it had appeared on a few bibliographies of important twentieth-century books. Faculty who had included the book on such lists were brought before the regents, who pestered the professors about where they were born and where they were educated and their marital status and, most important, how *The Big Money* had ended up on reading lists. Henry Nash Smith, "The Controversy at the University of Texas, 1939–1945: A Documentary History," paper presented to Student Committee for Academic Freedom, University of Texas, August 13, 1945, 14–15, Homer Price Rainey Papers, Dolph Briscoe Center for American History, Digital Collections.

9. Davis, *J. Frank Dobie*, 153.

10. *AAS*, August 1, 1943.

11. Smith, "Controversy at the University of Texas," 16–17.

12. *WP*, November 27, 1944.

13. *NYT*, February 15, 1945.

14. Bernard DeVoto, "The Dark Age in Texas," *Harpers*, August 1, 1945.

15. Smith, "Controversy at the University of Texas," 21; *AAS*, November 18, 1944.

16. While the term "cowboy conservatism" has popped up occasionally over the past several decades, often used to describe Ronald Reagan's (and George W. Bush's) performative westernness, it was first used to describe Texas right-wing politics in Jeff Roche, "Cowboy Conservatism: High Plains Politics, 1933–1972," PhD diss., University of New Mexico, 2001; and the essay "Cowboy Conservatism," in *The Conservative Sixties*, ed. David Farber and Jeff Roche (Peter Lang, 2003).

17. Buckley would argue that the curriculum and educational philosophy of Yale should reflect the attitudes and beliefs of the university's alumni and governing body. William F. Buckley, *God and Man at Yale: The Superstitions of Academic Freedom* (Regnery, 1951).

18. J. Evetts Haley, "The University of Texas and the Issue," Subseries B, Miscellaneous Writings, Series IV, Literary Productions, Haley Papers.

19. Haley, "University of Texas and the Issue," 26–27.

20. *AT*, January 12, 1950. All of Haley's columns can be found in the Haley Library. For the convenience of readers, I've cited instead newspapers where they can be found online.

21. Don E. Carleton, *Red Scare! Right-Wing Hysteria, Fifties Fanaticism, and Their Legacy in Texas* (Texas Monthly Press, 1985).

22. Theodore White, "Texas: Land of Wealth and Fear," *The Reporter*, May 25, 1954.

23. A single Dallas fundraising dinner one year netted the Wisconsin senator $100,000.

24. Texas Tory Talk appeared in the *Amarillo Daily News*, *Amarillo Globe Times* and *Sunday News Globe*, *Big Spring Herald*, *Marshall News Messenger*, *Paris News*, *San Angelo Standard-Times*, *Snyder Daily News*, and *Wichita Falls Times*.

25. *AGN*, December 29, 1950.

26. *AGN*, December 29, 1950.

27. *WDT*, November 23, 1950. Quote from *PN*, October 8, 1950.

28. *WDT*, June 24, 1951.

29. *PN*, November 12, 1950.

30. *SAST*, December 31, 1950; J. Evetts Haley, interview with Bill Wilkerson, December 5, 1982, Subseries J, Interviews, Series IV, Literary Productions, Haley Papers.

31. *WFT*, February 11, 1951.

32. In his later years, he would claim that it was FDR's interference with the economy that drove him to turn on the president.

33. *PN*, December 10, 1950. In 1954, during the Geneva Accords, Haley wrote Senator Price Daniel about Vietnam: "Are we going to sit here and let another administration carry us into war in Asia, and slow and certain suicide through gradual debilitation, without a fight? All of Asia is already Communistic. What the hell does this little peninsula amount to now compared to the maintenance of our own strength and invulnerability?" Haley to Daniels, April 23, 1954, Box 20, File 14, J. Evetts Haley, Bonner Feller Papers, University of Oregon.

34. *PN*, May 1, 1951.

35. One December day, as he held forth on Truman, Acheson, and Korea at a cattle auction at the Amarillo Stockyards, he got so worked up that he prepared a statement and had it signed by his listeners—a collection of "cowpunchers, truckers, buyers, and handlers of cattle"—and telegrammed it to the Texas congressional delegation: "Let's Work for America First, Last and All the Time." *LAJ*, December 23, 1950.

36. *PN*, December 10, 1950.

37. J. Evetts Haley, "Patriotism in Our Own Hour of Decision," Speeches, Subseries F, Literary Productions, Series IV, Haley Papers. See also the coverage in *ADN*, November 21, 1951.

38. He was married to Minta Ellis Maedgen, who founded Lubbock's Women for Hoover club in 1928.

39. Memo, copy of original agreement between C. E. Maedgen and Clifford B. Jones, Institute of Americanism, Box 34, Clifford B. Jones, SWC (hereafter cited as Institute of Americanism, Jones Papers, SWC).

40. W. C. Holden, "Proposed Foundation for Fostering Americanism," Institute of Americanism, Jones Papers, SWC.

41. Jones to Arnspringer, February 27, 1952; Jones to Haight, February 22, 1952; Jones to Bailey and to Teetor, February 29, 1952; Maedgen to Benson, November 13 and December 22, 1951; Wiggins to Benson, January 25, 1952; Green to Wiggins, January 22, 1952, U 147.26 President's Office Records, 1936–1964 and undated, Box 7, Folder 29, Maedgen, Southwest Collection/Special Collections Library, Texas Tech University, Lubbock, Texas (hereafter cited as Institute of Americanism, Maedgen, SWC).

42. Interestingly, one of the early names batted about was that of intellectual historian Henry Nash Smith, a native Texan who had graduated from SMU and UT and

who had taught at both schools. Recommenders praised Smith as one of the most distinguished thinkers on American life and culture in the country. Smith, however, was also an outspoken critic of threats to academic freedom. One former SMU colleague suggested in a private letter to Tech vice-president E. N. Jones that Smith might not be the person best qualified to "teach the kind of fundamental Americanism that your Foundation might want taught." Trent Root to E. N. Jones, April 18, 1952, Institute of Americanism, Maedgen.

43. W. C. Holden, "Memo Proposal to Maedgen (1951), Institute of Americanism, Jones Papers, SWC. See also J. Evetts Haley, "The Institute of Americanism," Haley File, Jones Papers, SWC; W. C. Holden, interview with Jimmy Skaggs, May 3 and 6, 1968, General Oral Histories, SWC.

44. *LAJ*, June 1, 1952.

45. He meant the part about still being a rancher; earlier that year he had expanded his holdings and negotiated a sweetheart deal to run the Institute that gave him summers off to tend to his ranches and did not require him to teach or have any regular campus responsibilities. Memorandum outlining Haley's duties and the goals of the Institute, n.d. (probably May 1952); Haley to Wiggins, May 9, 1952, Institute of Americanism, Maedgen.

46. *LAJ*, September 5, 1952.

47. "Minutes, Texas Technological College Meeting of Board of Directors, 1952–1953," Board of Regents, 1953–1954, Texas Tech University Archives, SWC.

48. *LEJ*, October 1 and 28, 1952.

49. Charlie Flagg, the protagonist of Elmer Kelton's heartbreaking novel *The Time It Never Rained*, a man defined by his refusal to accept federal aid during the 1950s drought, was the embodiment of this mindset.

50. *Wichita Falls Record News*, October 21, 1952.

51. Fifield was a critical figure in the early days of the modern right wing. From his pulpit at the Los Angeles Congregationalist Church, one of the wealthiest congregations in the country, he developed a theology termed Christian Libertarianism. Herbert Hoover was a fan, as was oil tycoon J. Howard Pew. Kevin M. Kruse, *One Nation Under God: How Corporate America Invented Christian America* (Basic Books, 2015), 3–26.

52. J. Evetts Haley, "Americanism without Apology," Speeches, Literary Productions, Haley Papers.

53. It was a busy and exciting month for Haley. In addition to his public talks, his latest book on the frontier days of Fort Concho had just come out and he attended several book signings.

54. W. C. Holden, interview with Jimmy Skaggs, SWC.

55. Haley had mentioned the potential value of such a survey in a phone conversation with the governor. But that was the extent of Allan Shivers's involvement. Haley and Shivers were political allies.

56. Ernest Poteet to E. N. Jones and Logan Wilson to Jones, February 19, 1953, Box 7, Folder 28, Institute of Americanism Papers, Texas Tech President's Office Records, 1936–1964, SWC (hereafter cited as Institute of Americanism, President, SWC). There are literally dozens of communications complaining about the survey in this file. Jones, who as Tech's vice-president had been involved in the search for the Institute of Americanism's director, had become Tech's president in the summer of 1952 when then-president Wiggins resigned suddenly to go into banking.

57. Haley got a decent return rate at Tech, but it was probably weighed a little heavy toward the disgruntled. Anyone who has worked in higher education in the past seventy-five years will find the results familiar: the Department of Education was an impe-

rialistic blob with an overstuffed curriculum that left its graduates underprepared; a preoccupation with sports; lowered standards; an intellectual joke masquerading as a business school; costly, trendy buildings; not enough parking; a constantly expanding bloat of an administration filled with brainless bureaucrats creating needless work for themselves and others (like the survey). "Report on Texas Technological College by the Institute of Americanism," Institute of Americanism, Jones Papers, SWC.

58. E. N. Jones, Office Memorandum, "Conference with Mr. C. E. Maedgen, Sr., Relative to Institute of Americanism," June 4, 1953, Institute of Americanism, President, SWC. Jones seemed genuinely perplexed as to what to do about Haley's lack of engagement with the larger Texas Tech academic community. See Jones to Haley, September 20, 1952, and Haley to Jones, June 6, 1953.

59. *LEJ*, February 15, 1954.

60. *LEJ*, February 25, 1954. Most audiences were townspeople.

61. *LA*, March 18, 1954. Armstrong's biggest applause came after he said that for him "Americanism" also meant Texas Tech joining the Southwest Conference.

62. His appearance was cosponsored by Tech's Department of History. Nevins gave two other public talks while in Lubbock. The book *Ford: The Times, the Man, the Company* (Scribner, 1954) is an excellent work of business history.

63. *LAJ*, April 8 and 9, 1954.

64. Frazier Hunt's *Douglas MacArthur: The Untold Story* was originally published by conservative outlet Devin-Adair in 1954.

65. Haley to Fellers, January 7, February 15, March 18, 1954, J. Evetts Haley, Bonner Fellers Papers, Hoover Institution, Stanford University. Haley and Clifford B. Jones would both be named to For America's policy committee when the organization formed in the fall.

66. *LAJ*, May 5, 1954.

67. *LAJ*, May 6, 1954.

68. *LEJ*, May 14, 1954.

69. A law passed in Texas in the spring of 1954 that required an additional three hours of government in all state colleges made adding an additional six hours of Americanism almost impossible for many departments, especially those in agriculture and engineering.

70. Rushing and Nall, *Evolution of a University*, 110–111.

71. In the late 1950s, the Bureau of Economic Understanding would be joined by the equally conservative Texas Educational Association in spending hundreds of thousands of dollars to teach Americanism in West Texas schools. *AAS*, March 6, 1960; *TO*, January 1, 1960.

72. Other members included the editor of the ultraconservative *Midland Times*, a wealthy cotton oil tycoon, and the man who ran Plainview's largest grain elevator complex.

73. In a report on the Tech board, the American Association of University Professors was shocked at how little the board understood the basic systems that governed higher education. "It seems fair to state, therefore, that because of their relative inexperience in administration of higher education, some Board members were not accustomed to examining such concepts as academic freedom and the proper relationship of a board of control to an administration and a faculty." Ralph C. Barnhart and Joseph C. Pray, "Texas Technological College," *AAUP Bulletin* (March 1958): 183.

74. *ARN*, July 15, 1957.

75. The AAUP concluded that Greenberg's research into segregation and his "questionable attitudes on the subject of race relations" had been the primary motivation for his dismissal. Barnhart and Pray, "Texas Technological College," 180.

76. Rushing and Nall, *Evolution of a University*, 114–116; *TO*, August 2, 23, and 30, 1957, May 2, 1958; David M. Welborn, "An Ex–Hired Hand on Why He Left," *TO*, January 8, 1965; C. Vann Woodward, "The Unreported Crisis in the Southern Colleges," *Harper's*, October 1, 1962, 82–89.

77. *DMN*, July 20, 1957.

78. Within a few years, Baggarly adopted "Haleyites" as an all-purpose descriptor for the extremist right. *TH*, July 18, 1957; *Castro County News* (Dimmit, TX), July 17, 1957.

79. *NYT*, August 18, 1957. Haley and Clifford B. Jones had already cooked up a plan wherein the men could appear before the board, be heard, and then dismissed without comment. As Jones explained in a letter to Haley, that was the strategy the board had used twenty years earlier when it fired a faculty member it suspected to be a socialist. Jones to Haley, July 18, 1957, Correspondence, Haley Papers.

80. Mrs. H. G. McCleary to Charles Thompson, Chair, Texas Tech Board of Directors, July 26, 1955, Political Interests, Haley Papers.

81. Barnhart and Pray, "Texas Technological College," 174.

82. Barnhart and Pray, "Texas Technological College," 176.

83. J. Evetts Haley, "States' Rights the Issue," Box 4, Governor's Campaign (1956), Subseries C, Political Interests, Haley Papers.

84. *FWST*, March 1, 1956; *CN*, March 7, 1956; *LAJ*, March 1, 1956.

85. Haley finished a distant fourth in a six-candidate race. He trailed the third-place finisher, Pappy O'Daniel, taking one last shot at relevance. The winner, Price Daniel, widely considered a tool of big business, outpolled Haley 7:1.

86. Several other members of the Texas delegation did not sign the document. They included Lyndon Johnson and West Texas's other two representatives George Mahon and J. T. Rutherford. As the *Beaumont (TX) Enterprise* (July 31, 1956) explained: "Many sections of the state have very few Negroes . . . it is hard to get excited about a problem that does not exist on the local level."

87. The standard account is Robin Duff Ladino, *Desegregating Texas Schools: Eisenhower, Shivers, and the Crisis at Mansfield High* (University of Texas Press, 1996).

88. Daniel lost the case, *Sweatt v. Painter*, 339 U.S. 629 (1950).

89. There were two other minor candidates in the race.

90. The Supreme Court, responding in something close to real time to a series of last-minute massive resistance laws by the state of Arkansas, already under a court-ordered mandate to integrate schools, struck down Interposition in 1958 once and for all. See *Cooper v. Aaron*, 358 U.S. 1 (1958).

91. *CN*, April 12, 1956.

92. In another metaphor he liked, Haley compared the Constitution to an agreement reached by a rancher and his managers. The three branches of government are the managers. If one of them made a new rule that broke the original rules of the compact, the other partners could ignore the rule and dismiss that manager. *AGT* April 4, 1956.

93. *Brownwood Bulletin*, June 15, 1956.

94. Chandler A. Robinson, *J. Evetts Haley and the Passing of the Old West* (Jenkins, 1978), 21.

95. *DMN*, June 10, 1956.

96. It was an interesting but unlikely coincidence that Haley announced his candidacy just days after President Eisenhower vetoed an oil industry–written bill that would have removed federal utility rate controls from oil and gas. With support from western free-marketeers like Barry Goldwater, northeastern Republicans who wanted cheap natural gas in the winter for their constituents, and knee-jerk southern antistatists, the bill

had passed both the House and the Senate and was about to bestow multimillion-dollar windfall profits on oil tycoons like Hunt. President Eisenhower, who supported the bill, was forced to veto it when the ham-handed bribery by oil lobbyists went public. (They were literally stuffing envelopes with $100 bills and handing them out to members of Congress.) Eisenhower couldn't believe the "arrogance."

97. *TO*, June 27, 1956.

11. Brainwashed

1. Davis, *J. Frank Dobie*, 97–98.

2. E. Merrill Root, *Brainwashing in the High Schools: An Examination of Eleven American History Textbooks* (Devin-Adair, 1958).

3. See, for example, E. Merrill Root, "Darkness at Noon in American Colleges," *Human Events* (July 1952); and Root, *Collectivism on the Campus* (Devin-Adair, 1956).

4. Root was the first person whom the TFA contacted when it began its campaign. Root to Haley, August 26, 1960; Root to Haley, September 15, 1960, Texans for America, Haley Papers.

5. For more information and context for these events, see Allan O. Kownslar, *The Great Texas Social Studies Textbook War of 1961–1962* (Texas A&M University Press, 2019).

6. The immediate precursor to the organization was a segregationist group—the Conservative Texans—formed immediately after the *Brown II* decision in late spring 1955. Haley was a member.

7. *FWST*, September 20, 1957.

8. *FWST*, September 22, 1957. This was two days *before* President Eisenhower sent in the U.S. Army and federalized the Arkansas National Guard.

9. The Committee on Correspondence Issue Papers for any given month are in Committee on Correspondence, "Issue Papers," Subseries B, Texans for America, Box 2, Series III, Political Files, Haley Papers. Quotes from "Issue Papers," January 20, 1960.

10. Haley to Venable, March 6, 1960; Haley to Rodgers, March 8, 1960; Haley to Patriot, October 1, 1959, Texans for America, Box One; *Dallas Morning News*, undated 1959 clipping, Texans for America, Box 2, Haley Papers.

11. Quotes from February 1958 issue, Texans for America, Box 3, Haley Papers.

12. *TO*, May 9, 1958.

13. *Texans for America News* (October 1959), Texans for America, Box 3, Haley Papers. Other compilations that Lowman published with Circuit Riders between 1956 and 1962 included *658 Clergymen and Laymen Connected with the National Council of Churches* (1962), *660 Baptist Clergymen* (1960), *1411 Protestant Episcopal Rectors* (1956), *2,109 Methodist Ministers* (1958), and *30 of the 95 Men who Gave Us the Revised Standard Version of the Bible* (1960).

14. *Dan Smoot Report*, February 8, 1960.

15. Yes, that SMU. The one in University Park in Dallas.

16. Harold Lord Varney, "Southern Methodist University Pampers Leftism," *American Mercury* (January 1960): 22. Varney argued that the SMU problem stemmed from the undue influence of northern industrialists moving to the city. See also David Austin Walsh, "The Right-Wing Popular Front: The Far Right and American Conservatism in the 1950s," *JAH* (September 2020).

17. "Sometimes," Boller later quipped, "I thought I was being cold-hearted in trying to deprive reactionaries of their beloved Communist Party." See Boller, "An American Irrelevance: CP, USA," *Southwest Review* (Autumn 1960); and "The 'Dallas Morning News' and Communist Russia," *SWSSQ* (March 1961). Quote from Boller, *Memoirs of an Obscure Professor* (Texas Christian University Press, 1992), 23, 24.

18. "Issue Papers," August 24, 1960, "Committee on Correspondence," Texans for America, Box 2; Haley to Texans Committee for Education, July 12, 1961; Haley to R. A. Kilpatrick, August 18, 1961, Texans for America, Box 2, Haley Papers.

19. Moon to Haley, September 10, 1960, August 29, 1960; Moon to Haley, draft, "TFA Criteria for Textbooks 1961," Texans for America, Box 2, Haley Papers.

20. Adopting this aggressive interpretive approach to evaluation was necessary because, in reality, publishers had tailored their textbooks for years to the conservative Texas market, making them models of blandness. For an enlightening critique, see Hillel Black's comments on the Texas schoolbook market in his *The American Schoolbook* (Morrow, 1967), 142–161.

21. Ilanon Moon, "Textbook Criteria for Young Americans," Texans for America, Box 2; Moon to Haley, draft, "TFA Criteria for Textbooks 1961," Haley Papers. Haley would repeat the "American Side" phrase ad nauseum over the next few months. See also Haley's statement on the criteria in the *Texas Observer*, May 13, 1961.

22. George Parker to Roger Harlan, July 26, 1961; "Reports," Texans for America, Box 2, Haley Papers.

23. *LA*, September 15, 1961.

24. Another reason for Haley's rejection of this book came out over the course of his testimony: it was the book's "integration sentiment" that was too subtle for teachers who "don't have the critical ability to evaluate subtle communist influences." *TO*, November 18, 1960. Criticism of *The Stockman's Handbook* Textbooks, TFA, Haley Papers; R. K. Harlan, "Instructions," May 31, 1961, Texans for America, Box 2, Haley Papers.

25. Mel and Norma Gabler, *the* power couple of the textbook watchdog set, added that since the new math had been tried with great success in "AFRICA," it most likely meant that "UNESCO is involved." The Mel Gablers, "Textbook Criteria", n.d., Texans for America, Box 2, Haley Papers.

26. Moon to Haley, August 29, 1960; Harlan, "Instructions"; George Parker to Harlan, July 26, 1961, "Reports," Texans for America, Box 2, Haley Papers. *DMN*, November 21, 1961.

27. *TO*, November 18, 1960, May 13, 1961; *AAS*, October 6, 1961; *OA*, February 9, 1962.

28. Quoted in *Victoria (TX) Advocate*, November 14, 1961.

29. Bob Sherrill, "Books Scorched by Haley Critics," *TO*, September 22, 1961. Sherrill added that the "Haleyites" wanted "textbook authors to look with special favor on General MacArthur (especially in his role of wanting to bomb China in the Korean War), Chiang Kai-Shek, J. Edgar Hoover, Herbert Hoover, the memory of Calvin Coolidge, what they consider to be the 'traditional' presentation of Christianity, the 'traditional' presentation of national heroes, nationalism, 'patriotic wars,' the memory of Senator Joe McCarthy, Senator Connolly, laissez faire, republicanism (as distinguished from democracy), and government subsidies to business."

30. John Edward Weems et al., "Talking Back to the Censors," and John Howard Griffin, "Current Trends in Censorship," *Southwest Review* (Summer 1962), Griffin quote on 200.

31. *TO*, November 17, 1961.

32. John Edward Weems, "Talking Back to the Censors," 201; *Texas Observer*, October 20 and November 17, 1961; *AAS*, October 26, 1961.

33. "J. Frank Dobie," Texans for America, Haley Papers.

34. Bass quoted in *ADN*, February 26, 1962.

35. Some balance was restored at the following meeting, when a group of UT profes-

sors who spoke out against censorship and extolled the free exchange of ideas in schools. What students needed, they assured, was a vigorous history education and not just "tears-in-my-eyes" patriotic indoctrination. *TO*, December 8, 1961, January 19, 1962, January 26, 1962.

36. *TO*, February 2, 1962; Davis, *J. Frank Dobie*, 228–229.

37. Davis, *J. Frank Dobie*, 229.

38. *ADN*, February 11, 14, 16, and 17, 1962, October 6, 1961; *AGT*, January 31, 1962; *TO*, March 2, 1962.

39. *TO*, March 2, 1962; *AGT*, February 26, 1962.

40. *TO*, March 2, 1962; *AGT*, February 26, 1962.

41. Roberts would later sue Boots for slander over the remark, seeking $85,000 in damages. Boots claimed that she made the remark based on her belief that Roberts had over his political career "adopted Communist techniques and espoused Communist causes" and because—and this is Bircher logic at work—his actions were "consistent with established communist policy of public profession of patriotism while secretly striving to undermine and destroy capitalism through aiding and abetting the Communist conspiracy." Moreover, she added that Roberts, employing an old communist trick, was using freedom of speech and the hearings to "ridicule, embarrass, harass and smear those citizens of Texas who protested the insidious implantation of the Communist philosophy in the minds of the children attending our Texas schools and official contribution to moral delinquency through school libraries, which ridiculed the Supreme Being, recognized by the Christian world, emphasized and glamorized immorality and sexual license in such lewd, lascivious, foul and vulgar language." Roberts later dropped the suit. *AGT*, April 19, 1962.

42. *ADN*, 27 February 1962, *AGT*, February 27, 1962.

43. John Alaniz, "Textbook Report," reprinted in Kownslar, *Great Texas Social Studies War*, 200. Roberts's report came to similar conclusions.

44. *EPHP*, June 1, 1962.

45. *AAS*, February 18, 1962.

BOOK THREE. COWBOY CONSERVATISM

12. Birchtown

1. The *Lubbock Avalanche-Journal* (March 24, 1961) estimated that the city had upward of twenty chapters in early 1961.

2. Arnold Forster and Benjamin Epstein, *Danger on the Right* (Random House, 1964), 13.

3. *AGN*, August 7, 1960.

4. *ADN*, August 15, 16, 1960.

5. Jonathan Soffer, "The National Association of Manufacturers and the Militarization of American Conservatism," *BHR* (Winter 2001): 781–782.

6. The JBS origin story has oft been told. A solid and thorough account of Welch and the JBS can be found in Edward H. Miller, *A Conspiratorial Life: Robert Welch, the John Birch Society, and the Revolution of American Conservatism* (University of Chicago Press, 2023).

7. For an insider's look at how the society worked, see Gerald Schomp, *Birchism Was My Business* (Macmillan, 1970).

8. Welch once wrote that it was his "firm belief that Dwight Eisenhower is a dedicated, conscious agent of the Communist conspiracy." Welch, *The Politician* (privately printed, 1958), 267.

9. In the John Birch Society's basic manual, the *Blue Book*, Welch lays out ten different

program types: establishing and patronizing the organization's American Opinion book-stores (based on Christian Science Reading Rooms, ubiquitous in small-city America); consuming conservative media; letter-writing campaigns; developing issue-specific front groups; maintaining and supporting conservative speaker programs; and the frightening ongoing program to "expose" the advances made by communists at the local level to "shock" "brainwashed" Americans into action. Basically, accusing people in the community of being communists. *The Blue Book of the John Birch Society* (Western Islands, 1961), 46–71.

10. No shortage of these sorts of texts were produced in the 1960s. The statistics cited were culled from Raymond E. Wolfinger, Barbara Kaye Wolfinger, Kenneth Prewitt, and Sheilah Rosenhack, "America's Radical Right: Politics and Ideology," *Ideology and Discontent*, ed. David Apter (Free Press, 1964); Sheilah Koeppen, "The Radical Right and the Politics of Consensus," in *The American Right Wing*, ed. Robert Schoenberger (Holt, Rinehart and Winston 1969); Barbara S. Stone, "The John Birch Society: A Profile," *Journal of Politics* (February 1974).

11. Fred Grupp Jr., "The Political Perspectives of Birch Society Members," in *American Right Wing*, 90.

12. Between 1926 and 1960, the three major Amarillo newspapers—the *Globe*, the *Daily News*, and the *Times*—came under the control of S. B. Whittenburg. The *Daily News* was the morning paper.

13. John Michael Haynes, "Wes Izzard: Voice of the Golden Spread," MA thesis, Texas Tech University, 1991; Dixon quoted in Robert Sherrill, "Panhandle Center of Ultra Writers," *TO*, February 23, 1962.

14. Izzard was such a committed booster that he took to criticizing Randolph Marcy's 1852 report of his exploration across the region for its lack of enthusiasm for the Panhandle.

15. *ADN*, November 22, 1960.

16. Quoted in A. G. Mojtabai, *Blessed Assurance: At Home with the Bomb in Amarillo, Texas* (1986; reprinted, Syracuse University Press, 1997), 190.

17. *LEJ*, May 6, 1959; *ADN*, September 28, 1960; *PDN*, December 3, 1960.

18. *TH*, December 28, 1961; *TO*, March 30, 1962. For Reagan's speech, see *AGT*, March 1, 1962.

19. *AGT*, January 14, 1959.

20. Olin Hinkle, "Panhandle Hugs Its Conservatism," *AAS*, April 16, 1961.

21. As Terry Isaacs points out, in "Politics, Religion, and the Blue Book: The John Birch Society in Eastern New Mexico and West Texas, 1960–1965," *NMHR* (January 1996), any West Texas businessman just going about his professional obligations would have been exposed to a constant stream of right-wing propaganda.

22. *ARN*, March 17, 1961; Jimmy Woolridge (high school student) to editor, *ARN*, May 3, 1961.

23. Welch, *Blue Book*, 50.

24. Social theorist Talcott Parsons, commenting on the far right in the early 1960s, noticed that the biggest difference between McCarthyism and Birchism was the latter's strength in the Southwest, "the nearest thing left to a frontier . . . [where people] still cherish the illusion that the old frontier is alive." Parsons, "Social Strains in America," in *The Radical Right*, ed. Daniel Bell (Doubleday and Company, 1963), 195–199 (quotes from 196).

25. Quoted in Jonathan Schoenwald, *Time for Choosing: The Rise of Modern American Conservatism* (Oxford University Press, 2003), 66–67. Historian Richard White, consid-

ering the "current weirdness" of western antistatism in the mid-1990s, came to the same conclusion. White, "The Current Weirdness in the West," *WHQ* (1997).

26. Mann would work for the JBS for two decades.

27. *OA*, November 4, 6, 1960. My biographical sketch of Mann, sometimes misidentified as "Buck McMann," was drawn from stories in the *Odessa American* across the 1950s and early 1960s.

28. For thorough descriptions of the coordinators' role, see Schomp, *Birchism Was My Business,* and Schoenwald, *Time for Choosing,* 81.

29. As the textbook hearings demonstrated, there was plenty of overlap between the JBS and the TFA.

30. Robert Sherrod, "The Toughest Guy in the Air Force," *Saturday Evening Post,* March 27, 1955.

31. *NYT,* July 21, 1961. Secretary of Defense Robert McNamara ended the program, prompting apoplectic sputtering from the right wing about muzzling the generals. J. Frank Cook, *The Warfare State* (Macmillan, 1964), 266–272. Fulbright read the entire story into the *Congressional Record.* 107 Cong. Rec. 14433–14439 (1961), quotes from 14433, 14434.

32. The story broke after a confused airman showed the report to his pastor, asking for clarification. Soon it was national news; the *Washington Post* carried front-page stories on February 17 and 20, 1960. Hargis would milk his role in the controversy for years. "Air Force Manuals" in *CQ Almanac 1960* (Congressional Quarterly, 1960), 11-52.

33. "The Investigation: Operation Abolition," *Time,* March 17, 1961; Stephen J. Whitfield, *Culture of the Cold War,* 1st ed. (Johns Hopkins University Press, 1991), 124. Jerry Lee believed the film to be gospel, an unimpeachable source that "documented" the communist conspiracy. The American Legion and DAR also screened the film widely. *AGT,* March 17, 1961.

34. Screening the film at WT in May 1961, Evetts Haley almost got in a fistfight with a history professor who questioned its veracity and intentions. The next day, when the men met in the president's office to smooth things over, Evetts Jr. ambushed the professor and Haley sucker-punched him. The men were pulled apart by campus police. The best coverage of the scuffle can be found in *ARN* and *CN,* April 29, 1961.

35. *AGN,* March 17, 1961.

36. *ARN,* March 18, 1961.

37. *AGT,* March 8, 1961.

38. Capital letters and boldfacing in original. Lee also believed that communists were going into the public libraries, checking out anticommunist books, and failing to return them to keep vital information from the hands of patriotic Americans.

39. *AGT,* March 17, 1961. The ministers, though letting it be known that they had no intention of getting into "a running battle of words in the press," responded with a several hundred–word, point-by-point refutation of Lee's claims (even the outlandish ones) and deposited their sources with the *Amarillo Globe-Times* for reference. *AGT,* April 21, 1961.

40. Al Dewlen, *Servants of Corruption* (Doubleday, 1971).

41. Isaacs, "Politics, Religion, and the Blue Book," 64; Donald Janson and Bernard Eismann, *The Far Right* (McGraw Hill, 1963), 214.

42. *ARN,* March 18, 1961; *NYT,* November 1, 1962; Janson and Eismann, *The Far Right,* 214; *TO,* March 25, 1961; Isaacs, "Politics, Religion, and the Blue Book," 63 (quote); Paul Timmons, ed., *The Centennial Book of the Polk Street United Methodist Church, Amarillo, Texas, 1888–1988* (Polk Street United Methodist Church, 1989), 86. Quotes from *NYT,* November 1, 1962.

43. Darren Dochuk, *From Bible Belt to Sunbelt: Plain-Folk Religion, Grassroots Politics, and the Rise of Evangelical Conservatism* (W. W. Norton, 2011), xiv–xv.

44. According to the most recent census from the Association of Religion Data Archives, as of 2020 there were over three hundred separate congregations in the larger Amarillo area. Almost a quarter of them were nondenominational evangelical Protestant churches. See "Randall County, Texas, Potter County, Texas—County Membership Report (2020)," ARDA, accessed February 20, 2025, www.thearda.com/us-religion/census/congregational -membership?y=2020&t=0&c=48381&c=48375.

45. Quoted in Mojtabai, *Blessed Assurance*, 220.

46. From an advertisement promoting Welch's appearance in Amarillo. *AGT*, April 14, 1961.

47. This dispensationalist interpretation, in which the Bible unfolds along a specific historical path with the United States and Soviet Union fighting the final battle for control of humanity, would be a foundational premise of the Moral Majority in the 1980s.

48. Unsigned letter to editor, *AGT*, May 10, 1961.

49. The UPI's Barbara Bundschu wrote a seven-part investigative report on the Society that appeared in papers across the country. Gene Blake of the *Los Angeles Times* produced a five-part series that appeared in the first two weeks of March 1961.

50. "The Americanists," *Time*, March 10, 1961, 21. R. C. Hoiles produced his own multipart pro-JBS series of articles that appeared in his Freedom Newspaper chain, including the *Pampa News* and the *Odessa American*.

51. Ben Ezzell, untitled essay on the John Birch Society, *Texas Monthly* (March 1990); Ezzell, *The Editor's Ass and Other Tales from 50 Years behind the Desk of Editor Ben Ezzell* (Canadian Record, 1986); and Ezzell, "The John Birch Society: A Threat to America?" *Canadian Record*, March 9, 1961.

52. *AGT*, April 14, 1961.

53. Two of the officers were in plain clothes and mingled in the crowd.

54. *AGT*, April 20, 1961.

55. *ADN* and *AGT*, April 16 and 17, 1961.

56. Americanism Committee, American Legion, Waldo M. Slaton Post no. 140, *The Truth About the Foreign Policy Association* (1960). Dan Smoot repeated the one-worlders charges in *The Invisible Government* (Dan Smoot Report, 1962).

57. *AGT*, February 15, 1961.

58. *AGT*, March 28, 1961. Seale's positions on a variety of issues were clearly revealed in a series of front-page statements to questions posed to the candidates by the *AGT* in the last few days of March 1961.

59. *AGT*, May 24, June 20, and July 28, 1961.

60. It was part of a larger compact meant to clean the waste flowing into the Canadian River.

61. The city manager, N. V. Moss, the man who had to make the city run, was flummoxed. The money, he tried to assure the commission, had already been paid in federal income taxes, and making sure the Canadian River ran clean was absolutely within the proper purview of the federal government. *AGT*, August 25, 1961.

62. *AGT*, August 25, 1961.

63. Reprinted in *AGT* September 12, 1961. Through September, the letters to the editor were full of praise for the action.

64. *TO*, October 12, 1962.

65. *TO*, May 2, 1962.

66. Seale's team scoured Rogers's two thousand floor votes in Congress, looking for opportunities to demonstrate that he was not a true conservative. They turned up only eight possibilities. Willie Morris, "A Little Humility?" *TO*, November 9, 1962.

67. *TH*, March 1, 1962; "Panhandle Birchers Poured It On and Lost," *TO*, November 16, 1962.

68. *TO*, November 9, 1962.

69. *NYT*, November 1, 1962; *TO*, November 9, 1962.

70. *Union County Leader* (Clayton, NM), March 11, 1964.

71. The event, including Haley's wisecrack, was the subject of several national stories, including the lede of a multipage story on the far right in *Newsweek*, December 4, 1961.

72. *AGT*, June 23, 1963. For an example of the ad, see the *Jefferson City News and Tribune*, July 28, 1963. For some of Stroud's other efforts, see *AG*, November 16, 1967; *BNH*, November 11, 1966; *ADN*, November 7, 1967. See also Buck Ramsey, "Is Amarillo Ready for Self-Government?" *TO*, December 8, 1967.

73. *CN*, May 14, 1964.

74. Amarillo had a sweetheart deal for natural gas, negotiated decades earlier by Mayor Ernest Thompson.

75. Ramsey, "Is Amarillo Ready for Self-Government?" For more on Stroud's first few months in office, see *AGT*, June 4, 6, 27, 28, 29, August 21, 22, October 6, 26, and November 22, 24, 1967. *Globe-Times* editor Tommy Thompson paid particular attention to Stroud in those years.

76. *AGT*, August 16 and 18, 1967; Ramsey, "Is Amarillo Ready for Self-Government?"; L. O'Brien Thompson, interview with Monte Monroe, May 27, 2005, Southwest Collection Interviews, SWC.

77. C. F. to editor, *AGT*, February 20, 1969.

13. The West Texas Crowd

1. For most of the first half of the twentieth century, the Texas GOP was run first by Cecil Lyon and later by R. B. Creager.

2. His family was among the thousands who trekked from the Piedmont South to Parker County in the 1880s.

3. Billy Hathorn, "Orville Bullington," *WTHAY* (2018).

4. Roger M. Olien, *From Token to Triumph: The Texas Republicans since 1920* (Southern Methodist University Press, 1982), 63–64; Paul D. Casdorph, *A History of the Republican Party in Texas, 1865–1965* (Pemberton Press, 1965), 142–143; Michael L. Antle, "The Rise of the Republicans: Party Realignment in Twentieth Century Texas," PhD diss., University of North Texas, 2012. The standard bearer of 1930 was a nobody named William Talbot.

5. While some think that Bullington was a member or even a founder of the Jeffersonian Democrats, I have found no evidence that this was the case, though the aims of both Bullington's Republican Party and the Jeffersonian Democrats certainly aligned.

6. A summary biography can be found in George N. Green and John Kushma, "John Tower," in *Profiles in Power: Twentieth-Century Texans in Washington*, ed. Kenneth E. Hendrickson, Michael L. Collins, and Patrick L. Cox (University of Texas Press, 2004), 195–224.

7. Now Midwestern State University, it was originally an offshoot of the Wichita Falls public school system. When Tower arrived on campus, there were only a couple dozen faculty and a few hundred students.

8. He later claimed that much of this philosophy was first honed as he argued late in the night with the socialist and Marxist students at the London School of Economics in the early 1950s.

9. John G. Tower, "The Conservative Worker in Britain: Why a Working Man Supports the Tories," MA thesis, Southern Methodist University, 1953.

10. *FWST*, August 19, 1956.

11. "Civil Rights Planks in the Party Platforms, 1960," *Current History* (October 1960): 237–240; Green and Kushma, "John Tower"; Perlstein, *Before the Storm*, 86–89.

12. Tower, *A Program for Conservatives* (Macfadden-Bartell, 1962) 19–20 (quote on 19).

13. Tower, *A Program for Conservatives*, 51–65.

14. Tower, *Consequences: A Personal and Political Memoir* (Little, Brown, 1991), 14.

15. Viguerie would go on to become a foundational figure of the New Right of the 1970s and 1980s.

16. Consider, for example, the 1960 senatorial race, when John Tower earned more votes in Midland County alone than LBJ could muster in Borden, Glasscock, Irion, King, Loving, Sterling, Armstrong, Hartley, Kent, Lipscomb, Oldham, Roberts, Sherman, Briscoe, Foard, Concho, Hansford, Kimble, Mason, and Schleicher counties combined.

17. Goldwater was unaware, however, that the book was one part of a larger strategy meant to deny Richard Nixon the Republican nomination later that summer.

18. Perlstein, *Before the Storm*, 64.

19. Barry Goldwater, *The Conscience of a Conservative* (Victor, 1961), 1.

20. Naomi H. Kincaid, review, *ARN*, September 18, 1960.

21. Richard Brooks, interview with author, July 17, 2000.

22. Pragmatists always, most of the big-money oil men who donated millions to right-wing causes hedged their bets and didn't try to challenge Lyndon Johnson, the head of the state party and one of the most powerful men in the U.S. government.

23. The sheer size of Texas and the number of its major media markets make it an extremely expensive place to run a statewide campaign.

24. Olien, *From Token to Triumph*, 175.

25. Most commenters on the Texas GOP in those days remarked on the youth and energy of its local activists. But this youth movement was apparent all over the Sunbelt.

26. Brooks interview.

27. *FWST*, August 27, 1960; *Tyler Telegraph*, August 25, 1960.

28. *PDN*, August 25, 1960.

29. Earl Black and Merle Black, *The Rise of Southern Republicans* (Harvard University Press, 2002), 90.

30. Strangely enough, this was the second time Blakley had been named to the U.S. Senate. He had held Price Daniel's old seat for three months after Daniel had resigned to run for governor.

31. Tower, *Consequences*, 19. John R. Knaggs, *Two-Party Texas: The John Tower Era* (Eakin Press, 1985), 7.

32. *TO*, February 11, 1961.

33. *OA*, February 12, 1961.

34. Blakley garnered 18 percent of the vote. Future House Speaker Jim Wright finished third, followed by Wilson, Maverick, and Gonzalez.

35. *TO*, October 13, 1961.

36. Tower, *Consequences*, 166.

37. Tower, *Consequences*, 25.

38. The ad made a particular point to remind voters that Eisenhower had supported Texas's claim to the Tidelands.

39. Quoted in Meg McKain Grier, *Grassroots Women: A Memoir of the Texas Republican Party* (Wingscape Press, 2001), 60.

40. A strange and, in this case, literal footnote to the election involved liberal Demo-

crats who helped elect Tower by voting *for* the conservative Republican as part of a too-clever-by-half plan to help create a viable Republican Party in Texas that would drain the right-wingers from the Democratic Party and, the thinking went, allow the state and the state party to move to the left.

41. He was, for example, the featured speaker at the National Association of Real Estate Boards in Los Angeles (which often featured right-wing presenters), where he explained to the five thousand attendees how to defeat the "international communist conspiracy." *Los Angeles Times*, November 17, 1961.

42. John G. Tower, *A Program for Conservatives* (Macfadden-Bartell, 1962).

43. Laveta Larie Amsler, "Ed Foreman: A Conservative Republican," MA thesis, Texas Tech University, 1969.

44. A nice set of biographical notes can be found in 110 Cong. Rec. 1253 (January 7-29, 1964).

45. Michael Barone put it this way: "In vivid contrast to the Hispanic part of New Mexico is the area called Little Texas. With small cities, plenty of oil wells, vast cattle ranches, and desolate military bases, this region resembles economically and culturally the adjacent High Plains of West Texas." Michael Barone and Grant Ujifusa, *The Almanac of American Politics, 1984* (National Journal, 1984), 762.

46. In 2013, two Roosevelt County clerks resigned their posts rather than issue marriage licenses to same-sex couples.

47. The president of Eastern New Mexico University was so impressed by Schwarz when he visited in the early 1950s (long before the Australian was famous) that he arranged for him to stay in the state for ten more days, setting him up with speaking engagements all over New Mexico. Hubert Villeneuve, *Teaching Anticommunism: Fred Schwarz and American Postwar Conservatism* (McGill-Queen's University Press, 2020), 48.

48. Ed Foreman, "Role of Brine Important in Petroleum," *OA*, October 13, 1957.

49. He called his talk "Job Security." *OA*, August 10, 1960.

50. Paid for by the du Ponts, the film was sponsored by the Western Oil and Gas Association, the Rocky Mountain Oil and Gas Association, the Independent Petroleum Association of America, the Mid-Continent Oil and Gas Association, and the American Petroleum Institute. *OA*, November 6, 1960.

51. *OA*, February 26, 1961.

52. *EPT*, June 19, 1961.

53. *Human Events* covered the emerging Texas Republican Party carefully in those years. In its August 11, 1962, issue, the magazine described Foreman as a Goldwater Republican.

54. *LAJ*, October 11 and 21, 1961.

55. *OA*, April 20, 1962.

56. Dunn was also responsible for a major JBS project: the Americanism Bookshelf program, wherein local members donated right-wing books to local school libraries in towns too small to support an American Opinion bookstore. He also had a thing for cloak-and-dagger operations and liked to ride around with the police at night harassing people who, he thought, were out later than they needed to be. (An old buddy who had become chief named him official police surgeon, with a badge and everything.) He was active in Haley's Texans for America. After Dunn took it over, the *Pecos Independent* heaped effusive praise on the TFA's efforts in the textbook fight. Dunn's personal papers are housed at the Haley Library. See FBI File, John Birch Society, San Diego, Report, 90–92, Internet Archive, accessed January 21, 2025, https://archive.org/stream/JohnBirchSociety/JBS -San%20Diego-1_djvu.txt.

57. *TO*, June 1, 1962; the quoted statement was run in the first issue of the paper under its new ownership. *Pecos Independent*, July 5, 1960.

58. *Pecos Independent*, February 12, 1962.

59. *TO*, June 1, 1962; Stephen Bates, "Mixed Motives behind a Pulitzer," *Journalism History* (2019): 208.

60. The story is well told in Bates, "Mixed Motives behind Pulitzer."

61. KSEL made the promise after the station manager took one too many phone calls from listeners complaining that they were "sick of hearing about Estes." *OA*, July 8, 1962.

62. *EPT*, May 25, 1962; *OA*, July 8, 1962.

63. Quoted in Rebecca Miller, "The Birchers, the Doctor, and the Wheeler Dealer," MA thesis, Texas Tech University, 1994, 63.

64. *EPT*, November 4, 1962.

65. Jim O'Brien, "Mr. Wrong Deeds Goes to Washington," *Big Bend Sentinel* (Marfa, TX), November 7, 1963.

66. Foreman, who had apparently planned on a long career in D.C., had sold all his Texas businesses. Back home, he went into the concrete business in Las Cruces with his brother. In 1968, he got the itch again and this time ran for Congress from New Mexico's 2nd District and won. Again, his outspoken conservatism cost him, and he was defeated after serving just a single term.

14. Viva! Olé!

1. *AGT*, July 15, 1964.

2. Barry Goldwater, with Jack Casserly, *Goldwater* (Doubleday, 1988), 210.

3. *PDN*, September 19, 1962; *EPHP*, September 20, 1962.

4. Knaggs, *Two-Party Texas*, 33.

5. *Time*, October 27, 1961; Kenneth Ingwalson, "Resignation Rallies in Texas," *Human Events*, October 6, 1961; "Where Democrats Are Walking Out of the Party," *U.S. News and World Report*, November 6, 1961, 71; *FWST*, November 8, 1961.

6. *TO*, October 13, 1961.

7. Jon Ford, "Barry Key for Texas GOP in '64," *SAEN*, September 22, 1963.

8. Knaggs, *Two-Party Texas*, 52. Grier, *Grassroots Women*, is an indispensable source on Tower (see 66).

9. Michelle Nickerson, "Women, Domesticity, and Postwar Conservatism," *OAH Magazine of History* (January 2003), is a short introduction to the larger arguments the author makes in the excellent *Mothers of Conservatism: Women and the Postwar Right* (Princeton University Press, 2012) and in "Moral Mothers and Goldwater Gals," in *The Conservative Sixties*.

10. Quoted in Grier, *Grassroots Women*, 55. See also Judith McArthur and Harold Smith, *Texas through Women's Eyes* (University of Texas Press, 2010), 162–164.

11. McArthur and Smith, *Texas through Women's Eyes*, 163.

12. Historian Sean Wilentz, in his introduction to an updated edition of the book, described it as a "topographical map of the changed political terrain of the late 1960s." Kevin Phillips, *The Emerging Republican Majority*, (Princeton University Press, 2014), x.

13. Phillips, *Emerging Republican Majority*, 318.

14. Between 1920 and 1960, more people in Arizona had been born in Texas than any state other than Arizona. James Gregory, "Texas Migration History 1850–2022" and "Arizona Migration History, 1860–2022, America's Great Migrations Project, University of Washington, accessed February 21, 2025, https://depts.washington.edu/moving1/; "Where We Came From and Where We Went, State by State, Interactive Map," *NYT*, August 13, 2014, https://www.nytimes.com/interactive/2014/08/13/upshot/where-people-in-each-state

-were-born.html#Texas. Also helpful in understanding this cultural-demographic phenomenon are James N. Gregory, *American Exodus: The Dust Bowl Migration and Okie Culture in California* (Oxford University Press, 1991), especially 142–154; Gregory, *The Southern Diaspora: How the Great Migrations of Black and White Southerners Transformed America* (University of North Carolina Press, 2005), especially 155–157; and Dochuk, *From Bible Belt to Sunbelt*, 7–10, 20–21.

15. There are many good books on Goldwater. Among the very best are Robert A. Goldberg, *Goldwater* (Yale University Press, 1995); and Perlstein, *Before the Storm*.

16. Both editorials are reprinted in John Dean and Barry M. Goldwater Jr., eds., *Pure Goldwater* (Macmillan, 2008).

17. And she brought little else, arriving in Phoenix in 1903 with just a suitcase. Short of money, she had hitched a ride on a caboose for the last 140 miles.

18. Goldberg, *Goldwater*, 93–97 (quotes on 95, 96).

19. *AAS*, November 11, 1955.

20. For an insider's account of the entire campaign, see F. Clifton White, *Suite 3505: The Story of the Draft Goldwater Movement* (Arlington House, 1967).

21. Goldwater quoted in Perlstein, *Before the Storm*, 194.

22. White, *Suite 3505*, 142.

23. White, *Suite 3505*, 164–171.

24. *FWST*, June 16, 1964.

25. *Denton (TX) Record Chronicle*, June 17, 1964; *FWST*, June 17, 1964.

26. Haley's was one of three huge campaign books that season. The other two were Phyllis Schlafly's *A Choice, Not an Echo*, an "examination" of the Eastern Establishment's control of the American political system, and John Stormer's *None Dare Call It Treason*, a paranoid indictment of elites and Eisenhower Republicanism. They also sold in the millions and forever changed the media ecosystem of presidential elections.

27. The story of the 1948 senatorial election between Johnson and Stevenson is legendary and probably best told in Robert Caro's *The Years of Lyndon Johnson: Means of Ascent* (Alfred A. Knopf, 1990), even if Caro ignores Stevenson's extremist conservative views on race, federal power, and foreign policy. For a corrective, see Robert Dallek, *Lone Star Rising* (Oxford University Press, 1991). In the second primary, Johnson pulled off a miraculous last-minute victory over Stevenson when the "discovery" of uncounted ballots from South Texas (many cast by people who voted in alphabetical order, listed the local cemetery as their address, used the same pen to sign in, and wrote in identical handwriting) provided LBJ an eighty-seven-vote victory. A couple of friendly court decisions sealed the deal. Conservatives, who loved Stevenson, never got over it; they had never trusted Lyndon, and for a New Deal liberal to replace Pappy O'Daniel in the Senate was particularly galling.

28. The Kennedy assassination and the right-wing culture of Dallas were major influences in the development of Texas politics. No one explains it better than Edward Miller in *Nut Country: Right-Wing Dallas and the Birth of the Southern Strategy* (University of Chicago Press, 2015). Also helpful is Bill Minutaglio and Steven L. Davis, *Dallas, 1963* (Twelve, 2013).

29. Nita Stewart Haley, whom Evetts had met in college and who was his wife for thirty years, died of cancer five days before Christmas in 1958. Her death was devasting to Evetts Haley.

30. He also had a small team of volunteer researchers, including local rancher Thornton Dewey and his wife, Shirley Ann Dewey (who worked in Haley's Canyon office). *EPT*, September 20, 1964. For a description of the physical and emotional toll of the effort, see J. Evetts Haley Jr., "Preface," in Chandler A. Robinson, *J. Evetts Haley*, 19.

31. As becomes clear in the actual book, Haley saw Johnson as a violently vindictive man who would have no qualms about using the powers of the presidency to quash criticism and destroy his enemies.

32. Haley, interview with Bill Modisett, June 2, 1989, Subseries J, Series IV, Haley Papers; Donald Janson, "Extremist Book Sales Soar," *NYT*, October 4, 1964.

33. Robinson, *J. Evetts Haley*, 26; *AAS*, June 17, 1964; *FWST*, June 12, 1964. The CPT was shopping for a candidate who would "promote and espouse the principles of constitutional government," an easy-enough set of search parameters, but it had apparently found four who fit the bill: George Wallace; Curtis Dall, FDR's former son-in-law and a conspiracy theorist who thought the Illuminati were secretly running the world; Defenders of the American Constitution founder Pedro Del Valle, who believed that an international Jewish cabal was behind the communist plot of one-world government; and right-wing publisher W. Frank Horne.

34. Funnily enough, Haley's paranoia had created a logistical nightmare when the book took off. Convinced that Johnson would send in federal agents to destroy whatever copies of the book they could find, he had stashed boxes of the book in friends' garages all over Amarillo and Canyon. When the orders started piling up, he ended up having to hire WT students to drive around and pick up copies and ship them. He was also sure that his phone was tapped, that he was under surveillance, and that Johnson would use the IRS and post office against him. His FBI file, however, reveals that the Bureau had little interest in Haley. "J. Evetts Haley: Man and Book," *OA*, October 19, 1964; Haley, interview with Bill Modisett, July 13, 1989, Haley Papers.

35. *CN*, August 6, 1964.

36. *Childress (TX) Index*, July 21, 1964.

37. This appreciation for harangue dressed up as scholarship was the subject of much of political humorist and former U.S. Senator Al Franken's 2003 best seller, *Lies and the Lying Liars Who Tell Them* (Penguin, 2004).

38. Tom Anderson to Haley, July 30 and November 16, 1964; Tom Anderson to *Palo Duro Press*, December 10, 1964; Ida Darden to Haley, September 15, 1964; Haley to Robert Welch, "Memorandum Record of Orders as of August 27, 1964," all in Correspondence, Series V, Haley Papers; Robert Sherrill, "Looking at Lyndon—With a Bit of Blood in the Eye," *Miami Herald*, October 4, 1964.

39. Even when he is on more solid ground, as in his case for Johnson's having stolen, with the help of a South Texas political machine, the 1948 senatorial race from Coke Stevenson, Haley seemingly can't help but stretch the bounds of credulity to include in his story a preposterous conspiracy theory involving murder, prostitution, suspicious prison suicides, corrupt officials, and attempted and successful assassinations, and he even concludes the chapter by darkly hinting that the same forces that put Johnson in the Senate might have been involved in the Kennedy assassination. *ATLAL*, 21–54.

40. In this regard, the book continues to "inform" certain elements of the public about the former president. A quick glance at the reviews of the book on Amazon or Goodreads reveals that Haley continues to influence how people perceive Johnson. It's also popular with those convinced that the Kennedy assassination was part of some larger conspiracy.

41. Janson, "Extremist Book Sales Soar."

42. Parr quoted in Grier, *Grassroots Women*, 88.

43. Sherrill, "Looking at Lyndon."

44. Both quoted in *MNM*, October 11, 1964.

45. Dave Hickey, "Sweet Reason vs. Black Passion," *TO*, September 18, 1964.

46. Jim Mathis, "J. Evetts Haley: A Voice of Many Hatreds," *Houston Post*, October 12, 1964.

47. Pamphlet on *A Texan Looks at Lyndon*, LBJ-Humphrey Texas Campaign, J. Evetts Haley Papers, PPHM; Baggarly quoted in H. M. Baggarly, The *Texas Country Editor: H. M. Baggarly Takes a Grass-Roots Look at National Politics* (World Publishing, 1966), 319; *Shamrock Texan*, September 3, 1964; *Dallas Times-Herald*, September 29, 1964; *AG*, August 31, 1964; Randy Porter's essay, reprinted in *AG*, October 27, 1964.

48. *DMN*, September 26, 1964.

49. Haley quoted in Janson, "Extremist Book Sales Soar."

50. Most helpful in constructing these years of Bush's life were Jon Meacham, *Destiny and Power: The American Odyssey of George Herbert Walker Bush* (Random House, 2015); Herbert S. Parmet, *George Bush: The Life of a Lone Star Yankee* (Scribner, 1997); and Tom Wicker, *George Herbert Walker Bush* (Penguin, 2004). Also helpful is George Bush, *All the Best, George Bush: My Life in Letters and Other Writings* (Scribner, 2013).

51. The company published both *Redbook* and *McCall's*, magazines read by every young homemaker in America, including those in Midland.

52. The previous chair had attempted to purge the party of Birchers. "A Pandora's Box for Texas GOP," *TO*, April 28, 1962.

53. *TO*, October 30, 1964.

54. *FWST*, September 12, 1963; *Tyler (TX) Morning Telegraph*, September 12, 1963; *LAJ*, September 23, 1963.

55. The *Texas Observer* ran a solid exposé of the group in its February 14, 1959, issue.

56. It was editorials he penned for the *Dallas Morning News*, expressing these sorts of ideas, that got him fired as president of the University of Dallas. See Miller, *Nut Country*, 104–107. His campaign infrastructure was used in the early weeks of publication and distribution of *A Texan Looks at Lyndon*.

57. Bush, *All the Best*, 87.

58. *TO*, September 18, 1964.

59. *DMN*, October, 1964; *FWST*, November 1, 1964.

60. *DMN*, October 25, 1964.

61. Not to be confused with future Grateful Dead leader Jerry Garcia's band, the Black Mountain Boys, which was playing gigs in California that year as well.

62. *FWST*, October 9, 1964.

63. *TO*, September 18, 1964.

64. *DMN*, October 23, 1964.

65. *AAS*, October 23, 1964. Karl Rove would use the same trick when he ran William Clements's campaign for governor two decades later.

66. *ADN*, September 23, 1964.

15. Unintended Consequences: Civil Rights and West Texas Football

1. Tom Kerpansky, who played at WT, quoted in W. K. Stratton, *Backyard Brawl: Inside the Blood Feud between Texas and Texas A&M* (Crown, 2002), 68.

2. U.S. Bureau of the Census, *Negro Population by County: Supplemental Report*, Series PC (S1)-52 (Washington, DC: Government Printing Office 1966). As late as 1970, Amarillo, Midland, Odessa, and Lubbock were among the most racially segregated cities in the country, with 93 to 94 percent residential segregation; San Angelo was 90 percent. Sean-Shong Hwang and Steve H. Murdock, "Residential Segregation in Texas," *Social Science Quarterly* (1982).

3. Werner Grunbaum, a University of Houston political scientist, studied desegregation patterns in Texas and concluded that it was the areas of Texas with the lowest African American populations that were the least committed to massive resistance. Werner F. Grunbaum, "Desegregation in Texas," *Public Opinion Quarterly* (1964). Other polls and studies reached the same conclusion. See, for example, Amilcar Shabazz, *Advancing*

Democracy: African Americans and the Struggle for Access and Equity in Higher Education in Texas (University of North Carolina Press, 2004); *Southern School News* (May 1957).

4. *FWST*, February 12, 1960.

5. *Dallas Express*, September 8, 1956; Marty Kuhlman, Caprock Chronicles, *LAJ*, December 14, 2019. Neal's husband, Nat, a lifelong educator and former principle at Amarillo's Carver High School, would become the first African American on the faculty when he joined the Education Department in 1971. In 2020, West Texas A&M named a new gathering space at the student center the Nathaniel and Helen Neal Multicultural Suite.

6. The study, by Herbert Greenberg at Texas Tech, was the primary reason that Evetts Haley and other ultraconservative regents at Texas Tech fired the sociologist. In contrast to sports, half the students believed schools should have segregated water fountains and bathrooms. Herbert Greenberg, Arthur L. Chase, and Thomas M. Cannon, "Attitudes of White and Negro High School Students in a West Texas Town toward School Integration," *Journal of Applied Psychology* (February 1957): 27–31.

7. There is a haziness in the stories of Kerbel's early life, especially regarding his football career at the University of Oklahoma and his military career. This sketch was put together through stories published in his hometown newspaper, the *Seminole (OK) Producer*, from 1939 to 1955. He was known as "Morrie" Kerbel in his early life.

8. The best source on Kerbel was written by one of his former coaches. Jack Harris, *A Passion for Victory: The Coaching Life of Texas Legend Joe Kerbel* (Taylor, 1990). See also Ty Cashion, *Pigskin Pulpit: A Social History of Texas High School Football Coaches* (Texas State Historical Association, 1998).

9. Quoted in Kevin Sherrington, "Flashback," *DMN*, May 12, 2006.

10. Kerbel was a genius at recruiting. When trying to sign Mercury Morris, he apparently went to a local water ski park outside Amarillo, snapped some photos, and mailed them to Morris with a message about how lush and wet the area around Canyon was. When recruiting Duane Thomas, he showed up at the Thomases' front door in South Dallas with his entire family in tow, promised that the only thing he would offer Duane was a good education and a chance to play football (music to the ears of Duane's mother), and waited with the patience of Job while his mother nevertheless stopped Duane five times just as he was about to sign his letter of intent.

11. Pete Pedro, interview with author, July 7, 2000; Robert D. Jacobus, *Black Man in the Huddle: Stories from the Integration of Texas Football* (Texas A&M University Press, 2019); *AGN*, October 7, 2019.

12. Stratton, *Backyard Brawl*, 69.

13. Duane Thomas quoted in Harris, *Passion for Victory*, 153.

14. David Wolf, "Mercury, Wings and All," *Life*, October 18, 1968; Terry Funk and Scott E. Williams, *Terry Funk: More than Just Hardcore* (Skyhorse, 2012), 18; Logan quoted in *AGN*, October 7, 2019.

15. Four years later, Morris, along with former WT teammate Jesse Powell, would be members of the undefeated Miami Dolphins team that won the Super Bowl.

16. Larry Matysik and Barbara Goodish, *Brody: The Triumph and Tragedy of Wrestling's Rebel* (ECW Press, 2010).

17. David Bixenspan, "Examining the Connection Between College Football and Professional Wrestling," *Bleacher Report*, December 3, 2013.

18. Duane Thomas and Duane Zimmerman, *Duane Thomas and the Fall of America's Team* (Warner Books, 1988), 31.

19. Eugene Morris and Steve Fiffer, *Against the Grain* (McGraw Hill, 1988), 40–41; Thomas and Zimmerman, *Duane Thomas*, 33.

20. *TO*, April 26, 1968.

21. *CN*, April 11, 1968; Buck Ramsey, "The Panhandle," *TO*, April 26, 1968; Darrell Munsell, interview with author, July 6, 2000; Frederick Rathjen, interview with author, July 29, 2000; Carol Drerup, "History Professor Says Campus Activism Is Dead," *The Prairie*, November 10, 1978. See also Joe Bill Sherrod, interview with John T. McElyea, June 24, 1991, PPHM. Sherrod remembered his sixth-grade teacher making numerous negative comments about Dr. King.

22. The screaming matches between Kerbel and Duane Thomas were legendary. One afternoon during practice the coach kept hectoring Thomas for failing to run a play the way Kerbel wanted it run. A frustrated Thomas grew angrier and angrier and finally spiked the football, glared at Kerbel, yelled "Fuck you!" and stalked off. Kerbel was so floored he stood speechless for a few moments before finally sputtering at Thomas's back, "Well, fuck you back!" The latter was an all-purpose in-joke among Texas football coaches for years.

23. This is not meant to suggest in any way that Texas itself was not as devoted to the Lost Cause as the rest of the South. It was. Long before J. Evetts Haley and the Texans for America began their textbook-monitoring project, the United Daughters of the Confederacy (UDC) was making sure that the schoolchildren of Texas learned only what it deemed the proper interpretation of southern history and the Civil War. Every county in the eastern half of the state had a Confederate memorial of some sort or another, and the United Confederate Veterans, the Sons of Confederate Veterans, and the UDC were powerful and popular organizations.

24. In the mid-1970s, when Amarillo, under a court order, was forced to begin busing schoolchildren to end segregation in its schools, Tascosa was the site of several instances of racial violence and discrimination. Black students were forbidden to carry hair picks (the administration labeled them as weapons) or to wear Black Power gear. Racist graffiti was scratched on lockers and bathroom walls. According to one Black minister in Amarillo: "Black movements and organizations were suspect [to whites]. Even the music peculiar to black people was viewed as a Communist plot to degenerate white youths. Integration was a dirty word. Whites saw it as Red conspiracy to change the balance of White power to Black domination. Fear replaced reason. Hate supplanted love. Benign neglect led to polarization." "Busing: The Other Side," *Accent West* (January 1975): 20–23; quote from V. P. Perry, "Guest Opinion," *Accent West* (January 1975): 23.

25. *History and Catalogue of the Kappa Alpha Fraternity*, (Kappa Alpha Convention, 1891), xxiv.

26. Another former member once wrote, in a florid defense of lynching: "The problem of the hour is not how to prevent lynching in the South, but the larger question: How shall we destroy the crime which always has and always will provoke lynching? The answer which the mob returns to this vital question is already known. The mob answers it with the rope, the bullet, and sometimes, God save us! With the torch. And the mob is practical; its theory is effective to a large degree. The mob is to-day the sternest, the strongest, and the most effective restraint that the age holds for the control of rape." This was part of a lecture that John Temple Graves, one of Kappa Alpha's most prominent alumni, gave regularly on the Chautauqua circuit. Quoted in the *NYT*, August 12, 1903.

27. Anthony James, "Political Parties: College Social Fraternities, Manhood, and the Defense of Southern Traditionalism, 1945–1960," in *White Masculinity in the Recent South*, ed. Trent Watts (Louisiana State University Press, 2008), 76.

28. *CN*, May 9, 1968.

29. Thomas and Zimmerman, *Duane Thomas*, 29–42; Morris and Fiffer, *Against the Grain*, 32–51 (quote on 41); John Rhinehart, interview with author, May 21, 2000; Frederick Rathjen, interview with author, June 29, 2000; T. Paige Carruth, interview with author,

July 3, 2000; Carroll Wilson, interview with author, July 11, 2000; Louis Rizzuto, interview with author, June 29, 2000; Franklin Thomas, interview with author, July 16, 2000; *CN*, May 9 and 16, 1968.

30. Randall County Republican Party Platform, May 1968, Haley Papers.

31. See *Mapping Inequality: Redlining in New Deal America*, a digital mapping project by the University of Richmond that features maps and descriptions of the federal government's Home Owner's Loan Corporation. The maps and the philosophy behind them—that neighborhoods with large percentages of American Americans were "hazardous"—were among the most pernicious tools for the creation and sustaining of residential segregation in America. https://dsl.richmond.edu/panorama/redlining/#loc=5/39.508/-94.58.

32. For more on race in Dallas, see Jim Schutze, *The Accommodation: The Politics of Race in an American City* (La Reunion, 1986); and Michael Phillips, *White Metropolis: Race, Ethnicity, and Religion in Dallas, 1841–2001* (University of Texas Press, 2006).

33. Thomas, interview with author, July 16, 2000.

34. Thomas and Zimmerman, *Duane Thomas*, 37.

35. Thomas and Zimmerman, *Duane Thomas*, 37 (quote); Claudia Stuart, interview with author, July 25, 2000. Stuart's maiden name was Stewart.

36. *CN*, November 14, 1968.

37. *CN*, November 14, 1968.

38. *AGT*, March 6, 1969.

39. *AGT*, March 6 and 13, 1969; *CN*, March 2, 1969.

40. *The Prairie*, January 10, 1969.

41. *AGT*, April 18, 1969. The front page of the *Canyon News* in the edition that covered Afro-American Week featured a large photo of the Kappa Alpha fraternity, with the Confederate flag at full staff, doing a service project, with a smaller photo of the Afro-American Week speakers off to the right. *CN*, April 20, 1969.

42. *AGT*, February 20, 1969.

43. *The Prairie*, March 5, 1969.

44. *The Prairie*, April 23, 1969.

45. The 1970 Dallas Cowboys had 33 white players (most of whom were from the South) and only 13 African Americans on the team; 16 of the team's 22 starters were white.

46. He was also having money troubles, the consequence of a shady agent and an estranged spouse who had racked up debts while Thomas was in college.

47. It was the biggest story in pro football that summer. Most outlets, however, focused on Thomas's descriptions of Cowboys management rather than his descriptions of the larger racial issues in football. Joe Nick Patoski, *The Dallas Cowboys: The Outrageous History of the Biggest, Loudest, Most Hated, Best Loved Football Team in America* (2012; reprint, Back Bay Books, 2013), 255. The quotes were in every major newspaper in the country.

48. Hunter S. Thompson, *Fear and Loathing: on the Campaign Trail '72* (Warner, 1973), 74.

49. *CN*, March 15, 1970.

50. Franklin Thomas, interview with author.

51. *CN*, March 15, 1970.

52. *CN*, April 16, 19, 1970, Roger Scott quoted in April 19 edition.

53. Quoted in Thomas and Zimmerman, *Duane Thomas*, 119.

54. *AGT*, February 9, 1971.

55. Before coming to Permian, he had coached at Littlefield and Borger high schools, taking Borger to the state championship game, where they lost to Breckenridge.

56. In 1986, the team moved down to NCAA Division II. Between 2005 and 2013, it enjoyed some success under Coach Don Carthel. It never again produced a first-round draft pick. Kimbrough Stadium is now owned by the Canyon Independent School District. The new Buffalo Stadium, completed in 2019, seats 8,500, half the size of some of the larger high school venues in Texas.

16. Right-Wing Republicanism

1. Election results demonstrate Baggarly's influence. During his tenure as editor of the *Herald*, Swisher County remained one of the few Democratic strongholds in West Texas.

2. Baggarly took unique pleasure in public exchanges with Birchers who wrote to the *Herald*. His devasting responses critiqued the letters on everything from grammar to logic to historical context.

3. In one of his more brutal takedowns, Baggarly once explained the danger Izzard posed to West Texas:

> The *Amarillo News* radiates three of the more repulsive and obnoxious characteristics that can be possessed by an individual or publication.
>
> First, it reflects the conceit of a typical "know it all." The paper has the answers to all the world's problems. In one sentence it can tell us how to solve the problems of Communism, Castro, agriculture and Africa. It speaks with the precocious ninth grade science student telling the space agency how to put a man on the moon. Everybody's out of step except Wes [Izzard] and Louise [Evans, editorial page editor].
>
> Second, it reflects intellectual dishonesty. It sees only evil in its enemies and perfection in its friends. For example, since the name of John F. Kennedy was first mentioned as a Presidential possibility until this moment, the Amarillo paper has never seen even one commendable virtue, one commendable characteristic in this man or in any of his relatives. Even the person with no opinion concerning Kennedy or one only reasonably opposed to the President can recognize this as intellectual dishonesty because he knows that God never made a man as inept as Kennedy is painted by the Izzard-Evans team.
>
> Third, it reflects an underestimation of the intelligence of the Panhandle citizenry. Resentment boils within an individual when someone cast a reflection upon his intelligence by expecting to believe an obvious falsehood. And this is a well-known technique of the *Amarillo News*. It dishes out its deceptive information about Kennedy, Yarborough, Johnson, or others on its dirt list, in the spirit that "these hicks don't read anything but us and they'll fall for what we tell them like a child falls for Santa Claus."
>
> *TH*, February 15, 1962.

4. *TH*, May 12 and June 21, 1956, October 16, 1958, December 4, 1958, July 16, 1959, November 5, 1959, August 27, 1964, March 3, 1960.

5. *TH*, August 8, 1968.

6. A solid corrective to this narrative and interpretation is Matthew Dallek, *Birchers: How the John Birch Society Radicalized the American Right* (Basic Books, 2023). See also Rick Perlstein and Edward H. Miller, "The John Birch Society Never Left," *New Republic*, March 8, 2021.

7. *John Birch Society Bulletin* (May 1965): 10. That year, the JBS also prepared a sixteen-page advertising supplement for newspapers, "The John Birch Society: A Report," meant to reestablish the organization's reputation. It ran in the *Sunday ANG*, May 16.

8. In a rare instance when the JBS was behind the curve in anticommunist conspiracy theorizing, white supremacists in the South had been making this argument since the 1950s. Indeed, the citizens' councils insistence on the communist conspiracy behind the Civil Rights Movement had been a major link between the southern and western wings of the radical right in the 1950s and early 1960s. A good recent book on the citizens' councils is Stephanie Renee Rolph, *Resisting Equality: The Citizens' Council, 1954–1989* (Louisiana State University Press, 2018).

9. The book is still in print. It enjoys a 4.8-star average review on Amazon. Readers express their appreciation for "revealing" the "puppet masters" and the "hidden hands" pulling the levers of power, for uncovering facts apparently only available in the secret Jewish Encyclopedia of 1905, and for putting recent work by Ann Coulter and Paul Kengor in context.

10. The full-page ad appeared in hundreds and hundreds of newspapers across the country between 1965 and 1970.

11. Other regulars in the TACT stable of speakers were Birchers: Tom Anderson, Billy James Hargis, Clarence Manion, Edwin Walker, Robert Welch, and Alan Stang.

12. *FWST*, November 2, 1966.

13. *OA*, April 8, 1968.

14. Ads for screenings may be found in *EPT*, October 13, 1968 and *Childress Index*, October 14, 1968.

15. The median U.S. household income that year was $7,000. U.S. Census Reports, "Household Income in 1968," Series P-60, No. 65, October 31, 1969.

16. "I Was a Spy for the FBI," *Ebony* (March 1961), quote on 10; Julia C. Brown testimony, House Committee on Un-American Activities, "Communist Activities in the Cleveland, Ohio Area, June 4, 5, 1962; Julia Clarice Brown, *I Testify: My Years as an Undercover Agent for the FBI* (Western Islands, 1966). Western Islands was the John Birch Society's publishing company.

17. Young had a long career in Hollywood and is best known for playing Maxwell Scott, the newspaper reporter in *The Man Who Shot Liberty Valance*, who utters the most famous line in the film: "This is the West, sir; when the legend becomes fact, print the legend."

18. For more on Brown, see Veronica A. Wilson, "'To Tell All My People': Race, Representation, and John Birch Society Activist Julia Brown," in *Women of the Right*, ed. Kathleen M. Blee and Sandra McGee Deutsch (Penn State University Press, 2012), 242–256.

19. *SAEN*, November 13, 1963; *EPT*, March 23, 1965, *EPHP*, August 7, 1968. Quotes from *EPT*, August 14, 1968.

20. *OA*, August 15, 1968.

21. Phillips had been using his newspaper as basically a far-right broadside since the late 1940s, regularly railing against the United Nations, fluoride in public drinking water (a communist brainwashing tool), and communist textbooks, teachers, and preachers. His 1952 essay "We Owe a Debt" was an early-1950s classic of underground right-wing paranoid literature, outlining Soviet plans to begin executing Americans according to a prepared list.

22. The *Canyon News*, edited by an RCRP member, covered its rise well in the 1960s, as did Wes Izzard in the *Amarillo Daily News*.

23. Grier, *Grassroots Women*, 89; *ADN*, May 11, 1964; *CN*, May 14, 1964.

24. Rogers, who had run unopposed in the May primary, had left the local party scrambling. *AGT*, August 1, 1966

25. *CN*, May 19, 1966.

26. Haley speeches to Republican Party of Randall County, October 2, 1967, JEH—Speeches—To Republican Party of Randall County, Series IV, Literary Productions, Subseries F, Speeches, Haley Papers.

27. Over fifty Academy Award winners appeared on the program. Tomas Kellner, "Lights, Electricity, Action: When Ronald Reagan Hosted 'General Electric Theater,'" GE News (February 2019).

28. Ronald Reagan, *An American Life* (Simon and Schuster, 2011), 126–131.

29. Moving into the old and slightly dilapidated governor's mansion after Reagan won the 1966 California gubernatorial race was simply too big an adjustment for the Reagans, who had grown accustomed to living in a home with literally every modern convenience. They moved out after only four months and rented a house in Sacramento during his eight years in office. In his last term, Reagan approved the construction of a new governor's mansion, a modern 12,000-square-foot home that, like the GE house, was fully modern. Joan Didion described it: "It is simply and rather astonishingly an enlarged version of a very common kind of California tract house, a monument not to colossal ego [as many Reagan critics attested] but to a weird absence of ego, a case study in architecture of limited possibilities, insistently and malevolently 'democratic,' flattened out, mediocre, and 'open' and as devoid of privacy or personal eccentricity as the lobby area in a Ramada Inn. It is the architecture of 'background music.'" Joan Didion, "Many Mansions," in *The White Album* (Simon and Schuster, 1979), 69.

30. Timothy Raphael, *The President Electric: Ronald Reagan and the Politics of Performance* (University of Michigan Press, 2009), 183; "The Body Electric: GE, TV, and the Reagan Brand," *TDR: The Drama Review* (June 2009): 120–121.

31. Reagan's GE years are well covered in Thomas W. Evans, *The Education of Ronald Reagan: The General Electric Years and the Untold Story of His Conversion to Conservatism* (Columbia University Press, 2006).

32. *ARN*, April 12, 1959.

33. Over the course of that year, "The Speech" existed in three forms: "What Price Freedom?" "Losing Freedom by Installments," and "A Time for Choosing."

34. It was this speech that the Amarillo NBC affiliate broadcast in place of Chet Huntley's special program "America's Farm Problem," described earlier. The original Freedom Forum was an offshoot of Fred Schwarz's Christian Anticommunist Crusade.

35. Texas Regular and Pappy O'Daniel sponsor E. B. Germany used his weekly column, carried all over Texas, to reprint Reagan's Freedom Forum address. Corporate sponsors rebroadcast the speech in most major markets over the next few weeks, including the Dallas–Fort Worth CBS station that ran it during the *GE Theater* time slot.

36. *Mexia Daily News*, November 18, 1963.

37. Wuthnow, *Rough Country*, 552n59.

38. This was the movie that the TFA demanded be shown before the San Antonio hearings of the Textbook Committee. *The Blue Book of the John Birch Society, 1963*, 440.

39. Description provided by the Christian Americanism Crusade, in *Kerrville (TX) Mountain Sun*, May 29, 1963.

40. Among the others were *Operation Abolition, Communist Imperialism, Communism and Coexistence* (by the Truth about Communism team). *AAS*, September 8, 1964.

41. *AGT*, October 28, 1964.

42. Matthew Dallek, *The Right Moment: Ronald Reagan's First Victory and the Decisive Turning Point in American Politics*, (Oxford University Press, 2004) x.

43. *The Berkeley Revolution*, produced and directed by Bill Richardson, written by Gary Allen, distributed by Constructive Action, 1966; *OA*, March 19, 1966; Bart L. Verhoeven,

"The Rearguard of Freedom: The John Birch Society and the Development of Modern Conservatism in the United States, 1958–1968," PhD diss., University of Nottingham, 2015, 137–138.

44. Gerard J. De Groot, "'A Goddamned Electable Person': The 1966 California Gubernatorial Campaign of Ronald Reagan," *History* (1997): 429–448, and "Ronald Reagan and Student Unrest in California, 1966–1970," *Pacific Historical Review* (1996): 107–129; William J. Rorabaugh, *Berkeley at War: the 1960s* (Oxford University Press, 1989); Kurt Schuparra, *Triumph of the Right: The Rise of the California Conservative Movement, 1945–1966* (M. E. Sharpe, 1998); Michelle Reeves, "'Obey the Rules or Get Out': Ronald Reagan's 1966 Gubernatorial Campaign and the 'Trouble in Berkeley,'" *Southern California Quarterly* (2010): 275–305; and Curtis Marez, "Ronald Reagan, the College Movie: Political Demonology, Academic Freedom, and the University of California," *Critical Ethnic Studies* (2016): 148–80.

45. Reeves, "'Obey the Rules or Get Out.'"

46. Haley to J. C. Barnes, September 29, 1967, Correspondence; JEH to Coombs, January 31, 1968, both in Correspondence, Haley Papers.

47. To be honest, Haley was a minor nuisance compared to Houston's Nancy Palm, or "Napalm Nancy." She was brilliant, tough, organized, ruthless, and totally obsessed with a Reagan presidential campaign.

48. Two insider accounts provide excellent coverage of the Texas GOP during this time: Wayne J. Thorburn, *Red State: An Insider's Story of How the GOP Came to Dominate Texas Politics* (University of Texas Press, 2014) and Knaggs, *Two-Party Texas*.

49. These sorts of conflicts were erupting at every level in the Texas GOP, and nationwide, that year.

50. *AGT*, May 1, 1968; Dick Brooks, interview with author, July 17, 2000; Grier, *Grassroots Women*, 89–90.

51. Among the planks presented were some of Haley's typically long-winded condemnations of the welfare state, politicians who "pandered to the minority vote," LBJ's "no-win" policy in Vietnam, and a demand for the guarantee of local control of law enforcement. There were the usual collection of Bircher demands: end foreign aid, farm and poverty programs, trim government expenditures, and support local police. The platform also included this gem: "Whereas continued pursuit of . . . concentration of authority will inevitably rob the states, the cities, and the counties of all vestiges of local authority and hence ability to protect the lives, the properties, and the rights of the citizens at home . . . [and since] these policies would appear to have been designed to destroy respect for local government and authority, and thereby destroying law and order generally, . . . we demand that Congress return to the states and the local jurisdictions that complete control of our policy and the enforcement of law, as guaranteed in the Constitution." RCRP Resolutions, 1968; Precinct Resolutions, RCRP, May 4, 1968, both in Haley Papers; *CN*, May 9 and 16, 1968.

52. Other stops on the "southern solicitation" strategy included Arkansas, Virginia, Kentucky, and Maryland, where he met with large numbers of delegates. Lou Cannon, *Governor Reagan: His Rise to Power* (Public Affairs, 2003), 265–266; *NYT*, July 20, 1968.

53. *ADN*, July 20, 1968.

54. Food description from *ADN*, July 20, 1968.

55. Unidentified news clipping, April 5, 1942, Hazelwood Collection, Drawer One, PPHM; *Houston Post*, September 13, 1942; various news clippings Hazelwood Collection, Drawers 1 and 19, PPHM.

56. GH to Sheffy, June 10, 1941, Drawer One, Hazelwood Collection, PPHM.

57. *AAS*, March 22, 1966; *OA*, March 15, 1966; *Daily Texan*, March 15 and 16, 1966; *ADN*, March 16, 1966; TFA Report, May 23. 1966, Series III, Political Files, A, TFA, Box 2, Haley Papers; "Students: The Free-Sex Movement," *Time Magazine*, March 11, 1966.

58. Dale Simpson to editor, *LAJ*, March 20, 1966.

59. Mrs. R. E. W. to Grady Hazelwood, March 29, 1966; G. S. R. to Grady Hazelwood, March 23, 1966; J. F. G. to Grady Hazelwood, March 16, 1966; Hazelwood Collection, Drawer 19, PPHM.

60. In March 1968, Hazelwood sent Peter O'Donnell a personal check for $1,000 made out to the state GOP with a caveat: "This check may be cashed if, when and only if Gov. Ronald Reagan, of California is the official nominee of the Republican Party for the Presidency of the United States." Hazelwood to Peter O'Donnell, March 25, 1968; Hazelwood to Ronald Reagan, April 8, 1968, Hazelwood Collection, Drawer 23, PPHM.

61. Grady Hazelwood to Ronald Reagan, April 3, 1968, Hazelwood Collection, Drawer 24, PPHM.

62. Grady Hazelwood, speech, "Ronald Reagan Rally," Hazelwood Collection, Drawer 23, PPHM. See also coverage in the *ADN*, July 20, 1968.

63. Bush quoted in Meacham, *Destiny and Power*, 141.

64. The tiny *Gilmer Mirror* had a man on the scene who reported the convention for the paper in a series of articles that appeared in the August 15, 1968, edition.

65. *ADN*, August 9, 1968.

66. Marguerite Terrell to Grady Hazelwood, August 2, 1968, Hazelwood Collection Scrapbook, PPHM.

67. Quoted in Philip Crass, *The Wallace Factor* (Mason/Charter, 1976), 12.

68. *AAS*, October 28, 1967. *AG*, May 6, 1968; *ADN*, May 5, 1968. Many Birchers opposed Wallace in 1964, afraid he would bleed off support for Goldwater, but 1968 was a different story. Haley to Tom Anderson, June 26, 1964, Correspondence, Haley Papers.

69. She had also been the Bush family's pediatrician when they lived in Midland.

70. B'nai B'rith, Press Release, September 13, 1968, Cong. Rec. 31578–31580.

71. SAC Baltimore to SAC Oklahoma City, March 18, 1974, Glenn O. Young FBI File, https://archive.org/details/YOUNGGlennO.OklahomaCity1571011/page/n1/mode/2up.

72. *Waco Tribune*, August 17, 1968; *FWST*, August 18, 1968; *NYT*, August 25, 1968.

73. *AGT*, October 18, 1968; Dick Brooks, interview with author.

74. Walter L. Shelly, "Political Profiles of the Nixon, Humphrey, and Wallace Voters in the Texas Panhandle, 1968: A Study in Voting Behavior," PhD diss., Texas Tech University, 1972, 91–94.

75. Bryan Poff's Republican opponent had pulled out of the race a few weeks earlier.

CODA

1. One of Haley's oldest friends, W. C. Holden, tells the story of visiting Nita Haley in the hospital when she looked up from Don Quixote to say: "Going up and down the country chasing—attacking windmills—chasing windmills. That's Evetts. He's done it all of his life. He does just about as much good as ole Don Quixote, because he's after things that there's no hope for." William Curry Holden, interview with Jimmy Skaggs, May 3 and 6, 1968, Reel 7, Transcript 9, SWC.

2. For a demonstration of this argument, even going so far as to lump the western half of the state in with the rest of the South, see Michael Lind, *Made in Texas: George W. Bush and the Southern Takeover of American Politics* (Basic Books, 2002).

3. Joining the three West Texas congressional districts in the Top Ten most reliably

Republican districts in the 114th Congress were the Georgia 9th and 14th, the Alabama 4th and 6th, and the 1st Districts of Louisiana and Tennessee. As this book was going to press, one could already spot a post–New Right regional shift as Republican strength gathered in the Appalachian districts of Ohio, West Virginia, Kentucky, and Pennsylvania.

4. Reagan's first big primary victory was in late March in North Carolina. The press reported it as a major upset. But it wasn't really; Reagan's campaign in the Tar Heel State, run by Jesse Helms, was a preview of what would happen in Texas. He ran a right-wing campaign designed specifically to appeal to the ultraconservatives who dominated the North Carolina GOP. He did the same across the South, with great success. In Florida, which had a stronger GOP than most of the rest of the South, Reagan picked up a third of the delegates. He dominated in South Carolina, Alabama, and Georgia. He also won Arkansas and split the vote in Tennessee.

5. Probably the best thing ever written about Bentsen is Al Reinhart, "The Unveiling of Lloyd Bentsen," *Texas Monthly* (December 1974).

6. His plan failed; Bentsen got steamrolled by Georgia governor Jimmy Carter in Texas. His national campaign, seemingly based mostly on his gray-templed and gray-suited gravitas, had lost so much traction by May, he never had a chance. Carter would go on to win Texas in the general election in November. No Democratic presidential candidate has won Texas since.

7. Unfortunately, the race was then and is still too often framed within an Establishment vs. Upstarts narrative structure that focuses on party leaders rather than voters and that assumes a level of control over the party by its leadership that belies the evidence. This structure is all too often accompanied by an introduction of Reagan that fails to acknowledge his longtime popularity among Texas conservatives. See Wayne J. Thornburn, *Red State: An Insider's Story of How the GOP Came to Dominate Texas Politics* (University of Texas Press, 2014); Sean P. Cunningham, *Cowboy Conservatism: Texas and the Rise of the Modern Right* (University Press of Kentucky, 2010); and Cunningham, "The 1976 GOP Primary: Ford, Reagan, and the Battle that Transformed Political Campaigns in Texas" *ETHJ* (2003) for three examples. Even Gilbert Garcia's excellent *Reagan's Comeback: Four Weeks in Texas That Changed American Politics Forever* (Trinity University Press, 2012), the definitive history of Reagan's 1976 efforts in Texas, hints at this set-up.

8. When Reagan officially began his candidacy, Barry Goldwater took over his programming.

9. During the segment, which aired in March 1975, Carson kept pushing Reagan about whether he would run as a third-party candidate.

10. Garcia, *Reagan's Comeback*, 97.

11. Like many Birchers in those years, Angelo was a regular letter writer to local newspapers, particularly in his case the *San Angelo Standard-Times*, where he defended the JBS and railed against communist plots. For two examples, see *SAST*, March 23, 1961, and December 3, 1963. He also exhibited the brand of snarky, sneering humor that would come to define many on the right. His funny response letter as mayor to a request by the Department of Housing and Urban Development for a parking permit at the Midland Airport was widely distributed in John Birch circles in August 1976, and a copy eventually made its way onto the editorial page of the *Bakersfield Californian*, August 21, 1976.

12. *SAST*, February 3, 1976.

13. *Corpus Christi Caller*, April 15, 1976.

14. Haley used the money for huge newspaper ad campaigns promoting Reagan and educating voters on how they could support him in the primary. Federal Election Commission, news release, October 27, 1976.

15. He lost those by a total of 223 to 130.

16. *Denton Record-Chronicle*, May 2, 1976; *AGN*, Sunday, May 2, 1976.

17. Another of its four at-large delegates was a proto-Libertarian representative from Lake Jackson named Ron Paul.

18. Many of these issues had been on the primary ballot, where they passed in numbers that almost directly corresponded to Reagan's votes.

19. That same month, *Texas Monthly* (June 1976) named Haley the state's "Best Old Coot."

20. *Denton Record-Chronicle*, July 15, 1976. A UPI story about Haley showed up in newspapers across the state that summer. The longer versions included Haley's claim of having been fired from the University of Texas in 1936. See *Plano Daily Star-Courier*, July 21, 1976.

21. Stephen Harrigan, "Whoever Said It Was a Grand Old Party?" *Texas Monthly* (October 1976); John Dean, "Rituals of the Herd," *Rolling Stone*, October 7, 1976; Adam Wren, "It Was Riotous: An Oral History of the GOP's Last Open Convention," *Politico*, April 5, 2016.

VERY SELECT BIBLIOGRAPHY

Nick Hornby structures his hilarious and heartbreaking novel *High Fidelity* around descriptions of Rob Fleming's Top Five all-time romantic breakups. Making "Top Five" lists is a thing that Rob Fleming, the novel's narrator-protagonist does, the primary means of communication for him and the other music- (and film- and television-) obsessed know-it-alls who hang around Rob's record store. Top Five albums by blind artists, Top Five Dustin Hoffman movies, Top Five songs for your funeral, Top Five songs for a wet Monday morning, and so on. The endless meditations of an expert class.

Historians are like that. Obsessives, whose hunger for expertise leads them not just to seek knowledge and understanding but to also accumulate scholarship. We can be ruthless, inexhaustible builders of bibliographies. The working reference catalog I assembled for *The Conservative Frontier* has over 1,600 entries. Which is a lot. Culling our libraries into digestible "suggestions for further reading" requires tough calls and great discipline.

I have decided to follow the lead of the gang at Championship Vinyl and organize this book's bibliography by making Top Five lists. These lists are not meant to be comprehensive but rather biographical, pointing out those important stops on my intellectual journey across the conservative frontier. Besides, in our wired world, bibliography builders don't need me to help them find books or articles or websites on the subjects covered here. Finding sources and interpretations has never been easier. Instead, these are the carefully culled lists of those books and other sources that had the most influence on my thinking or understanding of a subject or time. These were the works that put me in a particular frame of mind.

There are Top Five lists for each chapter and a few extra on larger and more personal subjects. Each section has two different lists: one specifically on academic or scholarly texts (almost always books) and a second, more eclectic group that might include books, novels, articles, dissertations, paintings, albums, poems, exhibits, or other sources. Also, sometimes I cheat.

To make this list as wide as possible within its constraints, I have tried to avoid duplication.

Specific references can be found in the book's endnotes. A fuller bibliography, also organized by chapter and theme, is available at jeffroche.net..

Top Five Archives
Panhandle-Plains Historical Museum, Canyon, Texas
Southwest Collection, Texas Tech University, Lubbock
Haley Memorial Library and History Center, Midland, Texas
LBJ Presidential Library, Austin
Research Collection for Conservative and Libertarian Studies, University of Oregon
    Libraries, Eugene

Top Five Go-To Resources

Encyclopedia of the Great Plains, http://plainshumanities.unl.edu/encyclopedia/

Handbook of Texas Online, https://www.tshaonline.org/handbook

It is close to impossible to describe how valuable this resource is for Texas history. There is not a subject in this book about which I did not consult *The Handbook of Texas Online.* It is a breathtakingly remarkable tool.

The Portal to Texas History, University of North Texas, https://texashistory.unt.edu/

Texas Observer Online Archives, https://www.texasobserver.org/archives-search/

Texas Monthly Online Archives, https://www.texasmonthly.com/archives/

EXPOSITION

Top Five Books

Paul Howard Carlson, *Deep Time and the Texas High Plains: History and Geology*, 2005

Pekka Hämäläinen, *The Comanche Empire*, 2009

John Miller Morris, *El Llano Estacado: Exploration and Imagination on the High Plains of Texas and New Mexico, 1536–1860*, 1997

Frederick W. Rathjen, *The Texas Panhandle Frontier*, 1973

David J. Weber, *The Spanish Frontier in North America*, 1994

Top Five Other

John L. Allen, "The Garden-Desert Continuum: Competing Views of the Great Plains in the Nineteenth Century," *Great Plains Quarterly*, 1985

Pedro Reyes Castañeda, *The Journey of Coronado, 1540–1542: From the City of Mexico to the Grand Cañon of the Colorado and the Buffalo Plains of Texas, Kansas, and Nebraska, as Told by Himself and His Followers* (1545), 1904

Dan Flores, "The Great Plains 'Wilderness' as a Human-Shaped Environment," *Great Plains Research*, 1999

W. B. Parker, *Notes Taken during the Expedition Commanded by Capt. R. B. Marcy, U.S.A., through Unexplored Texas, in the Summer and Fall of 1854*, 1856

John Wesley Powell, Geographical and Geological Survey of the Rocky Mountain Region (U.S.), *Report on the Lands of the Arid Region of the United States, with a More Detailed Account of the Lands of Utah. With Maps*, 1879

1. THE RISE AND FALL OF THE CATTLE KINGDOM

Top Five Books

J. Evetts Haley, *Charles Goodnight, Cowman and Plainsman*, 1936

Laura V. Hamner, *Short Grass and Longhorns*, 1943

Terry G. Jordan, *Trails to Texas: Southern Roots of Western Cattle Ranching*, 1981

Jacqueline M. Moore, *Cow Boys and Cattle Men: Class and Masculinities on the Texas Frontier, 1865–1900*, 2011

Ernest Staples Osgood, *The Day of the Cattleman*, 1929

Joshua Specht, *Red Meat Republic: A Hoof-to-Table History of How Beef Changed America*, 2019

Top Five Other

Sjoerd Beugelsdijk, "Entrepreneurial Culture, Regional Innovativeness and Economic Growth," *Journal of Evolutionary Economics* (2007)

John L. McCarty, *Maverick Town: The Story of Old Tascosa*, 1946

Joseph G. McCoy, *Historic Sketches of the Cattle Trade of the West and Southwest*, 1874

Reviel Netz, *Barbed Wire: An Ecology of Modernity*, 2009

Jerome C. Smiley, *Prose and Poetry of the Live Stock Industry of the United States, with Outlines of the Origin and Ancient History of Our Live Stock Animals*, 1905

Richard White, "Animals and Enterprise," in *The Oxford History of the American West*, 1994

2. AGRICULTURAL WONDERLAND

Top Five Books

Jan Blodgett, *Land of Bright Promise: Advertising the Texas Panhandle and South Plains, 1870–1917*, 1988

B. R. Brunson, *The Texas Land and Development Company: A Panhandle Promotion, 1912–1956*, 1970

David B. Gracy, *Littlefield Lands: Colonization on the Texas Plains, 1912–1920*, 1968

Frieda Knobloch, *The Culture of Wilderness: Agriculture as Colonization in the American West*, 1996

Allan Kulikoff, *The Agrarian Origins of American Capitalism*, 1992

Lester Fields Sheffy, *The Life and Times of Timothy Dwight Hobart, 1855–1935*, 1950

Top Five Other

Isaiah Bowman, "Jordan Country," *Geographical Review*, 1931

John Brinckerhoff Jackson, *Discovering the Vernacular Landscape*, 1984

Thomas Lloyd Miller, *The Public Lands of Texas, 1519–1970*, 1972

"The Rise and Fall of the Soash Empire: A West Texas Hard Luck Story," Baylor Digital Collections Blog, accessed June 23, 2023, https://blogs.baylor.edu/digitalcollections/2012/11/15/the-rise-and-fall-of-the-soash-empire-a-west-texas-hard-luck-story/

Yi-fu Tuan, *Topophilia: A Study of Environmental Perception, Attitudes, and Values*, 1990

3. CAPITALIST UTOPIA

Top Five Books

Charles Dudley Eaves and C. Alan Hutchinson, *Post City, Texas: C. W. Post's Colonizing Activities in West Texas*, 1952

Timothy Miller, *The Quest for Utopia in Twentieth-Century America*, Vol. 1: *1900–1960*, 1998

Chad Pearson, *Reform or Repression: Organizing America's Anti-union Movement*, 2016

Martin J. Sklar, *The Corporate Reconstruction of American Capitalism, 1890–1916: The Market, the Law, and Politics*, 1988

Stephen V. Ward, *Selling Places: The Marketing and Promotion of Towns and Cities, 1850–2000*, 1998

Top Five Other

Karen Kaye Bilbrey, "Historic Buildings in C. W. Post's Model Town, Post, Texas," MA thesis, University of Texas, 2010

T. C. Boyle, *The Road to Wellville*, 1993

Digitized Maps, Architectural Drawings, Blueprints, and more available online at the Double U Company Collection, Southwest Collection, Texas Tech University, https://swco-ir.tdl.org/handle/10605/1695

William K. Howard, director, *The Power and the Glory* (film), 1933
Written by Preston Sturges, grandson-in-law of C. W. Post. The main character of the film, played by Spencer Tracy, is based on Post.

Peyton Paxson, "Charles William Post: The Mass Marketing of Health and Welfare," PhD diss., Boston University, 1993

4. WEST TEXAS NATIONALISM

Top Five Books

Benedict Anderson, *Imagined Communities: Reflections on the Origin and Spread of Nationalism*, 2006

Glen Sample Ely, *Where the West Begins: Debating Texas Identity*, 2011

Greg Grandin, *The End of the Myth: From the Frontier to the Border Wall in the Mind of America*, 2019

Kerwin Lee Klein, *Frontiers of Historical Imagination: Narrating the European Conquest of Native America, 1890–1990*, 1999

David M. Wrobel, *Promised Lands: Promotion, Memory, and the Creation of the American West*, 2002

Top Five Other

Mody C. Boatright, "The Myth of Frontier Individualism," *Southwestern Social Science Quarterly*, 1941

Donna Haraway, "Teddy Bear Patriarchy: Taxidermy in the Garden of Eden, New York City, 1908–1936," *Social Text*, 1984

Walter Prescott Webb, "Some Historians of the Plains Region," *Amarillo News and Globe*, August 14, 1938

Virtual Tour, Pioneer Hall, Panhandle Plains Historical Museum, https://www.virtually -anywhere.net/tours/wtamu/pphm/vtour/index.html?startscene=scenePioneerHall

Donald W. Whisenhunt, *The Five States of Texas: An Immodest Proposal*, 1987

5. BOOSTER POLITICS ASCENDANT

Top Five Books

Norman D. Brown, *Hood, Bonnet, and Little Brown Jug: Texas Politics, 1921–1928*, 1984

Lewis L. Gould, *Progressives and Prohibitionists: Texas Democrats in the Wilson Era*, 1973

Joseph L. Locke, *Making the Bible Belt: Texas Prohibitionists and the Politicization of Southern Religion*, 2017

Judith N. McArthur, *Creating the New Woman: The Rise of Southern Women's Progressive Culture in Texas, 1893–1918*, 1998

Lisa McGirr, *The War on Alcohol: Prohibition and the Rise of the American State*, 2016

Top Five Other

Cary W. De Wit, "Women's Sense of Place on the American High Plains," *Great Plains Quarterly*, 2001

Richard Hofstadter, *The Progressive Historians: Turner, Beard, Parrington*, 1968

Herbert Hoover, *American Individualism*, 1923

Katherine Jellison, *Entitled to Power: Farm Women and Technology, 1913–1963*, 1993

"Votes for Women!" (online exhibit), Texas State Library and Archives Commission, accessed January 29, 2025, https://www.tsl.texas.gov/exhibits/suffrage/index.html

Phebe K. Warner, *Selected Editorials*, 1964

6. RUIN

Top Five Books

Paul Bonnifield, *The Dust Bowl: Men, Dirt, and Depression*, 1979

Hannah Holleman, *Dust Bowls of Empire: Imperialism, Environmental Politics, and the Injustice of "Green" Capitalism*, 2018

Vance Johnson, *Heaven's Tableland: The Dust Bowl Story*, 1947

Brad Lookingbill, *Dust Bowl, U.S.A: Depression America and the Ecological Imagination, 1929–1941*, 2001

Donald Worster, *Dust Bowl: The Southern Plains in the 1930s*, 1979

Top Five Other

Ruby Winona Adams, "Social Behavior in a Drought-Stricken Texas Panhandle Community," MA thesis, University of Texas, 1939

William Cronon, "A Place for Stories: Nature, History, and Narrative," *Journal of American History*, 1992

Alexandre Houge, Paintings, Erosion Series: "Drouth Stricken Area" (1934), "Wind Erosion" (1935), "Drouth Survivors" (1936), "Erosion" (1937), "Mother Earth Laid Bare" (1938), "Road to Rhome" (1938), "The Crucified Land" (1939), "Avalanche by Wind" (1944), "Soil and Subsoil" (1946)

Archibald MacLeish, *Land of the Free*, 1938

Siegfried D. Schubert et al., "On the Cause of the 1930s Dust Bowl," *Science*, 2004

Top Five Contemporary Pieces

Avis D. Carlson, "Dust Blowing," *Harper's Magazine*, July 1935

Walter Davenport, "Land Where Our Children Die," *Collier's*, September 18, 1937

Caroline A. Henderson, "Spring in the Dust Bowl," *Atlantic Monthly*, June 1937

John L. McCarty, "Dust of the Past," transcript of KGNC Radio program, aired November 18, 1941, McCarthy Papers, Amarillo Public Library, Amarillo, TX.

John L. McCarty, "Thou Shalt Not Bear False Witness," *Amarillo Daily News*, September 13, 1937

7. NEW DEAL AGONISTES

Top Five Books

Jefferson Cowie, *The Great Exception: The New Deal and the Limits of American Politics*, 2016

Lionel V. Patenaude, *Texans, Politics, and the New Deal*, 1983

Catherine McNicol Stock, *Main Street in Crisis: The Great Depression and the Old Middle Class on the Northern Plains*, 1997

Sarah T. Phillips, *This Land, This Nation: Conservation, Rural America, and the New Deal*, 2007

Geoffrey S. Smith, *To Save a Nation: American Countersubversives, the New Deal, and the Coming of World War II*, 1973

Keith Joseph Volanto, *Texas, Cotton, and the New Deal*, 2005

Top Five Other

James O. Cade, *The New Deal on Cartwheels*, 1936

Great Plains Committee, *The Future of the Great Plains*, 1937

The Living New Deal (maps), https://livingnewdeal.org/maps-and-sites/

John Opie, "Moral Geography in High Plains History," *Geographical Review*, 1998

Rexford Guy Tugwell, "The Problem of Agriculture," *Political Science Quarterly*, 1924

Walter Prescott Webb, *Divided We Stand: the Crisis of a Frontierless Democracy*, 1937

8. THE ORIGINS OF THE TEXAS RIGHT

Top Five Books

George Norris Green, *The Establishment in Texas Politics: The Primitive Years, 1938–1957*, 1979

Seth Shepard McKay, *Texas Politics, 1906–1944*, 1952

Kim Phillips-Fein, *Invisible Hands: The Businessmen's Crusade against the New Deal*, 2010

Leo P. Ribuffo, *The Old Christian Right: The Protestant Far Right from the Great Depression to the Cold War*, 1983

Jason Morgan Ward, *Defending White Democracy: The Making of a Segregationist Movement and the Remaking of Racial Politics, 1936–1965*, 2011

Top Five Other

Stetson Kennedy, *Southern Exposure: Making the South Safe for Democracy*, 1946

Kevin C. Motl, "Under the Influence: The Texas Business Men's Association and the Campaign against Reform, 1906–1915," *Southwestern Historical Quarterly*, 2006

Vance Muse III, "Making Peace with Grandfather," *Texas Monthly*, February 1986

Matthew Avery Sutton, "Was FDR the Antichrist? The Birth of Fundamentalist Anti-liberalism in a Global Age," *Journal of American History*, 2012

George Wolfskill, *The Revolt of the Conservatives: A History of the American Liberty League, 1934–1940*, 1962

9. THE RIGHT-WING POPULISM OF PAPPY O'DANIEL

Top Five Books

Darren E. Grem, *The Blessings of Business: How Corporations Shaped Conservative Christianity*, 2016

Isaac William Martin, *Rich People's Movements: Grassroots Campaigns to Untax the One Percent*, 2013

Seth Shepard McKay, *W. Lee O'Daniel and Texas Politics, 1938–1942*, 1944

Theodore Saloutos, *Twentieth-Century Populism*, 1951

George Brown Tindall, *The Emergence of the New South, 1913–1945*, 1967

Top Five Other

Bill Crawford, *Please Pass the Biscuits, Pappy: Pictures of Governor W. Lee "Pappy" O'Daniel*, 2004

Walter Davenport, "Where's Them Biscuits, Pappy?" *Collier's Weekly*, January 6, 1940, and "Savior from Texas," *Collier's*, August 18, 1945

The Essential Bob Wills, 1935–1947, Columbia Records, 1992

Helen Fuller, "The Christian American Cabal," *New Republic*, January 25, 1943

James Yauger, "A Rhetorical Study of Selected Radio Speeches of Governor W. Lee O'Daniel of Texas on Behalf of Social Security Legislation, 1939–1941," PhD dissertation, Louisiana State University, 1968

10. RANCHER/SCHOLAR/REACTIONARY

Top Five Books

William F. Buckley, *God and Man at Yale: The Superstitions of Academic Freedom*, 1951

Don E. Carleton, *Red Scare! Right-Wing Hysteria, Fifties Fanaticism, and Their Legacy in Texas*, 1985

George Fuermann, *Reluctant Empire*, 1957

Chandler A. Robinson, *J. Evetts Haley and the Passing of the Old West: A Bibliography of*

His Writings, with a Collection of Essays upon His Character, Genius, Personality, Skills, and Accomplishments, 1978

Richard M. Weaver, *Ideas Have Consequences*, 1976

Top Five Other

Guy Story Brown, "J. Evetts Haley and the Mind of the South," *Abbeville (TX) Review*, January 3, 2017

John S. Huntington, "'The Voice of Many Hatreds': J. Evetts Haley and Texas Ultraconservatism," *Western Historical Quarterly*, 2017

Elmer Kelton, *The Time It Never Rained*, 1973

James Evetts Haley and Evetts Haley, *J. Evetts Haley, KSJ: Cowman, Historian, Texan: The Legacy: A Collection of Essays in Remembrance of J. Evetts Haley*, 1996

B. Byron Price, "J. Evetts Haley," in *Writing the Story of Texas*, edited by Patrick L. Cox and Kenneth E. Hendrickson, 2013

Stacey Sprague, "James Evetts Haley and the New Deal: Laying the Foundations for the Modern Republican Party in Texas," PhD dissertation, University of North Texas, 2004

11. BRAINWASHED

Top Five Books

Gail Collins, *As Texas Goes . . . : How the Lone Star State Hijacked the American Agenda*, 2012

Matthew W. Dunne, *A Cold War State of Mind: Brainwashing and Postwar American Society*, 2013

Jill Lepore, *The Whites of Their Eyes: The Tea Party's Revolution and the Battle over American History*, 2010

James W. Loewen, *Lies My Teacher Told Me: Everything Your American History Textbook Got Wrong*, 1995

Jack Nelson and Gene Roberts Jr., *The Censors and the Schools*, 1963

Top Five Other

Paul F. Boller, *Memoirs of an Obscure Professor and Other Essays*, 1992

Robert Cashby, director, *The Ultimate Weapon*, film starring Ronald Reagan, 1962, and Allen Rivkin, director, *Prisoner of War*, film starring Ronald Reagan, 1954

E. Merrill Root, *Brainwashing in the High Schools: An Examination of Eleven American History Textbooks*, 1958

Texas House of Representatives, Textbook Investigating Committee Recordings, 1962, https://tsl.access.preservica.com/uncategorized/SOc8d43be5-5cb1-467a-b6bf -e2679ab7dbad/

Texas Observer, 1961–1962

Charles S. Young, "Missing Action: POW Films, Brainwashing and the Korean War, 1954–1968." *Historical Journal of Film, Radio, and Television*, 1998

12. BIRCHTOWN

Top Five Books

Matthew Dallek, *Birchers: How the John Birch Society Radicalized the American Right*, 2023

Arnold Forster and Benjamin R. Epstein, *Danger on the Right*, 1964

Edward H. Miller, *A Conspiratorial Life: Robert Welch, the John Birch Society, and the Revolution of American Conservatism*, 2023

Michelle M. Nickerson, *Mothers of Conservatism: Women and the Postwar Right*, 2012
Irwin Suall, *The American Ultras: The Extreme Right and the Military-Industrial Complex*, 1962

Top Five Other
Richard Hofstadter, "The Paranoid Style in American Politics," *Harper's Magazine*, November 1964
Terry Isaacs, "Politics, Religion, and the Blue Book: The John Birch Society in Eastern New Mexico and West Texas, 1960–1965," *New Mexico Historical Review*, 1996
Dan Kelly, "Birchismo," *The Baffler*, December 1999
Willie Morris, "Cell 772; Or, Life among the Extremists," *Commentary*, October 1964
Carroll Wilson, "The Blue Book of Birchers," *Accent West*, July 1981

13. THE WEST TEXAS CROWD

Top Five Books
Paul D. Casdorph, *A History of the Republican Party in Texas, 1865–1965*, 1965
Barry M. Goldwater, *The Conscience of a Conservative*, 1960
John R. Knaggs, *Two-Party Texas: The John Tower Era, 1961–1984*, 1985
Roger M. Olien, *From Token to Triumph: The Texas Republicans, since 1920*, 1982
John G. Tower, *Consequences: A Personal and Political Memoir*, 1991

Top Five Other
Sean P. Cunningham, "John Tower, Texas, and the Rise of the Republican South," in *Seeking a New Majority*, 2013
John Tower Campaign Ads, 1961, Texas Archive of the Moving Image, https://texasarchive.org/
Phil Ochs, "The Ballad of Billie Sol," recorded mid-1960s, released 1986
Jan Jarboe Russell, "Billie Sol Estes Has a Deal for You," *Texas Monthly*, November 1989
John G. Tower, *A Program for Conservatives*, 1962

14. VIVA! OLÉ!

Top Five Books
John Bainbridge, *The Super-Americans: A Picture of Life in the United States, as Brought into Focus, Bigger than Life, in the Land of the Millionaires—Texas*, 1962
Mary C. Brennan, *Turning Right in the Sixties: The Conservative Capture of the GOP*, 2007
Robert Alan Goldberg, *Barry Goldwater*, 1997
Richard H. Rovere, *The Goldwater Caper*, 1965
Nancy Beck Young, *Two Suns of the Southwest: Lyndon Johnson, Barry Goldwater, and the 1964 Battle between Liberalism and Conservatism*, 2019

Top Five Other
David Danzig, "Conservatism after Goldwater," *Commentary*, March 1965
Richard Hofstadter, "Goldwater and Pseudo-Conservative Politics" and "Pseudo-Conservatism Revisited—1965," in *The Paranoid Style in American Politics*, 1965
Harry Hurt III, "George Bush, Plucky Lad," *Texas Monthly*, June 1983
KHOU-TV, "Texas Republican Convention, 1964," 8:56, Texas Archive of the Moving Image, https://texasarchive.org/
Elizabeth Tandy Shermer, "Origins of the Conservative Ascendancy: Barry Goldwater's Early Senate Career and the De-legitimization of Organized Labor," *Journal of American History*, 2008

15. UNINTENDED CONSEQUENCES

Top Five Books

Buzz Bissinger, *Friday Night Lights: A Town, a Team, and a Dream*, 1990

Ty Cashion, *Pigskin Pulpit: A Social History of Texas High School Football Coaches*, 1998

James W. Loewen, *Sundown Towns: A Hidden Dimension of American Racism*, 2005

Jim Schutze, *The Accommodation: The Politics of Race in an American City*, 1986

Amilcar Shabazz, *Advancing Democracy: African Americans and the Struggle for Access and Equity in Higher Education in Texas*, 2004

Top Five Other

Gary Cartwright, "The Lonely Blues of Duane Thomas," *Texas Monthly*, February 1973

Don DeLillo, *End Zone*, 1972

Ben Fountain, *Billy Lynn's Long Halftime Walk*, 2012

Peter Gent, *North Dallas Forty*, 1973

Jan Reid, "Big D, Why Hast Thou Forsaken Me?," *Esquire*, September 1997

Duane Thomas, "Highlight Reel," YouTube, 26:56, posted by Classic Sports, June 21, 2020, www.youtube.com/watch?v=5bS1zHiAuJg&t=404s

16. RIGHT-WING REPUBLICANISM

Top Five Books

Timothy Paul Bowman, *You Will Never Be One of Us: A Teacher, a Texas Town, and the Rural Roots of Radical Conservatism*, 2022

Chandler Davidson, *Race and Class in Texas Politics*, 1990

Geoffrey M. Kabaservice, *Rule and Ruin: The Downfall of Moderation and the Destruction of the Republican Party, from Eisenhower to the Tea Party*, 2012

Carl Oglesby, *The Yankee and Cowboy War: Conspiracies from Dallas to Watergate*, 1976

Wayne J. Thorburn, *Red State: An Insider's Story of How the GOP Came to Dominate Texas Politics*, 2014

Top Five Other

Paul Friedman, "The Metaphysics of the John Birch Society," *North American Review*, January 1968

Norman Mailer, "Nixon in Miami," in *Miami and the Siege of Chicago*, 1968

Rick Perlstein and Edward H. Miller, "The John Birch Society Never Left," *New Republic*, March 8, 2021

Ronald Reagan, "A Time for Choosing," October 27, 1964, YouTube, 29:07, posted by Ronald Reagan Presidential Foundation and Institute, April 2, 2009, https://www.youtube.com/watch?v=qXBswFfh6AY

Michael Paul Rogin, "Ronald Reagan, the Movie," *Radical History Review*, 1987

CODA

Top Five Books

Gilbert Garcia, *Reagan's Comeback: Four Weeks in Texas That Changed American Politics Forever*, 2012

Michael Lind, *Made in Texas: George W. Bush and the Southern Takeover of American Politics*, 2003

Rick Perlstein, *The Invisible Bridge: The Fall of Nixon and the Rise of Reagan*, 2014

Daniel K. Williams, *The Election of the Evangelical: Jimmy Carter, Gerald Ford, and the Presidential Contest of 1976*, 2020

Jules Witcover, *Marathon: The Pursuit of the Presidency, 1972–1976*, 1977

Top Five Other

Gary Cartwright, *Blood Will Tell: The Murder Trials of T. Cullen Davis*, 1979

Blake A. Ellis, "An Alternative Politics: Texas Baptists and the Rise of the Christian Right, 1975–1985," *Southwestern Historical Quarterly*, 2009

Frances Fitzgerald, "The Triumphs of the New Right," *New York Review of Books*, 1981

Alan Taylor, "America in the 1970s: Texas" Photographs, *The Atlantic*, July 25, 2013

The Tonight Show Starring Johnny Carson, with special guest Ronald Reagan, January 3, 1975, YouTube, https://www.youtube.com/watch?v=xrNKguJLUYE

TOP TEN SUBJECT LISTS

Top Ten Books on Right-Wing Conservatives

Darren Dochuk, *From Bible Belt to Sunbelt: Plain-Folk Religion, Grassroots Politics, and the Rise of Evangelical Conservatism*, 2011

David Farber, *The Rise and Fall of Modern American Conservatism: A Short History*, 2010

Thomas Frank, *What's the Matter with Kansas? How Conservatives Won the Heart of America*, 2005

Godfrey Hodgson, *The World Turned Right Side Up: A History of the Conservative Ascendancy in America*, 1996

John S. Huntington, *Far-Right Vanguard: The Radical Roots of Modern Conservatism*, 2021

Allan J. Lichtman, *White Protestant Nation: The Rise of the American Conservative Movement*, 2008

Michelle M. Nickerson, *Mothers of Conservatism: Women and the Postwar Right*, 2012

The Rick Perlstein Tetralogy: *Before the Storm* (2001), *Nixonland* (2008), *The Invisible Bridge* (2014), *Reaganland* (2020)

Kim Phillips-Fein, *Invisible Hands: The Making of the Conservative Movement from the New Deal to Reagan*, 2009

Corey Robin, *The Reactionary Mind: Conservatism from Edmund Burke to Sarah Palin*, 2011

Top Ten Books on Texas (Right-Wing) Politics

Norman D. Brown, *Hood, Bonnet, and Little Brown Jug: Texas Politics, 1921–1928*, 1984

Don E. Carleton, *Red Scare! Right-Wing Hysteria Fifties Fanaticism and Their Legacy in Texas*, 1985

David O'Donald Cullen and Kyle Grant Wilkison, eds., *The Texas Right: The Radical Roots of Lone Star Conservatism*, 2014

Chandler Davidson, *Race and Class in Texas Politics*, 1990

Ricky F. Dobbs, *Yellow Dogs and Republicans: Allan Shivers and Texas Two-Party Politics*, 2005

George Norris Green, *The Establishment in Texas Politics: The Primitive Years, 1938–1957*, 1979

Mike Kingston, Sam Attlesey, and Mary G. Crawford, *The Texas Almanac's Political History of Texas*, 1992

Michael Lind, *Made in Texas: George W. Bush and the Southern Takeover of American Politics*, 2003

Edward H. Miller, *Nut Country: Right-Wing Dallas and the Birth of the Southern Strategy*, 2015

Robert Wuthnow, *Rough Country: How Texas Became America's Most Powerful Bible-Belt State*, 2014

Top Ten Books on West Texas

Margaret A. Bickers, *Red Water, Black Gold: The Canadian River in Western Texas, 1920–1999*, 2014

Nate Blakeslee, *Tulia: Race, Cocaine, and Corruption in a Small Texas Town*, 2006

Paul Howard Carlson and Bruce A. Glasrud, eds., *West Texas: A History of the Giant Side of the State*, 2014

John C. Dawson Sr., *High Plains Yesterdays: From XIT Days through Drouth and Depression*, 1985

Glen Sample Ely, *Where the West Begins: Debating Texas Identity*, 2011

Dan L. Flores, *Caprock Canyonlands: Journeys into the Heart of the Southern Plains*, 1990

Donald E. Green, *Land of the Underground Rain: Irrigation on the Texas High Plains, 1910–70*, 1981

Willie Newbury Lewis, *Between Sun and Sod*, 1938

Larry McMutry, *In a Narrow Grave*, 1968

A. G. Mojtabai, *Blessed Assurance: At Home with the Bomb in Amarillo, Texas*, 1997

Walter Prescott Webb, *The Great Plains*, 1931

MORE TOP FIVE OR TEN OR SO LISTS

Top Five West Texas Novels

Elmer Kelton, *The Time It Never Rained*

Cormac McCarthy, *All the Pretty Horses*

Larry McMurtry, *Horseman, Pass By*

Annie Proulx, *That Old Ace in the Hole*

Dorothy Scarborough, *The Wind*

Top Ten West Texas Musical Artists

Josh Abbott

John Bauman (and the other Panhandlers)

Joe "King" Carrasco

Summer Dean

Joe Ely (and the other Flatlanders)

Buddy Holly

Waylon Jennings

Amanda Shires

Tanya Tucker

Bob Wills

Top Ten West Texas Songs

Terry Allen, "Amarillo Highway" (especially the Robert Earl Keen live version)

John Baumann, "Bible Belt"

Ryan Culwell, "Flatlands"

Mac Davis, "Lubbock Texas in My Rearview Mirror"

Waylon Jennings, "Bob Wills Is Still the King"

Lyle Lovett, "West Texas Highway"

The Panhandlers, "West Texas is the Best Texas"

Saint Motel, "Van Horn"

George Strait, "West Texas Town" (a better dance number than the other one)

Bob Wills and his Texas Playboys, "I'm a Ding Dong Daddy from Dumas"

Top Five Joe Ely West Texas Songs

"Because of the Wind"

"Boxcars"

"I Had My Hopes Up High"

"Ranches and Rivers"

"West Texas Waltz"

PHOTO CREDITS

160   Photo by Arthur Rothstein; FSA/OWI Collection (LC-USF34-005229-E), Library of Congress, Prints and Photographs Division
192   Fort Worth Star-Telegram Collection, courtesy of Special Collections, The University of Texas at Arlington Libraries
195   Lubbock History Collection (wr.c.12N.2.8.1.1), courtesy of Southwest Collection / Special Collections Library, Texas Tech University, Lubbock, Texas
219   Bob Kesterson Photograph Collection, courtesy of the Panhandle-Plains Historical Museum, Canyon, Texas
230   Archival collections, courtesy of the Haley Memorial Library and History Center, Midland, Texas
290   What the Camera Saw Collection: Photographs by Jim Cochran Collection, courtesy of Midwestern State University, Wichita Falls, Texas
321   Winston Reeves Photograph Collection (wr.c.12N.2.8.1.1), courtesy of Southwest Collection / Special Collections Library, Texas Tech University, Lubbock
322   Winston Reeves Photograph Collection (wr.c.124N.2.8.7.4), courtesy of Southwest Collection / Special Collections Library, Texas Tech University, Lubbock
338   West Texas State University, University Photographer Collection, courtesy of the Panhandle-Plains Historical Museum, Canyon, Texas
343   West Texas State University, University Photographer Collection, courtesy of the Panhandle-Plains Historical Museum, Canyon, Texas
381   Archival collections, courtesy of the Haley Memorial Library and History Center, Midland, Texas

INDEX

Photos and illustrations are indicated by italicized page numbers